GOLDWYN

A BIOGRAPHY

A. SCOTT BERG

PAN BOOKS

First published 1989 by Alfred A. Knopf Inc., New York

First published in Great Britain 1989 by Hamish Hamilton

This edition published 1999 by Pan Books
an imprint of Macmillan Publishers Limited
25 Eccleston Place, London SW1W 9NF
Basingstoke and Oxford
Associated companies throughout the world
www.macmillan.co.uk

ISBN 0 330 39248 4

3 5 7 9 8 6 4 2

A CIP catalogue record for this book is available
from the British Library.

Printed and bound in Great Britain by
Mackays of Chatham plc, Chatham, Kent

"A thorough job of research . . . interesting but little-known facts are brought to light. . . . How this boy of the ghetto transformed himself into that film-baron fashion plate is the real meat of the story. . . . One is left to wonder if, fame and riches aside, Goldwyn wasn't motivated not so much by the mere will to survive, which exists everywhere, as by the iron-and-granite will to be great, to reach for and possess power."

—*Chicago Tribune*

"Richly detailed, at once a biography of Samuel Goldwyn and a business history of Hollywood—Berg is especially good on the backgrounds of film deals. It is also a biography of the inner dreams that energized the great era of Hollywood."

—*Vogue*

"Thoroughly engrossing . . . The book is peppered with hundreds of Goldwyn's famous and infamous malapropisms, dozens of anecdotes about his critical and commercial failures as well as his outstanding successes, and details of his relationships with, among scores of others, Eddie Cantor, Ronald Colman, Merle Oberon, Gary Cooper, George Cukor, William Wyler, Billy Wilder."

—*Publishers Weekly*

"Meticulously researched . . . Besides discovering stars like Gary Cooper, David Niven and Ronald Colman . . . Goldwyn invented the 'package': He was the first to buy the book, hire the screenwriter, stars, crew and director. His fifty-year career established the model for today's independent producer."

—*Harper's Bazaar*

"Berg has done a painstaking job of re-creating this epic life. . . . We see Goldwyn-the-lonely-tyrant-of-tinsel-town working with the most brilliant writers, directors, and stars."

—*Cosmopolitan*

(continued on next page)

"Does something no other Hollywood history has ever accomplished: this book *explains* Hollywood, is the best single-volume education in the movie business. . . . In the long run, Berg's book, meticulous, restrained, yet passionately empathetic to Goldwyn and the contract players of his life, will certainly take the cake among Hollywood histories of the age."

—*Manhattan Inc.*

"Whether you own a thousand film books or nary a one, room ought to be made for *Goldwyn*. . . . The films we watch now, with either gritted teeth or contented smiles, are the products of an industry that ended up taking its shape from the psyche of this tumultuous man."

—*GQ*

"Superb . . . a complex portrait of a man and an era. There has never before been a Hollywood biography as profound as this."

—*Playboy*

"As meticulous, as sterling in quality and as large in scope as independent movie producer Samuel Goldwyn always (but not always very accurately) claimed his movies were."

—*People*

"It's a great place to start reading about the movies. . . . Cukor said of the gregarious mogul, 'He acted as though every part were given just for him.' Thus does he dominate Berg's big, rich, graceful biography. One hates to close it for the last time as one hates to see Goldwyn and his larger-than-life moviemaking come to an end again. Berg's achievement is spectacularly rewarding."

—*The Washington Post Book World*

ALSO BY A. SCOTT BERG

Lindbergh
Max Perkins: Editor of Genius

to

Katharine Hepburn, Kevin McCormick,
and Irene Mayer Selznick

I met a traveler from an antique land
Who said: Two vast and trunkless legs of stone
Stand in the desert. Near them, on the sand,
Half sunk, a shattered visage lies, whose frown,
And wrinkled lip, and sneer of cold command,
Tell that its sculptor well those passions read
Which yet survive, stamped on these lifeless things,
The hand that mocked them and the heart that fed:
And on the pedestal these words appear:
"My name is Ozymandias, king of kings:
Look on my works, ye Mighty, and despair!"
Nothing beside remains. Round the decay
Of that colossal wreck, boundless and bare
The lone and level sands stretch far away.

—SHELLEY, "Ozymandias"

CONTENTS

GOLDWYN

PART ONE

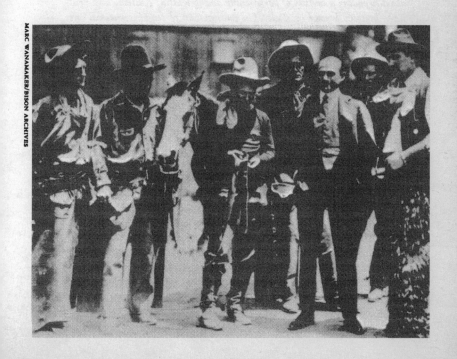

. . . and the children of Israel dispersed, embarking on an endless cycle of settlement and influence that invoked persecution and expulsion.

The Hebrews suffered at the hands of the Egyptians, the Chaldeans, the Romans. Through the Middle Ages they continued to search for a homeland, only to be expelled from England in the 1290s, France in the 1390s, Spain in the 1490s. Into central Europe they poured.

In 1791, Russia established a Pale of Settlement, that portion of their land in which Jews were permitted to reside. Much of Poland—which was about to endure a century of partitioning among Russia, Austria, and Prussia—lay just beyond the Pale. The continuation of Jewish communal life, forever threatened, found hope in a charismatic new religious movement there.

Hasidism emphasized piety over learning. Aglow with mysticism, this folk gospel preached that God smiled upon the ignorant as well as the wise and that one's devotion could best be expressed through passionate prayer. By the nineteenth century, most of Poland's Orthodox Jewry belonged to the sect. The Jewish faith, bound by laws and tradition, proved imperishable. By 1876, the thriving city of Warsaw, on the left bank of the Vistula, found that one third of its 300,000 citizens was Jewish.

In 1881, a new czar took hold of Russia; Alexander III imposed on the Jews conditions as intolerable as any they had yet experienced. . . .

1 Exodus

S AMUEL GOLDWYN was not born on August 27, 1882.

For most of his life he swore it was his day of birth, but both the name and the date were fabrications. He promulgated other distortions of the truth as well, liberties he took for dramatic effect. He spent years covering his tracks, erasing those details of his origins that embarrassed him. The reason, he revealed to a psychotherapist at the pinnacle of his career, was that ever since childhood he "wanted to be somebody." Starting at an early age, Samuel Goldwyn invented himself.

Schmuel Gelbfisz was born in Warsaw, probably in July 1879. Records vary, and Jews were known to falsify their sons' birth dates to protect them from future conscription in the czar's army. He was the eldest child of Hannah and Aaron David Gelbfisz, Hasidic Jews. The family had lived in Poland for generations, but their surname was new. Not until 1797 were the Jews of Warsaw ordered to adopt patronymics. Many fashioned names from house signs, which were often hieroglyphs painted in a single color. The picture of an animal might refer to part of a family's history or simply represent a family member's trade. In Poland, the spellings of these names were often a mixture of languages. "I'm sure there was a fishmonger somewhere back there," said one Gelbfisz descendant; and his house sign, as the German first syllable indicates, was painted yellow.

Aaron had been a rabbinical student in his youth but went to work at an early age to support his new family. A sickly and gentle man, he had a handsome face with fine, even features. He liked to read. Goldwyn remembered him as "a sensitive fella." He struggled with a small store that sold "antiques"—mostly secondhand goods and junk. Fluent in several languages, he supplemented his measly income by reading and writing letters for his neighbors.

His wife, Hannah Reban Jarecka, was born in 1855, three years after her husband. Except for their religious beliefs and their mutual birthplace, Warsaw, they were essentially opposites. Hannah was a tall brunette, so stout that she was known as *lange Hannah*—Big Hannah. She had piercing eyes and squashed features, a combination that produced a constant scowl; and she tended to shout rather than speak. One granddaughter remembered, "She wore the pain of many generations of suffering." Like many women of her period, she ruled the house.

The Gelbfiszes, whose marriage had been arranged according to tradition, did not especially care for each other. Within sixteen years, they produced five more children—Mania (born in 1884), Barel (later known as Bernard, who was born the following year), Natalia (called Nettie, born in 1889), Ben (born in 1890), and Sally (born in 1894). Hannah showed a stringent affection for her family.

In 1882, the Jewish population of Warsaw reached 130,000; it was the largest Jewish community in Europe. A generation later, the Jewish population there had almost trebled. Natural increase was responsible for only part of this growth; immigration made up the rest. After the Russian pogroms of 1881, tens of thousands of Jews had fled to Warsaw from all corners of the Russias.

The age-old history of ambivalence toward Jews caught up to Poland. The country needed them, for they contributed to the nation's economy and growing mercantile class; but when they succeeded, the Gentile population felt the need to punish them, and subjected them to higher taxes, restrictive laws, violent attacks.

The Gelbfisz family of eight lived in two rooms of a flat on a crowded street in the Jewish sector of Warsaw, one narrow building wedged against another. Fear surrounded them. The three boys shared one hard bed. "You can't visualize how we lived," Ben recalled years later. "All I can see is pogroms." The Gelbfiszes never starved, but once they survived an entire week on a handful of potatoes. In a vulnerable moment, Goldwyn volunteered three adjectives to describe his life in Poland: "poor, poor, poor." Almost everything under the sun disappointed Hannah; and she complained constantly of her plight, making life miserable for her husband.

Aaron Gelbfisz periodically disappeared, abandoning his family for days, sometimes months, at a time. Fortunately, a few relatives could assist, especially Hannah's brother, who had scraped together enough money to invest in a small block of apartments. When there was not enough food to spread among her children, Hannah farmed Schmuel out to her husband's parents. He adored them.

Schmuel's grandparents Zalman and Perele Gelbfisz lived in a tenement on nearby Brovarna Street, in much cozier surroundings than Schmuel was accustomed to. Zalman was a *mohel,* the man who circumcised male babies on the eighth day after birth in the ritual known as *Brith Milah.* As such, he held the respect of his community and had the carriage of an aristocrat. He had squirreled away some savings and retired. Schmuel admired the old man's haughtiness; and he began to model himself after him—the only dominant male figure in his life—especially in his inability to control his own volatile temper.

Like most Jewish children in Warsaw, Schmuel attended *cheder,* in black cap and *payess,* and received an Orthodox Jewish education. He could read and write Hebrew, and he spoke some Polish, except at home. Yiddish was his mother tongue. One day after school when he was still very young, Schmuel was playing with a bunch of friends in the street. A well-dressed young man rode past on horseback, followed by a lackey on a donkey. The servant pitched a handful of coins onto the cobblestones, and all the children scrambled to gather them. Long after spending his share, Schmuel held on to that image of a man too rich to carry his own money.

During one of his extended visits with his grandparents, in 1895, Schmuel was suddenly summoned home. His father had returned from a trip with excruciating pains in his stomach and difficulty breathing. After a short illness, Aaron Gelbfisz died at the age of forty-three, saddling Hannah with the responsibility of six children, the youngest of whom was eleven months old. The eldest, fifteen-year-old Schmuel, would hardly go another day thereafter without catching himself coughing or thinking he felt pain in his stomach.

As life grew harder for the fatherless household, increased support came from Schmuel's mother's family. One of the Jarecka aunts provided a cheaper dwelling for them, a little cash, and various jobs over the years for the children, according to age and ability. Schmuel's brother Ben, for example, kept her accounts.

Schmuel saw that his mother, although still young, planned to settle into widowhood, to be supported by her children. Her sons would become laborers or bookkeepers, her daughters secretaries or seamstresses; and she would spend her final years indulging in her favorite pastime, *oko*—a game like poker, which she played every day.

As for Schmuel, he realized he had been dealt a bad hand. Upon the death of Aaron, he began to cut himself off from people—even his family—becoming indifferent, often bitter. Schmuel felt deprived of a father and blamed his mother for "killing" him. For years, he admired the way she had kept her large family together under adverse conditions. Now he felt neglected and forced into unendurable circumstances—all of which he attributed to her. For the rest of his life, Sam Goldwyn, encountering a baleful situation, would shake his head and say, "You don't know how many rotten mothers there are in the world."

At age sixteen, Schmuel, his mother's eldest son, assessed his future in Warsaw. His responsibilities had suddenly increased sevenfold, and life in the Jewish ghetto showed no signs of improving. The tall, skinny teenager, with his doleful eyes, saw only hopelessness around him, and the probability that as a Jew he would serve as cannon fodder in the czar's army. His face—with its jutting jaw and mashed nose—had already experienced many fights. He had become what was often referred to as a "miniature Jew," those Jewish youths who carried the burdens of adults. He felt too young to assume those responsibilities but old enough to act on a fantasy he had been fostering.

"When I was a kid . . ." Goldwyn later admitted, "the only place I wanted to go was to America. I had heard them talking about America, about how people were free in America. . . . Even then America, actually only the name of a faraway country, was a vision of paradise." Because of the prohibitive cost, Schmuel knew he would have to make his journey in stages. His mother had a married sister in Birmingham, England; that was his first milestone if he intended ever to cross an ocean.

Schmuel took one of his father's suits to a tailor, who altered it to the boy's narrow frame. He sold off the rest of the clothes that he thought had any value. The old clothes grubstaked his future. *Lange Hannah* had long sensed Schmuel's restlessness, but upon learning of his plans, she wailed for days. At the same time, eleven-year-old Mania remembered, her mother wanted him to go. Even at that age, she felt her mother believed Schmuel was the member of the family most likely to survive, that with prayer he might make it to America. He might even prosper enough to help the rest of his family toward a better life.

Schmuel stopped off at his grandparents' flat. His grandfather was out playing chess; his grandmother asked if he wanted supper or to spend the night. Schmuel replied that he had come over "just to kiss you." Then he left Warsaw for the port of Hamburg as tens of thousands of Jewish pilgrims did—he walked.

Between 1880 and 1910, one and a half million Jews joined wagon trains of pushcarts leaving Eastern Europe. In the 1880s alone, the family of Louis B. Mayer left Demre, near Vilna, in Lithuania; Lewis Zeleznick (later Selznick) ran away from Kiev; William Fox (formerly Fuchs) emigrated from Tulcheva, Hungary; the Warner family uprooted itself from Krasnashiltz, Poland, near the Russian border; Adolph Zukor abandoned Ricse, Hungary; and Carl Laemmle left Württemberg, Germany—gamblers with nothing to lose, all from within a five-hundred-mile radius of Warsaw.

In 1895, Schmuel Gelbfisz walked alone, almost three hundred miles due west to the Oder River. There he paid someone to row him across; half the fare was for the ferrying, half for smuggling him out of the Russian empire into Germany, past police who guarded the border on both sides. "This took most of the little money in my pocket," Goldwyn later recounted, "and then I tumbled into the water, got a good soaking, and lost the rest." He walked another two hundred miles to Hamburg.

He was drawn to the harbor, a maelstrom of activity. Emigrants speaking German, Russian, Polish, Lithuanian, and Latvian piled onto ships in pursuit of happiness. Schmuel got by on his Yiddish. He stood on the dock, penniless, and watched the throngs of those able to proceed. Gazing at the boats departing for England, he considered stowing away.

Schmuel was not completely alone in Hamburg. His mother had given him the name of a family that had moved there from Warsaw. The boy wandered the streets until he found the storefront bearing the name Liebglid. "I stormed into the shop with my ragged clothes and dirty, tear-stained face," Goldwyn remembered, "and told the proprietor my story. 'I can't go back,' I cried, 'I am on my way to America and I won't go back.'" The comforting shoulder offered him belonged to Jacob Liebglid, a young glovemaker who had left Poland only a few years earlier for many of the same reasons Gelbfisz had. In Hamburg, Liebglid had cut out a tolerable life for himself.

Schmuel was put to work and stayed for several weeks, learning the rudiments of glovemaking. He realized he could remain in Hamburg and become a glovemaker like Liebglid; but he refused to settle. He insisted he had to move on. Liebglid canvassed the Jewish neighborhood, raising the eighteen shillings necessary to put Schmuel on a boat train to London.

Great Britain was at the zenith of empire, but poverty was the same everywhere. Schmuel scrounged around London to subsist. He lived off scraps and stolen food, and he slept for three nights in the bushes of Hyde Park. Finding all doors in London closed to him, he pressed on to his relatives, who would at least provide him with food and shelter.

The next leg of his odyssey was the 120-mile walk from London to the Midlands. He lived for two days on a single loaf of bread. In Birmingham,

he found the ghetto, and his mother's sister and her husband, Mark Lin-
denshat, a foreman in a factory that made fireplace tools. They welcomed
him, but they could not support him.

With little meat on his bones and speaking but a few words of English,
Schmuel became an apprentice to a blacksmith. His job was to pump the
bellows with his feet. "This did not last long, however," he admitted years
later, "because I lacked the strength to keep up a good fire." He was discharged and was subsequently let go from several other backbreaking jobs
in the industrial city.

Schmuel later admitted that he often cried openly in front of his relatives. Convincing himself that he would never be strong enough for any
physical labor, he often took to his bed. "I was too weak to do the work
and they didn't understand," Goldwyn later admitted to his son; "that's
why I was crying."

The overburdened Lindenshats packed him off to other relatives, Dora
and Isaac Salberg. Dora claimed that she taught the boy how to use a
handkerchief and a knife and fork. She also took credit for anglicizing
his name, translating Schmuel Gelbfisz to Samuel Goldfish. She explained
the disadvantages of emphasizing his Jewish heritage. People began to call
him Sam.

In 1897, the United Kingdom of Great Britain and Ireland celebrated
the Queen's Diamond Jubilee. The pomp of the occasion threw into greater
relief Goldfish's miserable circumstances. It also helped shape his taste,
converting him into a lifelong Anglophile. He coveted the best that was
British—manners, clothes, speech, looks, and, especially, an air of self-
confidence.

For a while, Sam Goldfish sold sponges. Isaac Salberg, having failed in
business in Birmingham, packed up one day and moved to South Africa.
Before leaving, he had invested a small sum of money in a sponge dealer-
ship. Goldfish was supposed to peddle the wares and return the original
investment to the company. It never saw a farthing.

Goldwyn later claimed that while staying with the Salbergs he was
struck by a quote from Benjamin Franklin in a reader from which he was
studying English. The essay was called "Information for Those Who
Would Remove to America"; the phrase was: "America, where people do
not inquire of a stranger, 'What is he?' but 'What can he do?'" By the fall
of 1898, Sam Goldfish felt the urge to move on. He journeyed another
hundred miles, northwest to Liverpool.

Years later, Goldwyn told his son that when he arrived in Liverpool he
did not have enough money to pay for a transoceanic passage and that he

was sitting on a bench crying when a man approached to comfort him. "I'm so unhappy. I don't know what to do," he blubbered. The cavalier Englishman allegedly said, "Why don't you to go America; I'll give you the money." That was exactly the sort of fairy tale Goldwyn later liked people to believe about him. On other occasions, he said his aunt had passed a hat on his behalf. Dora Salberg always claimed that Sam skipped town with the sponge money. Goldwyn's future wife of forty-eight years said, "Sam always told me that he *stole* the money to get to America."

GOLDWYN could wax tearful about the vision of arriving in New York Harbor and seeing for the first time that Mother of Exiles welcoming the tired, the poor, and the huddled masses yearning to breathe free. But there is not a trace of his ever passing through Ellis Island, the immigration clearinghouse that had just been built to replace seam-split Castle Garden. There are no records of a Samuel Goldfish or Gelbfisz or any variant spelling either boarding a ship in England in the 1890s or disembarking in America. The nonexistence of the entry card required of every man, woman, and child who was processed at Ellis Island indicates that Sam Goldfish was not only a teenage runaway but also an illegal alien.

There are no records, either, of a Samuel Gelbfisz or Goldfish boarding a ship bound for Canada. This omission probably originates with a dockside clerk. On either side of the Atlantic—in immigration halls and shipping-line offices—it was the job of clerks with neat penmanship to record on a long list the name of every passenger who walked before them. This required reading the rudimentary scrawls of hundreds of passengers a day. The clerks often made their own adjustments or mistakes. Sam Goldfish, with little command of English, had poor handwriting. On his exit forms, the sloppy second syllable of his surname could easily have been read a number of ways.

At exactly this time, amid the thousands of outbound-passenger lists, a single entry fits his description. On one "Schedule A—Names and Description of Passengers" for the Dominion Line's *Labrador*, sailing from Liverpool to Canada in November 1898, passenger number 90 in steerage class is almost certainly he: "Sam Goldberg," age nineteen, a laborer born in Russia, whose ultimate destination was New York.

The *Labrador* was a schooner-rigged vessel, one of the largest sailing ships at sea. She was capable of carrying one hundred passengers in first class (called "Saloon" on Dominion Line ships), fifty in second class, and one thousand in what the *Labrador* called "third class." This was steerage.

One-way Saloon fare was ninety dollars. Steerage cost fifteen dollars, which rented an iron berth, a hammock, or, for some lucky passengers on the Dominion Line, cots. Most passengers used their clothes for bedding. Crowding in the airless, badly lighted ship's belly made most of them sick.

"Sam Goldberg"'s greatest advantage in sailing on the *Labrador* when he did was that only 128 other passengers occupied the space allotted for one thousand. That extra room carried its own price. The weather in England turned suddenly cold that week, and storms were forecast in the Atlantic. Practically all of the ship's passengers were male laborers between the ages of sixteen and thirty, the only souls hardy enough to brave a winter crossing.

The *Labrador* set sail in the late afternoon of November 26, 1898, heading northwest through the Irish Sea and the North Channel. The next day she picked up a few passengers in Londonderry, Ireland, then steamed due west. For the next eight days, the ship battled an angry sea.

The flight of the Jews from their homelands was more than cartographic. For most of them it was the first departure from the holy laws that had governed their lives, starting with their daily bread. There was no indication when or where the Jewish passengers would connect with another Jewish community; and there were limits to one's adherence to strict dietary laws. At what point does a religious man eat? Sam Goldfish's goal was no longer to be a good Jew; it was to become a good American, even if that meant sacrificing centuries of orthodoxy.

The *Labrador* pulled into the harbor of Halifax, Nova Scotia, at three-fifteen in the afternoon on December 4, 1898. The weather that greeted Goldfish was worse than he had left behind. A cold snap had stung eastern Canada; the most arctic December since 1871 gusted its way into New England and New York. "Goldberg" either jumped ship in Halifax or (if he had enough sense of Canadian geography) waited another day, until the *Labrador* anchored at Saint John, New Brunswick, leaving him sixty miles from the United States border.

Once he had his legs back, Goldfish took to the road again. Probably somewhere near Milltown, Maine, he crossed a snow-covered patch of land into America. Goldwyn affirmed on his Declaration for Naturalization five years later that the date was January 1, 1899. Many years after that, he admitted that upon entering the United States, he literally got down on his hands and knees and kissed the ground. He did not know a soul within four thousand miles.

In America, the landscape did not suddenly change, nor was nineteen-year-old Sam Goldfish any less cold or hungry. He felt he was not in the real America yet. "To me then," Goldwyn later recalled, "New York was America." Over the next month, he trudged through more snow than New England had seen in ten years. Sometime in late January 1899, he arrived in Manhattan, his head full of the stuff on which American dreams are made.

2 New York

THE GREAT METROPOLIS was a mare's nest, its slums as awful as Warsaw's, in some areas worse.

Samuel Goldfish scared up temporary lodging in a boardinghouse in the Bronx and a job delivering telegraph messages. Both were the result of *tzedaka*—that requirement of Jews to look after their own.

Making his rounds in Manhattan, Goldfish beheld some of America's wonders, riches beyond his imaginings. But he also saw poverty at every turn. On the Lower East Side, he encountered the most crowded living conditions he had ever seen. Communities of immigrants speaking their native tongues, with pushcarts and small shops, thrived as though entire city blocks from Eastern Europe had been set down there. Newspapers appeared to be in every European language but English.

Goldfish stumbled across the American Council of Nationalities. Someone there spoke of a place far beyond Manhattan with a growing population of Polish immigrants, a small town upstate where gloves were made. Factories were so hungry for labor, they would even provide transportation.

Goldwyn quickly considered whether he had exchanged one urban pen for another. He could remain in the relatively familiar surroundings of New York City, or he could gamble on the unknown in the hinterlands. Curiously, a special breed of those East European Jews who had come to America within a few years of Goldwyn's arrival chose to escape that most crowded Jewish ghetto, New York City: Louis B. Mayer became a scrap-metal and junk dealer in Saint John, New Brunswick, then moved to Haverhill, Massachusetts; Adolph Zukor became a furrier in Chicago; Lewis Selznick became a jeweler in Pittsburgh, Carl Laemmle a clothier in Oshkosh; the father of Jack, Harry, Sam, and Albert Warner became a cobbler, then opened a bicycle shop in Youngstown, Ohio; William Fox cut linings for men's suits and opened a cloth-sponging business, but extricated himself from the Lower East Side as soon as he could. For Sam Goldfish, the choice was clear.

The train trip was some 180 miles out of Pennsylvania Station on the New York Central Line, due north along the banks of the Hudson River until Albany, at which point the tracks elbowed westward into Fulton County. Each mile grew more rustic, even in winter affording beautiful glimpses of fields, forests, and valleys formed by the foothills of the Catskills, the Adirondacks, and the Mayfield Mountains. The train followed the Mohawk River for forty miles until it reached the town of Fonda. From there it was eight miles north (by electric railroad) to the twin cities of Johnstown and Gloversville.

Gloversville, New York, was a pretty community with broad streets lined by trees on both sides. The Cayadutta River ran right through the town, turning the wheels of mills and machinery. The population was pushing fifteen thousand people.

Into the nineteenth century, the area had become a convenient campground for travelers between New England and the expanding territories of Ohio. In 1803, one Ezekiel Case, who had journeyed as far west as Cincinnati, learned how to tan deerskins. He brought hides back to the area, where women cut and sewed them by hand into crude gloves and mittens. Land speculators cleared away acres of pinewoods, and the region became known as Stump City.

Another settler was a leather dresser from England, who found the waters of the nearby Mohawk River exceptional for softening hides. He shared his craft with anyone who wished to settle near him and learn. In 1825, an entire load of gloves left on a six-week trip to Boston. From that time "to the present," reads the official 1902 Board of Trade manual, "every variety of skins gathered from all quarters of the globe has been received and experimented with, so that at the present time there is no kind of glove that is not manufactured here." Stump City changed its name to Gloversville in 1828; it incorporated as a city in 1890.

Like the rest of the country, Gloversville received Jewish immigrants in two waves. Nathan Littauer, born in Breslau, Germany, in 1829, was the first Jewish settler in the region. He bought a storehouse and barn in the middle of town and opened his first dry-goods store. "After several years experimenting with the importing of finished leather gloves and lambskins for glove linings," reports *The Jewish History of Fulton County,* "Mr. Littauer established a glove factory in his building. The glove business was an immediate success and word went to the 'old country' that there was a need for glove workers." They came by the hundreds.

The German Jews were the first to convert the makeshift craft of glove-making into a business. After Littauer came men named Meyers and Deichsel and Levor and Rubin and Adler, then Lehr and Klopot and Bachner and Moses. They became moguls of a new industry. By the time Samuel Goldfish joined the 12,000 employed in the leading local industry, some $4 million worth of capital had been invested in the 125 factories in the area, which produced $15 million worth of gloves a year.

The city of Gloversville was divided into four segments by its two principal streets, Fulton running east and west, and Main extending north and south. Grand Victorian homes of the factory owners were located in the northeast quadrant. Upon his arrival, Sam Goldfish was given a room in a boardinghouse in the southwest corner of the city, literally on the wrong side of the tracks.

He lived just blocks from his job at Louis Meyers & Son, Glove Manufactory, a four-story stone building. There hundreds of animal skins went through several stages before becoming dozens of gloves. First, a man would "tax" the leather, figuring how many pairs of gloves could be made from a single hide; another would dampen the skins and stretch them; another would lay a pattern over the material and press gently, leaving light indentations of a double-image hand shape; with big, heavy shears, a man then cut around the pricked skin, stamping his identification number on the back; batches were sent into another part of the factory, the "making room," populated entirely with women, who sewed around the fingers and attached the fourchettes, those strips between each finger, which round them out; stitched gloves were delivered to the "laying off" room, where each glove was slipped over a cast-iron dummy of a hand and steamed; the pressed gloves were then sent to the "finishing room," where boys sewed on buttons or any other special touches. The gloves were inspected, wrapped in tissue paper, and banded together in pairs of six. Goldwyn's first job was sweeping all four floors of Louis Meyers & Son. His boss was one of Gloversville's leading citizens, Albert Aaron, who paid him three dollars for a six-day work week.

On Tuesday, October 3, 1899, Samuel Goldfish went to the county courthouse in Johnstown to register as a resident of the city of Gloversville and to petition to become a citizen of the United States. Where most applicants indicated what vessel they had sailed on, a clerk wrote: "Arrived in this country Jany 1st 1899." A few lines above that, Samuel Goldfish, in an undeveloped hand, swore that he was twenty years old, born in July 1879. It would be the last recorded time he would stick to those facts.

THE turn of the century was a good time for the glove business. Fulton County was producing almost half the heavy work gloves made in the United States and 95 percent of its fine dress gloves, then playing an important role in fashion. Job opportunities abounded. It was only weeks before Goldfish left Meyers for a job, as an apprentice cutter at Bacmo Gloves, one of the new, up-and-coming glove concerns in Gloversville, started by Joseph Bachner and Joseph Moses. Cutters were paid by the number of gloves they cut in a given week; the typical wage in 1900 was $1.20 for every dozen pairs. A good cutter could stamp his identification number into three dozen pairs a day.

Goldfish developed an attitude problem, the result of his frustration at having to work most of his days in silence. Barely able to express himself in English, he made no friends during his first year in Gloversville. At Bacmo, he paid attention to nothing but his work. One of his co-workers, Julia Flansburg, noticed that during his lunch break, Sam would eat out of a brown paper sack, speaking to practically nobody, then hasten back to the cutting room because time was money. Miss Flansburg remembered, "He wanted to find himself a rich girl. He once said he was saving for a fancy vacation, because that's where 'the live ones' were. He had no vices; he couldn't afford to, because he seemed to have his life all figured out."

There was one creeping sin in his life, which he never renounced. The moment Goldfish came into cash, he found it impossible not to gamble. In November 1899, he bet two dollars that Harvard would beat Yale that year in football. The game was a scoreless tie. Goldfish insisted he did not lose the bet, but in the end was forced to make good on it. One Jacob Sandler, then a young boy in town, recounted to Goldwyn many years later, "I overheard you bemoaning the loss of this $2.00 and started teasing you, and you chased me all the way around to the alley of the Windsor Hotel."

Inside the cutting room, Goldfish developed a reputation as a bully, a surly loner who pushed around anybody who got in his way. His co-workers did not like him, and they often pulled pranks on him, like gluing the blades of his shears together when he left the room. On a good day, Goldfish could cut only two dozen gloves at best. He was fired.

New companies sprang up in Gloversville almost every week. Any two people who thought they could mobilize enough workers to produce more gloves than they were producing by themselves on an assembly line invested their savings in equipment, took over some abandoned church or cellar, and hung out a shingle. Goldfish found a job as a cutter at the firm of Lehr and Nelson.

He realized that he was too weak ever to become a great glove-cutter. If his forearms were not going to get harder, he reasoned, the skins he was cutting would have to get softer. Goldfish took to arriving early at the factory every morning, so that he could lay his hands on the most buttery skins. If they were sitting in piles for other cutters, he simply exchanged one of his for one of theirs.

Goldwyn also made a friend at Lehr and Nelson, a son of one of the owners. Abram Lehr was a good-looking young man, Goldfish's age and even slighter in build. He had a nasal voice and an easy manner. Lehr's father wanted Abe to learn the glove business from the ground up. He became Goldfish's benchmate. Not having to prove himself as a glove-cutter and having a benchmate who did, Lehr struck a bargain with Goldfish: He would give Sam some of his hides each day, with the understanding that they were to be stamped with Lehr's identification number. If Goldfish worked an extra hour or two each day, Lehr could work that much less. Goldfish found the opportunity to earn extra money irresistible. Putting in thirteen-hour workdays, he began making close to twenty-five dollars a week.

When Samuel Lehr moved his son to another department, he caught on to the scheme and summoned Goldfish to his house. As Goldwyn recalled years later, "He asked me what made a youngster work so hard and what I was after in life. I was surprised that anyone would think of such a question. 'How can you get ahead, except by working harder than everyone else?' I demanded."

Feeling more secure financially, Goldfish made an effort to meet people. Women intimidated him. He was not especially comely—his hairline was receding, he had large, pointed ears, penetrating gray eyes, beneath dark brows, and a long nose. His surprisingly high-pitched voice knotted up in his larynx; his lips went through great contortions in trying to form words in English. His accent was thick and his manner was brash. He courted only Jewish girls, but he limited himself even there.

By 1900, Gloversville had a socially active Jewish population and a new synagogue. Goldfish had nothing to do with any of its activities. He was, in the words of Ralph Moses (whose family had participated in Gloversville's primary industry since the late nineteenth century), "a young man in a hurry." Goldwyn sensed that any associations at this time—religious or social—would only slow him down.

Whether Sam Goldfish chose to belong or not, it was part of the Jewish tradition for the community to take care of its own. Even Fulton County had its matchmakers. In 1900, one of these introduced the twenty-one-year-old Goldfish to a girl named Mary Cohen.

The daughter of a leatherworker, Mary was a tall, pretty girl with a pale complexion and light-brown hair. She had come to Gloversville with her parents from Osmania, a small town outside Vilna. Goldfish went to Mary's house on an appointed night and fell instantly in love with her. He aggressively pursued her for six months, but she never took to him. Her resistance only excited him.

The reason Mary Cohen did not fall for Sam Goldfish, said her son years later, "was that he was a more recent immigrant. My mother had come here and gone to school here, and was thoroughly Americanized. She had taken singing and dancing lessons. Here she had grown up in a small community with a relatively small Jewish population, and she was more sensitive to being an immigrant. . . ." His crude speech and manners never appealed to her. "She was a young American, and Sam Goldfish was not." He asked Mary Cohen to marry him. She refused, and they stopped seeing each other.

Goldfish decided to better himself. He enrolled in night school at the Gloversville Business College, a converted mansion at the north end of town. Three nights a week, he studied English. He never learned to hold a pen properly—he rested it between the second and third fingers of his right hand—but over the next two years he managed to transform his childish scrawl into penmanship that was quite readable, even flowery. He also picked up basic American values; such copybook maxims as "Haste makes waste," "Work overcomes all," and "Early to bed and early to rise" seasoned his speech for the rest of his life. Goldfish never fully grasped the English language, mostly because he was in such a hurry to implement those tools he had.

In 1901, after only two years in America, Sam Goldfish thought he had saved enough money to start his own glove business. He found a partner in his new friend Charles Sesonske, who was from Kiev and just Goldfish's age. Sesonske had apprenticed in this country to a jeweler, who then sent him to Albany to learn how to fit eyeglasses. A short time later, Sesonske had struck out on his own to Gloversville, where he worked as both a jeweler and an optician. He, too, had some money that was burning a hole in his pocket. The two speculators rented a few rooms in a building at 148 South Main Street, about a mile from Sam's residence at 148 North School Street. They hired a few cutters and a few women to sew and "lay off." For an initial investment of one hundred dollars, they could buy enough leather from an independent local tanner to get started. "Goldfish and Sesonske" lasted only a few months. The two partners had thought through the production phase of their business but not the distribution. They lost their entire investment. Sesonske went back to being a jeweler, and Goldfish—broke—cast about for a new job.

Just then the Elite Glove Company needed a foreman in its cutting department. Goldfish met the two owners—the brothers Ralph and Isaac Moses—and talked himself into the job. With only two years of cutting experience, Goldfish was suddenly overseeing a department of one hundred cutters, most of them older than himself. He moved into a slightly better rooming house, at 104 South Main Street.

Ralph A. Moses had a vision about his business. While most glove manufacturers would willingly make any kind of glove for any buyer, Moses wanted to produce only high-fashion gloves of the best leather. "My father wouldn't have the Elite name in second-echelon stores," noted Ralph Moses, Jr. The founder preferred to take pride in everything he produced. Goldfish saw how Moses had turned a new company into one of the most successful in Gloversville, how Elite Fitwell Gloves were earning a national reputation. The concept of "making fewer, better" stuck with Goldfish for the rest of his life.

The twenty-two-year-old foreman performed well, running his department with an iron hand. Part of Goldfish's job was to watch for new talent in town—an especially fast glove-cutter or seamstress or (what with America producing more ladies' gloves) a designer.

Even the lowliest employee lived decently in Gloversville. Bungalows rented for five dollars a week, and boardinghouses offered food and a room for as little as three dollars. There was little class distinction, and crime was virtually nonexistent. Gloversville had nine public schools, a public library, and two newspapers. The Littauer family built a hospital. The city also boasted a twelve-hundred-seat opera house—almost never dark, because of traveling companies—and a smaller legitimate theater. A new hotel dominated the skyline.

The Kingsborough Hotel, of brick and brownstone rising five stories above the center of town, was the most modern building for miles around. On the ground floor, five large arches with awnings faced Main Street— two big windows flanking each side of the main portal. A few steps led up to the magnificent mahogany lobby, which gave way to a café-bar over-looking the street. Potted palms and big leather chairs sat on marble floors; shiny brass spittoons were conveniently placed. At the far end of the building was the dining room, which, for the extravagant tariff of one dollar, reputedly served up the finest dinner in central New York. Each of the one hundred five guest chambers was an outside room, complete with the latest conveniences—steam heat, hot and cold water, electric lights, and a telephone. Forty-eight of the rooms were connected with baths.

Sam Goldfish walked by the Kingsborough often. What impressed him most was not the grandeur but the sight of "drummers"—the traveling salesmen—who used to sit with their feet up on the window ledge in the café, obviously on expense accounts, drinking whiskey and smoking cigars.

On Wednesday, April 13, 1904, Samuel Goldfish went to neighboring Johnstown and formally applied to become a citizen of the United States. He was told to return on the first Monday of the following month with someone who had known him for the past five years and who could vouch for his residency.

He reappeared on May 2, 1904, with Harry Galinsky, a retail merchant in Johnstown who had once worked for Isaac Moses. Two thirds of the way down a long sheet of paper, Samuel Goldfish signed an oath of allegiance to support the Constitution of the United States of America. A county judge signed the bottom of the document, thereby ordering "that the said Samuel Goldfish be and he is hereby admitted to be a Citizen of the United States of America."

AFTER five years, Goldfish had "taxed" the glove business. He figured that of the thousands in the industry, only the six or seven major producers were taking big money out of it. A dozen successful smaller producers, the independents, were making a little less. Everyone else took home small change. Everyone except those drummers who sat with their feet up on the windowsills of the Kingsborough Hotel. They worked on commission, and the sky seemed to be their limit. Goldfish realized that he had traveled as far as he could within the factory walls of the Elite Glove Company. If he wanted to get anywhere in the business, it would not be by moving up in Gloversville. He would have to move out into the world.

In 1904, Sam Goldfish went to Ralph Moses and announced his desire to be a glove salesman. The request was so brash, it took Moses a moment to compose himself and say no. "I know gloves inside out," Goldfish argued. "I've made them. I can sell them. I don't want any money except enough to travel from town to town. I'll go on streetcars instead of trains and I'll stay at YMCAs instead of hotels." Moses was not interested until Goldwyn said, "Give me the company's toughest territory—where it has never sold gloves before."

Moses gave him a list of small New England towns, starting with Pittsfield, Massachusetts. "The leading store there has never carried our goods," he explained. "If you can sell them, you can sell anyone, and I'll make you a regular salesman."

The next week, Goldfish rode interurban trolleys forty miles to Albany, and another forty miles due east, across the state line into the little city of Pittsfield, in the Berkshires. When he arrived at the target store, a secretary informed him that the buyer was out. Goldfish returned the next day and received the same message. Goldfish returned a third day, and the buyer finally met with him. He explained that he had done business with another firm for twenty years and that the Elite representative was wasting his time. "Maybe I am," Goldfish told him, "but I intend to sit here until you look at my gloves. You don't have to buy them, but you shouldn't turn me down without seeing what I've got to sell. You may be missing a bargain." Inside the office, Goldfish opened his sample case.

"Is this the way they will look when they are delivered, or is this just a special?" the buyer asked. Goldfish explained every detail of the gloves' construction and said that if the man did not like what he received, he could send them back. The buyer began by ordering six pairs of ladies' elbow-length gloves (which sold for twenty-four dollars a dozen). Goldfish left the store with orders for another three hundred dollars' worth of merchandise.

Ralph Moses made Goldfish Elite's salesman for New England and upstate New York and advanced him part of his salary for immediate travel expenses. That night, Goldfish walked to the Kingsborough Hotel. Upon entering the main corridor, he turned left into the high-ceilinged front room, where the drummers played poker. Feeling lucky, he sat down at one of the tables. When he rose a few hours later, he did not have a cent to his name.

A number of other rough-and-tumble Jewish-Americans like Goldfish were looking for instant returns on their money. A small group of them shared one vision in particular; and within a few years, several made career moves in the same direction. In 1903, furriers Marcus Loew and Adolph Zukor met and talked of investing together. They had their eyes on the lines of people who stood ready to drop coins into nickelodeons. They chose to invest in their dreams separately, buying into penny arcades with facilities for projecting motion pictures.

That same year, the Warner brothers had the identical vision in Ohio. In 1904, William Fox saw it in Brooklyn. In 1907, Louis B. Mayer bought a former burlesque house in Haverhill, Massachusetts, called the Gem, known locally as "The Germ"; he changed its name to the Orpheum.

In Chicago, Carl Laemmle slapped a fresh coat of paint on a building he bought cheap and called his emporium of entertainment White Front.

It was only a matter of a few years before these new theater owners would discover each other. A similarly self-confident Lewis Selznick moved his jewelry business to New York City and was soon trafficking among them. And on his new route in New England, Sam Goldfish was inevitably to run into the hard-nosed Louis Mayer, and soon the others.

"THESE are certainly Glove Days," read the first page of the July 1906 issue of *The Glovers' Review*, the monthly trade magazine published in Gloversville. The new young salesman for the Elite Glove Company—"Men and Women's Fine Gloves: chamois, cape, glace, and mocha" (an especially soft leather made from the pelts of Arabian goats)—could not have taken to the road at a more propitious moment. And by all reports, Goldfish sold gloves in New England towns where they had never sold before. He turned the loneliness of the road into high-horsepower sales drive. He compensated for his limited vocabulary by being relentlessly enthusiastic, persistent, and blunt.

Goldfish was quickly earning fifteen thousand dollars a year, one hundred times what he had made six years earlier. When he was feeling flush, he took the trolley to Saratoga for a few days of recreation. There he once saw Lillian Russell, in a blue velvet dress, with Diamond Jim Brady, gambling at the Canfield Club. Goldfish himself was steering clear of the gaming tables just then in an attempt to save some money for a future venture. Two personal debts were also weighing heavily.

Goldfish had long told himself that if he succeeded in America, he intended to give his brothers the same opportunities he'd had to struggle for. In the fall of 1906, he sent Bernard the money to sail—second class—to America; he arrived in Boston that December, via England. One year later, brother Benjamin sailed from Liban, Russia. Each assumed the surname Goldfish. Sam set them up as glove salesmen, turning over to them some of the smaller New England accounts he no longer had time to service. Constantly on the road, the three brothers hardly ever saw each other.

By December 1907, the Elite Glove Company was expanding from coast to coast, and Goldfish's territory grew with it. Philadelphia, Baltimore, Pittsburgh, and Washington were added to his New England territory.

The following June, he traveled to Europe, to inspect foreign product lines and to visit his mother. Unable to face Poland again, he sent her money to meet him in Karlsbad, where they would take the waters. For several days they visited, almost never leaving their hotel. Years later, Hannah told her granddaughter Adela that she could not believe the change in her son in less than ten years. The most striking proof of his success was his apparel: Sam had become a clotheshorse, fond of snazzy suits and smart shoes. Hannah Gelbfisz was proud.

Everybody else noted changes in Goldfish as well. The entire industry knew of him. When he returned to Gloversville from the road, he spent the night at the home of his boss, Ralph Moses. If he was staying in the Gloversville environs for a few weeks, he would take a room at Mrs. Jones's boardinghouse, where the proprietress cooked special meals for him. Goldfish maintained friendships with Charlie Sesonske, who had opened a successful jewelry shop, and Abe Lehr, who ran his own tanning factory, then became vice president of another booming glove company, called Dempster & Place.

Even women saw Goldfish through new eyes. He still came on too strong, but he had acquired the alluring aura of success. One town resident, Daisy Inch, wrote Goldwyn forty years later, "an evening was not complete unless we had a dance or two with 'Sammy.' (Always so full of fun.) At that time you were the best salesman the Elite Glove Co. ever had." Goldwyn never forgot Miss Inch, but she did not come within a mile of another young lady, with whom he had become smitten.

Her name was Bessie Ginzberg. A fair-skinned beauty with lustrous eyes, she had a deferential air; around men she turned kittenish. Her father was a Russian émigré who had come to America in steerage at the age of fourteen and sold matches in Maine before making a small fortune in the diamond business. They lived in Boston, where Bessie studied to be a concert pianist. Her mother was the sister of the Moses brothers in Gloversville.

Sam chased Bessie for months, but she kept him at bay for the same reasons most women did. She found his energy refreshing after her staid Bostonian beaus, but she still hoped to meet somebody more refined. She took up with another glover, a manufacturer named Harry Louis, who went into business with her uncle Joseph at the Bacmo Glove Company. Yet another rejection left Goldfish alone but undaunted.

In the summer of 1910, Bessie Ginzberg and her mother and Harry Louis were vacationing on Long Lake in the Adirondacks. There she caught the eye of an off-duty performer named Jesse Lasky, who had a cornet act with his sister, Blanche. The children of a shoe salesman who died young, the Laskys had grown up in San Jose, where they developed a decidedly different manner than that of most Jews who were their contemporaries.

They were fully assimilated Americans, flag-waving vaudevillians. Their act was a medley of army bugle calls. Jesse, with his sweet and doughy face, had auditioned as a child for John Philip Sousa. Later he sank his father's life insurance benefits into gold mines in the Klondike, then embarked on a stage career, shanghaiing his sister to be his partner. Jesse's head was always full of theatrical fantasies and get-rich-quick schemes. While on the road, he began managing acts he liked; in time, he put together his own shows, always thinking big and bigger. He was known throughout his life as the nicest guy in show business.

Up at Long Lake in the summer of 1910, there was nothing fainthearted about Jesse Lasky. In front of her mother and Harry Louis, he asked Bessie Ginzberg to dance and literally swept her off her feet. Over the next few days, they spent as much time together as possible. Harry Louis withdrew to Gloversville. The following December, Jesse and Bessie married in Boston. Unlike most of his former inamoratas, Bessie Ginzberg Lasky remained in contact with Sam Goldfish, even after she and her groom set up house in New York City.

The Elite Glove Company was moving to Manhattan too. After years of temporary offices in the city, they opened permanent sales headquarters there. Sam Goldfish was the leading candidate for the position of sales manager. The job would mean less travel, more prestige and money. He would become a stockholder in the private company and supervise all the East Coast drummers. All Sam Goldfish needed to complete the picture of success he had envisioned for himself was a wife.

On one of his next visits to New York City, Bessie Lasky invited Sam to dinner and introduced him to Jesse's sister. After years on the road playing cornet with her brother, Jesse noted, his sister was "becoming weary of theatrical activities, although she didn't hate the production end as she had the performing. Still, she frequently voiced a desire to marry a solid, staid businessman and have done with the frantic pace of show business." Upon meeting this sweet, dark-haired woman with sad eyes, Sam—almost completely bald and wearing a pince-nez—fell instantly in love. The only difference this time was that Blanche responded positively.

Each desperately yearned for the solace of marriage. For the thirty-one-year-old Goldfish it would end his years of solitude; for the twenty-seven-year-old Blanche Lasky it meant an end to the crowds. After years of constant rejection, Sam Goldfish had found somebody to love. He told everybody he knew of his good fortune.

The Laskys had mixed feelings. Jesse knew Blanche was anxious about being unwed, still having to live with her mother and brother and his wife; but he had always imagined someone who would adore her as he did.

Lasky asked around about Sam Goldfish. His theater-owning friend Louis B. Mayer, up in Massachusetts, had encountered Goldfish and told Lasky he must break up the wedding plans at all costs, that Sam Goldfish was no husband for any man's sister. Blanche told her fiancé of Mayer's advice; and four weeks after their announcement, she broke off the engagement.

Never one to take no for an answer, Goldfish sold himself to Blanche as he had never sold before. As Jesse Lasky, Jr., observed years later, "Sam Goldfish could be the most charming man in the world when he wanted to be." On May 8, 1910, Rabbi Rudolph Grossman married Blanche Lasky to Samuel Goldfish before the few immediate family members. The ceremony was performed in the newlyweds' large brownstone at 10 West Sixty-first Street, far from the crowded slums Sam Goldfish had first encountered in New York.

3 Synapsis

I T WAS a marriage of inconvenience, in trouble from the start.

Blanche never loved him, and Sam knew it. Except for their mutual desire to be married, they had almost nothing in common. Each strong and stubborn, toughened by years on the road, they were severely mismatched. Years later Goldwyn admitted to a therapist, "She couldn't stand the sight of me."

After years of living by himself, Sam was uncompromising in his ways, and he expected his wife to surrender to his demands. She craved affection, which he was totally unprepared to give. Blanche spent most of her days with her mother, a few blocks away, crying. This bad situation worsened in January 1912; on the twenty-fifth, a child, named Ruth, was born. "I was an accidental daughter," she affirmed many years later. "I know she didn't want my father's baby."

The Goldfishes' social life revolved around the Laskys and a few of their theatrical friends. Jesse and Bessie, also new parents, proved to be the best buffers between Sam and Blanche; but Sam always found Jesse Lasky a little foolish and never really liked him. Lasky fell further in Sam's estimation with his latest investment, his most extravagant theatrical venture yet, a production of the Folies-Bergère. "I lost everything I had accumulated—about $100,000—" Lasky recounted, "salvaging only the framed first dollar taken in at the box-office." For all the Goldfishes' marital contention, Blanche at least took comfort in being rid of show business.

"Despite doubts and dogmas; despite demagogues and defamers; despite

27

bugaboos and bugbears, business is better and improving," reported *The Glovers' Review* in the July 1912 issue. For Goldwyn's money, all those dangers to the prosperity of the glove business were wrapped up in one man—Woodrow Wilson. The President's solution to the rising costs of business was to lower tariffs, thereby promoting the importation of foreign goods. At noon on April 7, 1913, a special session of the Sixty-third Congress, called by President Wilson, convened. Congressman Oscar W. Underwood, of Alabama, introduced in the House of Representatives H.R. 10—a comprehensive bill to reduce tariff duties. It specified rates for each style and hide of glove, in some cases 60 percent reductions from existing duties. Sam Goldfish considered this a sop to big business and the first step toward stamping out scores of small concerns in Gloversville. He thought it paved the way for the largest glove manufacturers to become little more than glove importers.

On April 14, 1913, Gloversville and Johnstown, New York, shut down for the day in protest against the Underwood bill. Stores, offices, factories, and mills in the twin cities closed so that the employees might join in a "monster parade." Several thousand workers and merchants took to the streets, marching in sections behind large banners bearing their companies' names, all "in the common cause of striving to avert what they believe would mean disaster to the industry upon which the fifty thousand inhabitants of Fulton county are practically entirely dependent." The House passed the Underwood bill without changing a comma in the scheduling on gloves. There would be a summer's grace before the Senate doubtless passed the bill, thus clearing its enactment into law.

Goldfish worked through the season in the new Elite offices in Room 1405 at 100 Fifth Avenue, between Fifteenth and Sixteenth streets. Even in the summer torpor, he liked to walk home to his apartment. One especially hot, muggy afternoon that August, Goldfish altered his routine. He chanced into the Herald Square Theater on Thirty-fourth Street, which showed "flickers."

"Going into a nickelodeon wasn't considered in entirely good taste," Goldwyn remembered years later. Upon entering, he knew why. Inside the darkened theater, he was almost overcome by the heavy odor of peanuts and perspiration. For five or ten minutes at a time, images—cops and robbers and barroom slapstick—fluttered around on a crude idea of a screen. A cowboy on horseback, identified as "Broncho Billy," suddenly appeared, jumping onto a moving train.

Goldfish left the dingy three-hundred-seat theater and walked uptown. By the time he had reached the southwest corner of Central Park, his mind was made up. The same lightning bolt that had struck Zukor and

Laemmle and Fox and Loew and Mayer and the Warner brothers now elec-
trified him. He could not get that image of Broncho Billy out of his head.
It had, Goldwyn pinpointed years later, "brought me into a whole new,
exciting world and I wanted to be a part of it."

THOMAS EDISON was not the first to experiment with animated pictures.
Several Europeans had played with sequential photography of an action in
progress and with a novelty item called the zoetrope, or "wheel of life"—
a small cylinder with pictures that depicted movement when revolved on
a vertical spindle. In 1881, a young Englishman named William Kennedy
Laurie Dickson suddenly appeared in Menlo Park, New Jersey, and convinced Edison to take him on as an assistant. On October 17, 1888, their
work had advanced to the point where Edison could state, "I am experimenting upon an instrument which does for the Eye what the phonograph
does for the Ear, which is the recording and reproduction of things in
motion, and in such a form as to be both Cheap practical and convenient."
He called it a Kinetoscope.

In April 1894, motion pictures moved from the realm of science into
industry. Twenty-five Kinetoscopes were shipped to Atlantic City and Chicago and to a New York storefront at 1155 Broadway. Edison had not
worked out the synchronization of sound with the pictures, so the fifty-
foot loop of film passed before the viewers' eyes in silence, except for the
groans of the machinery. The price for sixteen seconds of "monkeyshines"
was twenty-five cents, the equivalent of a skilled worker's hourly wage.
The machines earned $120 their opening day.

The demand for motion picture projectors, film, and cameras was on,
and the supply kept pace. Once the novelty of their inventions wore off,
the film pioneers realized it was not the machinery that would lure audiences so much as the images they could offer. William Dickson left Edison
to start the American Mutoscope & Biograph Company; and, in 1896, one
of his machines projected on a screen footage of the Empire State Express
rounding a curve; the audience screamed in terror as the great New York
Central locomotive barreled toward them. Edison responded to Biograph's
films with such displays of action as *Sea Waves at Coney Island* and *Fire
Engines Responding to an Alarm.* One of Edison's cameramen, Edwin S. Porter, began creating such "story pictures" as *The Great Train Robbery.* Countless imitators followed.

Motion pictures packed in audiences everywhere. It seemed that anybody who invested in a storefront and projection equipment—like Zukor
or Loew—could make a killing. Harry Warner and his brothers opened a

theater in Newcastle, Pennsylvania. Its ninety-nine seats were rented by the day from the local undertaker. In 1905, nearly one hundred "nickelodeons" opened in Pittsburgh alone. These small operations gobbled up product on an almost daily basis, purchasing films outright. After they had saturated their audience, theater owners wanted to trade their films for others. Carl Laemmle established a "film exchange." It soon dawned on producers that they stood to make more money renting their pictures than selling them.

A number of Chicagoans realized the gains to be made at the front end of the business. Small-time actor G. M. Anderson (born Aronson) had made his bow in Porter's *Great Train Robbery*, then began to produce his own pictures. William N. Selig, who developed his own projector, also produced films, right in the Chicago tenderloin. On October 24, 1907, a local judge ruled that William Selig's camera had infringed on the Edison patents. Fearing subpoenas, several other filmmakers met at lunch in Chicago to discuss an arrangement they all might make with Edison.

An unexpectedly harmonious meeting in New Jersey resulted in the formation of the Motion Picture Patents company, by which all picturemakers could be licensed under the Edison patents in consideration of royalty payments. This "Trust" controlled most motion picture production through its participants' pooling of patents. They exerted as much strength over exhibition by threatening to cut off their supply of films to any theaters that bought outside product.

As the appetite for films increased, new cameras claiming new patents appeared. Pirating continued and independent film exchanges sprang up. In the summer of 1909, Carl Laemmle, finding it hard to keep his exchange adequately fed, decided to produce films himself. The Independent Motion Picture company—IMP, as the company was known from the start—got an immediate boost when Edwin Porter left Edison to produce its pictures.

The larger companies nurtured their output under greenhouse conditions, indoors. The Edison company built a studio in the Bronx; Biograph set up shop in a brownstone at 11 East Fourteenth Street in Manhattan. A procession of actors appeared regularly outside their doors, looking for work.

Among these ranks was a tall and lanky Kentuckian. David Wark Griffith had escaped his impoverished childhood by joining a traveling theater company as an actor and a hopeful playwright. He landed the part of a woodsman in Edwin Porter's *Rescued from an Eagle's Nest* at the Edison studios. Finding the door open to him at Biograph, he acted in the odd picture and sold several scenarios. In 1908, Biograph found itself short-handed in filling its orders and assigned a film to the thirty-three-year-old Griffith.

Griffith understood the intensity achieved by moving the camera close to an actor's face. He demanded a more naturalistic style of acting from the phenomenally gifted group of players that was at his disposal. Their names did not matter, because screen actors were not given billing. In time, however, certain performers appeared and reappeared in similar roles, and their faces began to register with an adoring public.

At first, only one thespian at the Biograph studio had distinguished herself from the rest of the chorus—Florence Lawrence. She was known only as the "Biograph Girl." In 1909, Carl Laemmle lured her away. After staging a publicity ruse about her alleged demise, he announced that the "Biograph Girl" was not dead but simply reborn as the "Imp Girl."

The next actor to command "movie fans'" attention was Florence Lawrence's successor as the "Biograph Girl," a Canadian named Gladys Smith. The public fell in love with this goldilocks of breathtaking innocence, who played a character known as "Little Mary." She had adopted the Christian name early in her stage career and traded in her surname for a family appellation, Pickford. Just as popular, at first, was G. M. Anderson, the bit player in *The Great Train Robbery*. After forming Essanay Productions, he starred in a series of weekly motion pictures—376 of them—portraying the American screen's first western hero, Broncho Billy.

SAM GOLDFISH walked directly from the nickelodeon on Thirty-fourth Street to his brother-in-law's apartment, passionate about launching a career in motion pictures. In those days of continuous vaudeville shows, theater owners used to run "flickers" every so often just to shoo patrons out of the theater; motion pictures were known in the trade as "chasers." Lasky asked how long Sam had been contemplating this idea. "About a half hour," Goldfish replied; "as long as it took me to get home. I've made a decision."

His initial thought was to become a theater owner. After pricing a few theaters, he assumed that producing films demanded less investment than exhibiting them.

For the rest of the summer of 1913, Sam Goldfish talked of little but Broncho Billy and the wide-open range of motion pictures. Jesse, still smarting from his experience with the Folies-Bergère, remained skeptical. His former cornet partner had had her fill of show business and offered absolutely no support. Not until the close of the season did Goldfish find somebody who would listen to him—a graduate of Harvard and Harvard Law School named Arthur Friend.

Friend's German-immigrant father, bored in the clothing business, had gone west in a covered wagon and sold shoes in Sacramento just when gold was discovered. Like most forty-niners, he went bust; then he traveled the country. In Boston, he found a wife, with whom he moved to Milwaukee and had eleven children. Arthur was a young boy when his father suddenly died.

Friend grew to six feet three inches and had caring, bespectacled eyes. Theatrical yearnings surfaced in college; and almost immediately after graduating from law school he returned to his hometown. Three years later, in 1909, he organized the Friend Players, a company that included Ruth Chatterton, Lenore Ulric, and Lowell Sherman. When his aspirations outgrew the city limits, he moved to New York, where he opened a law practice and fell in with a number of theatrical people. His passion for cards enabled him to meet a number of sharp young Jews who lived on the Upper West Side. Through a dentist, he came to play poker with Jesse Lasky and Sam Goldfish.

In late summer, the Goldfishes, the Laskys, and the Friends (Arthur had married an actress from Milwaukee) vacationed together in Naples, Maine. Jesse spent most of his time out on Sebago Lake, avoiding Sam's constant babbling about motion pictures. But Friend paid attention, especially to Goldfish's idea that a single filmed story could run longer than the present one or two reels.

Back in New York, Sam kept badgering his brother-in-law. He argued that there were great opportunities for producers who could serve up "something different from Western stuff and slap-stick comedies. . . . And why should your entertainment have to be so short? If it's a good story there's no reason why it couldn't run through five reels. . . . We could sell good films and long films all over the world."

At last Jesse responded. "I know a business that would be wonderful," he said, "—tamales. They make them in San Francisco. They are wonderful things. In the East you never hear about them." Lasky was convinced that if they "tied up the tamale concession in New York we could make a fortune."

"That's great," Goldfish replied. "Why don't you do the tamales? I'm going to do this." Then over lunch at the Hoffman House, a popular Broadway hangout, Goldfish used an old sales trick—"which is to show the other fellow how your idea will be to his advantage." Goldfish suggested calling the company the Jesse L. Lasky Feature Play Company.

"That sounds better than 'Lasky's Hot Tamales,' doesn't it?" he asked. Lasky finally agreed. Now they needed someone who knew how to make motion pictures.

Goldfish invited D. W. Griffith to lunch and put his ideas on the table. Griffith just sat there, his clear blue eyes peering out of his aquiline face in bemusement. "A very interesting project," he finally offered, "and if you can show me a bank deposit of two hundred and fifty thousand dollars I think we might talk."

Goldfish thought they should look elsewhere—for someone whose self-assuredness could compensate for any lack of experience. He and Lasky and Friend had just such a friend in common, Cecil Blount DeMille.

The de Mille family was already well known in theatrical circles. Cecil's father, Henry, was an actor turned writer who collaborated with David Belasco for many years. Cecil's brother, William, also became a successful playwright, and married the daughter of philosopher Henry George. Sometime after Henry de Mille died, his wife, Beatrice, took an office in the Knickerbocker Theater Building on Broadway and became an authors' representative, one of the leading play brokers of her day.

In 1910, Jesse Lasky had wanted to produce a musical, and he inquired about William's availability. Mrs. de Mille explained that he was heavily booked but that her other son was shaping into a good playwright. "Mr. Lasky could never be anything but urbane," Cecil B. DeMille recalled years later, "and he made it quite clear that he did not want Cecil; he wanted William. But . . . mother had a way with her; and mother had her way. When the converstion ended, Mr. Lasky, without quite knowing how it happened, was saddled with Cecil."

Already the younger de Mille was trying to step out of his brother's shadow: William, the intellectual, knew Shakespeare by heart; Cecil used to contend that "the greatest poem in the English language" was Kipling's "If." He compensated for his lack of depth with flair, overcoming his insecurities with a flamboyant personality. He took to capitalizing the *d* in his surname. He was full of derring-do and was willing to attempt anything. His first musical with Lasky, entitled *California,* was a mild success.

DeMille wrote a few more operettas for Lasky, and with their mutual "spirit of adventure," they became fast friends. After several years of Broadway, DeMille was eager for a change. "I was 32," DeMille recounted, "Jesse a year older. I was, quite seriously, thinking of going to Mexico to join a revolution. I forget what revolution was brewing or boiling at the time there. Any revolution would have done. . . ." Goldfish thought DeMille's participation in his motion picture venture would keep Lasky's dying interest alive.

At the grill at the Claridge Hotel on Forty-fourth Street, DeMille joined the Jesse L. Lasky Feature Play Company as director-general. They outlined the partnership on the back of their menu. "Jesse would head the company," DeMille remembered. "We were all glad to have his name on it, for his was the only one of our names which meant anything as a theatrical producer. I would make the picture, or pictures, if the company survived the first one. Sam Goldfish would sell them. Arthur Friend would handle the corporate and legal side."

A few wrinkles needed ironing out: DeMille had seen but one or two pictures in his life, to say nothing of never having directed; the Lasky Company had no idea what they were going to produce; and Samuel Goldfish was still sales manager for the Elite Glove Company.

If Goldfish had second thoughts about abandoning the glove trade, they were laid to rest on October 3, 1913. That night, President Wilson signed the tariff bill that the American glove industry had been dreading for a year. If that was not enough to convince Goldfish that it was time to change careers, his boss, Ralph Moses, provided the final stimulus.

"Sam," Moses said that fall, according to his son, "you're not the type of man who'll be a great man in this business. You want too much too fast. In the glove business, nothing comes fast." Despite Goldfish's phenomenal sales record, Moses said he would never become a partner in the family firm. Furthermore, the entire glove industry was stretched to its limits; it was already divided up among companies that were well established. In some instances, second generations of glove manufacturers were running their family businesses.

His head reeling over the possibilities of the motion picture business, Goldfish still showed up daily at his fourteenth-floor office on lower Fifth Avenue. There he discovered a way to import foreign gloves without paying duty. Goldfish ordered crates of the finest ladies' dress gloves from France, but instead of having them shipped in pairs, he requested that they be separated into boxes of right-hand gloves and left-hand gloves, each shipment sent to a different addressee at a different American port. Goldfish planned to let the parcels go unclaimed, leaving them to be auctioned after a few months by the two different port authorities. At each auction he would be the only bidder, for clearly hundreds of gloves for one hand were completely useless without their mates. Goldfish bought them for a song, matched them, and was able to sell highest-quality gloves far below market price.

Realizing he was never going to be a power broker in gloves, he served notice. He would remain with Elite through the end of the year. Moses wished him well in his new career. With some ten thousand dollars' savings to show for his fourteen years in gloves, the company's top salesman prepared for what he called his "first really big gamble."

Goldfish made an appointment with Thomas Edison himself and drove down to West Orange, where he encountered the inventor fussing in his laboratory in his efforts to synchronize sound with his motion pictures. Goldfish explained that he was about to enter the motion picture production business and he was sizing up the equipment on the market. Because of his deafness, Edison heard little of what Goldfish had to say; but he granted him permission to send his director to the Edison studios to see how films were made.

DeMille went to 188th Street near Bronx Park and watched an Edison director and cameraman set up a camera and point it toward a stone wall alongside a road. DeMille remembered: "The director called for action. The cameraman cranked. A girl emerged from a hedge, climbed the wall, and ran down the road, looking back in terror from time to time at some unseen pursuer. A man met her, stopped her, and they talked, in pantomime of course, with much emotive gesticulation." After a day of observation, DeMille reported to Lasky and Goldfish, "If that's the way they make pictures I think I will be knighted after the first year." He never returned for another lesson.

Years later, the other partners all credited Goldfish with charting the course their company should follow. The four men agreed their films should stand for quality, that they should not simply grind out two-reel sausages. "We determined to make it a policy of our company that all our pictures would be, as we called it, feature-length," said DeMille, "long enough to tell a real story, with the same elaboration of plot that an audience could expect from a stage play."

The company was severely undercapitalized at fifteen thousand dollars—half from Goldfish and half from Lasky; Friend was a partner by dint of his role as legal counsel, and DeMille because of his willingness to take a flier. Each drew one hundred dollars a week in salary. Lasky remained active in vaudeville—"and I didn't blame him," Goldwyn recalled—producing acts for the Keith-Albee circuit. It behooved Goldfish and DeMille to find a property to film. They turned to Broadway, hoping to get a minor stage success—one whose story had proved itself sound but whose film rights would come cheap.

DeMille thought *The Squaw Man*, a hit play by Edwin Milton Royle a few seasons back, suited them perfectly. It was a western with a love story, an infallible combination in Goldfish's mind because it would appeal to women as well as men; and it could be filmed outdoors, no small consideration to a band of gypsy filmmakers without a studio. One afternoon at the Lambs Club, Royle agreed to sell the rights for some four thousand dollars, a figure within their means.

Fortune smiled again, as Lasky and DeMille were able to lasso the matinee idol Dustin Farnum, who had triumphed on Broadway in *The Virginian*. This was no small stroke of luck, because Farnum was generally booked in a play, and few successful legitimate actors would appear in motion pictures, for fear of tarnishing their reputation. "Even unemployed actors would not consent to appear in films unless you guaranteed not to disclose their names on the screen or to the press," Lasky recalled. As company bursar, Goldfish pushed the idea of Farnum's working for shares in the company instead of salary. The actor was willing, as long as they stuck to the original idea of filming in Fort Lee, New Jersey, just across the Hudson River, where many one-reel westerns were shot. Plans changed because it was becoming well known that the Motion Picture Patents Trust had goon squads to bust up small, independent productions. Lasky, who realized that he had to maintain DeMille's interest in the project, urged moving the production to the real West. Farnum said he wanted to be paid in cash, up front, two hundred fifty dollars a week for five weeks.

The Lasky Company got Oscar Apfel, a young director who had worked for the Edison company, to watch over DeMille's shoulder. He would serve as both technical adviser and shotgun against any intruding members of the Trust. Albert Gandolfi was hired as cameraman. The only major decision still unresolved was the location for shooting the picture. They needed someplace out of town—far enough from the clutches of the Trust and western enough to suit the story's setting. Lasky, traveling with one of his vaudeville acts, Hermann the Great, had once seen some Indians in Flagstaff, Arizona.

In December 1913, DeMille, Apfel, Gandolfi, Farnum, and his dresser, Fred Kley, boarded a train for Flagstaff. Arthur Friend still had a lucrative law practice; Jesse Lasky had his career as a Broadway producer; Cecil B. DeMille, who had been feeling restless anyway, could always fall back on playwriting. As for Sam Goldfish, then thirty-four, his entire future was packed onto that train. Virtually his entire nest egg for the support of his wife and almost two-year-old baby was gone, putting an already shaky marriage in further jeopardy.

Sam went to Pennsylvania Station to see off the entourage. Cecil, with all his gear, arrived by chauffeur-driven car; the rest of his family regarded this venture, his niece Agnes recalled, as "the purest folly." At the last minute, the partners had tried to induce Cecil's brother, Bill, into investing five thousand dollars; but, as Cecil recalled, "he said he thought he had better keep his money to pay my fare home from the West when, as

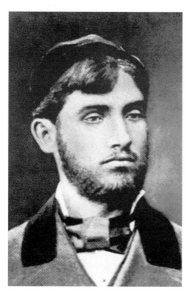

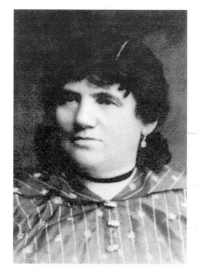

Samuel Goldwyn's parents, Aaron and
Hannah Gelbfisz, c. 1875.

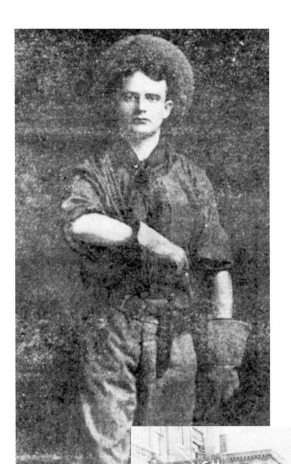

LEFT: Goldwyn, age twenty, in Gloversville, New York, where after his illegal entry into the United States in 1899 the newly named Samuel Goldfish became a factory worker. BELOW: Gloversville's Kingsborough Hotel at the turn of the century. To Sam Goldfish, it was the height of luxury.

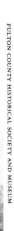

RIGHT: Blanche and her brother Jesse Lasky, 1905 — "The Musical Laskys" of vaudeville. To escape from show business, Blanche married Sam Goldfish, then the leading salesman for the Elite Glove Company. BELOW: The founders of Famous Players–Lasky (which became Paramount Pictures) in 1916. Left to right: Jesse Lasky, Adolph Zukor, Samuel Goldfish, Cecil B. DeMille, and Zukor's brother-in-law, Al Kaufman.

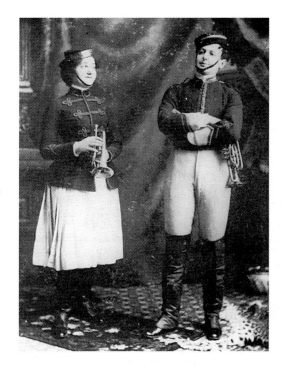

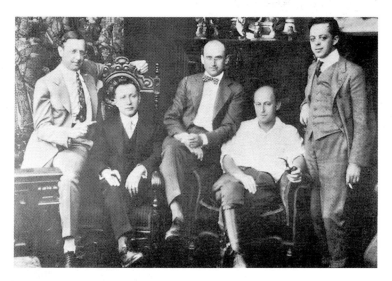

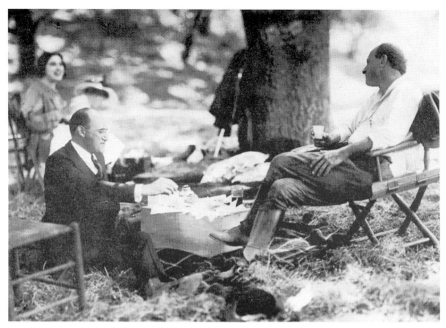

ABOVE: Sam Goldfish and DeMille on the set of *Joan the Woman*, Hollywood, 1916. Their star, Geraldine Farrar, is in the background. BELOW: With Farrar's co-star Hobart Bosworth.

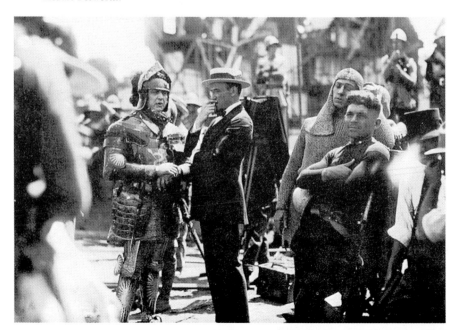

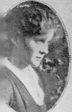
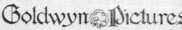
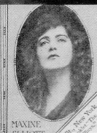
Sam Goldfish formed a new production company in 1916 with Edgar Selwyn
(INSET) and his brother, Archibald. A short time later, to the Selwyns' dismay,
Goldfish made the company name of Goldwyn his own.

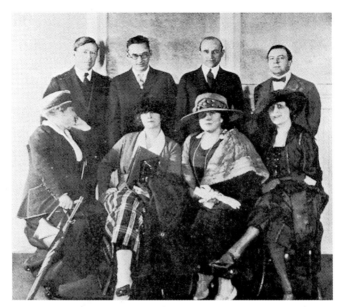

ABOVE: Goldwyn with seven of his Eminent Authors. Back row, left to right, LeRoy Scott, Gouverneur Morris, Goldwyn, Rupert Hughes; front row, Gertrude Atherton, Katherine Newlin Burt, Mary Roberts Rinehart, Rita Weiman. BELOW: Goldwyn and his new Culver City lot, flanked by Mabel Normand and Rupert Hughes on the left, Geraldine Farrar and Rex Beach on the right.

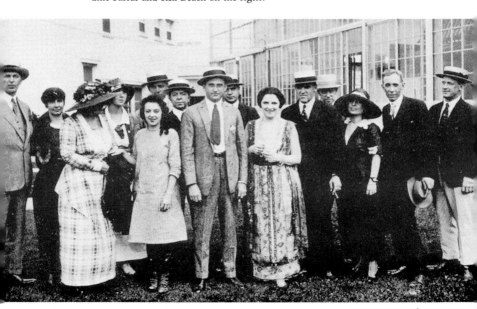

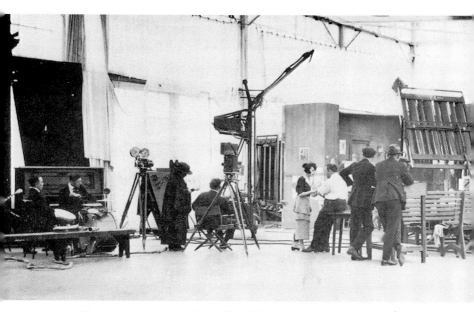

Mabel Normand conferring with Victor "Pops" Schertzinger, 1919. A jazz combo awaits the resumption of shooting. The silent screen's leading comedienne—part Cinderella, part lovable scamp (BELOW)—stole Goldwyn's heart . . . until one fateful weekend together in Saratoga.

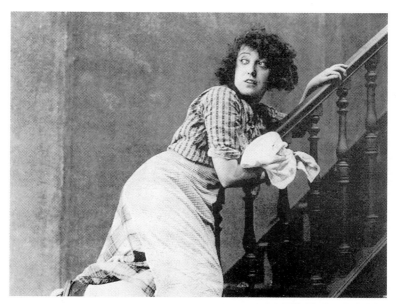

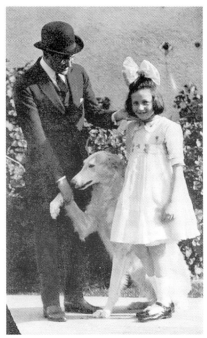 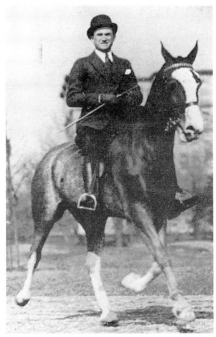

ABOVE LEFT: Goldwyn with his daughter, Ruth, c. 1920. After Sam divorced her mother, his visits with the child were infrequent. ABOVE RIGHT: Sam Goldwyn, ousted from the Goldwyn Company, took up horseback riding, tennis, and golf, and even commissioned the writing of his autobiography—all part of the process of "inventing himself," during the summer of 1922. BELOW: A Hollywood lunch for Dr. A. H. Giannini, the founder of the Bank of America and Goldwyn's financier. At head of table are Sol Lesser, Dr. Giannini, Joseph Schenck, and Mack Sennett; Jack Warner and B. P. Schulberg sit at the center of the far side of the table; Goldwyn sits fifth from the left on the near side.

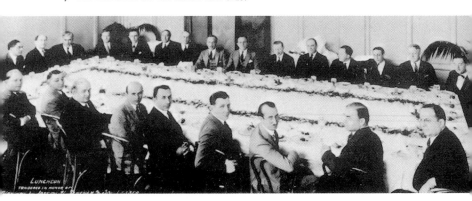

he confidently expected, the company folded up." Lasky was supposed to board the train but at the last minute backed out. As he recalled, "I had no great personal faith in the project and I couldn't see myself wasting time in Arizona when I had business to look after in the East. So I said good-by to the rest of them at the train and promised Cecil I'd come out if he needed me."

Blanche Lasky Goldfish was not among the well-wishers at the station. She wanted no part in this wild-goose chase. Throughout these last few weeks of frenzied preparation, the retired vaudevillian kept her distance and held her tongue. As the Santa Fe pulled out of the station, Sam Goldfish held his breath. His marriage and his career were riding on the boxcars rolling westward.

4 Dramatis Personae

I HAVE SINCE wondered whether a little more knowledge would have deterred them," mused William de Mille many years after his kid brother and the rest of the crew boarded the Arizona-bound train. "I am inclined to think not. Youth they had to a pronounced degree, and energy—ye gods! what energy!" De Mille's daughter Agnes thought it was more than that. Even as a child, she felt that what fired the hearts of the men in that enterprise was unmitigated greed—"pure lust for money and power."

By the time Cecil DeMille left New York, he had viewed several motion pictures and was "beginning to talk as an expert." Heading into the Arizona desert, the director-general and Oscar Apfel penciled twenty pages of script that combined Apfel's knowledge of motion pictures with DeMille's knowledge of dramatic construction. They hoped to get it typed in Arizona.

What DeMille encountered as the train pulled into the station in Flagstaff has been described as a siege of everything from rainstorms to blizzards to all-out war between cattlemen and sheepmen. In fact, it was a beautiful day—sunny and clear. The problem was that when he stepped off the train, he looked around and saw only dull flatlands, nothing like the West of his imaginings. He suddenly remembered tales he had heard of moviemaking in California. Before the train had watered up and whistled, DeMille and company were back on board. Through the "red and orange Indian mountains," they headed into the setting sun, until they reached Los Angeles.

It was like coming into Eden—temperate air, fragrant with orange blossoms, eucalyptus, and jasmine; palm trees here and there fanning the blue skies; geraniums, bougainvillea, roses, and poinsettias growing wild; the snow-capped San Gabriel Mountains looming over desert on one hand, valleys of citrus and grapes on the other, and yielding to the gentle slopes of the Santa Monica Mountains; then an unobstructed vista for miles, all the way to the Pacific Ocean. Three hundred thousand people called this loosely connected archipelago of communities home, four hundred square miles of land that held a century of avaricious history, brazen desire for the land and all its potential—gold, oil, water, railroads.

Upon arrival at the old Santa Fe depot, DeMille and crew took taxicabs to Los Angeles's finest hotel, the Alexandria, downtown at 210 West Fifth Street. They immediately attracted the attention that motion picture people and their equipment continue to draw. Two men in particular took special interest in the Easterners. L. L. Burns and Harry Revier owned and operated a small laboratory ten miles outside the city, near some space they thought might double as a studio. Burns and Revier drove DeMille through a great expanse of open country down a thoroughfare called Prospect Avenue, to "a broad, shady avenue" called Vine Street. There stood the "studio."

It was a barn—a large, L-shaped building of dark-green wood, stained with the droppings of pepper bark. It ran south on Vine and east along Selma Avenue, reaching back into a citrus grove. The owner of the barn, Jacob Stern, was willing to rent the space so long as he could garage his carriage and horses there.

Just when the New York office of the Jesse L. Lasky Feature Play Company assumed DeMille was capturing Arizona on film, a telegram from Cecil arrived, stating, as Lasky remembered: "FLAGSTAFF NO GOOD FOR OUR PURPOSE. HAVE PROCEEDED TO CALIFORNIA. WANT AUTHORITY TO RENT BARN IN PLACE CALLED HOLLYWOOD FOR $75 A MONTH. REGARDS TO SAM."

"Sam," Jesse remembered, "hit the ceiling." Lasky immediately defended DeMille's decision despite his own halfhearted belief. Goldfish insisted on calling the company home. Such unilateral decisionmaking was unacceptable; Goldfish had never liked the notion of their filming so far beyond his purview; and DeMille had a tendency toward excess that always troubled Goldfish. Then Sam realized the return trip would only cost additional time and money. The license to stay offered at least the chance of a film being made. "AUTHORIZE YOU TO RENT BARN," read the return wire, "BUT ON MONTH-TO-MONTH BASIS. DON'T MAKE ANY LONG COMMITMENT. REGARDS. JESSE AND SAM."

DeMille opened a motion picture studio. He hired a secretary, who, for fifteen dollars a week, provided her own typewriter. A partition was erected in the barn to create an office, and five stables became dressing rooms. A stage with canvas diffusers was constructed outside, and backdrops were painted. DeMille interviewed prospective actors right away and drew a large number of local talent, mostly cowboys and a few young actors who had appeared in one- and two-reel films. DeMille's ledger noted that he hired an extra named Hal Roach for five dollars a day and rejected Jane Darwell, because the actress was already commanding sixty dollars a week. Orange trees were dug up, and a big sign announcing the company's name was painted. The budget of *The Squaw Man* quickly ran up to $47,000, more than twice the company's assets. New York would somehow have to meet these needs.

Goldfish scrounged among his friends but found no backers. The Laskys were fast souring on the entire undertaking. Goldfish was able to borrow a few thousand dollars from a Philadelphia bank, but that only bandaged the financial hemorrhaging. The company's viability depended on a large transfusion of money.

Goldfish announced in the newspapers that the Lasky Company was going to produce a yearly slate of five-reel pictures, one a month, and that each state's rights for those films could be purchased in advance. In the matter of *The Squaw Man,* he guaranteed "a prospective epic of the screen for which theaters would be able to charge as much as 25 cents," top price those days. "The films you have seen so far are only rehearsals for what we're going to do," Goldwyn remembered saying. "The time is coming when the best plays and the best actors will be in pictures. This is going to be the greatest entertainment medium in the world."

Fortunately, Adolph Zukor had just successfully financed a five-reel version of *The Prisoner of Zenda.* Expansive motion picture stories were catching on with the public. Though the Trust filmmakers rejected this new idea as too expensive and referred to these lengthy films as "the feature craze," the independent exchanges were grabbing every new five-reeler they could.

Goldfish received immediate requests, starting with a California theater manager who plunked down four thousand dollars for the rights to show *The Squaw Man.* Then Goldfish began guaranteeing the Lasky Company's roster of a dozen films for the next year. He made deals with fourteen states' rights buyers, who made deposits on all twelve films. They did not realize they were in fact paying the costs of the first.

On December 29, 1913, a sunny Monday, DeMille gathered the members of his cast and crew outside the Stern barn for a group photograph. Then the shooting of motion pictures began—six days a week, so long as there was daylight, for a month. *The Squaw Man* was not, as has often been claimed, the first motion picture made in Hollywood. In fact, several small movie companies had filmed one- and two-reelers there for years; Griffith had made annual hegiras since 1910. The independents appreciated the distance from the Trust raiders and the proximity to Mexico in case they suddenly had to flee; more experienced filmmakers appreciated the profusion of sunlight and the variety of settings—snowy mountains, deserts, a city, and the sea all within a day's drive. *The Squaw Man,* which would use most of those locations, became the first *feature-length* film produced in Hollywood.

During one lull early in the shoot, DeMille noticed a crew member putting a lighted cigarette up to a discarded scrap of film and saw it vanish in a puff of smoke. Realizing how fragile these "permanent" pictures were, he made an extravagant request: that two negatives be taken of every scene in the picture—one to be kept in the barn and one in his home.

After a few days of shooting, DeMille entered the small, unlighted laboratory set up next to the barn, and before his eyes had adjusted to the darkness, he felt something underfoot. When he picked it up, his first panic-stricken thought was confirmed. All the footage of *The Squaw Man* to date had been scraped and torn and strewn. It would have been curtains for the Lasky Company had it not been for the extra negative at DeMille's house in Cahuenga Canyon. The perpetrator was never unmasked, but the director-general always assumed it was one of the people in that photograph taken on the first day of shooting, someone bribed by the Trust.

DeMille kept such catastrophes from the New York office. He already knew better than to trouble the company's treasurer with situations beyond his control. Besides, Goldfish was busy rustling up states' rights money. Once most of *The Squaw Man* was "in the can," DeMille invited Lasky to inspect his studio.

Lasky was present for the filming of the final shots of *The Squaw Man;* and in a few days it was completely assembled, as simple as that. The straightforward tale of an Indian maiden who saves the life of a British aristocrat, bears his child, then commits suicide required little more editing than the pasting together of each day's footage. DeMille and Lasky announced a screening of the film right in the barn for all who had worked on it and their families. Everybody connected with the film was there, except the company's legal counsel, Arthur Friend, and the man who had launched the entire venture and kept it afloat. Goldfish waited anxiously in New York for a telegram of good news.

Over fifty people gathered that night at the end of January 1914 in the big, drafty barn out in the desolate flats of Hollywood, coyotes howling all around them. The lights were turned out and the projector started to whir. "The title of 'The Squaw Man' went on the screen," DeMille remembered, "and promptly skittered off at the top of the screen. The actors appeared, and as promptly climbed out of sight, sometimes leaving their feet at the top of the screen and their heads peeking up from the bottom." They rewound the film and threaded the machine again. When they started it up, they encountered the same snag. The film looked all right, and there was no evidence of further sabotage, but the mysterious problem remained. The disheartened audience dispersed, leaving Lasky and DeMille alone to sulk over their ruination.

The thought of prison sentences passed through DeMille's mind, for Sam Goldfish had raised a lot of money that was tied up in a mile of worthless celluloid. Almost immediately after informing Sam of the catastrophe, Jesse left for San Francisco, where he was having trouble with one of his vaudeville acts at the Orpheum, Lasky's Redheads. He thanked God he had a career to fall back on.

Even in uncharted territory, Sam Goldfish never lost his sense of true north. He went straight to the top, this time calling on Sigmund Lubin of Philadelphia, an impish German-Jewish immigrant who had bought into the film business as early as 1896. Now in his sixties and known as "Pop," he was reputed to be the most knowledgeable man about film there was. He was also the one maverick member of the Motion Picture Patents Trust. Goldfish knew that Lubin had fought against the Edison company before the Trust was established; and he had since been known to rent out his Philadelphia rooftop studio to independents. Short of suing the Eastman Kodak Company for selling them defective film, Goldfish had nowhere else to turn.

"I got so emotional telling him my story," Goldwyn recounted years later, "I was practically in tears." Lubin sympathized. Contrary to Trust policy, he agreed to diagnose the problem. DeMille and Lasky (who rendezvoused in Chicago) went by train to Philadelphia with the tins containing *The Squaw Man*. They had not left DeMille's side for an instant during the cross-country journey; nor had DeMille's revolver. Arthur Friend came down from New York, and they converged upon Lubin's studio.

Pop Lubin held a piece of the negative up to the light and reeled it through his fingers. "The negative stock was defective, wasn't it?" offered Friend, girding his loins for legal battle. Lubin said there was no trouble with the stock, but he would have to examine the film in the next room. He left the officers of the Lasky Company for fifteen minutes, then returned with a broad grin.

Under Pop Lubin's questioning, DeMille revealed that in a moment of frugality he had purchased a secondhand, British-made machine for punching sprocket holes along the sides of the film. What DeMille had been too green to know was that his American equipment was regulated for film sprocketed at sixty-four holes per foot, while the British punched out sixty-five. In his drive to economize, Cecil had purchased unperforated positive stock and hand-punched the sprockets himself, each hole off the mark by a few microns. Lubin said his company could fix the film by pasting a strip of film over the edge of the negative and re-perforating it. Within days, the Lasky Company's first product was ready to market.

They had taken offices in the Longacre Theater Building on West Forty-eighth Street, at the heart of Broadway. On Tuesday morning, February 17, 1914, *The Squaw Man* had its first trade showing, in the theater downstairs. Goldfish had arranged the preview, packing the house with as many important journalists and buyers as he could gather. He had, of course, already sold a good share of the states' rights, but the company's future hinged on this audience's reaction.

Lasky and DeMille took seats in the rear of the little theater, "to watch for the moving of heads, the shifting of bodies, the coughs, the laughter at the wrong places, and the other unconscious signs which are always a more accurate gauge of audience reaction than what the viewers say or write about a picture." Sprocket holes constantly showed up on the muslin sheet that served as a screen; and the film broke six times in the next hour. But the six-reel story in 264 scenes entranced the audience. When the houselights came up, Goldfish found himself the center of adulation. He introduced Lasky and DeMille, who took their bows. Buyers swarmed around them. One was Louis B. Mayer, who said he would pay four thousand dollars for the rights to run the film in his theaters. Another was the undisputed leader of feature films, Adolph Zukor himself.

Until then, Goldfish had not met Zukor, but he had been so impressed by his life story that he often folded the more pathetic details of their similar backgrounds into his own autobiography. Zukor was but one year old when his father died in Hungary in 1874; his mother remarried but died eight years later. In 1888, he successfully pleaded with the Orphan's Bureau to let him emigrate to America. He apprenticed in a fur shop on the Lower East Side, and within four years he had moved to Chicago, where he became a furrier. Not until 1900 did a prosperous Zukor return to New York City.

In 1903, a penny arcade owner from Buffalo got Zukor to invest in a similar emporium in Manhattan. They opened their arcade on Fourteenth Street at Broadway. A few months later, Zukor converted the second floor into a motion picture theater. Within a few years, he had four-hundred-seat nickelodeons in Newark, Boston, and Philadelphia.

Zukor began to realize that the novelty of one- and two-reel chases and comedies had worn off. He concluded that "the only chance motion pictures had of being successful was if stories or plays could be produced which were like those on the stage or in magazines and novels. That way you could give something to the public that would hold their interest."

Opportunely, Zukor heard that Sarah Bernhardt had just closed in a successful European tour of a play called *Queen Elizabeth* and that its French producer wished to preserve the performance on film. Zukor agreed to finance the picture in exchange for the American rights. He cleverly exhibited the film in legitimate theaters during their dark afternoons.

"For the first time a movie had been reviewed and written about in the papers," Zukor would remember most of a century later. "They said Sarah Bernhardt had 'starred' in a motion picture." Its success set Zukor on a course of presenting "famous players in famous plays." He began to populate his films with stars from the stage who had proved their ability to fascinate audiences. When several of their vehicles did not go over as well in theaters as Zukor had expected, he realized, "The public attending motion pictures had never heard of or seen these theatrical stars. Matinee idols meant nothing to them at all. Finally we had to build our own stars."

THE public determined which screen deities would be placed or replaced in their pantheon; but the filmmakers decided which actors could even be considered. At first, only D. W. Griffith's opinions of talent mattered. But he tended to believe in his own mythology, putting more stock in his powers of attracting the public than in his actors'. Mack Sennett, once an unemployed actor, never forgot Griffith at the old Biograph brownstone on Fourteenth Street, toiling and grimacing "to make his actors and actresses act," all but turning them into marionettes whose movements were regulated by the lifting of his finger. He rehearsed their every smile and tear.

"Not until your name becomes a household word in every family—not only in America, but in the world, if the world feels it knows you and loves you—will you be a star in motion pictures," Griffith told Lillian

Gish. And though he was the first to recognize that possibility in James Kirkwood, Mack Sennett, Mabel Normand, and Mary Pickford, as well as Lillian Gish and her sister, Dorothy, he was just as ready to auction them off.

Adolph Zukor was the highest bidder. Having managed theaters, he had a sense of whom the audiences came to see. Although the one everybody called "Little Mary" was scarcely twenty years old—and hardly a famous player—Zukor saw something special in her performances on both stage and screen. But Mary was not convinced that motion pictures were good for her career.

Zukor knew what made Mary Pickford tick. She was a native of Toronto, the daughter of an unsteadily employed laborer who died before she was school age, leaving another daughter and a son to be supported by their mother, Charlotte. The young widow paid the mortgage by taking in boarders; one of them, an actor, spoke of getting jobs for the little girls in local stock companies. When Zukor met Charlotte Pickford, he suggested astronomical sums for her daughter's services. For five hundred dollars per week, Mary was his.

Zukor went after every actor he thought had star potential. Biograph was always an easy target for a raid. "Once you had worked with Mr. Griffith," Lillian Gish recalled, "other companies were always eager to hire you." All it took to lure most actors away was a bump up in salary.

In that moment the parallel aims of show business—art and commerce—diverged. "You can see that difference between Mr. Griffith and Adolph Zukor," observed Blanche Sweet, an actress who worked both sides of the street. "More than anybody else at the time, they embodied the artistic possibilities of motion pictures and the financial. Don't get me wrong, the Griffith pictures did very well at the box office, but he didn't know anything about money, and he was always broke." And many of Zukor's films were artistic successes. One of them needed money to make his films, the other needed films to make his money.

Once it dawned on these early producers that stars pulled audiences into theaters, there ensued a mad pursuit. Vitagraph signed the elegant Clara Kimball Young and the handsome Wallace Reid; comedies were created for a fat man called John Bunny. Rough-and-ready Tom Mix first rode into pictures for Selig. Essanay—"Broncho Billy" Anderson's company—signed a former sculptor's model who had won the *Ladies' World* "Hero Contest," Francis X. Bushman. Pathé made a star of Pearl White, who appeared in a successful series—each episode ending with a cliff-hanger—called *The Perils of Pauline*.

An erstwhile actor named Thomas Ince realized he had a greater future behind a camera than in front. He was directing at IMP when a former bookmaker named Adam Kessel and his friend from the track named Charles O. Baumann offered him the opportunity to make westerns in California. Ince enlisted a friend he had worked with on Broadway, a stone-faced Shakespearean actor named William S. Hart.

Baumann and Kessel, who formed a production company called Reliance, were lunching at Luchow's in New York in the late summer of 1912 when they noticed the tall and stocky Mack Sennett. Born Michael Sinnott in Canada, he had been directing at Biograph and thinking about the comic possibilities of policemen. "I kept right on telling D. W. Griffith that cops were funny," Sennett later recalled, because they had dignity—"and wherever there is dignity, comics can embroil it, embarrass it, flee from it, and thumb their noses at it. . . . I wanted to take a giant step and reduce cops to absurdities." Griffith failed to see the humor.

Kessel and Baumann offered Sennett the opportunity to direct his own films in his own fashion. They were all walking past Penn Station, trying to settle on a name for the company, when Sennett looked up and saw the Pennsylvania nickname on the building. By the end of the summer he was making "Keystone" comedies, with a sympathetic fatso named Roscoe Arbuckle and a number of Biograph stars he had nabbed, including a doe-eyed comedienne named Mabel Normand.

While still an extra at Griffith's studio, Mack Sennett had caught Karno's Pantomime Company, an English vaudeville troupe, and been especially impressed with a performer who portrayed a drunk in their show *A Night in an English Music Hall*. In 1913, when Sennett was building his troupe of players, he tracked down the five-foot-four-inch, twenty-four-year-old mime and offered him $150 a week to appear in motion pictures. Divinely inspired, Charles Chaplin picked up a pair of oversized shoes, a cane, and a cocked derby and developed a character right before Mack Sennett's camera eye. "You know this fellow is many-sided," Chaplin explained one day, "a tramp, a gentleman, a poet, a dreamer, a lonely fellow, always hopeful of romance and adventure."

BY the end of February 1914, *The Squaw Man* was in release. Within two weeks of its preview, only seventeen states did not have prints of the film running; a week later, only four states' rights remained unsold. The Lasky Company was on the map, having grossed by late spring close to $250,000. (Goldwyn swore all his life that Louis B. Mayer paid only half the $4,000 he contracted for that night in the Longacre Theater, the second strike against Mayer in Goldwyn's book.) Like all the other new production companies, the Lasky Company began to look for stars and properties.

Invariably they found themselves in Zukor's wake. Through Lasky's connections, they were able to reel in a number of minor Broadway successes, including a play called *Brewster's Millions;* it was a trifle about a playboy who stood to inherit many millions of dollars if he could spend one million within two months. For five thousand dollars, they purchased the film rights in perpetuity directly from the author, George Barr McCutcheon, and it was the second feature play from the Lasky Company.

DeMille became entrenched in studio operations on the West Coast, Lasky shuttled between coasts, and Goldfish minded the store in New York. In expanding, Goldfish held the company's reins, for it was he who had to generate income on a product that did not yet exist and whose quality could not be guaranteed.

The company seemed doomed yet again when *Brewster's Millions* was shot and assembled. Goldfish, alone in the theater with Lasky, ran it in New York just before his trade showing. For an hour, there was not a titter between them, and it was too late to do anything about it. It would just have to be shown to the buyers as it was.

Goldfish introduced the film and the houselights dimmed, but he could not bear to sit through the silence. He paced outside for most of the five reels, then returned to face an apathetic full house. The first sound that greeted him when he went through the lobby door was a roar of laughter. Another followed. Goldfish allegedly looked at the screen in disbelief, and looked again just to be certain it was their production of *Brewster's Millions*. He instantly realized the importance of screening motion pictures before audiences that were seeing the story unfold for the first time. He also understood that theatrical experiences are social situations and that certain emotions—especially laughter—are contagious.

These trade screenings proved doubly important for Goldfish. They were the only occasions during which he received any recognition. Except for those few times a year, Goldfish was practically invisible in the industry. Being a hidden partner gnawed at him, especially now that Jesse Lasky was dropping his vaudeville interests so that he could devote full time to motion pictures.

Goldfish wanted to be known the way Adolph Zukor was—or at least as several up-and-comers were: The Warner brothers—small-time exhibitors before opening an exchange (the Duquesne Amusement Supply Company)—began producing two-reel westerns; Louis B. Mayer was building his own film exchange as well as theaters; Carl Laemmle formed the Universal Film Manufacturing Company; and Lewis Selznick had sold himself to Laemmle as a general manager.

During the next year, the Lasky Company bought the screen rights to two dozen plays. Realizing that a good screenwriter was as crucial to their existence as a cameraman or actors, they approached DeMille's brother. William and Cecil discussed the importance of developing a technique of storytelling that would "follow the old dramatic principles, but adapt itself to a new medium; find its own compensations for its lack of words . . . to make a train of thought visible enough to be photographed." William de Mille went west for three months and stayed twenty years.

Oscar Apfel called the shots on most of the pictures until Cecil DeMille felt equipped to direct by himself. With two directors working at once, the Lasky Company could easily meet the increasing demand for their films; but DeMille wanted to decrease his output. Like Griffith, he became enchanted with the artistic possibilities of motion pictures. "As his flair for sweeping dramatic spectacle developed," Lasky recalled, "his shooting schedules stretched from five to six to seven and then eight weeks. He was responsible for many innovations in the interest of pictorial 'class.'"

Lighting intrigued DeMille. In 1914, while filming his brother's play *The Warrens of Virginia,* he experimented with bolts of black velvet, blocking out the sunlight streaming through windows when filming night scenes. As a result, he was the first director to depict interior night scenes that actually resembled night. When stage directions called for a light to be turned down, he would dim the lights on his set. He discovered that great effects could be achieved if the actors' faces were not always fully lighted. As Agnes de Mille observed of moviemaking in its paleozoic era, "Every picture broke boundaries."

When Goldfish caught his first glimpses of actors who were only partially visible, he fired off telegrams to the set in Hollywood, "demanding how in hell [they] expected him to sell a picture in which the lighting was so lousy that you couldn't even see the characters' faces half the time." Lasky was at DeMille's side in Hollywood when one such wire arrived. Cecil pondered for a moment, then, borrowing a phrase then popular at Griffith's studios, said, "Tell him it's Rembrandt lighting." That gave Goldfish an idea. "For Rembrandt lighting," he decided, "they pay double."

After the Lasky Company's first six months, Goldfish felt completely in the shadows himself. One of the spring issues of *Moving Picture World* boldly announced the production of *Brewster's Millions,* hailing Jesse Lasky as "America's Most Artistic Director," Oscar Apfel as "Acknowledged Peer of Directors and Genius of Innovators," and Cecil B. DeMille as "Master

Playwright, Director and Author of Numerous Dramatic Successes." Samuel Goldfish's name was nowhere to be found.

Never again was there such an omission. Goldfish planted his name in all subsequent announcements of the activities of the Lasky Company. One article simply referred to him as "head of the Jesse L. Lasky Feature Play Company."

Nobody was more mindful of the company's sudden prominence than W. W. Hodkinson. The operator of his own small motion picture theater in Ogden, Utah, he branched out, becoming a district manager for the Trust. After representing several western film exchanges, he dreamed of manifest destiny—a nationwide distribution company that would supply all forty-eight states with two new motion pictures every week. On an ink blotter, he sketched the trademark of a snow-capped mountain peak, which he thought best illustrated the name he had appropriated from a New York City apartment house, the Paramount.

Hodkinson wanted at least thirty-six pictures a year from the Lasky Company. According to their contract of June 1, 1914, Paramount agreed to pay on the day of release of each production the sum of $18,750 as an advance against 65 percent of the gross income of each picture. The advance was only a fraction of what it cost to produce a film, but it guaranteed income and demand for their product. The Lasky Company would, overnight, have to triple its output. The officers raised their salaries to $500 a week.

Ever since *The Squaw Man*, Adolph Zukor (who was supplying Paramount with one film per week) and Jesse Lasky had lunched regularly. Goldfish made a point of joining them. Lasky was charming and full of enthusiasm for show business; Goldfish, Zukor found, talked only of dollars and cents and knew next to nothing of the new personalities and plays then capturing filmgoers' attention. A short time later, in fact, Goldfish walked into Zukor's office and noticed him talking to a small girl in a simple navy suit. She was saying, "They've offered me five hundred for the use of my name, but do you really think that's enough? After all, it means a lot to those cold-cream people." When the girl left the office, Goldfish asked who she was. Zukor was stunned that he had not recognized Mary Pickford.

But Goldfish was a quick study, intrepid in his curiosity. In 1914, he and Zukor were both eager to sign Marguerite Clark, a dark-haired girl with waiflike innocence, who was giving Mary Pickford a run for her money at the box office. While she was on the auction block, an enraged Zukor got Goldfish on the phone. "Now I want to tell you something," he said. "I'm going to get her, no matter what I have to pay. So you'll do me a favor if you don't bid me up any higher." Goldfish agreed to withdraw if Zukor would allow her to appear in a filmed version of a successful play called *The Goose Girl,* which he had just acquired. Zukor reluctantly agreed.

Later that year, Goldfish pulled a coup so big it indicated that even he knew its magnitude. In the summer of 1914, David Belasco, the most renowned theatrical producer of the day, was selling the rights to ten of his plays for motion picture films. Zukor—the undisputed leader in transferring plays to the screen—had already formed a successful alliance with the other leading stage producer of the day, Daniel Frohman, and had the inside track. Through Belasco's business manager, Goldfish wangled a meeting with the great white-haired producer. Goldfish promoted his company with his customary zeal. Belasco was further impressed with the youth of the Lasky Company's partners. He agreed to sell his block of ten plays for $100,000 as an advance against 50 percent of the profits—one quarter up front. It was an exorbitant amount of money, but Goldfish knew the deal was worth it even if their company did not make a cent. The prestige of such plays as *Rose of the Rancho* and *The Girl of the Golden West* was just the magnet the company needed to attract more quality material and the best stars. Zukor—who was quietly buying up Paramount stock—had been bettered in the business of motion picture production for the first time. The Lasky Company, begun on a $25,000 shoestring, was now capitalized at ten times that amount.

Goldfish had been noticing the vast numbers of immigrants in movie audiences. Silent pictures offered them the opportunity to see all aspects of America, often idealized, without any language barrier. In fact, moving pictures, with their occasional captions in plain talk, proved good primers for learning English. Griffith often said the medium was "the universal language." The immigrant audiences convinced Goldfish that he could issue his films around the world. In the summer of 1914, he took a sales trip to Europe. Adolph Zukor asked Goldfish if he would promote Famous Players films over there as well.

Goldfish launched his campaign in England, whose film industry had made great artistic strides in recent years. But even at full throttle, the United Kingdom could barely supply one fourth of its public's demand for new films. Combining his own product with Zukor's, Goldfish signed with a distributor named J. D. Walker. Under their contract, the Americans would receive ten thousand dollars advance against 65 percent of the films' grosses. With the trail blazed, the rest of Goldfish's European journey was easy. Sweden, Norway, and Denmark promised to buy every picture Goldfish could offer, for some three thousand dollars each. Belgium,

Switzerland, and France all placed orders; Germany—with but twenty-five film companies of its own—guaranteed four thousand dollars per picture. Weeks later, an assassin's bullet in Sarajevo would set off gunfire in most of the countries in which Goldfish had just closed deals; but none of his business would be affected for a while.

Poland was never more than a short detour away, but again Goldfish got no closer to his homeland than Germany. He invited his mother to meet him in Berlin. On this visit—almost twenty years after he had run away—Hannah Gelbfisz's son was almost unrecognizable to her. Schmuel had grown into a tall, solid man—a little over five feet ten inches tall, weighing one hundred sixty pounds, with a perfectly erect carriage and the step of a Prussian officer. He was completely bald, except for a fringe of brown hair, and he wore a pince-nez.

Schmuel promised to send his mother photographs of his wife and his three-year-old daughter, whom she had never seen. He also assured her of a monthly allowance—enough money to support her and some of their poorer relatives. Hannah said that would enhance the social position of his sisters. Within the next few years, all three of them would find husbands. Schmuel's checks arrived every month like clockwork. The photographs were never mailed.

In truth, there was no family to capture in a portrait. In 1914, the Goldfishes separated. It was not just the new business that kept Sam so preoccupied. The time they spent together at their apartment at 808 West End Avenue—between Ninety-ninth and One Hundredth streets, in the same building as Jesse's family—was more difficult than their time apart. When Jesse realized that most of his work was to be accomplished in Los Angeles, he took his entire family with him—not only his mother, wife, and child, but also Blanche and the baby, Ruth. Jesse put them all up in the lively Hollywood Hotel.

Even before Blanche left him, Sam Goldfish dallied with other women. After years of sexual rejection, even from his wife, he had become, by virtue of his position and self-confidence, attractive to women who were once beyond his dreams. He had many love affairs, none of them of importance. Goldfish became known as a "chaser," a popular label for men in his profession who were always ostensibly "looking for new talent."

He *was* looking for new talent. In England, he met Edna Goodrich, one of the beautiful "Floradora girls," and enticed her to America with a promise of five thousand dollars for making one picture. He encountered the beautiful stage actress Fanny Ward one day in an elevator in the Hotel Claridge in New York and offered her a contract on the spot. A chance meeting at a restaurant led to the hiring of Wallace Reid.

Now that Goldfish was actively involved in the selection of stars and properties as well as the negotiating of their deals, he spent more time where the movies were being made.

The Lasky Company leased several hundred acres in the San Fernando Valley—a wide open, scrubby expanse with oaks and yucca plants—which became known as the Lasky Ranch. Their own team of real cowboys stocked their westerns. The company added to its real estate in Hollywood, renting the rest of the land from Selma Avenue to Sunset Boulevard, between Vine and El Centro. Their rent doubled to $150 a month, and they cleared away more orange groves near their barn to build additional dressing rooms for their growing list of players. ("Extras could be plucked like ripe tomatoes whenever needed, right outside the studio," Lasky remembered years later. "There were benches under the pepper trees in the middle of Vine Street and they became a gathering place for people who wanted jobs. A director could run halfway across the street and pick up a bit actor, an assistant director, or a prop man. Work was work, and when a fellow got a nod he didn't always know until he got on the set whether he'd be required to chew the scenery or push it around. If he wasn't particular, he worked oftener.") Several directors and actresses—including Blanche Sweet, the idol of young Lillian Gish—were signed to yearly contracts.

Miss Sweet was one of the first to notice Goldfish's increasing presence on the scene. "There he was back in New York feeling left out," she said, "so he'd go out to California to be seen. At first, he would be extremely polite, to command our respect. After all, he signed our paychecks. Then he came around to our dressing rooms and rattled the cages. It wasn't as if he had much control over what we were doing. Lasky and DeMille were there for that. He just wanted us to notice that he was there and know that he was the boss."

Although each Lasky Company film was earning more money faster than its Famous Players equivalent, it peeved Goldfish that he was not as successful as Zukor in acquiring talent. He had presented some actors, but he had not created a motion picture star. In early 1915, it struck Goldfish that he had not been looking in the right places.

While motion pictures were still toddling, the biggest stars in the world were to be found not in Broadway theaters but in opera houses. Popularity for a few film stars was snowballing, yet the greatest money and attention were commanded by operatic divas. None had more talent and beauty than the blue-eyed, black-haired Geraldine Farrar, then the most famous prima donna in America. Both Goldfish and Zukor bid for her services.

After closing her season at the Met in *Madama Butterfly,* Farrar wanted to rest. That the Lasky Company was making all their films in California while Zukor was producing in New York prompted the great soprano to invite Goldfish to her home in Manhattan. Even Lasky knew the idea of luring Geraldine Farrar to make a motion picture "was about as plausible as getting the Statue of Liberty to walk on water." But, as Lasky later said of his partner's irrefutable charm, "Sam has a touch of magic to him."

Farrar agreed to appear in three motion pictures for twenty thousand dollars. Goldfish knew the fee was ridiculously low, "for she could have got nearly double the amount for a concert tour of the same length of time that it would take to make the films." But the novelty of silent pictures appealed to her, especially that she could "perform" and still rest her voice. Goldfish promised her a reception in Hollywood greater than anything she had seen in the courts of Europe—including her own railroad car to Los Angeles, a furnished house, servants, and food during her stay.

Banner headlines followed Farrar's train as it crossed the continent. Legions of teenage followers, known as "Gerry-flappers," awaited her at every stop. Goldfish and Lasky were there at the Santa Fe depot in Los Angeles, along with five thousand schoolchildren, who were given a holiday so they might greet her en masse. As Farrar walked the carpet from her private railway coach to the waiting limousine, the youngsters tossed roses at her feet.

Hollywood was being built up—especially along Prospect Avenue, now Hollywood Boulevard; but, as Goldwyn remembered, it was still "a one-horse town in the West." For all the sudden fame of movie stars, Angelenos had never seen the likes of Farrar. The night following her arrival, the mayor of Los Angeles held a civic reception in her honor at the Hollywood Hotel—the first time, Goldfish noted, anybody connected with motion pictures had been accorded such a distinction. In a ballroom draped in bunting and reverberating with band music, two hundred specially invited guests paid homage. "I was prouder at that moment than I had ever been before," Goldwyn recalled years later. "To me, it was the crowning glory of my 'glorifying' days. There would, I told myself, be no more pinching and scraping—no more wondering whether we could afford a new star. We were firmly on the road to success."

For weeks, the singer had been asking Goldfish who was to be her leading man in her first film, *Maria Rosa.* He kept dodging the question because Farrar was notoriously "difficult," and he did not want to risk alienating her with an improper choice. Just before the mayor's banquet, Goldfish introduced her to Wallace Reid, one of the most striking figures in pictures—a twenty-three-year-old, fine-featured actor with blue eyes and a fatal streak of insecurity. For days before her arrival, Reid kept quailing, "What if she doesn't like me!"

She did—and so would the public, responding to a hunch that contributed to the evolution of screenwriting. In the stage version of *Maria Rosa*, the character to be portrayed by Reid had been killed before the curtain went up. Cecil DeMille recalled that his brother "thoughtfully changed all that. Instead of having Andres killed before the story started, he put him in prison, from which, of course, he escaped in time to come on the screen and achieve love's triumph in the expected happy ending." Such dramatic license for the sake of accommodating a star's power became a tradition in the medium, an important element in this collaborative art.

The greatest difficulty in Farrar's eight weeks with the company proved to be in adapting her most popular role, *Carmen*. The opera was considerably different from the Mérimée novel on which it was based; and the rights to the libretto were not available. The solution lay in William de Mille's rendering the story down to its most basic elements, those story points that were basic to both the book and the opera, thus upsetting neither opera lovers nor lawyers. Geraldine Farrar's filmed performance of *Carmen* remained a lifelong memory to the generation that saw it—even though nobody could hear a note of her singing.

The partners of the Lasky Company paid themselves one thousand dollars a week in salary. They could hardly work fast enough to keep up with the monthly demands of the Paramount Distributing Company. The biggest stars in the world were appearing in Goldfish's films, and hundreds of the most beautiful women in the world would sacrifice almost anything to be able to say the same. Goldfish's joy was as unbounded as Midas's in his first days with his newly acquired power.

Early in the fourth week of September, after returning from one of his extensive trips to Los Angeles, Goldfish was served with papers announcing the ordering of a referee in the case of Blanche Goldfish against Samuel Goldfish. The plaintiff contended that the defendant "has committed adultery without the consent, connivance, privity or procurement of the Plaintiff," who was therefore "entitled to a judgment in her favor dissolving the aforesaid marriage. . . ."

The papers came as no surprise. In fact, the decision to separate had been one of the few matters upon which Sam and Blanche agreed. Goldfish had only one great concern about the pending divorce—that it would jeopardize his business relationship with his wife's brother.

On September 23, 1915, the day after Blanche filed, Sam Goldfish and Jesse Lasky appeared in Arthur Friend's office. Both agreed "not to sell, assign or transfer any interest" in their company stock. Then they deposited all their shares in the Jesse L. Lasky Feature Play Company, Incorporated, in a safe-deposit box that required two keys, one belonging to each of them. Samuel Goldfish endorsed the agreement with his flamboyant signature, now bold with big loops and sharp jags.

It was a simple hedge against trouble in paradise.

5 Musical Chairs

OLLYWOOD was built on a dream.
In 1883, a real estate developer
named Horace Henderson Wilcox
moved with his wife, Daeida, to Los Angeles. He had been active in religious circles in his home state of Ohio before heading to Kansas, where he made a killing in land speculation and soapboxed for Prohibition. In Los Angeles, he bought a ranch eight miles northwest of the city center, flatland at the foot of easy mountains. He began subdividing his territory in 1887, selling it off in an attempt to create a utopia, a realm of Christian values—tempered by Methodism, steeped in Prohibitionism. The Wilcoxes offered a free parcel of land to any denomination that would erect a house of worship. All purveyors of alcoholic beverages were barred. It was said to be Daeida's idea to name this community of upstanding families Hollywood, after the country estate of friends back in Ohio.

When the "movies"—as participants in motion picture making were called—first arrived, Hollywood was still a natural wonderland. The bunches of red berries on the pepper trees swelled big as grapes, tufts of orange pansies and clusters of mariposa tulips dotted the hillsides. One afternoon, a sprightly Agnes de Mille counted seven different varieties of lupine, in gorgeous shades of pink and yellow and blue. Within a few years, much of that exotic foliage would disappear, never to be seen there again. Only the fittest would survive in Hollywood; the Wilcoxes' ideas for a model township never took root.

In 1916, only one out of nine marriages in America ended in divorce. On the fourteenth of March, one of Hollywood's future residents appeared at the County Court House in New York, where Judge Robert Wagner legally dissolved the wedlock between Blanche and Samuel Goldfish. Most terms of the decree were standard, including that which deemed it unlawful "for the said Samuel Goldfish . . . to marry any other person until the said Plaintiff shall be actually dead." He could always sidestep the law by crossing the state line to marry.

Custody of four-year-old Ruth was awarded to Blanche. Sam was granted permission to see her "on any reasonable occasion" until her tenth birthday, at which time he could "have her with him for a period of three months in each year for the purposes of travel," provided that period did not conflict with school. The alimony and child support payments were sufficient to command newspaper space in 1916, though, in fact, Blanche and Ruth were awarded a pittance of Goldfish's earnings. He was ordered to pay his ex-wife $100 "each and every week" during "her natural life" and the further sum of $2,600 per year "so long as the Plaintiff lives and remains unmarried." Yet another $2,600 was to be paid for Ruth's "use and benefit" until she reached the age of ten, at which time payments were to double. At age twenty-one, Ruth was to receive $5,000 per year in quarterly payments, due on the first of January, April, July, and October "of each and every year during the natural life."

Blanche reverted to her maiden name. She and Ruth remained at West End Avenue and Ninety-ninth Street until the following year, when all the Laskys packed up and moved into a large apartment ten blocks south. Sam had returned to his former bachelor quarters at 10 West Sixty-first Street.

It was only a matter of time before Goldfish spatted with the remaining Lasky in his life. He resented the title card "Jesse L. Lasky Presents" that introduced each of the company's features; and he realized he had spent the last three years building up his ex-brother-in-law's name. After one blowup between them, Arthur Friend intervened and drove Sam around Central Park to help him cool off. When his rage persisted, Friend just kept driving. "Why do you always fight?" Friend asked him somewhere on a road in the middle of Long Island. "Theodore Roosevelt taught me that a man has to fight," Goldfish replied, explaining his understanding of rugged individualism. "But you fight even when people agree with you," maintained Friend. "Yes," Goldfish agreed, "but Roosevelt teaches that the only things worth having are what you fight for."

Well into its third year, the Lasky Company was proving unable to contain the expansive egos of all its partners (except for Arthur Friend, who continued to practice law on the side). After another of Goldfish's outbursts, Lasky called a secret meeting and proposed his ouster. DeMille was a weak vote against, putting the balance into Friend's hand. "I'm willing to vote Sam out, if you will promise to stick to it," he said; "but I won't vote him out today and then vote him back in tomorrow. I know he'll break your hearts and you'll vote him right back."

The partners overthrew Goldfish that night and informed him the next morning. By dusk, he had bemoaned his way back to his desk in their new offices at 485 Fifth Avenue (at Forty-first Street). The company continued to prosper, boosted by the great box-office success of a racy "society picture," *The Cheat,* with Fanny Ward and a Japanese actor, Sessue Hayakawa, and of *The Arab,* which starred its playwright, Edgar Selwyn. Only Paramount's advances, skimpy alongside the rising costs of story material and stars, hampered the Lasky Company.

For months, Goldfish thought Zukor could be a way out of this quagmire. If their two companies joined forces, they would have the power to dictate better terms to Paramount. At first, Zukor did not see any advantage to pooling his greater assets; he just quietly continued buying Paramount stock. In the spring of 1916, Zukor suddenly told Goldfish he was willing to enter into the arrangement on a fifty-fifty basis—fully recognizing the Lasky Company's superior filmmaking and fully prepared to give his new partners complete access to his array of talent, notably Mary Pickford. On June 28, the merger with Zukor's Famous Players was complete. The truth was, Zukor had a hidden agenda.

Two weeks earlier, at a stockholders' meeting of the Paramount Picture Corporation, Zukor had replaced founder W. W. Hodkinson with his own man, Hiram Abrams. Zukor himself became president of this mighty distribution company and the newly merged Famous Players–Lasky Corporation. He allowed the first vice presidency of the production company to be filled by an officer of the Lasky Company. It was a bone both Goldfish and Lasky intended to fight over, and it fell upon DeMille to pull them apart. "I sympathized with Sam's position," DeMille recalled.

For three years he had been slaving successfully at the unglamorous job of selling the pictures directed by Cecil B. DeMille and presented to the public by Jesse L. Lasky. He and all the world read in the trade press about the "Lasky elegance" and about "DeMille as the foremost photo-dramatic producer in the world." Even if those lush phrases came from his own publicity department, Sam could not help feeling that his light was being hidden under a bushel, however elegant.

Nor was this presumptuous vanity on his part. Sam knew his worth. So did I, and I did not hesitate to tell him so.

Goldfish, promptly interpreting this back-patting as support, wired DeMille that he did not intend "to give Jesse his way on this" and urged Cecil to telegraph his vote immediately.

"If the election of First Vice President is a reward of merit purely then I consider that I am entitled to it!" DeMille wired the next day in jest. Then he added, "I believe the First Vice Presidency is offered to the Lasky Company because of the merit and efficiency of the company and not because of the value of any one member and that therefore the position should go to the President of this company and Jesse as such will have my vote. We entered into this deal as a unit and should continue as such . . . with a solid front and in the same ratio of positions as now exists." Zukor appeased Goldfish by naming him chairman of the board, which sounded powerful. Meantime, Zukor began buying theaters; he would soon be heading a full-service operation that manufactured, wholesaled, and retailed motion pictures.

For the next few weeks, each of the officers of the new company thought he had scored a great coup. Goldfish especially felt like the cock of the walk and dressed for success. Into fall, a chesterfield coat and homburg hat replaced his linen suits and straw boater; he added spats and chamois gloves to his wardrobe.

The executives all had adjoining offices overlooking Fifth Avenue. Lasky and Zukor agreed that their films made in the East would carry the screen credit "Adolph Zukor Presents" and those made in California would give Lasky billing. Goldfish was not long content. Zukor believed that Goldfish "disagreed many times only for the sake of argument," that his board chairman "liked operating in a turmoil."

The company stayed on an even keel through the summer, mostly because Goldfish went west. DeMille was directing Geraldine Farrar in *Joan the Woman;* at $300,000, it was the company's costliest production to date. Jeanie Macpherson, a former actress with Biograph, wrote a scenario that sought to "emphasize the humanity of Joan of Arc rather than project the conventional, and so frequently false, image of a saint." This telling of the story would serve as the model for many epic films DeMille would direct in the ensuing decades—"an absorbing personal story against a background of great historical events."

Viewing the "rushes" of a crowd scene one day, Goldfish felt something was wrong, but he could not put his finger on it. He asked that the film be screened a second time and noticed what had thrown him. Several extras, dressed as medieval soldiers, were chewing gum—an anachronism that had gone unnoticed during the filming. Goldfish ordered the day's work redone. It was.

A new no-nonsense, businesslike spirit suddenly charged the sets of motion pictures everywhere, as though a switch had been thrown. That juvenile sense of the adventure in filmmaking turned adult. "Summer camp was over," remembered Broadway actress Ina Claire, who had signed with the Lasky Company in 1915. She said it was because of *The Birth of a Nation,* whose influence affected everybody even tenuously connected to motion pictures.

For months, there had been rumors about Griffith's twelve-reel production in the works. Its success would lift all restraints of running time on a film. On February 8, 1915, Samuel Goldfish had been part of the premiere audience at Clune's Auditorium in Los Angeles roaring its approval.

The Birth of a Nation ran forty-four consecutive weeks at the Liberty Theater in New York, at an astronomical two dollars a head. Queues were so long that four other theaters were needed to accommodate the overflow. Close to one million people stood in line to see the film in that city alone. The picture stayed just as long in Boston and Chicago . . . and it played even longer in the South—twelve years continuously in some places, according to one source. By conservative estimates—for even then theaters and distributors tended to underreport actual box-office takes—*The Birth of a Nation* grossed at least $50 million in its first run, possibly 20 percent more than that. The motion picture industry was no longer nickels and dimes.

The business entered a period of natural selection—mergers, takeovers, buyouts, wildcatting, and raids—that would ultimately rid it of the weak. Those who remained would be the power brokers. The draconian Trust still loomed over the landscape, but all its production companies were falling prey to the new breed.

William Fox, among the first to fight the Trust, expanded his film distribution business and his chain of theaters. While *The Birth* was the talk of the nation, he produced *A Fool There Was,* based on Kipling's poem "The Vampire," in which Theodosia Goodman of Chicago played an unscrupulous seductress. The Fox publicity department transformed her into a woman of great mystery who had been born on the burning sands of the Sahara, Theda Bara. The film became a huge success, treading into taboo areas that motion pictures had previously dared not enter. Scores of local censorship panels united behind the aegis of the Trust; in 1909, a watchdog panel had been named, the National Board of Review.

While Theda Bara "vamped" in forty pictures over the next three years, displaying the immorality of women, Gilded Age America flocked to the ever-innocent Mary Pickford's monthly offerings in even greater numbers. In 1916, Zukor signed her to a million-dollar contract. Chaplin kept pace; and Harold Lloyd would soon follow.

D. W. Griffith, Thomas Ince, and Mack Sennett—the three undisputed masters of long-format motion pictures in drama, westerns, and comedy, respectively—formed the Triangle Film corporation and established two new stars: William S. Hart appeared in thirteen feature pictures and became the most celebrated cowboy in the world; Douglas Fairbanks would soon undo audiences completely with his cocky athleticism, playing pirates, swordsmen, adventurers, and lovers. Lewis Selznick of Universal suddenly resurfaced at World Special Films, having snatched Clara Kimball Young from Vitagraph. A distributor from Pittsburgh named Richard Rowland built Metro Pictures Corporation. The secretary of the new company was the successful Massachusetts theater owner Louis B. Mayer. After grossing close to one million dollars off the New England states' rights to *The Birth*, Mayer, too, decided to enter that select company of men, mostly in their mid-thirties, who ran motion picture production companies. He began with a serial starring Francis X. Bushman.

As salaries, admission prices, and the films themselves enlarged, so, too, did the exhibition halls. One colossal edifice after another was erected, completely dwarfing America's seventeen thousand small theaters. By 1915, over two dozen motion picture palaces had been built in the United States. The Exeter Street Theater in Boston could accommodate 900 patrons; the Orpheum organization built the Palace in Los Angeles for 1,950 patrons. The Strand opened in New York City with plush seats for 2,985. A motion picture's success could depend on the theater manager, the screen impresario. Foremost among them was Samuel Rothapfel, known to the world as "Roxy."

Starting at the Strand, Roxy raised motion picture exhibition to extravagant heights. In such "temples of the silent drama" as the Rialto, the Rivoli, and the Criterion, Roxy presented an entire program of entertainment, complete with music, built around a feature-length motion picture. Composers were hired to create elaborate scores for the films. Without a word being spoken, the art form of motion pictures became as complete—and as voiceless—as ballet.

"While we were burning Joan of Arc at the stake," Cecil DeMille recalled of the hot summer of 1916, "another and more explosive fire was growing in the New York offices." It sparked up from the friction between

Sam Goldfish and Adolph Zukor. "A chairman of the board," Zukor recounted, "does not ordinarily concern himself with the day-to-day details of operation," not in Zukor's mind anyway. He had, in fact, created the sinecure just to keep Goldfish out of his way. But wherever Sam saw an inch of latitude, he took a mile. He liberally interpreted his title as license to rule over all aspects of the company's business.

Zukor had just completed a contract with Jack Pickford, Mary's actor brother, for five hundred dollars a week. Arbitrarily and unilaterally, Goldfish canceled it, asserting that the figure was too high. "His post didn't give him authority to do that," noted Zukor. "But . . . rules meant little to Sam when he was excited."

Within weeks of the merger, it was clear to everybody at Famous Players–Lasky that Goldfish was inventing pretexts to bring the matter of his jurisdiction to a head. He was almost methodical in booby-trapping all company business. Mary Pickford was keenly aware of the new strains the merger had put on Zukor. She had previously thought of Famous Players as her second family, and she called Zukor "Papa." Now, with all the problems of a large corporation filling his head, "he had become a house divided within himself," she observed. "In that strained atmosphere I now became involved in a rather unsavory issue"—the payment due on her new million-dollar contract.

"I went to see Mr. Zukor," Mary Pickford wrote in her memoirs, "to remind him of our agreement. In the discussion that ensued I saw Mr. Zukor put his hand under the desk and, I supposed, press a button." An office boy appeared, announcing that Mr. Goldfish wished to see Mary in his private office. "What's all this nonsense?" said Goldfish as, annoyed, she walked through the door. "It's not nonsense at all, Mr. Goldfish," she replied. "I made an agreement with Mr. Zukor that I scarcely think concerns you. I was put under contract by Famous Players. Mr. Zukor and I will decide it, if you don't mind—"

"Now you listen to me," he interrupted.

"And the next time," Pickford proceeded, without batting an eyelash, "please don't send the office boy for me. If you wish to see me, come yourself." She turned on her heels, thus initiating a lifelong relationship of intense mutual antipathy. One day shortly thereafter, Goldfish saw Miss Pickford in the street, coming into work. "My God," he said. "Ten thousand dollars a week and she's walking to the set yet. She should be running!"

Having successfully alienated his company's president and biggest star, he buried a land mine under the desk of his oldest colleague in the business. One day that summer, while Jesse Lasky was conferring with Mary Pickford about her picture *Less Than the Dust,* Sam appeared and blurted out, "Jesse, don't let Zukor butt in on this picture. He's okay as an executive, but we've always made better movies than Famous Players, so see that you keep the production reins in your hands!"

Lasky went to Canada for a vacation in August 1916. Upon his return, Zukor approached him with an ultimatum: Either Goldfish must leave the company or Zukor would. "I've never had a harder decision to make, and I had to make it alone," Lasky remembered. He hardly closed his eyes for the next forty-eight hours.

Although he believed Goldfish ("the one who had goaded me into the picture business in the first place") was a "brilliant strategist," Lasky wrote DeMille in Hollywood that Zukor was "an all around better businessman—has better foresight—is a better financier and has a broader and bigger grasp of the picture business . . . he is considered the biggest man in the motion picture industry and . . . his reputation for honesty and integrity is remarkable." Lasky felt that Arthur Friend worked more efficiently with Zukor than with Goldfish. And so, Lasky concluded, "I feel that we couldn't have a better man than Zukor as president of our new corporation."

Once Lasky rendered his verdict to Goldfish, his former brother-in-law surrendered so willingly as to suggest he knew perfectly well what he had been doing over the last three months.

Goldfish did not completely detonate his relationship with Famous Players–Lasky until he had constructed new plans for himself. On September 14, 1916, he resigned as chairman of the board of directors and also as a member of the executive committee of the corporation, but he still held stock and remained on the board.

"I have contemplated retiring from the active management of the Famous Players–Lasky corporation for some time in order to mature certain personal plans which are of great importance to me, and which I could not mature if I continued as one of the executives of the company," he told a reporter from *Motion Picture News.*

More than Sam's natural instinct to turn adversity into advantage drove him to think immediately of a new situation for himself. Over the preceding few years, anybody with enough drive could have dubbed himself president of a motion picture company. Now all the baronies were being parceled out, and one by one the thrones were being removed. If he wished to sit at this Round Table of film producers, he would have to assess his resources, cash in his stock, invest in properties and personnel, and establish a company. With Carl Laemmle at Universal; Adolph Zukor at Paramount and Famous Players–Lasky; Griffith, Ince, and Sennett at Triangle; Lewis Selznick at World, Louis B. Mayer, Marcus Loew, William Fox, and the Warner brothers already knighted; and Chaplin, Pickford, and Fairbanks reigning at their respective studios, Goldfish was obliged to make his decisions posthaste.

6 A Name for Himself

THE THEATER has long provided a home for misfits—adventurous strays and loners who find asylum in each other's company. It is not just the common search for fame and fortune or even fantasy that draws them all together. It is also the need for family.

A census of the motion picture industry's earliest population would reveal an inordinate number of victims of broken homes. Alcoholism coursed through their family trees. Griffith stars Mae Marsh, Blanche Sweet, Robert Harron, and the Gish sisters were all raised without fathers. Mary Pickford's father died when she was four; Douglas Fairbanks's—a half-Jewish lawyer named Charles Ulman—abandoned his wife when their boy was five; Charles Chaplin's—an itinerant vaudevillian who Charlie's brother Sydney insisted was a Jew originally named Kaplan—took to the road the year after Charlie was born. Griffith was ten when his father, a Civil War veteran, died; DeMille was twelve when he lost his. A promenade of fatherless actresses would continue across the decades. "From the very beginning," observed Lucille Ball, who would come to Hollywood a generation later with her mother, "the studios gave us Papas."

Almost to a man, the Hollywood moguls were Jewish immigrants with an instinct to surround themselves with family. It was a way to help one's own and protect oneself. Wherever possible, these men brought in their relatives: Adolph Zukor hired his wife's brother to manage his studio; Jack Cohn, upon leaving Universal as a film editor, ushered in his brother Harry, a song plugger, to serve as "Uncle Carl" Laemmle's secretary; the

Warners worked as a team during their early days of film production. Two Russian immigrant brothers, Nicholas and Joseph Schenck, first operated a drugstore on Third Avenue, then ran an amusement park in Upper Manhattan called Paradise Park. They attracted the attention of Marcus Loew, who incorporated them into the management of his expanding organization. *Mispoche*—family—was an unspoken want of the pioneer generation of movie people, especially the studio heads who had forsaken their fatherlands.

Except for Goldfish. Until he had created his own identity, he was too self-absorbed for family affairs. He had been an uncaring husband, and with each passing day he showed as little concern as a father. He almost never communicated with his family in Poland; and except for a $2,500 loan to each of them, he had little to do with his three siblings in America. The notion of an extended family through business (curiously, all his former partners—DeMille, Lasky, Friend, and Zukor—had grown up without fathers) seemed impossible unless Goldfish could be in absolute control, an undisputed paterfamilias.

The creation of a motion picture company was no longer a one-man job of opening a storefront operation. In fact, while Goldfish was plotting his future, "Papa" Zukor was expanding his motion picture interests. He appealed to Otto Kahn, head of the banking firm of Kuhn, Loeb & Company, for a loan of $10 million, all for the stock issue of a company that four years earlier had not even existed.

Toward the end of 1916, Goldfish redeemed his stock in the Zukor-controlled companies for $900,000. The cash settlement took some of the edge off his search for an entry into the industry, but it did not provide the open sesame. And it did nothing to lessen his anger toward those who had ousted him. For the rest of his life, Goldwyn could never let go of the feeling that Zukor was a "rat" and that Jesse "sold him out."

He moved into a new apartment at 255 West Eighty-fourth Street, only blocks from where Ruth was living with her mother and the rest of the Laskys; but he almost never took advantage of his visitation rights, consumed as he was with his career. "The secret of this man," Ruth said, "is that he always did what he wanted. Once he saw what he wanted to have next, he went in an absolutely straight line to get it."

That autumn, Goldfish reached out to two candidates for partnership— a pair of brothers with enough Broadway connections to make him forget about sole billing. Edgar Selwyn was born in Cincinnati in 1875 to a merchant who moved his family to Toronto, where another son, Archibald, was born. Both his parents died before Edgar was sixteen. He tramped to Chicago, where he saw no future. One winter night he jumped off a bridge into the Chicago River—actually, onto the river, for he landed on ice. Reaching the shore, he felt a gun at his head and was given an option of his money or his life. Selwyn said, "My life."

The two desperate men got to talking; and by dawn, the mugger had agreed to pawn his revolver and share half the proceeds with his intended victim. Selwyn left for New York, where he became an usher at the Herald Square Theater (the very place where Sam Goldfish would see his first motion picture) for fifty cents a night. Suddenly Selwyn had found his place in the world. "The theater strikes the Peter Pan in us all," he later said of his new career, speaking for himself and all the lost boys who found their way into it; "to make believe is the most glamorous thing on earth."

Selwyn grew to be a handsome five-foot-ten-inch man with black hair and brown eyes. He knocked about Broadway as an actor, picking up occasional supporting roles and doubling as assistant stage manager. He began to write plays. His brother Arch joined him in New York, and by 1912 they had gone into business together, the younger man looking out for Edgar's interests.

Edgar became a successful actor, starring mostly in his own works. He hobnobbed with the likes of H. G. Wells and Arnold Bennett. The Selwyns began to produce plays, one of which netted a million dollars in 1912. Edgar married a beautiful playwright named Margaret Mayo, who for years boasted that she was the only woman to have had a play produced in every spoken language in the world. Mary Pickford had offered sixty thousand dollars for the film rights to her hit romance *Polly of the Circus*.

Sam Goldfish had come to know the Selwyns when the Lasky Company starred Edgar in his play *The Arab*. Sam proposed a partnership. With his modest library of readily adaptable plays, Edgar Selwyn was interested; but Goldfish's reputation made him think twice. He went to Adolph Zukor and asked if he could give any reason why he should not enter into business with Goldfish. "As far as his honesty and integrity are concerned, there is none," Zukor stated. "But if you do, you'll be a most unhappy boy." Selwyn asked why. "Sam is like a Jersey cow that gives the finest milk," Zukor explained, "but before you can take the bucket away, he has kicked it over." The Selwyns called off the deal.

Goldfish railed for days but made little headway. Then, looking for the weak link, he approached Margaret Mayo and tried the ploy that had always worked for him in the past, a pitiful plea for basic human compassion—what Jews call *rachmones*. He pathetically described how he had created his first enterprise, all the while building up somebody else's name, only to have his powerful creation turn on him. Now here he was, alone and anonymous. To wring the last drop of pathos out of his jeremiad, Miss

Mayo reminded Goldfish years later, "you . . . told me of your determination not to be defeated by those whom you had helped to succeed."

He gave the performance of a lifetime; but beneath the histrionics lay the secret to Goldwyn's charm. His boundless enthusiasm—fueled by supreme self-confidence—created a sense of excitement, which made people want to be around him. "I altered my life's activities, and induced others to do likewise," Margaret Mayo recalled further. She got her husband and brother-in-law to go along, and they attracted another young, successful producer, Arthur L. Hopkins. Goldfish got each of the partners to invest $75,000. Margaret Mayo threw in *Polly of the Circus* and another play, for which she had been offered $75,000.

The biggest point left to decide was the name of the new association. Goldfish fully intended to promote his own name, and yet even he recognized that it was laughable. More often than not, he heard some wisecrack upon being introduced to somebody for the first time. Only recently, Sam had arrived late one night at a cabaret and was seated behind a glass partition in the rear of the house; he protested but was silenced by a man who said, "Behind glass is the place for a Goldfish." The gag quickly made its way into the Broadway columns.

The partners realized that several portmanteau words could be formed from the names Goldfish and Selwyn. They paired the more fortunate syllable of each, producing a company name that chimed with confidence. On November 19, 1916—two months and two days after the ax fell at Famous Players–Lasky—Goldwyn Pictures was incorporated in the state of New York. The company was capitalized for three million dollars, all of the hundred-dollar shares of stock being held by its founders. Goldwyn Pictures took offices at 485 Fifth Avenue, in the same L-shaped building the Lasky Company had started in. At first, Goldfish spent most of his time there, while the Selwyns kept up their play-producing business on Broadway. For years, show business wags joked about the abandoned syllables of their surnames.

"By the time I started the Goldwyn Company," a ghostwriter for Samuel Goldwyn wrote a few years later, "it was the player, not the play, which was the thing." Only a few of the hundreds of silent holy ghosts on the screen could regularly draw worshipers back to their shrine. The public was fond of creating new overnight favorites—a tragedienne (such as Nazimova), a cowboy (Tom Mix), a comic (Buster Keaton). Maidens galore were offered every week: Norma Talmadge signed with Lewis Selznick; Anita Stewart with Louis B. Mayer; Gloria Swanson and a bevy of what became known as "bathing beauties" with Mack Sennett. The dream of

every producer was to place a new star at the high altar of the trinity—
alongside the swashbuckler, the tramp, and the virgin named Mary.

Goldfish went on a shopping spree, but not randomly. A lesson he
learned in Gloversville guided him. The Elite Glove Company had specialized in fancy-dress gloves—making fewer better. "No one ever succeeded by thinking *down* to people," Goldfish realized. "Unless one 'thinks
up' constantly, the public will eventually reject them." He was determined
to produce only the top of the line. His archenemy was the model he
intended to emulate.

Zukor's production company was built on an international star (Bernhardt), a young innocent (Pickford), Broadway leading ladies (such as
Pauline Frederick), and now an opera star (Farrar). Within three months
of the formation of Goldwyn Pictures, the president had signed Maxine
Elliott (a renowned star of the English stage), Mae Marsh (the Biograph
star), Madge Kennedy (a famous player from Broadway), and Mary Garden
(Farrar's leading rival)—each to a six-figure contract. Holding four
queens, Sam Goldfish hoped to draw a joker.

Mabel Normand was born in Providence, Rhode Island, in 1892 to an
Irish mother and an alcoholic French father. "Her family was temperamental, improvident, and often in transit," noted Mack Sennett, whose
life was to become entangled in hers. Her parents and two siblings always
called her "Baby." Insecure from birth, she thought of herself as unintelli-
gent and unattractive. She compensated endlessly, becoming a tireless athlete, taking pratfalls for a laugh, peppering her talk with profanities—
anything to get people to like her.

At thirteen, encouraged by so many people telling her how pretty she
was, Mabel became an artists' model. She posed for Charles Dana Gibson
and James Montgomery Flagg, then for photographers in the booming
advertising business. She had a curvy figure and huge brown eyes with
long lashes, but she never developed enough confidence to take a compliment. She responded to praise with some goofy action, as though trying
to divert one's gaze from her looks.

One day in 1909, another model told her there was bigger money to be
earned at the Biograph studio, especially for girls with as much personality
as Mabel had. She immediately found work in the Biograph brownstone
on Fourteenth Street as an extra but did not attract much more attention
than that. Only a big, stocky Irishman who had been loitering around the
studio noticed her. "I was a hanger-on, leaning against a wall, hoping to
get noticed and put into the picture myself," remembered Mack Sennett
of Mabel's first day before a motion picture camera.

She was hired to play a page and carry a queen's train out of a room. She performed, grabbed her five dollars, then left, failing even to inquire if she should ever return. A week later, as Sennett remembered it, he bumped into her on Fifth Avenue. He told her she could have a future in motion pictures, if only by returning to film the scene that had been held in abeyance until the extra who played the queen's page could be found. That next shot called for the queen's entrance into the chamber, with the same page carrying the train.

Sennett became enamored of Mabel and spoke to her about someday directing his own pictures—in which she would star. Within a few years, Mabel became the focus of his comedies—the poor but good girl triumphing over "ruffians, villains, and amiable boobs." She delivered the screen's first pie in the face—Sennett remembered it as custard directed toward the crossed eyes of Ben Turpin; Minta Arbuckle said it was raspberry thrown at her husband, Fatty.

"Mabel was the moth to Mack's flame," said Madge Kennedy, who was to become her dressing-room mate. Mabel followed Sennett from Keystone to Triangle and stuck by him when his other stars accepted larger salaries elsewhere. Off camera she was less sure of herself. "Whenever she got too close to someone," Miss Kennedy observed, "she felt she had to pull back. Mabel thought of herself as 'the Ugly Duckling,' and she was afraid people would see her imperfections." For all her spunk in front of crowds, she was, in Miss Kennedy's eyes, "a frightened little creature." Alcohol removed the edge; cocaine made her fearless.

"The worst predicament of all is to fall in love with an actress with whom you are in business," Mack Sennett noted years later in pathetic retrospect. They got engaged and unengaged twenty times. On the eve of one of their phantom wedding days, Miss Normand discovered Sennett in the compromising company of another actress, Mae Busch. Mabel and Mack's personal relationship was never the same.

Sennett tried to make amends with extravagant baubles. He bought a patch of land on Sunset Boulevard and built the Mabel Normand Studio. She rejoined Sennett. After his success with the first feature-length comedy (*Tillie's Punctured Romance*, with Chaplin and Marie Dressler), Sennett proposed a similar venture for Mabel. He sank everything he owned into *Mickey*, the story of an innocent girl in New York. After the six reels were assembled, Baumann and Kessel notified Sennett that *Mickey* was a flop before it even opened, that they could not interest a single exhibitor in showing it. It was consigned to a shelf, and Mabel Normand's career was up for grabs.

Sam Goldfish had been smitten ever since Mack Sennett first allowed

Mabel Normand to show off in movies. He was not alone. In this early world of ephemeral stardom, Mabel Normand was one of the few genuine living legends to walk the earth. Every critic praised her as the greatest comedienne of the silent screen; "nobody," said Madge Kennedy, "had more heart." In real life she was even more alluring, a Lorelei who drove men wild. Chaplin rued decades later that he never got closer to a love affair with her than one passionate kiss on those "full lips that curled delicately at the corners of her mouth, expressing humor and all sorts of indulgence." Another man attempted suicide over her by trying to drown himself in a toilet bowl. "Many of us became queens overnight," said Miss Kennedy of the sudden status granted to motion picture stars, "but Mabel became a goddess."

The moment Goldfish learned that Mabel Normand was running from the clutches of Sennett, he fixated on her. He became, in the words of Blanche Sweet, Mabel's friend from their Biograph days, "a stark-raving, crazed, insane, lunatic madman." By the time Sennett arrived in New York to win her back again, he learned that Normand was poised to sign a five-year contract with Goldfish for $1,000 a week. Mack interceded, insisting that she ask for more money. After weeks of wrangling, Mabel wired Mack, "SIGNED TODAY. . . . START WORK SEPT. 1. COMPANY SAID I DIDN'T LOOK WELL. MUST REST AND GO AWAY UNTIL THEN. WINTER STUDIO FLORIDA. SO I WON'T BE ABLE TO PEEP AT YOU EVER AGAIN." The agreement was a one-year contract for $2,500 per week. To the man who had built Mabel her own studio and literally put her name in lights, this bargain-basement contract was like salt on his wounds.

After Goldfish signed two of Zukor's biggest stars, Geraldine Farrar and Pauline Frederick, the competition around town began knocking the Goldwyn Company as the "old ladies' home." The company president set out to bag some male actors.

For thirty years, Rex Beach reigned as one of the most popular novelists in the United States. Known for his "he-man" stories set on rugged frontiers, he struck discriminating critics as a poor man's Bret Harte or Jack London. He became the first popular author to take a great interest in the production of motion pictures. Goldfish offered the kind of contract generally reserved for a few stars, one that allowed Rex Beach to form his own production company and keep half the net profits of the films based on his books. Upon his signing a contract that called for three films a year, Goldwyn Pictures also signed Tom Moore—the handsomest of three Irish-born brothers who all took up movie acting. (One of them, Owen, married Mary Pickford.) Then Goldfish put Jack Pickford and Griffith star "Bobby" Harron into his all-star lineup.

Having watched Zukor soar to prominence by building an octopus of production, distribution, and exhibition, Goldfish insisted the Goldwyn Company immediately branch out. On April 25, 1917, the Goldwyn Distributing Corporation was established, capitalized at one million dollars. They opened a separate office at 509 Fifth Avenue, on the eleventh floor. The new company was given a twenty-five-year license to sell all Goldwyn pictures, exacting their fee from the profits at the standard rates of 35 percent domestically and 50 percent in foreign markets; they would receive 25 percent for any outright sales of Goldwyn films.

Goldfish spent money as though there were no tomorrow—opening offices to wholesale the Goldwyn product in Los Angeles, New York, Chicago, St. Louis, Seattle, Atlanta, and Boston. Over the next three years, branch offices were opened in another fourteen cities across the country. The company's goal was to produce a new film every two weeks.

A team of salesmen was assembled to peddle the product in each region; and Goldfish himself spent much of his time charting their marketing strategy. He knew he would not stand a chance competing against the major distributors head to head. Zukor, for example, could force theaters to rent an entire slate of mediocre films, just to get their hands on one Mary Pickford feature. So Goldfish emphasized that "Goldwyn *is not a program*." It was the company's intention to offer "a quality product, costing from four to five times more money than any other regularly or otherwise released productions to be found in the entire market. With the facilities we now have," he announced in a bulletin to his salesmen, "we could easily make one hundred or more productions of the so-called program pictures, but we have limited ourselves to 26 pictures."

The company hired a casting director named Robert B. McIntyre, two dozen players to fill in their stock company, ten scenarists, a playwright named Edith Ellis (who became the company's first "story editor"), a team of cameramen, and a dozen directors, headed by Clarence Badger and Victor L. "Pops" Schertzinger. The lesser directors could count on salaries of several hundred dollars a week; Hobart Henley got a year's contract at two thousand dollars a month; a bright hotshot director—such as Allan Dwan—would be hired on a picture-by-picture basis at one thousand dollars a week.

Arthur Hopkins, who was to oversee production, suggested hiring famous designers to create a look for the company's films. Goldfish appropriated the idea and put it into action. A team of four men came to work under the noted painter and muralist Hugo Ballin, a New Yorker who had studied art in Rome. For two hundred dollars a week, he introduced elaborate architecture and set design. A film could assume a visual point of view. The "Ballin touch," a philosophy of set design he passed on to Gold-fish, maintained the utmost in simplicity, understatement. "He eliminated useless detail," noted Kenneth MacGowan, who would one day work in Goldwyn's story department, before becoming a screenwriter and film his-torian. "He used large spaces of clear wall with restrained detail. In the decoration he began to suggest more of the habits and nature of the char-acters of the story than had until that time been attempted." (One of Bal-lin's assistants at Goldwyn, Cedric Gibbons, would later break away and create a far more lavish new style in Hollywood films.)

By the summer of 1917, all the departmental phalanxes of Goldwyn Pictures had been assembled. Even though Goldfish had decided that the company should make its films in New Jersey instead of California, he was usually too busy at one of its Fifth Avenue addresses to spend much time on the set. He needed a right-hand man, someone whom he could deputize and trust implicitly.

He looked to Gloversville—and offered a job to his first business part-ner, Charlie Sesonske, with whom he had tried to start a glove business back in 1901. The movies interested Sesonske, but he turned Goldfish down. Even with the promise of a large salary and an important position, Sesonske was not prepared to move to New York City.

Then Goldfish approached his first friend from the glove trade, Abe Lehr, the man who used to swap his best hides for an hour of Sam's over-time. Lehr had for years been vice president of Dempster and Place Glove Company in Gloversville, and he was ready to break away. Even more than business acumen, he had the equanimity to work alongside the paroxysmal Goldfish. When Sam offered him $26,000 a year as "Vice President in charge of Producing Operations of Goldwyn Pictures Corporation," Lehr accepted.

AT eight o'clock in the morning, a Pierce-Arrow limousine would arrive at Samuel Goldfish's new apartment at 310 West 86th Street, between West End Avenue and Riverside Drive. The chauffeur would drive the thousand-dollar-a-week executive to 125th Street and the Hudson River, where they boarded a ferry for the motion picture capital of the world. On the other side, the car would wind to the top of the Palisades, on which Fort Lee perched. The town's wide variety of scenery—woods, brooks, hills and valleys, swamps, meadows, and country lanes—coupled with its proximity to New York City made it desirable to motion picture makers.

The first studio in the borough had been erected just north of the town line, in Englewood Cliffs, in 1909. A half-dozen more studios quickly followed in Fort Lee. They were cavernous greenhouses, their walls and roofs made of glass panes for the flooding of as much sunlight as the New Jersey skies would permit. Employees, even the actors, generally worked from nine to five, six days a week. Most businesses in 1917 operated half days on Saturday, but knowing the importance of catching every minute of light, most everybody willingly worked those extra few hours on Saturday.

Famous Players had its studio just off the westernmost end of Main Street, about a mile through town. Where Zukor was, Goldfish was never far behind. He was renting facilities from Universal 250 yards away. A vast stage was housed in a steel-framed structure; and an abandoned barn became a rabbit warren of offices and dressing rooms, with thin wood partitions and no ceilings. A young girl from outside Altoona, Pennsylvania—Elda Furry, who went by the name Hedda and married the actor De Wolf Hopper—picked up one of her first film roles there. She remembered, "The cells where we dressed at Fort Lee were uncomfortable, cold, smelly! We didn't complain. It put granite in our spines."

As many as four different companies at once could camp on the stage in the big building. Each crew—consisting of the director, his assistant, the cameraman, and a still photographer—swarmed around a single camera, focusing on the scene. Dissonance filled the air.

Geraldine Farrar demanded a pianist and a violinist on the set to provide mood music, a string trio for especially dramatic scenes. Madge Kennedy liked a pianist to plink out the bouncy new tunes—"gay and lively was my tempo . . . and it was months before I learned my music man was a drug addict. At nine o'clock in the morning, even!" Mabel Normand liked it hot—a jazz combo blaring away.

On top of vying strains of music were the clashes of temperament, as motion picture companies were still collections of insecurity and ignorance. Abe Lehr had absolutely no experience in show business; Arthur Hopkins had never made a motion picture, and neither had the company's first star, Maxine Elliott. "It really was a case of the blind leading the blind," said Madge Kennedy; "and we were all really grateful for some voice of authority to speak, anybody who could lay down the law and help us get the job done."

"You have to remember Sam Goldfish was pretty much a nonentity in the picture business then," noted J. J. Cohn, who broke into motion pictures as a secretary, cashier, purchasing agent, and "gofer" for the Goldwyn Company. "He was just then making a name for himself. But make no mistake about it. He was the Goldwyn Company; and when he came onto the set with something to say, everybody stopped to listen."

In the interest of elevating the art of motion pictures, Arthur Hopkins suggested to Goldfish that they experiment with a new variation in the medium—a completely wordless film. Maxine Elliott's first motion picture, *Fighting Odds,* was just that: five reels of pantomime, unrelieved by title cards. In a moment of twelfth-hour jitters, Goldfish ordered titles stuffed in, which only underscored Miss Elliott's exaggerated acting. The Goldwyn Company had its first major flop on its hands.

Thaïs was not their salvation. Because Mary Garden had sung the definitive *Thaïs* of her day, it was determined to let her perform it the same way in film—except, of course, there would be no sound. During those scenes in which there had been arias to entrance audiences, Miss Garden simply stood in stiff poses, listing slightly, occasionally heaving a bosom.

Mary Garden was immediately cast into a second film, a short wartime love story called *The Splendid Sinner.* Her character shoots a man and goes off to war as a nurse; but she turns out to be a spy, and the Germans finally capture her and stand her before a firing squad. One afternoon during the three weeks of shooting particularly impressed her. Just before filming the scene in which the Kaiser's marksmen meted out their punishment, Miss Garden looked up and saw Sam Goldfish there among the props, examining "every one of the guns to be sure there were no real bullets in them."

Both Mary Garden ventures were fiascoes, which further alienated some theater owners, who thought they were renting a film with a pretty actress of a few years back named Mary Gardener. The singer bid the movies adieu, believing "that every actor and actress in the motion-picture business earn every sou they make."

Even for the seasoned professional, hazards always threatened to shut down Goldfish's business. Madge Kennedy, as stalwart a trouper as the Goldwyn Company had, recalled the dangers imposed by the rudimentary lighting in early filmmaking. "We'd do take after take standing before these klieg lights," she remembered, "and after each one, the still photographer would run right up to you, practically at your face, and shout, 'Hold it for a still!' Then a flash of light would go off right before your eyes." Miss Kennedy recurringly suffered from the temporary blindness that afflicted most silent-screen actors: "I'd be awakened in the middle of the night by a flash of bright, white light; and when I turned on the light in the room, I wouldn't be able to see, sometimes for several seconds." The danger of losing actors because of sightlessness was real; the remedy in those days was to balm the eyelids with castor oil or tea leaves. Actors would often repair to their dressing rooms and lie down, covering their eyes with slices of potatoes or cucumbers.

From the moment he established his new company, Goldfish relied strongly on the art of advertising. He asked an adman named Philip Good-man to design a trademark for the Goldwyn Company. Goldfish was in the market for something impressive, more along the lines of the Paramount summit than the Pathé rooster or the Metro parrot. Goodman passed the assignment on to his newest hireling, Howard Dietz—a Columbia University dropout. The Goldwyn offices overlooked the gleaming pink marble pair of recumbent lions that guarded the entrance of the New York Public Library, but Dietz forever maintained that he got the idea for a mascot from the lion cavorting on the cover of his former campus satire magazine, *The Jester.* Dietz did, however, dignify the lion by posing him like the library models and surrounding him in a crest of film proclaiming, in Latin, *Ars Gratia Artis*—Art for Art's Sake.

Under the lion's protection, Goldfish assembled his own "exploitation" department, to feed pictures and stories about the films to the media and to invent ideas that would lure "traffic" off the street and into theaters. Dozens of creative young men trained in Goldwyn's publicity offices over the years; but the company president always set the tone of all their advertising. That was never more plain than the day a young staff member in exploitation was summoned to Goldfish's office with photographs of their stars. Goldfish looked at them, then out of an oracular reverie uttered a single adjective for each star: Maxine Elliott was "dignified"; Mary Garden was "elegant"; Jane Cowl was "soulful"; Madge Kennedy, "winsome"; Geraldine Farrar, "glamorous"; Mae Marsh received a three-word appellation, "the whim girl." From then on, Goldfish wanted all their movies and the attendant advertising to promote those qualities.

Some of the actresses were in real life exactly as Goldfish saw them. Madge Kennedy, for example, was as winsome and sweet as the titles of her light Goldwyn comedies suggest: *The Perfect Lady, Baby Mine, Our Little Wife, Nearly Married, Day Dreams.* As for most of the other stars, extremely fictive minds were required to create stories that would live up to Goldfish's images.

The star whose press needed the most cosmetizing was the "vivacious" Mabel Normand, whose chemical dependencies were viewed by those who knew of them as the cause of her troubled life more than the effect. She was simply considered talented but irresponsible. One interview for a family magazine went very well until the reporter asked her hobbies. "I don't know," Mabel replied. "Say anything you like but don't say I like to work. That sounds like Mary Pickford, that prissy bitch. Just say I like to pinch babies and twist their legs. And get drunk."

Mabel was also absolutely unreliable. Her paychecks went uncashed for months at a time, totally throwing off the books of the Goldwyn Company. In the middle of shooting a picture, she often disappeared for hours, sometimes days. Her vulnerability made Goldfish's heart race.

In the summer of 1917, Mabel Normand hid out in Great Neck, Long Island, as much as possible. Hedda and De Wolf Hopper lived there and used to see a lot of Mabel—and her new constant suitor. "Wearing a man's sweater over a one-piece bathing suit—you'd have thought she had nothing on under the sweater—she rode a surfboard attached to Caley Bragg's high-powered boat around Long Island Sound," Hedda Hopper recollected. Miss Hopper also recalled one Sunday when Samuel Goldfish motored all the way to Great Neck to take Mabel to dinner. She had canceled the date in her own mind, thinking if she blocked it out she would not have to go through with it. By the time Goldfish arrived, Mabel had locked herself in a second-floor bedroom, refusing to descend the stairs. Goldfish sent one message after another, entreating her to come down. She kept refusing, ultimately telling him to go home. Around midnight, Sam left.

Mabel was Goldfish's companion at public functions for months. She avoided private encounters. He remained oblivious of her feelings for him, not knowing that when he was beyond earshot, she often performed a wicked impersonation of him, capturing the heavily accented, high-pitched words that got mangled in his throat. Anita Loos recalled a Christmas Eve party in Manhattan to which Mabel arrived late, without Sam, her hair mussed and her stockings ripped. Mabel "told the girls that she'd gone to St. Patrick's Cathedral and got roughed up in the crowd. She'd gone to pray to St. Anthony, she said, to please give Sam a good nose job for Christmas." He still looked the other way at her worsening drug addiction.

Goldfish assigned Abe Lehr to watch over and reprimand Mabel when necessary, anything to avoid having to scold her himself. Goldfish absolutely refused, Lehr remembered, "to help me keep her in line"—even though her habitual tardiness often kept an entire company and crew standing idle for hours. One day, Mabel picked up a troop of soldiers in her limousine so they would not be AWOL at Camp Merritt. Another time, her whereabouts were not known for days, until her name appeared in the newspapers under a Paris dateline. After her mood had swung, she would bubble forth, completely undoing Lehr's censure with charm.

As Goldfish noticed her fast living taking its toll on her natural luster, Lehr was instructed to monitor her nightlife. She accused him of spying. But on Lehr's next birthday, Mabel sent him an expensive watch with a humorous note. "Dear Mr. Leer," she wrote. "Wishing you many returns of the day. And now, damn you, you and your dicks can tell just what time I come in. Love, Mabel."

Goldfish had no way of knowing that his giving Mabel the big rush, as Mack Sennett had before him, only drove her to hide. Her unavailability made her more desirable.

Goldfish could think of no better way to prove his love for her than by glorifying her. He bought her private lessons in "charm"—manners and poise and other social graces. The lessons pleased her at first, recalled the scenarist Frances Marion, "then they began to irk when he curbed her natural instinct to stand spraddle-legged, rocking with laughter, and tossing in a few words usually scrawled on fences."

Goldfish wanted Miss Normand's first picture for him to be a serious drama, to prove she was a serious actress. In the spring of 1917, with American doughboys heading to Europe, he starred her in a drama about women on the home front, called *Joan of Plattsburg*. Once Goldfish's salesmen gave the film a disapproving look, he realized his heart was getting in the way of his mind. He postponed its release indefinitely, and retreated to the formula pictures that had served her in the past.

As if Goldfish did not have enough on his hands, Woodrow Wilson summoned the presidents of several American film companies to come to the aid of their country. A National Association of the Motion Pictures Industry was organized to help the war effort however it could. Pickford, Fairbanks, Chaplin, even Mabel Normand, toured the nation on behalf of Liberty Bonds. President Wilson invited Goldfish and two other motion picture company presidents to the White House and told them that "France was bleeding to death and that Russia was ready to give in," Goldwyn recalled of the meeting, "—that American efforts weren't understood in Europe. Wilson wanted a motion picture of American war efforts to be rushed to Europe to set aside fears that we weren't doing much." With but a few days to "prepare the documentation of America's great war effort," Goldfish sent his crews to capture the mobilization of the Red Cross and munitions industries on film. "The following Friday," Goldwyn recalled, "our films were on a boat, headed for Europe. They had a big morale effect when they were shown to Allied troops in the field."

In a less obvious but more profound way, so did the Goldwyn Company's feature films. All American products were gratefully received in Europe, especially motion pictures. The Allies and the neutral nations could not get enough of Charlie Chaplin and Norma Talmadge. Even in Germany, American movies drew vast audiences, sometimes playing on the same bill with anti-American propaganda. Shortly after Americans began fighting over there, motion picture companies could no longer procure space on ships to move their products, and the European market was closed off.

Business life on the home front got even tougher. The Goldwyn Company grew shorthanded because of the depletion of manpower. Governmental restrictions on fuel and electricity beset studios further. In order to conserve resources during the coal famine, commercial use of electric light was curtailed. To a business that in just a decade had grown dependent on artificial light, energy rationing spelled disaster. In December 1917, motion picture studios were ordered to work only half days through the winter. Without a hit picture, the Goldwyn Company would never survive; its only hope was in maintaining its present level of production.

His light halved, he doubled his space, renting the Norma Talmadge Studio on West 48th Street and the West End Studio on 125th Street. "GOLDWYN SURMOUNTS DIFFICULTY . . . Goldwyn Resourcefulness Won Out," read the headline of one trade magazine of the day.

The tide turned. In one film after another, Mabel Normand charmed the public. *Dodging a Million* was followed by *The Floor Below,* a quintessential role for her. She played Patsy O'Rourke, a copy girl in a large newspaper office—"a slave to duty and an ally to the spirit of mischief"—who is sent after a gang of burglars and six reels later ends up in the arms of handsome Tom Moore. In May 1918, Goldfish ordered the release of *Joan of Plattsburg.* Opening to a country engaged in the serious issues of war, the film became the company's first big hit. Mrs. Woodrow Wilson appeared at a screening of the film in Washington, sharing the stage with Mabel Normand.

Other Goldwyn stars caught on as well. Madge Kennedy scored in *The Kingdom of Youth,* the story of two newlyweds getting over their petty jealousies. Tom Moore starred in the film version of a successful play called *Thirty a Week.* "The plot of this picture is simply an every day occurrence, such as you have seen in real life yourself or read in newspapers," commented *Motion Picture News.* "Not one point is exaggerated. *He* is the chauffeur, *she* the daughter of his wealthy boss." Moore's co-star—in her second film—was the innocent-looking daughter of Alabama's senior senator, Tallulah Bankhead.

ONE of the first lessons Goldfish learned in show business was to make friends with the press. Beginning in 1914, *Photoplay* magazine, which began as a theater program and swelled almost overnight to a glossy magazine with a circulation of more than a half million, satisfied the nation's new mania for any chat about moviemaking, especially stars. Stacks of imitators followed. Most major newspapers began featuring photoplay departments. What began in the press as film criticism led to motion picture news. One writer at the Chicago *Record-Herald* had a new idea: Mae Tinee on the rival *Tribune* was writing a successful column reviewing motion pictures; "Why couldn't the *Herald*—with me, of course—go a step further and branch off into bits of gossip?" wondered Louella Parsons. In no time, Mrs. Parsons found herself, as she remembered, "in a nice little Seventh Heaven as a newspaperwoman covering the movie 'beat.' No longer did I have to be nice to the spoiled darlings of the sets and the front offices. They had to be nice to me. Ah, the power of the press was never sweeter!"

She was born Louella Oettinger, unhappy practically from birth. Her father died when she was very young, leaving her mother with little money. Forever fighting her weight, Lolly was a sad girl whose family laughed at her early literary aspirations. She secretly carried the shame of her family's skeleton—an alcoholic grandfather. When she was seventeen, she married an older man named John Parsons, but the relationship hardly lasted. Soon thereafter, the Chicago *Herald* was sold and Louella found herself without a job; she and her infant daughter moved to New York, where the *Telegraph* gave her the opportunity to continue her writing about the motion picture community. Louella Parsons's reporting evolved into tattling. The woman who confessed in her memoirs, "The first person I ever cared deeply and sincerely about was—myself," turned all her inner torment outward, on that growing colony of rich and beautiful people. The scoop became both her tool and her weapon: How much one revealed to her affected how much she would reveal to the public.

Sam Goldwyn was among the first to curry her favor. He met Louella Parsons at a luncheon the motion picture critics gave him in Chicago, when she was still writing there. He found her, as he admitted years later, "a most dynamic person with a genuine homey touch. She is a very down to earth human being who gives a great deal as a friend and who would never betray a confidence. . . . Her 'power,' if you want to call it that, comes mainly from the friendships she has made and kept over the years." Goldwyn was always careful to stay on her good side.

But not the support of columnists or all the advertising in the world could help Goldwyn Picures in its first year. Their overambitious investment in properties and stars mounted daily, far exceeding their returns. While war had failed to smite Goldfish, pestilence looked as though it would. A worldwide outbreak of influenza spread at last to America in the fall of 1918, killing hundreds of people a week. In some towns, public gathering places were padlocked; most patrons avoided theaters even where they were kept open. Ticket receipts dropped everywhere.

Goldfish put on his best corporate face. "Our second year of Goldwyn is GOING TO BE THE VITAL YEAR—THE TURNING-POINT YEAR—of this company's existence," he announced in his annual message to company employees. He had hoped to spread these encouraging words at a central convention of all the Goldwyn branch managers, to be held in New York City. But there simply was not enough money in the till for such a junket. In nineteen pages of mimeographed inspiration, he said, "war-time conditions make it urgently imperative that every Goldwyn manager and every Goldwyn man be on the job in the territory every minute of the time." Most of the surviving pioneer companies—World, Mutual, Essanay, Selig, and Pathé—barely kept their heads above water. Dozens of smaller companies sank that year.

Goldwyn's weekly payroll was $90,000. "How to meet it, here was the question which tortured every waking hour," he revealed years later. The largest single stockholder in the company, Goldfish was responsible for loans amounting to almost $900,000. He was dumbfounded one summer day in 1918 when Mabel Normand entered his Fifth Avenue office and handed over a long envelope containing her Liberty Bonds. "There are only fifty thousand dollars' worth of them," she said, "but if they will tide you over you may have them."

Madge Kennedy said, "Mabel was always giving everybody gifts"—a hundred-dollar beaded bag for a stenographer, a fur coat for the wife of a production assistant who got laid off—"she just wanted everyone to like her." But Goldfish viewed this grand gesture as a display of affection. He believed his weakness had attracted her in ways his strength had not.

For weeks, Goldfish moaned about his business; and this time when he pressed Miss Normand to spend a weekend alone with him, she agreed to go through with it. He chose Saratoga, the beautiful summer retreat in the Adirondacks, just outside Gloversville. Harry Alexander, a special assistant to Goldfish, said the boss's giddiness overtook the generally tense spirit of their offices.

The evening of their departure, as Goldfish waited at Pennsylvania Station for Mabel to arrive, he was no doubt braced for her canceling yet another rendezvous. This time she showed up, in what appeared to be a state of excitement. They scurried to make the train, met in the dining car for dinner, then went to Mabel's berth. In his hurried way, he began kissing her. Mabel pulled herself up and excused herself for a moment. When she returned, her ardent suitor had trouble even recognizing her. Mabel's entire mood had been altered; everything about her seemed speeded up. She appeared amorous toward him for the first time, but there was so much frenzy to her behavior that it was frightening. She looked at him with glazed eyes. Goldfish pulled back, retiring to his own berth. Mabel spent the entire weekend completely high on drugs, locked in her room most of the time. They returned to New York City in silence. From that weekend on, Mabel never looked the same to Goldfish. His feelings for her changed from satyric to sympathetic.

A few weeks later, Goldfish broke his ankle playing handball at the New York Athletic Club.

Predawn, when he invariably awakened from a restless sleep, was Goldfish's favorite time to think, to solve problems that would present themselves later in the day. Being laid up in bed gave him extra time to salvage the Goldwyn Company in his mind. One day, as he lay with his tarsals rigged up in a sling, his business partners came to call—bearing nothing but bad tidings. Bankruptcy at last seemed inevitable. Goldfish, in his hospital bed, just listened to his partners spell out their company's demise. "Gentlemen," he finally said, pressing his fingertips together, "I see nothing but roses." In his insomnia, Goldfish had dreamed up a plan. Before his partners arrived, he had summoned Erich Schay, the controller of the company, and asked how much ready money was sitting in each of their thirty branch offices. By pooling petty-cash accounts from each city, the Goldwyn Company would be able to scrape together the payroll money.

"And how about next week?" Schay asked. Goldfish merely shrugged his shoulders, confident that "something had to happen."

On November 7, 1918, word reached New York that Germany had accepted the Allies' terms of surrender. Four days later, in a railroad car in a forest north of Paris, the armistice was signed . . . and the Goldwyn Company was given a temporary stay of execution. Shipments of film sailed to Europe almost immediately.

Cash trickling in again, Goldfish considered moving film production to California: Triangle Films in Culver City was offering a lot of cheap space and light. It was an economy measure that would buy more time for his floundering company. It also meant putting a continent between the production and business ends of the company. Goldfish was especially reluctant this time, having worked so hard to give meaning to the name of Goldwyn. In everyone's eyes he embodied the entire company. In fact, mail often arrived at the office addressed to "Samuel Goldwyn." The Goldwyn Company switchboard plugged calls for that nonexistent person straight through to him.

On December 2, 1918, he petitioned to change his name. Two weeks later, Justice Thomas F. Donnelly ordered that "said Samuel Goldfish be and he hereby is authorized to assume the name of Samuel Goldwyn in place of his present name." The Selwyns spoke of suing Goldwyn for "stealing half our name," but they realized they had no case.

More than vanity prompted Goldfish to change his name. It was again survival. Goldwyn became an imaginary character through whom Schmuel Gelbfisz—just six months shy of turning forty—could live. Goldwyn's would be the face he would show the world.

He tried out the new character on his daughter Ruth, during his infrequent weekends with her. Goldwyn liked taking her to the Central Park Zoo. Uncomfortable at small talk, he would show her the lion's cage and talk about the animal as Ruthie's lion. Then he would wax eloquent on how her lion had been the inspiration for his company's symbol.

More often, Goldwyn made dates with Ruth and canceled them because of business. Despite all the gifts and sudden rushes of attention, the young girl saw right through him, becoming more reluctant with each visit ever to see him again. "I have not one memory of ever spending a single night under the same roof as my father," she said a lifetime later. "Not one. There are no family memories—no family anything—that include him so far as I'm concerned. He was not proud of me."

Young Ruth hammered out her own emotional armor. While still in elementary school, she assumed a posture that would protect her. "I grew up," she explained, "never expecting anything from anybody. That way I'd never get hurt."

Her father had his own way. For the rest of his life, whenever fear or anger or grief threatened to pull him under, he would indulge in a short crying jag, then pull through by saying to himself, "I've still got Goldwyn."

7 The Business of America

PAST THE New Amsterdam Theater's Pre-Raphaelite-style lobby awaited the *Ziegfeld Follies.* Appearing in the 1918 edition of the show—backed by Florenz Ziegfeld, Jr.,'s patented chorus line of beautiful women—were Marilyn Miller, Eddie Cantor, W. C. Fields, and a lariat-twirling Oklahoman who could drawl for hours in the most charming manner on whatever topic popped into his head. He especially liked poking at politicians. Will Rogers became, in the words of the producer's wife, Billie Burke, "Ziegfeld's greatest star." He never missed a performance, and he never failed to bring the house down. Producer and performer were bound only by a handshake.

Rex Beach was just then adapting his book *Laughing Bill Hyde* for Goldwyn Pictures. His wife thought their friend Will Rogers would be perfect to play the lead in this love and adventure story set in the Klondike gold fields. Rogers, who had never appeared before a motion picture camera, told her he didn't "know anything about the blamed thing. I thought pictures were made up of just three people: Mary Pickford, Charlie Chaplin, and Douglas Fairbanks." She said, "That's all right, you can learn." He liked the book enough to want to go along with the venture, so long as he did not have to renege on his promises to Ziegfeld.

Sam Goldwyn had mixed feelings about Will Rogers. "He knew that being a star on stage had nothing to do with becoming a star on the screen," said Arthur Mayer. But Goldwyn took a chance, and Will Rogers made *Laughing Bill Hyde* at the Fort Lee studio in the late summer of 1918, leaving the set each day in time to make his nightly curtain at the New Amsterdam.

Bridling Will Rogers for work in the movies seemed hopeless from the start—"they had to put a hitch on my upper lip to get me to smear paint all over my contour. Even that could not disguise this old, homely pan of mine." He felt like a complete rube. Hobart Henley, the director, explained the setup of the first scene to Rogers—"the scene where your old pal dies. You have broken out of jail, and he gets hurt and you are bringing him into the doctor's office at night to get him treated, and he dies. It's the dramatic scene of the whole opera." The actor cried, "But I haven't got out of jail yet!"

Laughing Bill Hyde, running a little longer than an hour, opened at the Rivoli Theater in New York City on September 30, 1918. *Motion Picture News* commented that "Will Rogers turns out to be such a fine actor, that you would never know he was acting." Box-office returns were modest, but Goldwyn had reason to give the actor another try. Word around town matched the December 1918 review in *Motion Pictures,* which said, "This is the very finest film released under the Goldwyn banner."

Will Rogers stayed with the *Follies* through the end of its New York run, then went on its annual tour of major American cities. He received $1,000 a week. Realizing Rogers had created a following in the hinterlands, Goldwyn caught up with him in Cleveland and offered a long-term, full-time contract—$2,250 a week for the first year, with an option for a second year at $3,000 per week. He would have to choose between stage and screen.

On September 30, 1918, Will Rogers signed with Goldwyn. He played at the New Amsterdam until Saturday night, May 31, 1919, fulfilling his obligations to Ziegfeld and leaving just enough time to pack up his wife, three children, horses, dogs, and goat and report to Goldwyn's new production headquarters in California.

By the spring of 1919, most motion picture production had transferred from Fort Lee to Mount Lee, the broad slope of the Santa Monica Mountains that loomed over Hollywood. There were over one hundred motion picture studios in the Los Angeles area by then—clustered mostly to the east and south of the hills, but sprinkled to the west as well. William Fox had established his first studio on what had originally been Colonel William N. Selig's lot in the Edendale area. Independent producer Louis B. Mayer moved his family from Massachusetts and began making movies on that lot as well. Carl Laemmle had officially opened a large Spanish mission of a studio in 1915 on Lankershim Boulevard, nestled in Cahuenga Pass, the wilds of the San Fernando Valley on one hand and the boom town of Hollywood on the other. Lacking easy access to the downtown film-processing laboratories, Universal City became a self-sufficient enclave, a second home to scores of cameramen, actors, directors, and writers. By 1917, it maintained its own fire department, police department, hospital, commissary, garages, and zoo.

Most of the action was in Hollywood, within walking distance of Famous Players–Lasky. Zukor had bought all the open land from Selma and Vine avenues to Argyle and Sunset Boulevard. What would become the Paramount studio on Melrose Avenue was originally built in 1918 by the Paralta Corporation. Dozens of small studios and laboratories sprang up on Sunset Boulevard between Gower and Beachwood Drive; Charlie Chaplin and his brother Sydney broke ground on their own studio in the 1400 block of La Brea Avenue, stretching north to Sunset. A few blocks above that, Hollywood Boulevard suddenly found itself lined with one- and two-story boxy buildings side by each, and a forest of telephone poles. In just the years since Sam Goldwyn had been in the motion picture business, the population of Hollywood had jumped from 12,000 to 35,000 people.

Far beyond this center of activity lay the city's newest real estate development, a community to the southwest. In 1915, a developer named Harry Culver had offered free land to anyone who would build a motion picture studio in this new city he was naming after himself. Thomas Ince had grabbed the sixteen-acre parcel of parched scrub to the south of a dirt road that became Washington Boulevard just as he and Griffith and Sennett were forming Triangle Films. By 1918, the three partners had disbanded. After a successful winter filming there, Sam Goldwyn purchased their modest but modern studio facilities for $325,000 in what was considered the backwater of Hollywood. With most of the Goldwyn actors and crews already in California, filming continued uninterrupted under the supervision of Abe Lehr.

Behind a three-story office building set back from Washington Boulevard stood six glass stages for filming. Scattered about were workshops, storerooms for properties and costumes, and areas for actors to make up. Goldwyn ordered new lawns rolled out, to tie the whole studio together into one tidy community. He offered Will Rogers an old building on the lot for stabling his livestock.

"Out in Hollywood, they say you're not a success unless you owe fifty thousand dollars to somebody, have five cars, can develop temperament without notice or reason at all, and have been mixed up in four divorce cases and two breach-of-promise cases," said Rogers. "Well, as a success in Hollywood, I'm a rank failure. . . . I hold only two distinctions in the movie business: ugliest fellow in 'em, and I still have the same wife I started with." By Will Rogers's standards, Sam Goldwyn was well on the road to success—with debts and divorce weighing heavily on his mind.

In March 1919, Blanche Lasky married Hector Turnbull, a tweedy Scotsman, who had been the dramatic critic for the New York *Herald Tribune*. "He was a man for all seasons," remembered Jesse Lasky, Jr., "a newspaperman, a boxer, war hero, and finally a novelist and film executive." After writing the stories for several pictures that Sam Goldfish had overseen, Turnbull had become New York story editor for Famous Players–Lasky. "He was quite perfect in every way," recalled Ruth, who had assumed her mother's maiden name, "—except he was an alcoholic. But after my father, that was easy to live with. He was an easy man to love."

Her father, on the other hand, became more remote than ever. He grew so disturbed over the news of Blanche's remarriage that he stopped all alimony and child-support payments. His divorce decree had ordered him to pay his ex-wife one hundred dollars a week for the rest of her life, an additional fifty dollars a week so long as she remained unmarried, and fifty dollars more for Ruth's support. Goldwyn saw things differently. She had a new husband to support them all, and this way, Goldwyn thought, he would be done with his ex-wife forever. By the end of the year, Blanche Lasky Turnbull had hired an attorney named Nathan Burkan to retrieve her back alimony.

His own attorneys found Goldwyn's position untenable. They told him he could not arbitrarily stop payments, not even of the fifty dollars a week that were to end upon Blanche's remarriage; only the court could order that. He was persuaded at least to maintain child-support payments while the case dragged into the following year. In October 1920, the Appellate Division of the New York State Supreme Court would instruct Goldwyn to make the back payments and to keep up his future ones as previously determined. But he would quickly resume his dilatory ways.

Although Blanche restrained herself from discussing the child's father, seven-year-old Ruth could not help picking up fragments and choosing sides. In the spring of 1919, the Turnbulls went to San Francisco for several weeks, before moving to Los Angeles.

Their relocation drove Goldwyn into a panic. He had not spent a fraction of the time with his daughter to which he was legally entitled, but he liked knowing she was available when it was convenient for him. In May, returning from one of his visits to what Will Rogers called "the celluloid coast," Goldwyn stopped off in San Francisco and tried to pack as much love as he could into two days with Ruth. They talked of writing letters to each other, an obligation his sensitive daughter took seriously.

Ruth missed her father. She said as much in a series of extremely touching letters that usually closed with "Love from your sweet heart," a line of
X's, and her name—Ruth Lasky.

He always replied promptly, with a formally typed, dictated letter, addressed to Ruth Goldwyn. So long as he felt he had recovered some ground
with his daughter, he was extremely loving, even gushy. "Father is very,
very lonesome for his little sweetheart," he wrote her on May 13, 1919.

> I don't remember enjoying anything in my life as much as I did being
> with you in San Francisco for two days. You are a wonderful little
> darling and I love you better than anything in the world.
>
> I am looking forward to the day when I can be with my little
> sweetheart all the time because I love you so much that I want to be
> with you.
>
> All the love there is, I send to my little darling, with a million
> kisses.

If, however, so much as a few weeks passed without her writing to him,
Goldwyn reproached the girl, gently at first.

The correspondence quickly revealed Goldwyn's dismay with their re-
lationship. He felt he was giving more than he was getting. "I WROTE YOU
TWO LETTERS WITHIN LAST TWO WEEKS," he wired Ruth on May 26.
"FATHER NEVER FORGETS YOU. I THINK OF YOU EVERY MINUTE OF THE
DAY BECAUSE I LOVE YOU BETTER THAN EVERYONE ELSE IN THE WORLD.
YOU ARE A WONDERFUL LITTLE DARLING AND I ADORE MY LITTLE BABY
MORE THAN I EVER DID." Ruth would write back of her activities—swimming and horseback riding—but it rankled Goldwyn to read of another
man's rocking the cradle he never did. He found an ally in Ruth's nurse,
an Irish Catholic named Catherine McDonough, to whom he sent a private
fund from which Ruth could buy special items she really wanted—"as
presents from me," he wrote Ruth. There was always a big tip for Catherine as well.

By the end of the year, Goldwyn's letters to Ruth were following the
pattern of his visits. There simply was no time for him to maintain a full-
time relationship with anyone, certainly not while his company was sinking. Goldwyn Pictures Corporation had all but broken even in 1918, but
in 1919 they suffered a $100,000 loss.

"The war for motion picture supremacy had moved on to new battle-
grounds," observed Terry Ramsaye. "Now in its next phase it was becoming an issue of theatre seats, real estate investment and large scale financial
investments." Companies bigger than Goldwyn's—such as Fox and the

new First National Exhibitors' Circuit—got bigger still. Adolph Zukor's spreading empire now included Paramount-Artcraft, Famous Players–Lasky, and Select (out of which he had aced Lewis Selznick, practically into obscurity). Then Zukor joined forces with William Randolph Hearst, who had established Cosmopolitan Productions to showcase the talents of his mistress, Marion Davies. Douglas Fairbanks, William S. Hart, Wallace Reid, Dorothy Gish, Marguerite Clark, and Gloria Swanson all fell under Zukor's aegis. D. W. Griffith, who had gone bankrupt producing *Intolerance,* found himself signing on to make films for Artcraft Pictures in 1917. Zukor showed his understanding of the business by purchasing flagship theaters in all the major cities.

Companies smaller than Goldwyn's, and some that were just starting up, were surpassing him. Metro Pictures, for example, had been reduced to producing the cheap "program" filler between main features; but in the summer of 1919, their president, Richard Rowland, and his attorney, J. Robert Rubin, went to Zukor to propose that Metro join his team. "The only reason I'd have to take you in," he reportedly told the two, "would be to put you out of business." After being shown the door, Rowland and Rubin called on another former furrier. Marcus Loew's chain of theaters had grown considerably over the past five years. Loew had picture houses from Atlanta to Boston, from New Orleans to Hamilton, Ontario, plus a few new ones in New York. When he decided to acquire some theaters on the West Coast, he refinanced his company, securing a loan just short of $10 million. Loew, like Zukor, saw that the only way to be a superpower in motion pictures was to combine production with exhibition.

Loew's Incorporated bought Metro Pictures Corporation—which owned a charming lot of green-shuttered buildings at Cahuenga Boulevard and Romaine Street in Hollywood—for $3 million, half in Loew's stock. A darkened New York office went with the deal, along with a modest roster of talent, notably the alluring new star Nazimova. Loew had a long way to go in order to catch up to Zukor, but at least he had a factory in which to make the goods.

In just seven years, motion picture actors had risen from obscure employees to international idols. The most ambitious were establishing their own production companies. Benjamin P. Schulberg, who began as a press agent for Zukor and became a studio executive, thought the biggest stars in pictures should form an organization and distribute their own pictures, thus retaining the bulk of the profits they generated.

In a series of conferences, Pickford, Fairbanks, Chaplin, William S. Hart, and director Griffith kicked the idea around. Hart immediately dropped out of the discussions, citing his loyalty to Zukor (who was paying him $200,000 per picture). The lawyers for the others drew up papers establishing a corporation. On February 5, 1919, the four undisputed giants in motion pictures affixed their autographs, agreeing to "become associated with each other in the marketing of motion pictures and to set up a company with headquarters in New York having the name United Artists Corporation."

The "big four" set their distribution fee at 20 percent of the gross domestically and 30 percent foreign, thereby operating more as a service organization than as an investment; the rates were lower than those charged by Zukor or First National or even Goldwyn. Hiram Abrams, who had been running Paramount's theaters, fell out with Zukor and became general manager, B. P. Schulberg his right-hand man. Thus, even a handful of artists were staking a greater claim than Goldwyn in competing against the corporations that controlled the American motion picture market. "So," remarked Richard Rowland when he first heard of United Artists, "the lunatics have taken charge of the asylum."

Goldwyn's stars steadily dimmed. Geraldine Farrar's next few vehicles were box-office failures, so he suggested she stay off the screen for a while, even though her contract guaranteed an annual $125,000 over the next two years. Farrar, the ultimate professional, took out her contract and ripped it up right before Goldwyn's eyes. Pauline Frederick cost him much more money; she appeared in several expensive failures before her contract expired.

Mabel Normand's career began wasting away at an accelerated pace. Even the posed stills from her pictures indicated the ravages of drugs— her weight fluctuated wildly and there was a deadness in her once vibrant eyes. Goldwyn asked Abe Lehr to dine with her at least once a week.

Mabel was losing her timing, but at the moment she was the company's salvation. Goldwyn summoned her to New York. After her next three pictures, *Upstairs*, *Jinx* (in which the twenty-four-year-old Mabel played a circus orphan half her age), and *Pinto*, he acknowledged the change in her. Renting space at the Erbograph Studios at 146th Street and Seventh Avenue, Goldwyn starred her in *The Slim Princess*.

It was another "Cinderella" picture, of which the public was tiring. Photographs from the production reveal that Mabel had taken the title to unhealthy extremes; she looked drawn and emaciated. Goldwyn followed that with *What Happened to Rosa?*, the silly story of a hosiery clerk who believes she is the reincarnation of a famous Spanish dancer. Then she made *Head Over Heels*, a film so muddled that Goldwyn could not even release it. Her cocaine addiction had sucked her completely into its vortex.

Men were still in her thrall. Actor-director William Desmond Taylor pursued her. She was seen in the company of matinee idol Lew Cody, known around town as the Butterfly Man, because he always dressed so beautifully. And Mack Sennett, who had not given up the chase, went to see Sam Goldwyn. Sennett was desperate to spring Mabel Normand from the remaining eighteen months of her contract and to make one more Cinderella story. "I thought if I could get her for 'Molly O' I could keep her forever," Sennett later admitted. "She's a pretty expensive luxury, isn't she?" he said to Goldwyn. "Mabel Normand is the most valuable property in Hollywood," Goldwyn replied. But he let her go for $20,000. Over the next few years he saw drugs, scandals, and poor health bring her career to its knees.

One by one, the residents of Goldwyn's "old ladies' home" were laid to rest. Only Chaplin, Fairbanks, and Pickford (pushing thirty and divorcing her husband, Owen Moore, but still playing the title roles of *Pollyanna* and *Little Lord Fauntleroy*) seemed to hold the audience's interest longer than a few years. Public taste kept changing, constantly demanding new and different types. At the Goldwyn studios, the burden would have to be borne by the cowboy from Oklahoma.

Will Rogers arrived in Los Angeles "rearin' to go." Over the next three years, he appeared in a dozen pictures, most with the same basic plot: An amiable fellow, usually a cowpoke in the South or the West, is thrust into a situation in which he must overcome his faintheartedness.

Rogers did not draw at the box office. Women made up the majority of moviegoers, and they preferred strong, handsome types. The titles of Rogers's next two years' motion pictures reveal Goldwyn's attempt to put across the charm of his character with the suggestion of romance for the ladies: *Jes' Call Me Jim, Cupid the Cowpuncher, Honest Hutch, Guile of Women, Boys Will Be Boys,* and *An Unwilling Hero.* As with the early cinema's operatic stars, the success of some performers was as much auditory as visual. For all Will Rogers's charm, his pictures fell flat without the benefit of his voice.

In its descending spiral, the Goldwyn Company could not seriously compete against the other studios by chasing the same stars. Rex Beach suggested that people went to the movies—above all—to see stories, not stars. So instead of currying "famous players," Goldwyn established a new division of his company: Eminent Authors.

"Just classy writers," Arthur Mayer remembered the barely literate Goldwyn telling a cadre of salesmen. "Goldwyn's got just classy writers." Rex Beach culled the list: Gertrude Atherton, a California novelist and the great-grandniece of Benjamin Franklin, who wrote romantic and historical novels; Gouverneur Morris, the great-grandson of one of America's founding fathers, who wrote action dramas; Rupert Hughes, a novelist and short-story writer (whose brother established a successful tool company that would be handed down to Rupert's nephew Howard); Mary Roberts Rinehart, best known for her detective fiction; Basil King, a Canadian-born novelist and the rector of Christ Church in Cambridge, Massachusetts; and short-story writer Leroy Scott. They were all among the most popular writers of their day.

They granted Goldwyn the motion picture rights to any works they might write during the term of the contract. He (and his partner in this venture, Rex Beach) would have ninety days to decide whether or not they wanted to film the work. If they did, the author would receive a $10,000 advance against one third of the film's earnings. With most Goldwyn films costing $80,000 apiece and hit pictures earning in the high six figures, the authors easily stood to become even more affluent than eminent.

The first week of July, the Goldwyn advertising department heralded Eminent Authors in a thirty-two-page brochure that was stapled into *Motion Picture News* and *Moving Picture World.* Goldwyn took pride in its being "the largest and most elaborate insert ever used in the industry." (Zukor responded to the announcement by signing Somerset Maugham, Arnold Bennett, Sir Gilbert Parker, and Elinor Glyn, a glamorous redhead from England, whose personality was as sensational as her novels.) To make good on all the claims in his advertisement, Goldwyn had to put his entire portfolio of stock (including 11,148 shares of Goldwyn Pictures Corporation, then valued at $100 per share) down as collateral against $200,000 worth of loans.

Most serious authors proved unsuccessful in silent films. The language of books simply was not that of motion pictures. Few prose writers ever got the hang of it. Once a studio owned the rights to a story, there was little more for the author to do. Studio executives told Mary Roberts Rinehart of "the vast gulf between the picture audience and the reading public," then passed one of her books on to the scenario department to translate into a motion picture.

One by one, the Eminent Authors came to Hollywood to try, in Mrs. Rinehart's phrase, to "beat the game"; but just as quickly they returned to their typewriters at home, where they could be masters of their literature, not slaves to illiterates.

Of the original Eminent Authors, only Rex Beach and Rupert Hughes delivered both the prestige and the audiences Goldwyn sought. One of Hughes's efforts, a soapy mother-love melodrama called *The Old Nest,* earned nearly a million dollars for the Goldwyn Company. Goldwyn salesman Arthur Mayer was instructed never to sell that film without "wrapping around the exhibitor's neck" three or four Will Rogers features. The Goldwyn Company posted a third-year loss of $82,937.10.

"I am not in a very good humour these days," Goldwyn wrote Abe Lehr on June 9, 1919, "as I have been very nervous but I have never allowed it to get the best of me." In fact, Goldwyn was assembling a "big deal" to resuscitate his company—one that was "liable to give us the exclusive rights to every famous success produced on Broadway."

That summer, the Goldwyn Company refinanced itself by negotiating deals with a handful of the most industrious producers on Broadway. Lee and J. J. Shubert, Sam H. Harris, and Al H. Woods (who specialized in "comedy cheapies") each bought into the company for $125,000. For shares of voting stock, they granted exclusive options to the picture rights of their plays. If Goldwyn chose to film any of the plays, he and the respective producer would agree on the purchase price. Goldwyn's company was still undercapitalized and lacked outlets for its product; but for the first time, he had preemption on most of the major hits on Broadway. The price for this infusion of money and material was high. Each new partner subtracted from Goldwyn's power.

An even bigger investor was standing in the wings. Al Woods's wife had a cousin who was about to change the fate of the Goldwyn Company.

Frank Joseph Godsol was a darkly handsome man-about-town, a fabled character who first hit New York just before the war. Tall and trim, he exuded so much confidence that people were inclined to overlook his checkered past. Since 1912 he had been making deals for the Shubert organization at home and abroad. In addition to his interests in an Italian studio, he owned and managed several theaters on the Continent. But word had it that Godsol (born Goldsoll, in Cleveland) had promised the French army dozens of healthy horses and delivered spavined mules. He had also promoted a product called Tecla pearls, which he insisted were so "much superior to the original" that he never advertised their being artificial. He was currently under review of the French Council of War. People saw in Godsol what they wanted to see. Goldwyn discerned a self-made man with aspirations and a taste for luxury, someone in many ways like himself.

Godsol drove a Hispano-Suiza, smoked large coronas, traveled with a retinue of valets, maids, secretaries, a bookie, and always a beautiful actress. He played bridge for a dollar a point; and he was, noted one observer, "willing to wager on any proposition." His pockets literally bulging with money, he was looking for a new business venture, a vulnerable motion picture company he could raid. He beguiled Goldwyn with two magic words: theaters and money.

No business had flourished during the four winters of war so much as Du Pont of Delaware, manufacturers of munitions and gunpowder. The company earned over one billion dollars in gross income between 1914 and 1918, profits close to sixty million dollars each of those years. The company established a Development Department, investing in plastics, enamels, rubber, dyes, paints, varnishes, and heavy chemicals. Just when Goldwyn was considering buying only Du Pont raw film, Godsol interested two members of the du Pont family in motion pictures.

Godsol catalyzed a deal, and the Goldwyn Company entered the world of big business. He directed an immediate increase in its capital stock to one million shares. With Godsol and the du Ponts came barons from Wilmington, the president of the Chase National Bank, and an officer of the Central Union Trust Company. The turn of a page, and the Goldwyn Company books went from tens of thousands of dollars in red ink to five million in the black.

Even with so august a board, Goldwyn was not about to fall again into the ceremonial position of chairman. He demanded a voting trust agreement that gave him veto power over any further consolidation or mergers involving the Goldwyn Company, and he was named president of the company. Godsol accepted the ceremonial title. The two men were to receive identical salaries—one thousand dollars a week. Godsol said he would serve his first year for one dollar.

On December 17, 1919, Goldwyn wrote Abe Lehr:

> The last deal we made has placed us in the position where everyone in the industry envies us. The Goldwyn Company stands as solid as the rock of Gibraltar in the eyes of the public, as well as in the banks. We have today $5,000,000 in cash in the banks, which is more than any picture company in the world has laying in the banks, and that balance puts us in a position where we have a credit of like amount. In other words, if we needed $10,000,000 cash tomorrow, we could get it, and further, it is understood should we need $10,000,000 or $15,000,000 more the DuPont and Chase people will find it for us.

Security became him, brightening his entire outlook. "You and I are integral parts of the Fifth greatest industry in the world," Goldwyn wrote his employees in his fourth annual message. With visions of grandeur, Goldwyn articulated his credo, watchwords by which he lived for the rest of his professional life:

> *Every* picture we make is intended to be a Big picture. We feel when we start that it will be a knockout—and we strain every nerve to

make it a hit. But in creative work it simply can't be done and never will be done. If out of sixty pictures we get six or seven big hits we pat ourselves on the back. If out of these hits we get two or three knockouts you can't hold us. So when you see a Goldwyn picture no matter how you like it just consider that a lot of hard working men and women put all they had in it to make it successful and if they failed it is only human. But one thing we certainly try mighty hard to do [Goldwyn emphasized], and that is to make *every* Goldwyn picture, clean, [and] "classy" . . .

For $50,000, Goldwyn purchased twenty acres adjacent to the Culver City studio. He commissioned architect Stephen Merritt to design a new administration building, and all around it a complex of edifices and avenues. The cozy studio was transformed into an Olympian mill. Behind Ince's Corinthian columns rose a walled city, running almost a half mile along Washington Boulevard, a make-believe world in miniature. Within two years, the Goldwyn lot contained forty-two buildings; Russian, southern, Alaskan, Spanish, French, Chinese, western, and New York streets were reconstructed; J. J. Cohn, who was brought to Culver City and managed the lot for the next four decades, exaggerated only slightly when he said, "Rome was built in a day."

With more money on hand, Goldwyn believed he could bring greater luster to his notion of Eminent Authors. After Kipling and Shaw, Maurice Maeterlinck was possibly the most honored writer alive. Known primarily for his fantasies, melancholy legends, and works of natural history—*The Blue Bird, Pelléas and Mélisande,* and *The Life of the Bee*—Maeterlinck arrived in New York at the start of the new decade for a nationwide lecture tour. He could not speak English, so his speeches had to be written out phonetically. Before a packed house at Carnegie Hall, the Belgian appeared, his script in hand—with "ainded" written for the word "ended," and "ichou" for "issue." Halfway through the lecture, Maeterlinck got as confused as his audience and walked off the stage.

A concert impresario from Boston named Henry Russell entered Maeterlinck's life, determined to make the most of the situation. He thought the universal language of film might be just the idiom for him and that Sam Goldwyn, famous for hiring "just classy writers," seemed the right studio head. Russell became Maeterlinck's agent and brought him to Goldwyn's office; the latter had summoned his publicity man Howard Dietz (who could speak some French). As Dietz recounted, "Goldwyn listed the stipend of his eminent authors in order to give Maeterlinck the feeling that he would share the rarefied atmosphere of American literary lights and American substantial terms." As Goldwyn reeled off the roster of his eminences, from Gertrude Atherton to Booth Tarkington, he drew a blank stare from Maeterlinck. "What is he," Goldwyn asked Dietz, "a dumbbell?"

Once Goldwyn began to talk money, Maeterlinck showed signs of comprehension. The poet-playwright agreed to the basic Eminent Authors contract. One unique clause reflected Goldwyn's second thoughts. The "dumbbell" was to submit a rough sketch of his story to the producer before proceeding to a final script. If Goldwyn could not get a shootable scenario out of the Nobel Prize winner, he would only be out the initial $5,000 advance. Goldwyn intended to get at least that much back in publicity, starting with a whistle-stop train trip across the country.

Goldwyn was in Culver City to greet Maeterlinck and to meet his every need. This included a house on a sunny hilltop. "I feel proud to have allied to the production forces of my organization, the brain and inspired pen of Maurice Maeterlinck and to establish as a policy of Goldwyn the desire to secure the greatest creative brains from the world's literati," Goldwyn announced to a group of exhibitors.

One of early Hollywood's chestnuts is that Maeterlinck's first screenwriting was an adaptation of his *Life of the Bee* and that upon its submission, Goldwyn ran out of his office screaming, "My God, the hero is a bee!" But Howard Dietz remembered Maeterlinck's going two months before getting a page written, and that was an abstract story entitled "The Power of Light." All Goldwyn remembered of the author's first scenario was that it was a useless notion about a little boy and a mattress and a lot of blue feathers. Still, Goldwyn liked having Maeterlinck on the lot. He made a point of introducing him to all the press and any visiting dignitaries as "the greatest writer on earth. He's the guy who wrote *The Birds and the Bees*."

Goldwyn urged Maeterlinck to watch some movies. Day after day, the Belgian sat in projection rooms, absorbing action pictures. His next scenario, Goldwyn recalled, started with "the lid slowly rising from a sewer in a street of Paris; up from the sewer came the face of a gory and bedraggled female Apache with a dagger gripped between her teeth." Maeterlinck's Hollywood career "ainded" there. Goldwyn accompanied the writer to the train station. On the platform, Sam patted him on the shoulder and said, "Don't worry, Maurice. You'll make good yet."

Goldwyn sailed to Europe on the *Mauretania* on March 23, 1920, for almost two months of business. He hated to leave with so many irons in the fire—especially his pending offer to buy the opulent five-thousand-seat Capitol Theater in New York—but the trip was necessary. The Continent had reopened as a major film market, and he could not trust anybody else to close these deals, which would serve as boilerplate terms for many years to come. His representative was stuck in negotiations with William Maxwell Aitken, better known as Lord Beaverbrook—the newspaper tycoon, British minister of information, and controller of 80 percent of England's first-run cinemas. Goldwyn also had every intention of visiting the greatest living playwright in the English language. He was cheered to learn that his publicity director was a friend of the novelist Hugh de Selincourt, who was a friend of George Bernard Shaw . . . and that Mr. Goldwyn had been invited to tea.

Shaw—sixty-four years old, between *Heartbreak House* and *Back to Methuselah*—had rejected out of hand the offers of countless motion picture people. Goldwyn's entreaties appealed to him. Mr. and Mrs. Shaw entertained Goldwyn at their apartment on Adelphi Terrace and struck him as "contented and settled as a hardware merchant of Topeka and his wife."

"To my surprise," Goldwyn recalled, "I learned that he was a picture enthusiast. He told me that there were two people whose films he never missed—Charlie Chaplin and Mary Pickford. Regarding the former, he was especially enthusiastic." Goldwyn assured Shaw that he would treat his plays with velvet gloves, that their integrity would be preserved at all costs, commercial considerations be damned.

The precise words at their parting were known only to the two of them, but the next day a newspaperman called on Shaw to learn the outcome of his conversation with the American film magnate. "Everything is all right," Shaw reported. "There is only one difference between Mr. Goldwyn and me. Whereas he is after art I am after money." Both men dined out on the epigram for years. Shaw had not heard the last of Sam Goldwyn. He would be back every few years to press his case.

Goldwyn was no more successful when he called on H. G. Wells, who also had him to tea. He suggested that Wells visit California and write some stories for his company. "Oh," the writer said, "I should like to come, for I know I should enjoy the California sunshine and meeting Charlie Chaplin. The only trouble with me is that I never could write on order. I haven't been able to do it for magazines or publishers and I should certainly fail abjectly when it came to doing it for the screen." Goldwyn left on the table an offer of a trip to California as his guest, with no obligation other than to "look over the situation." Wells never took him up on it. As Goldwyn left Wells's house that afternoon for his room at the Savoy Hotel, he was momentarily struck by the fact that only twenty-five years earlier, as an illiterate Polish immigrant, he had scavenged these same streets of London, hungry and penniless.

Goldwyn was more successful on the mainland. He drummed up business for Goldwyn Pictures—especially his newest film, *The Penalty*, a tour de force for actor Lon Chaney, from a story by Gouveneur Morris. In Germany, he saw an intriguing German picture directed by Robert Wiene, *The Cabinet of Dr. Caligari*, and became its American distributor.

The film struck many discerning viewers as the first demonstration since *The Birth of a Nation* of the expanding potential of the motion picture camera. It provided a new look at how motion pictures could photograph life and tell stories. All aspects of the film were stylized. Sets were painted, for example, without straight horizontal and vertical lines; mechanical movements by the principal actors and contrasts of light and shadow added to the film's terror. It was the talk of the Continent, the rage among intellectuals. No one was more amazed than Erich Pommer—the head of UFA, the German film trust—that this cheaply made film proved a masterpiece, not to mention a big box-office attraction in Germany. Goldwyn figured the film would perform similarly at home.

Goldwyn was due to arrive in New York on Sunday, May 16, 1920, at which time he intended to conclude his negotiating for the Capitol Theater. Aboard ship, he picked up a newspaper and read that the deal had been closed. When he reached the office, he asked how the company was going to finance the deal and was told "that everything had been taken care of." When he pressed for further information, Joe Godsol explained that in Goldwyn's absence, the B. F. Keith theater interests had driven hard to buy the house for themselves; so Godsol seized it. The result was less an outright purchase than a merger: For $1.9 million, the Goldwyn Corporation bought a half interest in the Capitol Theater, which in turn received exclusive exhibition of Goldwyn films in first run. A substantial portion of the purchase was to be made in company stock, thus doubling the number of directors under Godsol's chairmanship.

Goldwyn had never had any trouble with Edgar Selwyn, and he had even accepted dealing with Lee Shubert and Joe Godsol and Eugene du Pont, and all their associates. Now there was Capitol Theater builder Messmore Kendall and his faction to contend with—General T. Coleman du Pont, mining magnate Colonel William Braden, Major Edward Bowes (the theater's general manager), even the president of the United Cigar Stores Company. One middle-management employee warned company newcomer Harry Alexander, "If you want to keep your job around here, you'll have to run between the raindrops."

Across the hall from Goldwyn's austerely furnished office, Joe Godsol moved in, laying down elegant Oriental rugs and hanging up European paintings. Periodically, he slipped the building's elevator starter a crisp five-dollar bill, so that the lift would be at his beck and call. "I have been unusually busy, busier than I have ever been before, in fact, too much so, as I find I am unusually nervous and unable to sleep nights," Goldwyn wrote Abe Lehr, the only person in the world to whom he could confide about personal matters. "Never in my life have I given as much to an enterprise as I have to this one. It is a matter of pride with me to see this thing a very big success. You will appreciate it is not the easiest thing in the world to have a lot of new associates and keep everyone happy." Goldwyn cleared his desk every night, locking his papers in his wall safe.

Godsol tried to unnerve Goldwyn at every turn. He often threw statistics in his face that showed how poorly Goldwyn pictures were performing. At the March 19 board of directors meeting, Goldwyn was told that the company was spending too much money on production. "We are cutting down in our home office in every direction and of course it is up to you that this is done at the studio without affecting the quality of our pictures," he notified Lehr as soon as the meeting ended. Meantime, the Goldwyn Corporation built itself up as a motion picture conglomerate—buying into the Ascher Theater chain in the Midwest, Bishop Cass Theaters in the Rockies, and the Miller Amusement Company's theaters in Los Angeles—all of which, Goldwyn thought, would rescue his company.

The president and the chairman of the board crossed swords over every matter. When they were in the same city, Godsol thought nothing of storming unannounced into Goldwyn's office with his complaints; when Goldwyn was on a business trip—three to the West Coast and one abroad in 1920 alone—Godsol had his say in telegrams, running on for pages about press releases, production, distribution, exhibition, mergers, actors, bankers, and more—all within weeks of his joining the company.

After a month, Godsol got vicious. He scheduled important board meetings when Goldwyn was out of town, and he continued to make decisions unilaterally, in the name of exigency. Then he sicked Goldwyn's allies against each other on budgetary matters. Most difficult for Goldwyn was "to sit at executive meetings and listen to the criticism of those who have not the slightest idea of the motion picture business."

On Thursday, September 2, 1920—less than a year after Godsol's arrival—Samuel Goldwyn was backed into a vote of confidence; he "tendered his resignation as President of the corporation, as a member of the executive committee of the board, as voting trustee under the voting trust agreement dated October 10, 1919, and as president or other officer and director of all subsidiary corporations." The resignation was accepted.

Messmore Kendall, the most level head in the boardroom, was put in charge of the corporation until a committee of five had elected Goldwyn's successor. The meeting was adjourned until the following week.

When the September 8 meeting was postponed until September 28, Goldwyn decided to await the verdict in White Sulphur Springs, a hundred miles northwest of New York City. "I should like to hear from you at least once a week," Goldwyn wrote Lehr, "as I am naturally keenly interested in the progress the studio is making, as well as the progress you are making with the new management." His emotions rendered raw from his months as the company punching bag—"I had to stop making pictures and spend all my time explaining things," he later recalled of the period— he admitted to Lehr, "This whole affair has been the most severe blow I have ever had but I hope to profit by the experience. The only consolation I have is that I am getting all these knocks while I am still young enough to stand them."

Messmore Kendall found the board of directors at odds on every proposition, not just those regarding Samuel Goldwyn. "The meetings were most unfriendly," he remembered, "and any proposition advanced by one Director was immediately taboo to the other faction." The September 28 meeting accomplished little more than to move to adjourn until October 5. The committee of five needed more time to compose a financial plan for the rescue of the corporation. Because of Goldwyn's "familiarity with the affairs of the company," Kendall asked him to draft a proposal.

He labored faithfully and brought out an elaborate plan which he had prepared [Kendall recalled]. He was still a member of the Board of Directors although no longer President. He started to read his recommendation when he was interrupted by a Director who had a very substantial investment in the Goldwyn Company.

"Before you read that, Sam, I want to tell you now I am against it."

"But you have not heard what I have to recommend," protested Goldwyn.

"I don't care what you recommend, without hearing it I am against it."

When Kendall could stand the disputes no longer, he stepped down, recommending that the company be put back in the hands that created it.

On October 22, 1920, the board obliged, renaming Samuel Goldwyn president for two years. But, it ruled:

. . . Mr. Godsol shall accept the office of chairman of the board and
the by-laws of the corporation shall be amended so that the chairman
of the board shall have all the powers now vested in the president of
this corporation.

. . . Mr. Goldwyn . . . shall perform such duties only as shall be
assigned to him by the board under the direction of the chairman of
the board.

. . . Mr. Goldwyn shall immediately enter into an agreement modi-
fying the voting trust agreement of October 10, 1919 that the voting
trustees may vote for the consolidation or merger of the corporation
without his consent . . .

Regarding the business at large, nothing had changed: His salary was the
same and he was back in his office. But Goldwyn knew he had been busted
to employee. He was a lame-duck president who had to pass every decision
before his board—even which stories could be filmed and which stars
should be hired.

Godsol immediately took hold of the production slate by submitting
scripts to the marketing department of the company. "I have always contended that the Sales Organization should pass on stories—at least whenever possible—and I still feel strongly that this should be done," Godsol
informed Goldwyn. "They should be given the opportunity to tell us
whether or not stories we contemplate making are of the type demanded
by exhibitors."

"Goldwyn became too arty for the rest of them," said Arthur Mayer.
When the company president expressed interest in bringing to America
some of the brilliant young German directors, notably Ernst Lubitsch, an
adviser on the operating staff squashed the idea. Because Abe Lehr was not
empowered to authorize even ten-dollar salary raises, the nuts-and-bolts
members of the Culver City crew were walking out. By the end of 1921,
the core of the Goldwyn editorial department, including Elmer Rice, had
moved to the Lasky Studio.

The board of directors had even more ammunition against Goldwyn
when *The Cabinet of Dr. Caligari* opened. Audiences at the Capitol Theater
in April 1921 booed and demanded their money back. No less a figure
than Carl Sandburg championed the film when it opened in the Midwest,
writing in the May 12 edition of the Chicago *Daily News:* "It is a healthy
thing for Hollywood, Culver City, Universal City, and all other places
where movie film is being produced, that this photoplay has come along
at this time. It is sure to have healthy hunches and show new possibilities

in style and method to our American Producers." Its quality was lost on Godsol. "We want pictures to make good, not be good!" became his new refrain.

Monday morning, May 9, Goldwyn could not get himself out of bed. An ambulance took him to the hospital, but the doctors promptly sent him home, saying he was suffering from nervous exhaustion. Goldwyn had a maid and a butler to look after him but nobody to care for him. He summoned his secretary, Rae Lipnick—five feet tall and all business—to his bedside at 44 West Seventy-seventh Street. He wanted this medical business hushed up, except for one telegram—to Mabel Normand. "SAW MISTER GOLDWYN AT HIS HOME YESTERDAY," Miss Lipnick wired. "HE SUGGESTED I WIRE YOU THAT IT WOULD BE USELESS TO TELEPHONE AS HE CANNOT SPEAK ON TELEPHONE HE IS OUT OF HOSPITAL AND GOING THROUGH TWO WEEK REST CURE TO RESTORE HIS HEALTH HE HAS SUFFERED NERVOUS BREAKDOWN. . . ." It was not as desperate as all that, as the wire further indicated: "WILL BE WELL AGAIN IN TWO WEEKS HE EXPECTS TO BE IN CALIFORNIA EARLY IN JUNE." Goldwyn simply needed to lie low and think.

Miss Lipnick's wire to Abe Lehr the next day reported the situation more accurately. Mabel sent a bouquet of flowers, and Lehr sent assurances from Culver City that "THERE IS NO OCCASION FOR HIM TO WORRY ABOUT THE SITUATION HERE AS EVERYTHING POSSIBLE IS BEING DONE THAT IS FOR THE INTEREST OF THE COMPANY." Those small doses of attention worked wonders. On Friday, Goldwyn himself wired Lehr: "AM FEELING MUCH IMPROVED THINK BY BEING IN BED ANOTHER WEEK I WILL BE IN EXCELLENT SHAPE."

A good crisis was still the best elixir for Goldwyn, and the next one jolted him back to his desk, where he worked hand in hand with Joe Godsol. A tide of recession washed across the motion picture industry in late May 1921, threatening to pull the Goldwyn Company under altogether. Company disbursements were approximately $170,000 per week, almost twice its receipts. The Ascher Theaters, their chain in the Rockies, lost $17,000 in one week; the next week, it lost $20,000.

The meter ticked away. Every Thursday at noon, the man who delivered the Kodak film stock arrived. If he did not get paid, he did not leave the next week's supply. Employees' checks were to be handed out on Saturdays. During one payroll crunch, Goldwyn ordered his export manager to make deals on the early Fort Lee pictures at whatever price. Rumors of mergers with Zukor or Laemmle, even with Lewis Selznick, flared up regularly.

The Goldwyn Company cut its costs across the board by 22 percent. From Culver City, Goldwyn reported to his board that practically all the large-salaried contracts had been canceled or permitted to expire, "and the organization which we have left is so small it is very difficult to find any place where substantial cuts can be made." Their once lustrous chart of stars had been reduced to newcomers taking home two-hundred-dollar paychecks. Business worsened.

In February 1922, Godsol was in Los Angeles when news arrived that the French Council of War had dismissed all charges brought against him in the matter of animal-selling and that he had been completely vindicated. Goldwyn sent a gracious day letter to Godsol at the Hotel Ambassador, saying "I NEVER HAD ANY DOUBT AS TO THE OUTCOME."

Everyone smiled through gritted teeth. From the moment Godsol returned to New York, Goldwyn encountered behavior as hostile as any he had experienced. "When he comes into the room he stands with his hand on the knob of the door ready to leave," Goldwyn confided to Lehr in a long, whining memorandum; "he avoids me more than ever. When he first returned I told him I would like to have a talk with him and he asked me to postpone it for a week or two." Sam Goldwyn realized he had been taken by the consummate con man, one of the few men in the business who could make him look like a piker.

When the board of directors convened on Friday, March 10, 1922— with a loss of $686,827.50 posted for the preceding year, and an even bigger one rolling up for the present year—Goldwyn was all but under house arrest. He had no allies present. A kangaroo court was called to order.

That night, Arthur Mayer was killing time at the office, until his girlfriend finished performing in a Broadway play. In the hallway he bumped into Joe Godsol, who, impressed with the young employee's working overtime, escorted him to Goldwyn's oak-paneled office. A workman was scraping the glass pane on the door, scratching away the gold letters of Mr. Goldwyn's name. Godsol reached into his pocket, pulled out a cigar "as thick as three thumbs," stuffed it into Mayer's mouth, and said, "Goldwyn and Goldwyn Pictures are no longer synonymous!"

8 Elba

"T HERE WAS a sickness in Hollywood, but it was a sickness that infected the whole postwar world," stated Cecil B. DeMille, one of the city's great moralists. He believed the "crumbling of standards" was aggravated in America by Prohibition. Others felt it was the release of nervous energy after the war, that Americans especially were atingle over their victory. The restlessness seemed especially manifest in the movie capital, that haven for the nation's most beautiful flaming youths.

Hollywood's quintessential observer of all this lust was the flamboyant English author Elinor Glyn. As more of her romantic stories were being adapted to the screen, she spent more time at the studios. One day, Wallace Reid was walking off a set when Miss Glyn hailed him. "My dear boy," she said, "you're really very wonderful to look at. And, besides, you know you have—It." The golden lad, still in his twenties, was confused. "Oh, that is my word," she explained. "It!" she repeated in her mellifluous contralto. "Don't you see, that one syllable expresses everything—all the difference there is between people. You either have It or you haven't." As the title of one of her novellas, "It" became a popular idiom, a demure way of saying what seemed to be on everybody's mind and lips in those days, "sex appeal."

King Vidor, not long in Hollywood and eager to become a director, thought the sexuality of this torrid zone was more than skin-deep.

The mysteries inherent in this new art created a feeling of isolation on the part of its performers. They spoke a silent language, a different language from the orange growers who surrounded them, but they felt a camaraderie with all the other members of their clan. This bond gave them the assurance that they could create their own laws, devise their own moralistic codes, establish their own habits and behavior. This isolation made them feel temporary, reckless. No doubt that subconsciously they feared the magical bubble would soon burst and they would run scurrying back to their Brooklyns, their carnival shows and their villages to continue an existence more closely allied to life as it was—rather than as it was imagined.

These special people could also defy laws of time and space, for their souls were presented around the world and would be preserved through the ages. People asked even barely recognizable motion picture actors for their autographs. Stars of greater popularity were treated like royalty. When Madge Kennedy traveled to the Orient, she was received by the emperor of Japan. After Mary Pickford and Douglas Fairbanks married, they toured Europe, where they were mobbed in every city. In Moscow, a crowd of 300,000 met them at the train station.

Chaplin, Pickford, and Fairbanks maintained their preeminence for the better part of a decade; but with the concupiscent fervor sweeping the nation, their virginal antics had lost some of their allure. A new image stole the breath of the public—a tall, swarthy Italian with slick black hair and fiery almond-shaped eyes. His tango in *The Four Horsemen of the Apocalypse* set hearts aflutter. In *The Sheik*, he was decked out in dashing desert garb; and when he swept Agnes Ayres off her feet and into his tent, his nostrils flaring, women in the audience swooned. In the words of Chaplin, "no man had greater attraction for women than Valentino."

"By this time," observed Anita Loos, who had been in Los Angeles writing since the arrival of the first big motion picture companies, "the stars were moving out of the Hollywood Hotel and beginning to live in their own private houses with servants, most of whom were their peers in everything but sex appeal—which pinpoints the reason for the film capital's mass misbehavior. To place in the limelight a great number of people who ordinarily would be chambermaids and chauffeurs, give them unlimited power and instant wealth is bound to produce a lively and diverting result." It became the wonderland through the looking glass: Gardeners, acrobats, and hat models strutted as kings and queens. In no other arena did rewards so vast come so fast. Few could adjust to the sudden wealth and fame. Infidelity and bootleg liquor went with the territory.

The world accepted Charlie Chaplin's marrying seventeen-year-old Mildred Harris and divorcing her two years later, then marrying a sixteen-year-old, Lita Grey. Movie fans quickly got over the respective divorces of Douglas Fairbanks and Mary Pickford, noted Mary's friend Carmel Myers, "because it was what everybody wanted. The world got the happy ending they had been rooting for." But the press could not ignore the nearly dead body of pretty Virginia Rappe found in Fatty Arbuckle's suite at the St. Francis Hotel in San Francisco in 1921. A jury completely exonerated him of the young actress's subsequent death, but public opinion kept Adolph Zukor and Jesse Lasky from releasing three completed films or from hiring him to act thereafter. Without appearing before a camera again, Arbuckle died in 1933 in ignominious oblivion.

Drugs suddenly took the life of Wallace Reid. After Zukor's press department vainly tried to conceal the truth, they admitted that the star had been addicted to morphine. Abe Lehr wrote Goldwyn that their former star Tom Moore was flat broke and no longer hirable because of booze. The same was true for Jack Pickford. His wife, a bright young Goldwyn star named Olive Thomas, killed herself in 1920, as did Robert Harron, the handsome juvenile in many of Griffith's landmark films.

For years, Hollywood's misbehavior had titillated the public. Now all the backsliding disgusted them. Many fans boycotted anything that came out of that slough. Box-office figures plummeted between 1921 and 1923—precisely when Goldwyn was most desperate for business.

Filmmakers wondered how to woo patrons back to their theaters. They could clean up their acts by reverting to the sappy melodramas that had long been boring audiences, or they could throw more logs on the fires of passion and produce films that presented life as it actually was. By depicting sin in all its evil they thought they could have it both ways, pandering and preaching at the same time. Cecil B. DeMille wielded the mightiest double-edged sword of all. In his 1923 biblical epic, *The Ten Commandments,* he presented saturnalia at its most salacious, all under the punitive gaze of the Lord. In 1921 alone, legislators introduced nearly one hundred censorship bills in thirty-seven states. One day, Louis B. Mayer confided to King Vidor, "If this keeps up there won't be any motion picture industry."

Hollywood decided to clean house. There already existed a National Association of the Motion Picture Industry; but the heads of the largest film companies recognized the need for somebody outside the industry to regulate its activities. Lewis Selznick—who had been demoted in the busi-

ness to distributing a biweekly newsreel—proposed an unlikely candidate
for the job, a member of the Harding administration.

"Beyond the fact that I had arranged for the newsreels to have propor-
tionate coverage with the press during the campaign, I had never been
identified with any phase of motion pictures," recalled Will H. Hays, an
unsuspecting jug-eared Hoosier. "I was an Indiana lawyer who had become
Republican national chairman, then Postmaster General. Just that." Hays
had been born in 1879 in Sullivan, Indiana. To his parents, he later recalled, "the Christian life meant the Ten Commandments, self-discipline,
faith in time of trouble, worship, the Bible, and the Golden Rule."

In early December 1921, Selznick and Saul Rogers, William Fox's lawyer, circulated a round-robin letter among the heads of a dozen motion
picture concerns. In it, Samuel Goldwyn (while still president of Goldwyn
Pictures), along with a dozen other company heads, requested that Hays
ask the President to relieve him of his present duties so that he might head
a "national association of motion picture producers and distributors."

On December 17, Hays met the signatories at Delmonico's in New
York. He wanted the holidays in Indiana to ponder the offer. Christmas
morning, Hays made up his mind. Sitting at breakfast, he overheard an
argument among his six-year-old son and two cousins who were trying on
the cowboy outfits Hays had bought them. "I want to be William S.
Hart," cried young Bill Hays. "No, I'm going to be him!" contradicted
one of the cousins. "No, I am!" yelled the other. "You can be Doug, and
Bill can be the bad guy." Hays realized "that the great motion picture
industry might as easily become a corrupting as a beneficial influence on
our future generations." On January 14, 1922, he agreed to serve as president of the Motion Picture Producers and Distributors of America, Inc.
Quipsters called him "Czar of all the Rushes."

While the MPPDA began to heal the wounds of Hollywood—establishing fair contracts between distributors and theaters, setting standards for
films, overcoming local censorship movements, and wiping up after the
major scandals—Samuel Goldwyn withdrew into solitary exile on West
Seventy-seventh Street, seeing nobody except his servants. Miss Lipnick
set up a makeshift office in his apartment. "I've got some thinking to do,"
he explained to the few granted admittance to his bedroom, then he would
wail that all his competitors were "going after a sick man."

Goldwyn instructed Miss Lipnick to scout the summer real estate rentals on Long Island—among the thousand-dollar-a-month estates. He
settled on a mansion at Elm's Point in Great Neck, which he would share
with Broadway producer Arthur Hammerstein.

The most terrible aspect of the Goldwyn ouster was the swiftness with

which Godsol had acted. Even though business had been poor, Goldwyn
had been negotiating in good faith with several promising filmmakers up
to the eleventh hour. Marshall Neilan, the successful director of such Mary
Pickford hits as *Rebecca of Sunnybrook Farm* and *Daddy Long Legs*, was about
to sign with him to direct his wife, Blanche Sweet, in *Tess of the
d'Urbervilles;* Goldwyn was closing a deal with Erich von Stroheim, an
Austrian actor-writer-director, who wanted to transform Frank Norris's
novel *McTeague* into an epic motion picture called *Greed;* and he was obtaining the rights to General Lew Wallace's *Ben-Hur—A Tale of the Christ.*

Goldwyn sought the counsel of Max D. Steuer, the prominent theatrical
attorney. He informed Goldwyn that the recent overthrow sounded illegal
and that if Goldwyn wanted to force the board to hold another election, it
could probably be done. Even so, Goldwyn realized he had few allies. He
received letters from but a handful of employees—Harry Alexander, Arthur Mayer, Howard Dietz; they would move on with the Goldwyn Company and in time to other careers. (Dietz led a dazzling double life—for
years the chief of publicity and advertising for MGM, all the while writing
Broadway musicals, including the charming lyrics to such standards as
"Dancing in the Dark," "That's Entertainment," and "By Myself.") Only
Abe Lehr was constantly there for Goldwyn, assuring him, "YOUR SITUA-
TION IS NOT AS DARK AS YOU PROBABLY FEEL IT TO BE." But Lehr was
also still part of the Goldwyn organization. He had no option but to ride
the wave that had carried him to the Pacific coast. As for Sam Goldwyn,
he would have to determine his future as he almost always had—by
himself.

Goldwyn decided not to challenge the election; it was best to divorce
himself from the company altogether. "I can make more money being foot-
loose than I could ever hope to make out of the Goldwyn situation," he
wrote Lehr. His 9.5 percent interest—then worth some $600,000—
would be plenty of seed money.

Having devoted most of his motion picture career to sales, Goldwyn
now realized that the production of films was "just too important to leave
to others." Twice burned by his desire to expand, he also saw the advantages of keeping things as small as possible. "There are two kinds of producers," he recounted years later: "One is a film manufacturer who turns
out many pictures, some of them good, more of them not so good. I once
tried being a film manufacturer but I didn't like it. There were too many
pictures going out under my name which were not satisfactory to me.
Since then, I've tried to be the other kind of producer, making fewer
pictures but each one the best I could make it."

Unfortunately, the industry was finding little room in those days for the producer of quality films who did not want to work within a studio. To bankers and exhibitors, the word "independent" was becoming synonymous with "fly-by-night." Once Goldwyn realized no "big personalities" were rushing into business with him, he decided to sit out the summer. His ambition was to redefine the reputation—if not the role—of the independent producer.

On May 15, Goldwyn moved into his mansion in Long Island. "To keep busy," he wrote Abe Lehr nine days later, "I conceived the brilliant idea to write my memoirs of the movies, which is practically my reminiscences of the last ten years, and giving a description of the different stars and authors and my various experiences with them." The idea of writing an autobiography probably originated with Goldwyn's former fellow board member at the Goldwyn Company, publisher George H. Doran, who agreed to print it. When Arthur Hammerstein heard that his housemate, already famous around town for his slips of the tongue, was going to write a book, he asked, "Who's going to translate it for you?"

Goldwyn had the last laugh. On top of the book advance, *Pictorial Review,* with its two million circulation, agreed to serialize it, paying a thousand dollars for each of six installments. They recommended a writer named Corinne Lowe to write the book. "Feel certain that I can make enough money to keep the wolf from the door for a while," Goldwyn wrote Abe Lehr.

Lehr tried to talk Goldwyn out of the memoirs, not realizing that *Behind the Screen* was another phase in Goldwyn's process of self-invention. The book would not only allow him to appear publicly as a literate, even literary, figure; it would also enable him to rewrite his history, expunging the mistakes of his past.

Goldwyn contributed little to his 263-page autobiography. He supplied Miss Lowe with half-truths or glamorous stretches of fact, shedding just enough light on himself to cast Horatio Alger's shadow across the entire book.

The stars he knew were discussed only in superlatives, all to burnish his own reputation. Such celebrities as Valentino and child favorite Jackie Coogan, with whom Goldwyn had little or no connection, had whole chapters written about them—gilt by association. An autographed picture of Mr. and Mrs. Douglas Fairbanks served as the book's frontispiece, suggesting an intimacy that did not exist.

Behind the Screen, one of the first "histories" of the infant art form, sold a respectable seven thousand copies. It even received pleasant notices—all of which added an air of legitimacy to Goldwyn's new gentlemanly mien.

Great Neck had become Broadway's playground—summer home to Lillian Russell, George M. Cohan, and the Ziegfeld crowd. For Goldwyn it was the workshop where he added the finishing touches to his character. He bought a seven-year-old chestnut gelding and became a fair horseman; he learned to swim in Long Island Sound; he picked up a little tennis. During the season, he became better acquainted with his idol, Florenz Ziegfeld, and with the newest *Follies* star, Eddie Cantor. He played back-gammon with newspaper magnate Herbert Bayard Swope; and he took up golf with Harpo Marx, who had just moved onto the Swope estate, after his struggling vaudeville act with his brothers had at last scored on Broadway.

Without the legions of employees he was used to ordering, Goldwyn unleashed his temper on his valet and chauffeur. He did not know how to operate an automobile, but he was a vociferous backseat driver. One day that summer, after all the yammering he could stand, the uniformed chauffeur drove Goldwyn to the middle of nowhere on the Jericho Turn-pike, in the outback of Long Island. He stopped the car, got out, an-nounced that he was quitting, and ran off, leaving Goldwyn alone. Goldwyn learned to drive that summer, all but rounding out his self-portrait as the complete country gentleman.

"Being down here and having an opportunity to think a great deal about my future," he wrote Abe Lehr in August 1922, "I have come to the conclusion that the thing for me to do is to either get a star that is good for three or four pictures a year . . . or get a great director and make about three pictures a year with him or get a real big story and start off by doing a big picture . . . unless something else should come up in the meantime that would also yield money."

Goldwyn could put together a production easily enough, but he would need somebody to distribute it. The concept of United Artists—an asso-ciation of small independents who made "special" films—appealed to him. He knew they desperately needed product, what with Chaplin still under contract to First National and the remaining founders coming up with but two pictures a year. He tried to horn his way into a deal Fairbanks was making with Jackie Coogan. It all fell apart because Mr. and Mrs. Coogan wanted nothing to do with Sam Goldwyn. Neither did Mrs. Fairbanks.

A shrewd businesswoman—"and a tough little Mick," said David Rose, a lifelong friend of both Goldwyn and Fairbanks—Mary Pickford also liked her whiskey. When she drank too much, she often turned anti-Semitic. "That's the Jew in you that's saying that," she would cry whenever Fairbanks tried to defend any of the Jewish moguls. She spoke of Sam Goldwyn as Shylock. Even with such million-dollar hits as Griffith's *Way Down East*, Fairbanks's *The Three Musketeers*, and Pickford's *Little Lord*

Fauntleroy, the infant United Artists looked as though it might never get to its feet, so dire was its need for product. But remembering Goldwyn's behavior with Adolph Zukor, Mary Pickford promised herself to avoid doing business with him at all costs.

If anybody could help him, Goldwyn thought, it was his friend Chaplin, with whom he frequently double-dated. Chaplin had, in fact, met his first wife through Goldwyn, whose beach house he continued to use as a trysting place. If Chaplin could not get him into United Artists, he might at least put in a good word at First National. Goldwyn asked Abe Lehr to suggest nonchalantly that Chaplin give Goldwyn a dinner some night, inviting important people in distribution. Lehr discouraged the idea. He said Chaplin was engrossed in an intense love affair with actress Pola Negri that "USES UP ALL OF HIS TIME AND MAKES HIM EVEN MORE UNRELIABLE AND ERRATIC THAN FORMERLY." In spite of Chaplin's affection for Goldwyn, Lehr also let fall, "PERHAPS YOU ARE NOT AWARE THAT . . . HE FREQUENTLY ENTERTAINS DINNER PARTIES WITH BURLESQUE OF YOUR SPEECHES AS TO FUTURE OF INDUSTRY. ETC." Goldwyn got the message.

To anyone who would listen, Goldwyn insisted that there was a "conspiracy" against him. In fact, it was nothing so melodramatic. He had not made that many enemies in his ten years in the motion picture business; and a lot of people liked him. Quite simply, nobody wanted to work with him. "My name," Goldwyn later imparted to his analyst when speaking of this standstill in his career, "was Sam Mud."

If nobody who entered the business with him required his expertise, he would turn to people who did. Fortunately, the motion picture colony was swarming with a new generation of fresh talent. In a medium with no old masters—Edwin S. Porter had quietly disappeared from the scene, directing his last film in 1915; and Griffith, as beset by financial woes as ever, struggled to make one picture a year—the job of capturing action on celluloid was about to be placed in the hands of a few dozen men practically born with the century, mostly rough-and-ready Gentiles (many of them hard-drinking Irishmen), who would get on-the-job training.

Some had been actors—Frank Borzage, John Ford, George Marshall, Raoul Walsh, and Henry King, all born around 1890. William Wellman from Boston had recently been in France with the Lafayette Flying Corps. On leave in Paris one night, he wandered into a café, heard noises in a back room, and barged in on General Pershing dining with two high-ranking officers. After the war, he married a Goldwyn ingenue, Helene Chadwick, and was holding down a lowly production job the day Pershing came to visit the studio. Pershing happened to remember him, and they had a brief chat in front of all the studio personnel. What Goldwyn mistook for their intimacy led to a promotion for the handsome man in his mid-twenties. Wellman was made an assistant director.

Almost all the others of Wellman's generation of directors had a similar lucky break. They were men in the right place at the right time. Allan Dwan, Howard Hawks, and Gregory La Cava got onto movie sets because of an ability to write scenarios, then worked their way into directors' chairs. Lewis Milestone could edit film. Victor Fleming, the oldest of the new wave of directors—born in 1883—knew how to operate a camera, as did George Stevens, born in 1904. While Stevens trained under Hal Roach, Frank Capra, a Sicilian born in 1897, apprenticed to Mack Sennett, directing Harry Langdon comedies. Sam Wood was an assistant to DeMille. Clarence Brown went from being an electrical engineer to directing Valentino in *The Eagle*.

No sooner had his flivver arrived in Hollywood than King Vidor was poking around D. W. Griffith's enormous set for *Intolerance*, a Babylonian square surrounded by palaces and massive walls. He made friends with the guards and got to watch "the great D. W." at work. He began at Universal as a company clerk for twelve dollars a week. "Men who had never been inside a studio," Vidor realized, "were given directing assignments on pure bluff. They wouldn't have the slightest notion of what a camera could do. Some of these ne'er-do-wells would turn out several pictures before being discovered; by the time busy executives got around to viewing their initial efforts they would be well into their third film."

When the recession in Hollywood threw Vidor onto the street, he bounced from one independent producer to another. He tried running his own small studio, and when that failed, landed at the "tottering" Goldwyn Company. Vidor remembered "the studio workers expressed their precarious position with the phrase, 'In Godsol We Trust.'"

Erich von Stroheim, Joseph von Sternberg, and Victor Seastrom made pilgrimages from overseas to work in the movie capital. Ernst Lubitsch quickly became one of the most admired directors in town because of his sly and sophisticated "touch." Another foreign director to make his name in Hollywood was George Fitzmaurice, an Irishman born in Paris in 1895, who had set up Famous Players–Lasky's London studios. In late 1922, attorney Neil S. McCarthy suggested a venture between him and Goldwyn. Like Goldwyn, Fitzmaurice was an elegant dresser, and his films reflected both aspirations and style. Unlike Goldwyn, he was a gourmand and oenophile, with good looks—a full head of dark, slick-backed hair, intense eyes, and a neatly trimmed chevron of a mustache.

Fitzmaurice was receptive to the notion of a partnership. Goldwyn would select, finance, and sell their productions; Fitzmaurice would direct and cast, and develop the scenarios. He wanted to be an equal partner in the films' net earnings and receive a salary of $2,000 a week. "FEEL THAT I KNOW FITZ VERY WELL," McCarthy wired Goldwyn, "AND THAT HE IS HONORABLE AND DEPENDABLE AND OF HIGHEST INTEGRITY." By the end of the year, both men had agreed to a partnership, starting February 16, 1923, once Fitzmaurice's contract with Lasky expired. That gave Goldwyn little time to scare up material, financing, and a distributor.

Fitzmaurice recommended a play Paramount had filmed in 1915, Sir Hall Caine's *The Eternal City*. The rights could be purchased from the author; and Fitzmaurice's wife, an attractive writer named Ouida Bergere, had already suggested updating this love story, set against post-Risorgimento Rome, to Mussolini's Italy. A sturdy drama fraught with timeliness would certainly make for a debut worthy of the name he had established over the last five years, but Goldwyn doubted the commercial possibilities of such a film. His financial instincts told him to debut with a splashy comedy, one that would assure distributors and exhibitors that the prestigious Goldwyn name also meant money in the bank.

Goldwyn had his eye on the "Potash and Perlmutter" stories, a series about two quarreling partners in the garment business. Goldwyn had known the stories since his glove days, when the works of the author, Montague Glass, appeared in *The Glovers' Review.* More recently, Glass had woven several vignettes with his ethnic characters into a play. It was a hit on Broadway in 1905 and even bigger in its 1913 revival. Most people in the movie business had a natural aversion to any material so blatantly Jewish. Goldwyn recognized its possibilities in a nation whose immigrant population had soared in the last twenty years.

He bought the film rights to both properties. In so doing, he established a pattern for his production slate that he would follow most of his career, alternating a serious drama with a light comedy.

Goldwyn needed a distributor and $200,000 to start up his new business. He turned for help to the same man the United Artists were trying to lure to their company, the producer insiders called "Honest Joe." Joseph Schenck—with a big potato nose and saggy jowls—was reputed to have the best connections in town. Since resigning in 1917 from the Loew organization—where his brother Nick was company secretary—he had quietly ruled over his own expanding duchy.

He began simply by managing the career of his wife, Norma Talmadge. She called him "Daddy," and he hired the best writers, directors, and designers to highlight her considerable beauty and talent. She caught on. *Secrets* and *Camille* made her a major star, with a big contract from First National to release her films. Schenck worked as hard for her sister Constance and their sister Natalie's husband, Buster Keaton. Meantime, Schenck bought a controlling interest in the United Studios in Hollywood and stock in West Coast Theaters.

Nobody admired Schenck's initiative more than Dr. A. H. Giannini, founder of the Bank of Italy. As early as 1909, Giannini had been interested in the motion picture business. That year, the San Francisco banker opened his first out-of-town branch in San Jose and loaned $500 to Sol L. Lesser to invest in a nickelodeon on Fillmore Street. Seven years later, Lesser had a regular line of credit with the bank and headed All Features Distributors. In 1918, the Bank of Italy loaned $50,000 to Famous Players–Lasky. In 1919, Giannini took over the East River National Bank on Broadway, just a few blocks south of Fourteenth Street, the cradle of the moving picture business. After a few years of small loans to the early producers, "Doc" Giannini loaned $250,000 to First National, which put up a film, *The Kid,* as security. Joe Schenck's credit line expanded with his empire. When Giannini opened Los Angeles branches of his Bank of Italy, he named Schenck to the advisory board, along with Cecil B. DeMille. "Since the banks were becoming more and more interested in motion pictures," DeMille recounted, "I thought it would be a good idea to have a foot in their camp; and a new bank in Hollywood apparently thought it would be good to have a motion picture man among its officers."

Schenck opened talks between Goldwyn and both First National and Giannini's Commercial National Bank. Goldwyn's old friend Cecil DeMille came to his aid as well. He had never forgotten his career debt to Sam Goldwyn; and in 1923, he repaid it.

Sam's request for $200,000, DeMille recalled, "had been turned down by a number of the soundest bankers.

> It was a big loan, bigger than any that had yet come across my new desk in the Cherokee Avenue branch of the Commercial Bank. In the Giannini empire, it was expected that requests for unusually large loans would be submitted to headquarters in San Francisco. But I knew Sam; and I approved the loan.

DeMille took the next train north.

In Giannini's new office building on Powell Street in San Francisco, the two men sat down to discuss the Goldwyn loan. The hearty Italian said, "No good, C. B. He has no assets." DeMille said that in fact he had already okayed the loan, and Giannini let out a roar. "You say Sam Goldwyn has no assets," offered DeMille in defense. "You're right. He hasn't. He has no assets, except talent, which is the only asset worth anything in the motion picture business. I made that loan on talent and on character." DeMille asked whether he had the authority to make such judgments or whether he should resign. Giannini turned to DeMille and said, "It's all right, C. B. But don't do it too often!"

First National also came through for Goldwyn, offering him a distribution contract. They would not change company policy for Goldwyn by allowing him to review all contracts they made for his films with the exhibitors, but Goldwyn signed anyway. There were compromises to be made with Fitzmaurice as well, namely the director's insistence that he receive top billing in advertising. They agreed to release their films as "George Fitzmaurice Productions, presented by Samuel Goldwyn."

Goldwyn Pictures Corporation protested when they learned that their founder was about to form Samuel Goldwyn, Incorporated. In September 1923, they filed an action in the United States District Court to enjoin Goldwyn from "using the legend 'Samuel Goldwyn presents' in his First National releases, on the grounds that the name Goldwyn had been used by [their] company since the 1916 incorporation, and before Samuel Goldfish became Samuel Goldwyn." They maintained that they owned the rights to that name, especially important just then, while they were shopping for new partners. Years later, tears would literally roll down Goldwyn's face whenever he thought of what he called that "black period" of his life, that time when "they wouldn't let me have my name!"

On October 18, Federal Judge Learned Hand rendered his decision. "A self-made man," he proclaimed, "may prefer a self-made name." He decreed that Goldwyn was entitled to use it so long as he made clear his dissociation from his former company. He was required to run the banner "Samuel Goldwyn Presents" before the title of his pictures, and the disclaimer "Presented by Samuel Goldwyn (not now connected with Goldwyn Pictures)" elsewhere in the advertising copy. Most people assumed he was posting his name everywhere for vanity's sake, but he insisted he was simply complying with the law.

Samuel Goldwyn, Inc., opened for business at 383 Madison Avenue, the same building out of which First National operated. Goldwyn intended to keep his base of operations in New York City, but from the beginning he was tugged in several directions.

In 1923, moviemakers were raving about one place—Italy. Its film industry, trying to recover from the war, offered inexpensive skilled technicians and fully equipped facilities. Goldwyn had already sampled the troubles that could beset a business when its production and business ends were separated. But the potential savings and the guarantee of authenticity in this instance seemed more than he could resist. Reluctantly he allowed

George Fitzmaurice's company of *The Eternal City* to journey to Italy (where Goldwyn's former company was preparing *Ben-Hur.*). Along with the glamorous leading lady, Barbara La Marr, sailed a cast that included Lionel Barrymore and Richard Bennett. The latter's teenage daughter Joan would have a walk-on in the movie as a pageboy. A square-jawed English newcomer named Ronald Colman, in Rome filming *The White Sister* with Lillian Gish for director Henry King, also got a bit part. Still unknown to the world, he was mistaken by those who had seen footage of him as some "new Italian actor."

In addition to its stars, advertisements for *The Eternal City* boasted "20,000 others." One mob scene clearly depicted two men standing on the balcony of the royal palace—none other than King Victor Emmanuel and Benito Mussolini. When the Fascisti caught wind of the film and demanded its confiscation, Fitzmaurice and his crew quickly left the country; Arthur Miller, the cameraman, smuggled the negative safely out of Italy. It was Goldwyn's first experience filming abroad and his last.

Closer to the home office, Goldwyn oversaw the New York production of *Potash and Perlmutter.* It fit more into the mold of most of the 180 films that he had already supervised. He proceeded cautiously, signing Barney Bernard and Alexander Carr, the stars of the 1913 Broadway revival of the play, to recreate their roles, and Clarence Badger, a veteran of the Madge Kennedy and Will Rogers comedies, to direct. Of the filmmakers, only the scenarist was new to Goldwyn, and his choice left little to chance.

The one aspect of motion pictures in which women had made the greatest strides—indeed, in which they had led the way—was in screenwriting. Anita Loos had sold over one hundred scripts (mostly to Griffith at the old Biograph Company) by the time she was twenty-two; Jeanie Macpherson had been supplying Cecil DeMille with scenarios for years; Louis B. Mayer had relied on Bess Meredyth and Kathleen Norris to provide stories for him. The Goldwyn Company was banking heavily on June Mathis. They were all self-assured young women, much better read than anybody for whom they worked. Most had entered the business as actresses, then recognized they could get farther on their brains than on their looks.

By the early twenties, none had achieved greater success than Frances Marion. A San Franciscan, born in 1887, she had gone to Hollywood to paint theatrical posters and found herself appearing in Mary Pickford's *A Girl of Yesterday*. She discovered she had a knack for writing and became one of Paramount's most important scenarists. By the 1920s, she was freelancing. In 1922, she wrote eight motion pictures. Her sixth assignment in 1923 was adapting the Montague Glass play for Sam Goldwyn. The plot involved Abe Potash and Morris Perlmutter's hiring a new fitter, a poor Russian violinist who falls in love with Potash's daughter, Irma. After much tribulation and a trial (for murder), all ends well.

On Thursday, September 6, 1923, the comedy passed its first test at the Rivoli Theater in Baltimore. Two Sundays later, it began a successful run at the Mark Strand Theater in New York. "'Potash and Perlmutter' has been fashioned into a good movie comedy, far better than one would expect," commented *Variety*. The *New York Times* heaped highest praise, noting, "the picture has as many laughs as a Chaplin comedy."

The Eternal City opened on January 20, 1924, also a Sunday night, at the Strand. Again Goldwyn triumphed—critically and financially.

Meantime, Goldwyn Company stock sank to 8¼. After another unsuccessful financial reorganization, Joe Godsol was asked to take a temporary vacation in Florida. That January, he bumped into Lee Shubert, an early Goldwyn investor, who suggested that Godsol talk to another man wintering in Palm Beach. Marcus Loew was there deciding whether to build up his production capacity at Metro Pictures or to bail out.

The Goldwyn Company, with its refurbished studio, its roster of relatively inexpensive talent under contract, and its modest string of theaters, looked attractive to Loew. His major reservation was that he had nobody to operate the studio. He was suffering from a heart condition, and Nick Schenck was running the larger parent organization; neither Joe Engel at Metro nor Abe Lehr at Goldwyn seemed strong enough for the position. Loew's legal counsel, Robert Rubin, recommended his friend Louis B. Mayer, who had built up an impressive studio for himself in just a few years.

In April 1924, the merger of the three companies was made public. The first phase of the transaction involved Loew's buying up the Goldwyn Company stock, giving him control of the Metro-Goldwyn Corporation. For $75,000, he absorbed Mayer's business and included his name in the company's title. The short, barrel-chested Mayer became vice president and general manager of the new organization; his young associate, Irving Thalberg, became second vice president and "supervisor of production." They decided to retain the Goldwyn Company's leonine logo.

All parties enthusiastically supported the merger—save one. Samuel Goldwyn did not approve of the deal, and he did not approve of being recompensed with preferred stock of the new corporation. He especially objected to Louis B. Mayer, with whom there had been bad blood since the days when Mayer submitted his opinion regarding Goldwyn's engagement to Blanche Lasky. For one million dollars, Goldwyn was bought out of the company that would thereafter bear his name. On April 25, 1924—

in front of stars and reporters—Abe Lehr handed a large ceremonial key to the big studio on Washington Boulevard to Louis B. Mayer.

The merger conformed to a consolidation trend in American business. By the end of the twenties, two hundred companies would control one half the nation's corporate wealth.

Famous Players–Lasky continued to acquire theaters and stars (including Valentino types Ricardo Cortez and Rod La Rocque). It was soon reestablished as Paramount Pictures Corporation. Fox Film Corporation cashed in on the dark, handsome looks of John Gilbert and a Mexican youth named Luis Alonso, who acted under the name Gilbert Roland. Buying into West Coast Theaters, Fox went from two exhibition halls to one hundred fifty, then five hundred. In 1920, they grossed $12,605,725 and netted $1,413,542; five years later, those corporate earnings had practically doubled. In 1923, Harry, Albert, Sam, and Jack Warner expanded into production on the West Coast, establishing Warner Brothers Pictures, Incorporated. Under Sam and Jack's supervision, their Hollywood studio signed Ernst Lubitsch, John Barrymore, and one of the decade's biggest draws at the box office, an Alsatian sheep dog called Rin Tin Tin—many of whose heartwarming runs to the rescue were being written by a twenty-two-year-old Nebraskan, Darryl Francis Zanuck. Now Metro-Goldwyn-Mayer ("Controlled by Loew's Inc.," read the bottom of the big new sign towering over Culver City) promised to become the largest corporation of studios and theaters in the world.

No longer a manufacturer of programs of films, Goldwyn was committed to independent production, one picture at a time. It was virtually impossible to compete against the big corporations for properties to film. In the flush of his first two marginal successes, Goldwyn thought of several stories at MGM that he had brought in but that were lying fallow. To obtain those rights meant going hat in hand to Louis B. Mayer. Weeks passed before Goldwyn swallowed his pride. On his next trip to Los Angeles, he made an appointment with Mayer.

Goldwyn arrived at his former Culver City headquarters and drove past guards and workers who had recently been his employees. At Mayer's office he discovered his own former secretary, who announced his arrival to her boss. He waited for what seemed an interminable amount of time before he was ushered in. Goldwyn stood in front of a big desk, at which Mayer sat signing checks out of a large book. "Yes?" he asked flatly, without stopping what he was doing, without looking up, without offering the man before him a chair. At last, Mayer sat back and faced his petitioner. "What have you got on your mind?" he asked. Goldwyn controlled his temper and began to plead his case. Halfway through his appeal, he started to sputter, "Louis . . . you're . . . a son of a bitch!" He stormed out of the office, determined to have nothing more to do with the company.

Over the decades, this second great motion picture complex he had helped establish became the best-known studio in the world. The sandwiching of "Goldwyn" in the celebrated trio of names caused no end of confusion or of publicity for the man himself. Goldwyn never passed himself off as being a member of the company, but he never denied it either—especially if it could help him get a room in a foreign hotel or a table at a crowded restaurant. Because of his enmity toward Louis B. Mayer, he never included the man's name when he spoke of the new organization. To his dying day he referred to MGM as the "Metro-Goldwyn Company."

Joe Godsol disappeared from the scene as mysteriously as he had entered. He stole to Europe, and died in Switzerland in 1935, leaving a large estate.

In the new world of corporate Hollywood, Sam Goldwyn became the first of the great independent American film producers. The year after Learned Hand's decision, MGM agreed that he could present films without disclaiming his association with Goldwyn Pictures Corporation. If at all possible, he wanted to remain in business by himself, with neither stockholders nor partners. He intended to become the industry's "rebel," a lone wolf—one of the few in the history of the industry who could state at the end of his career: "My pictures were my own. I financed them myself and answered solely to my self. My mistakes and my successes were my own."

9 Leading Ladies

BEAUTY HAS BEEN a passport across social borders since time immemorial. Naturally, women who thought they bore it descended upon Hollywood. If they projected an image that enough people wanted to look at, they might become powerful goddesses in their own right. If not, they could still sway men of influence. That writhing between Beauty and Power, as ancient as Aphrodite and Zeus, created the electricity that sparked all of Hollywood.

"God makes stars," Samuel Goldwyn declared. "It's up to producers to find them." By the mid-twenties, studio moguls could explore the world in search of Beauty without ever leaving their screening rooms. Hollywood was the magnet for every pretty girl who had ever been told she "ought to be in pictures." Actresses who had made films abroad could be considered for American stardom without their even knowing it.

In the fall of 1924, Louis B. Mayer left for Rome to salvage MGM's production of *Ben-Hur,* then foundering in extravagant chaos. He took his wife and his two daughters, aged seventeen and nineteen, to visit other capitals of Europe as well. One Sunday afternoon in Berlin, the Mayers sat in a projection room to watch *The Atonement of Gösta Berling,* a new film directed by the Swedish director Mauritz Stiller. A fellow Swede, MGM director Victor Seastrom, had urged Mayer to sign Stiller. "The only advance reservation my father had about him," recalled Mayer's younger daughter, Irene, "was the stipulation that he wouldn't come to Hollywood without his new leading lady, an obstacle my father thought he could overcome." The protégée was the nineteen-year-old daughter of an un-skilled Stockholm laborer named Karl Gustafsson and his plump wife, Anna. Their Greta had dropped out of school, become a latherer in bar-bershops, then clerked in the millinery department of the PUB depart-ment store. Appearing in two promotional films for PUB, she was soon accepted as a scholarship student at the Royal Dramatic Theater's training school. Stiller saw her and changed her surname to Garbo.

As her image flickered before Mayer's eyes, Irene Mayer remembered, "Miss Garbo overcame him in the first reel. It was her eyes. He said, 'She reminds me of Norma Talmadge.' There was no resemblance, but what they had in common and what he must have meant was the capacity to convey feeling through their eyes. Dad said, 'I'll take Stiller, all right. As for the girl, I want her even more than Stiller. I can make a star out of her.'" Mayer met them both that afternoon in his suite at the Adlon Hotel.

A few months later, Greta Garbo sailed for New York. Publicity stills were taken of her leaning against the rail of the *Drottingholm*—"slender, smart, beautifully groomed," a white cloche hat framing her immortal eyes and sculpted face. "It was," Mayer's younger daughter later noted, "the Garbo the world was to know." The producer cultivated her image, on the screen and off, creating the greatest legend in motion pictures, a singular mystique. She brought to the world a new standard by which beauty was measured. The impact of this new deity on Western culture was not lost on the other motion picture moguls.

SAM GOLDWYN'S next two films—distributed by First National in May and September of 1924—copied the pattern of his first pair. He selected a dramatic love story—Joseph Hergesheimer's *Cytherea*—and another Pot-ash and Perlmutter comedy. Frances Marion wrote both scenarios. Gold-wyn took offices at First National's United Studios at 5341 Melrose Avenue in Hollywood, where he assembled a staff to work on his pictures. As soon as Abe Lehr's contract with the Goldwyn Company expired, he reassumed his position as Sam Goldwyn's delegate in Hollywood. The producer also hired the dapper little man from Price Waterhouse & Company who had been auditing his books—James A. Mulvey—to run the New York office. Mulvey quickly became his most trusted business confidant. He spent the next forty years working in the wings; and Goldwyn never made a business move without first consulting him.

In Hollywood with Potash and Perlmutter is the story of two Jewish gar-ment manufacturers trying to be movie producers, who will get financing if they hire the banker's girlfriend. Nothing unusual happened during the months of preproduction on the picture: The star dropped dead; First National—which had final approval of all Goldwyn's productions before putting up any money—threatened to withdraw its backing; and only days before shooting, Goldwyn was without a leading lady.

Goldwyn's second film that year was *Cytherea,* the scorchy story of a love-starved man in his forties. It was controversial source material for a motion picture, especially then, what with Will Hays looking over producers' shoulders. Women's clubs throughout the country waged a letter-writing campaign against Goldwyn. "TAKE NO CHANCES ON DOING ANYTHING THAT SEEMS CENSORABLE," Goldwyn wired George Fitzmaurice. Frances Marion managed to expurgate some of the spicier sections without losing the central story of passion and fantasy. Goldwyn further distracted the film's detractors by promoting its great scientific and artistic innovation. In several dream sequences, *Cytherea* dissolved into a new process called Technicolor. The eight-reel drama (which featured Constance Bennett in her first Hollywood role, as a vampy niece) was a modest success at the box office and impressed most critics with its sophistication.

At age forty-five, Sam Goldwyn was playing out his own version of *Cytherea.* He was forever auditioning pretty girls. Since Mabel Normand, he had not fallen seriously in love with anyone, but he courted many beautiful ingenues. In the early twenties, Sam Goldwyn was known in New York for being at every important opening night. He was caricatured more than once in the pages of *Vanity Fair* as one of the celebrities always apt to be on view at premieres among the show business four hundred. He was just as well known for taking unbridled liberties with women on first (and usually last) dates.

Goldwyn's clumsy manhandling of women especially amused Charlie Chaplin. One day in New York, he conspired with theater owner Sid Grauman on an elaborate practical joke. Charlie told Sam he had a beautiful girl to whom he wanted to introduce him, someone rich and pretty but quite shy. Chaplin suggested a carriage ride around Central Park that evening. He and his mystery lady, wearing a dark veil, picked Goldwyn up at his new apartment at 125 East Sixty-third Street. In the warm evening, the three of them rode in the hansom cab through Central Park, the girl saying little. Goldwyn kept trying to loosen her up by putting his arms around her. When he started to nuzzle her, she threw back her veil, revealing Sid Grauman in drag. Grauman and Chaplin never forgot the incident. Neither did Goldwyn. He turned crimson whenever Chaplin retold the story, which he seemed to do at any dinner party at which Goldwyn was present.

In 1924, the object of Goldwyn's desire became the dark-eyed Florence

Vidor, who in the words of her recently divorced husband "was beginning to be known as 'the first lady of the screen.'" Sam Goldwyn fell for her "stateliness." He came on strong, showering her with gifts. They were seen together for a few months. "I know Sam wanted to marry her," said King Vidor years later; "but Florence could never have taken Sam seriously as a lover."

Goldwyn was looking hard for love. At Easter, he sent a twenty-five-dollar basket of lilies to the twenty-eight-year-old Miss Vidor; and he instructed his secretary at United Studios to "send my baby . . . a nice basket for about $10." Once Miss Vidor realized the seriousness of Goldwyn's intentions, she stopped seeing him. The sole surviving recipient of Goldwyn's love remained his "baby"—Ruth, who was suddenly twelve.

Her father had in five years hardly set eyes on her, as Ruth became a sore reminder of the love that was missing in his life. Smart and pretty, the square-shouldered girl grew to be the tallest pupil in her class at the Hollywood School for Girls—a private school that taught Edith and Irene Mayer, Agnes de Mille, Harlean Carpenter (who would later act under her mother's maiden name, as Jean Harlow), and a few boys, including Douglas Fairbanks, Jr., and Joel McCrea. Ruth instinctively distanced herself from her father a little more each year. Being his child, she commented years later, "was like playing a game in which nobody told you the rules: There would be the great proclamations of love, then off with your head. And you never knew what word would set him off. He'd cry at corn and laugh at pratfalls—the perfect audience. But those feelings were only skin deep, because when it came to people—to real emotions—he knew nothing. . . . You could be dying of a broken heart, and he wouldn't ever know."

Ruth's elementary school years were peripatetic. Her stepfather, Hector Turnbull, traveled constantly between the two branches of Paramount Studios. As a child of divorce, she was often ostracized by her schoolmates. They derided her for all her surnames—Goldfish, Lasky, Goldwyn, Turnbull. Fortunately, she grew up in a loving environment, surrounded by supportive relatives. From the time of the divorce, Blanche never mentioned Sam Goldwyn's name; to Ruth, she would refer to him as "your father."

After Blanche's remarriage, Goldwyn let most of a year go by without making a single child support payment.

When in 1921 the Turnbulls had planned a trip to Europe with Ruth, Goldwyn had agreed to her being gone for three months. Upon reconsideration, it occurred to him, as he wired his lawyer, "THAT I HAVE NO ASSURANCE THEY WILL RETURN BY THAT TIME AS TURNBULL IS JUST AS

LIKELY TO REMAIN THERE FOR A YEAR AS HE IS FOR THREE MONTHS."
He did not want to see Ruth; he simply did not want to lose her. The
lawyer had advised taking no action until Goldwyn cleared up his support
payments. He did neither.

In July 1923, Goldwyn wrote Ruth that he hoped to get to Los Angeles
in September to see her. Until then, he asked her to send a picture of
herself, "as I am very anxious to know what you look like now. You seem
to change so much every time I see you." In August, he wrote Ruth a long
paragraph about the joys of his vacation in Saranac Lake and repeated his
request for a picture.

By the end of September—after sending her books and asking if she
wanted a new Kodak—Goldwyn's patience had been exhausted:

> In my last letter I wrote you about some pictures of yourself but
> up to now I have not received any answer. I wish you would go to
> the photographers at the very earliest time you can and have some
> pictures taken. As I wrote you I am very anxious to see how you look
> as I have not seen you for such a long time that it seems like years.

He suspected sabotage in his crumbling relationship with Ruth. September 28:

> Do you open every letter that I send to you, or does some one else
> open the letter before you read it? . . . Darling, this is the first time
> I have asked you to definitely answer my letters and unless I receive
> an answer I might have to bring you on to New York and spend a
> few months with me here so as to make sure that you realize that
> Father loves you and is anxious to look after you and do everything
> in the world for you.

Ruth sent her father a snapshot of her with her dog—"as I don't care
about having a big photograph taken as they are never any good as I always
look to [sic] self-conscious." She explained that she tried to answer all his
questions, "but it is hard work to write such long letters so often when I
am going to school and having to practice every afternoon after school
beside music and tennis lessons. You don't seem to think that I ought to
play.

"I got the three books you sent," Ruth added, "but I had already read
one of them and the other two were too grown up for me, and anyway I
don't need any books." If her father could not read her sentiments between

the lines, her next paragraph spelled it out: "I see all of your letters but of course I like to show any letters I get to Mother as we have no secrets and all children have their letters opened for them."

"I am in receipt of your letter and judging by the tone of it you are no longer the sweet, wonderful little girl of mine that you have always been," he dictated, in a tone that meant business.

> I am surprised that you would write a letter like this to your Father, whom you know loves you better than anything else in this world. . . . Of course I want you to play and have a good time; I would do anything in this world to help you have a good time, but I am sure that you want me to be happy also, and I can only be happy if I hear from you often and know all about the things you are doing.

Goldwyn called her "negligent" for failing to remember him on his last birthday. And he still wanted a proper photograph.

Ruth not only held her ground, she gained some, calling her father on his neglectful behavior.

> I realize that I should have come out to see you oftener than I have [he replied], but unfortunately I have had to work very hard within the last year and it has not been easy for me to leave New York. . . .
>
> I am sure that when we spend a few months together (which I expect very shortly to be able to arrange) you will find out for yourself that I am just as nice a Father as you used to think I was. . . . Please, dear, do not write to me the way you have; you hurt my feelings when you do that and I am sure you do not want to hurt me as I would rather do anything in the world than hurt your feelings.

The photograph was never mentioned again.

Goldwyn spent the Christmas holidays on the West Coast. A single moment during that visit affected the future of their entire relationship. It occurred over lunch, when Ruth's fork punctured the skin of her baked potato in the dining room at the Ambassador Hotel. The potato seemed undercooked to Goldwyn. He called the waiter over, then the headwaiter, and finally the maître d', carrying on for fifteen minutes over a potato that Ruth found perfectly edible. The whole incident proved so "upsetting and embarrassing" that from then on she wanted him at arm's length.

Spurned by every woman in his life, Goldwyn was not about to let go of Ruth. "I am determined to have her live with me if it is only for sixty days," Goldwyn instructed Nathan Burkan, who had been Blanche's divorce lawyer but whom Goldwyn had dragooned into acting as counsel on several business deals. On his next trip to California, in February 1924, Goldwyn found Ruth distant to the point of near total absence. "She has been just as mean as she can possibly be," Goldwyn wrote Burkan. "She always has something to do that is more important than seeing me, and I am so disgusted that I feel there are only two things for me to do: One is to entirely ignore the child, to feel that she does not belong to me and I am not to see her—the other is to insist on my rights."

Europe had become an important market for Goldwyn again, a place to sell his growing list of films and shop for talent—another undiscovered Garbo. He had also received a letter from his mother (sent in English by a professional letter writer), who reminded him that they had not seen each other in years. Her son's two hundred dollars a month allowed Hannah Gelbfisz to live in some luxury in Warsaw; but since the war, she had suffered from cardiopulmonary disorders and "general nervous disease." "Do not forget that I am not young already . . . and that my greatest and only desire now, when, thanks to you, my existence is assured, is to see you," she told her son.

At his next reunion with Ruth, at the Astor Hotel in Times Square in New York, Goldwyn mapped out his plans to take her abroad. As he spoke, Ruth could only think of "weeks of 'baked potatoes.'" After hearing out the offer, she looked up and said, "No, thanks." Ruth would never forget her father's turning "apoplectic." He threw the twelve-year-old girl out of the Astor Hotel and resolved never to see or speak to her again. From that moment, all legal actions toward spending time with her stopped, his support payments ceased, their correspondence ended.

FOR the better part of the year, Goldwyn had been negotiating for the rights to his biggest property yet, *Stella Dallas,* a contemporary American melodrama built around the growing crisis of broken homes. Olive Higgins Prouty's best-selling novel was a shameless tearjerker about a mother's love and the extremes of self-sacrifice: Stella Martin marries a dejected Stephen Dallas, her social superior. They have a daughter, Laurel, the only joy in their doomed relationship. Stephen drifts to New York, leaving Stella to raise the girl alone. Years later, he returns to ask for a divorce. He wishes to marry his former sweetheart, socialite Helen Morrison, and raise Laurel, offering her all the advantages Stella cannot. For her daughter's sake, Stella agrees; but the girl refuses to leave her mother. Out of devotion to her, Stella marries a boor, to drive the girl into her father's arms. After a few years in society, Laurel becomes embarrassed by her mother's common behavior. She does not even invite her to her wedding to the handsome Richard Grosvenor. Instead of barging in on the occasion, Stella Dallas stands in the rain, behind an iron gate outside the house where the wedding is taking place. She watches through the window . . . as a policeman pokes her along on her way. The themes of love lost reverberated doubly for Sam Goldwyn—the selfless mother he never had, the daughter he had discarded.

Once the rights were his, Goldwyn found George Fitzmaurice and Frances Marion so eager to make the film that they offered to forgo their salaries and share in profits. Before that, Miss Marion wrote three scenarios for Goldwyn (at $10,000 apiece), which Fitzmaurice would direct, in 1924 alone. They were all part of Goldwyn's burning desire to establish a leading lady.

Goldwyn had purchased three serious dramatic properties as vehicles for three beautiful young actresses. For the leading man in the first of them, Goldwyn was impressed with the stolid good looks of the young actor opposite Lillian Gish in *The White Sister,* Ronald Colman. Not even aware that Colman had played a bit part in his own *Eternal City,* Goldwyn in New York wired Fitzmaurice in Hollywood about the little-known actor: "PERSONALLY THINK HE LOOKS VERY FOREIGN BUT THEY CLAIM HE CAN SHAVE HIS MUSTACHE AND LOOK THE JUVENILE PART AS HE IS ONLY THIRTY YEARS OLD." Fitzmaurice thought Colman was an excellent choice. "I HAVE NO OBJECTION TO HIS FOREIGN LOOKS OR MUSTACHE," Fitzmaurice added. "AS YOU KNOW FOREIGN LEADING MEN VERY POPULAR IN AMERICA." Colman ended up starring in all three pictures.

Each role enhanced his screen stature, as each asked Colman to choose between two women—one always wholesome, the other a scheming vamp. In *Tarnish,* May McAvoy played a hard-working stenographer in love with her boss, whom she woos away from a gold-digging manicurist. In *A Thief in Paradise,* Colman played a derelict beachcomber conned into posing as the son of a millionaire; a socialite, played by Doris Kenyon, and a femme fatale, Aileen Pringle, vie for his affections. In *His Supreme Moment,* Colman played an earnest engineer torn between a caring actress and a carefree silk stocking. He ends up with the former, Blanche Sweet, who later recalled that her co-star used to require a few swigs of liquor before playing his love scenes. Goldwyn never worked with any of the leading ladies again. He put his commanding new leading man under long-term contract.

Each of the movies was filmed in six weeks, for $250,000. They were marginal successes at the box office, pulling in enough money to encourage A. H. Giannini to extend further loans to Goldwyn.

In January 1925, Goldwyn left for Europe—alone. He traveled by train from capital to capital, as far east as Germany. Sam had been sending extra money to his mother each year so that she could escape the cold by vacationing in Murano. That winter, she forwent the trip to Italy and met her son in Berlin. "Lange Hannah" Gelbfisz and her daughter Mania and granddaughter Adela journeyed from Warsaw. Sam's sister Sally crossed the Channel from England to act as interpreter, for the family had heard that Schmuel had become "a famous millionaire who spoke only English."

They reunited at the Adlon in Berlin. Sam's days were filled with business, but he took all his dinners in his mother's suite. For the better part of a week, Hannah Gelbfisz never once left her room. Young Adela felt resentful that "Uncle Sam was ashamed of us." Years later, he confided to a therapist that that was not the case. He said he had been trying to protect his mother from her own embarrassment.

Over the four days, Goldwyn spoke only Yiddish to his relatives. He assured his mother that his three siblings in America—Ben, Bernard, and Nettie—were all happily married and that he looked after them. (Ben, in fact, had been a manager for the old Goldwyn Distribution Company in Denver; and Sam would soon bring him into his new operation.) He sent a generous allowance every month to his sister Sally in Birmingham. During their visit, Mania Lebensold said to her brother that she wanted to move her family from Poland to Palestine, but Sam vetoed the idea. "Your husband will never make a living there," he insisted, "with all those Jews living together."

On his last afternoon in Berlin, Sam went upstairs to the suite where the family was sequestered and handed a roll of money to his sister Sally. In English he said, "Take Mother out and buy her a fur coat." Hannah received the translation and replied in Yiddish, "I don't want anything. I just want to sit and look at your face." Almost every chance she had, Hannah would walk over to Sam and squeeze his face between her palms. Staring tearily into his eyes, she said over and over, *"Shayner Yid. Shayner Yid"*—"Beautiful Jew."

Sam would not be able to dine with his family that night, because he was the guest of honor at a dinner the American ambassador was giving at the hotel. Shortly before the reception, he instructed his mother to put on her best dress. He escorted her downstairs and right up to the ambassador. *"Das ist mein mutter,"* he said. He promenaded her once around the room, full of important people in evening clothes, then accompanied her to the lobby, where he kissed her on each cheek and instructed a bellman to show her back to her suite. His mother felt as though she had danced at the ball.

Hannah Gelbfisz returned to Warsaw full of tales about her regal reception in Germany. That May, an intestinal disorder flared up, and she died. Goldwyn hardly ever spoke of the woman again, and then it was only to vilify her. He even invented a story about her having remarried all too hastily upon the death of her husband, which in Goldwyn's mind justified his loathing for her.

GOLDWYN left the Adlon Hotel—where the gods did not favor him with a Greto Garbo, as they had Louis B. Mayer just the year before—for Budapest. After a press conference at the Ritz Hotel, he asked a newspaperman to join him for a walk. As they strolled past a shop window that displayed picture postcards, a photograph of one particularly beautiful woman jumped out at Goldwyn. He asked who she was. Employing the Hungarian form of address, in which the surname is given first, the journalist replied, "Banky Vilma."

Vilma Banky, a twenty-seven-year-old blonde with enormous violet eyes, had been born in Nogyrodog, not far from Budapest. She had creamy skin, a heart-shaped mouth, and pronounced cheekbones—definitely more Pickford than Garbo. Goldwyn learned that she was a motion picture actress, with experience in Austria and at UFA in Germany; she was currently working at a small studio across the Danube. The reporter said he could arrange for them to meet on the set the next day.

"I appeared," Goldwyn remembered, ". . .and was met by all the studio dignitaries—such as there were—by the Mayor of the city and by an assorted group of other officials. But the real object of my visit—Banky Vilma—was not present." Goldwyn's inquiries regarding her whereabouts were evaded.

As they left the studio, the journalist told Goldwyn, "If you will be at your hotel tonight, I will bring Banky Vilma around to see you." Goldwyn canceled his appointments for the evening and waited at the hotel, but the actress never showed up. He was scheduled to depart from Budapest the next morning at eight o'clock but, upon leaving the hotel, was informed that he had not yet received the necessary police permit. "I was much annoyed and started raising a certain amount of fuss with Budapest officialdom," Goldwyn later recalled. The permit came through, delaying his departure to two o'clock that afternoon.

When word reached the eager newspaperman that Goldwyn was still in town, he phoned to say he was sure he could line up Banky Vilma for lunch.

12:00 o'clock came, no Banky Vilma; 1:00 o'clock, still no Banky
Vilma; 1:30, ditto. Finally, disgusted with everything about Budapest I left for the train, [Goldwyn recalled].

I arrived five or ten minutes before train time and while I was on
the platform watching my bags go on I saw the little newspaperman
come pounding his way towards me. He reached me breathless. "I've
got Banky Vilma outside at the gate," he said. I answered, "Tell her
to go home—I am busy and leaving on this train in ten minutes."
The little newspaperman looked as down-hearted as anyone I have
seen. "Please," he begged, "if you can come for just a minute and say
hello you would do me a great favor. It would embarrass me terribly,
after all I have gone through, if you would not do even that." I did
not feel much like doing this but I agreed to go down to the gate to
say hello—but that was going to be all.

Goldwyn missed his train. "I needed only one glimpse at Banky Vilma
to know that this was one of the great beauties of the age and that she
would be a great star," he recounted. Her current producers, fearful of
losing her, had crossed all the wires to prevent their meeting. Goldwyn
did not leave Budapest without committing her to a five-year contract. He
instructed her to go immediately to Paris, where money would be deposited with a couturier to outfit her properly. Then he wanted her to sail to
America. From that moment on, Vilma Banky later admitted, "I never
knew what hit me."

Goldwyn already had her debut vehicle picked out, the filming of a hit
play by Guy Bolton. *The Dark Angel* is a lachrymose melodrama about
Hilary Trent, an Englishman blinded in the war, who nobly prefers that
his fiancée, Kitty Vane, think him dead. On her wedding day, Kitty learns
that Hilary is alive and seeks him out. Not wishing to burden her with
his tragedy, he memorizes his surroundings and convincingly performs as
a perfectly sighted person who rejects her. In leaving, Kitty extends her
hand, which he cannot see. Confused, she is intercepted by Hilary's secretary, who reveals the man's blindness. Kitty rushes back into his arms. The
role of Hilary seemed tailor-made for Ronald Colman. He would receive
top billing for the first time. Goldwyn already saw his dark, handsome
looks complementing the fair loveliness of Vilma Banky.

Between her arrival on the S.S. *Aquitania* at Ellis Island on March 10,
1925, and the commencement of photography on *The Dark Angel* one
month later, Goldwyn wished to make Vilma Banky known nationwide as
the greatest star ever to arrive on American shores. He wanted her available
for any number of interviews and photographic sessions. Unfortunately,

his Hungarian star spoke not a word of English and was by European standards *zaftig;* by Goldwyn's, she was ten pounds overweight.

Goldwyn met Miss Banky stateside and was appalled at the dowdy clothes she had selected in Paris. Before presenting her to the press, he sent her to a dressmaker to whom he used to sell gloves and ordered her to "dress her properly and to burn the clothes she's brought." Then, as though instructing a parrot, he gave Vilma Banky (whom he called "Wilma") four words of English, the only words she was to speak until she reached Hollywood. Goldwyn thought it would create a cute publicity hook and help her reduce if all she could say was "Lamp chops and pineapple."

Goldwyn knew that the quickest way to spread Vilma Banky's name was to give an exclusive to Louella Parsons of the Hearst syndicate. In exchange for the scoop, Goldwyn told Miss Parsons, "I would be grateful indeed if you handled this from a standpoint of news for the news columns, rather than as a motion picture story." He urged her to "surround the idea with an air of secrecy," taking details he gave her (which included the actress's spuriously noble birth) as facts she had dug up. Several days after Louella's news article, Goldwyn and his press team blanketed the country with stories and photographs. Every major fan magazine ran a story and awaited an interview.

Goldwyn spent two weeks in March squiring Vilma Banky around town. They were seen somewhere different every night. One evening over dinner at the Colony, magazine publisher Condé Nast could not help stopping at Goldwyn's table; he playfully chided him for not having responded to the invitation to his next party. Goldwyn said he would be there with Miss Banky.

Condé Nast had two months earlier moved into a spectacular apartment at 1040 Fifth Avenue, a penthouse at the corner of Eighty-fifth Street. In almost half a dozen parties already, Nast had broken in his thirty-room urban palace, gathering the most brilliant lights from the worlds of theater, literature, and society. A paragon of elegance, the host graced all his soirees with an abundance of young beauties.

It was a typical evening at home for Nast that last week in March when Sam Goldwyn arrived with Vilma Banky. Among the few hundred milling guests were Gloria Swanson and her husband of two months, the Marquis de la Falaise, playwright Marc Connelly, and two of that year's new beauties, the red-haired Howard sisters.

The host's son, Coudert, had been courting the younger sister, nineteen-year-old Constance; and Condé Nast himself was said to be interested in marrying twenty-one-year-old Frances. After dinner, on the dance floor with Vilma Banky, Sam Goldwyn caught a glimpse of her. "I saw a stunning redhead dancing with some man," Goldwyn recalled more than forty years later, "and I quickly cut in and made him dance with Banky Vilma." Goldwyn felt at once that "opportunity" was tapping him on the shoulder. And, he said, "I did not have to be tapped twice."

In fact, it was not the first time he had seen Frances Howard. A few years earlier, she had screen-tested for the Goldwyn Company in New York, and Goldwyn had admonished his casting director for having wasted the time and money on her. Shortly thereafter, Goldwyn bumped into Miss Howard, who had snipped her ginger tresses for a part. "You used to be fairly good-looking," he said. "Now that you've gone and bobbed your hair, you're terrible."

Under Condé Nast's crystal chandeliers, however, Sam Goldwyn saw Frances Howard in an entirely new light. Whether it was the shrewdness he detected in her cerulean eyes (set closely together), the authority with which she carried her slim figure, or just knowing that Condé Nast was smitten with her, Sam Goldwyn fell instantly in love. He did not know yet that, like him, she was a survivor. Rumored to be one of the Howards of Virginia, a daughter of the American Revolution, an heiress who had turned to the stage, Frances—like the man looking her over—was in the process of inventing herself.

She was born Frances Howard McLaughlin on June 4, 1903, in Omaha, Nebraska, the eldest of four children. Her mother, Helen Victoria Howard (known as Bonnie), was the youngest daughter of well-heeled Kansas landowners living just outside Wichita. They were not one of America's first families. The favorite niece of thirteen uncles, Bonnie was constantly fussed over—becoming, in the words of one of her granddaughters, "a spoiled brat and troublemaker." When she debuted in Chicago, her parents hired one of the city's most celebrated cultural figures to make the arrangements, Florenz Ziegfeld, father of the future impresario.

Bonnie had many gentleman callers, but she chased one of her older sister's suitors, the handsome Charles Douglas McLaughlin, from Batavia, New York, just outside Rochester. His mother was a daughter of the Irish nationalist Daniel O'Connell; his father's clan were landed gentry and horse breeders, with a weakness for alcohol. Bonnie had been raised a Quaker, but she converted to Catholicism for her fiancé. When she married, her uncle William lavished china and furniture, then stocks and bonds, on her, a dowry worth close to one million dollars. She insisted on luxury, and always wanted everything to be, as she said, "perfect—fine as silk."

Her husband met her every whim, for a while. With his brothers,

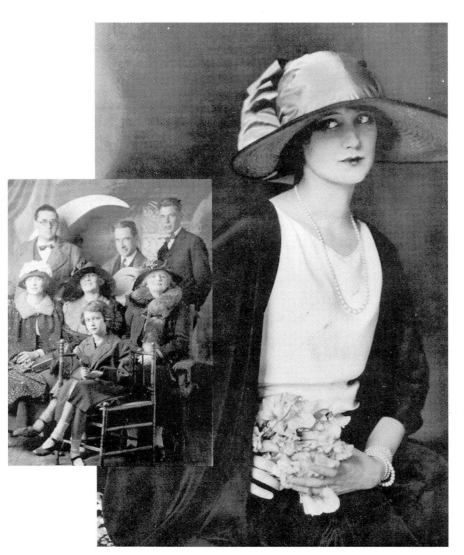

Frances Howard, as photographed in 1924 by Edward Steichen for *Vogue*.
INSET: The budding actress in 1920 (second row, left) sits in front of the
great love of her life, George Cukor, then manager of the Lyceum Players
in Rochester. Frances's sister Dede sits in front and their mother, Bonnie,
to the right.

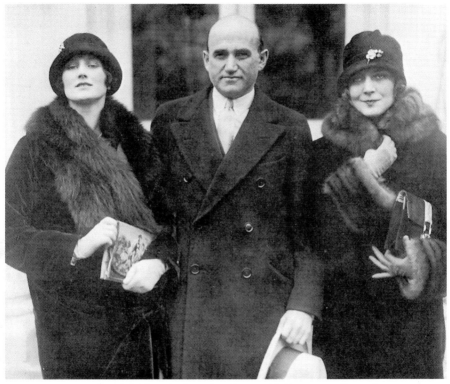

ABOVE: Samuel Goldwyn in the spring of 1925 with his two new discoveries: Frances Howard, whom he would marry, and Vilma Banky, whom he would turn into a star. OPPOSITE: In 1926 Goldwyn gave Gary Cooper his first important role, in *The Winning of Barbara Worth*. INSET: On the Nevada set of the film with director Henry King.

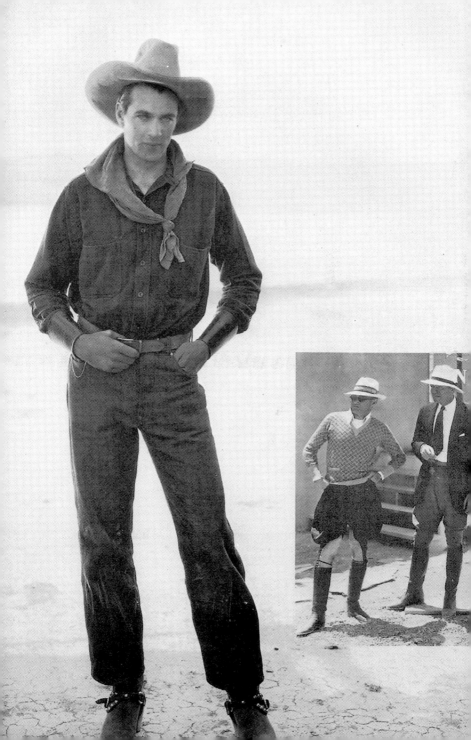

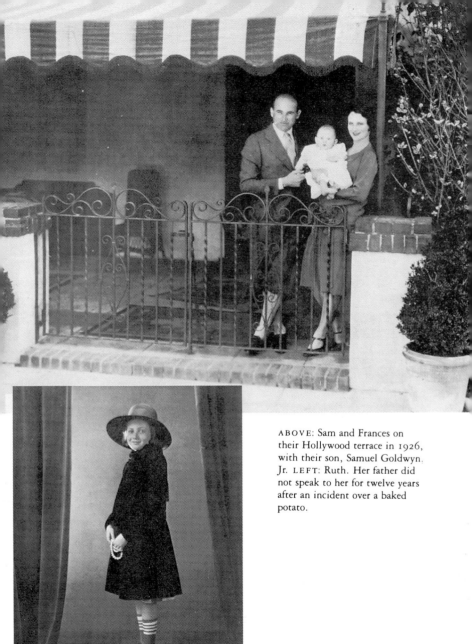

ABOVE: Sam and Frances on their Hollywood terrace in 1926, with their son, Samuel Goldwyn. Jr. LEFT: Ruth. Her father did not speak to her for twelve years after an incident over a baked potato.

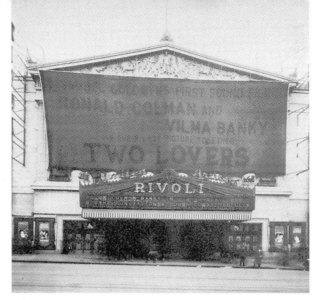

ABOVE: *Two Lovers*, starring Vilma Banky. The addition of sound quickly killed the Hungarian actress's career. BELOW: Left to right, Goldwyn, Joseph Schenck, Frances Goldwyn, and writer Sidney Howard in 1929, promoting *Bulldog Drummond*, the picture that successfully carried Ronald Colman from stardom on the silent screen into the talkies.

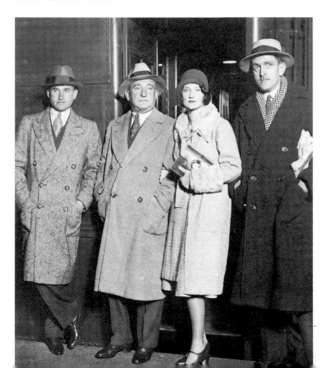

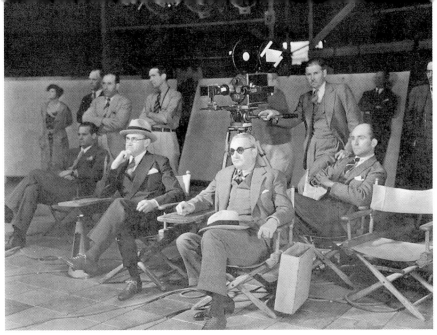

ABOVE: Goldwyn, Florenz Ziegfeld, and Goldwyn's associate Arthur Hornblow, Jr., on the set of *Whoopee!* The smash musical made a movie star of Eddie Cantor and marked the end of Ziegfeld's career. BELOW: Eddie Cantor (right) "serves tea" to Goldwyn, who was consulting with Sinclair Lewis in 1931, when the producer was adapting *Arrowsmith* for the screen.

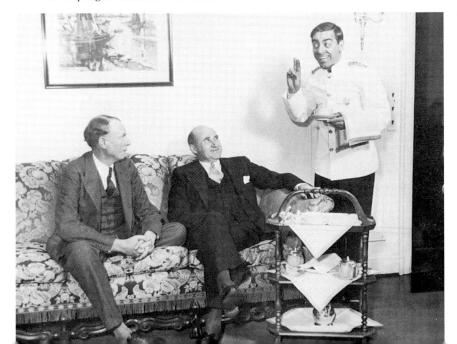

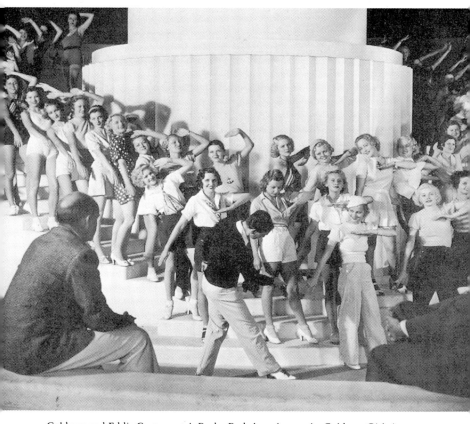

Goldwyn and Eddie Cantor watch Busby Berkeley rehearse the Goldwyn Girls in a number from *Roman Scandals* (1933). The eager blonde (lower right) is Lucille Ball.

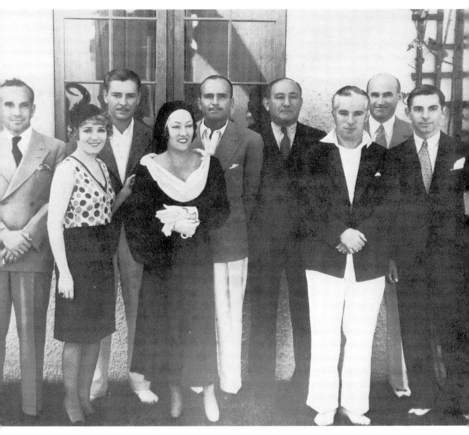

United Artists stars and partners in 1931. Left to right: Al Jolson, Mary Pickford, Ronald Colman, Gloria Swanson, Douglas Fairbanks, Joseph Schenck, Charlie Chaplin, Goldwyn, and Eddie Cantor. Within a few years Schenck would leave to merge his Twentieth Century Productions with Fox, and all the stars would fade from the screen—except for Goldwyn's Colman and Cantor, whose films kept the studio alive in the early years of the Depression.

Charles McLaughlin established a successful business in women's shoes. At the turn of the century, he oversaw the building of their plant in Omaha, where his first child, Frances, was born. After a few years, the McLaughlins moved to Chicago, where Charles directed the door-to-door distribution of their product. Frances attended an unmerciful Catholic boarding school there. She was allowed to bathe but once a week, and then she had to enter the tub clothed, peeling off her frock only as she immersed herself in the water. When she began to develop physically, the nuns bound her chest and cautioned her to eat less. They inculcated her with the belief that the Jews killed Christ.

While barely in her teens, Frances moved with her family—there were three other children: Mary Virginia (who went by the name Dede), Christine Helen Victoria (Constance), and a son named for his father—to Rochester, into a large white Victorian house, which sat behind a picket fence. Charles provided his wife with servants and tried to smooth over their difficult marriage with furs and jewels. His brothers had been operating their business out of the nearby village of Brockport, and they seemed to be running it into the ground. In truth, they were embezzling, and they left Charles holding the bag. McLaughlin struggled to make good on a raft of bad debts. In an effort to save the family name, he let go of the staff, the furnishings, the house, his wife's entire legacy. "We had everything," Bonnie stated years later, "then nothing."

McLaughlin took to liquor and often to the road. Starting in the morning, he would imbibe at least a bottle of whiskey a day. His once-pampered wife had worked up so much resentment against what he had done to her, she made it impossible for him to come home. Bonnie made the girls assume her maiden name, and she overtly neglected her ill-yclept son. (She had long resented him anyway, because he was born with a defective ear.) Frances always looked forward to her father's coming home, but a few years later he died—drunk, broke, and alone—at the age of forty-seven.

Frances came to realize that her father was less emotionally disturbed than her mother. Most people had long dismissed Bonnie's extreme vanity as simply odd behavior. When her husband "stole her fortune," something snapped inside. Bonnie's looks began to go, and she took to concocting beauty creams and cabbage-juice tonics. She pitted her daughters against each other and banished her son from the house as soon as she could. She could not bring herself to utter the word "Jew." She called them "Orientals."

Unable to cope, Bonnie reverted to a second childhood. All the girls were sent to work—even eleven-year-old Constance, who had to dodge truant officers so that she could peddle her mother's beauty creams. Bonnie's dementia was hardest on Frances, leaving deep emotional scars. She teased the child with feathers to the point of cruelty, and Frances grew up with a lifelong dread of birds; Bonnie once locked her in a room of a burning house, which made Frances pyrophobic. Frances felt guilty about ever enjoying herself too much—she regarded even food as more a luxury than a necessity. She had a nervous desire to see that everything was "perfect—fine as silk"—if only on the outside. She lived in mortal fear of "losing everything."

Even more than Schmuel Gelbfisz, who had also been rushed into adulthood, Frances became the family caretaker. She needed to be needed. Despite her conflicted feelings, she put upon herself all responsibility for the welfare of her mother and sisters, whatever the cost, for the rest of their lives.

Bonnie McLaughlin depended on the kindness of strangers. Moving her family into a small apartment in a brownstone boardinghouse on West Eighty-fifth Street near Amsterdam Avenue in Manhattan, she called on the Ziegfeld boy to see if he could not help her children with their careers. Ziegfeld got sixteen-year-old Frances a part in the road-show chorus of a musical entitled *Oh! My Dear.* After its run, Ziegfeld asked her to be in the chorus of another musical, but she refused. She said she wanted to act. Ziegfeld's wife, Billie Burke, was about to open in a Booth Tarkington comedy, *Intimate Strangers.* The small part of a pretty young flapper had not yet been cast.

Billie Burke took a shine to Frances Howard. She helped get her the role in the fall of 1921 and got her over her fear of bobbing her hair, as the part required. The show ran a respectable ninety-one performances and was scheduled to go on the road.

In the spring, the cast was called for a rehearsal at Tuxedo Hall, on Madison Avenue and Fifty-ninth Street, in preparation for their opening in Syracuse. That day, Frances Howard met the stage manager of the upstate theater and they fell in love.

"We had to rehearse in another hall," recalled that stage manager, who had been stagestruck since childhood, "and my job was to tell the actors to proceed to another hall over on Sixth Avenue. Suddenly this dazzlingly pretty girl walked in—she was very pretty and very friendly. 'I'm here,' she said. In fact, she was the prettiest girl I had ever seen—a beautiful figure, lovely face, and beautiful skin. And there was something very respectable about her, very elegant. She was soignée."

The stage manager volunteered to accompany the actress across town. During the course of their two streetcar rides, he discovered that she was "really intelligent and had a rather cultivated way of talking, as though she paid attention to every word that came out of her mouth." By the time they arrived at Forty-second Street and Sixth Avenue, they had become "fast friends."

At first glance, George Cukor was not an especially attractive man. He was short and pudgy, with a prominent beak, thick lips, and spectacles. But he had a razor-sharp wit and a way of throwing his whole body into his every fast-spoken word. A second-generation American of Jewish-Hungarian descent, he was the most sensitive and knowledgeable man Frances Howard had ever met. His enthusiasm was matched by his generosity in sharing what he knew about theater and literature and music. They spent all their time as part of the Knickerbocker Players (which included Florence Eldridge) in Syracuse together, living down the hall from each other in a boardinghouse. Cukor, a lonely outcast who was picked on by most of the company, delighted in the attentions of somebody so beautiful. He became the first person to get Frances to question the way she had been raised; he said she should start living for herself and less for her family. "How do you put up with all these terrible people?" he asked, referring to Bonnie and one of the daughters, who was growing up with many of the same superficial values.

For the next two years, Frances Howard was almost never out of work. She moved on with her stage manager to Rochester, where he became manager of the Lyceum Players and began directing. Other work came up for her—acting in a play under Gilbert Miller's direction in Toronto, modeling for such photographers as Edward Steichen and Baron de Meyer in New York. Home again became Rochester, where she played ingenues in Cukor's plays. They lived in neighboring rooms in another boardinghouse.

Their feelings for each other were profound—it was the greatest love of either of their lives. Several of his friends later insisted that Frances was the only woman he ever truly loved. He even asked her to marry him. But George Cukor was homosexual, at a time when such a fact could only be whispered. He was not the answer to Frances Howard's prayers.

Professionally, good fortune struck both the young actress and the director, four years her senior. Their apprenticeships in Rochester—where Louis Calhern and Miriam Hopkins were part of the company—led to bigger success in New York. Frances introduced Cukor to Gilbert Miller, and almost overnight he was directing the likes of Ethel Barrymore, Laurette Taylor, and Dorothy Gish in plays by Zoë Akins and Somerset Maugham. Frances snatched the lead in *The Best People,* playing another flapper. She suffered from stage fright, and her performances were wooden;

but Jesse Lasky, who was part of the opening-night audience at the Lyceum
Theater, was so impressed with her beauty that he signed her to a five-year
movie contract.

Living with her family on West Eighty-fifth Street, Frances turned over
most of her money to support them. She made two films at Paramount's
Long Island studios before getting the lead in *The Swan*, the story of a girl
groomed to marry a crown prince. She busied herself outside the family
apartment as much as possible. George Cukor, living on the East Side,
often rescued her—"anything to keep her away from that ass of a mother
. . . and that crappy beauty cream!"

Frances dated tentatively. She went occasionally to the theater or a
nightclub with a young art director she had met at the Paramount studio;
and Curt Gerling, a Rochester boy who was attending the University of
Pennsylvania, pursued her. He would take the train to New York for weekends, even though he knew he would have a lot of free time while Frances
was onstage. He spent it with Mrs. McLaughlin, stirring up gin in the
basement. Frances did not become seriously involved with anybody—except George Cukor, her mentor and protector. "She was never highly
sexed," he said; "and I'm absolutely certain that the night Sam Goldwyn
first danced with her, he danced with a virgin."

Condé Nast's party in March 1925 was Frances Howard's first "big social
affair." For the occasion she bought an elegant white crepe dress for $310,
a great extravagance for a twenty-one-year-old more comfortable in a hair
shirt. Before the night was over, Goldwyn asked Miss Howard if he might
see her again. She thought he had "a diamond-in-the-rough charm" and
said she would be delighted. Vilma Banky remembered leaving Condé
Nast's that night with Sam Goldwyn absolutely aglow. "I thought it was
because of me," she said decades later, "because I had done so well."

The next day, Miss Banky left for Hollywood, a whistle-stop tour that
received all the press coverage Goldwyn had dreamed of. Even with his
obsession to make a star of Vilma Banky, the producer could not get
Frances Howard out of his head. The night after Condé Nast's party, he
took her to a nightclub, the Golden Eagle, where he wasted no time. "I
don't believe in beating around the bush," he said. "You and I must be
married."

"That's ridiculous," Frances told him. "I don't know you at all. We've
only met once, and briefly. Besides, I'm going to Hollywood to be in the
movies."

"Good," he said. "But first we should get married, because if we're not
married, anyone as young and beautiful as you running around Hollywood
with me, well, people will take it for granted that you're my . . .

girl. . . . You don't know what evil minds people in Hollywood have." Without hesitating, he proposed again. She said she needed time.

For most of his life, Sam Goldwyn had considered himself (as he admitted to a therapist) physically unattractive. This hard assessment fueled his powerful professional drive; but it also rendered him virtually sexless— the one aspect of his character about which he always felt defensive. After years of scaring women off in response to their scaring him, he was not about to lost this rare beauty—who radiated her own weak sex drive. Feeling at ease with her, he became insistent. "You don't have to think about it," he said, "because that is what you are going to do. You are going to marry me."

"Sam was ambitious, engaging and forthright," was Frances's assessment. He dismissed his first marriage by saying, "When a picture is over, it's over. The same with a marriage." He confessed that he was "lonesome and needed a wife, someone he could trust and confide in."

"Right off the bat," Frances later confessed, "I thought to myself, Why not?"

The next morning, she raced crosstown to tell George Cukor about the preceding forty-eight hours. "You know," she hemmed, "I've met Sam Goldwyn." Cukor was impressed. He said it would not be long before she was mingling in Hollywood's inner circles. "Sam Goldwyn wants to marry me," she added. He fell silent. "What do you think?" she asked.

He paused for a moment and said, "Marry him, Frances. You'll never get a better part!"

"I didn't think she was a very gifted actress, and she certainly never thought much of herself as an actress," Cukor related many years later. "Frances was ambitious and enormously practical," he said. "Everything she could see about him, she admired enormously, and what she could not she thought she could live with. I always thought it would be a 'proper marriage.' Not a romantic one, but one that would work. And I think Frances thought the same." As she occasionally admitted to a handful of intimates, "I have a cash register where my heart should be."

Frances accepted Goldwyn's proposal, but both thought it best to keep silent about the engagement. After a week, he got cold feet and tried to back out, citing the difference in their religion as just one of many problems. Frances would not hear of it. "You asked me to marry you, and you're going to," she said. "So just make up your mind to that." She insisted their children would be raised as Catholics. The next day, Goldwyn slipped an engagement ring on her finger.

"Then we told Mother," Frances remembered. "This meant I faced disbelief, logical opposition, tears and an explosion." Sam—almost exactly

Bonnie's age—received most of the fallout, but he stood fast. "Even if you do marry," Frances's mother insisted, "it won't last." Frances said it would. Sam said he hoped it would. "Well, it won't," Bonnie kept repeating. Frances sat down and tuned her mother out by cocking her head skyward, drumming her fingers, and chanting, "Wait and see."

Bonnie had every intention of busting up this engagement as soon as possible. Not only was Sam Goldwyn twice her daughter's age, but he was an "Oriental," who had already been married. Frances had met enough Jews in the theater (including George Cukor) to realize they did not have horns; she subscribed instead to the more positive stereotypes of the day, which made Goldwyn most appealing—Jews were good with money and they did not drink. He made Frances feel that she might never have to worry about losing her house again, and that he could help provide for her sisters and Bonnie. He certainly seemed formidable enough to protect her from her mother. A few days later, Sam and Frances and Bonnie went to Jersey City to obtain a wedding license. Mrs. McLaughlin never once acknowledged Goldwyn's presence. Above the rumble of the train as it tunneled beneath the Hudson, she could be heard murmuring, "My daughter will not marry Sam Goldwyn."

Goldwyn set their wedding date for Thursday, April 23, 1925—four weeks from the night they had met. He asked Edgar Selwyn to stand as his best man and swore him to secrecy because he did not want the event to be a circus of publicity. Selwyn agreed not to breathe a word.

The night before their wedding, Frances asked Sam to pick up a copy of *The New Yorker* for the limousine ride to New Jersey. Between his present residence at the Ambassador Hotel on Park Avenue and Frances's apartment, Goldwyn thumbed through the tenth number of the smart new periodical, which was becoming the rage of the young artistic crowd in Manhattan. In the "Motion Pictures" column was a disparaging review of Goldwyn's latest offering, *His Supreme Moment*, with Ronald Colman.

Closer to the front of the magazine, on page thirteen, came a more shocking discovery. One of the first of *The New Yorker*'s celebrated "profiles" was entitled "The Celluloid Prince." Staring out from the center of the page was a caricature of Goldwyn himself, casting a shrewd, squinty eye straight ahead, while the other eye looked off to the side, beneath a skeptical, high-arched brow.

He did not know at the time that his own press agent, Carl Brandt, had planted the story. The two-page article called him "a great man," noting: "There are so many stupid people in the movies who cannot see beyond their noses, narrow-minded and timid little men, that Mr. Goldwyn stands out from among them a dramatic figure—an inspired buccaneer." The rest of Goldwyn's fairy-tale rise from glovemaker to "a great Prince of the Movies" was not the sort of thing a man would want a bride with butterflies in her stomach to read on her way to their wedding.

Now he has a valet and dresses and looks like a gentleman, but to hear him speak is a shock. He shouts in a vocabulary of ten words— words used by a prize fighter who has gone into the cloak and suit business and upon whose nodular tones an expressman has let fall a half ton case of goods. If after an interview you are a bit raw, he won't know it. . . .

. . . In the matter of pictures he has the master's instinct for reaching at the heart of humanity, but he often loses his way. His own intuitions are crystal clear, but with a mind capable of deduction he has no confidence in his own convictions and will swallow verbatim the logic of others. Thus he will make up his mind and change it simultaneously, and since like all geniuses his intuitions are his best bets, he is, so to speak, his own worst enemy.

When Goldwyn arrived at West Eighty-fifth Street, he hid the magazine. Frances entered the car, and he apologized for not having been able to get hold of a copy. Frances detected his dissembling and demanded to see it. She read the piece in silence all the way to Jersey City. Her mother and George Cukor rode in a car behind them.

"We've got to stop this," Bonnie said to George, who she had hoped would be her son-in-law. "It's going to be all right," he kept assuring her. As the long car pulled up to the city hall, a horde of reporters and photographers swarmed around the couple. Edgar Selwyn worked his way through the crowd and said, "Hey, Sam, I thought you didn't want any publicity." Goldwyn sheepishly replied, "Can I control the press?" Frances let out a whoop of laughter, and the two of them marched into the chambers of Judge Leo S. Sullivan; the best man, the mother of the bride, and Cukor trailed.

After the vows were recited, Mr. and Mrs. Samuel Goldwyn and their small wedding party returned to New York. Twenty guests toasted the bride and groom at a champagne breakfast at the Ritz Hotel, then the beaming benedict took his bride to his office on Madison Avenue. He proudly showed her off and bade his office staff farewell. There were hugs and tears all around, as Frances looked on. Then they caught their train. "Mr. Goldwyn," the *Jersey Journal* stated, "is going to Hollywood to make one or two pictures."

10 Canaan

ONLY FOUR DAYS out of New York, the honeymoon was over. As they crossed the Arizona desert, Frances's new husband confessed, "There's one thing I want you to know . . . I've had two failures in business, and I haven't got any money. But with you at my side, I'll make some." Goldwyn's financial picture was not as bleak as he painted. While most of his money was tied up in his new company, he did have five-figure savings accounts in several Giannini banks, an active portfolio of stocks, and a few hundred thousand dollars' profit on paper from his most recent productions. To prove that his greatest assets would always be the films that lay ahead, he described how he had survived the treacherous road behind him. "I was," he said, "on the brink of an abscess."

Frances, with her chronic fears of "losing everything," listened nervously. Her mind wandered to that week's *New Yorker,* which had called her husband "the epitome of the movies, and heir apparent to its great future achievements." Now when he said, "In this business it's dog eat dog, and nobody's going to eat me," she believed him. She resolved to stand behind her man.

About noon on the last day of April 1925, the Goldwyns stepped off the Chief downtown at the Santa Fe terminal. It was a hot, sunny day. Frances looked in awe at everything around her—first noticing the distant mountains "crouching on one side, spikes of oil wells poking up on the other." Orange trees, practically growing alongside the tracks, perfumed her walk along the platform to the entourage of business associates awaiting them. "Lots of people smiled at me," she remembered. "Then we got into a car and drove miles and miles over the slickest cleanest pavements I'd ever seen."

Frances's first glimpses of the city between the depot and her new home were as fantastic as her childhood fantasies of the place. Amid the boxy office structures and tile-roofed stucco dwellings, a fanciful skyline was developing, a potpourri of architecture in this vast conglomeration of loosely connected communities. The mid-twenties occasioned a boom in the building of motion picture palaces—in the styles of Spanish missions, Egyptian and Mayan temples, even a Chinese pagoda.

As the Goldwyns' car headed west on Hollywood Boulevard, off to the right, looking like a tiara across the forehead of Mount Lee, thirteen letters, each four stories high, spread the distance of a city block to announce a new real estate development—HOLLYWOODLAND. Many show business personalities were building sumptuous houses and swimming pools right into what were being called the Hollywood Hills. The noontime crowd down along the flat boulevard was as nonchalant as it was outlandish: "Bathing beauties, extras in evening attire, Indians in full war regalia, Orientals, Biblical characters poured out from near-by studios to snatch a hasty luncheon before returning to the impatient cameras." Frances's head was spinning. Sam told her they were invited to a dinner party that night.

She hardly had time to consider the significance of the evening when their car crossed La Brea Avenue. Hollywood Boulevard suddenly turned residential and quiet. Along both sides of the street dwelt many families unassociated with motion pictures, though within the boulevard's heavy scent of eucalyptus and orange blossoms lived Joe Schenck and Norma Talmadge, Pola Negri, and the Jesse Laskys. On what Irene Mayer Selznick remembered as "the perkiest corner" of this neighborhood, the northeast corner of Hollywood and Camino Palmero, the mother of actress Betty Compson owned a house that had more character than any other on the street. This quasi-Norman farmhouse, with an imitation thatched roof, sat a dozen steps above street level; "it was lovely and tidy," recalled Irene Selznick, "giving the impression that the people who lived there weren't being grand, but were prosperous in a conservative way." Sam Goldwyn rented the house and lived there with his bride for the next few years.

Frances had barely arrived, it seemed, when she was standing in her best dress—pink chiffon embroidered with tiny imitation shells—in the doorway of Richard Rowland, the head of First National. "My fingers were icy," Frances remembered. "So, incidentally, were my toes. And my throat had gone dry. Indeed, I felt exactly the way I always did just before my stage entrance on an opening night—only worse." Sam poked her hard in the back. "I was me again," she recalled twenty-five years later, "wild to meet and know Hollywood and be liked by it. Getting to know it was to take long. But I certainly met a lot of it, all in one glittering burst": Constance and Norma Talmadge, Pola Negri in a silver lamé turban; John Gilbert, Ernst Lubitsch, and Sam's former crush, Florence Vidor. The new Mrs. Goldwyn's biggest thrill came when she discovered that one of her dinner partners was Earle Williams, the "dream prince" whose photograph she used to clip from *Photoplay* and keep in a candy box during her grammar school days.

By the end of the evening, everyone in the room had shrunk in her eyes to a mere mortal. She felt something less than that. "A man was talking about a barbecue he had been to the Sunday before," Frances never forgot; "another man asked who'd been there. A string of names was mentioned. Half were stars; half, though I didn't particularly notice it at the moment, were male names. . . . Then in a throw-away tone, came the addition, 'And some wives, a'course.'" During the rest of dinner, nothing registered with her except a voice inside saying, "You're not Frances Howard, who was going to be a great actress on the stage—the real stage, where you have to be a good actress to be a quarter as famous as these people here. You suddenly up and got married. You chucked what you'd been working like a beaver for ever since you were fifteen. Yes, you did! And you can't pretend you didn't agree to stop being an actress to become a—just a wife, any more than you can pretend you didn't help Sam along to proposing to you. Because you did—both. So now you're what you wanted to be. You're just another—'some wives, a'course.'" Her ego, she later admitted, shriveled "to nothing."

After her first night in Hollywood, two women rushed to Frances's aid. One was Margaret Talmadge, the wisecracking mother of Norma and Constance, an abandoned wife who had become the most successful stage mother in motion pictures. Known to the Hollywood crowd as Peg, she responded to Frances's no-nonsense attitude and unclouded desire to make good. The other booster was Sam's devoted employee Frances Marion, the town's most celebrated scenarist and cook. They taught her the responsibilities of being a Hollywood hostess.

She started by learning how to keep a menu book, lists of all her company and the meals served. It saw that people would get the same dish twice only if it had been noted as a special favorite. Each guest's cocktail was recorded, so a return visitor never had to order it. She learned where to shop for clothes and flowers and food. "And while I was still trying to learn the difference between shoulder, rack and leg of lamb, brisket of beef and filet, the price of peas versus asparagus," Frances later wrote in the

Woman's Home Companion, "before I discovered how to get wet glass marks off table tops, before I had sense enough to be nervous or hesitant—already I was giving dinner parties, half of which were thrown at me on wickedly short notice."

Frances had barely settled into her new life when Sam arrived home from the nearby United Studios and casually announced that he had invited an extra man—the former ambassador to Spain—to a dinner Frances had been planning for weeks. She flew into a tizzy but pulled off the entire evening to her husband's great satisfaction—until the women retired to the living room for coffee. From the dining room, Frances heard a stentorian voice boom, "Sam. The dinner was all right. But, if you'd have spent five cents more, I could have had a good cigar." For years, Sam would caution Frances before each party not to buy any more cigars from a drugstore.

In this most private enclave of the pampered nouveau riche, where everybody was out to impress everybody else, the rise or fall of a dessert could eventually affect the culture of the world. Or so it seemed. "Tonight's wink across a room could be tomorrow's star," said King Vidor. "The way Colleen Moore wore her hair at a party in Hollywood would change the way women across America would wear theirs in two years." Frances Goldwyn understood the solemnity of her position. "She smoothed Sam's rough edges," remembered Carmel Myers, a rabbi's daughter recently back from Rome, where she played Iras in MGM's *Ben-Hur.*

There seemed to be some celebration in Hollywood every night, each event more extravagant than the last. Many of the Hollywood parties in the spring of 1925 were given in Sam Goldwyn's honor—to meet his new wife and his new Hungarian discovery. Within weeks, Frances knew the entire crowd, having bumped into the same people everywhere. On June 26, 1925, Chaplin's *Gold Rush* premiered at Grauman's Egyptian Theater; and Goldwyn challenged his bride with the task of throwing an after-screening party in Chaplin's honor. Less than two months in Hollywood, and this twenty-two-year-old former ingenue found herself inviting Pickford and Fairbanks, William Randolph Hearst and Marion Davies, Norma Talmadge and Joe Schenck, Constance Talmadge, the Buster Keatons, John Barrymore, Gloria Swanson and her marquis, Sid Grauman, Louella Parsons, Fred Niblo (about to direct the climactic chariot sequence of *Ben-Hur* in Culver City), George Fitzmaurice, and Florence Vidor to her house. Goldwyn's secretary ordered the liquor from the bootlegger, "$300 worth of stuff."

Gradually the venue of these revolving galas shifted to a remote outpost of baronial mansions several miles to the west of Hollywood. It was accessible only by the unpaved extension of Sunset Boulevard, which snaked its way to the sea. The 4,500 acres of the original land parcel deeded by the governor of Mexico was named El Rancho Rodeo de las Aquas—The Land of the Gathering Waters—its borders having been carved by the winter rainwater that streamed down Benedict and Coldwater canyons into the flats below. By the arrival of the twentieth century, the land had passed through several owners, never attracting much of a population. In 1906, Burton S. Green drilled for oil and came up with water; forming the Rodeo Land & Water Company, he began selling off parcels. He named the hilly terrain after a town President Taft had recently visited in Massachusetts.

Green knew he needed a lure to Beverly Hills, some sign of civilization. At Sunset Boulevard, in the delta where the two canyon riverbeds met, he built a three-story hotel in 1912—a huge T-shaped mission-style edifice of thick stucco, which he painted pink. For years, the Beverly Hills Hotel stood alone in the wilderness, a folly. It began to draw Angelenos eager to hide away or cut up on Saturday, away from the public glare. A nearby town tried to build itself up. "In those days Beverly Hills looked like an abandoned real-estate development," recalled Charlie Chaplin. "Sidewalks ran along and disappeared into open fields and lampposts with white globes adorned empty streets; most of the globes were missing, shot off by passing revelers from roadhouses."

In the scrubby, coyote-filled hills, on a knoll high above the back of the hotel, an attorney built a weekend hunting lodge. As the neighboring population swelled to six hundred, he sold that two-story bungalow atop Summit Drive to Douglas Fairbanks, who built a stately home around it. The four-story mansion, Tudor in influence, had its own screening room, billiard room, and bowling alley. After Mary Pickford married Fairbanks, they moved into his bachelor pad, for which the press found a euphonious sobriquet in the first syllables of their last names.

Pickfair became the social hub of the world, attracting such titled houseguests as the King of Spain, the Queen of Siam, and the "Sultan of Swat." Hollywood nobility flocked to its doors as the reigning stars began building their own dream palaces in its backyard. Gloria Swanson bought a "Renaissance" palazzo down Crescent Drive near Sunset Boulevard. Will Rogers moved his family and animals to several acres on Beverly Drive. Chaplin built an estate on Summit Drive, as did cowboy Tom Mix. By 1925, the population had risen to 7,500. Lots that had sold for $500 in 1920 were fetching $70,000. Just before moving into the Compson house on Hollywood Boulevard, Sam Goldwyn had tried to rent a place in Pickfair's shadow, on Lexington Road, but Marion Davies's mother grabbed it for herself and her daughter.

The Spanish-style house was a place for Marion to hang her hat when she was working. Between pictures and on weekends, she played hostess for William Randolph Hearst and as many as fifty guests at his castle at San Simeon, California, halfway between Los Angeles and San Francisco. By the mid-twenties, she was also holding court on the sands of Santa Monica, at her three-story colonial mansion.

Within a stone's throw of the Davies beach house—at the foot of the steep palisades, along Ocean Front—was a tract of twenty far more modest houses. With the lure of its prime shoreline and the frequent presence of Mr. Hearst himself, this quarter-mile strand became the summer haven of the Hollywood elite.

In the first years of their marriage, the Goldwyns rented a place at the beach every summer. Their neighbors included the Jesse Laskys and the Louis B. Mayers. Any given weekend in the summer was sure to draw, it seemed, every Hollywood star to the beach. Watching over the proceedings—between heated card games and ocean dips—was a minyan of moguls, men who controlled most of the lives and fortunes of the guests at play. There, on a quarter-mile strip of ancient sand by a pacific sea, lolled a handful of tribal chieftains. Little more than a quarter century earlier, most of them had been wretches living within five hundred miles of each other in Eastern Europe, strangers destined to be forever bound by their common dreams. Surely this was the promised land.

"The Goldwyns, recently married," recalled Louis Mayer's daughter Irene of those days on the beach, "were forbidden fruit. My father detested Sam and Sam detested my father. My father thought Sam's wife, Frances, was a marvelous woman; her only defect was her lack of judgment in marrying Sam." Both Mayer girls—but a few years younger than Frances—forged their own private friendships with the Goldwyns. Louis B. gently approached the new member of the innermost social circle.

"In the first few years after I arrived in Hollywood," Frances remembered, "Sam and I would sometimes meet Mr. and Mrs. Mayer at a social or industry occasion. Sam and Louis would ignore each other, but Louis would talk to me. Once he said, 'Frances, Sam will have nothing to do with me. But I'd like to know you better. Why don't you come to the studio and have lunch with me?'" Frances agreed if she could get her husband's permission.

Everyone stared that afternoon when Frances Goldwyn walked into the MGM dining room by Mayer's side. "They couldn't believe I was there because the whole town knew about the feud between my husband and Louis." The lunch was nothing more than civil, the conversation polite. "All during lunch Louis complained about Hollywood," she recalled.

"Mostly he complained that it was too chilly at night. I suggested he wear an overcoat. When I got home and told Sam that my conversation with Louis had been superficial and nonsensical and that Louis' prime worry was the weather, Sam laughed and shook his head. He said, 'Now I realize more than ever the secret of becoming a success in this business. No partners!'"

Except for Frances. "She had a mind of her own and was correct in thinking she would have her hands full as Sam's wife," Irene Mayer Selznick later wrote in her memoirs. "She catered to him, but she also took him in hand and started to mend some of his broken fences, even to the point of inviting my parents to dinner, short-lived as those occasional truces would be."

More and more, Sam included Frances in his activities. At first, he did not solicit her opinion. It was frustrating, as Frances later revealed in a letter to him: "I would go to the studio with you many a morning, see the rushes—just to see them, not to be asked what I thought. Then I'd run off to the market, be shown a cut of beef, but again not be able to criticize." In private, Frances had her husband's ear. Once he realized that her instincts for her survival were synonymous with his, he listened. "Frances became Sam's protector," said George Cukor. "She had a built-in device that detected crap. She knew just who to let into his life and who to keep out." In the words of one longtime observer of the Goldwyn marriage: "Frances made the trains run on time."

She promptly adopted his schedule. From the beginning of her marriage, Frances knew that her husband wanted a male heir. Although she had little interest in bearing children, Frances found herself pregnant after eight months of marriage. The day she went to the gynecologist to confirm her suspicion, she asked Louella Parsons to accompany her. Frances was a quick study.

"EVERYBODY is so temperamental and childish in this business, that in order to get on I suppose I shall have to adopt an attitude of complete indifference, and develop a tough hide so that all their words will roll off and leave me entirely uneffected [sic]," wrote Sam Goldwyn's new secretary. And she had not even met her boss yet. In the early spring of 1925, Valeria Belletti had lucked into the job while he was in Europe. She wrote her best friend back in New York:

Mr. Lehr . . . told me that as Mr. Goldwyn's secretary I would have to look very smart and dress well. He told me that if I needed any money for this purpose, he would be glad to give it to me, and pay him back when I could. . . . Really, it is astounding how free people are with their money here. . . . Of course, I have to keep my hair marcelled, but in view of the salary I'm being paid, I can easily do it.

At the end of the first week in May, her first week with her new employer, Miss Belletti wrote her friend, "Well, Mr. Goldwyn hasn't 'jumped down my throat' yet. I don't particularly like him, but I don't think he's any worse than the others." After a few weeks, though, she was ready to quit. Frances changed her mind. "I think it's terrible the way he comes in in the morning and doesn't even say 'Good morning' to you," she said to Miss Belletti one day. Then she assured the secretary that her husband was extremely pleased with her work, even though he had not said so. Frances left her feeling so good, she thought of hitting her boss up for a raise.

She knew best to wait. Goldwyn was about to sink over half a million dollars into his next year's slate of pictures, aimed largely at building up Vilma Banky into his first female star, someone to share the marquee with Ronald Colman. Miss Belletti also smelled a crisis brewing between Goldwyn and his distributor.

After Goldwyn's first years of steady success, First National relinquished their creative control over the properties he was adapting, but they would not let him near their financial books. He had hardly seen a cent of profit, because of First National's overhead charges and delayed payments. When *A Thief in Paradise* became one of the year's top ten box-office attractions and First National's accounting of the film's profits did not square with Goldwyn's, he sued over the $75,000 discrepancy. He was, in fact, willing to settle out of court and strike a new deal with First National.

First National did not want to continue distributing Goldwyn's films. Even cooking the books, they found too little money to be made off a man who produced so few films. Neither of the companies he helped establish—MGM and Paramount—was interested in his product, nor was Fox. He turned to United Artists, who did not especially want him but were as desperate as he was.

After more than five years in business, United Artists still seemed an idea whose time had not come. Since completing his own contract with First National in 1923, Chaplin had released only one picture through United Artists; Pickford and Fairbanks had delivered but one picture apiece per year; D. W. Griffith—whose last two productions, *America* and *Isn't Life Wonderful?*, were financial disappointments—pulled out of the company and signed with Paramount. United Artists' grosses were a fraction of those of the major distributors, and they were operating at six-figure losses. The three remaining partners were on the verge of folding up their enterprise.

In late 1924, they succeeded in bringing the dynamic Joe Schenck into the company as a stock-owning partner and chairman of the board. He promised to deliver at least six Norma Talmadge pictures, but he knew he needed more product. He signed Gloria Swanson to produce a block of films, and he gave a contract to Valentino, who had temporarily retired from the screen after the disappointing results of *Blood and Sand* and *Monsieur Beaucaire*. To help save United Artists, Chaplin urged Joe Schenck to consider doing business with his friend of almost ten years, Sam Goldwyn.

In fact, Schenck had been one of the first people Goldwyn called when his contract with First National expired. That May, Sam and Joe dined, and as Goldwyn reported to his attorney, "I told him that I was ready to talk business with United Artists." He said he could deliver them two Fitzmaurice productions, a Potash and Perlmutter comedy, and two films directed by Henry King. In return, he wanted a unit of stock and to become a director of the corporation. A week later, Schenck informed Goldwyn that "there was no chance of getting the stock as the directors were opposed to it."

Each of the united artists had veto power, and Mary Pickford exercised hers. She could not forget those early days when Zukor and Goldwyn were associates. Schenck promised Goldwyn he would raise the matter again in the near future. Goldwyn sought the advice of his chief backer. "Now just a parting word, Sam," Giannini wrote on May 22, 1925. "Do not be too anxious to make too good a contract. . . . If you can tie up with United Artists, do so immediately. If you cannot do that and First National is willing to take you—even on the old terms, I would suggest that you return." When Goldwyn's lawyer informed him that the First National dispute would consume time and money for years, the producer pulled out for $150,000, a pittance for eight pictures that had grossed several million dollars.

Goldwyn told Schenck he would settle for a compromise offer from United Artists, but that he hoped Joe would still campaign for the directorship as well. Schenck brought all his partners around on the matter of distributing Goldwyn's films. They even granted him the right to approve the exhibition contracts. On the vote to extend a directorship, Mary Pickford used her blackball.

Sam Goldwyn's contract with United Artists was drafted in the summer of 1925. It called for him to supply at least two and no more than five pictures per year. The splits of the gross receipts were on a par with those of all the United Artists partners (75 percent going to the producers and

25 percent to the corporation). He was also accorded the right to control the advertising for his films. Samuel Goldwyn still did not have the power of the United Artists superstars, but to the eyes of the world, it looked that way.

THE DARK ANGEL began filming on June 15, 1925, at United Studios. By then, the Great War had become a popular subject for films, novels, and plays in America; but they were mostly sentimental treatments. *What Price Glory?* was one of the first works to break that mold. King Vidor persuaded its author, Laurence Stallings, to write a story for him to direct on screen. The result was *The Big Parade*. It captured a new sense of realism on film, not only in its treatment of the subject matter but in the level of the acting. The "Great Lover," John Gilbert, was Vidor's leading man, and the director "decided that in his new character of down-to-earth doughboy, he would use no makeup and wear an ill-fitting uniform. Dirty fingernails and a sweaty, begrimed face were to take the place of perfectly made-up skin texture." The film became the biggest-grossing picture of the decade and "skyrocketed John Gilbert to the height of popularity."

George Fitzmaurice had the same artistic ambitions for *The Dark Angel*. Working with so sentimental a story, he knew he needed to take a harsher approach than he had previously on his "society pictures." He invented several haunting touches. One of his scenes depicted bereaved parents searching the depleted ranks of returning troops, only to see ghosts of dead soldiers clad in white uniforms slowly rising. "This effect is corking," said *Variety*, "as is the phantom of the Dark Angel, Death, flying over the battlefields and then into the quiet English home of Kitty."

Enabling Fitzmaurice to capture these effects was the newest recruit to the Goldwyn ranks, a talented cameraman named George S. Barnes. Born in Pasadena in 1893, Barnes attended Glendale High School, then sold automobiles and played violin in a theater orchestra pit before applying for jobs at all the early film studios. Little experience was necessary in 1917, when he began as an assistant at the old Ince company. "George Barnes was one of the first cameramen to be subjective with his instrument," said King Vidor. "Without gimmicks, he played with lights and shadows and camera positions. He made the audience see things in ways that were never ordinary." The results—love scenes as well as battle scenes—were everywhere evident in *The Dark Angel*.

The performances of Goldwyn's actors were no less remarkable. "As the picture progressed," the film's scenarist, Frances Marion, later recounted, "it was fascinating to watch the scenes between Vilma and Ronnie Colman.

He spoke his lines in a deep, rich voice and with the authority of an actor schooled in the theatre. Hesitant in speech, struggling to master our difficult language, Vilma responded in a mixture of pidgin English and Hungarian. When we saw them together on the screen we realized how clever Sam had been to sign this lovely blonde girl and to team her with his dark-eyed star." Vilma had slimmed down for the part, but Goldwyn constantly fretted over her difficulty maintaining her weight. He never knew that she supplemented her "lamb chops and pineapple" diet with jars of homemade goulash, which she snacked on all through the day.

The Dark Angel finished shooting July 30, 1925. Three weeks later, Goldwyn previewed the eight-reel film in Venice, California, a seaside resort built in 1905, complete with bridged canals, an amusement pier, bathhouses, dance halls, and an entire street in the style of the Italian Renaissance. Goldwyn's supporters turned out that night in full force— Joe Schenck and Norma Talmadge, Hearst and Marion Davies, Elinor Glyn, even Valentino. So stunning was Vilma Banky in her debut that the Sheik himself told Joe Schenck he wanted Miss Banky to be his leading lady in his next picture, *The Eagle*.

Valentino seemed to have an off-camera interest in his new co-star as well. "You remember I told you that Valentino had picked Vilma as his leading lady," Goldwyn's secretary tattled to her friend back in New York. "Well it seems they are going around together quite a bit." This was a publicity break better than any Goldwyn could have imagined, but he told Miss Banky "that she must not do anything that will in any way ruin her reputation."

Goldwyn hired a publicity director named Ray Coffin to capitalize on the romantic appeal of his new star. The month before the October 11 opening of *The Dark Angel,* they promulgated a complete fiction about a baron from Budapest who had proposed marriage to Vilma and wanted her back, especially now that she was consorting with Valentino. The story got such a big play that the Goldwyn organization had to hire a European actor to hold a press conference.

Recently I saw reports in the papers that Valentino is separated from his wife [he said]. He plays with my darling and is famous for his attractiveness. Is my darling under his spell? Or is Goldwyn bribing her with an immense salary in order to keep her loveliness for his pictures and away from me. . . . Just think, she has so far forgotten her old country that she actually suggests my joining the Hollywood colony. As if a member of a noble family could possibly become an actor.

Overnight, the Hungarian actress would be installed in the world's most royal order—movie star.

Ironically, Goldwyn's publicity ploys were not completely necessary. Vilma Banky's work spoke for itself. "I HAVE JUST SEEN THE DARK ANGEL AND IT IS ALL YOU PROMISED AND MORE," wired Louella Parsons, the most powerful member of Hollywood's fourth estate, soon to supervise all the Sunday motion picture departments of all the Hearst newspapers. "VILMA BANKY WILL PROVE A SENSATION SHE HAS BEAUTY ABILITY AND A PERSONALITY THAT IS DIFFERENT I AM DELIGHTED WITH HER SYMPATHETIC PORTRAYAL OF THE GIRL AND WITH THE CHARACTER SHE HAS CREATED I HAVE ALWAYS HAD A WARM SPOT IN MY HEART FOR RONALD COLMAN AND HE CERTAINLY JUSTIFIES MY FAITH IN HIM."

The reaction from all quarters was unanimous. The *New York Times* said: "Vilma Banky is not only a radiant beauty, but also an actress who performs with ease and charm. Her loveliness will be a feature in any screen story in which she appears, as nobody will be surprised at a hero falling victim to her soft pleading eyes." Richard Halliday assured his two million readers in *Liberty* magazine that "'The Dark Angel' will disappoint no one. It is one of the most important films. It places on view to advantage Samuel Goldwyn's commendable new discovery, Vilma Banky." Theater owner Sid Grauman predicted that Vilma Banky would become "a great star." Elinor Glyn said she "has 'IT!'"

Vilma Banky was soon receiving two thousand fan letters a month. Without his next script for her completed, Goldwyn happily loaned her again to play Valentino's flame, in *The Son of the Sheik*. Goldwyn ripped up his original contract with Vilma Banky and paid her one thousand dollars a week. Frances Marion got a big raise too, Goldwyn's way of enticing her into writing the next Potash and Perlmutter comedy, *Partners Again*—in which the hapless twosome took on the automobile industry.

Goldwyn closed out his deal with First National in a blaze of glory, but that was a flicker alongside his first drama for United Artists. From the moment he had heard the story of *Stella Dallas,* Goldwyn believed it was bound to be his greatest motion picture to date. "The episodic plot moves forward through a series of strained coincidences, misunderstandings, overheard conversations," noted film historian Richard Griffith. But Sam Goldwyn—his own life in conflict over a daughter and divorce—had been obsessed with the story, even though he did not have the $15,000 on hand to afford it. He persuaded his attorney to put up the cash on his behalf and hold the rights as collateral.

"Everyone was surprised that Sam chose a simple story like 'Stella Dallas' at a time when the public seemed to be clamoring for spectacles or lurid melodrama," recalled Frances Marion. "The audiences had just shuddered through another grotesque performance of Lon Chaney in 'The Phantom of The Opera.' They were also attracted to the most overanimated young leading man ever seen on the screen, John Gilbert. Obviously he was a rival as well as a marked contrast to Ronald Colman." Goldwyn got Henry King to direct *Stella Dallas* for $75,000 and 25 percent of the profits.

"It's a beautiful woman's story," Goldwyn told Frances Marion as she broke ground on the scenario. "I'm starring Ronald Colman in it." She knew he meant to exploit the marquee value of his popular male star now, even though his part would be but a featured role; but she could not resist saying, "As a female impersonator." Goldwyn and King practically came to that necessity. For all the strength of the title role, Henry King recalled, "we couldn't give the part away . . . except to actresses Sam didn't want."

While almost seventy-five screen tests were made and rejected, a thirty-four-year-old actress named Belle Bennett—who had played small roles in two earlier Goldwyn pictures—began lobbying for the part. "I want 'Stella Dallas' more than any thing in this world, just now," she handwrote Sam Goldwyn. "You know (as well as all directors and producers *know*) that I can *play it* also *can* make up for *any part* from *fourteen* to *eighty.*" After a number of Broadway actresses—from Laurette Taylor to Estelle Winwood—turned him down, Goldwyn let Miss Bennett audition. Her test literally moved him to tears.

On his last trip to Paris, Sam Goldwyn had seen a seventeen-year-old American-born actress named Lois Moran. Her dewy beauty—which would inspire F. Scott Fitzgerald to create Rosemary Hoyt in *Tender Is the Night*—made her ideal for the pivotal role of Stella's daughter. Jean Hersholt, as the boor Stella married on the rebound, and Alice Joyce, as Stephen Dallas's socialite second wife, filled out the rest of the cast, alongside eighteen-year-old Douglas Fairbanks, Jr., in one of his first roles. Director King instructed young Fairbanks to grow a mustache. The day the actor's father learned that it was for his role in the picture, he rang King on the telephone. "Henry," said that year's "Son of Zorro," "remember that I'm still in pictures. Don't make Junior look too old." King assured the forty-two-year-old star—who no longer stripped quite to the waist in his pictures—that the mustache would only make the boy look younger, a callow touch.

"This was going to be Goldwyn's masterpiece," recalled Henry King. "That's what he kept telling Frances Marion and me. And he put his money where his mouth was. Everything was first cabin on that picture." Miss Marion concurred: "If a player proved inadequate for the role, he permitted Henry King to throw out every foot of film already shot and retake the scenes. Because of this urge for perfection, which often piled cost upon costs, his bankers grew anxious." The shooting schedule stretched to a lavish nine weeks. When the budget went beyond Goldwyn's $350,000 credit line, he appealed to Dr. Giannini himself. Moved by the producer's enthusiasm as much as for the project itself, Giannini chipped in the necessary funds from his own pocket—for 10 percent of the film's profits and the promise that Goldwyn would not borrow any more money for one year.

Henry King directed *Stella Dallas* in an understated manner, telling his story mostly in medium shots, cutting to close-ups for punctuation. "In those days we had faith in our material, faith in our actors, and faith in our audiences," he said. "We didn't feel we had to cut back and forth sixty times a minute to hold the viewer's eye. The secret of the silent camera— and I think this holds just as true for motion pictures with sound—is restraint. Human emotion can be the most exciting action there is."

The most convincing illustration of King's words occurs in the birthday sequence of *Stella Dallas:* Stella and Laurel wait in vain for Laurel's classmates to arrive at her party, unaware that all the schoolchildren have been told not to show up. Laurel dams up her feelings as she realizes there will be no guests. The camera holds on her as she takes a spoonful of ice cream. Not until her first taste do tears stream down her face.

No matter how many times he saw that scene, Sam Goldwyn never failed to burst into tears himself. While *Stella Dallas* was being assembled, he showed the scene to Ernst Lubitsch. The German director praised Henry King's work but "questioned the wisdom of spotting so intense a scene in the first half of the picture." He wondered how it could be topped. Goldwyn merely grinned and ordered the projectionist to run the finale of the picture, the beautifully composed sequence of Stella Dallas in the rain, staring into the living room of the Dallas home on Fifth Avenue as her daughter and young Richard Grosvenor (Fairbanks junior) take their wedding vows.

The whole of a motion picture does not always equal the sum of its parts. On Sunday the fifth of September, less than two weeks after shooting was completed, the filmmakers ran the rough cut of *Stella Dallas.* When the lights came up, they all looked at each other in disappointment. Henry King walked out of the projection room, dejected. Goldwyn's secretary was practically in tears because the picture looked like such a "flop."

Stella Dallas had slipped from pathos into bathos. Each scene ran too long and there was not enough relief between the heavy emotional moments. Fortunately, Goldwyn had a top editor under contract, Stuart Heisler, who had been in the business since 1914. King reminded himself that the themes of the story were so basic, "they didn't need circles drawn around them."

He and Heisler worked around the clock for two weeks, knowing that Goldwyn was leaving soon for New York to arrange for the exhibition of the picture. On the morning of Saturday the nineteenth, aware that Goldwyn and his wife and the Lehrs were expecting to screen the final edited version in just a few hours, King went home to his cottage at the Ambassador Hotel and fell into bed. He was awakened by the telephone: Goldwyn insisted that he would not run the film without King there. The director said he had not had more than a few hours' sleep in the last fortnight. Goldwyn said he would start the film, but he expected King to be there when it finished. King was just making his way to the projection room when Goldwyn swung the door open. He was shaking, and his face was white. "Henry," he called out, "you've ruined me, ruined me!" King asked what he meant. "Look at Mrs. Lehr over there," he said. "Look at Frances. They can't talk either." Goldwyn himself started to cry. "We'll talk about it Monday," he said, walking with his wife to his car. "Henry," he shouted in leaving. "Go home and get some sleep. You look terrible!"

After a few more days of fine-tuning and last-minute title writing, Goldwyn previewed the film in San Bernardino, and Pasadena. The audiences' reactions convinced him that almost two thirds of the title cards and two complete scenes would have to be thrown out. By the end of September, Goldwyn stood confidently behind *Stella Dallas*.

The head of his new distribution company lacked his enthusiasm. Joe Schenck thought *Stella Dallas* was "a great woman's picture," but he did not believe it would have the universal appeal necessary for it to play at a big legitimate theater for two dollars a ticket. He suggested that Goldwyn release the picture in as many theaters as would book it and spend twenty thousand dollars in advertising. Goldwyn trusted his own instincts and booked George White's Apollo Theater on Forty-second Street for three shows daily. His former partner from the Capitol Theater, Samuel Rothafel—who had broken ground on his great monument to motion picture exhibition, the Roxy—staged the premiere.

By October, most of Hollywood's elite had seen the film at special previews or in private screening rooms. The reaction to *Stella Dallas* was unprecedented. Ethel Barrymore wrote Goldwyn that it was "the best moving picture I have ever seen. Best in its direction, acting, restraint, taste and appeal." Elinor Glyn pronounced it "wonderful," assuring Goldwyn that it "will wring every mother's heart!" As Goldwyn had suspected, men fell even harder for it: "Few things have affected me as much in my life as did 'Stella Dallas,'" wrote Douglas Fairbanks. "A FRIEND OF MINE WHO HAS SEEN THE PICTURE THREE TIMES ENJOYED IT AS MUCH LAST NIGHT AS I DID MYSELF SEEING IT FOR THE FIRST TIME," wired Chaplin. "*Stella Dallas* . . . is, in my opinion, one of the few great screen achievements," declared Cecil B. DeMille. "You have literally taken a slice of life and transferred it to the screen in a highly entertaining, and at the same time artistic manner," wrote Harold Lloyd. Goldwyn worked the celebrities' tributes into various forms of advertising.

The most important reaction to *Stella Dallas* came at the final preview in Los Angeles. The following noon, William Randolph Hearst appeared at the studio, only to be told that Goldwyn was at lunch. Hearst had grown fond of the Goldwyns—inviting them on his yacht and to "the ranch" for weekends—so he lingered around the office. When he returned, Hearst gave Goldwyn an unsealed note addressed to Arthur Brisbane, editorial writer and publisher of the New York *Mirror*, which he suggested Goldwyn deliver in person. In it, he urged Brisbane to ask Louella Parsons "to do all she can for the picture"; and he made it clear that he wanted his most influential newspapers to discuss *Stella Dallas* "helpfully." Brisbane wrote about *Stella Dallas* for weeks.

The film's top-billed star, however, had been getting short shrift, and he resented it. Despite Ronald Colman's strong appearances in both of Goldwyn's latest hits, Belle Bennett, Lois Moran, and Vilma Banky were receiving all the attention. Without a film ready for the handsome $2,000-a-week leading man, Goldwyn loaned him out, netting three times what he was paying him. One of the ironclad conditions for borrowing the actor was the agreement to advertise "Ronald Colman through courtesy of Samuel Goldwyn."

His first loanout was Ernst Lubitsch's adaptation of *Lady Windermere's Fan* at Warner Brothers. *Photoplay* reported that the director never failed to get in a dig at the man holding the actor's contract. "Mr. Colman," he would instruct the actor, "you walk across the room, you stop by the table, you pick up the book, then you look into the eyes of Miss McAvoy by courtesy of Sam Goldwyn!" Colman next played opposite Norma Talmadge in *Kiki*, one of the most popular films of the decade. The title role in Jesse Lasky's *Beau Geste* followed. It, too, became a smash hit. Even though outside employers were making better use of the actor than Goldwyn had, within the first two years of his contract Ronald Colman had risen from bit player to one of Hollywood's most popular leading men. He received close to five thousand fan letters every month—reputedly more than any actor except John Gilbert.

Vilma Banky was not far behind. After her back-to-back pictures opposite Valentino, she was fetching $50,000 per picture for Goldwyn. Gossip about the romantic co-stars ebbed once Pola Negri made her play for Valentino. Frances Goldwyn remembered her husband's irritation, because he had tried his "darnedest at playing cupid." To maintain the lease on all that free fan-magazine space, the Goldwyn publicity department churned up romantic stories linking Banky and Colman. They were completely fictitious. Miss Banky had her eye on another of Miss Negri's former lovers.

A Chicago-born actor, Rod La Rocque (his real name), had worked for the old Goldwyn Company in Fort Lee. Then DeMille signed him, and *The Ten Commandments* made him a star; he became Paramount's second-string leading man. In 1925, Zukor and Lasky could not come to terms with DeMille over his new contract. DeMille signed instead with the Producers Distributing Corporation and bought himself a motion picture lot of his own—the Ince studio in Culver City, which was sold upon the sudden death of the film pioneer. Just when Goldwyn's contract with First National and his lease at United Studios expired, DeMille asked if he wished to rent office space. Goldwyn moved his base of operations into the new DeMille Studios, a huge white colonial mansion down Washington Boulevard from MGM, where a black man in uniform stood outside the main entrance, ran down the steps to greet every guest, escorted him or her to the front door, then bowed before opening it. Within the walls of this plantation, Rod La Rocque began courting Vilma Banky. "Of course we couldn't tell Sam Goldwyn at first," remembered Miss Banky; "he would have killed us. You couldn't fall in love until he told you to fall in love."

Goldwyn unwittingly kept them apart with a project he had found to reunite his two biggest stars—*The Winning of Barbara Worth*. Harold Bell Wright had written this epic about the Colorado River flood of 1908 and sold close to three million copies. Jefferson Worth is a banker traveling across the desert with a young boy named Abe Lee and a civil engineer who dreams of harnessing the river and making the desert "blossom like a rose." They survive a devastating sandstorm but discover a family less fortunate. The banker rescues a four-year-old girl, Barbara, and raises her. By the time she is seventeen, the eastern engineering interests have returned to reclaim the land and develop the town called Barbara Worth. Among them is Willard Holmes, an able engineer, ignorant in the ways of the desert. Abe Lee, grown to manhood, has also become an engineer and knows every cactus for miles around. Both men compete for Barbara's hand, as they struggle to tame the river and the land. "Fifteen years ago I came to the west and this country took me to her heart and was kind to me," Sam Goldwyn was quoted in some publicity bunkum. "Since then I have always wished for an opportunity to repay. I found it in this story of Harold Bell Wright's." It cost him $125,000 for the story rights alone.

In the first months of 1926, Goldwyn dispatched Henry King to scout locations and told Frances Marion, "MANY CHARACTERS HAVE TO BE ELIMINATED AND LOVE STORY HAS TO BE BROUGHT OUT BEFORE BIG PICTURE CAN BE MADE OF IT." She cleverly truncated the early years of exposition into a prologue, making the romantic triangle the heart of the motion picture. In addition to a sandstorm and a climactic flood, Miss Marion's continuity afforded King the opportunity to stage practically every scene before some breathtaking vista.

"A rock is a rock, and a tree is a tree. Shoot it in Griffith Park!" was a popular aphorism making the rounds in Hollywood, falsely attributed to Sam Goldwyn. In fact, those words were uttered by a producer named Abe Stern—who also said, "Our comedies are not to be laughed at"—and expressed the opposite of Goldwyn's attitude. After trekking across the sands of California, Arizona, and New Mexico, Henry King found the location he wanted in the Black Rock desert near Oregon, between the towns of Gerlach and Winnemucca, Nevada. The area was so arid that no fauna inhabited it. King believed Goldwyn approved of the distant location only because the director was also a profit participant, not about to fritter money away.

A spur track was constructed, linking the main line of the Western Pacific to the new city of Barbara Worth, Nevada. A mess hall was built to feed the thousand and more residents of the tent city alongside the movie set. A well was drilled 185 feet below the desert, and a complete plumbing and sanitation system was installed. Goldwyn spared no expense, as his vision of the film surpassed anything common sense might have dictated. "I DON'T WANT TO MAKE COMPARISON WITH OTHER PICTURES," Goldwyn wired Hiram Abrams in April 1926, "BUT I SEE SOMETHING BIGGER NOW IN BARBARA WORTH THAN I EVER DREAMED OF." After a week of interior shooting in Culver City, Goldwyn went to inspect the city he had financed and the hundreds of laborers, crew members, actors, and extras.

"Here I am 'in the great open spaces' where men are men and the only woman here is Vilma Banky," Goldwyn wrote from Barbara Worth, Nevada, to the town's banker in fact, Dr. Giannini. "This is really a remarkable place—I don't think I have ever seen a desert that has the desolateness and expresses more what Harold Bell Wright calls the palm of God's hand than the location right here." The heat was fierce, some days throbbing upward to 130 degrees. Desert sandstorms kicked up regularly at noon for two hours, filling the air with alkali as fine as talcum powder. Production progressed with hardly a hitch.

Other than a sandstorm blowing away the Barbara Hotel one afternoon before its cue, the greatest mishap in the making of *Barbara Worth* occurred at Warner Brothers in Hollywood. Ernst Lubitsch ran over schedule on his film *The Honeymoon Express* and did not release an actor named Harold Goodwin, who was cast in the role of Abe Lee. There would have been a great to-do had Goldwyn's secretary not ridden to the rescue.

Valeria Belletti would have quit her job months earlier were it not for the perquisites. She especially enjoyed the premieres she often got to attend and chatting with the stars who dropped in on the office. She was constantly falling for the handsome actors. That summer, while walking on the lot, she caught sight of a cowboy who took her breath away.

He was six feet two inches tall, weighed a lean one hundred eighty pounds, had a rugged face softened by big sensitive blue eyes, a sensual mouth, and an unruly hank of brown hair. He had been born in Helena in 1901, the second son of a Montana State Supreme Court justice. He later spent several years in England, where his mother convalesced from an illness, then returned to his family's ranch. In 1921, he entered Grinnell College in Iowa; summers, he was a guide at Yellowstone National Park. In 1924, the young man's father resigned from the bench to administer the estates of two cousins in California. His son, named Frank, joined him and his mother there.

After weeks of odd jobs, Frank encountered two friends from Montana ambling down Hollywood Boulevard in cowboy garb. They told him they picked up as much as ten dollars a day riding and performing stunts in westerns. The friends began to take him along on their rounds. They introduced him to casting directors and moseyed around Gower Street in Hollywood—the section called "Poverty Row," where scores of small motion picture outfits regularly rounded up herds of drugstore cowboys to appear as extras in their cheap two- and five-reel westerns. He did have one great edge over the thousands of other desperadoes who stalked the streets of Hollywood: Women fell at his feet.

A stunt-riding actress named Marilyn Mills got him cast in a picture she made in 1925, called *Tricks*. She thought he looked interesting enough to recommend to a woman named Nan Collins, who had worked in studio casting before becoming a motion picture agent. Miss Collins thought she could scare up work for him if he would invest seventy-five dollars in a demonstration reel—a screen test that showed off his equestrian skills. "He came down Poverty Row riding a horse, pulled the horse to a stop, made a very gallant dismount, threw the reins over the post, entered the saloon door, turned around, looked at the camera and walked in," was the way Henry King remembered it. Because several local actors already shared the cowboy's name, Nan Collins urged Judge Cooper's son Frank to adopt the name of her hometown in Indiana—Gary.

Cowboys were such a glut on the market, many dreamed of just getting inside a studio, a chance to be seen. Impressing a secretary generally counted for little. But Valeria Belletti used every bit of influence she could to give her crush a break. When she discovered Goldwyn was not interested in her opinion, she worked on everybody else, starting with the women. She raved to Frances Marion and to Frances Goldwyn before going to Robert McIntyre, the head of casting, and finally to Henry King. The director ran Cooper's audition reel and said to McIntyre, "At least he can ride a horse."

Cooper, who had been loitering outside the casting office, got to meet King and said he wanted to play the role of Abe Lee in *Barbara Worth*. The director explained that the role had been filled but offered to take him to Nevada as one of the background riders. When asked to list his previous credits on the Goldwyn questionnaire he filled out on June 13, 1926, he listed only that he had the "Male lead" in *Lightnin' Wins*. He failed to note that the lead was actually a dog.

Days before the *Barbara Worth* company moved to Nevada, Henry King had to film a scene between Barbara Worth and Abe Lee that required at least the body of the actor. Harold Goodwin still had not shown up. King put Gary Cooper in Abe's costume. "All you have to do," he told the cowboy, "is to keep your eyes on Vilma Banky." From eight in the morning until noon, no matter where Vilma Banky went—"whether we were shooting or not"—his eyes stayed glued to her. Cooper played a few more scenes with his back to the camera, until King thought to himself, "if he can do the scene at the hotel—where he rides across the desert for twenty-four hours to bring the news to Mr. Worth—then I'm not going to wait on the man from Warner Brothers."

King met Cooper on the set the next morning at seven and rehearsed him for his first big scene:

> . . . the first thing I did was talk to the boy. I wet his face and covered it with fuller's earth, and I walked and I talked. Tired— tired—tired. That was my subject. Tired—tired—tired. I walked around with him and I talked about how one feels when one is exhausted. Why *I* wasn't exhausted, I'll never know. I kept him walking between scenes, then I'd go back on the set. When I'd rehearsed

those people, I'd go back to him. I worked with him for an hour
before I asked him on the set.

Just as King was about to shoot the scene, Irving Sindler, the property
master, announced that Mr. Goldwyn—who respected the set as the director's domain—wanted to see him. King went to the other side of a huge
black curtain he had mounted to block off the playing area. "Henry," the
producer said, "when you're spending a dollar of my money, you're spending a dollar of your money. You're going to put that damn cowboy in one
of the biggest parts in the picture."

King said he had no choice. They had finished every scene up to their
leaving for Nevada, and waiting for another actor would only cost more
money than the attempt with Cooper. "This is a big dramatic scene,"
Goldwyn insisted, "and no damn cowboy can play it." He buzzed off, "mad
as a hornet." King called for "action" on the set and signaled Sindler to tap
Cooper off camera. "I didn't think he was going to make it," recalled the
propman more than fifty years later. "Cooper could barely knock on the
door. The knock was so quiet they could hardly hear it on the other side."
Then Colman stood up, opened the door, and revealed what the director
called "the most pathetic case I've ever seen in my life." The actor gasped
his line as he fell for the floor. Colman grabbed him, just inches from
smacking his face. King called "Cut," and for George Barnes and his assistant—a twenty-one-year-old named Gregg Toland—to move in with
their equipment right away for Cooper's close-up.

Irving Sindler popped onto the set, announcing that Mr. Goldwyn
wished to see the director again. In exasperation, King walked around the
huge black mantle. "Henry," Goldwyn said, "you're always trying to tease
me. Why didn't you tell me that man was a great actor?" King said,
"Because he isn't. He's a cowboy from Montana."

"Henry," Goldwyn disagreed, "he's the greatest actor I have ever seen in
my life."

"How do you know," King asked.

"Because I was peeping through a hole in the curtain."

Goldwyn would later cut the scene for fear of Cooper's overshadowing
Colman—but only after raising his pay to sixty-five dollars a week and
offering him a five-year contract. Before papers were drawn, word that
Cooper was no ordinary cowboy was already spreading.

In the next month, Cooper heard that Sam Goldwyn was casting somebody else for the second male lead in his next picture. Nan Collins began
shopping her client around town. Paramount signed him with the promise

of putting him in a western immediately. On that lot, another woman succumbed to his charms and got him out of his western gear.

Paramount's leading ingenue fell head over heels for him. A pert little beauty from Brooklyn, Clara Bow proved to be the screen's quintessential flapper. The studio was about to promote her around the world as "The IT Girl," the embodiment, said Elinor Glyn, of everything the word stood for. She met Cooper at a studio party, and they launched into a torrid romance. She urged the Paramount bosses to slot him between his westerns into her pictures—*Children of Divorce, IT,* and William Wellman's aerial spectacular of World War I, *Wings.* Goldwyn would not have a crack at casting Cooper again for another nine years. By then it would cost him more each week than it would have cost to have him for the entire year of 1927.

The struggle between Ronald Colman and Gary Cooper in *Barbara Worth* proved to be over more than Vilma Banky's affections. Two different schools of acting squared off against each other. Colman was a starchy successor to the leading man that had evolved in motion pictures from the matinee idols of the nineteenth-century stage. "Coop was the new idea," recalled Henry King. "Everything about him was natural—the way he acted, the way he walked, the way he stood there." As Goldwyn put it: "He is an unintentional actor. He never gives the impression of giving a performance."

Flappers still wanted their "sheiks" sleek. Proof came less than two weeks after the *Barbara Worth* company had dismantled its tent city on the sands of Nevada. In mid-August, peritonitis struck Valentino down. Movie fans anxiously stood by as he lay in New York's Polyclinic Hospital. "BOTH MRS. GOLDWYN AND MYSELF ARE HOPING FROM THE BOTTOM OF OUR HEARTS FOR QUICK RECOVERY AND EVERYONE IN HOLLYWOOD FEELS SAME GOD BLESS YOU," Sam wired the patient. Five days later—on August 23—he instructed James Mulvey in his New York office to send fifty dollars' worth of flowers to Valentino. Before placing the order, Mulvey wired back, "VALENTINO DIED AT NOON." Over 100,000 people paid their respects at Frank Campbell's funeral parlor in New York City. The headlines could not but make his last picture, released in the hysteria of his funeral, a titanic hit, grossing in the millions. Most moviegoers' last romantic vision of Valentino was as the Son of the Sheik, his arms around Vilma Banky. On August 26, Goldwyn announced that he was insuring his leading lady for $500,000 with the Morrison Insurance Company of Los Angeles.

Three of Goldwyn's next four films were tandem vehicles for Banky and Ronald Colman—European costume melodramas. In each of them

—*The Night of Love, The Magic Flame* and *Two Lovers*—Colman presses himself upon her, then must plot against a tyrannical duke and correct several misunderstandings before he and Vilma Banky can unite in true love. (Goldwyn's fourth offering that year was *The Devil Dancer,* a silly tale set in Tibet, built around the stunt casting of Gilda Gray, a Polish-born dancer who popularized that year's dance craze, the Shimmy.)

Colman and Banky became one of the most successful teams in screen history, "good chemistry" that rivaled MGM's mating John Gilbert with Greta Garbo and Fox's pairing Charles Farrell with Janet Gaynor. United Artists very likely would have gone under had Goldwyn not supplied one third of their product of the preceding two years. Joe Schenck's plan of bringing outside producers such as Goldwyn into United Artists salved their problems, but it would not solve them. They were still a small-time distribution company without dibs on a single major first-run theater in the country. Meantime, the major motion picture corporations kept building their empires on theaters, through acquisition and construction. Zukor's Publix Theatres Corporation had amassed one thousand theaters; Loew had one hundred fifty to his name; Fox's West Coast theaters numbered eight hundred; and the Warner brothers were scraping money together to buy shares in First National.

In 1926, Goldwyn teamed with Pickford, Fairbanks, and Schenck to create United Artists Theatre Circuit, Inc. (Chaplin was not interested in investing.) Realizing they could never compete against their larger rivals, they tended to enter into partnerships with other companies. In Louisville, for example, they bought a half interest in a Loew's theater; in New York, they bought into the Rivoli and the Rialto. In Hollywood, they partnered with Sid Grauman at his Chinese Theater.

To defray the costs of its expansion, United Artists floated stock in a finance company called Art Cinema Corporation. Goldwyn subscribed. When Art Cinema moved onto the Pickford-Fairbanks lot, another subsidiary corporation acquired a ten-year lease on the land and invested one million dollars in building stages, dressing rooms, and an administration building. Goldwyn found himself part owner of the rechristened United Artists Studio.

Goldwyn offered to buy a block of preferred stock if he could, at last, be made a partner of the struggling company. He had successfully insinuated himself in its workings since his arrival, and his films continued to open regularly and earn money. The Fairbankses still balked, but they were at least willing to listen.

All Goldwyn's recent corporate investments had been heavy gambles beyond his means, as his profits still remained more on paper than in his pocket. *Stella Dallas,* for example, was his highest-grossing silent film, his company's take amounting to $1,110,134.85. From that, almost $700,000 worth of production costs had to be deducted. Goldwyn had to lop off royalties to his profit participants—25 percent for Henry King, 10 percent apiece to Abe Lehr and Dr. Giannini. Finally, Goldwyn had to pay off the interest on his bank loans. By the time he had cleared his debt on one picture, he was in hock on the next. He was eating caviar but living hand to mouth.

Into this world of affluent insecurity entered Goldwyn's second child. At four-fifteen on the morning of September 7, 1926, Frances gave birth at the Los Angeles Good Samaritan Hospital to an eight-pound son. "Ashkenazic Jews"—those from Central and Eastern Europe—"don't name their newborns for the living," explained Rabbi Edgar F. Magnin, who began his career in Los Angeles in 1915, oversaw the building of Los Angeles's Wilshire Boulevard Temple in 1929, and towered over Hollywood's religious life for close to seventy years. "It isn't law. It's a mystical tradition, because naming after the living casts a kind of evil eye." But it was a special tribe that brought motion pictures to southern California. Rabbi Magnin said, "They were men who made all that money and realized they were still a bunch of Goddamned Jews. So they looked for other ways to cover it up." In an industry whose scions already included Jesse Lasky, Jr., Jack Warner, Jr., and Carl Laemmle, Jr., the infant was named Samuel Goldwyn, Jr. He was called Sammy.

"Los Angeles was different with respect to the Jews, because the show people regarded themselves as different," observed Rabbi Magnin, a grandson of the clothier I. Magnin. "The city had its downtown Jews, who were merchants and lawyers; and then there was the theatrical community. In other cities the divisions were usually between the German Jews who looked down on the Eastern European Jews, because they didn't have enough education or refinement; but there was at least some mixing. Not here. This crowd was different . . . because they wanted it that way. My mother called them 'movie kikes.'"

Although they quickly adopted new ways, the moguls clung to their Old World values. They wanted their sons to be educated and their daughters to marry nice Jewish boys. "What do I have to do?" Louis B. Mayer ranted as his eldest daughter, Edith, entered her twenties with no marriage prospects. "It isn't enough that I'm L. B. Mayer!" The Laemmles prayed for Irving Thalberg to marry their daughter Rosabelle. The wife of another mogul used to wash her daughter's hair with eggs and lemon to lighten it, and scrub her skin with bleach.

Except for broad Jewish stereotypes, clearly designated Jewish roles were generally assigned to Gentile actors. Years earlier, when Sam Goldfish had interviewed Carmel Myers, he insisted he could make the sixteen-year-old a big star but that she would have to change her name. A rabbi's daughter, she asked why. "Oh, Carmel," he tried to explain, "there's so much anti-Semitism in the world. Why play into their hands?" Years later, Carmel Myers admitted, "Sam Goldwyn was just trying to give me good advice. He knew none of the other moguls was about to make a leading lady out of a Jewess named Myers."

Rabbi Magnin suggested that the concerted effort of the moguls to closet their Jewishness was more than "just wanting to be good Americans." The daily busloads to Los Angeles of hopeful starlets reminded them of the most basic reason "to wish they didn't have to be Jewish." He said, "Sleeping with a pretty Gentile girl made them feel, if only for a few minutes, 'I'm half Gentile.' No wonder they made idols out of *shiksa* goddesses. They worshipped those blue-eyed blondes they were forbidden to have."

As Frances had insisted, upon her engagement, Sammy was hers to raise as a Catholic. It was her small offering to the Church, which she no longer attended, out of shame. She felt she was living in sin, having married a divorced Jew. Sam willingly conceded the boy's religion; but he had no idea that one afternoon, when he was in New York on business, Frances and her mother would take Sammy to a church and have him baptized.

Goldwyn's only say in the baby's rearing was his insistence on the hiring of Catherine McDonough, the strong Irish Catholic who had been Ruth's baby nurse. Her presence added untold tension to an already neurasthenic situation for the twenty-three-year-old lady of the house. Her lifelong admirer George Cukor admitted, "Frances was never cut out to be a mother."

Within just eighteen months, Frances had become part of the Hollywood community. Yet she always stayed apart, casting a cold eye on the others. In the autumn of 1926, she saw signs that the old order was toppling. Movies were suffering at the box office again, owing in part to the phenomenal growth of radio. In an effort to lure audiences into their resplendent picture houses, producers danced around the Hays Office's rules of decency. Censorship boards cropped up everywhere, passing local ordinances and waging newspaper campaigns against films. Talk of organized labor kicked up in Los Angeles. Union leaders targeted the motion picture industry, with its high visibility, as the obvious shop to close. Attempts to organize screenwriters and screen actors failed in late 1926; but by the end of the year, nine major film companies had signed a Studio Basic Agreement with unions representing the film business's blue-collar workers—carpenters, electricians, painters, and stagehands.

The most unsettling talk of the town was over synchronization of sound with motion pictures. There had been crude attempts at such an invention ever since Edison first tinkered with sound cylinders. In 1906, Dr. Lee De Forest invented a three-filament, gas-filled Audion tube. Western Electric purchased the rights, and with further development, produced equipment able to amplify sound 130 times its original volume. The Bell Telephone Laboratories experimented with large disks that reproduced sound.

The Warner brothers, like all independent filmmakers, went to great lengths to get their product into theaters. In search of some novelty to rescue their sinking company, they joined forces with Western Electric and Bell in forming the Vitaphone Corporation. The company would produce sixteen-inch disks with prerecorded music to accompany their reels of film. Vitaphone debuted on Friday, August 6, 1926, at the Warner Theater in New York City. Will Hays appeared on screen, and his voice could be heard as he welcomed the audience; seven musical selections followed, then John Barrymore in *Don Juan*, with a complete musical accompaniment. Reviews hailed this experiment in sound. Its success suggested that first-class music could accompany films everywhere, even into remote theaters where an upright piano had passed for an orchestra. "The Vitaphone premiere passed off without accident," noted Will Hays, "but it didn't set the world on fire." Adolph Zukor sat down in front and said, "It's a fad, it won't last."

While the Warner brothers perfected their gizmo, William Fox bought a German process of recording sound directly onto the film. He tried it on his Movietone newsreels. On May 21, 1927, he sprang his invention on the American public. The day before, he had sent one of his crews with sound recorders to Roosevelt Field, to film the takeoff of a shy Minnesotan in his flying crate. By the time the "Spirit of St. Louis" had landed at Le Bourget Airport in Paris, Fox had his newsreel of the departure ready to exhibit. Thousands jammed into the Roxy that night, where they not only saw the plane take flight but also heard the coughing of Lindy's motor. They cheered wildly.

Still, Vitaphone emitted more noise than music; and the conversion of a theater to accommodate Fox's Movietone was thought to cost $20,000. "I have no fear that scraping, screeching, rasping sound film will ever disturb our peaceful motion-picture theaters," wrote Louella Parsons. "The industry is too wise to spend fortunes for machines, new equipment, and soundstages to project noise that the customers do not want to hear. The public has no intention of paying good money to be so annoyed!"

Movies were trying to talk. Terry Ramsaye observed in his 1926 history of the silent cinema "that the average motion picture of 1909–1910 contained only eighty feet of titles per reel of a thousand feet. The same screen footage today requires ordinarily close to two hundred and fifty feet of titles. The screen story of today cannot all be told by the camera." Mary Pickford's 1926 release, *Sparrows*, had five writers collaborating; her 1927 offering *My Best Girl* (in which Charles "Buddy" Rogers gave Mary her first grownup onscreen kiss) required the audience to read almost as much as watch. Screenwriters could no longer get away with merely writing continuity to string pictures together. They had to write convincing dialogue.

While the motion picture industry's adolescence was at its most painful, Goldwyn received a telegram from nine of Hollywood's godfathers—including producers Schenck, Schulberg, and Thalberg. It was an invitation, which read in part:

A NUMBER OF REPRESENTATIVE MEMBERS OF THE MOTION PICTURE INDUSTRY ARE ORGANIZING A CLUB TEMPORARILY KNOWN AS THE MAYFAIR FOR THE PURPOSE OF ESTABLISHING A SOCIAL ORGANIZA- TION TRULY REPRESENTATIVE OF THE BEST ELEMENTS IN THE IN- DUSTRY AND FOR THE FURTHER PURPOSE OF MAINTAINING CERTAIN SOCIAL AND PROFESSIONAL IDEALS AND OF RECOGNIZING AND PAY- ING TRIBUTE TO SPECIAL TALENT AND ACHIEVEMENT IN EVERY DE- PARTMENT OF PICTURE ACTIVITIES.

"To lend dignity to the institution," the telegram of October 7, 1926, stated further, the club was establishing an honorary board of governors, on which they hoped to seat Goldwyn. Within weeks, the notion of the Mayfair Club had developed into that of a formal institution, an organi- zation that could bind potentially warring factions within the industry in crises of labor, technology, and censorship.

On January 11, 1927, three dozen actors, directors, writers, producers, and technical personnel convened at the Ambassador Hotel and founded the Academy of Motion Picture Arts and Sciences. Sam Goldwyn did not attend, Henry King later suggested, because "he wasn't a joiner. He was a professional hold-out." Among the original committees formed in May 1927 was one to create annual awards of merit. It was another two years before their first awards were presented.

Until then, all of Hollywood royalty flocked to many celebrations in honor of their own. King Vidor married Eleanor Boardman in an MGM-family ceremony at Marion Davies's Beverly Hills house. Irving Thalberg married Norma Shearer, and subsequently named their firstborn Irving Thalberg, Jr. Lewis Selznick had recently gone bust, and his son David had moved to Hollywood to ennoble the family name. At a Mayfair dance—"those glittering affairs held periodically for the Hollywood elite in the Biltmore ballroom"—ringing in 1927, he met Louis B. Mayer's daughter Irene. They were married in 1930, one month after another producer, William Goetz, walked Edith Mayer down the aisle.

In the spring of 1927, Goldwyn turned a potentially ruinous situation into the nuptials of the season. Vilma Banky had fallen in love—not with Ronald Colman, as Goldwyn's publicity department ballyhooed, but with Rod La Rocque. At a small dinner party at the Abe Lehrs', the couple announced their desire to steal away to Santa Barbara and marry in the mission. Actress Bebe Daniels excused herself from the table and called Louella Parsons.

"How could you do this to me?" Goldwyn demanded of his star the next morning. "I brought you to this country. I acted like a father. I protected you. What are you, ashamed? You want to go someplace and hide, disappear?" Goldwyn calmed down when she agreed to let him throw the wedding. He was determined to make it Hollywood's grandest bridal ceremony.

"The wedding of Vilma Banky and Rod La Rocque at the Church of the Good Shepherd in Beverly Hills on Sunday, June 26, will be a film affair," read the first of the formal newspaper announcements, after two months of gossip and feature stories about the wedding. Constance Talmadge, Bebe Daniels, Mrs. Harold Lloyd, Rod La Rocque's sister, Mildred, Abe Lehr's wife, Ann, and Frances Goldwyn made up the bridal party. George Fitzmaurice and actors Donald Crisp, Jack Holt, Victor Varconi, Harold Lloyd, and Ronald Colman were ushers. Vilma Banky's parents would not be journeying from Hungary, so Goldwyn would give the bride away. He asked Cecil B. DeMille to be best man, even though La Rocque and his producer-director were in the middle of a contract dispute. Sam pointed out that because the wedding would be on a Sunday, neither man's legal position would be jeopardized for those few hours.

Six hundred guests were invited to the church on the corner of Santa Monica Boulevard and Bedford Drive that fourth Sunday afternoon in June. Goldwyn had ordered scaffolding so that news cameras could capture on film the arrival of every notable. Thousands of fans lined the streets of

Beverly Hills to catch a glimpse of the guests. Traffic stopped when Tom Mix, in a purple cowboy outfit, drove up in his own open carriage behind a team of four horses.

The church was bedecked with thousands of dollars' worth of flowers for the ceremony. A fifty-voice choir sang. After the service, Goldwyn had arranged for the wedding party to pose for photographs on the steps of the church, while throngs cheered from behind police-enforced cordons. Vilma Banky looked radiant, wearing her lace cap and wedding veil from *The Dark Angel*. It had to be returned to the Goldwyn wardrobe department after the wedding.

Those who witnessed the ceremony met another six hundred guests at the Beverly Hills Hotel. For decades thereafter, it was rumored that Goldwyn had only prop food on display at the reception. In fact, guests in the Crystal Room filed past huge buffet tables marked by spotlights shining down on two papier-mâché turkeys. In front of them was an endless supply of turkey and salads and lobster and shrimp—"an abundance of everything," recalled La Rocque. There was dancing to Dr. Louis Furedi's society orchestra, adding another hundred dollars to what Goldwyn estimated was $25,000 out of his pocket. Pretty May McAvoy, who soon married a United Artists executive and remained in Hollywood for the next half century, said of her hometown's glamour, "After the Banky–La Rocque wedding, it was all downhill."

THAT very month, Miss McAvoy was filming *The Jazz Singer*. After George Jessel walked out on the project, the Warner brothers had approached Al Jolson—a rabbi's son, born Asa Yoelson. He was willing to take the role for very little cash, investing the bulk of his fee into the production and in Warners stock.

Jolson, who had never appeared before a motion picture camera, was privately coached by May McAvoy. She reminded him that in his silent dramatic scenes he did not have to "play to the second balcony." When it came to the musical numbers, however, there was no holding Jolson back. After an exuberant rendition of "Dirty Hands, Dirty Face!" the irrepressible Jolson could not keep himself from blurting out a few unscripted words to lead him into his next number. "Wait a minute, wait a minute!" he ad-libbed. "You ain't heard nothing yet! Wait a minute, I tell ya, you ain't heard nothing. You want to hear 'Toot, Toot, Tootsie'? All right, hold on."

The final version of the film included a few other improvised speeches between several Jolson numbers. After the gala opening of *The Jazz Singer* at the Warner Theater in New York on October 7, 1927, May McAvoy could not help sneaking into theaters day after day as the film was being run. She pinned herself against a wall in the dark and watched the faces in the crowd. In that moment just before "Toot, Toot, Tootsie," she remembered, "A miracle occurred. Moving pictures really came alive. To see the expressions on their faces, when Joley spoke to them . . . you'd have thought they were listening to the voice of God."

ON October 11, 1927, a telegram informed Goldwyn that he had been made a director of the United Artists Corporation. "I LOOK FORWARD WITH REAL PLEASURE TO A LONG ASSOCIATION WITH YOU AND AS I HAVE OFTEN TOLD YOU YOU WILL FIND ME A LOYAL LIEUTENANT," he wired Joe Schenck in reply to the news. No future in motion pictures seemed more secure than Goldwyn's, now financially linked to the foremost screen pantomimists of the world—Pickford, Fairbanks, Chaplin . . . and his own Ronald Colman and Vilma Banky. From where he sat—in his manor house in Hollywood, with his beautiful wife and a son to perpetuate his name—he could see only palmy days ahead, nothing to disrupt the dynastic dreams he had worked most of his forty-eight years to build.

PART
TWO

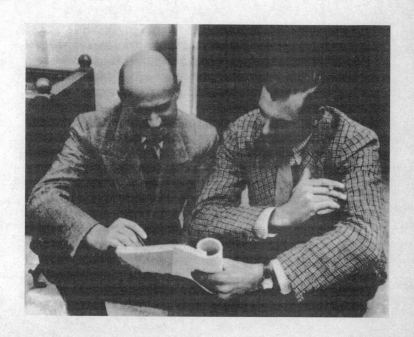

PART TWO

11 Interregnum

FOR YEARS, Frances Goldwyn would flirt with the idea of writing a novel about Hollywood, a murder mystery. Her opening scene was going to be the Los Angeles premiere of *The Jazz Singer*. George Cukor remembered Frances's calling that night "the most important event in cultural history since Martin Luther nailed his theses on the church door."

All of Hollywood turned out that Wednesday evening, December 28, 1927, the Goldwyns (attending with the Irving Thalbergs) among them. After the eighty-nine-minute film had run, the audience sat stunned. They were less spontaneous than the New York premiere audience, which had leapt to its feet and applauded for several minutes.

As thunderous clapping finally brought the houselights up, Frances looked around at the celebrities who had become her friends over the last two years. Afterward she swore she saw "terror in all their faces"—the fear that "the game they had been playing for years was finally over." There was a great buzz of excitement in the lobby, but she was sure there was dead silence in every car driving home. "I know there was in ours," she told Cukor.

Only recently, D. W. Griffith had insisted, "Speaking movies are impossible. When a century has passed, all thought of our so-called 'talking pictures' will have been abandoned." Mary Pickford had said, "Adding sound to movies would be like putting lipstick on the Venus de Milo." King Vidor had believed "talking motion pictures would never take the place of silent film. It was unimaginable to some of us, because silent pictures were an art form complete unto themselves."

The "Bible of the business," *Variety*, recorded the gradual spread of *The Jazz Singer*'s influence. The twenty-two-year-old weekly tabloid was already becoming renowned for its reporting show business news in esoteric lingo composed of snappy abbreviations and slangy metaphors. *The Jazz Singer* never commanded one of its bold banner headlines. It was just another film that had opened during the second week of October 1927, with only its gimmick of synchronized songs and a Broadway star making his motion picture debut to boast of. The handwriting on Hollywood's wall became visible over the next three months in the fine print of *Variety*'s pages that tallied the film's grosses as it opened across the country.

"Another twice daily entrant made its presence felt at Warner's, where 'The Jazz Singer' premiered Thursday and got $9,900 in two and a half days," reported the October 12 edition of the trade journal. MGM's *The Big Parade*, in its third week at the Capitol Theater in New York, Paramount's *Wings*, in its ninth week at the Criterion, *King of Kings*, entering its twenty-fifth week at the Gaiety, and even Goldwyn's *The Magic Flame* at the Rialto, in its third week, all posted higher numbers. The following week, however, "Goldwyn's romantic opus" fell off 18 percent, while *The Jazz Singer* held its own.

"MAGIC FLAME LOOP'S REAL PUNCH . . . The Colman-Banky necking team is no flash in the pan," observed *Variety* when Goldwyn's film opened in Chicago. As in New York, it followed the pattern of most pictures: It was strongest in its first week, attendance dropped steadily over the next two weeks, and it closed within the month. Meantime, *The Jazz Singer* proved to have what became known in the trade as "legs," the ability to run a long time. The Warner Brothers film repeated its pattern when it opened in Philadelphia, Baltimore, St. Louis, Milwaukee, Seattle, and Tacoma. Vitaphone may have started out as a novelty, but there was no stopping the film's word of mouth.

Other events knelled a new era in Hollywood. Sam Warner, the brother most responsible for his family's buying into Vitaphone, died at forty on September 5, two days before *The Jazz Singer* opened in New York. His brothers Harry, Albert, and Jack had rushed to be at his deathbed, but were on board the train out of New York when he died, and were present at neither the birth of talking pictures nor the death of the man behind the occasion. Rabbi Magnin conducted the funeral services.

On September 6, Marcus Loew died at fifty-seven. Memorial services for the motion picture business's first trailblazer were held on a studio stage. Louis B. Mayer fought back tears in describing Loew as "Christ-like," then introduced Rabbi Magnin. Will Rogers later observed that what he always liked about Marcus Loew was his basic attitude about motion pictures: "He made more money out of them than anybody. . . . But he always said, 'I don't know what they are all about, and the more I learn about them, the less I know.'"

HOLLYWOOD retooled. By the summer of 1928, most major film companies had signed an agreement with Electrical Research Products, Incorporated (known as ERPI), a subsidiary of American Telephone and Telegraph. In order to obtain sound equipment, each studio had to pay ERPI a royalty on every negative film it produced, then distribute its pictures only to theaters "wired for sound" by Western Electric, another AT&T subsidiary.

Having already fought one great patents war, Hollywood drew battle lines anew. The Radio Corporation of America developed with General Electric and Westinghouse laboratories its own sound system, called Photophone. RCA's David Sarnoff merged his Photophone with the Keith-Albee-Orpheum circuit of vaudeville theaters and the Film Booking Office of America, a distribution company run by Joseph P. Kennedy.

Germany's electric companies declared war on the United States, claiming their patents had been infringed upon. Within two years, lawsuits had been filed around the globe. In 1930, ERPI, RCA, and the German combine signed an armistice known as the Paris Agreement, forming a cartel and dividing the world among themselves.

Goldwyn went along with the rest of his United Artists partners and signed ERPI's Recording License Agreement. He listened at length to a young scientific whiz named Gordon Sawyer, whom Schenck had hired to install their studio's sound system. Sawyer, a quiet man with a Bachelor of Science degree in engineering from the University of California at Los Angeles, had recently traveled around the country, supervising the building of radio broadcasting studios. Over the years, he would develop such ingenious innovations in sound as planting small microphones on the actors' bodies as well as the traveling microphone boom. He ended up in Goldwyn's employ for the next forty years; but it was months before Goldwyn knew what to do with him.

Sam Goldwyn maintained his policy of watchful waiting, as he prepared to split up his successful love team of Vilma Banky and Ronald Colman—an attempt to reap twice the rewards. *Two Lovers,* the last of their films together, was ready for release, and a new project for each of them was on the drawing board. Goldwyn had no plans to convert them into talking pictures. Even if he completely believed in the changing art form, twenty thousand theaters in the country (10 percent of which were under Zukor's aegis) still had to be refitted for sound, and film producers were obligated to them while making the changeover. "By the fall of 1929—two years after *The Jazz Singer*," Zukor remembered, "—only about one-fourth of them had managed it. Therefore we continued to produce silent pictures."

Most vulnerable during this transitional period were the silent players. As if an actor's life was not tough enough already, a recent census revealed that there were 120 motion picture directors available to work at the various studios, "requiring if all are actively engaged, a daily maximum of 1,200 players." By the end of 1927, the movie colony was home to 4,000 principals, each wondering whether he would survive the reformation.

Early sound equipment tended to render voices slightly higher and thinner, thus favoring the deep-toned. When young Jean Arthur listened to the playback of her voice test, Adolph Zukor recalled, she cried in despair, "A foghorn!" But Zukor recognized a likability to that "foghorn quality which made her a greater star than she might have become on the silent screen"; her voice was her most salient feature. Upon hearing his voice, William Powell bolted out the door, shouting that he "planned to go into hiding." Again, the addition of sound would only enhance his screen presence.

Most silent-screen stars did not fare so well. B. P. Schulberg's son Budd remembered the tragedy of his father's great discovery, Clara Bow. Not only did the stationary sound cameras stifle her charming, impromptu movements but, as he remembered, "Millions of adoring fans heard for the first time the flat, nasal Brooklynese we who knew her had always associated with her." The Talmadge sisters suffered similarly; after but a few attempts at talking pictures, they bowed out gracefully.

If a regional twang could kill a career, a foreign accent was sure to toll disaster. Adolph Zukor was desperate about the future of Pola Negri; Carl Laemmle worried about Conrad Veidt; Louis B. Mayer had Ramon Novarro to consider, as well as his stunning Swede. Along with Chaplin, Garbo remained the most conspicuously silent star. In one MGM film after another, Mayer kept her from speaking. In *The Single Standard*, Garbo shambled through the rain and a title card spoke for her: "I am walking alone because I want to be alone." The public imagined how the mysterious actress might utter the line.

Sam Goldwyn lost plenty of sleep, his entire career resting on the shoulders of a bashful Englishman and a Hungarian whose English was barely intelligible. He deliberated a full six months (during which time *Variety* reported the consistently rewarding grosses of pictures with sound) before committing himself to the future.

Having pocketed one million dollars from his Banky-Colman pictures, Goldwyn was ready to borrow again, this time to invest in establishing separate followings for his two stars. Frances Marion found time between the five scenarios she did for MGM that year to write a story for Sam Goldwyn's first film in which Banky's name alone would be billed above the title.

The Awakening, as *Variety* reviewed it, was "a pinch of 'The White Sister,' a seasoning of 'The Scarlet Letter,' a large chunk of all the war pictures since 1918, and several slices of small-time baloney." The story of an Alsatian belle torn between the French fiancé she does not love and the German officer she does, strained credibility at every turn. It revealed just how far silent-screen plots had been stretched in order to hold an audience. Through it all, Vilma Banky held her own as a star. Its sound track included the singing of "Marie," written by Goldwyn's friend Irving Berlin, which became a hit tune. *The Awakening* cost $762,000, and after deducting costs of distribution, prints, and advertising, Samuel Goldwyn, Inc., pocketed a $50,000 profit from the film's run—hardly the six-figure grosses Banky and Colman used to pull in together, but enough to encourage Goldwyn to develop another film for her—a talking picture. Ironically, Goldwyn encountered more resistance to "talkies" from his other star, that reedy-voiced Englishman with impeccable diction.

Abe Lehr had recently sent a brief legal document to all Goldwyn contract actors, an amendment covering sound pictures. "I would rather not sign this," Ronald Colman replied on August 5, 1928. "Except as a scientific achievement, I am not sympathetic to this 'sound business.' I feel, as so many do, that this is a mechanical resource, that it is a retrogressive and temporary digression in so far as it affects the art of motion picture acting,—in short that it does not properly belong to my particular work (of which naturally I must be the best judge)."

Goldwyn did not push his leading man into talking pictures. He cast him instead as a traditional silent hero in an adaptation of Joseph Conrad's *The Rescue*. At a cost of $800,000, it became the first film with Ronald Colman's name above the title to lose money. *The Rescue* did far less business than Vilma Banky's *The Awakening*.

Filmmakers and their audiences alike suffered through two years of Hollywood's identity crisis. Most of the films released in 1928 and 1929 were in fact hard on the ear. Many were an equal strain on the eyes, as established methods of acting metamorphosed awkwardly. Mary Pickford and Douglas Fairbanks played out their own marital strife in a talking version of *The Taming of the Shrew.* It was an unfortunate wedding of Shakespearean acting and the broad pantomime they had practiced so successfully for fifteen years. Gloria Swanson was trapped in an overwrought production called *Queen Kelly,* which producer Joseph Kennedy shut down in mid-filming when the budget reached $800,000. The plot about a convent girl's love affair with the consort of the mad queen of Cobourg-Nassau wrecked the career of everybody involved. The star and the director, Erich von Stroheim, were practically banished from the screen.

Miriam Hopkins, Helen Morgan, Jeanette MacDonald, Tallulah Bankhead, and Kay Francis paraded before microphones at Paramount's studio in Astoria, in hopes of making the grade. So did Walter Huston and the Marx Brothers. Any number of famous voices from the stages of New York—Ethel Merman, George Burns and Gracie Allen, Ginger Rogers, Charles Ruggles, George Jessel, Jack Benny, Eddie Cantor, Lillian Roth, Ruth Etting, and Rudy Vallee—acted in a series of one-reel sound shorts, also made on Long Island. Goldwyn's most promising test for a new leading man during these years of frantic auditioning was of twenty-four-year-old Robert Montgomery. The reports from New York were favorable but warned Goldwyn that the young man's neck was too long. Goldwyn saw the tests and decreed, "His neck is not too long; his collars are too short." He ordered new shirts for the actor and new tests as well. Unfortunately, MGM saw the second test and signed Montgomery to a contract before Goldwyn's people had drawn one up.

Producers felt that talking actors required a new kind of director, and so they combed theaters for those who had thus far steered clear of Hollywood. Rouben Mamoulian, a thirty-year-old Russian émigré, had been staging opera in Rochester before Paramount lured him to the West Coast. On his recommendation, Jesse Lasky hired George Cukor to direct one-reelers; and Frances Goldwyn proudly introduced him around town. "There was a great demand in Hollywood for anyone who knew anything about the theater, who could help the actors speak the 'titles,' as they called the dialogue at first," recalled George Cukor years later. "A whole bunch of us was transported to California." Cukor later summed up his theatrical experience as little more than the strategic planting of Ethel Barrymore's whisky bottles onstage, so that she could sip her way through a performance. But in 1929 he let Hollywood believe he was a seasoned man of the theater. Within months of his arrival, he advanced from dialogue director on *All Quiet on the Western Front* to directing features at Paramount. For the first few years of her marriage, Frances Goldwyn had constantly urged her husband to bring her friend to Hollywood. Sam extended genuine offers and Cukor repeatedly dodged them. "I knew better," he confessed, "than to let working for Sam ever get between Frances and me."

Even successful directors fell by the wayside along with the scores of discarded actors. In the middle of this transitional period, Cecil B. DeMille filmed a morality tale, *The Godless Girl,* which not even the addition of a sound track could save. Having lost his studio, he signed a contract for three pictures at MGM. The last of them was a talking remake of *The Squaw Man.* When that flopped at the box office as badly as his last silent picture, DeMille found himself unemployable in Hollywood, "washed up." He left for Europe and considered looking for work there.

For two years, Hollywood went topsy-turvy with hirings and firings. The most conspicuous rising star was Harry Cohn, twelve years younger than Sam Goldwyn and cut from even coarser cloth. After breaking away from song plugging into movies, as Carl Laemmle's secretary, Cohn, his brother Jack, and Joseph Brandt formed the CBC Sales Corporation on Poverty Row. Their low-budget shorts and two-reel comedies earned their studio the nickname "Corned Beef and Cabbage."

Cohn was the son of a German tailor and a Russian mother. He grew up with the same ruthless drive and sloppy sentiment of the moguls born in the old country; but his unabashed vulgarity sometimes made even them blush. In 1924, Cohn changed the name of his company to Columbia, in an effort to upgrade at least its reputation. The new gag around town was "Columbia, the Germ of the Ocean." In 1928, Cohn hired Frank Capra, a young director at loose ends after several years directing comic shorts. With the days of the silent clowns dying out, Cohn broke in Capra with a series of "quickie" feature films budgeted at $20,000, then graduated him to more serious material. By the time soundstages were erected on Columbia's lot, Frank Capra was their leading director, the man who might rid them of their Poverty Row reputation. Cohn became well known for what he called his "foolproof device" for judging a picture's quality: "If my ass squirms," he once said, "it's bad. If my ass doesn't squirm, it's good. It's as simple as that."

George Cukor, who later directed at Columbia, said, "The Sam Goldwyns and L. B. Mayers and Jack Warners all produced by the seat of their pants too; Harry Cohn just had the bad taste to say it." In a 1928 interview, Cohn commented on his profession by noting the "most important point I can stress is that any man with a normal degree of intelligence knows as much as the other fellow in six months. It is an open business."

That was never more true than in the twilight of the silent era. At Paramount Studios alone, a lot of men (noticeably better educated than their predecessors) made their marks during this period of flux. Twenty-six-year-old David O. Selznick had got no closer to his adolescent dream of attending Yale than taking some extension courses at Columbia University; but he was a ravenous reader. After quarreling with Thalberg at MGM, he became B. P. Schulberg's executive assistant. While still in his twenties, Dartmouth graduate Walter Wanger—smart and suave—was named general manager of production for Paramount on both coasts. Herman Mankiewicz, the son of a German intellectual who taught at New York City College, graduated from Columbia before he was twenty, became a foreign correspondent, theater critic, playwright, and head of Paramount's scenario department before he was thirty. His kid brother, Joseph, also a Columbia alumnus, followed three years later, writing silent film titles, then dialogue, for Paramount in his early twenties.

A few Gentiles made their presence known in town as well. Howard Hughes—a lanky Texan with a hearing deficiency, and an heir to a tool company—began producing his own pictures at age twenty-three. A former art student from Kansas City who moved to Hollywood in his early twenties began drawing an amusing character, a mouse named Mortimer; the next year, twenty-seven-year-old Walt Disney changed the rodent's name to Mickey. Disney integrated music with his animated pictures, starting a series called "Silly Symphonies." He set up shop in the Silverlake district of Los Angeles.

Hollywood's gradual embracing of sound caused a flurry of expansion, especially of the most successful studios. Stock certificates were flying every which way. Warner Brothers merged with First National and moved into a new studio the latter company had built on farmland in Burbank. William Fox built his Fox Movietone Studios in an area between Beverly Hills and Culver City. He was quietly buying up Loew's stock, which would affect MGM, then erecting soundstages a short ride away from the new Fox lot. Joseph Kennedy muscled into the Pathé organization, which he merged with the Keith-Albee-Orpheum theater chain and David Sarnoff's Radio Corporation of America. In late October 1928, Radio-Keith-Orpheum Corporation was born. RKO moved into studios on Gower Street in Hollywood and promptly invested half a million dollars in construction for talking pictures.

Down the block, on Melrose Avenue, were the United Studios, which Paramount Pictures Corporation (the name Famous Players–Lasky started to use) bought. Their Publix theater chain was actively buying up other circuits—paying part in cash, the rest in rising Paramount stock. "As a sentimental salute to our beginnings," Jesse Lasky insisted on moving the original *Squaw Man* barn—only fifteen years after he and Sam Goldwyn had first rented it—to the new Paramount lot. He plopped it down in the middle of the vast studio so as "never to lose sight of the modest way we started." For years, it sat there uselessly, a relic.

In 1929, Sam Goldwyn moved into new offices on the United Artists lot. The former Pickford-Fairbanks Studio, with the back of its two-story office building forming the only wall against the traffic of Hollywood, ran the 7200 block of Santa Monica Boulevard. It had an eastern entrance on quiet Formosa Avenue. More modest than most of the major movie factories in Los Angeles, the homey lot was often referred to as "Doug and Mary's."

As the fortunes of the actor partners of United Artists—Pickford, Fairbanks, Swanson, and Chaplin (who did not release a single picture between 1928 and *City Lights* in 1931)—faded, the fate of the company fell into the hands of its full-time producers, Joe Schenck and Sam Goldwyn. To meet the demand for product, Goldwyn needed an associate. He hired Arthur Hornblow, Jr., a bright young man who, more than anybody, enabled him to become a successful producer of talking pictures.

Hornblow was the debonair son of the managing editor of *Theater Arts Monthly.* A Dartmouth graduate, young Hornblow was erudite, epicurean, and exacting. A playwright and producer, he had adapted Edouard Bourdet's controversial play about lesbianism, *The Captive,* for the Broadway stage, for which he got carted off to jail on opening night. Now that motion pictures were starting to talk, they intrigued him.

"All I really like, all I care about," Sam Goldwyn later told Hornblow's third wife, Leonora, "is class. That's why I liked Arter." Goldwyn never got closer than that to pronouncing his most indispensable employee's first name; but it was better than the job he did on Arthur's last name—which usually came out "Hornbloom." Hornblow immediately felt that Goldwyn himself possessed that class he so desperately sought, that "Sam was really a Polish prince who no doubt had been left in the woods as an infant." Years later, Hornblow would note that all the studio heads were "monsters," Sam included. "The only difference was that Sam laughed . . . even at himself."

Hornblow's first assignment was to develop material for the talking-picture debuts of Vilma Banky and Ronald Colman. Goldwyn believed the only way to determine their futures was to put each of them to the ultimate test. He provided Banky with daily English lessons; and Colman had already lost much of his accent in just the few years he had lived in America. Then Hornblow and Goldwyn read *Variety* as though it were a Ouija board, looking for trends.

"KIDDING KISSERS IN TALKERS BURNS UP FANS OF SCREEN'S BEST LOVERS," read a page-one headline in 1929. The problem came from the new realism that sound brought to a scene. As *Variety* explained: "In the silents when a lover would whisper like a ventriloquist, lips apart and unmoved, and roll his eyes passionately, preparatory to the clinch and then kiss, it looked pretty natural and was believable. The build-up to the kiss now makes a gag of the kiss." Many leading men got hooted off the screen.

Hornblow persuaded Goldwyn that his primary concern should be the proper presentation of his actors. He believed audiences should meet their new talking stars in roles that came close to revealing who they actually were, displaying their distinctiveness rather than disguising it. Ronald Colman, he suggested, was a reserved Englishman who would elicit laughs if he continued appearing as a passionate Latin lover. Vilma Banky was a simple, beautiful Hungarian immigrant, who should not be passed off as an exotic woman of mystery, a Garbo.

Goldwyn had a "screen play" of his next film for Vilma Banky, a silent picture—almost one hundred pages laying out the film's 384 shots and 150 title cards. Under Arthur Hornblow's supervision, this Cinderella story of an innocent immigrant who landed a job flipping flapjacks at Child's restaurant and fell in love with a millionaire passing himself off as a chauffeur would be adapted to include talking. Several scenes with spoken dialogue were patched in. The eleven pages of lines contained but a few words for the female lead.

On Friday, January 11, 1929, while the sound sequences were in rehearsal, Goldwyn screened the first assembly of the film, *This Is Heaven*, and was thrown into a quandary. He felt it was "so fine and complete in that form" that it could stand perfectly well as a silent film. He was convinced that "pictures either had to be entirely silent or all talkie and that part silent pictures were doomed to failure"; but he was afraid of going down on a sinking ship. *Variety* was already printing rumors that Vilma Banky's accent was so thick that he could not put her in talkies.

Goldwyn ordered three spoken sequences stuffed into the ninety-minute film. The idea was to give Banky a simple but endearing scene at the opening, in which to introduce her voice to the audience, a snappier exchange of dialogue in the fourth reel, and a wordier scene in the final reel. After they were recorded, Goldwyn sat on the film for several months, debating whether or not he should even release it.

He turned all his attention to his first all-talking picture. Despite Ronald Colman's own reservations about the suitability of his voice for motion pictures, Goldwyn admired his diction and knew that the former stage actor could handle genuine scenes of dialogue. Colman was also Goldwyn's only leading man under contract. At the producer's command, Arthur Hornblow tried to wrest the rights to *Arms and the Man* from George Bernard Shaw. The playwright resisted, sticking to his much-quoted policy that he was only interested in money while Mr. Goldwyn was interested in "art."

Arthur Hornblow found the perfect solution to Goldwyn's immediate problems in a writer who was interested in both. Sidney Howard was one of the most dashing figures on the Broadway scene in the late twenties. A scrappy northern Californian with wide gray eyes and a neat stripe of a mustache, Howard had studied playwriting at Harvard, served in the war as both an ambulance driver and the captain of a bombing squadron, then written book reviews for *Life* before beginning his career as a playwright. *They Knew What They Wanted*, an exploration of sexual mores that was bold for its day, won the Pulitzer Prize in 1925 (and later became the basis for the Frank Loesser musical *The Most Happy Fella*). He followed that with another hit *Lucky Sam McCarver*, then two more great successes (*Ned McCobb's Daughter* and *The Silver Cord*), produced by the Theatre Guild within a month of each other. Subject to bouts of depression, he was unhappily married to an elegant and talented actress, Clare Eames, whom he divorced; then he married Polly Damrosch, of the distinguished musical family.

Sidney Howard had steadily declined propositions to write for films. When Arthur Hornblow came to call, they began to talk about several works that might be adapted to the new medium. Howard admitted that the addition of sound created the "opportunity to make tremendously important [pictures] of a wholly new kind." Mindful of Goldwyn's reluctance to produce a love story for Ronald Colman's first talking picture, they agreed that a wonderful "talkie" could be made from the character of Bulldog Drummond, which had already proved successful in a series of novels, on stage, and in a score of silent pictures. Although Colman lacked the bulldoggish physical attributes of Hugh Drummond, he was wanting in none of the urbanity required of the former army officer turned detective.

In fact, Goldwyn owned the rights to this story and had solid adaptations for both silent and sound versions. The latter script differed from the former only in the occasional expansion of a title card into a volley of dialogue. Goldwyn felt the talking version of the script needed brushing up, a playwright's hand. Hornblow talked Howard into accepting that job for $10,000 with the mutual promise of developing future films together at a higher salary. "It was a real coup," recalled George Cukor. "After O'Neill, Sidney Howard was the most renowned playwright in America, and here Sam Goldwyn had him writing for the movies. Sam was extremely clever that way, because he not only got unusually good scripts for the time, but also enormous publicity."

Most early talking pictures suffered from monotony, visual and verbal. Because the camera was housed behind glass and actors were planted near microphones, there was little motion except for the actors' mouths. Monta Bell, one of the leading directors during these transitional years, also pointed out that "in the early stages of talking pictures the producers and the public wanted them to talk, so we let them talk and at length. Much too lengthily." If a refinement to pictures was to take hold, Bell believed, "All lines spoken [should] be for the purpose of furthering the story" and visual tedium could be relieved only by "making the screen continuously interesting."

Toward that end, Goldwyn assembled a team of filmmakers as creative as they were experienced. He had George Barnes photographing, assisted once again by his imaginative protégé, Gregg Toland. Although the motion picture camera was still partially paralyzed, the two of them never stopped experimenting with unusual camera angles, lighting, and composition.

In casting *Bulldog Drummond*'s leading lady, Goldwyn took a chance on a beauty making her sound-feature debut, an actress he had not seen since her childhood appearance as a page in his production of *The Eternal City*. In the intervening six years, Joan Bennett had bloomed into a stunning blonde with exquisite features. She had recently made several screen tests at Paramount's Astoria studio, in which her stage-trained voice came across as lovely as her photographed image. Over the next few months, all the studios saw her tests; but as Miss Bennett later remarked, "Sam was the only one who picked up on me."

At Goldwyn's insistence, the director, F. Richard Jones, rehearsed the actors for several weeks, as though it were a play—a Griffith procedure that had long since fallen into disuse. Such run-throughs became standard practice on Goldwyn talking pictures for the rest of his career. On January 28, 1929, cameras rolled film—twenty-four frames per second instead of the silent equipment's sixteen (which accounts for the frenzied gallop of old silent footage when viewed on modern equipment). Film studios still operated on a six-day week, and *Bulldog Drummond* was put "in the can" by March 18.

The film met all Goldwyn's requirements. Although it appears static by modern standards, Monta Bell (who had nothing to do with the production) remembered it as one of the handful of "moving" pictures of that year. The damsel-in-distress mystery has no love scenes to speak of: Joan Bennett utters "I love you" in the film's final seconds, just before she and Colman embrace and fall behind a trick doorway. At a total negative cost of $550,000, it was one of the least expensive films Goldwyn had produced in years, three quarters the cost of the Colman-Banky epics. Striking prints and advertising the film (plus interest on Goldwyn's bank loan) would make the total outlay just under $700,000.

The film's greatest unbudgeted expense occurred after its editors had assembled a rough cut. In the opening scene, set in a London club, an elderly waiter, "with the manner of a graveyard Sexton, is passing with a tray of drinkables" and drops a spoon. "Tinkle of spoon dropping," reads the sound effects cue. A "Peppery Colonel" harrumphs, "The eternal din around this club is an outrage." After sitting through the entire two-hour screening, Goldwyn asked his staff, "What is that word 'din'?" He was told it meant noise.

"Then why didn't the writer say 'noise'?" he demanded. When Goldwyn did not hear a satisfactory answer, he ordered the entire scene redone. The sets had already been dismantled and the actors had been dismissed; but Goldwyn said, "It makes no difference. We have to re-shoot it. The word is archaic."

While the set was being reconstructed and the actors rehired, Goldwyn carried on about the use of this peculiar word . . . until nobody less than William Randolph Hearst himself assured him that "din" was not archaic. Goldwyn ordered the rebuilt set dismantled and the actors dismissed.

Both *Bulldog Drummond* and *This Is Heaven* opened in New York in May 1929. The future of Vilma Banky's picture was instantly clear. Goldwyn's instincts about the public's not buying part-talking pictures had been correct; and the star's heavy accent became the discussion of every review. He took a $200,000 bath on the $600,000 picture.

Goldwyn might have stuck by Vilma Banky had she been more diligent about her speech lessons. Instead, he dropped all plans for future films with her. He tried to get her to pay the fifty dollars a week for the vocal coach, but she refused. "My face belongs to the screen," she said, "but my voice belongs to Goldwyn." Abe Lehr and Arthur Hornblow discussed the possibility of an indefinite suspension of her $5,000-a-week salary until some new project for her presented itself, but she refused to let that one picture seal her fate. She asserted that she was still willing to work, even if Goldwyn had to farm her out to another studio.

Irving Thalberg borrowed her for one picture at MGM; but her co-star, Edward G. Robinson, later remembered that "it did not take long to realize that Miss Banky was seriously out of her depth. The glorious creature . . . was seized with stage fright and inability."

After that, she entertained thoughts of making films in Europe. Goldwyn could not have cared less. He no longer even went through the motions of maintaining her speech lessons or seeing that she was properly groomed in public. In 1930, he summoned her to his office and said, "Vilma, you have two years to go on your contract at $5,000 a week. Now you go to the bank every week and you get your money." Goldwyn never saw her again.

"I have just reached a decision to quit pictures entirely and become once and for all Mrs. Rod La Rocque," Vilma Banky announced at a press conference. "We are so happy. We will never, never part, I know. I am an American citizen now and I am ever so happy." She lived for most of the next fifty years in Beverly Hills with her husband. He, too, gradually disappeared from motion pictures. "Oh, Wilma was so dumb," Goldwyn said to Leonora Hornblow many decades later; then, with the sweetest look, he added, "but she was so adorable."

She was also one of the lucky ones, with a half-million dollars to invest and a happy marriage. Most of the other silent-screen victims, observed Budd Schulberg, succumbed to gradual suicide: "Behind the locked doors of their Beverly Hills mansions, the talkie drop-outs searched for an answer to their fears and frustrations in the amber bottles their bootleggers hauled to the back door by the case."

Ronald Colman was another of the lucky few. With that first showing of *Bulldog Drummond* at the Apollo Theater in New York City, his stock as a screen personality skyrocketed. He became the first big silent film star to emerge an even bigger talking star. Sam and Frances Goldwyn asked Colman to accompany them to the black-tie opening of the film in Manhattan, and at the film's conclusion the star was swept to the stage by the audience's thunderous ovation. A beaming Goldwyn joined him and shared in the bows. The critical praise for the film was unanimous, practically every reviewer extolling Colman's cultivated voice and easy manner. In the June 10, 1929, issue of *Film Weekly,* Goldwyn proclaimed, "What Chaplin is to the silent film, Colman will be to sound!"

Goldwyn could back his boast. Pickford, Fairbanks, and Chaplin still attracted their legions into theaters, but Colman was outdrawing them, grossing over a million dollars for Goldwyn's company in less than a year of play dates. *Bulldog Drummond* earned another half-million the next year, netting Goldwyn three quarters of a million dollars—almost as much profit as all his independent silent films put together.

After months of planning and postponements, the first Academy Awards, for the film year 1927–28, were presented on May 16, 1929, at a black-tie dinner in the Blossom Room of the Hollywood Roosevelt Hotel. After the two hundred seventy guests had dined on squab and lobster, awards were presented in eleven categories—with special awards given to

Chaplin "for versatility and genius in writing, acting, directing and producing 'The Circus,'" and to Warner Brothers for producing "the outstanding pioneer talking picture, which has revolutionized the industry." Each winner was handed a thirteen-and-one-half-inch, eight-and-one-half-pound statue of gold-plated Britannia metal, designed by Cedric Gibbons, in the shape of a man standing atop a reel of film, holding a sword in front of him.

Hollywood came out of its spin, completing its changeover to sound. By the end of 1929, the sixty leading film studios had recording apparatus, and more than five thousand theaters across the country were equipped to reproduce sound. Theaters welcomed an additional ten million weekly patrons. Four out of the five Best Picture nominees for the 1928–29 year were talkies. Thalberg starred Greta Garbo in Eugene O'Neill's *Anna Christie,* and he lured her faithfuls and many new converts just by placing two words above the title on the theater marquees: "GARBO TALKS." After that—with the exception of Chaplin's *City Lights* and *Modern Times*—silent films became ancient history.

AFTER several years in their rented house on Hollywood Boulevard and Camino Palmero, the Goldwyns bought a place of their own, just a block away on the northeast corner of Franklin Avenue and Camino Palmero, near the dead end of the palm-tree-lined street. It was a two-story Italianate house, 6,500 square feet, which had been constructed in 1916 and valued then at $21,000. The outside of the house at 1800 Camino Palmero featured an impressive symmetrical facade and an entrance portico with Doric columns. Dozens of leaded glass windows adorned each side of the square stucco house.

The ground floor had large, nicely proportioned rooms, all trimmed in heavy, dark wood. The wainscoted dining room stretched from one side of the foyer, the living room from the other. A wide central staircase with three perpendicular banisters led up to a complex of suites. Two of the corners were occupied by adjoining bathrooms and bedrooms, one for Sammy and one for Catherine, the governess who had looked after Ruth. The master suite had its own dressing room, a large bedroom, and a modern bathroom, strictly for Frances's use. "My mother," noted Sammy years later, "would never share a bathroom with anyone."

The back of the house gave way to a lovely yard and a swimming pool that had been built in 1918, one of the first in the area. Beyond that was a "sun house," a pavilion Goldwyn promptly designated his cardroom. A large garage, complete with apartment, housed a vintage Rolls-Royce—driven only by the chauffeur, a German veteran of the war—and a blue Packard, which Goldwyn himself took out for short jaunts.

It was an impressive piece of property in what had become the established residential area of the Hollywood community. Outside his bedroom, on the second floor of this solidly built mansion, Samuel Goldwyn at age fifty could stand on the balustraded balcony, the Doheny estate on the hill above him and a magnificent vista of most of Los Angeles below. Herbert Hoover had barely moved into the White House, assuring the continuation of national prosperity, and Sam Goldwyn was voting Republican now. Financially, he was no Jesse Lasky—who *Variety* had recently calculated was the eighth richest man in show business, worth some twenty million dollars. But with neither partners nor stockholders, Goldwyn's had become a million-dollar motion picture production company. He was square with his bank loans; he had a savings account in six figures; and he had hundreds of thousands of dollars tied up in the stock market. Having pulled through even this latest career cataclysm, Samuel Goldwyn had never felt so secure in his life. Frances resisted giving in to the feeling.

The last week of October 1929, the New York stock market collapsed. On Wednesday the thirtieth, *Variety* capsulized the tragedy in the most famous headline in its history: "WALL ST. LAYS AN EGG."

12 Making Whoopee

S AM GOLDWYN—with no partners and no stockholders (except for some token company shares to such loyal employees as Abe Lehr and James Mulvey)—was successfully overseeing an autonomous small studio.

The crash dented his finances but hardly daunted him. Most of his investments in the preceding few years had been in himself—in Samuel Goldwyn, Incorporated, of California; in the heavy-beamed house that stood at 1800 Camino Palmero; in $130,000 worth of life insurance. His books at the start of 1930 showed a surplus of over $1 million in cash in his business account; the rest of his assets equaled that much again.

Each studio steeled itself for the unknown fate of the thirties, finding safety in assuming an identity, a style of film the public could count on. RKO stock steadily declined over the next two years, but that did not stop the company's producing a new picture practically every week for its theaters. David Sarnoff hired thirty-year-old David Selznick, who had recently resigned from Paramount. Selznick, in his own words, "sold him the idea . . . that the whole system of assembly-line-production picture studios was absurd, and that the business had to be broken into small producing units." He created the title "executive producer," under which such men as Kenneth MacGowan and Merian C. Cooper supervised pictures for RKO, creating its image of a smart outfit that produced sophisticated films. Goldwyn took an immediate interest in Selznick, to see if he might succeed where his father had failed.

Fox stock fell gradually, but the company kept its production up, projecting plucky optimism in its wholesome films—vehicles for Janet Gaynor and Charles Farrell, Will Rogers, and a propman named Marion Michael Morrison, who was suddenly the star of Raoul Walsh's *The Big Trail* and renamed John Wayne. In 1930, Fox also introduced a new tough guy in a trifle about an ex-convict, *Up the River;* Spencer Tracy would play heavies for the next few years.

Warner Brothers ripped many of their ideas for movies off the front pages. They ground national headlines about gangsters, unemployment, civic corruption, and juvenile delinquency into hard-hitting, naturalistic dramas. Mervyn LeRoy directed such gangster epics as *Little Caesar* and *I Am a Fugitive from a Chain Gang,* making stars out of Edward G. Robinson and Paul Muni. In 1931, Cagney squashed a grapefruit in Mae Clarke's face and became the screen's public enemy number one.

Louis B. Mayer and Irving Thalberg competed constantly for control of MGM, but there was always consensus about their making "beautiful pictures for beautiful people." The company stock fell from 64 to 50 within weeks of the crash, but Garbo, Joan Crawford, Norma Shearer, and platinum-blond Jean Harlow helped the company live up to its motto. Over the years, their leading men (especially Clark Gable) proved just as glamorous. Sam Goldwyn marveled at MGM's efficacy, how they built their success on "two big ideas—they had great stories and they created great personalities," each in service of the other.

Except for a few of Lubitsch's sophisticated comedies, Paramount remained decidedly middlebrow—schmaltzy musicals, romantic dramas, and western epics under the direction of Cecil B. DeMille, who was back in their fold. Jesse Lasky signed Marlene Dietrich, a German blonde with shapely legs and cheekbones to rival Garbo's. Two other Paramount players proved deft in all genres, from costume melodrama to farce—Miriam Hopkins and Paris-born Claudette Colbert, who helped define femininity for her generation with her chic manner. For all their mass production, Paramount was feeling the ground beneath them shake. Hundreds of their newly acquired theaters had been purchased partly with cash, the rest in company stock to be redeemed later at a fixed price—one well above the new stock-market value of the company.

"Uncle Carl Laemmle/has a very large faemmle," ribbed poet Ogden Nash. But in several instances, Laemmle relatives were raising Universal Studios from its bog of mediocrity. William Wyler, the son of a cousin in Alsace, learned his craft directing silent western shorts; he suddenly found himself directing Charles Bickford, Walter Huston, and John Barrymore.

(An ingenue named Bette Davis tested for him, but made no impression.) When sixty-six-year-old "Uncle Carl" handed the keys to Universal City over to his son in 1929, twenty-one-year-old Carl Laemmle, Jr., brought new vigor to the lot. He signed a British director named James Whale, who ushered the macabre film into the talking era with *Frankenstein*. And "Junior"'s production of *All Quiet on the Western Front*—the ninth film to be directed by the Russian-émigré Lewis Milestone—won Academy Awards for Best Picture and Best Direction in 1929–30.

Independent Sam Goldwyn was determined to make films the way he had for the last seven years, one at a time. He could not do otherwise, for he had only one star, Ronald Colman, whom he was promoting as motion pictures' "King of Romance." Within thirteen months, the producer starred him in no less than three movies, each a bit more amatory, as both sound equipment and Colman's status as a screen lover improved. The first picture was an adaptation of a recent best-seller that Sidney Howard had liked, *Condemned to Devil's Island*. The hero is a convicted thief imprisoned in the French Guianan penal colony, who falls in love with the wife of the fiendish warden. After his escape and surrender, and the warden's death, she promises to meet him in Paris upon completion of his prison term. In the film's final shots, she does.

Howard's final script was nothing so lofty as he had originally hoped. The title got shrunk to *Condemned* and the psychology of the story with it. This simplistic melodrama offered little more than a chance for Colman to display a broader acting range than he had previously shown. In the interest of making his character as attractive as possible, several pieces of comedic business were tossed into the production. Upon completing the film, Colman at last realized how liberating the addition of sound was for him. "It has let me play a character who has a sense of humor!" he told *Film Weekly*. "I have played sombre roles for so long—it was a relief to play a man who smiled not only at the things about him but also a little at himself."

Condemned opened at the Selwyn Theater in New York the first week of November 1929, and then at a glamorous preview, complete with klieg lights and a national radio broadcast of interviews with the stars, at Grauman's Chinese. Thoughts of a depression seemed thousands of miles away from the throngs who crowded Christmas-decorated Hollywood Boulevard that night. The steady arrival of limousines, their passengers in furs and jewels, was the nation's assurance that its gods were in their heaven and all was right with the world.

The film netted the Goldwyn Company almost $350,000, half what it made on *Bulldog Drummond,* but enough to instill confidence. For Colman's next picture, Goldwyn harked back to a role more akin to the Drummond character.

Raffles had been a war-horse of the London stage since 1903. Based on the 1899 novel *The Amateur Cracksman,* by Ernest William Hornung, it is the story of an elegant, cricket-playing burglar, determined to reform for love's sake but drawn into another heist when a friend becomes suicidal over a debt. The gentleman thief (first portrayed on screen by John Barrymore in 1917, and destined to become the prototype of one of motion pictures' most durable stock characters) manages to get a diamond necklace into the hands of his friend, who collects a handsome reward. Taking for himself only his ladylove's promise that she will join him, Raffles departs for a new life in Paris.

"The day of the director is over and that of the author and playwright has arrived," Goldwyn announced as he was getting his slate of talking pictures under way. With scripts detailing every camera angle and vocal inflection, and Goldwyn overseeing every piece of costume, construction, and casting, directors on his sets were reduced to technicians. Invariably, they became his whipping boys.

Arthur Hornblow was generally dispatched to the set after watching the dailies with the boss. Goldwyn would utter his irritations, and Hornblow would translate them into specific objections for the director to dispense among the cast and crew. On rare occasions Goldwyn invaded the director's territory. "You could always hear him coming," recalled Bruce "Lucky" Humberstone, who served as assistant director on *Raffles* and several Goldwyn pictures thereafter, "because he walked heavy on his heels, very fast. You could be anywhere on the sound stage, and off in the distance you'd hear those footsteps. They'd get louder and louder, and pretty soon there wouldn't be another sound on the set, only his heels hitting the floor, and you knew somebody's goose was cooked."

On *Raffles,* it was that of Harry D'Arrast, the director, a hot-tempered Basque. After but a few days of filming, Goldwyn did not like what he saw. "I think it was all playing too fast for Goldwyn, and he had trouble making out some of the words," recalled Humberstone. "Harry D'Arrast said that comedy had to be played at a certain speed, but Goldwyn didn't think it fit in with Colman's style." Invectives flew. "You and I don't speak the same language, Mr. Goldwyn," the director allegedly said. "I'm sorry, Mr. D'Arrast," replied Goldwyn, "but it's my money that's buying the language!" D'Arrast was fired, and George Fitzmaurice (who continued to direct for Goldwyn after their partnership dissolved) was on the job the next morning. His leading lady was Kay Francis, who had just appeared in the Marx Brothers' first film, *The Cocoanuts*.

With practically all the nation's theaters now wired for sound, *Raffles* was the last picture Goldwyn produced in both a silent and a talking version. It grossed more than $1 million, $200,000 in profit. "Considering the condition of the country," Goldwyn wrote Abe Lehr in a memorandum dated October 2, 1930, "I think this is marvelous." Goldwyn continued his search for properties and a leading lady worthy of his star.

In 1930, the master of Russian cinema, Sergei Eisenstein, entertained several offers from American studios. He accepted Jesse Lasky's invitation from Paramount. After failing to get both his story of the California gold rush and his adaptation of Dreiser's *An American Tragedy* approved by the feuding Lasky and Schulberg, Eisenstein backed out of the deal and met with other film potentates. Sam Goldwyn was reputed to have said to him, "I've seen your film 'Potemkin' and admire it very much. What I would like is for you to do something of the same kind, but a little cheaper, for Ronald Colman." After a great misadventure making a film in Mexico, Eisenstein kissed Hollywood goodbye and returned to a far less vagarious life under Stalin.

Goldwyn found his next project for Colman in London, where he and the star went for the opening of *Bulldog Drummond*. He canvassed the West End for some play he might bring back. Through Arthur Hornblow he met with one of England's most successful playwrights, Frederick Lonsdale, whose drawing room comedies, paragons of literate wit, had been the rage of London for almost a decade. Goldwyn was as charmed with the forty-nine-year-old writer as he was with a story Lonsdale created, one that was perfect for Ronald Colman.

The Devil to Pay is the story of a lovable cad, the black sheep of an English titled family who is as loose with his money as he is with his women. But when Willie Leeland meets socialite Dorothy Hope, he renounces all others, even his former girlfriend, Mary Crayle. Unfortunately, Dorothy jumps to the incorrect conclusion that the wastrel playboy is nothing more than a mountebank after her money. Goldwyn paid Lonsdale $25,000 for the story and screenplay, plus a percentage of the producer's gross. He also picked up the tab for Lonsdale's visit to California, including a $350-a-month suite at the new Beverly Wilshire Hotel, a Florentine palazzo in the middle of the business district of Beverly Hills. Lonsdale thanked Goldwyn for "one of the happiest business associations I have ever had."

Not until Goldwyn had seen the first two weeks of shooting did he decide to stop the entire production. Lonsdale's story, steeped in English manners, was coming out tepid and weak—underdressed sets, inconsistent accents among the actors, none of the nuance Goldwyn felt was necessary to make the picture convincing. This time, director Irving Cummings heard the heavy heels of Mr. Goldwyn on the set. Again George Fitzmaurice filled in.

The ingenue in the film, Constance Cummings, was also dismissed, largely because of her strong American accent. Her replacement was an eighteen-year-old from Salt Lake City. Like so many girls who drifted into the movies, Gretchen Young had been abandoned by her father. Her mother moved to Los Angeles, where she ran a boardinghouse and sent Gretchen out to pick up money working as an extra in films. In *Naughty But Nice,* she had a role large enough to get billing. The star, Colleen Moore, arbitrarily changed Gretchen's name to Loretta.

Dialogue and diction coaches were brought in to help Miss Young with her accent, especially in putting *g*'s on the ends of her gerunds. In her scenes with Colman, she found herself literally tongue-tied, not yet over her childhood crush on him. She got through the part, but Goldwyn saw nothing in her performance to warrant his working with her again. It was almost two decades before he rehired her, and then it was on the eve of her winning an Academy Award.

The most interesting career to unfold in *The Devil to Pay* was that of the actress playing Ronald Colman's rejected girlfriend. The former Myrna Williams from Crow Creek Valley, Montana (another Los Angeles transplant to have lost her father while still a child), Myrna Loy was steadily advancing from vampy Oriental sirens to trampy "other women." Goldwyn put a blond wig on her and liked her performance enough to ask for her the next time he needed a femme fatale.

The Devil to Pay cost more and earned less than Goldwyn had expected, not making back its investment until the following year, when the film was marketed worldwide. Big studios with theater chains could afford the occasional film with a short shelf life; they always had two new films to fill their houses the next week anyway. Goldwyn could not afford to waste his stars on pictures that were simply no better or worse than the hundreds manufactured each year. He realized that he could survive only by capitalizing on his smallness, in being sui generis. "He had to make every film special somehow," noted Samuel Goldwyn, Jr. "It wasn't enough to produce just a film. It had to be an event." Determined to become Hollywood's most prestigious impresario, he turned to the only showman he had ever dreamed of imitating.

. . .

FLORENZ ZIEGFELD'S career had inspired Goldwyn even in his glove days. He marveled at the producer's zeal, how he was always planning his next show, whether it followed a failure or a success. He admired Ziegfeld's methods of producing and promoting with dignity—and turning a fancy profit at it.

Ziegfeld closed out the twenties on one of the most impressive rolls in theater history. Besides the annual *Follies*, his 1927 production of Jerome Kern and Oscar Hammerstein's *Show Boat* was instantly recognized as a theatrical milestone. He followed that with the hugely successful Gershwin musical *Rosalie* and Rudolf Friml's *The Three Musketeers*. Then he bought Owen Davis's play *The Nervous Wreck*, about a hypochondriac who goes west for his health, only to find himself caught up in the confusion brought on by a group of cowgirls, Indians, and an ingenue whose red-skinned lover happily turns out to be a paleface after all. Ziegfeld brought in William Anthony McGuire and tunesmiths Gus Kahn and Walter Donaldson to spin it into a musical for his biggest star, Eddie Cantor. The result was *Whoopee!*

Ziegfeld's irrepressible flair spilled into his offstage life. His love affairs with the greatest beauties of the day—Olive Thomas, Marilyn Miller, Anna Held—were legendary. The day after meeting Billie Burke, he sent not flowers but an entire shop, including the decorative orange trees that had stood in the window. Budgets were for bookkeepers; he was interested in results. *Whoopee!*'s dazzling costumes, scenery, showgirls, score, and star made it a smash hit of the 1928–29 season, keeping Ziegfeld on top for another year.

Then the stock market crashed. Ziegfeld had never discussed his investments with his wife, because she did not have a head for money matters. But Billie Burke could not fail to grasp the gravity of their situation that night in late 1929 when he returned extremely late from the theater to their mansion in Hastings-on-Hudson and "sat down heavily on the edge of my bed looking utterly wretched and weary." There had been setbacks in the past, from which he had always recovered, but she had never seen her husband like this before. Through great struggling sobs, he cried, "I'm through. Nothing can save me." He had lost more than a million dollars in what Billie Burke later referred to as "the Wall Street unpleasantness." But he did have some assets he had not yet fully considered.

Whoopee! was precisely the sort of property Sam Goldwyn was looking for. A proven hit on Broadway, it boasted the tasteful extravagance with which he liked to associate himself; and it offered the opportunity to present a new star to the talking screen—the eye-rolling Cantor, who could sell a song as well as a joke.

Ziegfeld was warier of Hollywood than ever. Film producers had already abducted his biggest discoveries: W. C. Fields and Mae West were on the verge of their great fame at Paramount; Will Roger's popularity was soaring at Fox; Fanny Brice was making musicals for Warners.

Once sound was perfected, "song-and-dance movies" had quickly surfeited the public's appetite. In 1929, they proliferated so fast that the idea of plotting them was often cast to the winds. Revues, sometimes legitimized by a thin strand of a story, were slapped together. The industry churned out "nightclub musicals" and "Broadway musicals"; the movie capital even turned its cameras on itself and created "Hollywood musicals"—such as MGM's *Hollywood Revue of 1929,* in which Buster Keaton, Marion Davies, and a chorus in slickers burst into "Singin' in the Rain" alongside Joan Crawford. Hollywood's Roosevelt Hotel, Goldwyn later recalled, "was filled with refugees from Tin Pan Alley."

Paramount tried to dignify their musicals with the strains of European operetta, thereby creating stars out of Maurice Chevalier and Jeanette Mac-Donald; MGM hired a baritone from the Metropolitan Opera, Lawrence Tibbett. Hollywood produced two hundred musicals between 1928 and 1930. "The glut of musicals got so bad," Goldwyn recalled of 1930, "that some theaters were advertising: 'This picture has no music.' The Santa Fe Chief was now crowded with songwriters heading back to Tin Pan Alley."

Goldwyn chose that moment to make *Whoopee!*—his first musical—with Eddie Cantor and a seven-figure budget. The producer had acquired hit properties in the past, but never one this expensive. Goldwyn himself admitted, "I was told on every side that I was 'insane,'" that the "public is fed up with musicals. You'll lose your shirt putting that much money into a picture with Eddie Cantor. He was out here in silents, and he didn't click. They sent him back to Broadway." Cantor also presented an unspoken ethnic problem. Broadway audiences, a largely Jewish crowd, readily bought Cantor's act with its throwaway lines in Yiddish; but the moviegoing public had not yet embraced so overtly Jewish a performer.

Goldwyn reasoned that Cantor had flopped in his silent pictures at Paramount because, as with Will Rogers, "you have to hear him to appreciate him." Paramount had already approached Ziegfeld, eager to make *Whoopee!* with Cantor at their Astoria studio, by the time Goldwyn came to plead for the rights. That day, Ziegfeld called the star to his office, and Cantor remembered Goldwyn's arguing "that if a picture could be made well in Long Island it could be made ten times better in California, where there was greater experience, top technicians, and the natural scenery (horses

and Indians) indispensable to a Western—which 'Whoopee' in part was."
Goldwyn said he was even willing to film the picture in Arizona, because
"you need Indians and there you can get 'em right from the reservoir."

Disregarding the occasional malapropism, Cantor found that Goldwyn
"talked with complete confidence and know-how." The star made up his
mind on the spot "that if I was going into talkies, this Goldwyn was
for me."

Ziegfeld had his reservations. He did not want to relinquish the property without maintaining control over the film, and he knew Goldwyn's
history with previous partners. Goldwyn's doubts ran just as deep, for he
had happily produced on his own since 1923. But each of the producers
needed to make the deal.

It was a simple swap of cash for cachet. Upon the formation of Z & G
Productions, one partner quickly emerged as more equal than the other.
Goldwyn gave the desperate Ziegfeld the ambiguous title of co-producer
and little else. He agreed to relieve him of considerable financial burden
by assuming the contracts of as many Ziegfeld personnel as he could employ. He also paid Ziegfeld for his rights to the play and for his services as
producer and he promised him 20 percent of the profits. At that, Ziegfeld
would have to take second position as a profit participant—after Eddie
Cantor, who was signed to reprise his role as the nervous Henry Williams
for $100,000 plus 10 percent of the profits.

While the Ziegfeld orchard was ripe for the picking, Goldwyn caught
his new partner's latest British import, Noel Coward's *Bitter Sweet,* and was
thoroughly taken with its star, a blue-eyed blonde named Evelyn Laye.
Without even having a property in mind for her, he signed her to a contract. To turn the film debut of Britain's leading musical comedy star into
an event, Arthur Hornblow helped Goldwyn get Louis Bromfield—a best-
selling, Pulitzer Prize–winning novelist—to write the story for an operetta. He threw together a trifle in which a flower girl in Budapest
masquerades as a cabaret singer, falls in love with a prince, and evades his
premarital sexual advances by singing duets with him. Goldwyn's in-house
Pulitzer Prize winner, Sidney Howard, agreed to write the screenplay. Rudolf Friml wrote the music.

With three Ronald Colman productions for the year also in the works,
Goldwyn had reached his loan limits at Dr. Giannini's Bank of America.
He asked Joe Schenck for one million dollars, figuring Art Cinema would
bankroll Goldwyn's productions to keep up UA's supply of product. For
half the profits, Art Cinema agreed to fund both musicals. Then Schenck
learned that the Goldwyn budgets demanded close to two million dollars.
Schenck told Goldwyn he never would have agreed to both pictures had

he known their costs would run so high. He asked Goldwyn to excuse him from one of the films. Within two weeks, Sam chose one and arranged for the Bank of America to back the other. The financial plan confirmed that Goldwyn's primary goal in making *Whoopee!* was prestige more than proceeds. Even if the film recouped its negative costs, any profits beyond Cantor's and Ziegfeld's shares now had to be split with Joseph Schenck.

From day one, Ziegfeld and Goldwyn argued over every detail of the film's making. One claimed expertise in mounting musicals, the other in making motion pictures. The project became an education for each of them. "Sam listened humbly to the Great Ziegfeld," writer Alva Johnston noted; "but when decisions were made, the Great Goldwyn made them." To make matters worse for Ziegfeld, one company executive explained, "Goldwyn is the kind of man who, if he understands what you tell him, thinks he thought of it himself."

While a small army was being assembled for the production of *Whoopee!*, Arthur Hornblow sent Goldwyn a detailed memorandum proposing a plan of "elemental military organization," which "if adhered to by everybody in the organization from the top to the bottom, will not only insure an orderly and prompt disposition of many technical problems, but also insures your being personally kept completely informed and in command of everything." It called for all aspects of the film to be assigned to one of five divisions—motion picture direction, art direction, dance direction, costume direction, and musical direction. The five division heads would meet every day, passing the notes of their sessions on to the commander in chief. In the three pages of single-spaced strategy, Florenz Ziegfeld's name was never mentioned.

Only the ampersand in Z & G Productions held the two partners together through the making of *Whoopee!* The tension of working with Goldwyn and the opening of a new show on Broadway led to Ziegfeld's being ordered by his doctor to go to Florida for a short rest—"to prevent a complete nervous breakdown." Even that did not stop the partners from bickering on all five production fronts. Western Union's wires burned for weeks. The arguments started when Ziegfeld suggested which women might co-star in *Whoopee!*—all big talents from the New York stage, including Lillian Roth, Adele Astaire, and Ruby Keeler. Goldwyn dismissed them all out of hand, insisting his partner's ideas were only causing "delays and heartaches."

"NOW FLO," Goldwyn wired when Ziegfeld announced he was on his way to Los Angeles, "AS TO YOUR COMING OUT HERE YOU KNOW I HAVE UNLIMITED RESPECT FOR YOUR TALENTS AS A PRODUCER BUT WHETHER YOU REALIZE IT OR NOT YOU ARE ENTIRELY UNFAMILIAR WITH MOTION

PICTURE REQUIREMENTS AND PROBLEMS STOP WHAT IS SCARING ME IS THAT WHEN I ANALYZE YOUR SUGGESTIONS I FIND THAT THEY ARE MADE WITHOUT ANY REGARD TO SCREEN REQUIREMENTS." Turning the casting into a crisis was just a gambit on Goldwyn's part. Many telegrams later, he revealed his real point: "YOU ARE ACCUSTOMED TO FOLLOW YOUR OWN IDEAS IN PRODUCING AND SINCE I CANNOT ACCEPT DIVIDED AUTHORITY I CANNOT IN ALL FRANKNESS SEE HOW YOUR COMING OUT OFFICIALLY AS A COPRODUCER COULD WORK OUT STOP THERE ARE MY HONEST FEELINGS CONCERNING YOUR PARTICIPATION IN THE MAKING OF WHOOPEE." Still, Goldwyn said, he would love Flo to make the trip—"NOT AT THE EXPENSE OF THE PRODUCTION BUT AS MY PERSONAL GUEST AND AS AN OBSERVER WITHOUT ANY RESPONSIBILITY ON YOUR PART." Ziegfeld returned to New York instead.

To mollify his partner and prove he was handling the material properly, Goldwyn arranged for his script writers to meet with the impresario. "I AM READY AND WILLING TO HELP YOU IN ANY WAY THAT I CAN," Ziegfeld wired Goldwyn on March 5, "BUT WHEN YOU BROUGHT ME THE TWO FELLOWS TO MY OFFICE AND THEY READ ME THEIR CONCEPTION OF WHOOPEE FOR A PICTURE ELIMINATING EVERYTHING IN IT THAT WAS ANY GOOD AND CONVINCING ME WITHOUT ANY QUESTION OF A DOUBT THAT THEY KNEW NOTHING ABOUT A MUSICAL SHOW I KNEW THEN THAT IT WOULD BE HUMANLY IMPOSSIBLE FOR ME TO GET MY CONCEPTION OF WHOOPEE ON THE SCREEN AND PUT IN A CAN THE SENSATION THAT I HAD PRODUCED FOR THE STAGE."

All the writers seemed to talk about was "motivation"—that every song or dance had to grow organically out of plot or character. All Ziegfeld could see of the screenwriters' work was that "WHEN THEY GET ALL THROUGH THEY HAVE MOTIVATED EVERYTHING THAT WAS ANY GOOD IN THE SHOW RIGHT OUT OF IT AND ALL THEY HAVE LEFT IS MOVING PICTURE TECHNIQUE." Of the original sixteen songs from *Whoopee!*, little more than the title song would make it to the screen. Several new tunes were written, including the infectious Charleston "My Baby Just Cares for Me." Sung by Cantor in blackface—unmotivated—it stands out as one of the most spontaneously joyous moments ever preserved on film.

When one of the writers pruned some of the stage-tested comedy routines, Goldwyn heard from yet another of the film's participants. "BELIEVE IT BEST FOR SUCCESS OF PICTURE THAT I HAVE A HAND IN WRITING OF SCRIPT," wired Eddie Cantor from Chicago, where he was touring in *Whoopee!* Goldwyn sent the writers to Chicago.

After considerable debate with Ziegfeld, Goldwyn finally agreed to another of Cantor's suggestions, his choice for the film's dance director.

Thirty-four-year-old William Enos had recently choreographed Earl Carroll's *Vanities* and, using the toe-tapping moniker Busby Berkeley, had danced in several Shubert productions. Goldwyn was hesitant to hire Berkeley because of an alleged drinking problem, but he did.

The night *Whoopee!* closed in Cleveland, Cantor and Berkeley went to Child's restaurant, where the choreographer sketched designs for the major dance numbers on the back of a menu. The next day, they boarded a train along with Conselman and director Thornton Freeland for Hollywood, where the young dance director was, in Cantor's words, "to revolutionize the making of musical films." They talked their way across the country, "for there were many changes to be made in transposing 'Whoopee' to the screen."

. . . the choreography had to be changed completely. Present a line of thirty-two girls on the stage and you have something highly effective. Present the same line on the screen and the camera has to move so far back the girls become inch-high midgets.

Berkeley already had in mind several techniques that were to become his trademarks, including the use of chorus girls making kaleidoscopic patterns when filmed from overhead. He had also dreamed up an ingeniously simple way of showing off the beauty of his dancing girls in their opening Stetson-hat number: The camera would hold on just one of them in close-up, and she would fall away, revealing another pretty girl, and so on down the line.

Ziegfeld came to Hollywood that April. "For Flo it was a letdown," observed Eddie Cantor. "Here was a man who was a potentate, who had created a domain and ruled it. Now, suddenly, he had little to do. But the advent of talkies had interested him in Hollywood as he had never been interested before—to the extent that he allowed me to call in a friend of mine to act as his agent and help promote a position for Flo in a major studio. Any studio would have engaged him save for one thing—they feared his fabulously expensive tastes." Ziegfeld realized that his Goldwyn connection was, in fact, the best he could get, even if that required kowtowing. Once Goldwyn realized that Ziegfeld had knuckled under, he assured him in a telegram: "DONT WORRY I WILL DO EVERYTHING IN MY POWER TO MAKE YOUR TRIP HERE AS PLEASANT AS I KNOW HOW." The Goldwyns introduced the Ziegfelds to the Hollywood community; but at work, Sam used Flo only for publicity purposes, starting with a big reception at the train station.

The Ziegfelds moved, at first, into a cottage in the Outpost Estates of

Hollywood, in the hills above the Goldwyns. But Flo, recalled his wife, "with his sure instinct for the lavish, immediately discarded this" in favor of a house just across the tennis court from Marion Davies's oceanside mansion. "Daddy and Mr. Goldwyn would talk for hours about show business," remembered Ziegfeld's daughter, Patricia, "but they were worlds apart in their outlooks. Mr. Goldwyn had his eye on the penny, Daddy on the effect, and they never managed to agree."

Ziegfeld did teach Goldwyn a lesson he would carry for the rest of his career, one of the secrets behind the success of the *Follies:* Women enjoyed looking at beautiful women in beautiful clothes, the glorification of their gender. Goldwyn decided to assemble his own chorus line, which he christened the Goldwyn Girls. He told the press his criteria were beauty, personality, talent, self-confidence, and ambition. "They must have one other characteristic," Goldwyn later told an interviewer. "I have always insisted that every Goldwyn Girl look as though she had just stepped out of a bathtub. There must be a kind of a radiant scrubbed cleanliness about them which rules out all artificiality."

Several of the first Goldwyn Girls quickly found their ways out of the chorus—Virginia Bruce, Claire Dodd, and Ernestine Mahoney (who, as Jean Howard, became one of the town's famous beauties and married a young, handsome agent, Charles Feldman). One other girl, with extremely shapely legs—only sixteen and living with her mother—was picked. Busby Berkeley saw Betty Grable as the first face to appear in the Stetson number. She stood out as a little more determined than the rest, already bent on stardom and compensating for her inexperience with hard work. Young Betty practiced dance routines alone in the rehearsal halls long after the other girls had gone home. "We all had that kind of energy," Jean Howard said, recalling those early days of the Depression, when Hollywood seemed to be the world's last oasis of luxury. "And, of course, we were all so grateful just to be working."

Most of the personnel at the studio at Santa Monica Boulevard and Formosa Avenue was suddenly new. Fresh faces of actors in their twenties had all but replaced the gods of the silent screen. In the three and a half years after the collapse on Wall Street, the four United Artists stars produced a total of six films—Gloria Swanson's last two, forgettable films for the company; two feeble talkies with Douglas Fairbanks (including his valedictory *Private Life of Don Juan*); Mary Pickford's final screen appearance, *Secrets,* in 1933; and Chaplin's *City Lights,* in 1931.

There were important changes behind the scenes as well. Goldwyn hired a thirty-five-year-old Canadian-born art director, a captain from the world war who had broken into movies as a set painter, then worked with von

Stroheim. His name was Richard Day. His versatility and sharp eye for realistic detail would make him one of the most indispensable members of the Goldwyn production team. He worked on all but one of Goldwyn's next thirty films, contributing as much as anybody to the understated elegance endemic to Goldwyn pictures. The United Artists music department, under the direction of fifty-one-year-old Hugo Riesenfeld, also needed new blood. A transfusion came from New York in February 1930, which affected every one of Samuel Goldwyn's films for the next decade and the very nature of music in films for generations to come.

Alfred Newman was born in 1900 in New Haven, Connecticut, the eldest of ten children of two Russian-Jewish immigrants. His father was a produce dealer; his mother, a cantor's daughter, encouraged her firstborn to study piano. One day, she sold Alfred's dog to make the weekly payment on the Emerson oak upright.

By the time he was eight, Alfred revealed prodigious talent at the keyboard, and several teachers offered him scholarships. He made his musical debut in 1916 and received auspicious notices. At the time of the birth of their tenth child, Luba and Michael Newman separated, leaving eighteen-year-old Alfred the family's breadwinner. Concert halls did not offer the quick financial returns of theaters, so Alfred took a job at the Strand, playing piano in brief pop concerts before nightly features and in the pit accompanying the films. At twenty, Newman had become the musical director of George White's *Scandals of 1920.* Revues gave way to bigger musicals, and through the twenties, Newman was conducting and arranging musicals by no less than the Gershwins, Harry Ruby, and Jerome Kern.

In November 1929, Rodgers and Hart's *Heads Up* opened, with Newman at the podium. The show was hardly into its run when Joseph Schenck offered him a three-month job as music director on Irving Berlin's projected new musical for United Artists, *Reaching for the Moon.* Berlin— who had led the caravan of Broadway composers from New York—was familiar with Newman's stylish arrangements and had recommended him.

Reaching for the Moon was in complete disarray when Newman arrived in Hollywood. The future of the film in doubt, producer Joseph Schenck offered Newman's services to Sam Goldwyn, who was looking for his own man to oversee Ziegfeld's music director.

Goldwyn appreciated music but knew absolutely nothing about it. That Irving Berlin, his gin rummy and backgammon partner from New York, liked Alfred Newman was enough recommendation for Goldwyn to hire him; that Newman had conducted the works of Gershwin made him in Goldwyn's eyes a genius. Newman agreed to work on *Whoopee!,* then stayed to work in Hollywood for another forty years.

Whoopee! was ready to film except for the hiring of the two female leads. Goldwyn claimed to be no longer interested in any of Ziegfeld's opinions, but at the last minute he engaged two actresses from the Broadway production. Ethel Shutta (whom Ziegfeld had proposed from the start) was signed to repeat her role as the comic love interest, and Goldwyn promoted Eleanor Hunt from the Ziegfeld chorus to leading lady. Players from the stage version filled the rest of the picture's featured roles.

Ziegfeld was present during the prerecording of songs and the filming of *Whoopee!* in his capacity as "technical adviser," but Goldwyn never solicited his advice. Even so, the film increasingly reflected Ziegfeld's taste, as Goldwyn absorbed his thoughts and made them his own. *Whoopee!*'s cast, costumes, and scenery all revealed the Ziegfeld touch. When the co-producers quarreled again about the importance of color to the production, Goldwyn heeded Ziegfeld and ordered the daring use of two-strip Technicolor, one of the earliest examples of the technique on film.

Although *Whoopee!*'s budget was an extravagant million dollars more than that of the average musical, it was so well rehearsed that director Thornton Freeland filmed it in forty-three days, $150,000 under budget. As one of the few Broadway musicals of the twenties to be adapted to the screen, *Whoopee!* remains one of the most telling fossils of that extinct genre—with all its nonsensical convolutions of plot, unexplained comedic star turns, and burstings into song. "'It's a Ziegfeld production, only better,' Goldwyn liked to say," recalled assistant director Lucky Humberstone.

Whoopee! also created a major movie star. Eddie Cantor became one of the few Broadway musical performers ever to attract a following onscreen. In presenting a goodhearted little chap (slightly better off than Chaplin's tramp) whose innocence leads him into life-threatening scrapes, he instinctively scaled down his performance once he stepped before the camera. His famous eye-rolling and hand-clapping became simple gestures, tossed off with ease. When the hypochondriacal Milquetoast pulled off his spectacles and strutted into the show's title song, Cantor seemed to pop right off the screen. His contagious optimism and charming self-deprecation suffused him with star power.

It pained Goldwyn to share the credit for *Whoopee!*'s success with Ziegfeld. The more he spoke of the film, the less frequently he mentioned his partner's name, until finally it never came up at all.

"THE critics in far away England who had condemned Hollywood with the labels of Sex, Sin and Divorce had named its problems without understanding their cause," observed Evelyn Laye, the star of Goldwyn's other musical that year. "You had to live among it to begin to understand." To an outsider like Miss Laye, the wealth and power Hollywood offered seemed so far beyond life as lived in the rest of the world that those who attained it were suddenly "a little apart, a little different from everyday people." What made it all interesting, she said, was that "neither the public, nor the film artists themselves, were used to this golden life which the moving camera and the synchronized microphone had opened up." Miss Laye found that everyone in Hollywood lived in fear of losing everything tomorrow, that the next picture was always one's last.

That was certainly the case at the Goldwyns', where marital and monetary strains were almost never discussed but could not be denied. He worked almost all the time, to the point that his house on Camino Palmero became little more than a place to sleep—in a room apart from Frances. His Sundays were spent in the pavilion behind the swimming pool, playing cards with Joe Schenck, MGM's Eddie Mannix, Zeppo and Harpo Marx, Sid Grauman, and Eddie Cantor. Trays of sandwiches were constantly refilled, while the men played gin rummy and poker and bridge for very high stakes. Goldwyn cheated shamelessly in every way possible; and when losing badly, he was known to hold the other players captive until dawn if necessary, until he was even again. One day Goldwyn won $155,000, and two weeks later he dropped $169,000. Frances never knew such amounts were changing hands, and she preferred not to know. "My mother was always afraid my father was going to gamble everything away," Sam Goldwyn, Jr., later recalled. On Sundays, she never set foot in her own backyard.

Come May, the game moved to the beach, along the "gold coast" down the street from Marion Davies's beach house. At 602 Ocean Front, in a house that would not have looked out of place on Cape Cod, the Goldwyns summered. The sturdy two-story home (with separate servants' quarters) had one large, shady patio between the coast highway and the main house and another on the ocean side. A white picket fence sat in the sand, staking out the Goldwyn property. Cards were dealt regularly on Sundays and any other day Goldwyn and at least one other shark played hooky. The Irving Berlins came to California every summer, and Irving became a regular. Frances, with her milky skin, never cared for the beach house. She spent most of her time sitting on the shady terrace under a straw hat, facing east, reading.

"My earliest memories are of him kissing me," remembered Sam Goldwyn, Jr. "Little Sammy" recalled most vividly his birthday on September 7, 1930. At seven o'clock in the morning, he tore down the stairs of the

Ocean Front house, screaming, "Daddy, I'm four years old!" Sam, already at the game table, halted him, saying, "Just a minute . . . till I finish this hand." A moment later, he yelled, "Goddamn it," threw all his cards down, then swept the boy into his arms and kissed him. "Actually," amended Sam Goldwyn, Jr., "my earliest memories are all of my father playing cards."

Joseph P. Kennedy, during his occasional forays to Hollywood, noted that except for Herman Mankiewicz, Sam Goldwyn was the only man "in Hollywood with a true family life." Kennedy did not see enough of the Goldwyns to perceive Frances's uneasiness over Sam's gambling and philandering. "Sam Goldwyn was not a fellow to make a pass in public," said Goldwyn Girl Jean Howard; "he had too much taste for that." But Lucky Humberstone stumbled into Goldwyn's office during the making of *Whoopee!* and discovered the producer in a compromising position with a girl who did not even get into the picture. Most of the girls on the lot had heard about Sam Goldwyn's "casting couch"; most of the men heehawed about it. Frances pretended not to know. Humberstone averred what most people said about Goldwyn, that "he really wasn't interested that much in fooling around, because he just didn't have the time for it. It was more like something he felt he had to do, because he was a mogul." He apologized to his beautiful young wife with expensive trinkets.

Frances forgave, but she could not forget, as her own childhood terror of abandonment and destitution was refueled. She talked of reviving her aborted acting career and went as far as making a screen test with Ronald Colman, but no farther. Instead, Goldwyn consciously included her more in his business. Frances had a good eye, and Goldwyn started to make use of it, allowing her to oversee the costumes on his pictures, then the sets; in time, she was reading scripts. He always felt he could trust her. "There was never a word of gossip about the Goldwyns," noted Irene Mayer Selznick. "They were a united front against the rest of the town, and Sam never had any better protection."

Frances even took to studying the budgets of her husband's films. Making herself hysterical over his constant indebtedness to the banks, she turned 1800 Camino Palmero into a madhouse whenever he had a film in production. Sammy never forgot his mother's "great sigh of relief" every time his father paid off a loan on one of his pictures. Her face would suddenly relax, and, for a few days anyway, she would rest assured that her house would not be taken from her.

Frances had good reason to be nervous in 1930. Her husband had more than $2 million tied up in three Ronald Colman pictures, and that much again in his two musicals, *Whoopee!* and *One Heavenly Night.* Goldwyn had gambled on the latter's making him the most money, because his profits on *Whoopee!* had to be parceled out so many ways.

That particular crapshoot cost him a fortune. Most of the critics mustered up some kind words for Evelyn Laye, but few could do the same for the rest of the production. The reviews were the worst Goldwyn had ever received, and *One Heavenly Night* incurred his biggest loss since his entering the business—over $300,000.

Whoopee! was a sensation. After two years of play dates, United Artists reported gross rentals on the film in excess of $2.3 million. Z & G Productions received 70 percent of that. After deducting the film's costs, and Cantor's and Ziegfeld's royalties, $216,000 profit remained, half of which went to Art Cinema, which had put up the money in the first place. The remaining half was profit for Goldwyn. That plus his Colman pictures gave Frances Goldwyn good reason to sleep soundly. Her husband had netted another million dollars that year.

Whoopee!, Goldwyn later noted immodestly, "brought the musical film back." After its success, all the studios renewed their search for musical performers who—like Cantor—could project their stage talents on the screen with effortless energy.

"The Ziegfeld of the Pacific" was a new title conferred on Goldwyn after *Whoopee!* A year earlier, the sobriquet would have flattered him; now it flustered him. Goldwyn swore to himself never to take on another partner. Except for bookkeeping, Z & G never did business again.

Ziegfeld complained about all the deductions in overhead and distribution from his checks, and he unsuccessfully tried to wangle 20 percent shares out of future Goldwyn-Cantor productions. Such sums would not have helped him regain his professional standing. He produced a few more shows, but he soon faced both fiscal and physical ruin. For the first time in more than twenty years, there was not a Ziegfeld opening on Broadway. Influenza and pneumonia got the better part of him; creditors got the rest. From his sickbed, he took to sending Goldwyn friendly but rambling telegrams, the subtext of which was his need to secure work for his wife in the movies. "I FEEL IT IN MY BONES SHE WILL BE A BIG HIT SHE IS A REAL COMEDIENNE," he wired Goldwyn in March 1932, complaining about the dearth of decisionmakers in the industry. Even after all they had gone through together, Ziegfeld wished Goldwyn would sign Billie Burke, because, he added, "YOU SEEM TO BE ONLY LIVE WIRE IN HOLLYWOOD." Goldwyn simply did not have a part available for her. The Ziegfelds' resources dwindled to little more than the royalty checks from *Whoopee!*

Frances had a private chat about her former patroness with George Cukor, who in his first years in Hollywood had created a stir as the director of such films as *The Royal Family of Broadway* and *What Price Hollywood?* David Selznick, who had been most instrumental in the early career of the quick-witted Cukor, signed him to direct *A Bill of Divorcement*, which had the role of a mother. Cukor called Billie Burke and offered her the part, which saved the house and the maid and enabled her to keep her invalid husband in some comfort. The Ziegfelds took the train to California— they occupied a private railway car. (On the same train sat yet another Hollywood-bound hopeful, Katharine Hepburn, whom Selznick had cast as the ingenue in his film.) Within a few weeks Florenz Ziegfeld died.

Friends rallied to Billie Burke's side, Sam Goldwyn the first among them. Ziegfeld had often talked of wanting his ashes scattered over the Amsterdam Roof, so Goldwyn immediately offered to provide a private railroad car to return Ziegfeld to New York. In the end, the widow chose a simple crypt at Forest Lawn. Will Rogers wrote the obsequies, saying, "Good-by, Flo, save a spot for me. You will put on a show up there someday that will knock their eye out."

Sam Goldwyn paid tribute in his own way to the man whose style had influenced him so strongly. Even though he still had no role to offer her, he put the widow Ziegfeld under personal contract. "Billie," he said, "let me act as your agent and your clearinghouse. I will get you parts in pictures and look after you, and whether you are working or not I will give you $300 a week so you won't have to worry." In fact, he ended up casting her only once. But he loaned her out over the years, raking in much more money—all of which he gave to her.

For a while, everyone assumed the nation's financial crisis would never affect motion pictures, that even in the darkest hours, the public would want their stars to brighten their lives. But movie attendance began to fall off, the studios' suffered, and the parent companies were being hit as hard as the rest of America's industries.

Hollywood became, more than ever, that place for only the toughest dreamers who believed in themselves.

13 Coming of Age

HOLLYWOOD was going belly up. Loew's stock dropped to a quarter of what it had been, as MGM's $10 million annual profits halved. RKO stock shriveled from 50 to 1⅞, and the company was forced to recapitalize. Universal suffered a similar fate. Fox Films, in the throes of reorganizing, stripped its founder of all power; within two and a half years, the stock, once traded at $100 per share, bottomed out at ¼. Warner Brothers barely held on. When Jesse Lasky went to cover some stock he had bought on margin, he discovered that $1.5 million worth of Paramount paper was worth only $37,500. He was banished from the lot and soon went bankrupt. Paramount fell into receivership.

United Artists had remained primarily a distribution company and prospered. Now, without a large studio and theater chain, it faced specializing itself out of business. Pickford, Fairbanks, and Griffith had all but retired, the last wallowing in drink and debt. Even the industrious Joe Schenck had become preoccupied with corporate business, as well as the dissolution of his marriage to Norma Talmadge. Without a steady flow of product, the company's profits tumbled in 1930 from $1.3 million to $300,000. United Artists' only rampart against doom was Art Cinema Corporation, the fund that had been established to keep them supplied with pictures.

On November 20, 1930, Schenck handed the Art Cinema checkbook to Goldwyn. Art Cinema would own the productions it financed, but the arrangement allowed Goldwyn to continue producing films under his own banner as well, thus making him most responsible for United Artists' earnings over the next year or two. With this power of the purse, Sam Goldwyn virtually controlled the company's product line.

Eighteen years after Goldwyn had seen his first Broncho Billy western, motion pictures entered a state of awkward adolescence. Just when films were mastering the mechanics of sound and bringing more complex material to the screen, the Depression forced most people to give up their regular moviegoing habits. Many writers of the day thought motion pictures could help the nation through the crisis by elevating its consciousness; they called for more reality and social responsibility in motion pictures.

Theodore Dreiser visited the film capital and discovered that even when studios set out to film such works as his *American Tragedy* or O'Neill's *Strange Interlude,* the decisionmakers were "not artists but business executives," men who pandered to "the intelligence, moral views, etc. of the masses." Dictates from the Hays Office helped create "Hollywood versions" of even classic works of literature.

Two days after taking hold of Art Cinema, Sam Goldwyn paid $150,000 for the motion picture rights to *Street Scene.* Arthur Hornblow, Jr., had talked Goldwyn into buying Elmer Rice's Pulitzer Prize-winning hit of the 1928–29 season. Goldwyn had balked before purchasing the urban drama, afraid it could not be made into a satisfying motion picture. *Street Scene* was a naturalistic slice of New York tenement life, one of the first American plays in which proletarians were depicted as heroes. The entire play was set outside a brownstone in New York City. One of the building's occupants, Anna Maurrant, is carrying on a love affair with Sankey, the milkman. Anna's suspicious husband returns to his apartment unexpectedly, finds Anna with Sankey, and shoots them both. Around the front stoop of the apartment, the play probes the squalid lives of all the building's tenants, especially the Maurrants' daughter, Rose. In the end, she flees with her boyfriend for a new beginning elsewhere.

Adultery and murder were red flags to the Hays Office; characters who were overtly Jewish had always been anathema to Hollywood producers; the play had but one exterior set, with no action other than people walking in and out of the building and stopping by the steps to talk; and Goldwyn himself had an aversion to stories that were in any way sordid. He believed people went to the movies—especially in the Depression—to see glamour, not the grime that was outside their windows every day. Arthur Hornblow convinced him that producing *Street Scene* would add the luster he wanted to his name. Hornblow suggested that the play was not Jewish so much as urban, and that it could all be modulated simply by casting a pretty Gentile actress as Rose.

Goldwyn promptly negotiated with Paramount for the services of a button-nosed, blue-eyed colleen called Nancy Carroll. Shortly before the contracts were signed, she suddenly became unavailable. Unknown to Goldwyn, Paramount's general manager, B. P. Schulberg, was trying to throw the part to another actress.

Sophia Kosow was the only child of Russian immigrants. After losing her father, young "Sylvia" was adopted by her mother's second husband, Dr. Sigmund Sidney. At fifteen, she studied at the Theatre Guild School and accelerated to Broadway. In 1930, she appeared in *Bad Girl,* which Schulberg saw with his wife, Adeline, who would soon open a successful talent agency. She raved about the girl. With the older generation of actresses bowing before the "new breed who could both dazzle and speak," said the Schulbergs' son Budd, "B.P. was anxious to keep his studio abreast of L.B.'s, and so it was logical that he would back Mother's judgment and sign young Sylvia before Mayer and Thalberg or the Warner Brothers snapped her up." Months later, young Budd found himself awakened by his parents' fighting; he heard his mother screaming about this "little *hoor*" and "cheap little *kike.*" B.P. had fallen in love with Sylvia Sidney while starring her in *City Streets,* a Dashiell Hammett gangland melodrama in which she played opposite Gary Cooper. By her next picture for Paramount, *An American Tragedy,* they had become Hollywood's number one topic of gossip.

Budd Schulberg noted that Miss Sidney's "New York waif-like quality . . . was coming into style with the Depression"; in fact, Elmer Rice had wanted her to play the ingenue in *Street Scene* onstage and recommended her for the film. "SYLVIA SIDNEY FINE ACTRESS BUT QUITE HOMELY," Joe Schenck warned Goldwyn in a wire from New York the instant he heard she was being considered. "STREET SCENE NOT ANY TOO COLORFUL IN STORY AND BACKGROUND STOP IN MY OPINION YOU SHOULD HAVE GOOD LOOKING PEOPLE." Fifty years later, Miss Sidney herself conceded, "He took a big chance with me. That was the craziest step in the world . . . taking someone in the process of being developed. But Goldwyn was a man who took chances. And Schulberg figured I should do it—that I'd come back pretty well established."

She returned to Paramount a better actress for the experience. The unusual production allotted almost two weeks for rehearsal—with Elmer Rice always present on Richard Day's authentic set, complete with elevated train station. Another twenty-three days were spent in front of the cameras.

Goldwyn recognized that the confines and the conscience of *Street Scene* demanded the talents of an extraordinary director. No American had made such vivid social statements on screen as King Vidor had in *The Big Parade*, *The Crowd*, and *Hallelujah* (with its all black cast)—all of which were Goldwyn favorites. And no director was more interested in new photographic technique, anything to liberate the camera from its tripod. "I think I was one of the few American directors to study what the Germans were doing in the late Twenties and early Thirties," said Vidor, referring to the experimentation of such cinematographers as Karl Freund and Fritz Arno Wagner.

Vidor was "anxious to work for a producer who was aiming high," but he thought *Street Scene*'s greatest strength as a play could be its primary weakness as a film:

it would be a mistake to tamper with the simple form and mood of the play and to try to transpose any of the action or scenes to the interior of the house or to any other interior settings. At the same time I feared that the static, immobile quality of that one stoop and that one section of sidewalk would offer little opportunity for movement. The result might prove monotonous.

In *Street Scene,* he decided,

we would never repeat a camera setup twice. If the setting couldn't change, the camera could. We would shoot down, up, across, from high, from low, from a boom, from a perambulator, and we would move back and include not only the sidewalk but the street as well. This flexibility would actually make the film more deserving of Elmer Rice's title than the play had been. The street, the sidewalk, the facade of the building would be our arena in which all the drama could happen.

This battle plan in mind, Vidor accepted the job, with George Barnes manning the camera.

Goldwyn populated most of his New York street with the original Broadway players. Eight of them came west, including John Qualen and Beulah Bondi, film novices who became two of the medium's most durable character actors. Goldwyn did not even meet Miss Bondi until the wrap party for *Street Scene*, and then it was to offer her a contract. "I was told if I wanted to have a career I would have to submit to the seven-year contract," she later recalled. "But I knew that those things meant seven years of slavery, so I didn't take it.

On Saturday at the end of the rehearsal period for *Street Scene*, Vidor gave a full-dress performance before a small audience that included Sam and Frances Goldwyn, Arthur Hornblow, and Helen Hayes, whom Goldwyn was courting for a future picture. Occasionally, Vidor would lean over and whisper how the camera would be moving, but Goldwyn could not have cared less. He kept shushing Vidor, saying he was busy watching the play. At the end, Vidor approached him for any comments. "He was telling Miss Hayes what a great picture 'Street Scene' was going to be," Vidor remembered. "She seemed to be in agreement, but suddenly Sam blurted out, 'If you don't believe me, come up to my office and I'll read you the letter I wrote to New York only this morning!'" Both Vidor and Miss Hayes swallowed their laughs. "You will be crazy about Sylvia Sidney— she is marvelous," Goldwyn wrote the skeptical Joe Schenck. "Believe me Joe, this is not said to make you feel good, but I truly believe everything I say."

Street Scene came in under its modest $584,000 budget, the cheapest Goldwyn picture in years. Because Vidor had choreographed so much of the camera movement before shooting began, he had cut most of the picture in his head. The only serious altercation in making the film came between producer and director over sound effects: Just as the play had been one of the first stage productions to include realistic sound effects throughout the performance, so too, Vidor hoped, the film would have a sound track rich with urban cacophony. Goldwyn violently refused. "At the time, he was right, of course," acknowledged King Vidor. "Movies were still being made in which you could barely make out some of the dialogue, and a lot of background noise was generally a sign of poor quality. Sam would never stand for that."

What *Street Scene* lacked in honks and sirens it more than made up for in music. In fact, the score of the picture remains its most enduring element. Movie music was going through its own metamorphosis in these first years of talking pictures, changing from constant accompaniment to more selective "commentative" use. Max Steiner, who was scoring as many as two motion pictures a month at RKO, recalled, "At this time, music for dramatic pictures was only used when it was actually required by the script. A constant fear prevailed among producers, directors and musicians, that they would be asked: Where does the music come from? Therefore they never used music unless it could be explained by the presence of a source like an orchestra, piano player, phonograph or radio, which was specified in the script." In time, filmgoers proved willing to suspend audio as well as visual disbelief.

Filmmakers realized the great power of silence in talking pictures. According to Max Steiner, producers and directors "began to add a little music here and there to support love scenes or silent sequences" in the spring of 1931. Alfred Newman's score of *Street Scene* that season helped the medium make the leap, illustrating how music might be utilized in the future.

Newman spent much time on the set during the making of the film, looking for places where he could "intersperse the dialogue with musical phraseology that [would have] the effect of intensifying each line." The tight eighty-minute film ended up with only five infusions of music, most notably a theme that brackets the story and creeps in in the middle of the picture as a kind of entr'acte at the start of a new day.

Newman's theme owed a lot to his idol, George Gershwin. The film opens with a montage of Manhattan, over which plays a brief brass fanfare that gives way to a lone clarinet warbling the same low trill and ascent of the scale that opens *Rhapsody in Blue*. A full orchestra then plays the main theme, sounding like a pastiche of Gershwin fragments—lush in melody but full of the flatted seventh tones characteristic of blues and the popular jazz of the day. Newman folded it all together into a lingering theme that has come to be synonymous with Manhattan mornings. He later incorporated its opening two bars—nine notes of yawning melody*—into a dozen other films.

Even without a single element of glamour to promote, Goldwyn got more advance publicity on this—his twenty-fifth film since starting his new company—than on any film he had yet produced. *Street Scene* firmly established Sylvia Sidney's career. She took several bows from the stage of New York's Rivoli Theater on the night of August 26, 1931, at what was another of Goldwyn's star-studded openings. The dozen New York newspapers were unanimous in their praise; and, to Goldwyn's surprise, *Street Scene* did respectable business.

Goldwyn, through Art Cinema, bought another Broadway hit, this time to complete the two-picture deal Joe Schenck had made in an attempt to get Gloria Swanson out of her career slump. *Tonight or Never* was an Americanized version of a popular Hungarian play about a temperamental

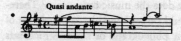

* Quasi andante

diva whose teacher (and fiancé) tells her that unless she ventures out and experiences life she will never become a great singer. She falls in love with a dashing gigolo, an impresario in disguise, who provides her with both love and a career. Goldwyn thought it was an ideal role for Swanson and that it would give him the chance to produce a film every bit as resplendent as *Street Scene* was drab.

After working with Ziegfeld, Goldwyn made it his contention that women went to movies to see how other women dressed. Many studio wardrobe departments were still headed by theater costumers, who were little more than seamstresses. Producers hired dress designers to make the clothes of important leading ladies in special productions. For many of Gloria Swanson's early films, Cecil B. DeMille had brought over a couturier from Paris. Sam Goldwyn outdid all his colleagues when he commissioned Gabrielle "Coco" Chanel—whom costume designer Irene Sharaff credits with nothing less than laying "the foundation of present fashion"— for her first Hollywood assignment.

Chanel and her retinue of dress cutters, seamstresses, and press secretaries arrived in New York in early March 1931. Their advance on Hollywood was delayed by Mademoiselle's bout with the grippe, but she rallied her way through Goldwyn's rigorous schedule of interviews and press receptions in New York. She even took him aback by grabbing all the headlines for herself. The newsworthiness of her work on *Tonight or Never,* she said, had nothing to do with motion pictures; it was that Chanel had at last come to America.

Shooting began in September 1931, under the direction of Mervyn LeRoy. He had broken into motion pictures less than ten years earlier, when his cousin Jesse Lasky gave him a train ticket to Hollywood and a job in his studio's wardrobe department. Most recently, LeRoy had directed the hit picture *Little Caesar* for Warner Brothers. Their studio in financial disarray, they gladly loaned out that year's hottest young director. Never having heard a first name like LeRoy's, Goldwyn called him "Moiphy."

Swanson's performance in *Tonight or Never* did not command the newspaper space her personal life did. (During the production, she and the Marquis de la Falaise divorced, and she eloped with the Irish playboy whose baby she was carrying.) Chanel's costumes drew raves; and the leading man, Melvyn Douglas, in his film debut, walked away with the best notices. When Miss Swanson went off to have her baby, Joe Schenck invoked several clauses in her contract and canceled it. She made one more picture, in England, with a young hopeful from the London stage, Laurence Olivier; but the film's failure meant a virtual end to her career as both a producer and a star. United Artists bought up her company stock and completely severed their relationship.

Goldwyn shopped on Broadway a third time that year. Zoë Akins's hit comedy *The Greeks Had a Word for It* had three choice female roles. At worst, it would provide Goldwyn with an opportunity to audition women for the vacancy in his operation since Vilma Banky's downfall. The bubbly farce followed a trio of gold diggers, known as the "Three Musketeers of Riverside Drive," on their quest for millionaires. Sidney Howard's script fleshed out the characters, playing up the girls' camaraderie while holding down the sexuality to the censors' standards. In fact, the simple allusion to "It" was enough to alarm Will Hays. In order to conform to the Hays Office's newly drafted code, Goldwyn changed the title of the movie to *The Greeks Had a Word for Them.*

Casting a picture invariably comes down to actors' availability. When Goldwyn found most stars under contract to the major studios and busy, he grew desperate. "He grabbed me in an elevator," remembered Ina Claire, who had not seen Goldwyn since he was called Goldfish. In the late spring of 1931, Goldwyn passed through New York and saw her at the Hotel Pierre. "I want to talk to you!" he called out, rushing to catch the elevator she was in. "You're my favorite actress, and I was just thinking about a great movie for you." In the time it took to get from the lobby to the tenth floor, Goldwyn had bolted through the pleasantries and offered her a contract. Miss Claire had no interest in a Hollywood career; but, as with so many others exposed to his charm, she said, "I liked Sam's enthusiasm and so I signed for a year with him."

Goldwyn told her she could play Schatze, the dizzy blonde with most of the script's zingers, but his eye still roved for more of a "bombshell" in the role. When he heard that Jean Harlow would be available, he set his heart on her, until both Frances Marion and Darryl Zanuck told him—as he wired Joe Schenck—"SHE PROBABLY WORST ACTRESS THEY HAVE EVER KNOWN STOP ZANUCK SAYS IT TOOK DAYS TO DO ONE SCENE WITH HER STOP MARION SAYS THEY HAD TO CUT HER ROLE [in *The Public Enemy*] DOWN TO HALF AND EVEN THEN DIFFICULT GETTING HER TO HANDLE IT STOP UNDER CIRCUMSTANCES I CANNOT AFFORD TO TAKE CHANCE USING HER IN GREEKS WHERE ROLE REQUIRES QUICK REPARTEE AND MARVEL-OUS ACTING . . ."

Then Goldwyn learned that Paramount was willing to loan him one of the most popular young women in town, if not yet to the public at large, Carole Lombard. Twenty-two and blonde, with big blue eyes, the former Jane Alice Peters, from Fort Wayne, Indiana, had lived in Los Angeles

most of her life with her divorced mother. When she was twelve, Allan
Dwan had spotted her playing baseball on the street with the neighborhood kids and put her in a picture. Five years later, she became one of
Mack Sennett's bathing beauties. Now Paramount did not quite know how
to exploit her, but they knew she had unthreatening glamour and sly
comic timing that made her appealing to both men and women. Ina Claire
was recast as Jean, the man-stealer of the group.

The role of Polaire, the most romantic of the threesome, went to Madge
Evans, a pretty actress who would play opposite Robert Montgomery,
James Cagney, Spencer Tracy, and Clark Gable in a series of forgettable
films in the thirties. Under the direction of Lowell Sherman—an actor
who also appeared in the film—shooting began August 21, 1931.

The first scenes were Lombard's, and after a few days she complained of
being ill. By the second week of shooting, she said she was so sick that
Lowell Sherman shut down the set for the day and drove her home. She
never returned, and her condition was never fully explained. (Aborting a
child by William Powell was the popular rumor.) Goldwyn gracefully sent
her roses to cheer her while she convalesced. "Regardless of newspapers
and talk," she wrote him back, "I do feel very badly about stopping the
picture. If it had been in my power to be back at work, I would have been
there." Ina Claire thought her co-star was more clever than anybody gave
her credit for: "Nobody believed she was sick. I think she knew it was a
lousy movie and she just wanted out." Goldwyn quickly replaced Lombard
with Joan Blondell, the daughter of a vaudevillian, whom Warners had
signed the year before. After *The Greeks,* she proceeded to play a number
of dizzy blondes and goodhearted gold diggers in Warner musicals.

"Believe me the 'Greeks' will be outstanding from the standpoint of
women's appeal and interest," Goldwyn wrote Joe Schenck, with his usual
self-confidence. "It will really be different from anything attempted in
Hollywood before by way of clothes, sets and women." But Carole Lombard proved to be the smartest of them all. Except for Joan Blondell, who
fell for the cameraman and became the fourth of George Barnes's seven
wives, *The Greeks Had a Word for Them* added little to anybody's life.

Ina Claire so disliked the way Goldwyn had tricked her into the movie,
by offering her a part she did not get to play, she asked him to tear up
their contract. He agreed—for ten thousand dollars. "It was," she said, "a
small price to be rid of him." Even the youngest Goldwyn Girl, who had
a walk-on in the film, was handed her papers shortly after the film flopped.
Except for one last chance in his next musical, Goldwyn saw no future for
the teenaged Betty Grable. She hacked around town for most of the decade, before she received a contract from Fox. They borrowed the *Greeks'*

formula time and again over the years, in such films as *Moon Over Miami* and *How to Marry a Millionaire,* often starring Betty Grable, who by then had become America's number one box-office attraction.

In his search for a female star, Goldwyn had plainly taken his one leading man, Ronald Colman, for granted. "Goldwyn's brash, uncouth manner had long grated upon Colman's natural reserve, despite the valuable intervention of 'buffer' Hornblow," observed the actor's daughter, Juliet. "Although their business partnership was of unaccountable mutual value over seven years, maintaining a balanced accord throughout required effort and self-control, neither of which Goldwyn supplied in quantity." By 1931, Goldwyn was casting Colman indiscriminately, settling for any script with a beginning, middle, and end that called for a well-spoken gentleman. That is exactly what he got between producing *Street Scene* and *The Greeks Had a Word for Them.*

On the same New York trip and in the same elevator in which he snared Ina Claire, Goldwyn bumped into Ben Hecht and Charles MacArthur. The two former Chicago newspapermen had recently teamed up as playwrights and taken Broadway by storm with their first play together, *The Front Page.* Each of the partners had a celebrated reputation of his own. Hecht was the author of a dozen books of fiction; MacArthur had written several plays and married Helen Hayes. Together, these two hard-drinking buddies were a powder keg of talent and trouble, currently in the midst of another play, *Twentieth Century.* It was then, Hecht later recalled, that "Charlie and I found ourselves in the ascending company of Sam Goldwyn. The yellow, billiard-ball head, the nutcracker jaws, the flossy tailoring, high-priced cologne, yodeling voice and barricaded eyes that were Sam Goldwyn greeted us en masse."

> "You are my two favorite authors," said Goldwyn. "I have a tremendous respect for your abilities. I really have. You can ask Frances. I want to engage you to write the next motion picture I am going to produce starring Ronald Colman. I intend to make it the finest thing I have done."

The two explained that they were not interested in movies just then, but Goldwyn ignored them and offered ten thousand dollars just for hearing a story from them that he liked. "And," Hecht remembered Goldwyn's continuing, "I say this in absolute sincerity, you should get another hundred and twenty-five thousand dollars for the kind of scenario you are going to write for me." Goldwyn had shrewdly scattered numbers big enough into his double-talk to attract the writers' attention.

Hecht and MacArthur went to Hollywood and unraveled a hypnotic tale about a gentleman thief hiding out in a North African oasis among a den of thieves. There Colman would fall in love with the beautiful grand-daughter of an embezzler. He would manage to steal the old man's stash of stolen francs out from under the noses of his fellow residents at the Saharan hideaway. Instead of absconding with either the girl or the cash, he nobly puts her on a plane with the money, to return it to its rightful owner, then makes his own getaway with his chum, Smiley. Goldwyn offered Hecht and MacArthur $25,000 to write the screenplay, plus 3.5 percent of the gross of the film. Each side thought it had put one over on the other.

The writers ensconced themselves in a wooden castle on a hill in Hol-lywood—"perched above a hundred pumping oil wells" and 250 turkeys, which the landlord bred. They moved in for an indefinite stay, often joined by their agent, Leland Hayward.

After a few weeks, word spread around town that not only were Hecht and MacArthur accepting other assignments but they had hoodwinked Sam Goldwyn. When he heard that MacArthur was showing up at MGM for still another job, Goldwyn demanded the pages for which he had paid. Not having committed a word to paper, Hecht challenged himself to write the entire script in a single day. He hired two stenographers and began dictating. Into the night Hecht rambled, adding the sort of twists and details that come out of desperation or exhaustion: The elderly embezzler became blind, the undercover agent for the local authorities became a sexy female agent. "Our hostelry was filled with European nobility wanted by the law for crimes of all sorts," recalled Hecht. "The lowest title among our miscreants was a countess. The rest went on up from that to dukes and princes. We figured Goldwyn, who was becoming a man of the world, would like that." Charlie MacArthur listened to Hecht's dictation for a half hour before leaving the room. "I can't stand bad writing," he said. By the time he awoke the next day, the scenario was complete. Leland Hayward tied a blue ribbon around it and delivered it to Goldwyn.

Ronald Colman had no choice but to appear in the films Goldwyn as-signed, no matter how inferior the material. Arthur Hornblow, Jr., ob-served that Colman became even more remote toward his employer than usual; but, professional that he was, Colman "entered into the filming in his precise, organized manner—always on time at the studio, always in command of the entire script on the first day. He continued to look casu-ally immaculate and was never anything but polite to cast and crew. Inside, however, he was fuming." Goldwyn sensibly hired George Fitz-maurice, who would direct Colman for the eighth time. For the embezzler's granddaughter, Goldwyn hired a brunette with several years of undistinguished experience, Fay Wray, whose hair he predictably bleached. "It was the talk of the studio that Ronnie was not speaking to Goldwyn," Fay Wray remembered, "and there was something rather admirable in the air he had, the fact that he could be doing pictures for Sam and still not tolerate any communication."

The Unholy Garden would forever stand as the worst blot on the records of everyone involved with it. Pare Lorentz, reviewing the film in the New York *Journal,* was completely bewildered at Hecht and MacArthur's even putting their names to such hash. John Cohen, in the New York *Sun,* said it was Colman's worst performance, his first "really mediocre picture." Years after its worldwide release, the film was still some $200,000 in the hole, the largest deficit on Goldwyn's books. It did not destroy Fay Wray's career altogether. Two years later, she became immortalized as the object of King Kong's affection.

In his next Colman picture, Goldwyn attempted to atone for all *The Unholy Garden*'s sins. He succeeded in every department, except in delivering an appropriate role for his star. It was Sidney Howard who first suggested that a film could be made of Sinclair Lewis's celebrated 1925 novel, *Arrowsmith.* Hollywood had not expressed the slightest interest in adapting the book, because of both its style and its substance. An episodic plot such as this—an idealistic doctor trains under a disillusioned but dedicated scientist, then moves to a small-town practice in North Dakota, the health department of a small city, an "institute" maintained by a wealthy couple, an isolated West Indian island, and a remote Vermont farm—tends to fight dramatic structure. The conflicts were intellectual, nothing at which one could aim a camera. The attitude among Hollywood filmmakers toward such works had long been one often falsely attributed to Sam Goldwyn: "If you want to send a message, call Western Union."

Sidney Howard said he could craft a gripping personal drama by truncating most of the story before Arrowsmith became a doctor in North Dakota, then focusing on the dramatic differences between his life there, at the McGurk Institute, and, finally, in the tropics, searching for the cure for bubonic plague. Those years would also include his courtship, marriage, and an extramarital dalliance. That Goldwyn might produce another script by his Pulitzer Prize–winning dramatist (an adaptation of a Pulitzer Prize–winning book by America's only Nobel laureate), that he could immediately rehire the blockful of fine actors who were completing their work on *Street Scene,* and that Ronald Colman could play the lead, were enough to spark his enthusiasm. While Charles MacArthur was in town, ostensibly working for him, Goldwyn chased his wife.

Helen Hayes had just finished filming her first talking picture, *The Sin of Madelon Claudet*. Although she had no following among filmgoers, Goldwyn was convinced *Arrowsmith* needed an actress of her caliber to put it over with the public. Miss Hayes had liked neither the experience of acting for the camera nor the routine of studio life. "I was bewildered by it all," she said, looking back. "It was not my way of doing things, and so I was a little leery of doing another, even though everybody was touting Sam Goldwyn as the best producer in town." It was that letter he mentioned on the *Street Scene* set, praising himself to the skies, that persuaded her. "He said, 'That's how good my pictures are,'" Miss Hayes recalled, "and it just won me over."

Goldwyn also got lucky off another studio's misfortune. In Fox's upheaval, they had suddenly come up short of projects for their contract director of ten years, John Ford. His agent did not have a difficult time talking Goldwyn into using the brilliant Irishman (born Sean O'Fearna), then just coming into his own.

Sidney Howard's script delivered everything he promised. He compressed scores of the novel's pages into a few expository scenes; and boy met girl on page eight. Curiously, the very elements that distinguished the screenplay in 1931 are those that eventually dated it. One of the first talking pictures to argue issues, it had its say in the most literal fashion. Almost every scene talked directly about one of the film's themes, with hardly a subtle or ironic word. Conversations became colloquies.

Martin Arrowsmith was an attractive hero, charming and intelligent. But forty-year-old Ronald Colman of Richmond, Surrey, was woefully miscast as the quixotic Midwesterner, especially ill-suited in his early scenes as a medical student. The actor knew it. As a result, Helen Hayes found her leading man "curiously distant and phlegmatic." Colman was always punctual and prepared, but he had taken to grousing about his life under the Goldwyn yoke. "Look at me," he said one day to Miss Hayes. "What do I do? I just bring the body to the studio and say my lines." She was "humiliated for him."

Colman's discontent showed up on the screen. He appeared either somnambulistic or stilted, especially stagy alongside the natural Miss Hayes. Myrna Loy played Joyce Lanyon, one of the last of her vampy supporting roles before MGM elevated her to leading-lady status.

"Then halfway through 'Arrowsmith' I played a dirty trick on Sam Goldwyn," confessed Helen Hayes. Her MGM picture was completed, and the studio previewed it in the gashouse district of Huntington Park, on a bill with *Red Dust*. "Here was this audience in leather jackets who had come to see Gable and Harlow," remembered Miss Hayes, "and then they got 'Madelon Claudet.'" Her tearjerking story of an unwed mother bombed that night. The studio considered not releasing it, until the leading lady's husband said the film only needed a new ending, which he would provide. With the star filming *Arrowsmith,* however, they could not reshoot it—until Helen Hayes said she would secretly moonlight over the next few Sundays. Without any days off, Miss Hayes found herself dragging through her work on the Goldwyn picture. One Saturday night at the Goldwyns', Sam caught her yawning. When the actress accidentally let fall that she had to get up early the next morning, Goldwyn pounced on the remark and would not let go until she admitted that she had been sneaking out to work on *Madelon Claudet.* Goldwyn stopped screaming at her only when Charles MacArthur "threatened never to cross Sam Goldwyn's threshold again. He swore he would never speak to the man."

The Sin of Madelon Claudet opened, and the leading lady received raves as well as the Academy Award for Best Actress. She had become a bona fide movie star by the time *Arrowsmith* reached the theaters. Charlie MacArthur stuck to his word and kept his distance from Sam Goldwyn for several years. Then, one summer day, the MacArthurs and their three-year-old daughter found themselves at Anita Loos's beach house, next door to the Goldwyns. The whole family ventured out onto the sand, when— Helen Hayes recalled—"suddenly Sam swooped down and grabbed up our child and ran off to his house with her. And we went chasing after him to recover our offspring. By the time we caught him, we were all laughing so hard that . . . well, Sam was always very dear after that."

Most of the reviews of *Arrowsmith* commented on the strain in accepting Ronald Colman in the title role but complimented the rest of the film. Richard Day's sets were lauded, as was John Ford's direction, which was just starting to find a style of its own at a time when "screen connoisseurs were beginning to wonder whether the medium would ever recover the visual eloquence it once enjoyed." In shot after shot, especially in Leora's death scene, observed film curator Richard Griffith, "they saw as beautifully developed a camera passage as any silent films had provided, and a unity of camera treatment throughout which was unknown in that day of shapeless talkies."

Many critics cited Goldwyn for his courage in producing the picture and thanked him for elevating the medium. The *New York Times* called him a man with "a desire to lead the public rather than follow it." Nobody believed the praise any more than Goldwyn himself. "The success of AR-ROWSMITH means as much to you as it does to me," Goldwyn wrote Irving Thalberg, whose proficiency and prosperity he admired more than anyone else's, "because you are continually trying to do the better things on the screen, and ARROWSMITH's success will ultimately encourage every producer of motion pictures to attempt the better things, instead of continuing to flood the country with so many of the bad pictures that are now being shown." The film broke even.

For the first time, Goldwyn found himself named as the producer of one of the year's best pictures. He did not win. But for Goldwyn, even this much recognition—placing him alongside King Vidor for producing *The Champ*, Adolph Zukor for *Shanghai Express*, Ernst Lubitsch for *One Hour with You* and *The Smiling Lieutenant*, Hal B. Wallis for *Five Star Final*, Winfield Sheehan for *Bad Girl*, and Irving Thalberg for that year's winner, *Grand Hotel*—was an honor he had long awaited. He would not be content until an Academy Award was his.

Goldwyn's next attempt further alienated his leading man. The protagonist of the hit play *Cynara* seemed at first glance as right a role for Ronald Colman as Arrowsmith had been wrong. "There are two things in the world you can trust—the Church of England and Jim Warlock," insists Clemency Warlock in describing her husband, a staid London barrister, seven years into his marriage. In his wife's absence, however, Jim Warlock drifts into innocent conversation with a shopgirl, only to find himself ensnared in an affair that results in her suicide. Throughout the ensuing scandal and inquest, Warlock adheres to his gentlemanly code. Instead of dredging up the girl's racy past, he silently suffers for his own transgression, sacrificing his career and marriage. He exiles himself to South Africa. As his ship sets sail, Clemency rushes aboard to be with him. The play's title was borrowed from a line of Ernest Dowson's poem "Cynara," then popular, which read: "I have been faithful to thee, Cynara, in my fashion." The Goldwyn advertising department noted in all its promotion that the title was pronounced "SIN-ara."

Therein lay the trouble. "Ronnie was not more difficult to cater for than other big stars," recounted Arthur Hornblow, Jr., but he wanted only "romantic, attractive roles to suit his image." The idea of Colman's playing an adulterer appalled the actor, as it did Goldwyn. But almost ten months had passed after the filming of *Arrowsmith,* and the producer was desperate to make the most of the final two years on his star's contract. "Finding material" seemed to be all Goldwyn talked about. One day, in fact, Harpo Marx came to the Goldwyns' house and found Sammy deep in the funny papers. "What are you reading, Sammy?" he asked. Said the boy, barely school age, "I'm looking for a Ronald Colman story, Mr. Marx." Goldwyn hired Frances Marion and King Vidor, who had just collaborated on *The Champ,* to write and direct *Cynara.* In his seventeenth picture for Goldwyn, Colman had never felt more ill at ease in a role. He believed his fans "were not willing to accept him as an actor if it detracted from his personality as a star."

One day during the filming of *Cynara,* Goldwyn's publicity chief, Lynn Farnol, was talking to movie columnist Sidney Skolsky. Farnol let slip that Ronald Colman often took a nip of liquor before performing his love scenes. He got carried away and said, "He believes that by getting more than slightly drunk, he plays love-scenes—well, more in love." Skolsky stretched that and wrote, "He feels that he looks better for pictures when moderately dissipated than when completely fit." Colman stormed into Goldwyn's office when the story appeared and demanded Farnol's firing. "I told him that I thought it was a mistake that the publicity man had made but that I did not think it was a thing that ought to cost a man his job and that I was not going to fire him," said Goldwyn. "As a matter of fact I knew that my publicity man, with whom Ronald had raised cain before he stormed into my office, had apologized to Ronald and offered to do anything within his power to correct the story." Days passed in silence, during which time Colman conferred with an attorney.

"RONALD COLMAN SUES GOLDWYN FOR MILLIONS," clarioned a six-column banner headline across page one of the September 13, 1932, Los Angeles *Herald-Express.* Photographs of the two principals filled the remaining two columns at the top of the page. Colman sought one million dollars in actual damages and an equal amount by way of punishment for Farnol's suggesting "that he was drunk and dissipated."

Goldwyn discussed the matter with the man he regarded as the ultimate authority on libel in America, his friend W. R. Hearst. "When a man has a weak case," Hearst handwrote in a six-page letter from San Simeon, "he generally sues for a large amount of money in the hope of frightening the defendant into a settlement." He did not believe Goldwyn had committed any libel against Colman; and even though Goldwyn was "in a sense responsible for the slander your employe committed," Hearst did not believe any jury would hold him "responsible in damages for all the loose talk of your employes."

Before any further ransom was demanded, Goldwyn hustled Colman into another film, even though he did not intend to release it for most of a year. *The Masquerader* had a hokey "Prince and the Pauper" gimmick, which enabled Colman to play dual roles—a journalist and his look-alike cousin, a drug-addicted Member of Parliament who becomes incapacitated in time of a national crisis. The double is secretly substituting for Sir John on the floor of Parliament when the actual M.P. dies in seclusion, forcing the masquerader to play the role for the rest of his life.

Goldwyn never worked with Colman again. The actor dropped his lawsuit and announced that he was "tired of making pictures." He said he wanted "a voice in the selection of stories in which he is to appear and also that he have something to say about the kind of publicity sent out about him." When Goldwyn gave him no satisfaction, Colman said he was returning to England and might make pictures there. Goldwyn reminded the actor that he was still under exclusive contract. Colman said he refused to appear in any more pictures for Goldwyn; the producer said he refused to let him work elsewhere. It was a stalemate.

In 1933, the Art Cinema division of United Artists folded, and a new company moved onto the lot. The dynamic Darryl F. Zanuck had left Warners and formed Twentieth Century Productions with Joe Schenck. (Louis B. Mayer helped finance this rival venture to ensure a position in the company for his son-in-law William Goetz.) As president of this new independent company, Schenck offered Colman a long-term contract. The actor refused it, noting, "As soon as I am free to do so, I shall free-lance. Should you have a story in mind that would suit me and attract me, I should like to make a picture for you. . . . As to the Goldwyn matter, I never expected any apology. A contradiction, or statement of correction was what we asked for, and it may quite likely be late for that now. In which, freedom from the contract becomes the chief consideration."

Because of Schenck's repeated favors to him over the years, Goldwyn said he would spring Colman from the rest of his contract—"unconditionally"—provided Colman would make one more picture with Goldwyn. "Personally, if you'd accept my advice in the spirit in which it is given," Schenck wrote Colman, vacationing in France, "I would say that it is important for you not to stay off the screen too long. You have a picture out now—THE MASQUERADER—which is a success and you ought to follow it up with another picture. . . . You may dislike his method of operation or his method of approach but you surely can stand it for one picture when you stood it for nine years, particularly now that you have had a good, long rest and your nerves are in a much better condition than when you left for Europe." Colman could not stand it, even at the risk of sacrificing his career. For almost two years, Ronald Colman—one of the biggest stars in the world—did not appear before a camera.

As soon as Colman had finished serving his Goldwyn time, Schenck and Zanuck offered him the ideal return vehicle, the aptly titled *Bulldog Drummond Strikes Back.* Free of Goldwyn, Colman's petrifying career sprang to life. He appeared in the series of roles for which he is still warmly remembered—Clive of India, Sidney Carton (doing a far, far better thing than he had ever done before), Robert Conway in *Lost Horizon, The Prisoner of*

Zenda, and François Villon (proclaiming, "If I were king . . .")—all in just the next four years.

Goldwyn's neglect drove another longtime employee from his organization. For almost four years, Arthur Hornblow, Jr., had been responsible for attracting almost every important Goldwyn property and writer; he had smoothed actors' feathers when Goldwyn had ruffled them; he had translated Goldwyn's garbled demands for improving his pictures into clear and concise suggestions to the artists involved. And after working day by day with Goldwyn on more than a dozen pictures, he had not once received a single credit on the screen. Hornblow broached this inequity with Goldwyn. But as Alva Johnston later recorded, "Sam's reaction to this was like that of Henry IV when he caught the Prince of Wales trying on the crown; he was wounded to the heart. The fact that Hornblow was entitled to screen credit, by all the canons of Hollywood, did not affect Sam. He was ready to give more money, European vacations, or anything except participation in the Goldwyn fame." Hornblow's was one of the few amicable departures in Goldwyn's life. They remained friends, as Hornblow went on to produce *Ruggles of Red Gap, Gaslight, The Asphalt Jungle, Witness for the Prosecution,* and *Oklahoma!* He never hesitated to call on Goldwyn for advice.

AMID his rotation of Ronald Colman dramas and Broadway adaptations for Art Cinema, Goldwyn had counted heavily on his cash crop, Eddie Cantor. While the financial and critical rewards of his other pictures fluctuated in the early thirties, big-budget Cantor extravaganzas became the staple of his production cycle.

Cantor had a story idea he had come up with in a Broadway midnight coffee shop, about his childhood friend Sidney Franklin, a kid from Brooklyn who had gone to Spain and become a world-class matador. Cantor could already picture a hilarious finale, with him alone in the ring with a ferocious bull. "Goldwyn," he remembered, "didn't think the public would go for anything Spanish at the time." Cantor disagreed. He pointed out the vast European market *Whoopee!* had opened up for both of them and said, "besides, to make a picture in which we did a ten-minute bull-fight sequence in pantomime—a universal language—how could we lose."

The producer committed instead to another story called *Palmy Days.* It reinforced the flimsy structure of *Whoopee!* and set in concrete the basic plot of all Goldwyn's future Cantor productions. The star would portray a mousy but adorable character named Eddie (this time Eddie Simpson, an unwitting assistant to a crooked palmist, mistakenly hired as an efficiency expert at a bakery), who bumps up against a gang of thugs. A secondary story would follow two young lovers, while Eddie becomes the apple of some brassy dame's eye—in this case, Charlotte Greenwood playing a physical culturist, whom Eddie refers to as a "physical torturist." Each picture would open with a big production number showing off the Goldwyn Girls, slip irrelevantly into a blackface number, usually about "his girl," and wind up with a slapstick chase, at the end of which everything is righted. *Palmy Days* grossed well over one million dollars.

Cantor renewed with Goldwyn for five more pictures over the next five years. After the success of *Palmy Days,* Goldwyn asked to see the Spanish story Cantor had worked up and bought it. On this picture, Goldwyn also tried a tactic Irving Thalberg would later adopt in working with the Marx Brothers. He sent Cantor, his songwriters, and Alfred Newman to San Francisco, where, four times a day for a week, the star tried out material in the huge Fox Theater. After "changing, revising, interpolating, [and] polishing" their script, based on public response, they received Goldwyn's authorization, and cameras rolled.

Betty Grable led the opening number, "The College Song"; another of the "coeds" was Paulette Goddard. Expelled from the university for raiding the girls' dormitory, Eddie Williams and his roommate, Ricardo (played by Robert Young), go to the latter's home in Mexico. Before leaving America, Eddie stumbles into a bank heist and is forced to cross the border. In Mexico, he is mistaken for a matador and must prove himself in the bull-ring. Goldwyn invited several friends to watch the filming of the bullfight sequence. Under wide sombreros, among the hundreds of extras, sat Harpo Marx, Harold Lloyd, Douglas Fairbanks, and Chaplin.

The million dollars Samuel Goldwyn had borrowed in order to make *The Kid from Spain* was the Bank of America's first seven-figure loan for a motion picture. Throughout the production, Goldwyn kept assuring Dr. Giannini that he was working overtime, pinching every penny. In a plea for sympathy, he told Giannini that only that morning Frances had remarked, "Sam, how drawn you look." "What she meant," Giannini corrected, "was overdrawn."

Frances was still tossing in bed at night as her husband seemed to be constantly robbing Peter to pay Paul, waiting for foreign sales of the last picture to help pay off the debt on the present one, whose returns would be applied toward financing the next. By 1932, Goldwyn was discernibly coming out ahead. An accounting of that year's first five months showed a profit close to $70,000, bringing the assets of Samuel Goldwyn, Inc., and its subsidiary companies just above $2 million. Most was tied up in his productions and United Artists stock; the rest of his portfolio, conservatively invested in utilities, had lost one third of its value in the last year. Goldwyn's personal account for day-to-day expenses was close to $200,000. His life was insured for $305,000 under nine different policies.

This Cantor picture did slightly less business than its predecessor, but it was still big box office. Goldwyn promptly paid back his Bank of America loan. Within a few years, he had a credit line of $4 million. That increase made Frances nervous. While her husband's primary interest in making money was to be afforded the luxury of making more movies, Frances still yearned for security.

As Hollywood continued building up into a prosperous business district, it became less fashionable as a residential area. Frances wondered whether her present property would hold its value. In the heart of the motion picture community—on a knoll just above the Beverly Hills Hotel and below Pickfair—she saw three lots on a short, winding private road off Coldwater Canyon called Laurel Lane. Director Wesley Ruggles lived in the one house already built (which tire magnate Leonard Firestone would later buy); a second lot would remain vacant for decades; and Frances Goldwyn persuaded her husband to buy the third—two and one-half acres full of promise.

With all her fears about spending money, she was completely in charge of constructing their house. She built the place piecemeal, whenever she saw enough money in the family cookie jar to pay for each job. Architect Douglas Honnold drew the plans, but she called on Richard Day and Alexander Gollitzen from the studio to cut corners wherever they could. Studio labor installed the guts of the house. "The result," observed Sam Goldwyn, Jr., "was that so much of the place—like the electrical wiring— was very Mickey Mouse." It would take more than two years before the Goldwyns could leave the Camino Palmero house in Hollywood.

Until then, Sam Goldwyn was front-page news—building his dream palace in Beverly Hills, receiving praise for the artistry of his pictures, tangling with prominent actors and writers. His scuffles with the English language became the delight of Hollywood columnists. The current favorite making the rounds followed several days of bad weather that held up filming on *The Kid from Spain:* Goldwyn told director Leo McCarey, "Tomorrow we shoot, whether it rains, whether it snows, whether it stinks." His active press department worked overtime seeing to it that whenever he appeared in print, he sounded eloquent and looked elegant.

Nobody took greater note of this new image than Goldwyn's daughter, Ruth. "He was loud and his clothes were loud," she remembered. "And then suddenly there he was beautifully and quietly dressed, and very courtly. It was all so strange; he seemed almost manufactured. And I used to ask myself, 'Is it possible he's my father?'"

To Ruth, her father was exactly the man he had been for most of the last decade, absent and hostile. He had nothing to do with her or her mother. For more than four years, Goldwyn had failed to make his weekly alimony and child support payments. Ruth's allowance was to double to five thousand dollars per annum upon her twenty-first birthday.

Ruth had grown into an attractive young woman, tall and slender. In her late teens, she studied art in Paris, where she met and fell in love with a gentle and good-looking artist named Henry McClure Capps. He went by the name Mac. "I was dying to marry him," Ruth recalled, "but to help me be sure, I sat down with a pencil and paper and made two columns and listed the pros and cons." The biggest liability she could jot down was "He'll never make a lot of money." After reading the words, she put her pencil to the opposing column and wrote, "Doesn't matter."

When Ruth told her mother's mother that she was marrying this Epis-copalian from Jacksonville, Illinois, old Sarah Lasky reared back. Religious only in her refusal to eat pork, she shouted, "You can't marry a Christian!" Ruth asked why and was told, "Because Jews make the best husbands!"

"You mean like my father?" Ruth snapped back, silencing her grandmother.

On January 20, 1932—five days short of her twentieth birthday—Ruth married Mac Capps. "We both had very small allowances," Ruth recalled of those years when they were starting out in New Haven, Connecticut, where he studied stage design at the Yale School of Drama; "but I honestly don't know how we ever ate."

Blanche Turnbull had found as much happiness as her newlywed daughter. The former vaudeville cornetist, who had ached all her adult life to be free of show business, was about to get her wish. Hector Turnbull had just managed to "goad the new head of Paramount into settling his contract for a considerable amount of cash." With this money, recalled Jesse Lasky, Jr., "he and Blanche planned to fulfill their dream of retiring to Pennsylvania on the old farm he had rebuilt with his own hands." Before moving, Blanche dragged her ex-husband into court, seeking $33,168.45 in back payments. "She had no feelings about him at that point," Ruth said. "Mother saved every penny from my father in a separate account for me."

Goldwyn claimed exemption from the payments because of custody violations of the divorce decree. He failed to mention that he had shown no interest in seeing his daughter for seven years, ever since the baked potato incident. Responding to the suit on January 25, 1932, Ruth's birthday,

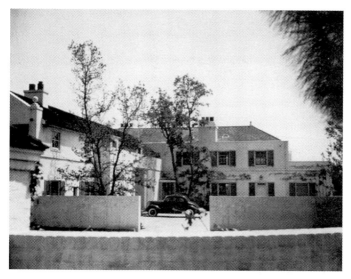

ABOVE: 1200 Laurel Lane, Beverly Hills, California, 1938. BELOW: Mrs. Irving Berlin and her daughter Mary Ellin, the closest friends of Mrs. Samuel Goldwyn and her son, Sammy.

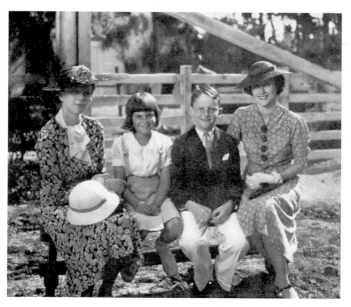

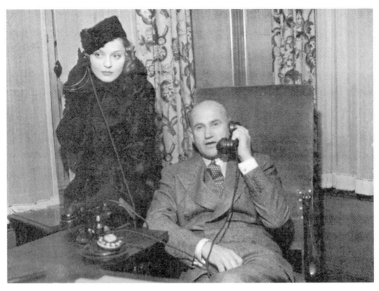

ABOVE: Goldwyn in 1932 with his "greatest discovery," Anna Sten. BELOW: The United Artists family in 1936: producers Douglas Fairbanks, Jr., Chaplin, Goldwyn, John Hay Whitney, David O. Selznick, Walter Wanger, Jesse Lasky, Douglas Fairbanks, and Roy Disney surround Mary Pickford.

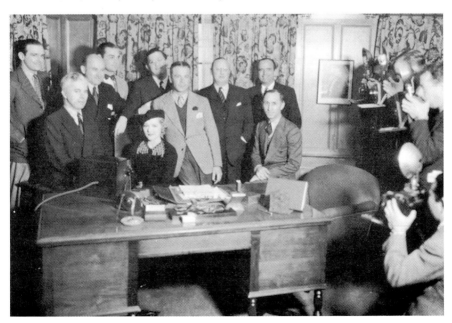

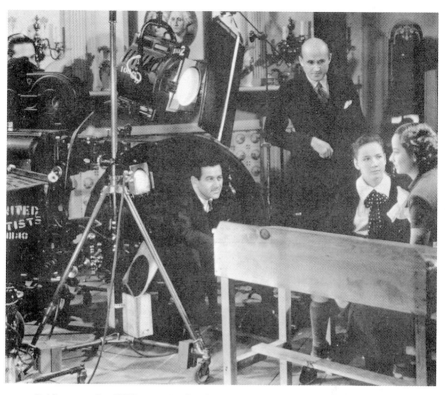

Goldwyn watches William Wyler direct Bonita Granville and Merle Oberon in *These Three*, the first of seven classic films on which producer and director would collaborate over the next ten years. Cameraman Gregg Toland looks on from the left.

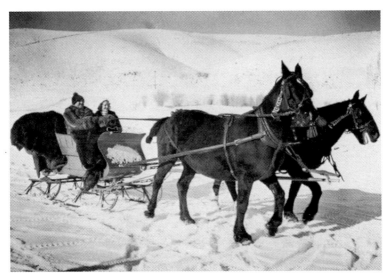

ABOVE: Sam recovered from a near-fatal illness in 1936 by spending the Christmas holidays with Frances in Sun Valley. BELOW: Goldwyn in 1937 with violinist Jascha Heifetz, around whom he created the film *They Shall Have Music*. Mrs. Heifetz was the former Florence Vidor, whom Goldwyn had courted in the 1920s.

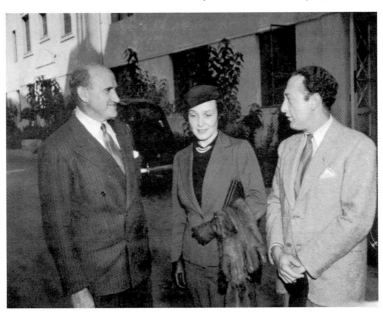

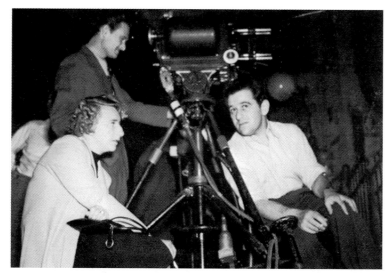

ABOVE: Lillian Hellman, Gregg Toland, and William Wyler—the core of Goldwyn's creative team in its heyday—on the set of *Dead End* (1937). BELOW: Goldwyn surveys the set of *The Hurricane* shortly before it was subjected to one of Hollywood's most spectacular displays of special effects.

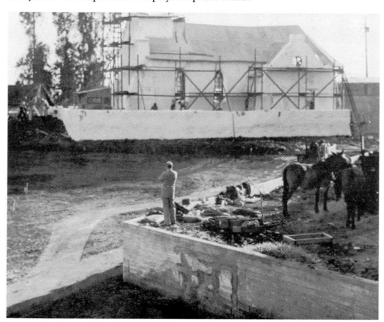

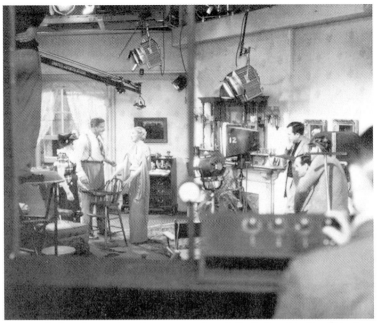

ABOVE: Barbara Stanwyck performs a scene from *Stella Dallas* with Alan Hale, in 1937, for director King Vidor. BELOW: Vidor and Goldwyn. After directing *Stella Dallas*, Vidor wrote a four-word note to himself, which he kept in his desk drawer for thirty years: "No more Goldwyn pictures."

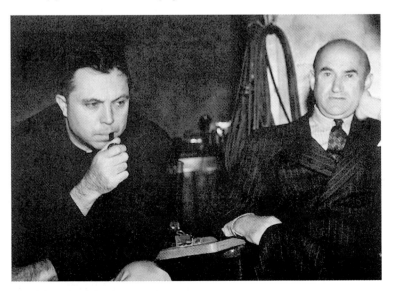

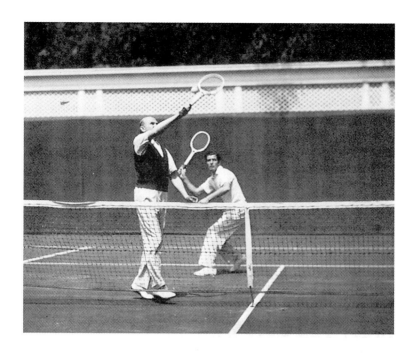

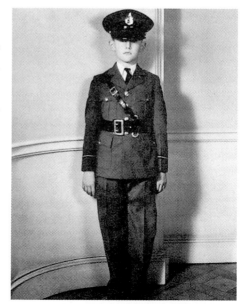

ABOVE: Goldwyn on the court at Laurel Lane, playing with champion Frank Shields, whom Goldwyn hoped to turn into a movie star. "Tennis you know," Goldwyn would yell at him. "Practice acting!"
RIGHT: Samuel Goldwyn, Jr., age nine, a cadet at Black-Foxe Academy, 1935.

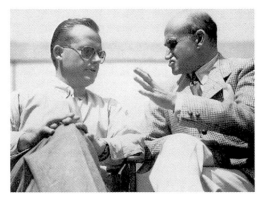

ABOVE: With the director Henry Potter, whose first picture was *Beloved Enemy,* 1936. BELOW: With his new stars Merle Oberon and David Niven, who were acting in *Beloved Enemy* and involved in a secret love affair, 1936.

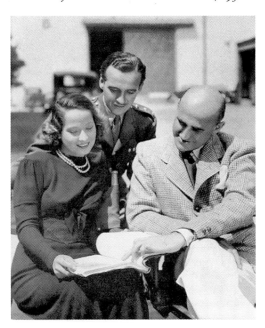

Goldwyn further claimed that her having a husband should exempt him from any further payments.

Goldwyn's pettifoggery took its toll on Blanche. Physically exhausted from weeks of legal battle, she agreed to settle out of court for $20,000 in cash. That was meant only to bring the records up to date, not to cancel future payments, to which she and Ruth were entitled for the rest of their respective lives. Living at the Ambassador Hotel in anticipation of her move east, Blanche contracted pneumonia. On March 3, 1932, the settlement papers were drawn up and Blanche signed them. Nine days later—while the documents were in the hands of Goldwyn's lawyers, awaiting his signature—Blanche died at the age of forty-nine.

Days passed, and Goldwyn still did not sign the agreement. It appeared he was trying to bury the whole matter with his ex-wife. Blanche's lawyer approached Ruth and said, "Your mother started this. I think you should finish it." She agreed, and the lawyer pressed for Goldwyn to affix his signature. On March 19, he complied and paid the $20,000.

Bereft of blood relations, Ruth started her own family. Within the first year of her marriage she was pregnant. By her sixth month, Ruth had celebrated her twenty-first birthday and her father had already missed the first two payments on the new $5,000 annual allowance due upon her coming of age. Ruth hired an attorney and served legal notice on her father. Both parties saw the opportunity to come to some kind of settlement, one that would cut the cord between them forever. Goldwyn informed James Mulvey, "For your personal information I would like to pay about $15,000 top."

On May 24, 1933—weeks into the lawyers' negotiating—Ruth handwrote a simple letter. "Dear Father," it said:

> You will probably think it strange to hear from me but I thought you might be interested to know that I am going to have a baby, in June.
>
> I am of course very pleased about it though it is difficult to get accustomed to the idea of being a mother.
>
> I daresay it will seem equally strange to you to think of being a grandfather.
>
> Your daughter
Ruth

Goldwyn's gut response was "to completely ignore the letter," believing that Ruth's lawyer had put her up to writing it. "If I had no lawsuit I would never answer the letter as I don't feel she is entitled to one," Goldwyn informed Mulvey, "and I don't intend to answer it." His attorneys also thought it was a ruse.

One month after Ruth's missive, McClure Capps wired the father-in-law he had never met: "RUTH HAD A BABY GIRL TONIGHT BOTH ARE SPLENDID." The birth signaled a weekend of truce to a month of lawyers' wrangling. Ruth's attorneys refused to budge from their demand for $25,000. First thing Monday morning, Goldwyn instructed Mulvey that he was "AGREEABLE TO PAY TWENTYFIVE THOUSAND BUT STRONGLY FEEL TWENTY THOUSAND SHOULD BE TOP." At the end of the day, Goldwyn asked Mulvey in a night letter to ascertain in which New York hospital Ruth was staying and to send flowers, with a card saying, "Am very happy for you. Father." The baby was named Blanche.

For the next three months, the lawyers haggled over $5,000. In mid-September, Goldwyn agreed to the $25,000, $10,000 on signing the agreement, the rest in quarterly payments without interest. On November 29, 1933, Ruth Capps signed quitclaims that forever discharged her father of all obligations.

The only trace of Ruth to remain in Goldwyn's life was her baby nurse, who still served as nanny to Sammy, then starting elementary school. Catherine McDonough had become a senile crone and a constant burr to Frances. She often filled the boy's ears with strange ravings. When they were alone, she would rant mysteriously about this girl Ruth, whom he had never heard of. One day in late 1932, she showed him a photograph in the newspaper of Governor Franklin D. Roosevelt and said, "This is a very bad man. If he comes to run this country, they'll take your father away." She would arbitrarily punish the boy by locking him in his bedroom closet. "But I didn't want to lose her," Sam Goldwyn, Jr., later recalled. He instinctively craved the insulation she provided against his father's overheated temper and his mother's icy reserve.

One day at Marion Davies's beach house, Sammy was in the oceanic pool when Catherine came out, screaming, "Nanny didn't give you permission!" She proceeded to "raise such hell" that Frances ran poolside, fearing bloody murder. When she learned the extent of the offense, she summoned all her courage and fired the woman on the spot. Sammy ran away in tears. Frances won the round, and the dismissal stuck. "Mother constantly spoke of that day," recalled Sam junior, "as her day of liberation."

Not long after that, Goldwyn prepared for a business trip, and Sammy pleaded with him not to leave. He cried "that this very bad man would keep him out of the country." In the boy's bedroom, Sam asked what he meant. He got to the bottom of the story and realized that Catherine had definitely overstayed her welcome. But he insisted on Sammy's thinking kindly of the old woman—"because she was wonderful with your sister." Sammy sat on his bed, stunned to learn that he had a sibling.

Sitting by his side, Goldwyn proceeded to tell him about Ruth. He spoke of her in the kindest way. "She's a wonderful girl," he said, his eyes starting to well up.

"When will I see her?" Sammy asked eagerly. For the longest time, Goldwyn sat in silence, tightening his lips, looking all around the room as though searching for answers.

When Sammy asked him again, his father began to sob.

14 "That Little Something Extra"

WHILE MOTION PICTURE attendance
steadily dropped, it seemed that a
handful of actresses was keeping the
major studios afloat. Bette Davis led Warner Brothers' fleet of films, appearing in eleven roles in 1932 alone. By the time she was eight, the
insuperable optimism of Fox's Shirley Temple had made her the number
one box-office attraction in America. Katharine Hepburn had become the
pride of RKO, making four films back to back in her first eighteen months
in Hollywood. Marlene Dietrich and Mae West kept Paramount breathing
hard. MGM met the public's appetite with a steady serving of Joan Crawford pictures; and they dangled a Garbo film before the public annually.
Without a leading man or leading lady to his name—except for the specialty act of Eddie Cantor, good for one production a year—Sam Goldwyn
was desperate for an actress around whom he could mobilize his production
army, a woman with star power, what George Cukor called "that little
something extra."

With a whole new generation of talking-picture personalities, Hollywood turned to the meatiest volumes on the shelves of source material,
confident of its ability to adapt history and the classics. Darryl Zanuck
produced *The House of Rothschild, Clive of India, Cardinal Richelieu,* and *Les
Misérables,* all within two years of founding Twentieth Century. At MGM,
Irving Thalberg's reputation continued to grow, with his film versions of
The Barretts of Wimpole Street, Mutiny on the Bounty, and *Rasputin and the
Empress,* starring John, Lionel, and Ethel Barrymore; he would soon hire

George Cukor to direct *Romeo and Juliet* and *Camille*. David O. Selznick left RKO in 1933 and produced *David Copperfield, Anna Karenina,* and *A Tale of Two Cities* in a single year on his father-in-law's lot. In 1935, he established his own company; under the Selznick-International shingle he made *Little Lord Fauntleroy, The Prisoner of Zenda,* and *Tom Sawyer.*

After thirty-four independent productions over the preceding ten years, Sam Goldwyn had not based a single film on a time-honored work of literature or an important historical figure. Most of his pictures had been translations of Broadway hits or recent popular novels. Sitting in his Hollywood office in early 1932, he suddenly seized upon the idea of producing a version of *The Brothers Karamazov*. The book itself could never have captured Goldwyn's attention; a woman's face staring out at him from the rotogravure section of a New York newspaper did. The actress's likeness was part of an advertisement for a German film of the novel that was playing at a small art theater off Broadway. Her name was Anna Sten.

She was born Anjuschka Stenski in Kiev in 1908. Another fatherless beauty, she found her way to that actors' mecca, the Moscow Art Theater. After several small roles in one of Stanislavsky's companies, she was admitted to the prestigious Mezhrabpom-Russ film studio. Anjuschka Stenski made several pictures and became the protégée of director Fedor Ozep. They married and went to Berlin, just as the Nazis were turning the German film industry into their propaganda factory. Ozep shortened his star's name and directed her in *The Brothers Karamazov.*

No prints of the film were available in Los Angeles, so Goldwyn wired his New York office to scare one up and rush it out by air express. The print arrived the day he was departing on a business trip to New York, literally minutes before he left the office. He hastened to his projection room and watched the first reel. The newspaper photograph had not done her justice. Anna Sten did not have the angular beauty of Garbo and Hepburn, then in vogue. She was the classic girl of Goldwyn's fantasies—a fair face, soft and round, with a slightly pug nose; huge, inviting eyes; cascades of flaxen hair; a curvaceous, fleshy body. When she opened her generous mouth, she spoke with a low, attractive throatiness. She moved with sensuous authority. Her acting was earthy and realistic. By the start of the second reel, Goldwyn had seen enough. He had not felt this way since first casting eyes on Vilma Banky. Racing for his train, he dispatched Lynn Farnol to Europe to sign her. Without even knowing if she could speak a word of English, he was determined to present her in an American version of *The Brothers Karamazov.*

Miss Sten had recently been in a minor automobile accident, and out of the other car had emerged an attractive man named Eugene Frenke.

As Miss Sten told it, they fell in love—rather the way people in the movies did. She left Ozep to marry Frenke, who would manage her career. When Goldwyn's agent called on them, she followed Frenke's lead and played dumb.

Goldwyn believed one got what one paid for, that spending more made something worth more. If he expected to launch Anna Sten into the stratosphere of stars, Goldwyn figured he should pay her as one. Sten and Frenke sat there mute as Farnol offered her a four-year contract—$1,500 per week for forty weeks of work the first year, $2,000 a week the second. They grabbed it.

The salary was nothing compared to the money Goldwyn would lay out to justify his expenditure. He intended to spend more promoting Anna Sten than had ever been invested in a new star. Ultimately, Anna Sten would have to pay the price.

While negotiating for the rights to the German version of *The Brothers Karamazov,* Goldwyn marshaled all his promotional forces into developing a public persona for Anna Sten. Above all, Goldwyn believed every star needed individuality. "Any time that an actor tries to imitate or copy another," he said in a local radio interview, "he is finished . . . the public never wants to see two stars of the same type."

Lynn Farnol, the chief engineer of Anna Sten's public facade, concurred. He told Goldwyn that "it would be a mistake to try to play [Anna Sten] up as a Greta Garbo–Marlene Dietrich. . . . For one thing, she doesn't exactly belong in the group, and the comparisons that would inevitably follow might not be good." Farnol suggested they build on her actual history as much as possible, that they capitalize on her being the first great star from the new Soviet Union. On March 7, 1932, Farnol wrote Goldwyn from Europe, reeling off Sten's many assets. He did not forget to add one liability: "She speaks . . . not a word of English."

With too much stardust in his eyes to see that as a problem, Goldwyn chose to turn Anna Sten into a mysterious fairy-tale princess. "The Passionate Peasant" was the title of the first major publicity piece he authorized. "The Soviet Cinderella," it read, "embarked in a sea-going pumpkin for a fling at Hollywood fame and fortune." Over the ensuing months, Goldwyn assumed that the world would be gripped by her allure as he was, spellbound by that countenance of timeless, enigmatic beauty. "She has the face," Goldwyn took to telling people, "of a spink."

Goldwyn urged the United Artists offices in Europe to keep Anna Sten under wraps. Because the first impression she would make in America was of such importance, Goldwyn sent her to Paris for Chanel to outfit her. While the *Europa* was at sea, Goldwyn cabled Farnol to "PLEASE GIVE

SOME THOUGHT TO AN EXPRESSION OR REMARK STEN MAY MAKE ON
ARRIVAL NEW YORK THAT WOULD BE OF SENSATIONAL NATURE BUT AT
SAME TIME NOT OFFENSIVE OR DETRIMENTAL TO HER PERSONALITY. . . .
GIVE THIS CAREFUL CONSIDERATION AND DISCUSS WITH OTHER GENIUSES
OF YOUR TYPE AND WIRE ME."

Farnol agreed that a piquant statement from Anna Sten would create
the kind of stir they all hoped for; but he also had the duty of reporting:
"HER KNOWLEDGE OF ENGLISH . . . IS STILL GROTESQUELY BAD AND
GROSSLY INADEQUATE FOR EVEN ORDINARY CONVERSATION." Without a
proper wardrobe, Farnol also found her "COMPARABLE ORDINARY PICTURE
PLAYER." Farnol arranged an unpretentious arrival. "Darling, sweetheart,"
Anna Sten told the crew of reporters waiting at the dock on April 18,
1932, "I lof you." Then, in her Chanel frock and hat and her own mussy
imitation-fur coat and rubber-soled tennis sneakers, she was hidden away
at the Hotel Pierre. Four days later, Farnol chaperoned Sten on the train
journey across America to Hollywood, where he had set up interviews only
with "people of assured sympathy and interest."

After journeying close to ten thousand miles, Anna Sten had the rug
pulled out from under her. Goldwyn announced that he was not going to
produce *The Brothers Karamazov* after all. He had gotten enraged over the
property's legal complications and had also been engaged in battle with
Ronald Colman, whom he had hoped to star. Goldwyn scrapped the project and told his staff to find a project worthy of a star. "You see," Goldwyn
would later explain, "she is such a dominating personality, it would have
been out of the question to cast her in secondary roles. . . . Either she
would be a star or nothing . . . the thing was to present her as brilliantly
as possible, and see whether or not the public would accept her. She could
not have been brought before them slowly. She wasn't the type."

Before leaving his employ, Arthur Hornblow had thrown the plots of
several classics at Goldwyn until he heard one he liked, *Nana*. Zola's girl
of the Parisian streets was just the sort of doomed heroine Garbo was making so popular. When Goldwyn heard that Nana had raised herself from
the gutter by becoming a chanteuse (which would allow his star to show
off her singing ability, like Dietrich), he was sold. Goldwyn's team of
writers spent the better part of a year breaking the massive book down
into a shootable film script. The process took longer than usual because of
Arthur Hornblow's absence. Two men were necessary to fill his shoes:
Twenty-seven-year-old Fred Kohlmar took over the production duties; and
an energetic man of letters named George Oppenheimer, who had helped
found the Viking Press, assumed the editorial responsibilities. Goldwyn
called him "Oppenheim."

Meantime, Anna Sten was stashed in a rented house in Santa Monica. She spent two hours each morning and each afternoon with an English teacher—"she was a German," recalled Miss Sten. "I don't know how I ever got out of it without a German accent. I never had any American teachers. My voice was given to me by God, not by Mr. Goldwyn. If he was worried about my accent, why did he give me a German teacher?" Goldwyn arranged for her to see at least three American motion pictures a week.

She endured more than a year of grooming. Fifty-one tests were made, to record not only the progress of her English but also her acting ability. Gregg Toland tried out every angle and lens for the optimal way of capturing her hair, her eyes, her costumes on film. Various makeups were tested under different lightings. "There were a good many jokes about Goldwyn with his accent instructing Sten with hers," noted George Oppenheimer, "but they were unfounded. Goldwyn backed up his confidence in his protégée with the best of everything—an English coach, dancing and singing teachers, speech instructors, a trainer and masseuse, since the lady had a tendency to put on weight and a rather unbridled appetite."

Goldwyn called on three of the foremost clothes designers to outfit her—Paramount's Travis Banton, Ziegfeld's John Harkrider, and MGM's leading stylist, Adrian. He went after no less a director than von Sternberg himself to stage her debut in American films. And he solicited Cole Porter to supply Nana with "a sexy recitative" along the lines of "Love for Sale" and a torch song in the manner of "What Is This Thing Called Love?" "YOU ARE THE ONE MAN IN THE WORLD TO WRITE TWO SONGS TO BE SUNG BY ANNA STEN IN HER FIRST PICTURE FOR ME," Goldwyn wired Porter in Paris in the spring of 1933. Porter refused, because he was composing a new musical; but he did salute the producer in the third refrain of his new show's title song:

> If Sam Goldwyn can with great conviction
> Instruct Anna Sten in diction,
> Then Anna shows
> Anything goes.

Goldwyn got Richard Rodgers and Lorenz Hart to write a minor-key lament called "That's Love."

WHILE the movies had done their best to keep America from fearing fear itself, times in Hollywood got harder. Even with theaters slashing ticket prices and adding a second film to the program—a double feature for the price of one—attendance in just the preceding two years had fallen off by one third, to some fifty million weekly viewers. After the new President launched his attack on the nation's economic crisis by closing the banks, studio leaders felt empowered to take drastic measures of their own.

Universal Studios suspended all their contracts by invoking the "national emergency" clause. Fox's 1,900 employees—from stars to messenger boys—volunteered to go on a four-week "salary holiday." Most other studio heads asked their workers for permission to cut wages by 50 percent for eight weeks, enough time to get through the emergency. All except one Goldwyn employee agreed to those terms. "This request comes at a time when I am in difficult financial straights [sic] because I have been here for ten months and during those ten months I have had lay-offs without pay for five and one-half months," Anna Sten wrote Goldwyn, then in New York. "I fully appreciate your own difficulties in the present crisis, and am willing to meet you half way by accepting half salary now, with the difference to be repaid me at a later date when conditions improve and you start my picture."

Sam Goldwyn was no doubt pleased to see the improvement in Anna Sten's English, but he fired off a telegram to her Beverly Hills house that minced no words:

YOU MUST REALIZE THAT THIS COUNTRY IS IN STATE OF PANIC AND CONDITIONS ARE MUCH MORE SERIOUS THAN CAN BE EXPLAINED IN TELEGRAM BUT ITS WELL YOU UNDERSTAND THAT LAST WEEK MY OWN PERSONAL RECEIPTS ON PICTURES WERE AFFECTED TO EXTENT OF EIGHTY THOUSAND DOLLARS THEREFORE ALL REASONS YOU ARE GIVING ME IN YOUR LETTER ARE GOING TO BE OF NO AVAIL STOP YOU WILL HAVE TO TAKE CUT JUST AS EVERYBODY CONNECTED WITH MOTION PICTURES WHETHER IN CALIFORNIA OR ANYWHERE ELSE IN COUNTRY. . . .

Anna Sten would not play ball. All she could see was "that I am asked to take a loss of $5,000 while you gain $5,000."

For weeks, the two Slavs engaged in a cold war marked by brinksmanship. Goldwyn accused her of lying about other stars who had refused to sign the agreement and threatened her with official actions he must take before the Motion Picture Academy. After a year of costly grooming, Sten knew perfectly well that Goldwyn was not about to jeopardize his investment. She claimed all these discussions were giving her heart trouble. In the end, Sten got her way.

Goldwyn's well-oiled machinery continued to crank out glowing publicity about her. He turned to his old friend Condé Nast, who agreed to a spread in *Vanity Fair*, with photographs by Edward Steichen. New stories of Goldwyn's dramatic discovery were released to all the syndicates.

By the summer of 1933, Goldwyn decided that *Nana* was ready to shoot. The Hays Office approved the script—so watered down from the original material that the credits would say the film had been "suggested by the novel by Emile Zola." Goldwyn engaged George Fitzmaurice, who had just directed Garbo in *Mata Hari*. Anna Sten took direction obediently but thought the film was "horrible." She later said, "It was not *Nana*, it was not me. I don't know what it was, but it wasn't exciting."

Into its fourth week, Goldwyn sat in the screening room for hours one afternoon, running the film over and over. Although he had invested close to $200,000 in Anna Sten and as much again in the film, he announced that he was shutting the picture down. The star asked for her release. Goldwyn assured her they were on the same side in this matter. The picture was "good enough" to play in theaters, he said, just not good enough to put her across as a star.

He commissioned veteran scenarist Willard Mack to pull together a more dramatic version of the script, he discharged the cast, and he paid off Fitzmaurice. It ended their relationship of eleven films over ten years. A few weeks later, Mack returned to Goldwyn's office and read the entire new script to him. Cameras were ordered to roll again. Lionel Atwill, fresh from the set of *Song of Songs*, opposite Dietrich, took over as leading man.

Goldwyn tried to hire George Cukor (then in the middle of his successful cycle of films for David Selznick at RKO), even though he felt the director had a tendency "to put lace panties on every scene." Frances, who fretted over her friend's career as much as her husband's, cautioned him against doing the picture. In addition to the chaos of the production, she thought the source material was too "artistic" and the star unproven. Cukor refused Goldwyn's offer, and the producer cursed him for weeks, saying Cukor was "biting the hand of the goose that laid the golden egg." When Cukor insisted he was too busy editing *Little Women*, Goldwyn turned to the director of *Christopher Strong*, Katharine Hepburn's second film.

For many years, Dorothy Arzner was the only woman directing at any of the major studios in Hollywood. She grew up in Hollywood, where her father owned a restaurant next to a theater, and found work at Famous Players–Lasky—as a typist, then as a script girl. After a few months, she moved into the cutting room, becoming one of the studio's most talented editors. She got to film a few shots for Valentino's *Blood and Sand,* and she began writing scripts in her spare time for Columbia. Upon submitting her next screenplay, Miss Arzner insisted that she would not sell it unless she could also direct it. Columbia accepted the deal, only to have her home studio better it when they heard Arzner might leave them. Goldwyn told her he thought *Christopher Strong* was the best picture of the year and that he hoped she could do as well with Sten as she had with Hepburn. Arzner had hoped for "a more important script" to help her in the task, but she accepted the challenge. "The only thing I could do," she later said of Sten, "was not let her talk so much."

Goldwyn's publicity machine went into overdrive, getting a lot of mileage out of his having junked $411,000 worth of film. When he liberally computed that starting *Nana* over again doubled his investment, Anna Sten suddenly became his "Million Dollar Discovery." Over one thousand newspapers carried his explanation: "When you are presenting a great star for the first time, and she is under contract to you for more than one picture, it is better to lose money on the first picture to make way for the second and third and so on."

Radio City Music Hall booked *Nana*—unprecedentedly guaranteeing Goldwyn a two-week run and 75 percent of the profits. "The country was Sten-conscious and eagerly awaited news of the opening," recalled George Oppenheimer. The Goldwyns had gone to New York for the February 1, 1934, premiere, in time to see Lynn Farnol's latest publicity effort. Every day for a week, the newspapers ran a different photograph of Sten in a seductive pose, captioned only with her name and an adjective: alluring, wistful, worldly, fascinating, mysterious, captivating. Then the name of the film was introduced into the ads, followed by such phrases as "America's Great New Star" and "A brilliant comet is born." W. R. Hearst pulled for his friend, splashing articles about Anna Sten all across his newspapers. Opening day of *Nana* broke all existing records at the Music Hall.

"IN SPITE OF FIRST BIG STORM HERE IN WEEKS," Goldwyn wired Abe Lehr on February 1, 1934, "PICTURE OPENED TO SENSATIONAL BUSINESS STOP THEY HAVE BEEN PACKED SINCE DOORS OPENED THOUSANDS OF PEOPLE STANDING IN LINE." In response to Alfred Newman's telegram of congratulations, Goldwyn wrote him on the fifth, "In all my years I have never known a woman to sweep . . . New York as she has. The line has never stopped at Radio City Music Hall since the picture opened. The success of STEN is the talk of New York." Goldwyn ordered the star hidden away, to add to her mystique. She went to Palm Springs incognito, and Goldwyn refused to let her be interviewed, not even by Louella Parsons.

The overnight reviews of *Nana* commented on the star's beauty but found the picture ordinary in every other respect. Practically all the criticism that followed (like the one in *Literary Digest*) pointed out Goldwyn's mistake in "presenting his young Ukrainian actress as one of those lyric, mysterious and studiously 'glamorous' screen personages that strive so desperately for the laurels of the great Garbo." Customers found the star as oversold as critics had found the movie overdone. The queues disappeared in the big cities and never even formed in the small towns. The film would not return its highly publicized cost. Zola's heirs applied to the French courts for permission to sue Goldwyn on the grounds that *Nana* had been "disfigured to a point where it is unrecognizable."

"Irrespective of how much I may lose on NANA," Goldwyn wrote Chicago theater owner John Balaban, "I am still going ahead and making and planning more Sten pictures."

Goldwyn's story department homed in on the actress's motherland for source material, settling on Tolstoy's auspiciously titled *Resurrection*. At first, the story of the spiritual regeneration of a young Russian nobleman hardly seemed grist for the movie mill. The novel had in fact reached the screen four times already, first in 1909, under Griffith's hand.

The broad strokes of the plot offered a strong role for Sten. A servant girl named Katusha is seduced by her mistress's nephew, Prince Dmitri, who leaves her pregnant and cavalierly joins his army regiment. She sinks into a life of prostitution in Moscow after the death of her child and soon stands trial for the murder of one of her customers. She meets Dmitri again in court, where he, about to marry into considerable money, is part of the jury unjustly condemning her to Siberia. He atones for all his wrongdoing by surrendering his property to his servants and joining her on the long march to exile, declaring, "All I ask is to live again with your forgiveness and your help and your love."

Goldwyn believed he had found the ideal director in Russian-born Rouben Mamoulian, who after years of experience in theater and film, had just directed Dietrich in *Song of Songs* and Garbo in *Queen Christina*. Tolstoy's *Resurrection* was one of his favorite books. Goldwyn told Mamoulian that despite its having been filmed several times already, "no one had ever understood the story in its true richness and drama," that it "has not been made until I make it."

Willard Mack was Goldwyn's first writer to adapt the Tolstoy novel. Of the old school of Hollywood scenarists, he detailed every piece of business and camera angle, so that the script "could be shot by the property man if we should all drop dead." Mamoulian was one of the new breed of directors who wanted the writer just to get the story down on paper in as few important speeches and scenes as were necessary. He liked to punch them up with his own strong visual style. Once Mack had the structure on paper, Mamoulian urged Goldwyn to give the pages to playwright Maxwell Anderson, whose adaptation of *What Price Glory?* and *All Quiet on the Western Front* combined poetic language with prosaic situations.

After several weeks, Goldwyn felt that Anderson was creating the characters out of marble more than flesh and blood. He called in Preston Sturges, a charming newcomer to Hollywood, "to bring out the people, emphasize the human as well as the class conflicts, and insert more lightness and humor." Sturges demanded $1,500 a week, a big enough jump in his asking price to make Goldwyn both distrust him and respect him. Sturges humanized the script with his special brand of banter. Goldwyn appreciated the contribution—what he once referred to as the "snappy nineteenth century dialogue." But after a few weeks he asked Mamoulian, "When can we get rid of this Sturgeon fella?"

Goldwyn hired one Leonard Praskins. His job was to blend the contrasting styles of his predecessors and to modulate the dialogue specifically for the voices of Anna Sten and Fredric March, whom he had been able to borrow from Irving Thalberg at MGM. March's career in pictures was just taking off after his winning the Academy Award for his performance in *Dr. Jekyll and Mr. Hyde,* and he was reluctant to appear second-billed opposite the possibly leprous Anna Sten. One hundred thousand dollars for a few weeks' work brought him around.

In late spring 1934, shooting of the picture, retitled *We Live Again,* began. Goldwyn then hired two of the director's friends from Broadway— Paul Green and Thornton Wilder—to give the script a final polish and to stay close at hand during production.

Fredric March was a dutiful soldier, making the most of his leaden supporting role and suffering in silence. One day, Goldwyn came on the set and found him morose. "Freddie," he said, trying to lift his spirits, "you got the best part in the picture." Then Goldwyn saw Sten sitting practically beside him. "And Anna," he added, without missing a beat, "you got the best part too."

Anderson, Praskins, and Sturges were the only writers to receive credit on the picture. The Screen Writers Guild had been formed in 1933, in an effort to put some teeth into what had previously been a more informal Writers Club. The Guild promptly composed a list of desires if not demands—that the industry become a guild shop, that contract writers not be lent between studios, that writers not be asked to write on speculation, that all writers working simultaneously on the same material be so notified by the producer, that blacklists be prohibited, and that writers receive screen credit according to their contribution to a picture. Over many years, those conditions would be met. For the time, producers still determined whose names they put on their films.

"Anna Sten shows dramatic ability of high order in a role less glamorous, but more exacting than her first," said *Variety* in its September 22, 1934, review of *We Live Again*. Within weeks of the opening, Anna Sten died again. "The public," Sam Goldwyn told George Cukor, "stayed away in droves."

Goldwyn was still not prepared to give up on her. Where the classics could not put Anna Sten across, Goldwyn figured, a new story with a strong leading man could. He had wanted to work with Gary Cooper ever since the cowboy slipped away after *The Winning of Barbara Worth*. In the ensuing eight years, Cooper had risen to stardom in thirty-seven pictures, his salary jacked to $6,000 a week plus whatever money he could pocket from the films he made off the Paramount lot. The Goldwyns invited Cooper and his new wife, Rocky (a former starlet, born Veronica Balfe), to dinner to discuss the possibility of his appearing with Anna Sten in an adaptation of a novel called *Barbary Coast*. By the time they had agreed on $75,000 for what would amount to a four-week job, Goldwyn had decided to put that costume piece in mothballs and to star Cooper opposite Sten in an original modern drama.

After more than a year with the assignment, George Oppenheimer found only one property for Anna Sten. *The Wedding Night*, by Edwin Knopf, was the love story between a jazz age novelist, who retreats to Connecticut to rediscover his muse, and a Polish peasant girl, the daughter of a neighboring tobacco farmer. The writer is already married to a socially ambitious wife in New York, and the girl is engaged to a local Polish farmer. A convenient snowstorm leads the reluctant lovers to kindle their feelings for each other. Manya, the beautiful Pole, proceeds with her marriage—only to race back to her new love on her wedding night. She trips to her death—providing an ending sure to appease the Furies at the Hays Office.

Goldwyn signed King Vidor to direct *The Wedding Night* as the first in a two-picture deal. Vidor looked forward to filming the Connecticut countryside and the colorful ritual of the Polish wedding that would be the climactic centerpiece of the film, but he dreaded working with the actors. Gary Cooper in the role of a Fitzgerald-like novelist seemed bad casting to Vidor; after hearing him mumble through a reading of the script, he "wondered how he could have carried his great success into the talkies." Anna Sten revealed more than a trace of an accent, as well as heavy gestures held over from her days in Russian silent pictures. The first day of shooting, Vidor discovered that Cooper could not get through a scene without forgetting some of the words, and it was difficult to make out those he remembered. After he saw the first day's rushes, however, Vidor discovered "a performance that overflowed with charm and personality."

Anna Sten had no such luck. While the film was still in preproduction, Vidor had protested to Goldwyn that there was "too much dialogue for Miss Sten's capabilities," that Garbo and Dietrich had proved most effective drawing out a long "Yes" or "No" in response to long speeches by the other actors. But Frank Capra had just bowled Hollywood over with *It Happened One Night*, in which Clark Gable and Claudette Colbert rattled off mouthfuls of dialogue at lightning pace. Goldwyn wanted Vidor to match that effect.

The challenge proved greatest in the scene in which Anna Sten was supposed to recite a few lines of Browning, which Cooper had inscribed in a book for her: "Earth's returns/ For whole centuries of folly, noise and sin!" No matter how much she practiced, she tripped between the first two words every time. Her tongue got twisted further when Goldwyn chose the moment they were rehearsing that scene to inspect the set. "He plunked into an empty chair close to the camera and peered anxiously at the two embarrassed lovers," recalled Vidor. Both actors gave all they had, but with Cooper's natural reticence and Sten's facial contortions as she spat out the words "Earse returzs," Goldwyn could not help interrupting the scene. He respectfully asked Vidor if he could have a word with the actors, then begged them to cooperate and concentrate. Goldwyn worked himself up over "the dwindling receipts at the box office" and said his whole career was staked on the success of this picture. "And I tell you," he said, reaching the climax of his speech, "that if this scene isn't the greatest love scene ever put on film the whole goddamned picture will go right up out of the sewer." He turned on his heels and marched out of the vast soundstage. Cooper turned to Vidor. "Did he say it, or didn't he?" he asked. "He said it," Vidor replied. The two of them burst into laughter. Vidor resumed rehearsal, but every time Anna Sten got to "Earse returzs," the set went to pieces. Behind her back, Gary Cooper called his co-star Anna Stench.

By the first weeks of 1935, *The Wedding Night* was filmed and assembled. The first preview was held in Glendale. Goldwyn emerged from the theater and huddled his creative team in a sidewalk conference. "You'll have to shoot the big love scene over," he said to Vidor. "That girl can't say 'earse.'"

Anna Sten received her best notices to date. Not only did Vidor photograph her at her most dreamy, but he extracted what he considered "an honest performance" from her. More than one critic commented that she had at last become something more than a publicity stunt. *Newsweek* noted that "the Ukrainian actress might someday live up to Goldwyn's opinion of her." When the public failed to embrace her the third time, Goldwyn decided that he could not afford to give her another chance. He told her they were through working together, and the picture became known around town as "Goldwyn's Last Sten." She said that she wanted out of their deal. With fifteen months left to run, at $2,500 a week, Anna Sten annulled their contract.

Miss Sten later claimed that she was "up for fabulous contracts after I left Goldwyn, but I think I was on the run." She and Frenke went to London, where they made one film together; and she answered the call of a minor studio, Grand National, a few years later for two pictures. Then she vanished from the public eye as quickly as she had materialized. Anna Sten became an asterisk in the annals of motion picture history. "Sam Goldwyn wanted to make her a star in the worst way," said Rouben Mamoulian. "That's just what he did. She never really had a chance."

" THE mention of Anna Sten's name made Frances apoplectic," said George Cukor, the only friend in whom Sam Goldwyn's wife confided about such matters. With her marriage entering its seventh year, she was just beginning to enjoy Sam's obvious pride in her rapid advance to the social fore and feel confident as Mrs. Samuel Goldwyn. During the flush months, she had started to acquire expensive silver and crystal while the new house on Laurel Lane was being constructed; she bought up china pieces of Napoleon's coffee service that Cartier had for sale. Then the two-million-dollar Sten debacle hit her in the pit of her stomach, making her feel exactly as she did when her father had lost everything, reducing the McLaughlins to mere subsistence.

"In the early days on Camino Palmero, I felt happy and secure, but then the atmosphere in the house changed and there was great hostility at home," remembered Samuel Goldwyn, Jr., who had been too young at the time to understand what was happening. The boy heard bits of arguments between his parents about money and women and gambling, and how his mother would not tolerate it any longer.

The Goldwyns loved their son dearly; and they beat their breasts about only wishing the best for him. But the deeds of Sam and Frances—both emotionally crippled by their own childhoods—often fell short of their desires. They wanted Sammy to have every advantage, but never handed to him on a silver platter—privilege without losing the common touch. They did not want to send the boy away, but they made almost no time for him at home. He does not recall eating a single dinner with his parents in the elegant wood-paneled dining room. (He took his meals in the kitchen, alone with the cook.)

In the westward migration of Hollywood's elite, the Gardner Street School was left with a racially mixed bag of students from middle-class families and lower—and Sammy Goldwyn. Although the school was a few blocks from home, Frances had her boy—in short pants, jacket, and tie—chauffeured there and back every day, sometimes in the Rolls-Royce. "The kids would tease me," Sam junior later recalled, "and I was always getting into fights." Some of the children picked on him for being Jewish, which stupefied him, because until he attended a friend's bar mitzvah at the age of thirteen, he had never been exposed to a trace of Hebraism. "Let 'em know they can't push you around," Sam kept urging, while Frances strictly forbade him ever to fight. A solution was found in a rigorous new military school at Melrose and Wilcox avenues, established by a retired army major and a former silent-screen actor, Earle Foxe. Seven-year-old Sammy, barely able to fill his uniform, was enrolled. "Black-Foxe," Goldwyn junior said fifty years later, "was sheer fucking hell."

"I loved Frances Goldwyn," George Cukor admitted to his dying days; she was a comforting confidante to this most sensitive man, the repeated victim of unrequited—sometimes heartbreaking—love affairs. "But," he said (with some frustration of his own), "she was one terrible, terrible mother. After a few years, she really lost interest in the boy. She looked after him, but she was never really interested in taking care of him." In making Sammy the daily charge of a school that prided itself on discipline, Frances felt she had done only what was best for her son.

Saturdays, the boy was Sam's. It was their day together and it was, as Sammy remembered, "the closest I ever was to my father." It usually meant ice cream and a movie at Grauman's Chinese. But after a while the boy realized that he was merely a "decoy." The two Samuel Goldwyns would walk down Hollywood Boulevard "and then he'd park me in a theater and disappear for a 'conference'"—the heaviest poker game in town. The regulars from the Sunday games at Goldwyn's and the Thursday games at Thalberg's played anything they could bet on. Besides the thrill of gambling, cards were a great source of relaxation for these semiliterate men, an easy way for nonverbal people to socialize.

Frances could only guess how much her husband was losing, extrapolating from the cost of the jewelry he would lay on her for no particular reason. Thinking ahead to her widowhood, she saw Sam squandering her pension fund. She would fly into a rage, then tuck away her jewelry—usually a five-to-ten-thousand-dollar piece from Cartier—her hedge against destitution.

Sam chased after starlets, enough for Frances to mention it to George Cukor. "She never complained, and she'd never discuss the situation," he said; "she'd just bring it up and drop it like a martyr." Sammy watched his mother's "hairshirt attitude" pull her through; in recalling that time, he said, "I could see my mother getting stronger." She began putting her foot down, and insisted that if she ever heard about his dallying with another woman or that he had gambled away any more money, she would walk out.

The threat worked. Sam agreed never to see any other women, but that did not stop him from looking. (In fact, most women felt safe around him, and allowed themselves to be charmed by his gallantry.) And what the Goldwyns lacked in passion for each other they made up for in respect. They almost never raised their voices to each other. When Frances saw one of Sam's tirades boiling up inside him, she could silence him with two words of Yiddish: "Schmuel," she would say, using his boyhood name, "shveig" ("Shut up!"). More and more he took to calling her "Mother."

Frances spent increasing amounts of time at the studio, working her way into all aspects of her husband's productions. The other wives in town respectfully noticed.

In late November 1934, Frances Goldwyn's dream house was completed, all to her own taste. She worked "like a beaver" for the next few weeks, applying the finishing touches. Sam had not seen the place since the earliest days of construction. One night in mid-December, they left the studio together, and she instructed the driver to take them home to Beverly Hills. At the top of their knoll off Coldwater Canyon awaited the gleaming white house with black trim, its two wings forming a welcoming obtuse angle. Inside, a generous foyer gave way to the public rooms, decorated in grays and mauves, pale green, and profusions of pink. Ahead lay a deep rose–colored dining room with a table that could seat twenty.

To the right of the foyer was the living room with its heavy green drapery and big pieces of upholstered furniture. At the far end was a small room just big enough for a card table and chairs. A small hallway in the foyer led past a bar into another large room, a paneled library that doubled as a screening room. Beyond that lay a guest suite that did not encourage long visits.

The library's outer doors opened onto an expansive patio. A lawn rolled to a large swimming pool and poolhouse, not visible from the main house. Below that, paths wove past a freshly planted cypress alley to a tennis court. Alone in the back stood a huge eucalyptus tree, with which Frances felt some kinship. Whenever her husband trampled on her feelings, she found comfort just in staring at the noble tree; "my proud lion," she called it.

Upon entering the house for the first time, Sam headed directly up the spiral staircase. To the left lay Sammy's room and, farther down the hall, service rooms and servants' quarters. To the right lay another long corridor. At one end was Frances's large bedroom suite; its narrow single bed, remembered Irene Selznick, "advertised, 'I don't sleep with my husband.'" At the other end was Sam's. Frances already had every article of clothing in its proper closet and drawer. Sam unblinkingly marched into his bathroom, complete with vanity mirror. A moment later he leaned over the banister and shouted to his wife downstairs, "Frances, there's no soap in my soap dish."

The house at 1200 Laurel Lane became not only where Frances resided but where she presided. She became one of the town's most celebrated hostesses, famous for the quality of her food, the efficiency of her servants, the sparkle of her guests. Her own wholesome American looks and unexpected wit made her a most desirable dinner companion.

The Goldwyns entertained regularly, sometimes as often as four times a week. There might be a half-dozen friends for dinner and a movie. An actor Sam was trying to hire might be invited for a private dinner, just the two men and their wives. The arrivals in Los Angeles of special friends—such as the Irving Berlins on their annual visit or the Goldwyns' latest social conquests, the Averell Harrimans—would warrant a dinner party for forty. New Year's Eve of 1935 brought Cole Porter, Lady Mendl, and the Gary Coopers together under the Goldwyns' new roof for a dinner of saddle of lamb, spinach salad, and vanilla éclairs with chocolate sauce. Harold Arlen, Jack Benny, Charles Boyer, Frank Capra, Marlene Dietrich, Clark Gable, the Gianninis, the Howard Hawkses, James Hilton, Sidney Howard, the Jesse Laskys, Myrna Loy, Ginger Rogers, the David Selznicks, the Walter Wangers, Jock Whitney, Loretta Young, and fifty others joined them for a champagne supper served at midnight. Frances specialized in throwing dinners for twelve, what George Cukor called "the hardest ticket in town." She and her husband sat opposite each other at the middle of the table, surrounded by only the most famous names in Hollywood. "You always knew where your career stood," remarked Katharine Hepburn (who shunned such dinner parties), "by where you sat at the Goldwyn table."

"Frances was charming and lovely to look at—very bright, cold, and tough as nails," recalled Dorothy Hirshon, the first wife of William S. Paley. "But you never saw that tough side in a social sense. Both she and

Sam always made an effort to get on with people if they thought it would be helpful. . . . I always thought Sam was calculating, but I didn't care. He was gracious and not without charm." Paley concurred. (He had met the Goldwyns aboard ship in 1928. At that time he saw almost nothing of Sam, who remained planted in the casino throughout the Atlantic crossing. Paley had found himself enormously attracted to the pretty young card widow and waltzed her from her position as "a decorative but inactive onlooker" onto the ballroom dance floor whenever possible. For years, each of them kept secret that the attractive Paley had tried to talk Frances into leaving Sam and marrying him.)

One summer day, Goldwyn was walking along the beach with the Paleys. Suddenly the radio tycoon pointed to some birds overhead and said, "Look at the gulls." Sam peered skyward and asked with some astonishment, "How do you know they're not boys?"

"Not a half dozen men have ever been able to keep the whole equation of pictures in their heads," wrote F. Scott Fitzgerald in *The Last Tycoon.* "And perhaps the closest a woman can come to the set-up is to try and understand one of those men." That seemed to be Frances Goldwyn's philosophy. But Mrs. Paley noted, "instead of just standing in his shadow, she turned her position into something. They had a real partnership . . . one in which I never felt little Sammy was included."

With so much financial tension in the air during the Anna Sten years, Goldwyn traveled more than ever. In his absence—and even when he was in town—Sammy was sent on Sunday mornings to Abe Lehr's house. There he got his first real taste of family life, as the parents and three children gathered for a huge sausage-and-waffle lunch. "It is," Sam junior later admitted, "one of the great memories of my childhood." The Lehr children felt sympathy for him, especially at everyone's calling him "Little Sammy Goldwyn, Jr."

"I grew up at a very young age," admitted Sam Goldwyn, Jr. He believed he was "underpampered," never having his own pony or elaborate birthday galas with all of Hollywood in attendance. He was allowed to go to the parties, but whenever he asked for something other Hollywood parents had lavished on their kids, his mother would admonish, "They have it this year, but let's see what they have next year."

Frances was forever instilling her values into her son. One day, while he was reading *Penrod and Sam,* Sammy shrieked with laughter at a scene with a scared "pickaninny" clambering up a tree. Frances scolded him for finding humor in that. "How would you like to be called a 'kike'?" she asked.

She was also allergic to people without a work ethic. In trying to immunize her son to the lot of rich playboys who swarmed around the town,

Frances constantly made work for Sammy around the house. Even though there was a team of gardeners to tend to the grounds, Sammy was given money for weeding. The chauffeur would pick him up after school and drive him on his newspaper route, while he tossed copies of the *Herald-Express* out the window. In time, Sammy was allowed to deliver his papers by himself. On his bicycle, he would ride down from Laurel Lane into the southern flats of Beverly Hills. "I had been so overprotected," he said, "it was freedom for me."

Sammy's most enduring friendship to emerge from his childhood was with Irving and Ellin Berlin's daughter Mary Ellin. They shared their summers with swimming lessons, tennis lessons, riding lessons, and French lessons. In retrospect, she admitted, "We really were two little rich brats." One afternoon, Mary Ellin, an avid reader of movie magazines, challenged Sammy to a contest, to see who could compile the longest list of famous people they had met. Mary Ellin easily came up with the most names. "But, my God," she said, "you should have seen the people on Sammy's list. They were the most famous people in the world, and even as a child he really knew them."

TOPPING his list those days was Eddie Cantor, as every third picture his father produced between 1931 and 1935 was a vehicle for the lovable "kid." Musicals had bounced back in favor in the mid-thirties, each studio providing its own brand to lift audiences from the depths of the Depression. Warner Brothers scored with their pavement-pounding backstage musicals full of Broadway ballyhoo and such Harry Warren songs as "Forty-second Street," and "We're in the Money." MGM specialized in lush, romantic operettas—Jeanette MacDonald and Nelson Eddy singing their hearts out. Other MGM musicals were already working up to the high gloss for which they would be known for decades to come. At Fox, Shirley Temple smiled through the tough times with such numbers as "Animal Crackers in My Soup" and "On the Good Ship Lollipop." RKO glided to new levels of sophistication by pairing Fred Astaire with Ginger Rogers in a series of musicals that featured top-drawer numbers from Jerome Kern, Irving Berlin, and the Gershwins. Walt Disney, releasing his cartoons through United Artists, cheered the nation in 1933 when his Three Little Pigs seemed to be laughing in the face of the Depression as they sang "Who's Afraid of the Big Bad Wolf?" And Goldwyn stuck to retailoring the same musical formula for Eddie Cantor, though it was becoming threadbare.

Goldwyn had recently chased the film rights to *Androcles and the Lion.*

When Shaw refused him yet again, Goldwyn tried to interest Robert Sherwood—who had written about Hannibal in his play *The Road to Rome*—and George S. Kaufman in writing an original story set in ancient Rome. Between 1930 and 1932, Kaufman had written six plays for Broadway, and every time Goldwyn saw him, he came closer to seducing him into a Hollywood contract. "I know, the minute I escape from your spell," Kaufman had said in a January 1932 letter, "that I don't really want to go into pictures. There is no one in the business with whom I would rather be associated, and I shall never take the plunge without coming first to you and asking if you want me." One of the most appealing aspects of Goldwyn's latest offer was that Kaufman and Sherwood would not have to work in Hollywood.

In March 1933, the team signed agreements for an original story and screenplay, each to receive $25,000—$2,500 upon execution of the agreement, $10,000 upon Goldwyn's receipt of "a full treatment script," and $12,500 for a draft complete with dialogue. Kaufman had had his share of experience with star comedians, so on this contract for his first original motion picture (after eighteen of his plays had been adapted for the screen) he insisted on a special clause, that he would never have to meet Eddie Cantor or listen to his views of the story.

After Sherwood and Kaufman completed their draft of *Roman Scandals*, Cantor learned that a story conference was to be held. He begged to attend. Goldwyn granted permission, provided that Cantor simply sit and listen. At the meeting the next day, Kaufman read the script aloud. When he concluded, Cantor asked if he might offer a suggestion. Goldwyn allowed the point of personal privilege; and as the producer himself related thirty years thence, "Three hours later, Cantor finished, having talked his way into an entirely new story." Kaufman walked out of the conference without uttering a word. A few hours after that, Goldwyn received a letter from Kaufman announcing that he and Sherwood were finished with the job. They returned to playwriting and awaited their final payment on *Roman Scandals*.

"I have no intention of paying any further money," Goldwyn wrote his attorneys, "and I am burning up over what they have done to me." He did not consider the script before him a complete draft. That did not stop Goldwyn from sending Kaufman an opening-night telegram months later, wishing him success with his new play. Kaufman wrote back that he was "puzzled about our exact personal relationship, as I am sure *you* must be. We are at disagreement as to a business point, and I feel so genuinely in the right in the matter that I cannot permit even our friendship to stand in the way of any future steps." Goldwyn assured him "that irrespective of how our business relations may eventuate, I shall never permit that to interfere with my deep affection for you." He still refused to write the checks.

Goldwyn probably would have taken offensive action of his own had the two writers not built a chassis of a story sturdy enough to send down his assembly line of writers. The result was an amusing variation on *A Connecticut Yankee in King Arthur's Court,* in which a mousy museum attendant is transported back to the Roman Empire.

As before, this Cantor picture found excuses for the self-deprecating character named Eddie ("I'm a failure; I can't even keep a job as a slave") to appear in blackface, frequently burst into song, undo the villain, and unite a pair of young lovers after a wild chariot race. He also got to sell the film's big number at the opening and the finale, rallying his Depression-weary neighbors in joyous song, "Build a Little Home." Goldwyn pulled out all his usual stops, surrounding Cantor with Richard Day's sets, Gregg Toland's photography, Alfred Newman's orchestrations, and his most gorgeous selection of Goldwyn Girls performing Busby Berkeley's choreography.

In his talent search for *Roman Scandals,* Goldwyn had asked Louella Parsons to write in her column that he was holding open auditions for "every girl from 16 to 25 who thinks she looks like a Roman beauty. They wouldn't have to make appointments," he told her. "They won't have to wait or to argue with the office boy. All that they do is to walk right in." Nine thousand hopeful girls walked before Goldwyn and his scouts. Seventy-five beauties were selected to appear in *Roman Scandals;* a dozen of them were designated Goldwyn Girls. A few days before rehearsals were to begin in Hollywood, the mother of one of those chosen in New York suddenly decided against her daughter's going into motion pictures, thus leaving a gap in the line.

It was one of those "hotter than hell" July Wednesdays when Lucille Ball, then a platinum-blond Hattie Carnegie model, was on her way to a lingerie shop to buy some underwear. She passed an agent friend on Seventh Avenue, and he said he had just heard that Sam Goldwyn was looking for one more "poster girl" for his new Eddie Cantor picture. The model—raised in Jamestown, New York, by her mother and grandfather—was trying to make it in the big city. She had already posed for a Chesterfield cigarette advertisement, and she bore a strong resemblance to Constance Bennett. She thought it would be hopeless even to pursue the job, as she had not even heard about the Goldwyn cattle call in the first place. The agent simply said, "Look, they need girls." Moments later, she was standing before James Mulvey, who asked if she could leave on Saturday for six weeks. The job lasted for six months and led to a middling career in motion pictures for the next seventeen years.

Upon reporting to the studio for her first day of work, Miss Ball realized that she was "the ugly duckling of the lot." Feeling inadequate, "embarrassed not to look like the other kids," she thought of Fanny Brice, who had gotten Ziegfeld audiences to look at her instead of the beauties. Tired of standing in the back row of the harem, she resorted to any stunt to stand out, anything for a laugh. When the Goldwyn Girls were supposed to strut before the cameras in precise step, Miss Ball limped across; she would cross her eyes when the camera passed before her; she overstuffed her brassiere with tissue. Somehow this twenty-two-year-old got it in her head that "it was all useful. They'd realize there's a girl out there not afraid to do anything." When Eddie Cantor suddenly decided one of the chorus girls—who wore little more than G-strings and long hemplike wigs—was needed to fall into some mud, the one self-described "skinny marink" stepped forward.

"Mr. Goldwyn was aware of what every one of us was doing," Lucille Ball recalled of her first days as a show girl; "and years later he always took pride in my having been a Goldwyn Girl." Of course, the chorine was never invited to the Goldwyns' house. She did not sit at the Goldwyn table until 1938, when she landed the female lead opposite the Marx Brothers in *Room Service*. "I ate my first artichoke at his place," she recalled. "I just stared at it and was about to attack it with my knife and fork when Harpo leaned over and whispered how to pull it apart." Through the years she and the Goldwyns became "more friendly." When Lucille Ball suddenly ascended to stardom in television, "Mr. Goldwyn was there recommending people and banks and other helpful things" to aid in the building of her entertainment empire.

The producer's take on *Roman Scandals* far exceeded a million dollars, and Goldwyn received a summons. Sherwood and Kaufman wanted the rest of their salary and their share of the profits. The case slogged through the courts for several years (during which time Kaufman wrote *A Night at the Opera* for MGM and several more Broadway hits, including *Stage Door* and *You Can't Take It with You*). The writers finally settled their claim for $20,000, most of which was absorbed by legal bills.

Another lawsuit over *Roman Scandals* had more drastic implications for Goldwyn's career, affecting not only his next two Cantor pictures but also his relationship with the film community at large. Ever since hiring Busby Berkeley to choreograph *Whoopee!*, Goldwyn had known of his late-night carousing. But Berkeley had always bounced back in the mornings. Then

Goldwyn began to find him listless day after day and hired private detectives to tail him after work. The gumshoes had to follow him no farther than the Warner Brothers gates.

In bringing Berkeley from Broadway to Hollywood, Goldwyn had not signed him to a long-term contract. Because there was but one Goldwyn musical a year, it made more sense for both parties to work on a picture-by-picture basis. Goldwyn had loaned Berkeley out to Warners, generously negotiating his deals and reviewing his contracts. Then one day in 1933, Berkeley arrived at Goldwyn's office, opened the door for his appointment, and just stood there. "I am ashamed to come in," he said. "I know you will be angry with me." At last Berkeley entered and blurted, "I have signed a long-term contract with Warner Brothers, and I am to direct pictures. . . . But I told Warner Brothers I was obligated to do the next Cantor picture." Warners honored that obligation—to a point. While Goldwyn was making *Roman Scandals*, they needed Berkeley to direct the dance numbers in *Footlight Parade*, which they secretly scheduled at night. Berkeley went for weeks on catnaps. Once his mediocre work on *Roman Scandals* was completed, he became the property of another studio.

What galled Goldwyn more than losing Berkeley was losing him to the Warner brothers, whom he considered the worst buccaneers in the motion picture business. Goldwyn had long suspected that their stock-market manipulations served only the siblings and not the shareholders; and he found them "guilty of the most reckless star-raiding that the industry has ever known." Goldwyn hauled Jack Warner before the Association of Motion Picture Producers to explain this pirating of Berkeley's services. Warner's only defense was: "What can I do about it?" When Goldwyn found no supporters, he rose angrily from his chair at the meeting and headed for the door. "Gentlemen," he said, resigning from the organization, "include me out!"

Busby Berkeley did get his chance to direct at Warner Brothers, then he moved on to slicker productions at MGM, leaving his singular mark on three dozen musicals.

With 10 percent of his films' grosses tacked onto his salary, Eddie Cantor became the highest-paid actor in motion pictures in 1934, earning $270,000. (Mae West was the highest-paid actress.) But tempers flared between him and Goldwyn after the release of every one of their pictures together. Each claimed the laurels for its success and declaimed the other's ingratitude. After months of disagreement over their next joint venture, they settled on the most convoluted Cantor plot yet. In *Kid Millions*, Eddie Wilson, Jr., inherits $77 million pillaged from Egyptian tombs by the archaeologist father he never knew. A number of heavies also pursue the fortune, including a Broadway song plugger, a colonel from the South, his niece, a shifty sheik, and his dizzy daughter. When Cantor saw the love story in the film again being thrown to a young couple, he pestered Goldwyn for a romantic interest of his own. "Eddie," Goldwyn said, "you've got no sex appeal."

"Sam," Eddie howled. "What do you mean, no sex appeal? How do you think I got my five daughters?"

Goldwyn allowed the writers to work up a comedy romance between Cantor and the sheik's daughter. Their committing "tramofatch"—the cursed sin of "kissing a sheik's daughter while riding a camel"—triggers the film's denouement. Eddie manages to escape an awaiting vat of boiling oil and winds up happily with his girlfriend, Toots, in Brooklyn, where he opens an ice cream factory. All that, plus a dozen musical numbers— including Irving Berlin's "Mandy"—would be packed into ninety minutes. Goldwyn hired Ethel Merman to play the song plugger and Ann Sothern, in but her second film, to play the colonel's niece. Her romantic lead was an amiable song-and-dance man from Broadway named George Murphy, in his motion picture debut.

For weeks, Goldwyn became preoccupied with the film's "Ice Cream Fantasy"—in which Cantor opens his ice cream factory for poor children. He was going to use the vibrant new three-strip Technicolor process. Almost daily, George Oppenheimer remembered, Goldwyn was on the phone to Dr. Herbert T. Kalmus, the Technicolor pioneer, harping on the same refrain: "The vanilla must look like the vanilla, the chocolate must look like the chocolate, the strawberry must look like the strawberry."

"For a month or more I heard this admonition so often," said Oppenheimer, "that I lost all taste for vanilla, chocolate, or strawberry ice cream." One Friday night, Goldwyn called a staff meeting. Richard Day led off, exhibiting drawings of his sets; Alfred Newman played some of *Kid Millions*'s songs—and Goldwyn fell into his cant that "the vanilla must look like vanilla." With that, he ushered his men into his private projection room to inspect a test Kalmus had prepared. "The lights went out," Oppenheimer remembered, "and on the screen, against a white background, there appeared a large and luscious Technicolor plate of chocolate ice cream. There was a moment's appreciative silence, broken by the smacking of Goldwyn's lips and his comment, 'Mmmm, strawberry.'"

Kid Millions opened to good reviews and good box office, but the air of excitement that surrounded the earlier Cantor pictures was gone. Goldwyn claimed that he had stuck to the formula that had proved so successful in the past and that it must be Cantor's overexposure on the radio that was threatening his popularity.

"People expect big pictures from us," an upset Cantor wrote Goldwyn. "True—but girls don't make them bigger. Neither do the goddamned juvenile and ingenue. Big sets, interesting personalities, good songs, interesting story, new situations are what we need. Half of our time is usually spent on the 'girl' lead. Let us concentrate on a story that gives us great excitement. On the stage for years I was and still am considered 'top man'—radio has accepted me as the head guy. Why do I have so much trouble in pictures?"

Strike Me Pink, filmed in 1935, would only add to his woes. More than a dozen writers worked the script over, starting from a *Saturday Evening Post* story called "Dreamland," set in an amusement park. It was standard Cantor fare, complete with gangsters and a final chase that took Eddie from a roller coaster ride to a hot-air balloon into the net of a troupe of acrobats. Harold Arlen wrote the songs, including a number called "First You Leave Me High, Then You Leave Me Low," which Goldwyn referred to as "First You Got Me Up, Then You Got Me Down."

Cantor felt Goldwyn's foolish consistency was costing the star everything he had worked for over the last five years. "It's like Babe Ruth up at bat," Cantor told Goldwyn. "The fact that he made a hit yesterday has nothing to do with today." Offering to make all kinds of concessions in his deal, just to "prolong my life on the screen," the comedian urged his producer to find a part for him that had nothing to do with the old Cantor "formula."

Cantor pleaded with Goldwyn to buy the rights to a new play called *Three Men on a Horse.* It was the story of a timid Brooklynite whose knack for picking winners at the track attracted gangsters of all sorts. The play had no music but plenty of laughs, which Cantor knew he could deliver. Warner Brothers beat them to the rights. When Goldwyn said he would not even consider loaning Cantor out to play the lead, the two stopped speaking to each other. Cracks about Goldwyn—attributed to Cantor—appeared in the newspaper columns. Cantor paid his way out of his contract and for a while forfeited Goldwyn's friendship. "I was hopping mad," said Cantor, "and so was he."

Cantor moved to Twentieth Century–Fox studios—a new company Darryl Zanuck and Joe Schenck created when they merged with Fox Films. He made a few more musicals; but even he conceded, "they never came up to the caliber of the Goldwyn pictures." Years began to pass between each of his films, until Cantor's career on screen quietly ended.

Without Cantor, Colman, and Sten, Goldwyn became desperate. He needed major motion picture personalities in order to survive alongside the major studios, all of which were establishing elaborate star systems.

Ten years earlier, Goldwyn had created his greatest star when he presented Vilma Banky in *The Dark Angel*. He believed its heroine, Kitty Vane, was a foolproof role—the "greatest ever written for [a] girl"— rigged with enough melodramatic tricks to put across any pretty face that could work up an eyeful of tears. He decided it was time to remount it, thereby launching another stellar career. Goldwyn had his eye on Madeleine Carroll, an English blonde who had made a picture for Fox. While several studios scrambled to sign her to a long-term contract, another beauty entered the scene, who took Goldwyn's breath away.

Estelle Merle O'Brien Thompson was the barely legitimate daughter of a coal-black nurse's assistant and an Irish mechanical engineer who had worked on the railways in India. In 1914, three years after her birth in Bombay, her father left his family to fight in the Great War. He died in the battle of the Somme. On the streets of Bombay, then Calcutta, Merle grew up quickly, developing into a teenager of exotic beauty. Beneath her dark hair and high forehead, two huge almond-shaped eyes illuminated her tawny skin. She had an inviting full mouth, a curvy figure, and velvety skin. A night with her was said to cost one hundred dollars. Through a series of liaisons, she found herself stepping out in European society, which had come to glitter with motion picture people.

In 1931, she fell in with Alexander Korda, another jackdaw strutting in peacock's feathers. Born Sándor Kellner in the heartland of Hungary, he journeyed first to Budapest. There he wrote for an independent daily newspaper, using the nom de plume Sursum Corda (Lift Up Your Hearts), then he graduated to a weekly cinema magazine. At twenty-five, he was directing his own films and running his own small studio. After stops in Vienna and Berlin, he made it to Hollywood, where his career screeched to a halt. Arriving in 1926, he discovered that an earlier generation of moguls had laid claim to all the territory. He directed several films under contracts to various studios, but only *The Private Life of Helen of Troy* had any impact, though it was considered too "European" to be much of a success. The cosmopolitan Korda never felt at home in Hollywood, where he found that the citizenry asked only two questions: "What did it gross?" and "Do you like orange juice?" His departure caused no more of a stir than his arrival.

After short stays in Paris and Berlin, he settled in London, where he set out to build his own empire. While his search for contract players was at its most fevered, he met the exotic Estelle Thompson, who had made a few appearances in moving pictures and was known alternately as Queenie

Thompson, Estelle O'Brien, and Merle O'Brien. Korda signed her to a contract, announcing his conquest as Stella Merle. She pleaded to use the surname O'Brien, but Korda thought it too common. When she came up with the variant Oberon, he agreed.

In 1933, Korda produced *The Private Life of Henry VIII*, in which Merle Oberon played the small role of Anne Boleyn. The success of that one film practically righted the course of the British film industry, putting Korda at its helm. Almost every producer in Hollywood wanted to hire the beheaded queen.

Just before leaving the presidency of United Artists, Joe Schenck proved most ardent. A bachelor on the loose since his divorce from Norma Talmadge, he suddenly placed a large diamond ring on Miss Oberon's finger and announced their engagement. United Artists signed a sixteen-picture deal with Korda's London Films.

Korda cast her next in *The Scarlet Pimpernel*, never foreseeing that she would fall in love with the married leading man, Hungarian-born Laszlo Stainer. As an effete romantic figure known as Leslie Howard, he was becoming one of the screen's heartthrobs. Although Korda held the ultimate power in determining what her next projects would be, Miss Oberon's moods were strong enough to sway decisions one way or another. After *The Scarlet Pimpernel*, he reluctantly agreed to let her go to Hollywood to film *Folies-Bergère* for Twentieth Century. She urged Howard to accept the part he had just been offered in Robert Sherwood's *Petrified Forest*, so he could join her there.

By the time she arrived in California, Merle Oberon's engagement had been called off and her diamond ring returned. At the start of 1935, she heard that Sam Goldwyn was looking for his lead in *The Dark Angel*. The original had been one of her favorite films as a child, and she immediately saw how the part could launch her in the States. Goldwyn was impressed with Merle Oberon and thought the remake would prove a strong showing for her and Leslie Howard. Back in England, Korda was entertaining the offers of several big producers for Oberon's services, Selznick among them. The star made it clear where her sentiments lay. "I CANNOT IMAGINE ANYTHING MORE WONDERFUL FOR ME IN MY CAREER THAN TO HAVE PICTURES PRODUCED BY YOU AND GOLDWYN," she cabled Korda that January. A few weeks later, she added, "DARK ANGEL GREAT FOR ME. . . . I WOULD DIE IF CARROLL GOT PART."

It was not hard to read Goldwyn's influence between the lines of Oberon's urgent messages. Korda received a cable from Goldwyn himself offering to "PRODUCE ONE MORE PICTURE WITH HER THIS YEAR FOLLOWING DARK ANGEL STOP ALSO RIGHT TO MAKE TWO PICTURES WITH HER DUR-

ING EACH SUCCEEDING YEAR SHE IS UNDER CONTRACT TO YOU." After several months, Korda and Goldwyn agreed upon a five-year contract that called for three pictures per year between them; the actress would start at $60,000 per picture and escalate to $100,000. The entire plan was designed to yield the former dance hostess over one million dollars by 1941.

During their negotiation, Goldwyn hired a director for *The Dark Angel*—Sidney Franklin, an Anglophile from San Francisco, who had become Norma Shearer's pet director in recent years. Goldwyn had two writers adapting the screenplay, working from Guy Bolton's original play and Frances Marion's silent-screen scenario. One was an Englishman named Mordaunt Shairp. The other was a former reader for Broadway producer Herman Shumlin and MGM, who had recently written a hit play, *The Children's Hour*. Her name was Lillian Hellman. She had accompanied Dashiell Hammett, who was writing the successful "Thin Man" series for MGM, to California and grabbed the offer to work on *The Dark Angel*. She and Shairp stuck close to the original story of the blind man returning from the war and trying to conceal his infirmity from his fiancée so that she will get on with a happier life married to his best friend. Even to a playwright with aspirations as serious as Hellman's, the job was irresistible, because it meant "easy money and easy hours." Work on the project—which Hellman referred to as an "old silly"—ambled into the spring.

By then Leslie Howard had returned to his wife, and he had no interest in the film. Goldwyn hired the stalwart Fredric March to play the wounded Alan Trent and Herbert Marshall to play the other man. When Sidney Franklin picked up bits of this casting news, he fired off an angry telegram to Goldwyn, then at the Waldorf-Astoria. "AM I TO UNDERSTAND THAT YOU ARE NEGOTIATING TO GET MERLE OBERON WITHOUT HOWARD STOP I CAN UNDERSTAND OBERON WITH HOWARD BUT I CANT VERY WELL UNDERSTAND OBERON ALONE STOP WITHOUT HOWARD AND WITH MARCH I WOULD WANT A GIRL THAT COULD GIVE ME A GREAT PERFORMANCE BY ACTING ABILITY AND EXPERIENCE STOP THE SOLE REASON I THOUGHT YOU WERE NEGOTIATING WITH OBERON WAS IN ORDER TO GET THE OTHER PERSON WITH HER." Further opposition came from Goldwyn's own staff—James Mulvey, Freddy Kohlmar, and a new story editor who had worked at the *Saturday Evening Post*, Merritt Hulburd. They felt, as one memorandum revealed, "that the leading girl for 'The Dark Angel' must depict a definite virginal quality, and that Merle Oberon does not and could not give a true impression of that quality. They think she is too exotic and sexy and if given the lead in 'The Dark Angel,' might destroy the essential qualities of that role."

Goldwyn thought them all wrong. So far as he was concerned, the men in the film were merely to support Merle Oberon. He thought her glamorous heat could be tamped down. While the producers of Oberon's other pictures always accentuated her features and figure, Goldwyn muted them. He saw to it that she was always dressed simply, usually in collared outfits; her hair was unlacquered, brushed back off her forehead; he ordered makeup that would lighten her coloring and do nothing to emphasize the slight slant in her eyes. In the words of one director who would later work with her, "Goldwyn wanted everything clean about Merle, as though she were the all-American girl."

Within months of Merle Oberon's signing with him, Goldwyn went on his biggest safari for stars since pictures started talking. He quickly bagged another leading lady, a leading man, and an extra with possibilities as a supporting player. The first was Miriam Hopkins, a vivacious blonde from Georgia with stage experience and five years of hits and misses in Hollywood to her credit. Mamoulian and Lubitsch had directed her in her best work—*Dr. Jekyll and Mr. Hyde, Design for Living,* and Hollywood's latest adaptation of a classic novel, *Becky Sharp,* the first all-Technicolor feature film. The haphazardness of her career appealed to Goldwyn, showing him the range of her talents and her potential for stardom if properly guided. Joel McCrea—an alumnus of the Hollywood School for Girls who used to ride around town on horseback—had become a strapping six foot two, with the wide-open good looks of the all-American boy. After attending Pomona College, he picked up cowboy roles, then got leads in such diverse RKO productions as *Bird of Paradise, The Most Dangerous Game,* and Sidney Howard's *The Silver Cord.* As with Miriam Hopkins, his versatility as much as his promise prompted Goldwyn to sign him to a long-term contract. Goldwyn thought his name was Joe McCrail.

Goldwyn's new potential supporting player was one of those young rogues Hollywood has always had in excess. David Niven had managed to charm his way into the town's most exclusive circles—Douglas Fairbanks's steam room on the United Artists lot, Darryl Zanuck's polo matches at the Uplifters Club, and through a letter of introduction from a friend in London, the home of Sam and Frances Goldwyn. "I asked him if he had ever acted before," Goldwyn recalled of his first meeting with the $2.50 extra in late 1934; "he told me that he had but that he had graduated from Sandhurst, been commissioned a Lieutenant in the British army and had worked, among other things, as a lumberjack and a wine salesman." Goldwyn thought he was "a handsome chap," but "did not see any place in motion pictures for him." He kept telling him "there was not a chance."

The cheery twenty-five-year-old continued to make friends—from the Santa Monica beach houses to the studios. British-born director Edmund

Goulding introduced him to Howard Hawks's agent-brother, William, who agreed to represent him. Niven got to make several screen tests, but producers in town were as nonplussed by the actor on screen as Goldwyn had predicted. Irving Thalberg thought there might be a nonspeaking role for him mutinying with Clark Gable on the *Bounty.* At a Friday-night card game, he dropped the actor's name as somebody he was thinking of signing.

The next night, Phyllis and Fred Astaire were dining at the Goldwyns'. "I saw them buzzing around mysteriously with my wife Frances but thought nothing of it," Goldwyn recalled. "After dinner we adjourned into the living room to see a picture as was the usual custom at my home. The lights went down, but instead of the picture that I had expected to see there came onto the screen a screen-test which had been made a short time before at M-G-M. The test had been directed by Eddie Goulding, and much to my surprise it was of our young friend—and to my much greater surprise I saw that he was quite a good actor." When the test finished running, Goldwyn asked Astaire to have David Niven come to his office.

"I'm giving you a seven-year contract," Goldwyn said in his high-pitched voice that Monday morning. "I'll pay you very little, and I won't put you in a Goldwyn picture till you've learned your job. Now you have a base. Go out and tell the studios you're under contract to Goldwyn, do anything they offer you, get experience, work hard, and in a year or so, if you're any good, I'll give you a role." Upon learning that he would be receiving one hundred dollars a week, Niven headed for the Ford Motor Company showroom on Hollywood Boulevard, where the new five-hundred-dollar models sat in the window. He pointed and said to a salesman, "I'll take that one."

After several years fussing over the script and casting of a project called *Barbary Coast,* Goldwyn believed he had at last a troupe of players to perform it. The Association of Motion Picture Producers had protested many times at the scandalous elements of this period gangster piece set in the underworld of gold-rush San Francisco. Goldwyn turned to Ben Hecht, who had slid as much past Joseph Breen, the chief censor, as anyone had. Of course, neither Hecht nor Goldwyn had forgotten their experience on *The Unholy Garden,* so the writer agreed to the assignment only if the producer promised to pay his wages on a daily basis, every afternoon in cash. Goldwyn agreed.

Howard Hawks had successfully directed Hecht's screenplays of *Twentieth Century* and (more relevant to the assignment at hand) *Scarface.* Hawks was a free-swinging man in his mid-thirties. His family had owned paper mills in the Midwest until his mother's health forced them to move to

California. After preparing at Exeter and attending Cornell, he returned to California, where he hung around movie sets. Hawks worked his way up from gathering props to directing one-reel comedies. He had most recently directed *Tiger Shark* with Edward G. Robinson, the man Goldwyn had just signed as the underworld chief in *Barbary Coast*. Hopkins and McCrea were cast as the young lovers, and David Niven got the one-line part of a Cockney sailor with a drooping mustache who was thrown out of a brothel window into the mud, only to have the stars, thirty vigilantes, and several donkeys walk over him.

One other bit player got his career rolling on *Barbary Coast,* a stumblebum who ended up as one of the medium's most enduring and endearing character actors. Hawks was casting the part of a grizzled barfly called Old Atrocity, when a production man said, "I know somebody exactly like that." Hawks told him to put the actor, Walter Brennan, into costume and give him some lines. When this scarecrow of a figure walked in, Hawks broke into laughter. The director asked if he was ready to recite his lines, and Brennan asked, "With or without?"

"With or without what?" Hawks inquired. "Teeth," said Brennan, and the part was his. He was supposed to work three days, but Hawks kept him around—dentureless—for a month. He would turn up in nine more Goldwyn pictures.

The moment *Barbary Coast* wrapped, Goldwyn walked his two romantic leads through wardrobe and into a neighboring soundstage. In *Splendor,* Joel McCrea, decked out in white tie and tails, played the scion of Manhattan aristocrats on their uppers. Instead of marrying the heiress his family has picked, he falls in love with Miriam Hopkins, a poor but principled girl. The pressures of their different backgrounds pull the couple apart, but he comes to his senses and takes a lowly job on the staff of a newspaper. In a rainstorm, he pours out his love and promises her a humble but honest married life together. "Darling," she says, beaming, "that would be such splendor!" The picture was not. It flopped critically and commercially.

Barbary Coast performed better on both counts, but not as much as the screenwriters would have liked. When Ben Hecht and Charles MacArthur saw the liberties Hawks had taken with their screenplay, they pleaded to "be absolved from the responsibility of authorship." Goldwyn kept their names in the credits, and it did not hurt their reputations any. They won the Academy Award for best screenplay of *The Scoundrel* that year . . . and they would be back working for Goldwyn just a few years later.

In the mid-thirties, many considered the latter the greater honor. Much of the Hollywood community had come to consider the Academy Awards bunk—capricious voting of apples against oranges. There were accusations of fraudulent tabulating and of too many foreign films and stars being honored. The major studio chiefs ordered their employees to vote strictly for the home product, and they campaigned for votes with advertisements in the trade papers. What had started as a family affair honoring their own was turning into a business event, which many guild members chose to boycott that year. The gold statuettes handed out as prizes were being referred to derogatorily by the pet name a librarian at the Academy, Margaret Herrick, pinned on them. She said they resembled her uncle, Oscar Pierce.

To stem the tide of unfavorable industry sentiment, the Academy turned the 1935 awards banquet—held in March 1936, at the Biltmore Hotel—into a testimonial to D. W. Griffith, who had retired to Kentucky. It also hired the accounting firm of Price Waterhouse to conduct the balloting. A number of stars did not show up, but most realized that the event still meant good publicity. For Sam Goldwyn, who had reached the top echelon of quality producers, the evening was an opportunity to stand alongside those men who produced ten times as many films as he did. He sat proudly with Merle Oberon, who had been nominated as Best Actress for *The Dark Angel*. Several Goldwyn craftsmen were also nominated that year, but Richard Day's art direction was the company's only winner. A few days later, Day made up a replica of his "Oscar," which he presented to his boss.

Goldwyn was touched, but it was a hollow consolation prize. The producer knew that the quality of his pictures had slumped in the last few years, and except for the Cantor pictures, so had his box-office receipts. His few stars under contract still offered only potential. He wanted a Bette Davis (that year's Best Actress winner), or a Claudette Colbert (who had won the year before), or a Katharine Hepburn (winner the year before that). Stuck in the horse latitudes, he wished for someone with "that little something extra."

For months, Joel McCrea had been trying to persuade Goldwyn that his beautiful new wife, who had played Meg in *Little Women*, was just such an actress. A couple of other parts led to her starring in a Jesse Lasky movie at Fox, a modern-day Cinderella tale. After arguing her case and getting nowhere, McCrea simply brought a print of that film to the studio and ran it for his producer. With McCrea by his side, Goldwyn sat in delight through all of *The Gay Deception*, starring Frances Dee.

And Sam Goldwyn's life was never the same again.

15 "The Goldwyn Touch"

HE COULD NOT HAVE BEEN less interested in Frances Dee.

When the lights came on in the projection room, Sam Goldwyn turned to Joel McCrea and asked, "Who directed this?" McCrea told him, "A funny little guy named Wyler."

William Wyler was born in Alsace-Lorraine in 1902, in a town called Mulhausen or Mulhouse, depending on which government laid claim to the territory that year. After the world war, Willy entertained the notion of studying business in Paris, anything to escape selling neckties in his father's haberdashery. He dreamed of America, the setting for fantastic tales he kept hearing about his mother's cousin Carl Laemmle. Not only had "Uncle Carl" miraculously turned his clothing business in Chicago into a film empire in Hollywood, but he had also taken it upon himself to sponsor people from the old country.

When her famous cousin next returned to Europe, Melanie Wyler met him in Zurich with her eighteen-year-old Willy in tow. "Uncle Carl" asked the youth, "Do you have ambition?" When he heard the kind of enthusiasm he had hoped for, he offered him passage to America and a twenty-five-dollar-a-week job, from which he would dock five dollars until the boat fare had been reimbursed. Wyler was "thunderstruck," because "in those days it was like making a trip to the moon!" Shortly after setting foot on American soil, he stopped a passerby and asked directions to the "street paved in gold."

Wyler shared quarters in a rooming house on East Eighty-sixth Street with another Laemmle protégé, a Czechoslovakian named Paul Kohner. The two worked as office boys in Universal's New York headquarters, on Broadway. With their working knowledge of several languages, they eagerly took it upon themselves to translate Universal's press releases from the Coast into German, French, and Czech, and they sent them to newspapers abroad. A few months later, Carl Laemmle caught sight of several articles about his company in these foreign journals and traced the deed back to Wyler and Kohner. He summoned them to his office, ready to deport them for ringing up these unauthorized expenditures. When he learned that the European market in fact wanted to pay them for more material, Laemmle put them in charge of Universal's new foreign publicity department.

After a year cooped up at 1600 Broadway, the adventurous Wyler told "Uncle Carl" that he wanted "to be where the action was." Laemmle made him an office boy at Universal City and advanced him the train fare, which also got paid back at the rate of five dollars per week. Wyler's expansive personality was right at home in the boom-town atmosphere of early-twenties Hollywood. He was an avid gambler, and he loved to tool around the city at top speeds on his motorcycle. He quickly moved out of an office on the lot into the prop room, then up the ladder of assistant directors. His primary task on Universal's production of *The Hunchback of Notre Dame*, with Lon Chaney, was to herd several hundred extras, shouting to them at the appropriate moment, "Pull up your tights and light your torches!" When the Metro-Goldwyn-Mayer company made *Ben-Hur* and needed assistants, Wyler performed similar duties in their Culver City colosseum. Back at Universal, Wyler asked for a chance to direct a two-reel western. His competence at that first twenty-minute formula picture earned him the right to make twenty more in their "Mustang" series. Each was filmed in a week and budgeted at two thousand dollars apiece, sixty dollars going to the director.

Winning those spurs led to six of Universal's "Blue Streak" five-reel westerns. "In those days it was like a school," Wyler said of his training ground. "I learned a great deal making little westerns because they all demanded action and the basis of motion pictures is really action." The framing of shots intrigued him from the beginning. "I used to spend nights," he remembered, "trying to think of new ways of getting on and off a horse."

Five-reelers gave way to feature films, and when sound came in, Wyler was one of the most experienced directors on the Universal lot. In 1933, he got to direct John Barrymore in Elmer Rice's *Counsellor-at-Law*. Although Wyler never completely lost his foreign accent, his hearing was sensitive to even the most subtle nuances in his adopted language. An inarticulate perfectionist, he frustrated performers because he could never state precisely what was lacking in a specific take, only that he wanted it "better."

In late 1934, Wyler was given the opportunity to direct Universal's budding new star, the sandy-throated Margaret Sullavan, in a Molnár play adapted by Preston Sturges, called *The Good Fairy*. He and the leading lady quarreled furiously on the set almost every day, and privately made up at night. A "handsomely homely dynamo," as Bette Davis later described him, he had a rapid-fire laugh that often gave way to a gap-toothed grin many women found irresistible. He and Margaret Sullavan married in November 1934.

For all his craftsmanship, Wyler had had little opportunity to develop his artistry. Married to a rising movie star, he became painfully aware of the professional quagmire in which he was stuck. He left Universal—"to become a bigger director, to get my teeth in big, important pictures, and become," he confessed, "as big as Maggie." Careers came first for each of them, and they were constantly at each other's throats. The marriage was not helped any when Wyler gave the first real indications of his directorial powers in *The Gay Deception* for Fox. By the time it opened, he and Sullavan had separated.

Wyler could have received no call more welcome than that from his agent, Leland Hayward (who soon married Margaret Sullavan), reporting that Samuel Goldwyn wanted to meet him. Goldwyn needed a director immediately for a property he had just purchased. "He couldn't have been more charming," Wyler remembered of their first meeting, in the summer of 1935, "but I thought he had lost his mind. He told me he wanted to make 'The Children's Hour.'"

In a 1930 anthology of true-crime stories called *Bad Companions* appeared William Roughead's "Closed Doors; or the Great Drumsheugh Case," a tale of a girls' school in Edinburgh that was forced to close because of a rumor that the owners were lesbians. Dashiell Hammett brought it to the attention of Lillian Hellman and suggested there might be a play in it. After several months, she had fictionalized the case into the three-act play *The Children's Hour*. Lee Shubert, who owned the Broadway theater in which it opened, sat in on a rehearsal of the confession scene—"the recognition of the love of one woman for another"—and said, "This play could land us all in jail." Instead, it made everybody connected with it rich, as it enjoyed a run of almost seven hundred performances. But there was not even an indication of the really big money that film rights brought. Article II of the Hays Office's Production Code—"Sex"—could not have been more explicit: "Pictures shall not infer that low forms of sex relationship are the accepted or common thing." Subsection 2 said, "Sex perversion"—as lesbianism was certainly considered in 1934—"or any inference of it is forbidden."

Lillian Hellman liked Sam Goldwyn. Remembering the time when she was writing *The Dark Angel,* she later said, "I think our early days together worked well because I was a difficult young woman who didn't care as much about money as the people around me and so, by accident, I took a right step within the first months of working for Mr. Goldwyn." After *The Children's Hour* proved to be a solid hit on Broadway, she discussed its film possibilities with him, only to have him "laugh right in my face." Then she explained to him that "nobody wanted to touch the movie rights because they all thought the play was about lesbianism." In fact, she said, "the play was about the power of a lie. The substance of the lie itself is of secondary importance . . . it could be anything powerful enough to stir up the drama of the play. When I wrote *The Children's Hour,* I simply thought lesbianism was the most insidious lie the child could spread." Goldwyn became the only bidder for the film rights, offering $40,000.

Upon hearing the news, Will Hays himself discussed the purchase with Goldwyn. Because of the widespread notoriety of Hellman's play, he ruled that the producer was:

(a) Not to use the title, THE CHILDREN'S HOUR;
(b) To make no reference, directly or indirectly, in either advertising or exploitation of the picture to be made . . . to the stage play THE CHILDREN'S HOUR;
(c) To remove from your finished production all possible suggestion of Lesbianism and any other matter which is likely to prove objectionable.

Miss Hellman altered the play into a more conventional love triangle. In the screen version, Karen and Martha, two teachers who have been best friends since college, decide to open a private school for girls in an old New England house, only to fall in love with the same man, young Dr. Cardin. He has eyes for Karen; but one of the students spreads the malicious rumor that he is having a secret affair with Martha. The future of the school, the women's friendship, and Karen's marriage to Dr. Cardin are all threatened, until the gossipmonger is brought to justice.

Once Goldwyn explained how he intended to present *The Children's Hour,* Wyler leapt at the opportunity to direct it. "Don't forget," Wyler recalled many years later, "Sam Goldwyn's name stood for something, for quality. I had been making second-class pictures, and Goldwyn was making first-class pictures, so it was a good step for me."

Just before offering a contract, Goldwyn had second thoughts. He hit it off remarkably well with Wyler, who was twenty-three years his junior; but he had seen only one of his pictures. He went to Irving Thalberg, who had known Wyler from their earliest days in the picture business, when they were both at Universal. Thalberg told Goldwyn that throughout those years of Wyler's apprenticeship, he was known on the lot as "Worthless Willy."

Within months of each other, both Wyler and Lillian Hellman signed three-year contracts with Goldwyn. The director's was straight yearly employment at $2,000 per week; the writer's called for her to write "screen adaptations of five stories, to be furnished and designated by us"—assignments guaranteeing ten weeks at $2,500 per week. Both contracts allowed the artists to work on other projects and at other studios if they did not conflict with Goldwyn's production plans. But there was one proviso Wyler and Hellman had to agree to, which was nothing short of signing themselves into indentured servitude—the standard clause in motion picture contracts of the day that called for "suspension and extension." It meant that each was free to refuse a project not to his liking, but the time that would have been given to the assignment would be tacked onto the contract, protracting its expiration date. Wyler's period of "suspension and extension" would be three months, Hellman's seven. If a writer or director did not care about the quality of the pictures on which his name would appear, these long-term contracts were extravagant opportunities for steady gainful employment in a depressed economy. An artist signed such documents with the faith that his employer would play fair, because by intentionally offering bad material in anticipation that it would be refused, a producer could legally keep people under contract forever.

Wyler and Hellman became fast friends, first in their optimism toward their new boss, ultimately to survive the experience. She was "not easy in any respect," said Wyler of the "strong-minded woman" who would come to serve as a conscience for him. Hellman found Wyler "the greatest American director." She said, "He had a wonderful pictorial sense—he knew how to pack so much into a shot that I felt I could leave certain things unsaid, knowing Willy would show them. We had to become friends," she remembered with a laugh, "because we were the only two people in the Goldwyn asylum who weren't completely loony."

In truth, the Goldwyn company was teeming with sound minds, including two of Hellman's friends from the East. One was George Haight,

a young alumnus of Yale, an aspiring playwright. He had become a Goldwyn executive when George Oppenheimer moved on. One of Haight's
schoolmates, Henry C. Potter—"prep-school handsome, respectable,
grandson of a bishop, an unexpected man for the world of the theatre or
Hollywood"—had also moved onto the lot, as Haight tried to help him
make the leap from directing plays to directing movies. A third Yalie,
Justus Baldwin Lawrence, known as "Jock," was the new "bright young
man" in charge of Goldwyn's publicity. Merritt Hulburd, from Philadelphia's Main Line, rounded out Goldwyn's staff. A shrewd and handsome
gentleman named David Rose, a former business associate of Douglas Fairbanks, became a business adviser and confidant.

Because of her literary connections, Goldwyn had become obsessed with
hiring George S. Kaufman's wife, Beatrice, as his New York story editor.
She had held editorial positions at several publishing houses and magazines
in the last few years. Now he wanted her to scout for new material on his
behalf—only months after the unpleasant settlement with her husband
over *Roman Scandals*. "The thing to do," Goldwyn said to Mrs. Kaufman
in persuading her to accept a job with him, "is to pretend it never happened. And then it never happened." With that, Goldwyn turned away,
then he turned back again, with wide-eyed innocence. "What's this about
a fight with your husband?" he said to Mrs. Kaufman. "It *never* happened!"
After such a performance, she could not resist the job. But she found that
his charm evaporated quickly, and she held the position less than a year.
"The truth is," Goldwyn's son admitted with hindsight, "he wasn't interested in developing good secondary people. He was always afraid of too
strong an organization, because then he'd have to watch out for them."

"Sam has had more fights than any other man in Hollywood," observed
Alva Johnston, who was sent by the *Saturday Evening Post* to profile Goldwyn. "Because he is a rebel and a trail blazer in the use of the English
language, he is the central figure of a great comic legend." After weeks of
research, Johnston found that even "most of those who hate him or laugh
at him will say, 'I admire Sam.'" Goldwyn's ability as a producer was sometimes discounted, "on the theory that he buys success." That was not the
whole story, Johnston discovered; there was an essence to Goldwyn's work:

"The Goldwyn touch" is not brilliance or sensationalism. It is something that manifests itself gradually in a picture; the characters are
consistent; the workmanship is honest; there are no tricks and short
cuts; the intelligence of the audience is never insulted.

Lillian Hellman worked through the summer of 1935 adapting *The Children's Hour* to the screen, using the working title "The Lie." Goldwyn and his story department considered the finished script one of the finest they had ever read. No other writers were brought in to polish it. In fact, the bulk of the script's editing was based on suggestions by Wyler, who found some of the scenes too wordy. The opening sequence of the film, for example, was several pages of dialogue revealing the friendship and backgrounds of Martha and Karen as they graduated from college. Wyler told Hellman how he could express the same information more effectively in just a few shots, hardly calling for a word to be spoken. The story department compiled lists of possible titles; it was not until the film was shot that Goldwyn selected *These Three*.

Goldwyn's trio of stars—Miriam Hopkins, Joel McCrea, and Merle Oberon—were bunched into their first film together and handed to the director. After testing dozens of children, Wyler did get to cast a terrifying twelve-year-old named Bonita Granville as Mary, the little liar. Except for her, he was unfavorably predisposed to his cast. All he had seen of Joel McCrea was of his running around in outdoorsy pictures; Miriam Hopkins's fabled temper scared him; and Merle Oberon herself knew she had never played a part that relied more on character than on costume.

Besides the added tension of working with the most challenging material of his career, Wyler felt that he was on trial. With this, his first dramatic film since leaving Universal, he was auditioning not only for Goldwyn but for the rest of Hollywood. Goldwyn understood why Wyler kept trying to postpone the start date of the picture.

For all his eschewal of his role in expanding the reach of the cinema, Wyler's motion pictures began to plumb new psychological depths. Lillian Hellman said he showed "that character could be action. He'd hold the camera on an actor's face for what seemed like forever, and then suddenly you'd see some look of recognition in an actor's eye or somebody would step out of a shadow into the light and you'd be shocked out of your seat." Many moments in *These Three* benefited from Wyler's interesting staging, particularly the scene in which Martha confesses to Karen her own love for Dr. Cardin. Wyler situated the camera at Miriam Hopkins's back, so that she might, in truth, have been revealing her love for Karen. The camera dwells instead on the reactions.

The thirty-three-year-old director worked with a crew entirely new to him, except for a film editor he had brought from Universal, Daniel Mandell, a former acrobat and strongman with the Ringling Brothers circus. Wyler found his cameraman, Gregg Toland, noticeably distant; and after several days Toland announced that he wanted to quit. The problem stemmed from Wyler's never having worked with a photographer who was anything more than a technician. He was in the habit of telling his cameramen where to place the equipment, how to move the camera, and how to light each scene. Here was a man who had learned at the feet of George Barnes and for years had been experimenting with lighting and camera technique of his own. (Goldwyn funded his development of new equipment.) Once Wyler understood Toland, he got him to stay, and the two developed one of the most extraordinary partnerships in Hollywood. "When he photographed something," Wyler said, "he wanted to go beyond lights and catch feelings."

The production went slowly. "I had always had somebody breathing down my neck telling me to move faster, that there was no time to get it right," said Wyler. "And one thing I have to say about Goldwyn is he wanted me to get things on film the way I wanted them." Wyler would shoot as many as forty takes with the same camera setup, printing but two or three of them. Another problem with Wyler, Joel McCrea recalled, was that "he tended to look out for one or two actors in a picture, and he would shit on the rest. He was crazy about the little girl, and Miriam knew how to take care of herself. But Merle didn't have that much experience and she started to panic."

She tried to convince McCrea and Hopkins that Bonita Granville was stealing the picture. "Merle came to me and we started talking about it," McCrea recalled years later, "and we agreed I should say something to Goldwyn. . . . Now, of course, Goldwyn never listened much, but I started to explain what I was doing up in his office. Goldwyn got awfully exasperated, and finally said, 'I'm having more trouble with you stars than Mussolini is with Utopia!'" McCrea returned to the set, forgetting why he had gone up in the first place.

After a week of filming, Wyler came to McCrea's dressing room. McCrea had already sensed the director's disappointment at his not being more of an actor. Before Wyler could get a word out, McCrea said, "Look, if I were directing this picture, I'd rather have Leslie Howard too." Wyler said, "Really?" McCrea assured him it was all right to feel that way, that he would still give it his all. Moved by the actor's candor, Wyler confessed, "You didn't know it, but I wanted Leslie Howard." McCrea said he did know; Goldwyn had told him.

"I told him not to!" Wyler cried.

"That doesn't make any difference," said McCrea. "I was at his house for dinner, and—"

"*I* haven't been invited to his house for dinner!" protested Wyler. After discussing the point that had brought him into the dressing room, he asked, "What's it like?" McCrea looked puzzled. "At the Goldwyns'?"

McCrea described his evening atop Laurel Lane. Clark Gable and Carole Lombard had been there, along with Paramount executives Y. Frank Freeman and Stanton Griffis, "and two or three other wheels." Sometime late into the meal, as though he just could not hold it in any longer, Goldwyn had said, "What is it with Willy Wyler? He must have an interest in some company that makes film or something. He does thirty-six takes and he prints one and six." Wyler felt safe enough with McCrea to confide why he worked that way. "I'm not sure of myself," he admitted.

Wyler's insecurity manifested itself in other ways as well, as his fears of permanently preserving mistakes became chronic. He developed stomachaches; he began to insist that his brother Robert or some trusted friend be hired on his films, if not to rewrite pages then to stand by his side to discuss them; he would approach each scene by shooting a loose master shot, then cover the scene by shooting every character from every possible angle.

Notwithstanding, Goldwyn's continual pleasure with the first rushes on *These Three* emboldened Wyler to stand up for what he believed. Goldwyn had the strength of character to change his mind, but never, Wyler observed, "until he saw you burst every blood vessel in your head. Even if he agreed with you, he'd intentionally disagree just to see how hard you'd argue your case." A rapport developed between the two men, partly because of their near-equal inability to express themselves. Deeper than that, after years of working almost exclusively with Gentile directors, Goldwyn had at last found a fellow European Jew with similar artistic aspirations.

"Mr. Goldwyn," as Wyler called him throughout his tenure, always kept the upper hand, but he harbored his own insecurities. In an early scene of *These Three*, Joel McCrea appeared as an apiarist, outfitted in protective mask and gear. Wyler filmed the scene as hundreds of bees were let loose, one of them attacking him. The next day, he was stunned to discover that the publicity department had released a feature story to *Variety* about the bees on the set of *These Three* and how one of them had stung Samuel Goldwyn.

From that moment on, competition between Wyler and Goldwyn steadily grew. "The big difference between them," said Danny Mandell, "was that Goldwyn could never admit that he was wrong." Wyler and Goldwyn had recently gone weeks barely speaking to each other because of the director's unusual staging of that "confession" scene, in which Miriam Hopkins stood with her back to the camera. Where Wyler believed he had cleverly captured multiple interpretations, Goldwyn saw only obfuscation. One Sunday while he was still in a rage over the problem, he forwent his usual card game and went to the studio to run the film over and over with Wyler until they could reach some solution. He brought Sammy along. For the better part of an hour, Goldwyn shrieked at his director, as Wyler insisted that the scene was perfectly clear. When he could stand no more, Wyler turned to the boy and said, "Sammy, do you understand what this scene is about?" Goldwyn's son explained in precise detail everything that the scene was meant to convey. Goldwyn simmered in silence until he blew his top and sputtered, "Since when are we making pictures for nine-year-olds?"

"He had an uncanny sense of knowing if something was wrong with a picture," Mandell said. "Then he'd drive everybody crazy until someone came up with what it was." The day after *These Three* previewed, his staff realized that Goldwyn had tossed all night over something he could not put his finger on. Wyler knew the trouble—a scene he wanted to shoot over, in which Mary blackmails another schoolgirl into being her conspirator. It showed how truly evil she was, thereby strengthening her as a villain. Wyler had underplayed it; but he did not say a word to Goldwyn, knowing the producer would disagree reflexively. Instead, Wyler conspired with Mandell. When they ran the film the next day, Mandell interrupted the screening right after the scene had played, according to plan. "I stopped the film, Mr. Goldwyn," Mandell said, "because of my integrity as a member of your staff. As an editor I can tell you this is the only weak scene in the entire picture." Goldwyn weighed this carefully, considering that the only solution for such a problem would be reshooting. "What do you think, Willy?" Goldwyn asked. "I think Danny has a point," he said, struggling to keep a straight face. The scene was reshot.

"I never knew what 'the Goldwyn touch' was," said Danny Mandell, who ended up editing practically all of Goldwyn's films for the next twenty-five years. "I think it was something a Goldwyn publicist made up." Said Wyler, "I don't recall his contributing anything other than buying good material and talent. It was all an attempt to make a name for himself as an artist. But as far as being creative, he was zero." And yet every decision as to which scenes were reshot or included in the picture required Goldwyn's approval; not a word of the script reached the screen without Goldwyn's okay; none of Richard Day's sets was built or Omar Kiam's costumes sewn until Goldwyn permitted; the successful Americanization of Merle Oberon was solely the result of Goldwyn's vision. The morning after one of the last previews of *These Three*, in February 1936, Goldwyn received an urgent memorandum from Alfred Newman, complaining about two places in which Mr. Wyler "rather whimsically, arbitrarily, and very vaguely" insisted that the music be cut. Goldwyn ruled that the music cues should stay. And whenever Danny Mandell was ready to quit working on a scene that still did not play right, Goldwyn could wheedle him into giving it one more attempt.

These Three gathered notices the likes of which Goldwyn had not received before. In language more thoughtful than the usual Hollywood superlatives, they treated the film with artistic respect, especially the demanding English critics. Graham Greene, who had become the regular film critic for the *Spectator,* wrote: "After ten minutes or so of the usual screen sentiment, quaintness and exaggeration, one began to watch with incredulous pleasure nothing less than life."

These Three was the fifth Goldwyn picture in the past ten United Artists releases. Ever since Joseph Schenck had resigned from United Artists in May 1935, Goldwyn's influence at UA had increased in other ways as well. Schenck's stockholdings were sold back to the company, giving Goldwyn a share equal to those of the rest of his partners. But Schenck sold Twentieth Century's stock in the United Artists Studio to Sam Goldwyn for $250,000. That meant that Mary Pickford and Douglas Fairbanks still held the real estate of their studio, but Goldwyn became the sole owner of everything that sat on it, including the stages and equipment.

Schenck's abdication also left a vacancy in power at United Artists, subjecting the company to a rapid succession of presidents. Al Lichtman was the first to find himself exposed to Goldwyn's constant attacks over the selling of their product. When he could stand the badgering no longer, he left, and Mary Pickford assumed the throne. She found Goldwyn no more of a friend in her court. After a few months, a compromise candidate, Dr. Giannini, was given the office, but Goldwyn did not even let up on his banker, rendering him but a caretaker until a real leader could take over.

"All my life I've been an adventurer, and have been in a lot of tough situations," Dr. Attilio Henry Giannini later reminisced. "But let me tell you, I never saw fights like the ones at U.A. board meetings in my life." He said that "criminations, recriminations, cusswords"—even physical violence—became standard boardroom procedure.

All fingers pointed at Goldwyn. Giannini said that once "he puts his name to a deal the deal is good." The problem with Goldwyn was that "out of 20 deals he starts, 18 will be frustrated." UA's counsel, Charles Schwartz, said that Goldwyn "nagged over everything." Regardless of who was right in any matter, Goldwyn would frustrate his opposition into submission. At one meeting, he called Douglas Fairbanks a crook, whereupon the retired swashbuckler vaulted across the table and grabbed Goldwyn by the throat. Giannini had to separate them. He took Goldwyn outside to calm him with a shot of whiskey. Moments later, Goldwyn returned to the meeting to make amends. "I can't prove anything," he said, "so I apologize."

The meetings always ended in a row—somebody against Goldwyn. The partners were angered because they felt they had established Samuel Goldwyn in the business, and that even if they were not making pictures anymore, "they were entitled to their fruits of ownership." Chaplin—who had endorsed Goldwyn's entrance into the company with a $150,000 loan—stopped showing up at meetings if Goldwyn was to be present. Soon the other owners sent proxies as well. When Goldwyn's contract with UA came up for ratification, he began demanding new terms, including a shorter contract with the company. When Giannini sided with the other partners against such preferential treatment, Goldwyn turned against him and proceeded to oppose any Giannini decision. The powerful banker became a lame duck.

In the marketplace, Chaplin's latest picture, *Modern Times*, released in February 1936, was a serious financial disappointment. David Selznick and Alexander Korda, recent additions to the company, could be counted on for a couple of releases that year. Even Mary Pickford, realizing the crunch her company was in, partnered with Jesse Lasky on two films. But none of them could improve United Artists' position with the exhibitors.

Goldwyn saw only one way they, as independent producers, could stand up to the major theater chains, and that was by bringing the best of the studio producers into their camp. For months Goldwyn entreated Irving Thalberg; and his UA partners backed him up by extending generous offers. The idea appealed to him. The frail MGM producer saw how he might truly flourish away from L. B. Mayer, the way Darryl Zanuck, for one, came into his own when he left the Warner brothers. But ultimately, UA could not offer Thalberg the security he already had. And so, as had been the case for five years, if United Artists was to chug along, it needed Sam Goldwyn to stoke its engine.

Goldwyn continued his pursuit of George Bernard Shaw, this time adding *Pygmalion* to his list of wants. The playwright was as contemptuous of Hollywood as ever and wrote Goldwyn that nobody out there had any "more notion of telling a story than a blind puppy [has] of composing a symphony." He was convinced that any of the studios would put his play in the hands of "the bellboy, in whose view life is a continual going up and down stairs and opening and shutting doors." Granting that Goldwyn was "a bit different from the ordinary Hollywood mental patient," Shaw said he would sell his plays for 10 percent of his films' grosses plus the right to alter the scripts and cut the pictures.

Goldwyn spent much of the year chasing trends instead: John Ford's *The Informer* had become one of 1935's great hits; so Goldwyn wanted his own story about Ireland's political turmoil. Ever since *It Happened One Night*, Goldwyn had been itching to come up with a "screwball comedy." Natural disasters had become a recent rage in films—a locust plague in *The Good Earth* and an earthquake in *San Francisco*—so Goldwyn snatched the rights to a new novel by *Mutiny on the Bounty*'s authors, Charles Nordhoff and James Norman Hall, *The Hurricane.* Having proved successful adding sound to *The Dark Angel,* Goldwyn figured he would remake his other great silent tearjerker, *Stella Dallas.*

Goldwyn also pursued two projects that imitated nothing currently playing at the movies. One was an Edna Ferber novel called *Come and Get It.* Goldwyn paid $100,000 for the rights to this lusty tale of Polish-Americans who worked in the lumber mills of Wisconsin. It followed the ruthless Barney Glasgow, who would let nothing stop him as he shinnied his way from lumberjack to logging king—not even his love for a beautiful dance-hall singer, Lotta. Years later, he meets the woman's granddaughter and falls for her, foolishly hoping to recapture lost time. Edna Ferber sold the book to Goldwyn, believing he understood the seriousness of her intentions in this book, that "it is primarily a story of the rape of America . . . a story of the destruction of forests and rivers by the whole-sale robber barons of that day."

Come and Get It had much of the spirit of *Barbary Coast.* Despite his trepidations about Howard Hawks's messing with scripts and letting actors improvise lines, Goldwyn had to admit the director had a way with brawling, sprawling stories. When he learned that Barney Glasgow was based in part on Hawks's grandfather, Goldwyn was convinced he was the right man for the job. Even Edna Ferber was impressed. After meeting with the charming Hawks, who said he wanted to fix a few details in Jane Murfin's tidy script, she felt confident enough to give him such license. Jules Furthman was brought in to rewrite the picture; it became the first of several celebrated collaborations with Hawks, who reveled in Furthman's cynicism and his "great ability to think of new ways of doing things."

Hawks began to exert his influence over Goldwyn in other ways as well. Although Miriam Hopkins had been announced to star in the dual roles of Lotta, she was not Hawks's type. He looked at countless tests of young starlets until he saw a UCLA graduate in a sixteen-millimeter student film. Her name was Antoinette Leeds, and she had a freshness Hawks liked, wholesome but sassy. Goldwyn put her under contract and changed her first name to Andrea. But even after agreeing that Miriam Hopkins was not right for the role of Lotta, he did not think Miss Leeds was equipped to carry a picture. He cast her in a supporting role. Before he knew it, Hawks was urging him to give the lead to a young actress with as little experience.

She was Frances Farmer, a leggy blonde of twenty-two, who auditioned for a small part in the film and bowled Hawks over. In her youth, she had stirred up trouble in her hometown, Seattle, when she won a national magazine competition with her essay "God Dies." At the University of Washington, she had entered another contest and won first prize, a trip to the Soviet Union. Returning through New York, the heavenly girl met some Paramount executives, who put her under contract. For all her great physical strength, young Frances was psychologically frail. Within her first few months, she made three films in rapid succession for Paramount; the sudden overload of all that fell upon her in Hollywood came close to crushing her. Before she walked out of Hawks's office, he said, "You ought to play the lead."

This Aryan goddess's beauty was not lost on Goldwyn either, but he doubted her ability to pull off the double roles. Hawks worked overtime with her. In her first test, she tried to become the character of the mother by using a lot of makeup; Hawks urged her to create the role from within. They cruised beer joints together one night, until they found a woman who Hawks thought was the same type as the character. He instructed the ingenue to return to the bar every night and become that woman. The screen test, said Hawks, was "fabulous. She was a blonde, a natural, but she just used a dark wig; that's all she put on. No change in make-up, just her face changed. Her whole attitude changed, her whole method of talking." Goldwyn was coming around to Hawks's way of thinking, a process hastened by bigger casting problems and the lack of time he had to give to the film's preparation.

Come and Get It needed a strong actor at the center. "Louis," Goldwyn boldly announced when he got his archrival, Mr. Mayer, on the telephone, "we're in trouble. You've got Spencer Tracy and I need him." Not even from an enemy would Mayer extort a lot of money for Tracy's services. After several years of the actor's playing petty racketeers and ordinary guys, L. B. was grooming him for more sympathetic, even heroic, roles. The next few years would see Tracy as priests, lawyers, newspapermen, and doughty fishermen. Hard-pressed for a dynamic Barney Glasgow, Goldwyn settled on Edward Arnold—not a major movie star but able to carry a picture.

Goldwyn was trying to accomplish as much as possible before leaving with Frances and Sammy for Europe. He meant to conduct business in

England and France that March, but the voyage was intended as a vacation, to calm his volcanic stomach. "Sam Goldwyn didn't get ulcers," King Vidor said, thinking back on the time when he was preparing *Stella Dallas*, his fourth film for him, "he gave them." In fact, Goldwyn—who had worried about stomachaches since his father's death—had recently been suffering from sharp abdominal pains, which his doctor tried to curb dietetically.

Goldwyn's most unusual property that season promised to be his most prestigious film to date. Back when Sidney Howard was writing *Arrowsmith* for Goldwyn, he had tipped the producer off to another Sinclair Lewis work, which he thought would make a wonderful motion picture, the 1929 novel *Dodsworth*. Howard said Goldwyn could buy the rights for $20,000. When the producer refused, he turned the book into a play, a smash hit starring Walter Huston. Now Goldwyn came around to buy the rights to film the story, only to find the price had jumped to $160,000. Howard pointed out that Goldwyn could have bought the same story just a few years earlier for a fraction of that. Goldwyn proved himself the shrewder for the waiting. "This way," he told Howard, "I buy a successful play. Before it was just a novel."

There were many reasons why no producers had shown interest in Lewis's book. *Dodsworth* was the story of a retired automobile manufacturer from the Midwest who retreats to Europe with his frivolous wife, Fran. While she skims along the surface of European society, dipping into one love affair after another, he earnestly attempts to absorb a culture other than his own. As his wife dallies with an English playboy, a Middle European banker, and an impoverished count, he falls in love with an American widow, Edith Cortwright. Fran stupidly thinks she will marry her count, until his forbidding mother confronts her. Then she wires for her husband to take her home to Zenith, Ohio, where Dodsworth discovers that his silly wife is none the wiser. He unexpectedly about-faces and returns to Edith and a happy future in Europe. It was more a story of character than of action; and all the lead roles were middle-aged, giving the studios opportunity neither to cast from their stables of glamorous young talent nor to appeal to the growing audience of young moviegoers. Where many producers saw *Dodsworth* as a tale of immorality, Goldwyn saw it as the "story of a man who held on to his pride—and then surrendered his soul to love." Sidney Howard wrote the screen adaptation.

Walter Huston, touring the country as Sam Dodsworth, desperately wanted to reprise the role on film. After a few dozen films, the public still did not recognize him as a movie star, but Goldwyn considered nobody else for the lead. He also cast the rest of the roles according to ability more than notability. Ruth Chatterton, in the waning of her short film career, got the part of Mrs. Dodsworth. Goldwyn's casting director, Robert McIntyre, recommended newcomer Rosalind Russell for the role of Edith Cortwright, but Goldwyn signed Mary Astor instead. He also felt it was time to elevate David Niven, who had spoken a few lines in films off the lot, to a featured role with actual scenes. He was cast as an English playboy, the first of Fran Dodsworth's lovers.

At the urging of Merritt Hulburd, who would be supervising the production of *Dodsworth*, Goldwyn had all but promised the project to director Gregory La Cava. After seeing William Wyler's display of talent in *These Three*, however, Goldwyn activated the option clause in his three-year contract by giving him *Dodsworth* to direct. His new favorite went to New York the week before the Goldwyns' March 4 departure on the *Berengaria*. He met with the producer and Sidney Howard, who liked him enough not to be put off by his obvious inability "to collaborate in the actual laying out or writing of the script." Wyler's shortcomings did not faze Goldwyn. He believed motion pictures were built best when there was a strong division of labor, compartmentalizing the artists.

One night before sailing, Goldwyn asked Wyler to join him and Frances at the Belasco Theater to see Sidney Kingsley's *Dead End*. The drama was set on a New York street, between the exclusive East River Terrace Apartments and a series of squalid tenement houses, not unlike *Street Scene*. As the curtain came down, Goldwyn turned to Wyler and asked what he thought of the play. "Great! Great!" he said between bravos. Before they had left their seats, Goldwyn asked if he would like to direct it. Wyler was beside himself with excitement. Goldwyn had heard that Selznick had recently bid $150,000 for the film rights; so the next day, Goldwyn closed a deal for $165,000. "That was the great thing about Goldwyn," Wyler said. "If there was some great material and he wanted it, he would just buy it, just like that." He put $25,000 down as good-faith money and embarked for Europe. His organization was stronger than it had ever been: Two pictures would start filming upon his return, three more would be ready shortly after that, followed by *Dead End*.

"SAMMY was wild with anticipation" over his first trip to Europe, Frances recalled, and Sam "was running him a close second." Frances, however, found herself subjected to inexplicable hysteria. She did not want to leave her new home. She tried to explain herself to her husband, but she could not get the words out. Sam called her "plain crazy" and complained of her moods. During the crossing he did not know she repeatedly locked herself in the bathroom and wept. She had simply been overcome with forebodings of doom because everything had been going so well.

"So we went to London, Paris, the south of France and always I felt trouble staring at me," Frances remembered. "Finally we took the ship for home. This was some relief, though not much." April 13, a Monday, she was in the cabin, packing, when her husband staggered in and said, "Frances, all of a sudden I'm awfully sick." He fell on his bed in pain and convulsed and vomited through most of the night. Once the ship docked, they went directly to Doctors Hospital in New York, where he was diagnosed as having intestinal toxemia. Frances felt instantly relieved when she saw Sam fighting with a nurse who insisted he drink a glass of bismuth. He had returned to his familiar dyspeptic self. His pain persisted, and the doctors recommended removing his gall bladder and appendix.

Frances was terrified. She dispatched Sammy to the West Coast, giving him so little information as to frighten him. Although she had agreed to let him change schools, she re-enrolled him in Black-Foxe Academy, to give the appearance that nothing had changed in their lives. He moved in with the Lehrs. For days, they and James Mulvey were the only people informed of Goldwyn's surgery.

Within a week, Goldwyn seemed better, "complaining of boredom." Frances allowed word of the operation out. Overnight, one hundred "get well" wires arrived, and flowers filled the room. His friends William Paley and Irving Berlin came to cheer him up, joking with him for several hours. Very early the next morning, Frances was summoned to the hospital. The stitches in Goldwyn's incision had burst, ostensibly from all the laughter. The problem went deeper than that. His entire system remained poisoned, and he suddenly sank into a serious decline. A doctor pulled Frances aside and told her that her husband had one, maybe two, hours to live. He parked her in the corridor, while they waited to see if the medication they had tried would work some wonders.

In the midst of her fright, James Mulvey raced down the hall with news of his own. "Frances," he said, "when Mr. Goldwyn made the deal for 'Dead End' he secured it with a down payment of twenty-five thousand dollars." Frances told him she could not be bothered with such thoughts just then. Mulvey said he could not wait any longer, that the remainder of the money due to secure the rights to the play had to be paid by noon that day or they would have to forfeit the property. It was eleven-thirty. "And if Mr. Goldwyn doesn't—" stammered Mulvey, "well, it's up to you, Frances."

The ever-cautious Frances Goldwyn was forced to fight her own instincts and do what her husband had done by nature almost every day of his life—gamble. "Pay the money, Mulvey," she said, as though she had just had some vision. "Sam's going to get well. He's going to make that picture. And it'll be good. I've got that faith in God and Sam Goldwyn."

Mulvey wrote the check. For days, Goldwyn lingered, getting neither better nor worse. While he was in extremis, Frances considered calling his twenty-four-year-old daughter, Ruth, then living in Los Angeles, whom he had not seen for more than a decade. But she did not.

The seriousness of Sam's condition was revealed only to a trusted few. Frances answered the well-wishing wires with calm responses, as though everything were all right. "My mother's attitude," Sam Goldwyn, Jr., said years later, thinking of other such moments of crisis in her life as well, "was never to let on that she and my father were in any danger. 'They must never know,' she would say. She was absolutely paranoid that if anybody ever found out that they were in danger, they would come and take her house away. *They* must never know!" It was, evidently, the major reason she had perfected the rights to *Dead End*.

On Monday, May 11, surgeons operated on Goldwyn a second time, removing several feet of decayed intestine. During the following three weeks, he recovered in the hospital, then he rested at the Waldorf-Astoria until he was able to return home. A half-dozen motion pictures hung in the balance—unknown to the hundreds of workers whose livelihoods would also be affected. Even after he had come out of the woods, Frances was committed to keeping the world from knowing how sick he had been. So all business—Eddie Cantor in the final throes of his leaving Goldwyn, Alexander Korda renegotiating Merle Oberon's contract, Merritt Hulburd supervising the final scripts and casting of *Dodsworth* and *Come and Get It*, the production staff scheduling the shooting of background footage of Tahiti for *The Hurricane*, Mary Pickford anxious to close United Artists' new partnership agreement with producer Walter Wanger, James Mulvey with the emergencies too big for him to handle alone—went through Frances.

Although it would be weeks before he could get to Los Angeles to oversee the commencement of photography on his next two pictures, Goldwyn ordered that it proceed. With nobody to oppose him, Howard Hawks began to turn *Come and Get It* into something all his own. He granted Jules Furthman new liberties with the script, and he cast the picture according to his taste. He started by giving the role of Swan Bostrom—a character Edna Ferber described as "the strongest man in the North woods"—to bony Walter Brennan. The director also put together his own shooting schedule and a budget $100,000 over what Goldwyn would have allowed. This news got Goldwyn's blood boiling. He felt Hawks was taking advantage of his infirmity.

Meantime, Merritt Hulburd wired Frances, the insecure William Wyler was "HESITANT AS USUAL BUT HAVE NO DOUBT OF HIS ABILITY TO START AROUND JUNE FIRST." After seeing *Dead End* that night with the Goldwyns, the director had spent several weeks in New York, during which time Sidney Howard discovered Wyler's unique gift for translating the verbal into the visual. He wrote Hulburd that Wyler's "presence in New York is not wasted . . . because I am feeding him sequences at a great rate and he is already hatching any number of good ideas on the earlier portions of the picture."

As the *Dodsworth* script progressed, Wyler's suggestions became more particular. He proved to have an uncanny ear for dialogue that was inappropriate or unnecessary. Wyler's strongest concern was that Howard "make Fran less of a bitch at the outset." Even as the story progressed, Wyler contended, Fran should show those elements of her personality that appealed to her husband in the first place. Otherwise he would appear as an unsympathetic fool for ever marrying her. Howard agreed.

Once shooting began, Wyler had to argue his feelings about Fran Dodsworth all over again. "It was like pulling teeth with her," he said of his experience with Ruth Chatterton. "She only wanted to play her as a selfish bitch, and I kept trying to make her see that Mrs. Dodsworth had a very good case for behaving the way she did. She'd been a good wife for twenty-five years, and raised their children, and now he's rich and retiring, and she wants to have a fling. She says to her husband, 'You're simply rushing at old age, Sam, and I'm not ready for that yet!' And that's true. In her mind, this was her last chance to live a little."

Wyler's fights with Miss Chatterton were monumental, ranging from sarcastic to sadistic. In the wide eyes of David Niven, the director was nothing less than a "Jekyll-and-Hyde character"—"kind, fun and cozy at all other times, he became a fiend the moment his bottom touched down in his director's chair. . . . He even managed to reduce the experienced Ruth Chatterton to such a state that she slapped his face and locked herself in her dressing room." Mary Astor contended that the problem grew from the leading lady's detesting her role, that "the character was that of a woman who is trying to hang onto her youth—which was exactly what Ruth herself was doing. It touched a nerve."

When Niven worked, the actor remembered, "it was perfectly normal for Willie to sit beneath the camera reading the Hollywood 'Reporter' and not even look up till I had plowed through the scene a couple of dozen times. 'Just do it again,' he'd say, turning a page."

More often than not, it was Wyler's "perfectionist" attitude that was running the production over budget, not his actors' lack of aptitude. He spent one entire afternoon, for example, shooting a scene of a crumpled letter being gently blown across a terrace. Miss Astor remembered, "He wanted it to go slowly for a way, then stop, and then flutter a little farther, and finally be caught up in a gust and blown over the edge of the balcony."

The Goldwyns returned to Beverly Hills on July 4, 1936, and the "fireworks" began immediately. At fifty-seven, Sam Goldwyn experienced a sudden change of life. His recent brush with death had brought him face to face with the ghost of his father—that "sensitive fella" who had died at forty-three. The visitation haunted him forever. From that day forward, Sam Goldwyn moaned constantly about his impending demise. A fear of germs and an obsession about cleanliness, which he had carried since his flight from the squalor of Poland, intensified. And now anyone who displeased him was out to get him; whoever defied him was trying to kill him. "I'm gonna die," he wailed whenever he did not get his way. Just when he thought the czar had stopped chasing him, Goldwyn found himself being pursued by the Grim Reaper. He took to his bed.

He had been recovering steadily since his operations, but the doctors said it would be weeks before he could go back to the studio. Frances supervised the conversion of their house into both hospital ward and office. She organized the domestic staff, team of nurses, and production personnel around a strict schedule that called mostly for her husband's resting. She read every book on diet that she could find, and she oversaw every forkful of his food. She pinned a St. Christopher's medal to his pajamas.

Once settled in, Goldwyn inspected the footage of his two films, both practically finished. The amount of excess film Wyler used upset Goldwyn; but the quality of *Dodsworth* pleased him enormously. Watching a rough assembly of *Come and Get It,* on the other hand, practically sent him through the roof.

Hawks had turned the film into something far afield of anything Goldwyn had ever imagined, into what would later prove to have all the earmarks of a Howard Hawks picture. He had shifted the primary focus of the story into a "buddy movie"—the story of two friends and a girl. What had once been intended to be Miriam Hopkins portraying a "little lame girl who sang so badly that the woodsmen hooted at her" got changed into Frances Farmer playing "a lusty wench." Goldwyn found every scene caked with bits of business, Hawks-inspired improvisation that detracted from the story. Character actors like Walter Brennan were allowed to steal scenes from the stars. Joel McCrea, who was meant to be second-billed in the film as Barney Glasgow's son, was lost altogether. "After I saw what [Hawks] had filmed," Goldwyn would later write Edna Ferber in an attempt to explain how her story got botched, "I suffered a relapse for a full two weeks; it upset me so."

In truth, he got on the case the next day. Against doctors' and Frances's orders, he went to the studio and confronted Hawks directly. "Writers should write and directors should direct!" rang Goldwyn's cry across the lot. Hawks said he was walking off the picture. Goldwyn said that suited him, because Hawks was fired. Goldwyn returned to his bed to think how the original story might be restored as much as possible. It dawned on him that *Dodsworth* had but a few shots to go.

Wyler received his first invitation to Laurel Lane. On a sweltering July afternoon, he was shown upstairs to the master bedroom, where he found Goldwyn in his pajamas, propped up in bed against a mound of pillows. Frances sat in a chair by his side, with what Wyler thought at first was a fan but was a fly swatter. Goldwyn said how pleased he was with *Dodsworth* and that he wanted Wyler to finish *Come and Get It*. Wyler protested that there was still more to do on *Dodsworth,* including the editing. Goldwyn assured him that could wait, and that he was not the editor anyway. Wyler said, "I can't just walk into another picture like that. It's Howard Hawks's picture." Goldwyn said Hawks had been fired. "Well, Mr. Goldwyn," protested Wyler, "I refuse to do it." Suddenly, Wyler later recalled, "he just exploded and Frances tried to calm him down. But he turned into a madman. He said I had to do this, that it was in my contract, and that if I didn't do it, he'd ruin my career." He got so mad that Frances started to beat him over his legs with the fly swatter. Wyler ran out of the house, straight to his lawyer, who told him Goldwyn was right. Refusal of the assignment would result in suspension from the lot. "And," Wyler realized, "I knew if he was getting somebody else to finish the Hawks picture, he'd get somebody else to finish mine."

Wyler spent two weeks on *Come and Get It*. His contribution to the film comes mostly in the last half hour, in which Hawks's raucous shenanigans settled down to several dramatic scenes, staged and shot with the straightforward simplicity that was the hallmark of Wyler's style. Wyler always thought the best parts of the film were the second-unit director's spectacular logging sequences, which opened the picture, and the film's first half, "which was Hawks all the way." Goldwyn saw things differently. In 1936—the year the Directors Guild of America was getting chartered— he had the authority to take Hawks's name off the film. He substituted Wyler's in all the publicity until the pinch-hit director said he would not allow it. Realizing it would look fishy to release a film without a director's name, he got Wyler to agree to a shared credit.

Goldwyn felt that he had salvaged the film. *Come and Get It* proved to be the high point in the film career of Frances Farmer, who soon found herself the victim of schizophrenia, sentenced to a lifetime in mental asylums. Edna Ferber wrote the producer "that I have the greatest admiration for the courage, sagacity and power of decision which you showed in throwing out the finished Hawks picture and undertaking the gigantic task of making what amounted to a new picture."

Goldwyn leapt from his "deathbed" on a second rescue mission that summer, this time because of a diary. Reporters had been staking out the United Artists Studio throughout the filming of *Dodsworth* because of Mary Astor, who was fighting to win back custody of the daughter she had surrendered the year before to facilitate her divorce from Dr. Franklyn Thorpe. After work each day, she left for night sessions in court. Another team of newsmen staked out her house. They did not catch up with her, for she was living at the studio, in a luxurious dressing-room apartment, complete with kitchen facilities. When *Dodsworth* finished filming, the trial went into day sessions. Then it came out that Mary Astor had kept a diary between 1929 and 1934, which contained "a rather overemotional account of a romantic interlude with George Kaufman in New York."

"The defense kept referring to the diary in oblique terms," insinuating it contained proof of her unfitness as a mother, recalled Miss Astor. She and her lawyer saw admitting the journal in evidence as their best defense. Somebody who knew that he figured prominently in the diary and did not wish that to happen released a forged diary into the surrounding hysteria. He hoped the threat of great scandal might provoke Hollywood's producers to persuade Miss Astor to drop her case or at least the notion of opening this Pandora's box. The forgery, said Miss Astor, "contained a 'box score' of practically every male big name in the business, and it was loaded with pornographic details. Fragments of this forgery were 'leaked' to the press." A warrant was put out for the arrest of the greatest sexual outlaw of the day, the homely George S. Kaufman.

Sam Goldwyn called a meeting in his office. Still ailing, he sat quietly before Harry Cohn, Jack Warner, Irving Thalberg, Jesse Lasky, A. H. Giannini, Louis B. Mayer, and their legal advisers, and Mary Astor with hers. Thalberg spoke for the producers, saying the actress was about to commit a grave error, that "the trial and the diary would create a vicious scandal. The scandal would give the industry a bad name," and she would probably lose both the case and the child. Miss Astor's attorney said he intended to proceed with the case as planned.

The next day in court, he asked the defense to produce the diary, only to discover that some pages had been removed. Because a mutilated document could not be submitted as evidence, the diary was thrown out altogether. Miss Astor later claimed that clinging to her dignified character of Edith Cortwright pulled her through the weeks of ordeal: "I sat a little straighter, I wore clean white gloves, and kept my hands quiet." Goldwyn was asked if he intended to exercise the morality clause in his contract. He thought for a moment and said, "A woman fighting for her child? This is good!" He stood behind Mary Astor.

So did the public. One night shortly after *Dodsworth* was released, Miss Astor, wearing scarves and dark glasses, sneaked into a theater. The moment the audience heard her first line, which was spoken offscreen, they burst into spontaneous applause. "Nothing has ever warmed me so much," recalled Miss Astor. The gavel finally came down on the trial, with Judge Knight dividing custody.

And *Dodsworth* proved to be Sam Goldwyn's most prestigious film to date. Nobel laureate Sinclair Lewis wired him, "I DO NOT SEE HOW A BETTER MOTION PICTURE COULD HAVE BEEN MADE FROM BOTH THE PLAY AND THE NOVEL THAN YOU HAVE MADE STOP I AM SO DELIGHTED WITH IT THAT I DON'T NEED THE FEEBLENESS OF ADJECTIVES TO EXPRESS MY PLEASURE." Unfortunately, the film failed at the box office, because—Goldwyn always believed—"it didn't have attractive people in it." That flaw ate at the producer. He thought for years of remaking it with an older Clark Gable, but he never did. By that time, the original had become a cult classic.

Dodsworth was nominated for seven Academy Awards, including Best Picture and Best Director. With *Come and Get It* nominated for Film Editing, Walter Brennan for the new category of Best Supporting Actor, and Bonita Granville for Best Supporting Actress, there was hardly a category in which a Goldwyn picture was not named. His films alone received as many nominations that year as any of the major studios—except for MGM, which had five of the ten films up for Best Picture. His only team members to walk away with Oscars were Brennan and Richard Day, for the second year in a row, this time for his sets in *Dodsworth*. No producer in Hollywood had maintained a higher profile for prestige, except Irving Thalberg, whose big entry in that year's sweepstakes was *Romeo and Juliet*. Thalberg's latest ventures—*Camille* with Garbo, *A Day at the Races,* and *The Good Earth*—were already projected favorites for the next year. Of all Goldwyn's rivals in the business, he considered Thalberg his closest friend. He still hoped to bring him over to United Artists.

Goldwyn remained bedridden through Labor Day 1936 and had to pass up a big industry gala at the Hollywood Bowl later in the week for a humanitarian organization. Irving Thalberg, nursing a cold, helped stage the "Everyman" pageant, rehearsing in heavy rains. The following Sunday, September 13, Thalberg was too much under the weather to attend MGM's annual picnic. His strep throat was rediagnosed as pneumonia. The next day he died.

All Hollywood mourned. On Wednesday, MGM shut down for the day. Mobs of fans appeared at the B'nai B'rith Temple to watch the arrival of almost every important figure in motion pictures. Clark Gable, Fredric March, and Douglas Fairbanks were among the ushers. Rabbi Edgar Magnin delivered the eulogy and read a message of sympathy from President Roosevelt. Work on the United Artists lot ceased for five minutes while the service was going on. William Wyler presided over ceremonies on the soundstage where he was directing retakes of *Dodsworth*. Goldwyn had been unable to attend any of the services. He wired Norma Shearer, "DARLING NORMA YOU HAVE LOST A WONDERFUL HUSBAND AND FATHER AND I HAVE LOST A GREAT FRIEND I FEEL VERY BADLY." At the end of the day, the bereaved widow came to Laurel Lane and sat at Sam's bedside.

Goldwyn suffered another loss in late 1936, when his most trusted employee and loyal friend from as far back as the workbenches in Gloversville tendered his resignation. After nineteen years in the film industry, Abe Lehr had been kicked upstairs as high as he could go in the Goldwyn organization: vice president and general manager. There were no challenges there, and at age fifty-six his health was starting to decline. Looking for a less demanding job, Lehr opened a small talent agency. Goldwyn threw business his way but found little reason to see him again.

Goldwyn's year rang out on a sour note. That Christmas, *Beloved Enemy* opened to sluggish business and reviews. George Haight had completely supervised this muddled Romeo and Juliet love story of a defiant Irish patriot leader (played by Brian Aherne) and the daughter of the Englishman sent to negotiate a peace settlement (Merle Oberon). David Niven was promoted to the level of secondary love interest. "Hank" Potter, after a year on the Goldwyn lot, at last got his chance to direct. He tried to hold the shaky plot together with several scenes of moonstruck speeches between the lovers, staring dreamily into space. Goldwyn had simply lacked the strength to rescue this film.

Samuel Goldwyn and his company sank into a depression. Sammy found his father in bed all the time, complaining, changing doctors, discussing only his death. In the event of such a catastrophe, Frances Goldwyn believed, everything they owned could be lost. Although her sisters had married, she still had her mother to provide for.

Frances saw the ghost of her father and became determined not to be deprived of her family's assets again. She marched into her husband's bedroom and began cursing him out in the most vile language ever to pass her lips. "Go ahead and die," she finally said, ". . . or get up out of that bed."

Sam and Frances gave themselves the month of January 1937 to revitalize themselves in the village of Sun Valley, Idaho, a sparsely populated "Alpine" resort built by their new friend Averell Harriman and the Union Pacific Railroad in an attempt to make America ski-conscious. Goldwyn returned to work, eager to take hold of his company once again. Every decision of every day became another contest against death, a struggle to survive.

SAMUEL GOLDWYN, INC., entered a reign of terror. It would not have another film before the cameras for several months, and an air of insanity fell over the company as their restless leader made up for their lack of motion with a flurry of commotion. The year was rampant with hirings of bright young associates, most of whose heads would roll before their two-year contracts had expired. One of these was Samuel Marx, who for the previous six years had been Thalberg's story editor. After Thalberg died, Marx went to Goldwyn and told him he was not looking to be a story editor again but that he wanted to get into production. Goldwyn was so "disarming" that when they got around to money, Marx cut his prior salary in half, just to accept a position with him. He found his first month of work there "paradise."

For another of Goldwyn's vague production jobs, Beatrice Kaufman recommended Garson Kanin, a self-described "twenty-four-year-old bundle of nerves who had been an early high-school dropout, a mediocre musician, a burlesque stooge, a stock clerk at Macy's, a drama student, a mildly successful minor New York actor, and the director of one Broadway failure." Goldwyn sat at his desk staring at young Kanin, who was eager to direct movies, thinking about opening the door to a Hollywood career for him. "Mr. Goldwyn, his right forefinger clamped firmly to the side of his nose, continued to study me through his small gray eyes," Kanin wrote of the crucial moment. After a long silence, Goldwyn clasped his hands under his chin and said, "in a high, penetrating voice, 'Sidney Howard tells me you're a very clever genius.'"

The next day, Goldwyn offered Kanin a seven-year contract, starting at $250 a week. Almost immediately Goldwyn took to calling his new assistant what sounded like "Tallboy." Not for weeks did the diminutive Kanin realize the nickname was a source of pride—Goldwyn's pronounciation of Thalberg. Kanin described his first month with Goldwyn as "euphoric."

By the second month of undefined duties, however, "Tallboy" realized that his chances of becoming a director there were remote. "Each of the major studios was making some seventy or eighty films a year," he said. "Goldwyn, however, made only two or three pictures a year. Each one was expensive and important and it was doubtful that he would ever entrust one to someone who had never before made a movie." Kanin suggested that he might direct some of the many tests for makeup, hairdressing, costumes, and acting that were done on the lot. Goldwyn said no, that that was a waste of time. Kanin persisted in explaining how it would allow him to practice his talents. "What's the matter with you?" Goldwyn asked him impatiently. "Jesus Christ, here you are, a young nobody, and you're getting this great opportunity, and you want to be a *test* director, f'Chrissake." Kanin said he did not want to be a test director, he wanted to be a director. "How can you be a director?" he asked. "You've never directed." Kanin said there had been a time when Willy Wyler and John Ford and Leo McCarey had never directed. Replied Goldwyn, "Don't you believe it."

Joshua Logan, just a few years out of Princeton, learned the hard way that directing tests for Sam Goldwyn was a cul-de-sac, not a road to bigger things. In 1936, he found himself confined to the lot and called a "genius" so long as his tests made the actors look better than Goldwyn had anticipated. The first day he saw a test of Logan's that was less than what he had expected, he fired him. Not only did Goldwyn never hire the future director of *South Pacific, Picnic, Bus Stop,* and *Sayonara,* but he denied for the rest of his life ever having worked with him.

Logan had at least escaped the mood swings that plagued those under contract to Goldwyn. Nobody was subjected to more of Goldwyn's emotional tyranny than Willy Wyler, who fought vigorously with him in an attempt to define the limits in their deepening father-son relationship. In gratitude for Wyler's having well served *Dodsworth* and saved *Come and Get It,* Goldwyn allowed Wyler his vacation as contracted and rewarded him unexpectedly with a few extra weeks—all at full pay. It was not until he was about to return from vacation that Wyler discovered the catch.

Ever since *It Happened One Night* captured Best Picture, Actor, Actress, Director, and Writing Oscars in 1934—thereby removing the "Poverty Row" label from Columbia Pictures—"screwball comedies" had become Hollywood's hottest novelty item. Usually goodhearted looks at the Depression, as seen through the lives of the irresponsible rich, they were irreverent battles of the sexes, marked by wisecracking dialogue usually paced at breakneck speed, farce falling just this side of slapstick.

Goldwyn had his contribution to the genre in the works for two years.

An original Ben Hecht story was worked over by almost a dozen writers, including Dorothy Parker and Alan Campbell. The plot ended up with all the traditional "screwball" elements, though in this film the usual character traits were assigned unexpectedly. *Woman Chases Man* is the story of a ne'er-do-well father whose overly practical son watches over the family fortune. The old man's latest harebrained scheme is a suburban development project for which he needs $100,000; his son refuses to give it to him. A fast-talking woman architect must break down the stuffy son, which she does with a lot of champagne. Goldwyn wanted Willy Wyler to direct the picture.

"The script," remembered Wyler, "was just plain stupid." Reaping praise at last as a serious director, he refused the assignment. Goldwyn contacted him by telephone in New York and appealed to Wyler as the friendly patron who had given him his first important pictures to direct. When that failed, Goldwyn called him an ingrate. Finally, he told Wyler that *These Three* and *Dodsworth* had not done such good business and that he was, in fact, untalented. Goldwyn carried on for the better part of an hour, as Wyler remembered it, "in the worst language I had ever heard. He said he was through with me and that I'd be finished in Hollywood." Wyler sent him a wire that afternoon:

> . . . AM STILL TRYING TO FIND SOMETHING PLEASANT ABOUT OUR CONVERSATION OF THIS MORNING STOP I HAD HOPED THAT AFTER MY FIRST YEAR WITH YOU WE COULD BOTH ENJOY A MUTUALLY HAPPY AND SUCCESSFUL ASSOCIATION BUT JUDGING FROM YOUR MANY COMPLAINTS TO ME ABOUT ME ITS EVIDENT THAT THIS IS NOT THE CASE STOP WELL FRANKLY I AM NOT VERY HAPPY EITHER SO WITH BOTH OF US UNHAPPY WITH EACH OTHER WHY NOT TERMINATE OUR AGREEMENT TO OUR MUTUAL BENEFIT STOP I SHALL ALWAYS BE GRATEFUL FOR THE OPPORTUNITIES YOU HAVE GIVEN ME BUT CANNOT FEEL THAT I HAVE FAILED YOU COMPLETELY STOP I WILL OF COURSE REFUND YOU ALL SALARIES RECEIVED DURING MY VACATION.

Goldwyn replied to Wyler as though there had been a misunderstanding. He wanted Wyler to stay under contract and direct *Dead End*. Until that script was ready, however, Wyler was suspended, and his contract time was extended. Goldwyn took back the five-thousand-dollar vacation bonus.

Woman Chases Man neatly followed the schema for "screwball comedy"—showing the Depression audience that the rich had troubles too, that they were just as starved for fun as the rest of the world. But these film farces also counted on the spark of improvisation, taking advantage of happy accidents on the set. Sam Goldwyn insisted on strict control, down to the pristine sound track. He even ordered one scene reshot because he thought the rustle of leaves in a tree was too distracting. Such precision, combined with his insistence that the director (a journeyman named John Blystone) and actors (Joel McCrea and Miriam Hopkins) adhere to the script, stifled the atmosphere necessary for the spontaneous combustion of comedy. *Woman Chases Man* was a complete dud with audiences and critics alike.

Miriam Hopkins had kicked and screamed over the last three years, but she had accepted all the parts and loanouts Goldwyn handed her. Contrary to his original intentions, he ended up starring her in only four pictures before her contract expired. She moved to Warner Brothers and never worked for Goldwyn again. The contract of her co-star in all her Goldwyn films was running out as well, and the producer still had not made the most of his talent either.

Goldwyn's next role for Joel McCrea might have been a breakthrough. In Sidney Kingsley's play *Dead End*, the hero had been a sensitive and moody cripple named Gimpty. An out-of-work architect, he had dreamed of rebuilding the slums and getting out of his rat's nest of a neighborhood. So did Drina, a hardworking girl who walked the picket line for higher wages so she could escape. She stayed around because of Gimpty, whose head was being turned by a gangster's mistress kept in the deluxe apartment at the end of the street. Baby Face Martin—Gimpty's childhood buddy, now a gangster—set the play's action in motion when he returned to his old neighborhood to visit his mother and former girlfriend, Francey, now a streetwalker.

Goldwyn wanted Sidney Howard to transfer the play to the screen; but Howard had just agreed to adapt a book for David Selznick, *Gone With the Wind*. Goldwyn's second choice was Lillian Hellman. At his insistence, Gimpty became another homogenized role for Joel McCrea—broad-shouldered Dave Connell, who instead of ratting on his old pal Baby Face, would take on the hoodlum himself. She was told to shift the focus of the film to Drina, thus creating a starring role for an actress. The gangster's mistress would become little more than a well-heeled woman living in the neighborhood, as Goldwyn insisted on veiling the references to her kept status. Francey would not have a social disease, only a ravaged look to show the toll of living on the streets. "Goldwyn said he wanted me to 'clean up the play,'" remembered Miss Hellman of her assignment. "What he meant was 'to cut off its balls.'"

Goldwyn considered nobody for the part of Drina but Sylvia Sidney, then under contract to Walter Wanger. For $75,000, she played the same optimistic city-dweller she had played in *Street Scene* and almost all her films since. "I was the highest paid laundress in the world," she said, summing up her career to that point. "In every picture I'd be ironing and my line would be, 'What would poppa say?'" Her only reluctance to *Dead End* was in working with William Wyler, who she had heard was "very sadistic with women."

Shooting was scheduled to begin in late February 1937 but got postponed a season when Miss Sidney slipped one afternoon at Elizabeth Arden's and fell against a table. Her face bloody and her nose bruised, she was rushed to Cedars of Lebanon Hospital, where she was sutured, bandaged, and given an eye patch. Without giving it a second thought, she reported to rehearsal later that day. "That's a movie star?" Wyler shouted when she walked onto the stage, without even inquiring what had happened. Word of Miss Sidney's accident reached Goldwyn's office, and he flew down to the set. "She's gotta go home," he said, fearful of what gossip columnists might write about this disfiguring of a glamour girl. He accompanied her back to her house and sat on her bed as she explained she would be out of commission for close to two months. She asked if they should sue Elizabeth Arden, and Goldwyn said, "No. That would just call attention. And for what?" Goldwyn kept her on salary during the layoff. By May, they were ready to roll film.

Wyler kept Miss Sidney on the verge of tears through the entire production. "He needled me and needled me," she remembered, "and he knew I had a concussion and my nose hurt. But that didn't stop him." His constant refrain to Sylvia Sidney was that he could get an actress for $150 who could do a better job; then he would ask her to try again. "He'd do thirty or forty takes of the same scene," she recounted. "How Goldwyn kept his temper with me, I'll never know. I'd say, 'I hate this goddamned picture,' and he'd come over to me and say, 'Don't cry. Villy is difficult. But he turns out good movies.'" *Dead End* alienated her enough to make her consider giving up motion pictures. But her performance was lauded as one of her best in a decade of distinguished appearances.

For the role of Baby Face Martin, Goldwyn wanted to borrow Hollywood's most popular gangster, James Cagney. But Cagney had also become Warner Brothers' private enemy number one, the first of their contract players to challenge the studio's ruthless long-term contracts. He took them to court on a technicality and won his case. While the studio appealed the decision, Goldwyn's counselors said there was no legal reason to avoid dealing with the actor; but they added, "it would be ill-advised for you to involve yourself in the Warner-Cagney fight for the sake of Cagney's services in one picture."

So Goldwyn tried George Raft, only to discover the actor found the role too nasty. In the screenplay the neighborhood gang of kids come to recognize Baby Face as a killer and start idolizing him. "I told Mr. Goldwyn how I would like to play the part," Raft later recalled. "I want a scene where I tell the kids how bad my life is, 'Just look at me crawling around like a rat, hiding. You don't want to hide all your life. Make something of yourself. Don't grow up like me.'" In another scene, Baby Face encounters his mother, who slaps his face and calls him a "yellow dog." "The way they had it," Raft said, "I was just supposed to walk away mad. I wanted to play it with a tear in my eye, so the audience would know that my mother is right and that I felt bad about my life as a criminal." Both Goldwyn and Wyler tried to pressure him into the part, but Raft turned it down.

Fortunately, there was a new mug among Hollywood's most wanted actors. After several lean years in movies, Humphrey Bogart had returned to the stage, where he created the role of gangster Duke Mantee in *The Petrified Forest*. His reprise of the role on film guaranteed him several more years as one of Hollywood's leading heavies. With Marjorie Main (in one of her first film roles) as his mother and Claire Trevor as Francey, Bogart took the part in *Dead End*. In but a few scenes, he etched one of his most indelible characterizations.

Most of the film's other featured players came from the original Broadway production. Leo Gorcey, Huntz Hall, Gabriel Dell, Bernard Punsley, Bobby Jordan, and Billy Halop became known as the Dead End Kids. After the picture was released, Warner Brothers rounded them up along with the rest of the big-time gangsters on their lot and produced a series of films around the teenage delinquents.

Part of *Dead End*'s problem lay in the set. Richard Day designed one of the most ingenious creations of his career—a realistic set that jammed slums right up against a luxury apartment, wooden docks, and an inlet of the East River into which the Dead End Kids could dive. It offered many different levels and angles with which Wyler and Toland could create visual interest. Except for three days of interior sequences, the entire picture was shot on the set. It cost one tenth of the film's $900,000 budget, but Goldwyn did not find it all good value for his money.

"This set is filthy!" he shouted just before the first day's shooting. Then he started picking up paper and garbage that had been carefully strewn about. "But, Mr. Goldwyn," protested Willy Wyler, "this is supposed to be a slum. It's part of what we're saying in this picture—that right next

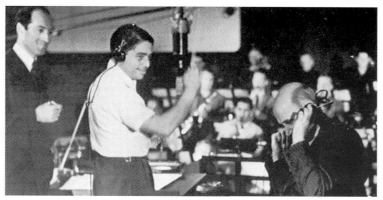

ABOVE: George Gershwin and music director Alfred Newman await Goldwyn's approval as he listens to music for *The Goldwyn Follies*. Some weeks later, after writing "Love Walked In" and "Our Love Is Here to Stay," Gershwin died. BELOW: Goldwyn (left) and Lillian Hellman on the lot.

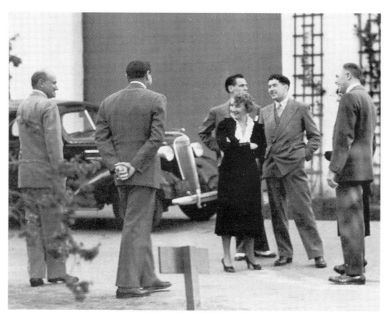

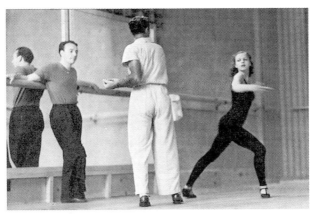

ABOVE: *The Goldwyn Follies* also boasted the talents of choreographer George Balanchine (leaning on barre) and ballerina Vera Zorina.

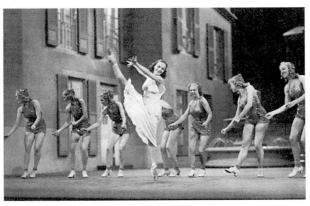

ABOVE: Goldwyn's infatuation with Zorina almost broke up his marriage. BELOW: Zorina rehearsing the "Water Nymph Ballet" sequence.

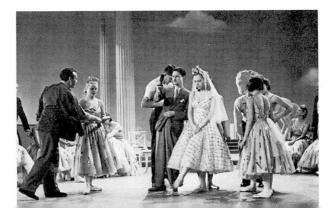

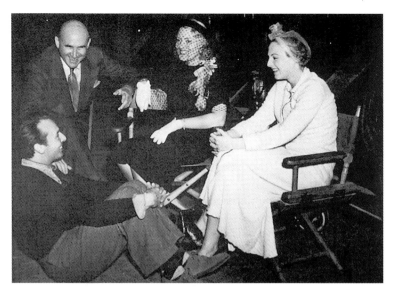

ABOVE: Zorina (right) had eyes only for Balanchine, whom she married the following year. Left to right: Balanchine, Goldwyn, Helen Jepson, and Zorina. BELOW: Eleanor Roosevelt on the Goldwyn lot with Goldwyn and her son James, then vice president of Goldwyn's company, 1939. Goldwyn was fond of saying, "The son of the President of the United States works for me."

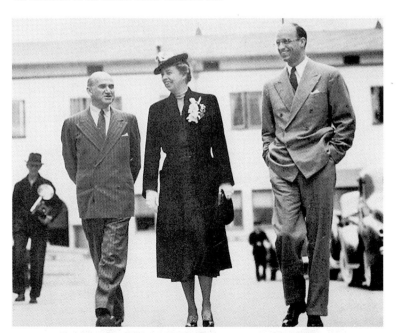

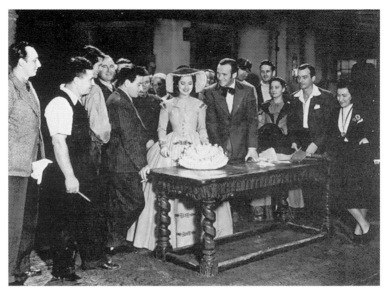

ABOVE: On the set of *Wuthering Heights*, 1939. One of the few harmonious moments—a celebration of Merle Oberon's birthday—in the midst of what was an ordeal for everybody involved. BELOW: Laurence Olivier, David Niven, and Donald Crisp on the steps; behind them, Merle Oberon talks with Gregg Toland; farther back and to the right, William Wyler sits behind the camera.

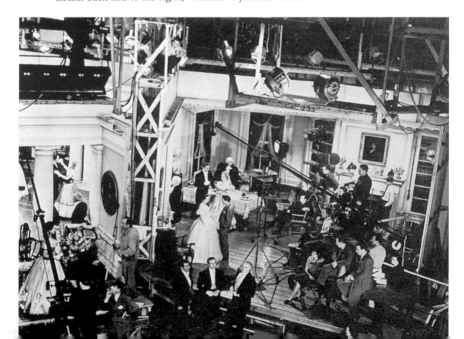

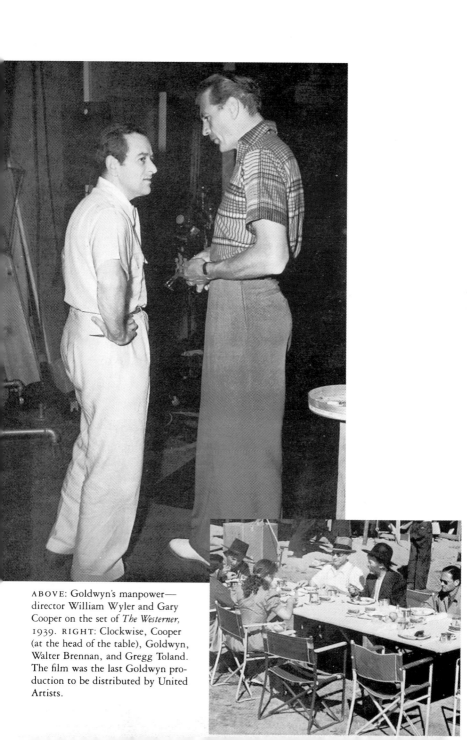

ABOVE: Goldwyn's manpower—
director William Wyler and Gary
Cooper on the set of *The Westerner*,
1939. RIGHT: Clockwise, Cooper
(at the head of the table), Goldwyn,
Walter Brennan, and Gregg Toland.
The film was the last Goldwyn production to be distributed by United
Artists.

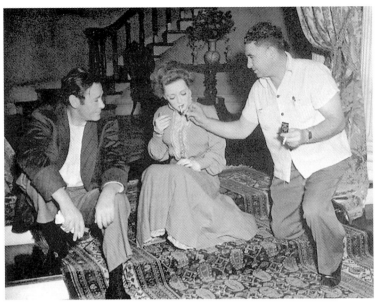

ABOVE: On the set of *The Little Foxes* (Goldwyn's first picture for RKO), 1941. Left to right: Herbert Marshall, Bette Davis, and property master Irving Sindler. BELOW: The same year, Goldwyn produced *Ball of Fire*. Left to right: Gary Cooper, Howard Hawks, Oscar Homolka, Barbara Stanwyck.

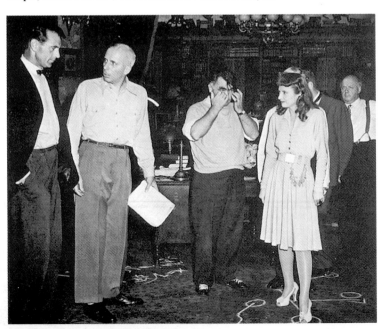

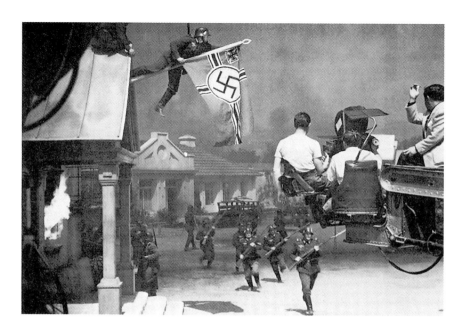

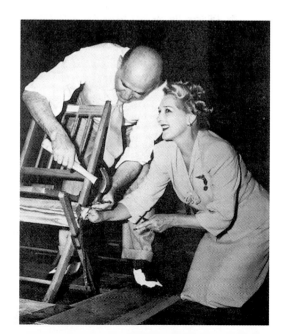

ABOVE: The set of *The North Star*, photographed by Margaret Bourke-White, 1943. Goldwyn would joke afterwards, "Whenever Stalin got depressed, he ran that picture." RIGHT: Mary Pickford, Goldwyn's enemy of twenty years, buried the hatchet long enough, in 1944, to help publicize the opening of *Up in Arms* at a makeshift theater in Reno, where Goldwyn dramatized the struggle of independent producers against the major studios' theater chains.

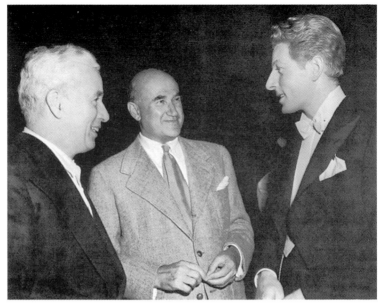

ABOVE: Goldwyn and his star Danny Kaye, whom he hailed as "the new Chaplin," with the original Chaplin. BELOW: Private Sam Goldwyn, Jr., with his parents— one of the happiest moments of their lives, 1944.

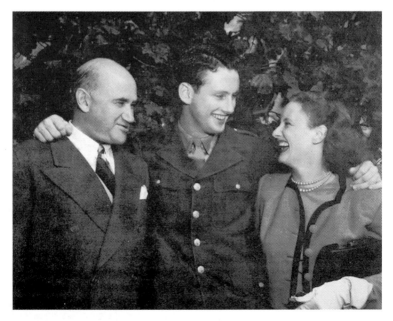

to a new modern apartment are all those old crummy buildings with dirt and garbage." Wyler recalled, "Goldwyn didn't like dirt. Everything in his pictures had to be clean. Like him. He'd sit in his office and you'd never see this man in shirt sleeves or his tie undone or anything like that. He was absolutely immaculate. And he said, 'There won't be any dirty slums—not in *my* picture!'" He took the debris he had collected and walked out. Wyler and Richard Day and propman Irving Sindler "dressed" the set with fresh garbage, but every morning Goldwyn would come onto the set and clean it away.

Goldwyn's insistence on an equally pristine sound track, with almost no city noises, gave the picture a certain deadness. But Goldwyn seemed to know what the public would buy. His slum may have lacked the tawdry authenticity of Warner Brothers' sets or even the forced colorful gaiety of the Fox and MGM decors, but his pictures had a distinctive look about them—a feel that was always tasteful, even in an East Side slum. *Dead End* made money, and the critics were practically unanimous in their praise.

And it was nominated for four Academy Awards, including Best Picture of 1937. For weeks many were touting *Dead End* as that year's film to beat. By Oscar night, Frances Goldwyn observed, her husband was "counting on it." He lost to Warners' *Life of Emile Zola* and was noticeably disappointed. Frances said she was too, but later she confessed, "I lied. For I really didn't give a darn." Her husband had two pictures nominated in other categories that year that were far more commercial.

The penultimate Oscar presented that evening—just before the new Irving G. Thalberg Memorial Award to the year's best producer went to Darryl Zanuck—was for Best Actress. Garbo (for *Camille*) was the inside favorite, but one of Goldwyn's leading ladies was offering the best odds that night at the Biltmore Hotel. Ironically, the actress's pride and the producer's prejudice had almost kept her from getting that plum role of Stella Dallas. Barbara Stanwyck, a former nightclub dancer who had starred in a score of films since 1929, had been director King Vidor's first choice from the start; but Goldwyn refused to hear of it. He considered such lesser stars as Ruth Chatterton and Gladys George and tested many women with even less drawing power. Goldwyn had finally given in to considering Stanwyck, but only if she would test for the part.

The actress refused. "There was no reason why she should've had to test," said her friend and former co-star Joel McCrea. "She'd made pictures for William Wellman, George Stevens, and John Ford. He could see what she could do." Zeppo Marx, who had left his brothers' act after *Duck Soup* because he got "sick and tired of being the stooge," became a talent agent, representing, among others, Stanwyck. He pleaded with McCrea to get her to test. McCrea in turn said to Stanwyck, "Listen, Barbara, you'll win an award for this picture. I'll underwrite the test myself." She at last submitted, only to have Sam Goldwyn tell her, as she recalled, "that he didn't think I was capable of doing it," that she was "too young for the part," and that she "didn't have any experience with children." King Vidor put in an entire day filming the birthday scene, in which Stella and her daughter Laurel wait in vain for the girl's friends to appear, not knowing word has been put out to boycott the party. Vidor remembered, "Stanwyck's test was undeniable. She put everyone else to shame." Still Goldwyn resisted.

McCrea went to the top man himself, selflessly pressing Stanwyck's cause. At last Goldwyn—whose taste in women had still kept him from discovering an important female star—blurted out his hesitation: "She's just got no sex appeal." McCrea exploded into laughter. "Well, you better not let Bob Taylor know that." Taylor was Hollywood's hottest new leading man, having just played in *Camille.* "He's nuts about her, and he thinks she has sex appeal."

Stanwyck got the part and delivered what most fans, and critics, and she herself, think is the performance of her lifetime—from her social-climbing beginnings to her standing in the rain trying to steal a glance at her daughter's society nuptials.

Stella Dallas was one of the great crowd-pleasers of 1937. It grossed more than $2 million, yielding a profit over $500,000 for Goldwyn. Its success gave life to a radio serial based on the characters, which would run on the National Broadcasting Company's network for close to twenty years. Both Stanwyck and Garbo lost the Oscar that year to Luise Rainer, for her performance in MGM's *The Good Earth.*

For all his nominations, the big studios shut Goldwyn out except in one category, Best Sound Recording—for *The Hurricane.* The South Seas adventure had been in the works for almost two years before its release, initially slated as a project for Howard Hawks. After clashing with him on *Come and Get It,* however, Goldwyn searched for another vigorous director who felt at home at sea. Fox's John Ford had read the Nordhoff and Hall novel three times before wiring Goldwyn from Honolulu during one of his many transoceanic sails, "AM MORE THAN EVER CONVINCED I SHOULD WORK WITH YOU ON IT STOP WISH YOU COULD CONVINCE DARRYL . . . REGARDLESS WHO MAKES PICTURE POSITIVE IT WILL BE SUPERB AND REBOUND TO YOUR GLORY." Goldwyn hired him for $100,000 plus one eighth of the film's profits.

Nordhoff and Hall's novel opens on the wedding day of Terangi, mate of a trading schooner, and Marama, daughter of a great chieftain, on the

South Pacific island of Manukura. Their honeymoon is interrupted when the schooner must set sail. In a Tahitian café, Terangi is provoked into striking a white man and is sentenced to six months in prison. Unable to endure captivity, he repeatedly attempts escape, and his sentence is extended to sixteen years. In desperation, he accidentally kills a guard and embarks alone on a six-hundred-mile ocean journey to his home and wife. From the outset, Terangi has had the sympathy of everyone on the island except Governor DeLaage, who is resigned to capturing Terangi and returning him to prison in Tahiti. Just as Terangi reaches the shores of Manukura, so too arrive the first winds of a swelling storm. The villagers scatter in fear, all except DeLaage, fixed on capturing the handsome native boy. Terangi could easily escape in the fury, but chooses to be with his people, lashing his wife and small child to a high tree. As the devastating hurricane reaches full force, Terangi also saves DeLaage's wife. In the dying winds, he and his family set out in a canoe to seek a new life on another island. DeLaage is reunited with his wife, whom he presumed dead with most of the islanders. As they see the fugitives paddling away, he watches them and says, "It is not Terangi—it is only a floating log." While Oliver H. P. Garrett was preparing the script for Goldwyn, Charles Nordhoff reread his story and realized he had "made a mistake in not sufficiently emphasizing the fact that the native hero was *not* a victim of injustice, but a victim of circumstance."

When John Ford joined Goldwyn in their first venture together since *Arrowsmith,* he brought along a screenwriter, a former reporter named Dudley Nichols. They had recently worked together on *The Informer,* each winning an Oscar. The success of their collaboration lay in the shared conviction that motion pictures should be based more on images than on words, that dialogue should be subordinate to action. Running against the current trend toward a lot of talking on the screen, Nichols's screenplay for *The Hurricane* contained about one third less dialogue than the average script. For all its merits, Goldwyn decided just before shooting that the script's opening and conclusion were weak. "Whenever my father was in trouble on a picture," said Sam Goldwyn, Jr., "he went to Ben Hecht." Hecht claimed to have completed his uncredited rewrite in two days.

Goldwyn had planned all along to star his own handsome beachboy, Joel McCrea. After six times before the Goldwyn cameras, McCrea was thrilled his producer was at last offering him the lead in a picture, but he felt the part called for somebody who looked more indigenous to Manukura than to Malibu. He went to Goldwyn and said, "Look, I think it's going to be a great picture. But there's a scene when the character enters, and all the white guys get up from the table. Now I don't look native. I look like an

Irish cop!" Goldwyn said, "I want to tell *you* something. An actor should be able to do anything—a pimp, a homosexual, anything."

"Now look," McCrea replied. "I never claimed to be an actor. I'm just a guy who rides a horse well." Goldwyn said, "Well, I'm paying you a lot of money to be an actor." Then the producer changed tack and asked McCrea who his favorite actor was. The big cowboy selected Leslie Howard. "Well," Goldwyn said, "*he* could play this."

"Yeah," said McCrea, "but who would you rather see play Buffalo Bill, him or me?"

Goldwyn ordered a full-scale talent hunt. Around that time, somebody working at the studio went to fill his car at a nearby service station and thought the strong and swarthy attendant looked the part of Terangi. He was an aspiring actor named Charlie Locher. Like hundreds of others, Locher—about to be renamed Jon Hall—paraded before Goldwyn and Ford and casting director Robert McIntyre; "but he was the first one," remembered Jock Lawrence, "who didn't look like an actor." Goldwyn asked him to remove his shirt and read a scene, then to wait in the anteroom. "I can take that boy and make something of him," said Ford. He got the part, and Joel McCrea was loaned out to Paramount.

In exchange, Paramount gave Goldwyn run of their seraglio of actresses to find his sultry Polynesian princess. One of their seventy-five-dollar-a-week contract players had recently gained attention for the fetching way in which she ran around in a sarong in *The Jungle Princess*. She was born Dorothy Kaumeyer and at seventeen became "Miss New Orleans." Later she became a singer with a band and got her break as an actress, using the surname Lamour. The group of men casting *The Hurricane* ran her film. Everyone said she looked "like a tart" except John Ford, who said, "I can do something with her."

A crew was sent to Pago Pago, in American Samoa, to film background footage, at a cost of $100,000. Native villages were built in Isthmus Harbor, on Catalina Island, for $150,000, and on the United Artists back lot—complete with a 200-yard-long lagoon—for another $150,000. James Basevi, the special-effects wizard who had devised the earthquakes and locust plagues for MGM's recent disaster sequences, was hired to create the film's climactic hurricane. It would cost $250,000 to destroy the sets. Mary Astor, cast as Madame De Laage, remembered weeks in which "we walked against winds, carefully calculated to blow at near hurricane level. Huge propellers kept us fighting for every step, with sand and water whipping our faces, sometimes leaving little pinpricks of blood on our cheeks from the stinging sand." Hoses and overhead sprinklers provided the great rains. A *Variety* correspondent spotted a number of native players actually cowering on the set as the storm reached the peak of its fury. Many were Samoans who had survived the islands' 1915 hurricane, the worst in their recent history. They said Goldwyn's was worse.

While filming on Catalina, Ford lived aboard his own 110-foot ketch, the *Araner,* which he had insisted that Goldwyn charter for him. The cantankerous director, whose prestige had jumped since he had worked for Goldwyn six years earlier, chose to ignore the producer as much as possible. After several weeks, Goldwyn worried that Ford was not making the most of his good-looking leads. So one morning he appeared on the set with Ira Gershwin, who was working on the lot. Ford was perched high above the village, preparing a crane shot. When he noticed Goldwyn, he halted all work and the crane lowered him to the ground. "There aren't any close-ups," Goldwyn complained. Ford could hardly believe he had descended to listen to such twaddle. After a moment of their eyeballing each other, Ford poked his boss in the navel and said, "Look, Goldwyn. When I want a long shot I aim the camera here." Jabbing him a little harder and higher in the stomach, he added, "When I want a medium shot, I aim here. And when I want a close-up," he said, now thumping away at his chest, "I'll put the camera here." Then he pushed Goldwyn toward the door.

"Well," said the producer to Gershwin on their way out, "at least I put the idea in his head." He did just that. Before the picture was over, Ford shot a number of close-ups of Lamour and happily spliced them into the film. After *The Hurricane,* Paramount considered her a star and wrapped her in a sarong at every opportunity.

The film's fifteen-minute hurricane sequence was so overpowering that most critics and audiences tended to overlook the hour and a half of melodrama that preceded it. *The Hurricane* became a box-office hit, one of United Artists' most successful releases in years, despite its nearly two-million-dollar cost. Alfred Newman's ubiquitous score for the film included a beguiling theme that came to be called "The Moon of Manakoora," an air widely imitated by other composers of South Seas pictures.

Goldwyn's publicity department proclaimed that Hollywood considered *The Hurricane* the "greatest of even the Goldwyn films because it, better than any other, shows clearly the famous 'Goldwyn Touch' of perfection."

EVER since film found its voice, the major studios had been producing revues to spotlight their contract players. After the first wave of musicals with Broadway backgrounds in the early thirties, movies turned for inspiration to that great new arena of popular entertainment—radio. In 1932,

Paramount produced *The Big Broadcast,* in which Bing Crosby, Kate Smith, and Burns and Allen saved a failing radio station. The studio served up a similar smorgasbord three years in a row in the middle of the decade, catering to the tastes of all audiences. *The Big Broadcast of 1938* featured Bob Hope in his movie debut, warbling "Thanks for the Memory" right after Norwegian soprano Kirsten Flagstad thundered Brünnhilde's battle cry. In 1937, Warner Brothers produced *Hollywood Hotel,* a story revolving around the town's celebrated radio program of the same name. It introduced what became movieland's anthem, "Hooray for Hollywood."

Upon the death of Florenz Ziegfeld, Goldwyn took it upon himself to uphold the tradition of producing an annual lavish revue. Announcements about *The Goldwyn Follies* began appearing as early as 1932. After discussing the project for five years with such talents as George Jean Nathan, Dorothy Parker, and Anita Loos, Goldwyn had settled only on a vague idea about a producer trying to hook a millionaire into backing a show. In time, the venue got changed to Hollywood. With that, Goldwyn chased the most colorful array of talent ever mounted in a single film.

He first approached Irving Berlin. But Berlin had been cheated at Goldwyn's card table enough times to know better than to get involved with him in this big a production. Selling him the occasional song was one thing; working through an entire picture was another. After Berlin gracefully bowed out, Goldwyn hired George and Ira Gershwin. No theatrical event had ever moved Goldwyn so much as their recent *Porgy and Bess;* and Goldwyn knew that the prestige alone of the Gershwin name was worth the tens of thousands of dollars he would pay them for a score.

From the radio, Goldwyn drafted comic Phil Baker, Jack Benny's tenor, Kenny Baker, and a new ventriloquist with his formally attired dummy, Edgar Bergen and Charlie McCarthy. In exchange for Joel McCrea's services, Twentieth Century–Fox offered Goldwyn an option on either Jack Haley or the Ritz Brothers. Goldwyn chose the three zanies. From the world of opera, he hired the Metropolitan's Helen Jepson and Charles Kullmann to sing arias from *La Traviata.*

The film's greatest distinction promised to be the inclusion of ballet. Goldwyn had attracted the Gershwins to his *Follies* by assuring them that the most celebrated new force in dance, the Russian émigré George Balanchine, would choreograph a ballet sequence for the film. George Gershwin intended to compose a new piece for the occasion. When the symptoms of apparent fatigue—headaches and vertigo—slowed him down, the idea shifted toward the creation of a ballet of his 1928 orchestral tone poem, "An American in Paris."

The star of the dance sequences would be a gifted ballerina (half-

German, half-Norwegian) with a strong face and a sensational figure. Born Eva Brigitta Hartwig, she had debuted at the age of six and danced with the Ballet Russe de Monte Carlo at seventeen. In 1936, at age nineteen, she performed in the London production of Rodgers and Hart's musical *On Your Toes*, using her stage name, Vera Zorina. On the strength of her reputation, her photographs, and the sales pitch of her agent, Louis Shurr, Goldwyn signed her to a seven-year contract.

"All I knew of Samuel Goldwyn was that he was the most distinguished producer in America," remembered Vera Zorina years later; "but there was only one reason I signed with him: George Balanchine was going to do the choreography. Otherwise, I'd never have gone to Hollywood." Upon reflection, she was impressed that Goldwyn had even heard of Balanchine and his small, budding ballet troupe, the Metropolitan Opera's American Ballet Company. "I think that's where Goldwyn's greatness as a producer came in," said the ballerina. "He was aware or at least well-advised. And he knew good advice when he heard it. That takes talent—to surround yourself with great talent and not be threatened."

Lacking only a screenplay to bind all the disparate elements of his *Follies*, Goldwyn called for his new favorite writer. In June 1937, George Haight's secretary ordered Lillian Hellman to report to the studio immediately for a conference about *The Goldwyn Follies*. Her working on that picture had never even been mentioned, so Hellman had no idea what she was in for.

"It was pure *Alice in Wonderland*," Hellman discovered upon arrival. Goldwyn sat at the far end of his office, presiding over an assembly of some of the greatest talent of the century. George Haight stood at his side, reminding Miss Hellman of the Mad Hatter's dormouse. Art director Richard Day was sitting alone on a long leather couch up against one of the walls, totally absorbed in his sketchpad. In a very large chair next to Goldwyn's desk was a very short man, whom she immediately recognized as Balanchine. Seated in two matching smaller chairs in the middle of the room were George and Ira Gershwin, their backs to everybody else. When Miss Hellman entered the room, not only was nobody speaking to anybody else, no two people were even looking at each other.

Static electricity charged the room. Goldwyn bobbed his head from artist to artist and then at the ceiling, as though he expected lightning to strike. By the time she had greeted each of the other guests, the host turned to Lillian Hellman and asked, "What are you doing here?" She pleaded ignorance. "Well, as long as you're here," he said, "why don't you write 'The Goldwyn Follies'?" Hellman caught on to his game and politely refused.

"Then what are you doing here?" Goldwyn asked. George Haight said that he had sent for her. "Well, that's fine," said Goldwyn. "You'll learn very nice, very quick. You'll write a great musical." She said she did not want to learn. "You'll get a raise," Goldwyn promised. "You'll like the Gershwins." George Balanchine started to hum an atonal ditty. "And it sure is wonderful to have a genius," said Goldwyn, leaning back in his chair, his hands locked behind his head, indicating Balanchine. With that, Richard Day looked up from his pad, and the Gershwins turned in their chairs. "I mean a bunch of geniuses," Goldwyn amended. "But all this modern music . . . it's so old-fashioned."

The Gershwins turned back around and muffled their laughter; Richard Day chortled into his sketchpad; Lillian Hellman bit her lower lip. Goldwyn instructed George Haight to take Balanchine to a screening room and run some Busby Berkeley musicals for him. "Who? Who?" Balanchine inquired eagerly. "Busby Berkeley," said Goldwyn. "Don't you know who Busby Berkeley is?" While George Haight described Goldwyn's former choreographer to his present one, Lillian Hellman pulled a chair alongside the Gershwins. In a low voice, Ira leaned over and told her that he and his brother and Balanchine had had a meeting at Goldwyn's house just the day before. They had all arrived and were in the living room, waiting for Sam to descend the stairs. After several minutes, Goldwyn appeared at the staircase in his bathrobe. "Hold on, fellas," he yelled down. "I'll be right there. And then we'll get into a cuddle."

Hellman exploded with laughter, prompting Goldwyn to dismiss everybody from the room. "You call yourselves geniuses?" he said as his talented team marched to the door. "I call you dumbbells!"

For the next week or two, George Gershwin jangled Goldwyn's nerves the most. The composer always seemed tired and dizzy. Goldwyn heard that he had been secretly keeping late nights with former Goldwyn Girl Paulette Goddard. Still, Gershwin showed up at his office on the lot to labor over two love songs, "Our Love Is Here to Stay" and "Love Walked In." Ira's lyrics were necessarily generic, because there was still not enough of a script to demand more specific sentiments. At this point, Goldwyn told Gershwin only that he wanted "hit songs you can whistle," just like the ones his friend Irving wrote.

One morning in late June 1937, George complained of a headache so severe that his brother had to phone him in sick. When this news reached the head office, Goldwyn ordered him off the payroll until his return.

Gershwin never made it back to the studio. What had been suspected were the results of fatigue (or possibly psychological malaise) proved more grave. He often lost his coordination, and he stumbled into moments of irrationality. With neuralgic pains on the right side of his face and an occasional ache at the top of his head, he took to bed. Playwright S. N. Behrman visited him, and Gershwin complained, "I had to live for this, that Sam Goldwyn should say to me: 'Why don't you write hits like Irving Berlin?'" On July 9, he fell into a sleep that deepened into a coma. At last the symptoms suggested a brain tumor, and emergency surgery was ordered. It was too late to remove the growth in the right temporal lobe. On Sunday, July 11, George Gershwin died.

For about a day, noted one observer, Goldwyn carried on as though he had lost his best friend. He talked of producing Gershwin's life story. Then he sprang right back to business. Because the Gershwin score was only half completed when George died, Ira recommended Vernon Duke, a Russian-born composer with a classical background, to complete the score. Goldwyn was not interested until he heard that Duke had written the hummable "April in Paris."

It was Duke's third day on the lot when Goldwyn asked to meet him. The producer, his left arm in a sling, said, "Sit down, Duke," then discoursed for three minutes on the task before him. He stressed the "honor of working on the greatest musical film of all time." Duke silently wondered if this really was the Goldwyn of legend, until the producer asked, "What songs did you write?" Duke dropped a few titles, and Goldwyn said, "Oh, yes, the song about April." Then he added, "That's good, but you won't get a firm footwork on the film industry until you've worked for me. Good-by, Duke." The new employee shook hands with the man he then *knew* was Goldwyn. Duke was told that Goldwyn's other hand had been injured while he bawled out his staff, banging his fist on the table. In truth, the producer had broken his forearm in a fall down the stairs of his Santa Monica beach house.

That afternoon, Duke's presence was requested on Stage 2. George Balanchine was about to unveil his "American in Paris" ballet. For weeks, Balanchine had been rehearsing the first full-length ballet created expressly for the screen, in privacy so strict that even Goldwyn had been prohibited from entering the dance studio.

Goldwyn perched himself in a high director's chair. Balanchine had small groups of three or four dancers in modernistic poses scattered about the stage. Off in a corner, the rehearsal pianist started to play "An American in Paris," and Balanchine began to narrate the story of the ballet, leading Goldwyn from his chair to the first cluster of dancers. Indicating his injured arm, Goldwyn said he preferred sitting in the chair, but Balanchine insisted that the producer accompany him through the ballet, step by step. "Goldwyn gave in," remembered Vernon Duke, ". . . and it was a rare sight to see the man piloted by George, made to crouch and squat, the better to view a couple wriggling on the floor or peer straight into a dancer's navel—'that's where camerra vill be shott!' George would exclaim triumphantly. With every succeeding episode, Goldwyn's face got redder and angrier; he complained loudly about his arm hurting after so much crouching and squatting, and refused to peer into any more navels. 'Bott I have more, Mr. Goldveen!' George exclaimed aghast. 'That's all right, George, I get the idea,' the producer said." He walked out, asking Balanchine to report to his office.

Goldwyn told Balanchine that his ballet was all very "artistic," but "that the miners in Harrisburg wouldn't understand it." Balanchine said, "I'm not President Roosevelt—what do I care about the miners in Harrisburg." Then the ballet master thought for a second and added, "Besides, there are no miners in Harrisburg; I know, because I've been there." Goldwyn just laughed and said he was sorry, that the "American in Paris" ballet was out. Balanchine stormed back to his apartment and prepared to return to New York City. When Vernon Duke caught up with him an hour later, Balanchine said if the dance was out, so was he. Duke called Fred Kohlmar, Goldwyn's assistant on this picture, who raced over to appease the dancemaster. Kohlmar explained that Goldwyn still wanted a ballet for his *Follies*, just one less abstract. Balanchine realized that he had done his work too well, choreographing not just the dancers but every camera angle— none of which Goldwyn wanted to see or hear about. He had simply walked onto the soundstage that afternoon expecting to sit through an enjoyable few minutes of ballet. Goldwyn was more intent than ever, Balanchine was told, on including ballet in his *Follies*. In fact, his heart was set on it.

Sam Goldwyn had fallen hopelessly in love with Vera Zorina. Still barred from the studio where Balanchine rehearsed his dancers, he used to sneak glances at her through the doorway whenever he could. He had countless tests made of her, which he watched over and over. He ordered a small mark on her face removed surgically and one of her teeth filed down and capped.

He built a new dressing room for her, an apartment so complete that she wondered why she even had to rent a house. He ran movie musicals for her, pointing out that for all Eleanor Powell's tap-dancing ability, she was a cold performer. "*You* gotta have *warmth*," he kept telling Zorina. And he had new dance numbers created for her. The first was a Romeo and Juliet story in which the rival families would be the jazzy Montagues and the square Capulets. Vernon Duke was also asked to write music for a second piece, called "Waternymph," in which Zorina could show off her dancing ability as well as what Duke called her "superhuman beauty."

Goldwyn was always on his best behavior with her. He tried to impress her in the nicest ways, dropping hints that he was a man of culture. One day he raced excitedly onto the set to tell her that he had just seen *One Hundred Men and a Girl* in which Deanna Durbin tried to persuade a great symphony conductor to form an orchestra of unemployed musicians. "It has that great music director—Dostoevski," he said proudly. "You mean Stokowski," Zorina gently corrected. "No, no," said Goldwyn, sure of himself, "Dostoevski"; and Zorina liked him for that. But all his subtle expressions of love for her were totally lost on the twenty-year-old ballerina. "My interests were somewhere else," she explained forty-five years later, when she first realized that Goldwyn had been tripping over himself to be near her. "I was falling in love with Balanchine. Not only did I love him, he was becoming my everything."

Goldwyn became a lovesick calf. One afternoon, Lillian Hellman saw him trot down the back stairs of his office and into a waiting taxi, only to return a few minutes later. The next day she observed the same unusual occurrence, this time realizing that his departure came just seconds after Zorina had driven off the lot. Word spread among the writers and executives in the building. After a week of this behavior, there were enough spectators to form an office pool. Each one chipped in a dollar, the pot going to whoever guessed the precise minute that Goldwyn's cab passed before the studio gate. This carried on several days a week for the better part of a month. One day, George Haight tailed Goldwyn's taxi, all the way to Zorina's little house in Beverly Hills. Haight reported that Goldwyn's cab had pulled to the curb a few doors down, and Goldwyn had craned his neck to watch her enter. Once she was inside, he returned to his office. Goldwyn's yearning was a secret only to Zorina, who had no idea she was being pursued.

Even Frances Goldwyn knew. She had no evidence of a love affair but plenty of signs of her husband's lust. Ever since the reaffirmation of their marriage contract—he vowing never to stray and she to stay—she had kept an eye out for any indiscretions. She never bothered to investigate the occasional peccadilloes she had heard about; but now she had something much more serious to deal with, worse than any infidelity: She had every reason to believe her husband was in love with Zorina. Sam constantly brought up her name in the most flattering way; Frances would catch him daydreaming; he came home with expensive trinkets for no special reason. She convinced herself that there was a love affair, and when she challenged her husband head-on, he protested far too much. Sam Goldwyn, Jr., remembered, "The only fights I ever remember my parents having with each other, real fights in which my mother threatened to leave him, were over Zorina."

The "affair" could not have come at a worse time. Frances was feeling overworked and underappreciated. Just recovering from the heavy burdens of Sam's illness, she was still supervising every detail of his domestic life. Zorina remained oblivious of the Goldwyns' family drama.

One night, Sam's dinner arrived at the table. Mushrooms were not on his prescribed diet, and the sight of them on his plate convinced him that Frances was out to poison him. She burst into tears at his accusations and fled upstairs, where she telephoned George Cukor to say she was leaving Sam. "She told me she could not take one more day with 'that man,'" Cukor recalled. Frances hung up and began emptying her closets and drawers, while Sam brooded in his bedroom at the far end of the hall. Within a few minutes, her bags were packed and she was descending the circular staircase at 1200 Laurel Lane. The doorbell rang. It was Cukor. He took one look at Frances and said, "Where the hell do you think you're going?" Cukor pointed her back upstairs, and Frances retreated, stifling her sobs all the way up. He joined her in her bedroom and helped her unpack. "And," said Cukor decades later, "that night was never mentioned again."

Frances bottled up her hysteria. From then on, if she even saw Sam defer to an attractive woman, she suspected the worst. Over the next few months, Frances started a private list of celebrated women she made herself believe were intimate with her husband. After Zorina, she enrolled Averell Harriman's wife, Marie, and Lillian Hellman. The playwright later swore, "I never wanted to sleep with Sam, and he didn't want sex from me. All he ever wanted was another good script."

Miss Hellman remembered telling Goldwyn to "go fuck himself" when he insisted she try writing *The Goldwyn Follies*. In truth, she took a crack at it, getting no closer to a cohesive story than her many predecessors. At last, Goldwyn turned to his usual standby.

Ben Hecht's script for Goldwyn was devoid of inspiration except in its send-up of the producer's recent "secret romance." An impeccably dressed Hollywood producer (to be played by Adolphe Menjou) named Oliver Merlin considers that his recent films have been failing at the box office because he no longer has his finger on the public's pulse. A naive girl from the country (Andrea Leeds) enters his life and observes that the great Merlin's films have lost the "common touch." He is so grateful for this diagnosis that he hires her as a private consultant, a confidante he calls Miss Humanity. He falls in love with her. But she is completely oblivious of his amorous intentions because she pines for a handsome singing hamburger slinger, whom she helps break into the movies. Merlin's pictures regain sudden popularity, and at a big cast party, he intends to announce his engagement to his unsuspecting inamorata, the woman behind his renewed success. When he discovers her love for the young singer, he turns the party into their celebration. "I'm so glad you and Hollywood turned out so nice," Miss Humanity tells Merlin at the end of the film.

The Goldwyn Follies of 1938 proved to be such a folly that the producer never again attempted a revue. It cost $1.8 million and ended up $727,500 in the hole, the most Sam Goldwyn had ever lost on a single picture. The Technicolor production contained several memorable moments, but they never added up to more than that.

The highlight for Goldwyn and the public alike was the "Waternymph" ballet, in which Zorina, swathed in a gold lamé tunic, rose from the bottom of a fountain that was the centerpiece of a stunning Richard Day set. It was a dazzling debut. Shortly after the film opened, Vera Zorina married George Balanchine, and she was in constant demand on both stage and screen. Sam Goldwyn loaned her out to other studios and permitted her to appear on Broadway, but he never worked with her again. The question of why a man so fervent to hire her would never put her in another film haunted Zorina for the rest of her career. It had been "humiliating" for this young, dedicated ballerina to think she had not performed adequately. Something so far removed from her dancing as the preservation of a marriage had never even occurred to her.

WHILE the ties that bound Sam and Frances Goldwyn tightened, his professional ties were slowly dissolved. After a year of Dr. Giannini's provisional government at United Artists—during which time Goldwyn produced one third of their American output—the company's firebrand staged a coup d'état. At a particularly testy directors' meeting, Goldwyn pounded his fists and exclaimed that Chaplin, Pickford, and Fairbanks were contributing next to nothing to the company and should renounce their interests. Goldwyn offered to buy each of them out, for $500,000 apiece. The once omnipotent monarchs of the silent era laughed at the offer but retired to another room to consider it. They returned to the table willing to accept $2 million each. Goldwyn could not afford that, so he sought an ally in the company's other leading supplier of films, Alexander Korda. According to UA's counsel, Charles Schwartz, "Sam persuaded Korda that he was being rooked, and that the two of them should band together to get the parasites out."

For the rest of the year, Goldwyn and Korda tried raising the money on two continents, putting the bite on such important investors as the Lehman brothers, the Rothschilds, and John Hay Whitney, the prominent New York socialite who had recently become president of Selznick International Pictures. They raised as much as $4 million, but Pickford, Fairbanks, and Chaplin stuck to their price, foreclosing further debate of a buyout.

If Goldwyn could not shake the partners down for their interests in United Artists, he would try to shake them up. He installed one of his cronies, Murray Silverstone, as head of distribution. This action, attorney Neil McCarthy wrote Douglas Fairbanks, "would indicate that Sam is in charge of the distribution of the company's pictures, whether or not he says that is true; and whether or not Sam states he would not want any man to favor his pictures over those of another, the men themselves are human beings."

Fairbanks and Chaplin never trusted Goldwyn, but there had always been some unspoken consanguinity; Pickford had long loathed him. In trying to get his way, Goldwyn knew he had to work on her. As he had in so many crises in the past, he persuaded Joe Schenck to work on his behalf. Even though Schenck was several years removed from United Artists, he took it upon himself to send a long letter to Mary Pickford. "A producer who spends between eight and nine million dollars a year has a perfect right and good reason to be apprehensive if he thinks the company, through which he distributes, is not properly managed," he wrote Mary Pickford in a long letter on March 16, 1938. He asserted that "Dr. Giannini does not concern himself intimately enough with the distributing end of the business as it cannot be done from Hollywood." Schenck said that "knowing United Artists as well as I do and knowing Sam as I do, I am convinced that he has no ulterior motive in what he wants to bring about."

According to attorney Charles Schwartz, Goldwyn "harassed and annoyed the bejesus out of Giannini, and finally persuaded Mary and Doug to throw Giannini out." Chaplin would not vote to remove him; in fact, he stopped talking to Goldwyn for instigating the ouster. Giannini resigned, and Silverstone was hired as general manager of United Artists. His first important assignment was to design a profit-sharing schedule. The Silverstone Plan included a record $500,000 dividend to be split among the five partners—enough to assuage Chaplin, Pickford, and Fairbanks—and a producers' fund from which bonuses would be paid according to the success of each picture—thus rewarding Goldwyn and Korda and such nonstockholding producers as Wanger and Selznick.

Goldwyn remained contentious, never content. With the three former giants of the company shoved into the background, he started to make life difficult for Alexander Korda (then struggling to keep his British film empire afloat), voting down propositions that might be to his advantage. Silverstone would be his next target.

The virulence with which Goldwyn dealt with his United Artists partners was one sure sign that he had fully recovered from his recent ailments. Another was the vigor with which he began discharging the bright young men around him. Over a period of months, he set traps for all his assistants so that they would plead to be set free. George Haight, for example, was the victim of subtle demotion. Goldwyn gave him increasingly demeaning tasks to perform and moved his office farther down the corridor of assistants until Haight was literally working out of what had once been a closet. When he could put up with no more, he went in for what he described as his "final surreal meeting" with Goldwyn. "How did it actually end?" Garson Kanin asked his colleague that day. "Did you shake hands, finally?"

"No," said Haight. "We shook *fists*."

For a year, Sam Marx had worked as Goldwyn's story editor, on the promise that he would be allowed to produce pictures. Goldwyn turned down practically every project Marx brought to him and excoriated him for every successful picture that other studios made. "Why haven't we got that?" he would ask.

"Part of the problem," Sam Marx remembered, "was that Goldwyn did not make many movies, so he was really not interested in *developing* material. He only wanted sure-fire stuff." Ernest Hemingway told Marx he would sell Sam Goldwyn the rights to his next work, about the Spanish Civil War, for $25,000. Marx was jubilant, only to have Goldwyn dismiss this piece of literary history in the making. "What are you trying to do—rob me? $25,000 for a book that isn't even written!"

One day at a production meeting, Goldwyn verbally attacked Marx for incompetence. The patrician Merritt Hulburd quietly excused himself. Goldwyn moved toward Marx and railed that all the writers and agents in town could not stand him, and that was why Marx had been unable to secure material for the company. Finally, he found the gall to say that the only reason Irving Thalberg had kept Marx on at MGM was that he felt sorry for him. The overt lie gave Marx room to breathe easy. He smiled. At the end of the week they met again and agreed to tear up their contract. After making one phone call to Harry Cohn, he reported for work at Columbia on Monday.

Merritt Hulburd postponed his appointment in Samarra simply by quitting. He returned to his desk at the *Saturday Evening Post* in Philadelphia, only to suffer a fatal stroke a short time later. Several of his friends attributed the death to his years of "shock treatments," sitting at the other end of Goldwyn's squawk box. Fred Kohlmar also walked out and would come into his own as a producer in the fifties, with such celebrated pictures as *Picnic, Pal Joey,* and *The Last Angry Man.*

Garson Kanin, too, realized that Goldwyn was not helping him attain his ambition. "I wanted to be a director," he recalled. "I had said so to Goldwyn five or six hundred times—so many times, in fact, that he had stopped listening." After several months, Abe Lastfogel of the William Morris Agency obtained a job offer for Kanin to direct a "B" picture at RKO, the bottom half of a double feature. They went to Goldwyn to secure Kanin's release. Goldwyn looked hurt when he heard the news. "Well," he said, "you're not the first one who stole money from me." For the chance to direct this one picture off the lot, Lastfogel said, his client was willing to pay back all the money Kanin had received in the past year. An insulted Goldwyn refused the offer and ultimately let Kanin go. Saying goodbye, he refused to shake "Tallboy"'s hand.

Shortly after Kanin's film, *A Man to Remember,* had opened, to respectable notices, he ran into Goldwyn at a party honoring William Wyler and his new bride, a beauty from Dallas named Margaret Tallichet. Goldwyn approached Kanin and said, "You dirty little bastard. You dirty, double-crossing little son of a bitch. . . . Why didn't you ever *tell* me you wanted to be a director?"

Wyler explained to Kanin that Goldwyn believed with all his heart that Kanin had never once mentioned his ambition. To think otherwise was to concede that he had blundered. "He's used bad judgment," Wyler elucidated, "so rather than admit this, he convinced himself you never mentioned it. I think it may be one of the main reasons for his success. To himself, he's never wrong. He's a god. Not a bad thing to be, especially if you live on earth." Kanin asked Wyler, "What makes you think he lives on earth?"

AFTER twenty-five years in the motion picture business, Goldwyn had the public believing he was someone special. Ben Hecht wrote that Goldwyn as a collaborator was inarticulate but stimulating, that he "filled the room with wonderful panic and beat at your mind like a man in front of a slot machine, shaking it for a jackpot." Alva Johnston, in his four-part *Saturday Evening Post* profile in the spring of 1937, wrote:

Patiently, diligently, he reaches into and searches $3000-a-week brains and $5000-a-week brains in the hope of finding something worthy of Goldwyn. He is a Flaubert—with the exception that the French genius tirelessly explored his own intellect for the perfect effect, while Goldwyn tirelessly explores the intellects that he has under contract. The results over a long period have justified Sam's methods.

William Wyler remembered reading Johnston's *The Great Goldwyn*, which Random House published after its appearance in the *Post*. It amused him and annoyed him. "Tell me," he asked in 1980, only half-joking, "which pictures have 'the Goldwyn touch' that I didn't direct?"

16 Annus Mirabilis

THE FEBRUARY 1, 1938, issue of American *Vogue* ran an article by Frank Crowninshield called "The New Left Wing in New York Society." It was about Manhattan's "Café Society," a "newly formed, colourful, prodigal, and highly publicized social army, the ranks of which are largely made up of rich, carefree, emancipated, and quite often, idle people." Bordering the opening two pages of the piece was a pen-and-ink montage by Cecil Beaton. On one side he sketched symbols of old money—a manor house, portraits of ancestors, classical music, volumes of Shakespeare and French poetry; on the other he drew satirical nightclub scenes, a blaring jazz band, scandalous newspaper headlines, and Walter Winchell's column. At the bottom of that page, in minuscule handwriting, Beaton's marginalia trespassed into vulgarity.

"M. R. Andrew ball at the El Morocco brought out all the damn kikes in town," read the microscopic caption to his cartoon of a magazine society page; and in print just as fine, he wrote "Party darling Love Kike" on a Western Union telegram. Then on some cards and telegrams in and around a box of orchids—legible only by turning the magazine upside down and putting one's nose to the page—Beaton wrote, "Why is Mrs. Selznick such a social wow? Why Mrs. Goldwyn etc. Why Mrs. L. B. Mayer?"

Walter Winchell learned of Beaton's act of veiled anti-Semitism as the first copies of the magazine were hitting the street, and he took *Vogue* to task in his column. Until then, publisher Condé Nast had not known of Beaton's cryptic comments. Some 150,000 copies had already been shipped, and nothing could be done about them; the remaining 130,000 were reprinted with the objectionable lines expunged. Cecil Beaton—one of *Vogue's* standard-bearers—was discharged, his work banned from the pages of all Condé Nast publications. Privately, Beaton referred to the incident as "a wretched little foible," a joke; three months later, he asked Nast to reinstate him. Three years would pass before Nast relented.

The incident blew over most of Hollywood virtually unnoticed. At 1200 Laurel Lane, however, it caused a cyclone of irrational behavior. The reason, said Sammy, was that "Mother realized that as far as the world was concerned, she was a Jewess."

Quite sensibly, Frances had recently discharged one of her household maids, Senta Schmidt, when she learned the German woman had been filling Sammy with pro-Hitler propaganda. Having had this "fifth column" living in her own home, Frances was now convinced that Nazis were everywhere. She accepted both her and Sam's having been publicly branded with Stars of David; but as Hitler began to overrun Austria and Czechoslovakia, she was determined that he would never get hold of her son. She prepared for a Nazi conquest of America by devising a scheme that would allow Sammy to assume a second identity. Her plan was to bring some of her son's clothes to the beach and let them wash on the shore, establishing that he had drowned. He would reappear, using another name, in Mexico, where money would be waiting for him—enough to last a lifetime if necessary. Sammy's father, most of whose relatives still lived within Hitler's reach, tried to reason with Frances, but on this subject there was no getting through to her. Like most American Jews then, on the subject of religion Sam Goldwyn silenced himself because "he didn't want to make waves."

The movie industry found its own way to respond to the rising tide of fascism. At the start of 1939, Will Hays, president of the Motion Picture Producers and Distributors of America, held a meeting in New York of representatives of leading educational institutions, religious and civic groups, women's clubs, youth organizations, and some of the members of the MPPDA's Public Relations Committee. They spoke of films as though they were part of the national archives, powerful symbols of the nation's strength, forceful weapons. The conferees called for: "the continuance and increase of those . . . treatments which have made the American motion picture a true product of democracy, by emphasizing in popular entertainments mankind's long struggle for freedom and the hopes and aspirations of free men everywhere." Will Hays himself sent a copy of the resolutions of that meeting to every important motion picture producer in the country, including Sam Goldwyn.

Few had profited more from the nine years of depression than the titans of Hollywood. They met a public demand, feeding the values of the American Dream to 80 million Americans a week. The business of movies alone employed 280,000 people and kept 17,500 theaters operating in more than 9,000 cities. The motion picture industry paid the federal government $100 million a year in taxes. Among the motion picture community's new contributors was a generation of European filmmakers, such refugees as Fritz Lang, William Dieterle, Otto Preminger, Billy Wilder, and Russian-born Anatole Litvak. They found themselves in the same town as Thomas and Heinrich Mann, Franz Werfel, Lion Feuchtwanger, and composer Arnold Schönberg—Jews who did not come to work in films . . . but mingled with members of the movie colony, imbuing Hollywood with an international flavor and intellectual fervor.

The Jews who ran Hollywood found new purpose in manufacturing their product. They poured their restless religious feelings into some six hundred films that year—infusing the very best human values, as spelled out in Will Hays's President's Report. Life, liberty, and the pursuit of happiness would be translated into tragic love stories, heroic adventures, and uplifting comedies tooled by craftsmen of the highest order. Nineteen thirty-nine—and a few monthly calendar leaves on either side—was a year of masterpieces, the greatest burst of creativity in Hollywood's history.

Leo, the MGM lion, was king of the Hollywood jungle. Harry Brandt, president of the powerful Independent Theatre Owners of America, had recently bought newspaper advertisements in which he labeled Greta Garbo, Joan Crawford, Marlene Dietrich, Mae West, Kay Francis, Edward Arnold, Fred Astaire, and Katharine Hepburn "poison at the box office" and urged studios not to make films with them anymore. Louis B. Mayer stood behind those who were under contract to him. That year, MGM presented Lubitsch's production of *Ninotchka,* luring audiences by announcing, "Garbo Laughs!" MGM also unleashed Joan Crawford in her first unsympathetic "bitch" role, in Clare Boothe's *The Women.* MGM's talented young actors peddled the values of "the American way of life." In addition to playing the title role in that year's production of *The Adventures of Huckleberry Finn,* Mickey Rooney was in the middle of a fifteen-picture cycle of films that depicted the Hardy family of Carvel, Idaho. Rooney's co-star in another picture he made that year, *Babes in Arms,* was Judy Garland; in 1939, she sold America on the philosophy "There's no place like home," after visiting a land over the rainbow in *The Wizard of Oz.* Admiration of strong, traditional values was nowhere more in evidence that year than in MGM's version of James Hilton's novel about British schooldays, *Goodbye, Mr. Chips*. It starred Robert Donat and, in her debut, a heavenly red-haired Anglo-Irish beauty named Greer Garson. The themes of patriotism and freedom got aired openly in *Idiot's Delight*, starring Norma Shearer, Edward Arnold, and Clark Gable. The "King" was also about to assume the most commanding male role of the year, Rhett Butler in *Gone With the Wind*. In exchange for his services, Louis B. Mayer won the rights to release the film from his son-in-law David Selznick.

As much as Mayer, Darryl Zanuck influenced the films his studio produced; and Twentieth Century–Fox also emerged in 1939 as a leader in popular entertainment that extolled American virtues. John Ford directed Henry Fonda in *Young Mr. Lincoln* and *Drums Along the Mohawk*. That same year, Fonda and Tyrone Power turned the lives of Frank and Jesse James into a touching family drama, Spencer Tracy went in search of Cedric Hardwicke in *Stanley and Livingstone*, Don Ameche composed some of America's most beloved songs in *Swanee River* and invented the telephone in *The Story of Alexander Graham Bell*. The studio saluted England in 1939 by pairing Basil Rathbone and Nigel Bruce in *The Adventures of Sherlock Holmes*. By the end of the year, production was under way on *The Grapes of Wrath*, with John Ford again directing Henry Fonda, as Tom Joad.

Warner Brothers' films in 1939 reflected the national spirit as well. Cagney and Bogart appeared in *The Roaring Twenties*, but it proved to be among the last of the studio's gangster pictures. Tough guy Edward G. Robinson turned G-man in *Confessions of a Nazi Spy*. The former "fugitive from a chain gang," Paul Muni, had become the cinema's most luminous impersonator of historical heroes—Pasteur, Zola, and, that year, Mexican revolutionary leader Juárez. In 1939 alone, Muni's co-star as Empress Carlota, Bette Davis, would appear as the queen in *Elizabeth and Essex* (opposite Errol Flynn) and as tragic victims in two of Warner Brothers' vintage "women's pictures"—*Dark Victory* (with George Brent) and *The Old Maid* (opposite Miriam Hopkins).

The drop in quality and quantity of Paramount's production that year revealed their ongoing economic turmoil, but a few big names kept the truth in their advertising: "If it's a Paramount picture, it's the best show in town." Adolph Zukor, in his mid-sixties, had been kicked upstairs as chairman of the board, but he kept his hand in production matters. Under him, DeMille limned "the story of the spanning of America by steel" in *Union Pacific*. Gary Cooper—who had made more than forty films for Paramount in ten years—appeared in *Beau Geste*.

No filmmaker captured the optimism of the human condition so vigorously as Frank Capra. In 1939, he draped all his favorite themes in Old

Glory in *Mr. Smith Goes to Washington,* again for Columbia Pictures. While James Stewart was playing Senator Jefferson Smith, Harry Cohn also had Cary Grant in Howard Hawks's *Only Angels Have Wings.*

The smaller studios contributed to the cornucopia of films in 1939 as well. Universal presented their treatment of law and order in *Destry Rides Again,* with Marlene Dietrich and James Stewart, who this time played a mild-mannered sheriff, Thomas Jefferson Destry. RKO offered such solid entertainments as Charles Laughton in *The Hunchback of Notre Dame,* Fred Astaire and Ginger Rogers in *The Story of Vernon and Irene Castle,* and *Love Affair,* with Irene Dunne and Charles Boyer, the screen's new "great lover." The studio also began distributing the films of Walt Disney. After six years with United Artists, Disney left for RKO's better terms on the eve of his completing *Snow White and the Seven Dwarfs,* the first feature-length cartoon. RKO had also just closed a deal with the force behind the Mercury Theatre, Orson Welles; they offered him the chance to write, direct, and star in a film of his choice. He began work on *Citizen Kane.*

United Artists remained the magnet for the industry's most prominent independent filmmakers. Walter Wanger produced the archetypal western *Stagecoach,* starring John Wayne. Hal Roach produced the second in his series of "Topper" pictures, then turned serious, hiring Lewis Milestone to direct an adaptation of Steinbeck's *Of Mice and Men.* Samuel Goldwyn's only full partner at United Artists to produce any films that year was Alexander Korda, who made *Prison Without Bars* and *The Four Feathers.* And David Selznick upheld his commitments to UA, completing *Made for Each Other,* a melodrama with James Stewart and Carole Lombard, and signing a contract for another four pictures. The first of them, released while *Gone With the Wind* was in production, was *Intermezzo,* a remake of a Swedish love story between a married violinist and his protégée, played by Ingrid Bergman. Simultaneously, Selznick imported Alfred Hitchcock from England to begin work on another best-seller he was adapting for the screen, Daphne du Maurier's *Rebecca.*

Irving Thalberg's death left a great void in Goldwyn's heart, which David Selznick began to fill. Goldwyn liked giving the prodigious producer—twenty-three years his junior—endless advice, mostly about the marketing of pictures. He felt more than recompensed just by the pleasure of Selznick's zestful company—especially at the card table, where the compulsive thirty-seven-year-old proved to be one of the town's pigeons. (Frances Goldwyn was already several steps ahead of her husband, having pursued Irene Selznick years earlier. It was inevitable that these two perspicacious women—each able to play all the Hollywood social games without ever losing the ability to laugh at them—would become fast friends for life, confidantes who discussed the inner workings of Hollywood during long walks around the Stone Canyon Reservoir.)

"No matter how much success he had," said Samuel Goldwyn, Jr., thinking especially of this period in his father's career, "he was still an outsider." Goldwyn's successful example of quality independent production was proving increasingly attractive to the most creative producers in town. Even so, the deck remained stacked against the independents. The major studios were still rich and powerful enough to control most of the important properties and actors. Unwilling to die, Goldwyn aggressively tried to change all that.

Throughout the thirties, as Gary Cooper steadily climbed to the top of the list of box-office stars, he and his wife found themselves increasingly frequent guests at the Goldwyn dinner table. Some evenings, the two couples just played bridge together. One night, Goldwyn kept Cooper in the dining room while the wives withdrew for coffee. He knew that Paramount had been negotiating a new contract with the actor, but Cooper said that nothing had been signed. Goldwyn offered to top anything they offered. Unknown to Zukor, the actor and his agent agreed to a six-picture deal with Goldwyn over six years, each film guaranteeing Cooper at least $150,000.

Goldwyn could not help announcing in *Variety* his "exclusive contract" with Gary Cooper. It was as ill-timed as it was untrue. Not only had the actor not completed his commitments to Paramount, but he would still be able to appear in other studios' films when Goldwyn was not employing him. Furthermore, Paramount claimed that the fine print in Cooper's present contract kept him from accepting another offer until he had rejected one from them. The matter fell into the hands of studio attorneys. Goldwyn knew the litigation would run on for several years, during which time he intended to make his few movies with Cooper while giving him plenty of time to honor any other contracts. The courts ultimately ruled the same. Shuttling between Hollywood lots, Cooper earned $482,819 in 1939, making him the top wage earner in the nation.

For months, Goldwyn looked in vain for projects for Cooper and Merle Oberon, who was growing as both a movie star and an actress. He announced their appearing in "Maximilian of Mexico," "Hans Christian Andersen," and a romance set in a mythical kingdom called "Graustark." All three productions were scrapped. His New York story editor, Miriam Howell, had tried to interest him in *Rebecca* and *Dark Victory* for Oberon, but Goldwyn was not interested. West Coast story editor Edwin Knopf met similar indifference when he pleaded with Goldwyn to option *The Grapes of Wrath* for Cooper. Lillian Hellman also urged Goldwyn to obtain the rights to the Steinbeck novel, which she was eager to adapt, but the "gloom and the sordidness of the background and the people plus a pro-Communist indication" made him shy away. After Fox bought it for John Ford, Goldwyn said to Hellman, "Let Zanuck make a mess of it."

Goldwyn might have done just that with another work that became a screen classic. To remove the stink of "poison" from her name, Katharine Hepburn retreated from Hollywood until she could find the right vehicle to chariot her back. In late 1938, playwright Philip Barry discussed with her a play he was calling *The Philadelphia Story.* She agreed to star in it and bought the film rights. After she had made a hit of the play on Broadway, producers pounded on her dressing room door. It was not enough, Hepburn told them, that she re-create the role on the screen; more important to her was whom they would provide for support. To reinstate herself with the public, Hepburn felt she needed on each arm a man with strong box-office appeal. Goldwyn was mad for the material. He offered Gary Cooper and sent Willy Wyler to Hepburn's town house in New York to discuss the play. In the end, Cooper felt he was wrong for the role—not that he could not portray the debonair Main Liner C. K. Dexter Haven, but because his presence in the film would rob the play of its suspense, the audience knowing that the heroine would inevitably end up with him. When Louis B. Mayer promised Cary Grant and James Stewart, Hepburn shook hands on a deal. "I AM HEARTBROKEN AND I HOPE WHAT I HAVE HEARD IS NOT SO," Goldwyn wired the star at the Shubert Theater. It was; and she made nine films for MGM in the next decade alone.

After months of deliberation, Goldwyn optioned Edna Ferber's *Nobody's in Town,* a short novel set in Manhattan. Sidney Howard agreed to write the screenplay, his first film assignment since completing his adaptation of *Gone With the Wind.* His correspondence with Goldwyn was full of old affection. Howard quickly got a draft on paper and pronounced "much of it fresh, lively, human and entertaining." Over the next few months, he intended to spend as much time as possible on his farm in Tyringham, Massachusetts, where he would rewrite the script. One day that August, he cranked a tractor while it was still in gear, and it crushed him to death. He had not completed the screenplay, nor did he ever see the final results of his work on Margaret Mitchell's novel. He left three children from his second marriage, to Polly Damrosch, and a daughter, Jennifer, from his first. *Nobody's in Town* never reached the screen.

Knowing that most stars' careers burned bright for but a few years, Goldwyn felt he had to strike while his irons were hot, even if his properties for them were not. In the mid-thirties, Douglas Fairbanks had dreamed up an idea of a film for himself about Marco Polo. When his popularity dimmed, he decided to produce the picture, perhaps starring his son. After divorcing Mary Pickford and marrying an English social climber, he came to Sam Goldwyn for assistance. Three meetings later, Fairbanks found Goldwyn taking over every aspect of the production. He begged his close friend David Rose, Goldwyn's new vice president and general manager, "to get him out of the deal." Goldwyn had no problems with that: He would simply produce the film alone.

He hired Robert Sherwood, who wrote a cheeky romantic adventure, built around the explorer's discoveries of spaghetti and fireworks and his teaching Oriental beauties the Western custom of kissing. At the court of Kublai Khan, the rakish Marco Polo falls for the royal daughter, Princess Kukachin. Part of the script's humor lay in its twentieth-century dialogue coming from the mouths of thirteenth-century characters. Goldwyn commandeered Gary Cooper into the role, the first film under his new contract. Sherwood thought Cooper was all wrong for the part as written.

A sure-handed director—someone who could bring out all the virility of the piece and have a good laugh about it at the same time—might mesh the sly script with the shy actor. John Cromwell, who had done just that with Ronald Colman in *The Prisoner of Zenda*, got the job. Seventeen-year-old Lana Turner had a bit part, as a Eurasian handmaiden. The naive young blonde was thrilled that Mervyn LeRoy had loaned her out for this, her third movie role; it made her think she just might have a career in motion pictures.

Merle Oberon, with her exotic Oriental looks, would have been the obvious choice to play the leading lady, Princess Kukachin. But she was in England, working for Korda, the part was too small, and Goldwyn still resisted drawing attention to her Asiatic features. Instead, he cast his newest discovery, a fair, high-foreheaded Norwegian named Sigrid Gurie, and promoted her as the "Norwegian Garbo." A month later, his twenty-seven-year-old "siren of the fjords" filed suit for divorce from a hitherto unsuspected husband, and news quickly broke that not only had Miss Gurie been married to an American luggagemaker but she had been born in Brooklyn—Flatbush, no less. The revelation stunned Goldwyn only momentarily. He told the press it was "the greatest hoax in movie history."

Shooting proceeded without incident for five days before Goldwyn realized that director John Cromwell was playing Sherwood's tongue-in-cheek script completely straight. A shouting match in Goldwyn's office ensued, from which the director emerged announcing his resignation. Goldwyn turned to Willy Wyler, who asserted that the problem was with the lead, that the role cried out "for a swashbuckler like Fairbanks or Errol Flynn. But Goldwyn said Cooper was the biggest star in the world and that he could play anything." Wyler refused the assignment and went to Europe, while his contract was "suspended and extended." Goldwyn pressed John Ford, mopping up after filming *The Hurricane*, into temporary service. He directed a blizzard sequence and a crossing of the Himalayas. At last Goldwyn signed Archie Mayo, who had no special qualifications for *The Adventures of Marco Polo* other than his availability.

The movie fell flat on its face. *Newsweek* commented that the $2 million production was "a disappointing case of touch and go with the Goldwyn touch." Few reviews were as kind. Even with the pull of Gary Cooper, the film ended up $700,000 in the hole, the first big slip in the actor's career. When Goldwyn rereleased the film in the forties, Sigrid Gurie's name was lost in the ad copy, and Lana Turner was billed as Cooper's co-star, despite her appearance on screen for no more than a few seconds. Following the $725,000 loss of *The Goldwyn Follies* in the company ledger, Samuel Goldwyn suffered his biggest dip in earnings.

Back on the Paramount lot, Cooper played a cosmopolitan millionaire opposite Claudette Colbert in an Ernst Lubitsch production called *Bluebeard's Eighth Wife*. The film's failure made Goldwyn anxious to get Cooper back into Stetson and chaps, preferably with Merle Oberon at his side. A fixture in Hollywood since the days of one-reel silent comedies, Leo McCarey, heard of Goldwyn's situation and provided the spur. "He could create hilarious situations, and imaginatively, almost inexhaustibly, develop those situations," said Garson Kanin. "He was not a writer, but he was a superlative talker, and in a time and place where there was a paucity of readers and a plethora of listeners, talkers were more effective (and more successful) than writers."

Goldwyn gathered his team of story editors and assistants to listen to McCarey's latest idea for a picture. None realized he told his whole story off the cuff. For the better part of an hour, he painted scenes that would show off stars, he invented comic situations, he described gags. McCarey's story boiled down to nothing more than the standard boy-meets-girl formula, involving a red-blooded cowboy and a blue-blooded daughter of a presidential candidate. It was called *The Cowboy and the Lady*. Goldwyn was not quite sure an entire plot had been revealed during the sales pitch, but he was ready to buy it.

The next morning, Goldwyn asked each of the men who had been present to tell the plot of *The Cowboy and the Lady*. After the ninth version, he had enough sense of what the story might be that he bought it for $50,000. That night, Kanin ran into McCarey and congratulated him. "Yeah," McCarey said, "but now the trouble is, I've got to write it down . . . and I can't remember what the hell I said." A dozen writers developed his twenty-five-page outline, including such literary talents as Anita Loos, Dorothy Parker, Robert Riskin (who had written most of Capra's classic films), and S. N. Behrman, who got screen credit.

Cooper never liked the script, but he was glad to get back in western gear. Merle Oberon buttered up Goldwyn with a gift of a black smoking jacket, in an attempt to get out of the picture. She consented to play in it only if she had a good director to guide her. Goldwyn offered his best. Wyler thought the script was "awful, just awful," but he could not afford another suspension. He weaseled out of the assignment legally.

Knowing his pace drove Goldwyn crazy, Wyler put in three days on the picture, using up more film than usual. Goldwyn discharged him. He kept Merle Oberon's feathers unruffled by promising a part in the picture to her current flame, David Niven, and letting her choose the new director. She picked Henry Potter, who had directed her in *Beloved Enemy*. He lasted most of the shooting, before Goldwyn replaced him. Niven's part was ultimately cut from the picture.

The Cowboy and the Lady cost $1.5 million and became Goldwyn's third loss in a row. After a year of requesting new stories in which his two stars could appear together, he now insisted they be kept apart.

His next project for Cooper was an out-and-out adventure film, practically all action. Robert Riskin and a battery of writers developed *The Real Glory*, the story of an American doctor and two soldiers of fortune (Broderick Crawford and David Niven, sporting a mustache) in the Philippines after the Spanish-American War. Cooper would play the mainstay of civility in a white community threatened by Moro terrorists run amok. In the course of an hour and a half, he would cure a cholera epidemic, blow up a crucial dam for an officer who had gone blind, challenge rapids, and win the final battle in the bloodiest sequence ever recorded in a Goldwyn picture.

The 1939 release of *The Real Glory*, on the heels of Cooper's great adventure performance in *Beau Geste* for Paramount that year, helped shore up the actor's slippage at the box office. But the actor knew Goldwyn had shoved him into three mediocre parts in a row, just to cash in on his name. He went to Goldwyn's general manager and pleaded to be let out of his contract. David Rose assuaged him with the promise of better pictures.

Merle Oberon, meanwhile, backed into the role of her life. Goldwyn had all but been conned into producing the film, but it would become his all-time favorite. Its route to the screen began in 1936, when Ben Hecht and Charles MacArthur summered on their friend Alexander Woollcott's private island in the middle of a lake near Bomoseen, Vermont. There, on speculation, they adapted *Wuthering Heights*. Knowing Woollcott was a hopeless snoop, they wrote ten pages of a dummy script, which they left for him to find—scenes of Heathcliff's lost year in the New World, written in what Hecht called "Ugh, ugh, heap big pow-wow dialogue" between Heathcliff and Chief Crooked Head. The prank kept Woollcott out of their hair for the eight days they needed to complete one of the best scripts of their years of collaboration.

Their version of *Wuthering Heights* neatly extracted the heart of the dark romance between Heathcliff, the waif from Liverpool who became the brooding stableboy, and Catherine Earnshaw, the bewitching girl of the moorlands. In stripping away many characters and telescoping the passage of time, the screenwriters preserved the intensity of the lovers at Wuthering Heights in all their twisted passion. The script was kicked around town for months, before Walter Wanger bought it for his two romantic leads, Charles Boyer and Sylvia Sidney.

But first Wanger had wanted the actors to appear in *Algiers* together, with Miss Sidney supporting the ingenue, Hedy Lamarr. Not only did the veteran actress think the stunning newcomer to American films would steal the picture; she thought her own role of the vengeful half-caste was yet "another tenement girl—this time in spangles." Already studying a Yorkshire accent for her part in *Wuthering Heights,* she refused to do *Algiers.* She and Wanger had a violent screaming match, after which he lost all interest in rewarding her with the part of Cathy. Then his second choice for the role, Katharine Hepburn, was labeled box-office poison, and he lost interest in the project. When Wanger muttered that he wanted "to put laughs in the picture," Hecht and MacArthur asked Sam Goldwyn to buy the script from him.

Goldwyn was not sure he wanted it. The script was relentlessly grim. Like the novel, it unraveled the story of the unconventional lovers in flashback, which confused him. He did not see why an audience would be pulling for a capricious, irresponsible girl or a hate-filled homeless boy from the streets of England who made good in America, only to seek his revenge. Goldwyn sent the script to Willy Wyler for his opinion. The director was ecstatic; he urgently recommended purchasing it but knew that was not enough to persuade the producer.

Wyler's latest picture had just opened to rave reviews. *Jezebel,* with Bette Davis, made on loanout to Warner Brothers, attempted to cash in on the nation's mania for the Old South. It beat *Gone With the Wind* to the screen by better than a year, and Bette Davis forever contended it was the role—her second to win an Oscar—that made her a star. Actress and director were both eager to work together again, and Wyler slipped her the script of *Wuthering Heights.* She asked Jack Warner to buy it for her. The director knew that was all Goldwyn needed to hear, but his plan partially backfired. Goldwyn was delighted to grab a property Warner wanted, but he knew Warner would never hand over his biggest star. Before buying the script, Goldwyn asked Wyler, "Can Merle play the part?"

The director had to admit she could. Wanger sold the screenplay to Goldwyn right out from under Sylvia Sidney's nose, in a moment of what she called "absolute vengeance." Goldwyn loaned him Sigrid Gurie for the secondary role in *Algiers*. And each producer thought he had outfoxed the other. The part of Cathy was Merle Oberon's.

Goldwyn wanted to do everything possible to brighten the story, but what fascinated Wyler about *Wuthering Heights* were its shadows. He discussed with Gregg Toland how they might capture the moodiness of the piece. The cinematographer suggested candlelike effects by subtly diffusing the light. He said characters' faces could be kept in partial darkness, then come into the light at climactic moments. He recommended low camera positions to capture the ceilings of the sets, thereby emphasizing the stifling confines and dour loneliness of Wuthering Heights. The film would be filmed in tight shots as much as possible, focusing on the characters' tension.

Even though the Hecht and MacArthur screenplay was beautifully laid out, Wyler had his usual preproduction jitters. He said the script was not ready, and he insisted that his close friend John Huston, who had patched parts of *Jezebel,* work on it for a few weeks. Once Huston had signed a contract, he and Wyler and Goldwyn met for a series of story conferences. They invariably ended up in shouting fests, as Goldwyn discovered Huston would have nothing to do with making Cathy and Heathcliff more "likable." Huston could stand the vociferation no longer. "Let's make a wager," he said; "each one of us puts up fifty dollars, and the first one who starts yelling loses." Wyler agreed and put his fifty dollars alongside Huston's. Goldwyn—who never carried money—went along, saying he was good for his. The three men completed their story conference in modulated tones, and in rising from the table, Goldwyn raked in the hundred dollars. Wyler asked what he was doing. "I win," Goldwyn said. "What do you mean, you win?" Wyler asked. "Well," said Goldwyn, trying to pocket the money, "I didn't yell."

When Goldwyn's sales department reported that they did not like the title *Wuthering Heights,* Goldwyn instructed his story department to better it. Wyler said such an idea was "crazy." Jock Lawrence came up with "The Wild Heart," "Dark Laughter," and "Bring Me the World," but told Goldwyn he would "be in for very bad condemnation if this title is changed because it is a classic. It is exactly as if Selznick would have dared to change

'David Copperfield' to 'A Little Boy in England' or 'Little Women' to 'Katy Wins Her Man.'" Goldwyn would allow the time period of the novel to be updated by several decades, because Regency costumes would not show off Merle Oberon's shoulders to their best advantage; but he did stick with Miss Brontë's title. Because his ear often led his mouth to pronounce words in ways that sounded more familiar, he always referred to the film as "Withering Heights."

While the script was being rewritten, Ben Hecht saw a film at home in New York, 21 Days, a Korda production that starred Vivien Leigh opposite an actor who had recently won kudos at the Old Vic, playing Hamlet. "I SAW LAWRENCE [sic] OLIVIER ON THE SCREEN LAST NIGHT," Hecht wired from Nyack, "AND THOUGHT HIM ONE OF THE MOST MAGNIFICENT ACTORS I HAVE EVER SEEN HE COULD RECITE HEATHCLIFF SITTING ON A BARREL OF HERRING AND BREAK YOUR HEART."

Merle Oberon seconded the opinion. But after a dozen appearances in British films, Olivier had not caught on with the moviegoing public. His last visit to Hollywood, in 1933, ended when Garbo herself banished him from the cast of Queen Christina. Olivier later admitted that he had "despised" the notion of acting in motion pictures, and he had no interest in returning to Hollywood just then because he was engaged in a love affair with Miss Leigh. At Goldwyn's dictation, Merle Oberon cabled Olivier in London: "I HEAR GOLDWYN WANTS YOU FOR WUTHERING HEIGHTS STOP THOUGHT YOU WOULD LIKE TO KNOW PART MAGNIFICENT BEST SCRIPT HAVE EVER READ ALSO HEAR HE WOULD LIKE VIVIEN FOR PART YOUR WIFE PICTURE TO BEGIN SEPTEMBER HOPE YOU WILL BE ABLE TO DO IT." Neither Goldwyn nor Oberon knew that Olivier did not think much of Merle's acting ability, and the thought of working with her made the proposition less appealing. Olivier was considering the role of Heathcliff only with the understanding that Vivien Leigh play Cathy.

Wyler went to London to hire an all-English cast, notably Olivier, whom Goldwyn was now bent on signing. For days, Wyler had no luck in bringing him around. Then, on July 7, 1938, he cabled Goldwyn: "HAVE FOUND HEATHCLIFF AMAZING YOUNG ENGLISH ACTOR . . . MUCH BETTER THAN OLIVIER." His name was Robert Newton. The rugged actor with fiery eyes and a crackling voice had appeared in only a few English films, but he seemed perfectly suited to play the character as Emily Brontë had written him. Goldwyn did not like his looks. He maintained that onscreen the role required a man of some physical beauty if the film was to work with audiences at all. At Merle Oberon's suggestion, Goldwyn tested Douglas Fairbanks, Jr., but found him as weak as he had found Newton ugly. "NEWTON OUT OF QUESTION," Goldwyn cabled Wyler back.

"PLEASE DO EVERYTHING POSSIBLE SELL OLIVIER PART AND PERSUADE HIM COME HERE WITH LEIGH ACT PROMPTLY."

Wyler took to dining with Olivier and Miss Leigh in their town house on Christchurch Street. One night, the host took Wyler to see *St. Martin's Lane,* one of the actress's films in current release. Wyler never doubted her ability, but at their next dinner together he said he could offer no better than the part of Isabella, the woman Heathcliff marries after Cathy has settled on Edgar Linton. Vivien Leigh plainly had her sights set on a big Hollywood film career and told Wyler point-blank that she would only accept the role of Cathy. Wyler contended that that was impossible, that the only reason Goldwyn was making the film was to showcase Merle Oberon. "Then I don't want any part," said Leigh. Wyler tried to explain the facts of studio life to her. "Look, Vivien," he said. "You're not known in the States. Nobody's ever heard of you there. Someday you might become known. But for your first role in an American film, you're never going to get a better part than Isabella!"

Wyler pushed for Robert Newton harder than ever, insisting that he was a "young Muni" and that even Alexander Korda thought he was ideal. Goldwyn agreed to additional tests with Newton, suggesting that a mustache might make him appear more like Ronald Colman. The director was now convinced. "NEWTON MAGNIFICENT HEATHCLIFF," he cabled Goldwyn; "HAS STRENGTH AND POWER WHICH OLIVIER LACKS STOP OLIVIER HAS UNAVOIDABLE WEAKNESS." He suggested that Goldwyn's first choice would make a much better Hindley—Cathy's lily-livered brother. "OLIVIER ALSO ADMITS NEWTON BETTER HEATHCLIFF," concluded Wyler, "WHY CANT YOU BELIEVE ME ABOUT NEWTON AM YOUR AGENT NOT HIS."

In all the ruckus, Olivier asked his dearest friend, Ralph Richardson, if he should take the role. Richardson said, "Yes. Bit of fame. Good." Without warning, Olivier announced his change of heart to Wyler, who cabled Goldwyn from aboard the *Queen Mary* on his return to America. "OLIVIER NOW VERY EAGER. CAN BE STALLED UNTIL MY ARRIVAL ALSO SOLD VIVIEN LEIGH ISABELLA." In the end, Goldwyn would not meet her price, and she chose not to accompany Olivier. He sailed alone.

After a few months, "blind with misery at being parted from Vivien," Olivier learned that his agent's brother, David Selznick, was ready to start shooting *Gone With the Wind* but still had not cast Scarlett O'Hara. The night the producer ordered the burning of forty acres of exterior sets on his back lot, which were doubling for battle-blazed Atlanta, she appeared with Myron Selznick. "David," he said, as flames illuminated Miss Leigh's face, "meet Scarlett O'Hara."

The colony of British actors in Hollywood—which had grown large enough since talking pictures to support a thriving cricket club—filled the cast of *Wuthering Heights*. Leo G. Carroll, Cecil Kellaway, Cecil Humphreys, and Miles Mander took the supporting roles. Jack Warner loaned out Irish-born Geraldine Fitzgerald (newly arrived in California) to play Isabella and Donald Crisp as Dr. Kenneth. Wyler imported Flora Robson from England to play the story's narrator, Ellen Dean. That left uncast only the role of Edgar Linton, what the poor bloke who ended up playing it would call the "actor's nightmare." In supporting the tempestuous leads, there was little for the character to do but simper and snivel. Goldwyn thought the role called for a "sympathetic, charming, and fine actor"; after three years of grooming, he thought David Niven had at last become worthy of such a break.

"But it's the most awful part ever written," Niven told Goldwyn, "and one of the most difficult; please don't make me do it." Goldwyn assured him he would have "the best director in the business." After the humiliation he had suffered at Wyler's hand on *Dodsworth*, Niven opted to refuse the part and go on suspension. "I could not afford it," Niven recounted later, ". . . but the combination of Edgar and Wyler was too daunting." Goldwyn sent Wyler to do his bidding again. A couple of weeks into Niven's forced vacation, Wyler invited him to dinner at Dave Chasen's restaurant. Over drinks, Niven called Wyler "a son of a bitch to work with." Wyler laughed and said he had changed, that Niven should join this wonderful cast. "It'll be a great picture and I'll make you great in it," he said assuringly. Niven acceded.

Amid the splendid scenic design of James Basevi, *Wuthering Heights* began shooting on December 5, 1938, near Chatsworth, California. Goldwyn had sent a crew to Yorkshire to film the moors, which he matched in the craggy barrens of Ventura County. Wuthering Heights was constructed atop one of the rolling hills, complete with hundreds of panes of hand-blown glass. Kilos of heather were imported from northern England and replanted in southern California among four-foot-high shoots of bristling broom. It drove horticulturists mad to see the inconsistency, but as Wyler noted, "it looked more like a field of heather than a field of heather." Animal lovers squawked when they read in a press release that the ducks and geese had been hired from a trainer who had snipped the fowls' vocal cords.

Of the three principals, Niven was most spared the director's rod; but if Wyler had changed, it was only for the worse. He made Niven play his first scene over forty times. More than once he reduced Merle Oberon to tears. Twice she ran from the set an emotional and physical wreck: her death scene and the scene in which she recognized that her spirit was as

dark as the "gypsy scum" she loved and had to declare, "I am Heathcliff."
Wyler humiliated her in his efforts to get her through these two most
difficult dramatic moments. When Cathy had to run out into a gale,
trying in vain to stop Heathcliff from riding off, the director came across
as nothing less than sadistic. Over and over, he ordered her into the pro-
peller-fanned winds, water hosed through the blades and whipping at her
face. Miss Oberon kept cowering in the tempest, but Wyler wanted her to
defy it, to be a part of it. After repeated takes, she would take no more.
Her shivers gave way to shakes; she began choking and vomiting. Fragile
in the best of times, Miss Oberon took to a hospital bed, where she ran a
fever for several days. Her absence cost the production thousands of dollars. When she returned, she refused to work under such adversity any
longer. But Wyler still had not got the shot the way he wanted it. Goldwyn authorized heaters to be rigged alongside the fans so that the water
was warmed before she had to stand up to the bitter storm.

Olivier most suffered the director's lashings, and not without cause. "I
was over-acting appallingly," the actor admitted forty-five years later. Time
and again, Wyler would catch him in the middle of some stagy posture or
extravagant gesture. One day he said, "For Christ sake, what do you think
you're doing? Do you think you're at the Opera House in Manchester or
something?" The classically trained actor was not one to leave the set in a
huff. He parried the insults and, in front of much of the cast and the entire
crew, lunged back, saying, "I suppose this anemic little medium can't take
great acting."

Olivier and Oberon never saw eye to eye. "I think she may have thought
that because I was a stage actor of considerable experience by that time, I
. . . looked upon her as a little pick-up by Korda," said Olivier, "which
she was." Their mutual animosity came to a head during one of their intense scenes together at Peniston Crag, their childhood "castle." Oberon
complained more than once that drops of Olivier's saliva were hitting her
in the face during the scene. "Why you amateur little bitch," Olivier
shouted, "what's a spit for Christsake between actors, you bloody little
idiot. How dare you speak to me . . ." Oberon ran to her dressing room
in tears. Wyler told Olivier to go after her and apologize. The actor refused, saying he would not be "insulted by snippets like that." Wyler
repeated his orders, because Olivier had called her an "amateur." He
pointed out that her standing in motion pictures was much higher than
his and that she knew plenty about acting for the camera—"a hell of a lot
more than you do."

After three weeks of shooting, Goldwyn's churning stomach told him
Wuthering Heights was lagging dangerously behind schedule and the per-

formances were below par. He found Wyler guilty of overshooting and overdirecting, and he wrote up all his charges in a letter on December 29, 1938. Goldwyn did not send the letter. He chose to face the accused and hear him out. No director in Hollywood would have subscribed more strongly to the notion of a director's self-effacement in his work; but Wyler explained that he was trying to create mood in *Wuthering Heights*, which could come only from shooting unusually. He repeatedly told Goldwyn "not to worry, that it would all piece together." Film editor Danny Mandell saved the day and, said Wyler years later, "I'm sure he saved my job."

Wyler got Mandell to work overtime so that Goldwyn would view as few unedited sequences as possible. The producer thought it "disgraceful," for example, when he saw the many camera angles from which the simple scene of Heathcliff's throwing himself on his pallet in the stable and thrusting his fists through the windowpanes was photographed. He felt— as he wrote in his unsent letter—it was "utterly impossible for me to permit you to continue tactics which you used in this scene." When Goldwyn saw the best of those shots spliced together, drawing in on an extreme close-up of Heathcliff, he appreciated the intense emotional effect Wyler had created.

After seeing the first days' rushes of Merle Oberon, Goldwyn realized that she was not fully equipped to play her heaviest dramatic moments in *Wuthering Heights*. He wanted the director to redo her deathbed scene, reminding him, "This is a somber scene and if you remember, I especially wanted Oberon beautifully gowned and beautifully photographed to help lighten it." Wyler could not have disagreed more. He believed that "when beautiful movie stars allow themselves to look terrible, people think they're really acting." Instead of cutting to gorgeous close-ups of Merle Oberon, Wyler and Mandell kept her in less glamorous longer shots as much as possible. After Goldwyn saw the death scene assembled, he wrote to the actress, congratulating her "on the finest scene you have done since you have been in pictures. . . . Your performance does not surprise me, as I knew you had it, but it will be a surprise to those who do not know you as well as I. I believe you should kiss Wyler for his direction of this scene."

Both Goldwyn and Wyler agreed that Olivier's performance was too hammy, and the director finally admitted to the producer that he did not know what to do about it. Goldwyn realized that the only solution was to turn Wyler from the actor's enemy into his ally. One day early in the shooting, Goldwyn appeared on the set. Olivier had been suffering from a case of athlete's foot so terrible that he could not squeeze his swollen foot into his shoes. He saw the producer and director conferring, periodically looking his way. Olivier imagined that if he hobbled over pathetically enough, Goldwyn would hold out his arm and say, "Willy, you must send this poor unfortunate fellow home. He looks dreadfully tired; we've got to rest him now." Olivier limped toward the producer and right on cue, Goldwyn held out his arm and rested his hand on the actor's shoulder. "Willy," Goldwyn said, "if this—this actor goes on playing the way he is, I close up the picture. Will you look at that actor's ugly face. He's dirty, his performance is rotten, it's stagey, it's just nothing. . . . I won't have it and if he doesn't improve, I'm gonna close up the picture." Wyler snapped to and said, "Right, Mr. Goldwyn. If you leave it to me . . ." Goldwyn needed to hear no more. "Now Willy," he said in leaving, "don't you pull your punches with this guy." From that moment on, Wyler hardly had to say another word to Olivier about his performance. "I was obedience itself," Olivier himself conceded, ". . . and very nice to Merle and very nice to Willy who was then prepared to teach me."

The improving performance did not stop Goldwyn from squeezing more out of Wyler. When they were alone, Goldwyn said that he had not been kidding: he thought Olivier looked ugly and too dirty. Wyler explained that he was playing a poor stableboy and was not supposed to look any better until later in the picture; he said the coarseness enhanced the chemistry with Merle Oberon. If Wyler was not present, Goldwyn was readier with compliments for the director's work. Samuel Goldwyn, Jr., remembered watching the wedding scene between Cathy and Linton, in which Wyler had improvised a sweet moment of a little girl's walking up to the bride with a bunch of white heather for good luck. Goldwyn simply smiled at the touch and clucked, "That's Willy."

But it was "that Goddamned Wyler" who was "trying to kill me"— bringing the picture in thirteen days over schedule, more than $100,000 over budget. By the end of shooting, Goldwyn was delighted with the performances—even Olivier's—but he found the rough cut frighteningly somber.

Few films cried out for music so much as *Wuthering Heights*. Unfortunately, Alfred Newman, after nine years as music director at United Artists and composer of twenty-three Goldwyn scores, had quit the week shooting of the film had started. The greatest booster in Newman's career had become his biggest hindrance. The UA producers were not coming up with enough pictures to keep him employed full-time; and Goldwyn was making as much money for himself every time he hired Newman out to another studio—$90,000 in 1936 and 1937 alone. When Darryl Zanuck said he wanted to install Newman as music director at Twentieth Century–Fox, where they produced a new picture every week, the composer eagerly accepted. Goldwyn never stopped thinking of Newman as his own employee and hired him to write the score of *Wuthering Heights* for $5,000. The hour and a quarter of music in the 103-minute movie would become a model of film scoring and one of the composer's own favorite works. The haunting melodies were perfectly wedded to the melodrama; Cathy's theme especially—with the otherworldly strains of humming female voices against dreamy strings—was guaranteed to wring every tear out of an audience.

Just two weeks after the last retakes had been shot, *Wuthering Heights* sneak-previewed in Riverside, and Goldwyn saw how wrong he could be. The audience's questionnaire cards were among the worst responses to a motion picture he had ever read. They found the story hard to follow and seemed to concur with Goldwyn's initial instincts to the material. He said, "People don't want to look at a corpse at the end of a picture." With most of the cast dispersed, saving the film seemed hopeless. It occurred to Jock Lawrence that Flora Robson, whose character related the story of Cathy and Heathcliff to a traveler, was still in town. He thought she could read several short, lyrical speeches that might be dropped in at the half-dozen confusing junctures—"just a little glue to hold the story together."

Providing a happy ending for the film seemed more difficult, until Goldwyn remarked that MGM's *Three Comrades* had recently managed to raise the dead, rejoining the departed friends in the form of spirits. If *Wuthering Heights* was such a great love story, Goldwyn saw no reason why Cathy and Heathcliff could not be shown as ghostly figures, united at last, walking hand in hand to heaven. Wyler refused to shoot it, insisting it violated the nature of the film. Besides, Olivier was performing onstage in New York and Merle Oberon had left for London. These were small stumbling blocks to Goldwyn. He got Henry Potter to run a camera on Olivier's and Oberon's doubles, filming from the rear. "It's a horrible shot," Wyler maintained, but Goldwyn simply superimposed it against the final frames of Peniston Crag before the fade-out. He took the doctored film to Santa Barbara for a second preview, and a burst of applause drowned out the last bars of the music over the end credits. "Well," Goldwyn remarked to the team huddled around him, "they understood it."

Still Goldwyn had a marketing problem on his hands. The salesmen were having difficulty booking so unconventional a film. The low marquee wattage of the cast did not help. The most alluring tag line his promotional staff could propose was: "The strangest love story ever told."

While *Wuthering Heights* had started with a strong script and no cast, his other major production in early 1939 had a world-renowned star already filmed and absolutely no story in which to slot his scenes. Ever since Goldwyn began collecting cultural icons for *The Goldwyn Follies,* he had fixated on the idea of putting Jascha Heifetz in the movies. But after a succession of writers had suggested dozens of plots, all Goldwyn had was the original germ—that Heifetz would portray himself and give a performance that would somehow affect the film's outcome.

Unfortunately, the violinist's schedule would not permit him to wait in Hollywood indefinitely while Goldwyn's writers fiddled with scripts. Knowing he would spend the summer of 1938 in California, he had signed a contract that gave Goldwyn any four weeks of that season for $75,000. The summer was drawing to a close, and Goldwyn was desperate for a story.

Finally, writer Irmgard von Cube provided what Goldwyn was looking for. The film's new focal point became an urban music school about to go under. Heifetz could be used twice—in a concert at Carnegie Hall that would inspire a juvenile delinquent to take up the violin, and later at a concert to benefit the school. The script was far from finished when Goldwyn hustled Heifetz onto a soundstage, where he performed works by Tchaikovsky, Saint-Saëns, and Mendelssohn. In September 1938, just before *Wuthering Heights* had gone before the cameras, Goldwyn conscripted Wyler.

Months later, John Howard Lawson submitted a script that was to Goldwyn's satisfaction. "The Restless Age," as the picture was then called, was meant to be a heartwarming drama with a social conscience. A series of coincidences—a young tough finding a violin, his subsequent discovery on the street of a ticket to a Heifetz concert, and his dog running into a music school—kicked off the story, in which music worked wonders on "kids with dirty faces and hungry hearts." Walter Brennan would play the good-souled taskmaster who teaches music to the underprivileged children for free. Joel McCrea (in yet another two-dimensional supporting role) and Andrea Leeds would provide the music school's predictable love story. By the time Goldwyn was ready to film the finale, Jascha Heifetz was back east.

Goldwyn offered him $10,000 to return for one week of filming, but Heifetz refused. His wife said he would accept nothing less than $25,000. The star got his price and rearranged his schedule so that he could film again in late March.

Goldwyn reluctantly put *They Shall Have Music,* as the film came to be called, into the hands of Archie Mayo, the man he had blamed for the failure of *The Adventures of Marco Polo.* In fact, Goldwyn had tried to fire him after that fiasco, but Mayo had a five-year contract. The producer tried torturing Mayo into leaving. He ordered the director to the studio at odd hours for no reason at all; he publicly dressed him down; he gave him such menial tasks as delivering cans of film from one cutting room to another.

"That's all right, Mr. Goldwyn," Mayo would say, biting the bullet, "so long as you pay me." A chagrined Mayo explained to Wyler that he had just bought a big house based on his contract, and he was sure the producer would let up on him at last. But Goldwyn seemed to resent him for being the only director in town who was available. One day he telephoned Mayo on the set. Joel McCrea was walking by as the director was obviously getting chewed out. After a moment, Mayo broke his silence and spoke back into the phone: "Maybe I am, Mr. Goldwyn, but I'm *your* son of a bitch!"

Within a week of its July 25, 1939, opening, many theater owners who had bought *They Shall Have Music* had dropped it to the position of second feature. It made half the money of even so unsuccessful a film as *The Cowboy and the Lady,* but it rang up incalculable prestige for Goldwyn. Among the powerful people he called his friends, he would long be remembered as the man who put Jascha Heifetz in the movies, the one Hollywood producer quixotic enough to try elevating the taste of the American public. Hearst and Paley, the Harrimans and the Swopes, all took notice. So did Arthur and Iphigene Sulzberger of the *New York Times,* whose friendship the Goldwyns had recently cultivated. Their hospitality whenever the Sulzbergers were in town was more than reciprocated in 1939.

For weeks before *They Shall Have Music* was released, the *Times* covered the production from every possible angle. When Goldwyn went to New York to open the picture, Lynn Farnol arranged for a *Times* reporter to meet him, in an effort to squeeze a few more column inches out of him. Thomas Pryor, the young interviewer, who later became the editor of *Daily Variety,* went to Goldwyn's suite in the Waldorf Towers for a drink. Goldwyn rhapsodized about his plans for bringing more serious music to the screen. "Next," he said, "I'm putting Toscanini and Stokowski together." When Goldwyn saw that Pryor was not taking any notes on this scoop, he added, "This is a front-page story." Pryor guessed that the two maestros would never even sit in the same room with each other. When he pressed Goldwyn for details, he discovered nothing had yet been negotiated. "Mr. Goldwyn," the young reporter said, "this is really just an idea you have." Goldwyn jumped up and asked, "You calling me a liar?" Pryor insisted he was not, simply looking for the evidence of a deal, which would make a good story. "You're calling me a liar!" Goldwyn now insisted. He shouted for his secretary to ring up the Sulzbergers. "I'm going to have you fired," he said. Pryor gulped his Scotch and left. Upon his return to the office, he learned that "the old man" was plenty mad at him, but that he still had his job. Because of his friendship with Sam Goldwyn, however, Arthur Sulzberger found himself sitting in the hot seat.

The next day, *They Shall Have Music* opened, and *Times* critic B. R. Crisler wrote a sarcastic review. He noted that "the screen debut of Jascha Heifetz . . . has been announced as Opus I in the musical works of Mr. Samuel Goldwyn" and that his temptation was to write about the superb music and "to skip lightly over the movie with some graceful side remark, such as 'All is not Goldwyn that glistens.'"

Sulzberger picked up a copy of that night's bulldog edition of the paper at a newsstand on his way home, and he "exploded." "What agitated him," said Pryor, "was the wise-guy attitude. Crisler hadn't disliked it respectfully." Still edgy over Pryor's treatment of his friend Goldwyn, Sulzberger raced back to the office, where he ordered one of the paper's second-string reviewers, Bosley Crowther, to rewrite the review. Crowther devoted more of his review to the brilliance of Heifetz's playing and gently dismissed the rest of the picture as a "tear-jerker." Somebody in the composing room at the *Times* tipped off Walter Winchell, at the *Mirror*. He ran an item that for the first time in history, the *New York Times* had changed reviews between editions. At four o'clock the next afternoon, Arthur Sulzberger summoned Pryor, Crowther, and Crisler to his office. "Gentlemen," he said, looking at each of them soberly, "I want to apologize. I did something last night I'll never do again."

GOLDWYN got more mileage that year out of friends in even higher places. One night in late 1938, President Roosevelt's eldest son, James, attended a large motion picture industry gathering at MGM. Sam Goldwyn approached him and asked young Roosevelt about his career plans. When the President's son said he did not know, Goldwyn invited him to his studio. Over lunch, he found before him a well-spoken, attractive thirty-one-year-old with some of his father's irrefutable charm and unlimited connections. Goldwyn offered him a vice presidency in his company, somehow replacing David Rose, who was looking to change jobs. "There was no question," admitted James Roosevelt many years later, "he created the job for me . . . so that Sam Goldwyn could say the son of the President of the United States worked for him."

On January 3, 1939, Roosevelt reported to his small pine-paneled office on the seventeenth floor of 729 Seventh Avenue, where United Artists had its Manhattan headquarters. He issued a formal statement to a crowd of journalists about how happy he was to be associated with Mr. Goldwyn. Then he told the reporters he did not know precisely what his duties would be.

Nor did Goldwyn know what Roosevelt's duties would be—only that he would tap him whenever the Roosevelt name might grease a stuck wheel. As much as possible, Goldwyn wanted him out from behind his desk, glad-handing bankers, exhibitors, and ambassadors. Just for announcing Roosevelt's hiring, Goldwyn received press coverage from coast to coast. Roosevelt's parents had always encouraged their children "to live our own lives," Jimmy later recounted; "but when this situation with Sam Goldwyn came up, I think they held their breath."

The other shoe never dropped. "He never once asked anything of me that related to my parents," Roosevelt added. In fact, Goldwyn became a contributor to FDR's future campaigns and a faithful listener to his fireside chats. He never failed to send a telegram after an especially rousing speech. "Hollywood at that time was not looked down on at all, and with the growing interest in national defense, it was about to rise to the great occasion," James Roosevelt observed. "In fact, Hollywood was potentially important to my father," he added, suggesting that the President might even have benefited from his son's connection.

Eleanor Roosevelt enjoyed her few encounters with Goldwyn. On April 13, 1939, she arrived at 1200 Laurel Lane for a small dinner before the premiere of *Wuthering Heights*. She joined Irving and Ellin Berlin, Norma Shearer, Merle Oberon with an escort, and a few others. As they filed into the courtyard to make their way to the theater, Frances said, "Sam, suppose you take Merle and go along with Mrs. Roosevelt. I'll see to the others and follow." Weeks later, Merle's escort would rebuke Frances for slighting him; but Frances knew just what she was doing.

Pandemonium greeted the Goldwyn party as they arrived at the Hollywood Pantages. Searchlights crisscrossed in the sky, photographers flashed pictures, and screaming mobs tried to push their way past the police lines. Just as Frances Goldwyn had envisioned, her husband strutted up the red carpet into the theater, Merle Oberon—in stunning clothes and jewels and carrying a bouquet of white orchids—on one arm, the First Lady on the other.

The screening was a triumph—"not a dry eye in the house," remembered James Roosevelt. The film elicited the same response in New York at the Rivoli Theater. Practically every review repeated those sentiments. "It is unquestionably one of the most distinguished pictures of the year," wrote Frank Nugent in the *New York Times*, "one of the finest ever produced by Mr. Goldwyn, and one you should decide to see." Critics sang the film's praises for months. "This is the one I'm going to be remembered by," Goldwyn told his wife and son.

Only Willy Wyler remembered the opening of *Wuthering Heights* as a bittersweet evening. He had come to accept the fact that the "perfectly awful" cloud-walking tag did not destroy the rest of the picture; but he would never get over Goldwyn's completely excluding him from the festivities. The Wylers had not been invited to dine at Laurel Lane or to appear in the photograph sessions in the lobby of the theater, not even to shake Mrs. Roosevelt's hand. "This was Goldwyn's evening," Wyler said forty years later, "and he didn't want to be reminded that I had anything to do with the picture." Indeed, whenever anyone spoke of William Wyler's *Wuthering Heights*, Goldwyn was quick to correct. "I made 'Withering Heights,'" he would say; "Wyler only directed it."

The film did brisk business in its opening weeks but lost its momentum by summer. Hospitals reported a rush of newborns being named Cathy that year; but it would not be until those babies approached their teens that *Wuthering Heights*, in rerelease, would show a profit. Discriminating audiences, however, championed the movie all year. Reviewers wrote enthusiastic follow-up articles; Mrs. Roosevelt heaped kind words on it in her newspaper column. When James Roosevelt went to England to host the London premiere, his father asked him to call on King George and Queen Elizabeth, in anticipation of their impending visit to America; Ambassador Joseph P. Kennedy planned his visit to Windsor Castle, and young Roosevelt arranged for their majesties to see *Wuthering Heights*. At the Paris premiere, his honored guests were the Duke and Duchess of Windsor. In less than a year, Jimmy Roosevelt would be off the payroll.

Two days after Christmas 1939, Goldwyn received the greatest gift of his career to date, a telegram from Kate Cameron, president of the New York Film Critics, announcing: "YOUR FINE PRODUCTION OF 'WUTHERING HEIGHTS' WAS VOTED THE BEST PICTURE OF THE YEAR." It was the first major award he had ever won, and it came in the toughest year of competition in motion picture history. The New York Film Critics had chosen to pass over the odds-on favorite, *Gone With the Wind*, which had opened in Atlanta only two weeks earlier, at a premiere as spectacular as the picture. Upon learning of his victory, Goldwyn wired Ben Hecht, "MOST OF THE CREDIT FOR WUTHERING HEIGHTS GOES TO YOU AND CHARLIE AS I HAVE ALWAYS FELT THAT IT WAS THE FINEST WRITING THAT WAS EVER HANDED TO ME SINCE I HAVE BEEN PRODUCING PICTURES." Visions of his first Oscar—the awards would be made in February—danced in his head.

Goldwyn had losses on his mind as well as gains. Beside the meager returns on *Wuthering Heights* and *They Shall Have Music*, he lost most of his talent that year. His leading lady and his most promising ingenue surrendered to that common desideratum of actresses—security. Merle Oberon did not give up motion picture acting, but she did realize that her best shot at a claim to English society lay in marrying the British film industry's leading figure, her longtime protector, Alexander Korda. The decision came at an opportune moment, because after *Wuthering Heights,* both Sam and Frances Goldwyn examined the financial returns of her pictures and decided it would be best for them if they could cancel her contract. When he politely raised the issue, Miss Oberon voluntarily withdrew from their arrangement, forgoing a settlement of any kind. It was so generous a gesture that Frances called her the next day, saying, "Merle, if there's ever anything we can do . . ." (Years later, there was: Miss Oberon was eager to own prints of her Goldwyn films, the cost for which she was' willing to pay. Frances telephoned again, this time to say that she simply could not allow copies of her husband's films to float around town.)

Following the September 1939 release of *The Real Glory,* Andrea Leeds also left Goldwyn to marry. Months later, after but a handful of appearances in films, which included her performance as the suicidal actress in *Stage Door,* she chose to retire from the screen.

Joel McCrea, at the end of his fourth year under contract, told Goldwyn that he wanted out. Worse than the producer's making a 600 percent profit off the actor on loanouts was that in seven pictures, Goldwyn had not once cast him effectively. With Gary Cooper making films for Goldwyn, McCrea knew he would never read a script that did not have Coop's fingerprints on it. "No one has ever asked to be out of a contract with Sam Goldwyn!" Sam Goldwyn yelled at McCrea. The actor knew that Ronald Colman had asked exactly the same thing, but he sat in silence as Goldwyn assured him that he would "never work in this town again." McCrea headed directly to Cecil DeMille, who put him before the cameras in *Union Pacific.* "Everybody has a little trouble with Sam," said DeMille. "What do you think Jesse and I went through?" Joel McCrea promptly came into his own as a leading man. The next year, Hitchcock cast him in *Foreign Correspondent,* then Preston Sturges created roles for him in *Sullivan's Travels* and *The Palm Beach Story.* McCrea enjoyed another twenty years of screen stardom as a western hero.

Goldwyn needed stars. While a wave of Anglophilia swept the country, he thought of remaking *Raffles,* which had helped put Ronald Colman across as a talking-picture star nine years earlier. No fewer than ten writers worked on the new script, updating the Edwardian comedy-thriller to modern times. A. J. Raffles would still be the suave gentleman thief trying to lay his hands on Lady Melrose's emeralds to bail out a school chum in debt; but contemporizing the play exaggerated the artificiality of the drawing-room genre so popular decades earlier. Working from Sidney Howard's 1930 screenplay, playwright John Van Druten brushed up a shooting script good enough to interest Cary Grant. Goldwyn found him willing to work for less than his regular pay because he liked the role so much. Sudden threats of another actor's defection, however, forced Goldwyn to reconsider his leading man.

After less than four years in Hollywood, David Niven was grateful to Goldwyn for the fact that he "had given me a chance when nobody else would touch me." But it was dawning on him that he, too, was getting his best parts in loanouts. Niven convinced himself that Goldwyn was taking advantage of him. His agent, Leland Hayward, said, "Leave Goldwyn to me. You're making a fortune for him. I'm going in there and ask for a lot of money and a contract for five years straight with no layoff and no options, a limited number of pictures and six weeks' guaranteed vacation."

Niven sat in the anteroom of Goldwyn's office as a confident Hayward walked into the meeting. Two minutes later, he was back with his client, who asked if their demands were met. "Not exactly," Hayward said. "Goldwyn has barred me from the lot. Now I can't even talk to him."

Niven and Goldwyn entered a "really ridiculous war of nerves"—ridiculous, the actor realized, because it was a losing battle. The producer snubbed him on the lot, suspended him for turning down another poor role, and complained that Niven had developed a swollen head. Louella Parsons spread the "news." Suspended without salary, Niven picked up some cash by performing on various radio programs. After several weeks, controller Reeves Espy informed Niven that according to their contract, Goldwyn was entitled to all moneys his contract player was earning—but that he would sportily settle for half. Niven's next radio show was with Bing Crosby, sponsored by Kraft Foods. "At the end of the show, as was often the custom," Niven recalled, "I was presented with a large hamper filled with all the Kraft products—cheeses, spreads and sardines." When he got home, he "meticulously removed half the spread from the jars, cut every cheese in half, every sardine in half; then with an envelope containing a check for half my salary from the show, I sent the lot to Goldwyn inside half the basket." Goldwyn sent for the actor.

In his office, the producer cheerily announced that he wanted to rip up the papers between them and replace them with a more remunerative seven-year contract. The lead in *Raffles* was Goldwyn's bait. Niven was stunned by the offer and even more by his agent's rejecting it. Hayward counseled Niven to play hard to get. "Your contract is running out," he said. "He doesn't want to lose you—he's just playing games. I know Sam. We'll get the deal we want."

Goldwyn had his own game plan. A few days later, he called Niven to the studio to appear in some costume tests for another movie. All morning, Niven noticed a man hovering nearby in white tie and tails. He was posing for still photographs halfway up a ladder, while holding a revolver in one hand and a strand of pearls in the other. He was obviously meant to look like Raffles. After lunch, Niven approached the man, who was posing for more pictures, and asked what he was doing. The young actor, a handsome thirty-year-old named Dana Andrews, was not sure himself. He had signed his own seven-year contract with Goldwyn earlier that year; and his instructions on his first major assignment were to wear the Raffles costume and follow Niven around having pictures taken. Niven signed his new contract without further hesitation. Goldwyn borrowed Olivia de Havilland from Jack Warner to play the romantic interest in *Raffles*, and the rest of the predominantly British cast was assembled by late summer.

Talk of a possible war had everybody on the set in jitters through the first weeks of filming. A tired Sam Wood—who had directed that year's valentine to Albion, *Goodbye, Mr. Chips*, as well as several sequences in *Gone With the Wind*—maintained a businesslike atmosphere through most of the shooting. Then on September 1, Hitler invaded Poland, and two days later England declared war on Germany. Confusion overcame the British colony in Hollywood, especially on the set of *Raffles*.

Goldwyn sounded his own alarm. He felt everybody's nerves were making the film play flat. He wanted a script doctor to pep up the love scenes. Edwin Knopf recommended a writer who was in town trying to finish a novel about Hollywood, its protagonist based loosely on Irving Thalberg. F. Scott Fitzgerald reported for work on the Goldwyn lot the first week of September, carrying a briefcase packed with Coca-Cola. He sat in a corner of the soundstage with his secretary, dashing off pages and handing them to the director. Between scenes, Niven talked to Fitzgerald of returning home to fight and his premonitions of not living through the war. After a week on the job, the author was thanked for his work with $1,200 and no screen credit. "You always knew where you stood with Goldwyn," Fitzgerald wrote in his notes for what became *The Last Tycoon*, "—nowhere."

With several weeks on the picture remaining, Niven, a former Highland Light Infantryman, announced to Goldwyn that he had been called to the colors and had to leave immediately. "Goldwyn, as usual, was far smarter than I gave him credit for," Niven remembered. "Within half an hour he had checked with the British Embassy in Washington and had been told that nobody outside the British Isles had yet been called up." In fact, Niven had long since resigned his commission and probably would never be asked to serve. But he genuinely felt silly parading about in costumes when he ought to be in uniform.

Goldwyn felt good about *Raffles*, mostly that Niven had proved he could carry a picture. But just when Goldwyn was at last able to reap the benefits of having developed a certifiable new star, Niven returned home to join the Royal Air Force, unable to shake the "nasty feeling" that he might never see Hollywood again. "If when I get home," Niven wrote Goldwyn in valediction, "I am told that they definitely have nothing for me to do, then the streak of light half way across the world will be Niven returning to Goldwyn!" Complained Goldwyn upon his departure, "Movies aren't enough! Now I've got the whole World War on my hands!"

Meantime, Goldwyn was engaged in battle against his own allies, the United Artists. Flanked by James Mulvey, James Roosevelt, and his attorney, Richard Dwight, he had marched into the annual stockholders meeting on January 16, 1939, and dropped a bombshell. Chaplin had sent his legal proxy; but Korda, Pickford, and Fairbanks were present when Dwight opened the meeting with a brief statement. It was an ultimatum based on his client's feeling trapped in a blind alley: Like the old Goldwyn Company, UA lacked sufficient outlets for its product. Goldwyn, he said, wanted to be made its sole voting trustee. He did not want their stock, just the right to vote it, thus enfranchising him to elect his own board of directors. Without that power, Goldwyn did not see how he could deliver any more pictures to United Artists. He wanted all or he wanted out, and he intended to veto every proposition of his fellow stockholders until he got his way.

Everyone sat in "shocked silence" until Chaplin's attorney, Charles Schwartz, asked if he was serious. Dwight assured the stockholders that he was. Schwartz replied that his client would release Goldwyn from his United Artists contract, which had another three years to go, if he would surrender his stock—then worth some $500,000. Alexander Korda expressed equal astonishment at Goldwyn's demands, and said he would agree to Schwartz's settlement plan. Goldwyn, of course, refused.

And he rejected everything else that was put before him that day. Formal adoption of the Silverstone Plan reached the floor, the very scheme he had helped devise by which producers would be rewarded for their productivity. Goldwyn alone said nay, though its passage would have earned him $200,000. As a business formality, Fairbanks requested permission to form a new company with outside capital, which would make pictures for UA to distribute. Goldwyn said he would veto that unless Fairbanks agreed to this new voting trust. "Sam," Fairbanks said, "I've been your friend for many years, and now that I ask this thing, you attach this condition. Surely you don't mean it?" Goldwyn simply replied, "Yes, I do." Fairbanks left the room without another word.

Korda requested permission to substitute pictures from his new company for those owed by his London Films—another technicality. Goldwyn dissented.

The partners overrode Goldwyn on all the day's proposals, insisting that these measures did not even require a vote. But the man everybody in Hollywood had been warned never to take on as a partner had made his point. The meeting adjourned with Charles Schwartz shouting at Goldwyn, "Get out, you punk . . . and take your 'Murdering Heights' with you."

The United Artists partners could not ignore the fact that Goldwyn's fifty pictures had been the mainstay of United Artists for the last fourteen years. But Murray Silverstone told a reporter from *Fortune* that if they let Goldwyn dominate the company, UA "would lose every producer it has." Even Goldwyn's friend David Selznick went on record saying there would be no "producer-parity" if Goldwyn gained complete control of the company. Dr. Giannini asserted that such successful filmmakers as Frank Capra, Leo McCarey, and Gregory La Cava would have come into UA had they not feared fighting with Goldwyn; it was well known around town that Walt Disney had left UA because of him.

Two months after the board meeting, Goldwyn filed suit in the New York Supreme Court for a release from his United Artists distribution contract. The formation of Korda's and Fairbanks's new companies, allowing them to benefit from the Silverstone Plan, and permitting Korda to submit films from his new company, Goldwyn claimed, constituted breaches in his contract. Technicalities drove the case from one bench to another, until it landed in a federal court in April 1939. It went through legal gyrations for months, then got temporarily stuck when Douglas Fairbanks suddenly died in his sleep in December 1939.

Mindful that he owned everything that sat on the United Artists lot (even though Pickford and Fairbanks owned the property), Goldwyn asked his advisers if there was anything to prevent his changing the studio's name. They said there was not. One morning in 1939, the United Artists switchboard operators arrived for work and received orders to answer the telephones with the name of its owner—"Samuel Goldwyn Studios." When "March of Time" came to film Goldwyn for some newsreel about the movies, he suddenly noticed a prop behind him, clearly marked "United Artists"; he ordered them to reshoot the interview without the prop. The United Artists brass plate at the entrance of 1041 Formosa Avenue was replaced with one bearing the name of the building's landlord.

Having just turned sixty, Sam Goldwyn began asserting himself with greater authority than ever. Still inventing himself, he set out to prove once and for all that he was a force in the industry, different from the hundreds of other independent producers—the "little promoters," as he called them. From his corner office at Samuel Goldwyn Studios, he took on all comers—not just his UA partners but the industry at large. For years, Goldwyn had individuated himself by taking unpopular stands; the odd magazine piece on some controversial issue occasionally appeared under his byline. Throughout his years of legal battles with United Artists, he launched an argosy of press releases, each aimed at some common business practice of the major studios that he found offensive.

He raged against "block booking," that system by which theaters bought a studio's entire yearly output. He called for the "abolition of the deadliest menace that has ever faced the motion picture industry—the practice of having two feature pictures on one program." As early as 1934, Goldwyn had been exclaiming that the next important development in motion pictures would be not the perfection of color but the advent of television. In 1939, he was the only producer to stand up at the meetings of the Association of Motion Picture Producers and address the fact that "television has made tremendous strides technically . . . [and] the television people are doing everything possible to keep the picture people out of their industry because they naturally foresee a conflict of interest."

Goldwyn went public with none of these visionary positions for the amelioration of society. "If you look at every one of those issues," his son later observed, "you'll see that they posed a threat to him, a small independent film producer. Getting support for those stands he took was the only way he saw that he could survive."

Goldwyn reveled in his high visibility. A picture and quote of Sam Goldwyn became essential to any article on Hollywood, totemic. "Boy," he told a photographer that year at a big industry bash after *Life* had recently published an unflattering pose of him, "I don't care how you take my picture just as long as you spell my name right."

WHILE the professional Goldwyn became more public, the personal man became more private, cut off, severing even the strands that bound him to his family. Sam and Frances continued to provide for each other, but their love seldom overstepped into intimacy. Emotionally, they lived separate lives. George Cukor, who often suffered pangs of resentment over the Goldwyn marriage pact, said, "Frances settled for bread and pretended it was cake." Sammy, entering his teens, scraped for crumbs.

Dinner at the Goldwyn house was served promptly at seven, prepared by a Swedish cook. Sam Goldwyn, Jr., remembered almost always dining with his parents in the Laurel Lane house—except for the two or three nights a week when they were invited out and the two or three nights a week when they entertained. He was permitted to join the company if the guests were the Harpo Marxes, the Fred Astaires, or A. C. "Blumy" Blumenthal, a pint-sized dynamo who was the brain behind some of the industry's biggest real estate and stock deals. Family fare was "very simple, beautiful food": soup almost every night; broiled chicken, pot roast, or lamb stew served with salad; a light dessert, berries or applesauce. Thursday was cook's night off, and the three Goldwyns usually went to Romanoff's or Chasen's.

"The table conversation," Sam Goldwyn, Jr., remembered, "would begin with the crimes of the day—somebody who was trying to kill him." His father enjoyed starting the meal with some horrific tale of Hollywood—preferably at Louis B. Mayer's expense. Then he would run through the rest of his activities. Before leaving the table for a card game, he would mechanically inquire about his son's day. "No matter what I said about school made him express his great fear that I didn't VALUE EDUCATION," Sammy later recalled. "I could never quite satisfy him that I was getting an education."

Goldwyn did not even notice that his son was becoming a passionate reader. "My mother gave me the joy of books," said Sam Goldwyn, Jr.; "my father gave me the power of books. But ours was not a home in which culture played a part. Movies were our life, not books." As her husband got more caught up in himself, Frances found much solace in literature. She devoured every word she could find about French history, especially Marie Antoinette. She and Sammy often spoke to each other in French, but Sam resented it. As Sammy explained, "He didn't like things going on that he didn't understand."

Publicly they kept Sammy on a short leash. "Frances used to trot him out at parties," remembered Mrs. Albert Lasker, "—long after the days when she would dress him up in his little party outfits. And Sam liked to make fun of him, sometimes to the boy's face."

By 1939, Sammy had left Black-Foxe Academy and enrolled at Beverly Hills High School. Even there, he found his surname was more of a liability than an asset. But he began making friends as he grew into a tall, handsome young man. He swam on the school team, setting records in the breast stroke. After coming home from several meets repeatedly triumphant, he later recalled, "I was feeling very up. And my father gave me a terrible lecture about the elation of victory. He warned me to be careful. He loved victory, but he said if you enjoyed something too much it could be a serious problem. And then he'd tell me, 'Success ruins more people in this business than failure.'"

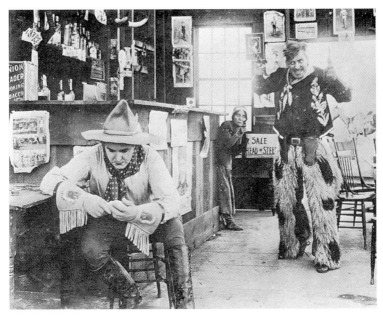

ABOVE: *The Squaw Man,* 1914, Dustin Farnum, Red Wing, and Billy Elmer.
BELOW: *The Winning of Barbara Worth,* 1926, Vilma Banky and Ronald Colman.

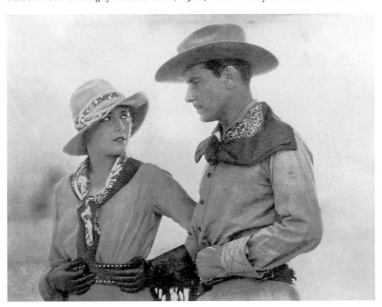

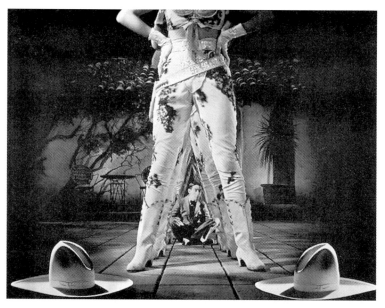

ABOVE: *Whoopee!*, 1930, Eddie Cantor. BELOW: *These Three*, 1935, Alma Kruger, Merle Oberon, Bonita Granville, Miriam Hopkins, and Joel McCrea.

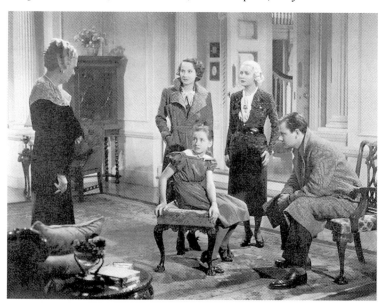

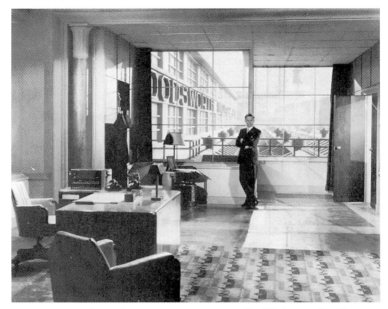

ABOVE: *Dodsworth,* 1936, Walter Huston. BELOW: *Dead End,* 1937, Leo Gorcey, Huntz Hall, Bobby Jordan, and Gabriel Dell.

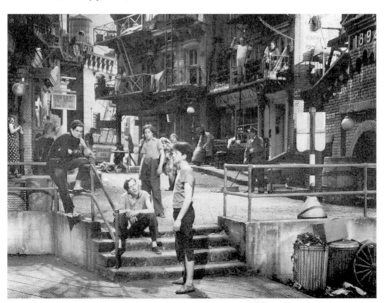

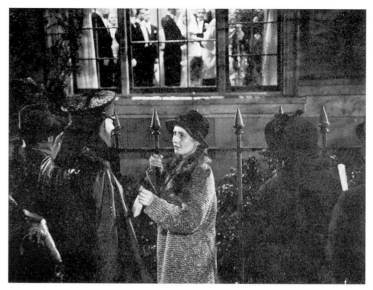

ABOVE: *Stella Dallas*, 1937, Barbara Stanwyck. BELOW: *Wuthering Heights*, 1939, Laurence Olivier and Merle Oberon.

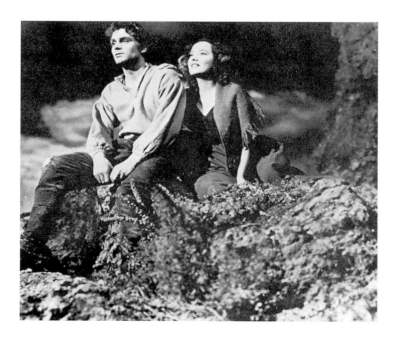

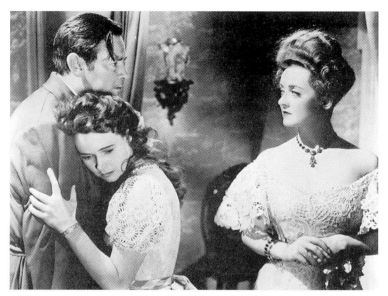

ABOVE: *The Little Foxes,* 1941, Herbert Marshall, Teresa Wright, and Bette Davis.
BELOW: *Ball of Fire,* 1941, Henry Travers, Aubrey Mather, Oscar Homolka,
Leonid Kinskey, S. Z. Sakall, Tully Marshall, Richard Haydn, Gary Cooper, and
Barbara Stanwyck.

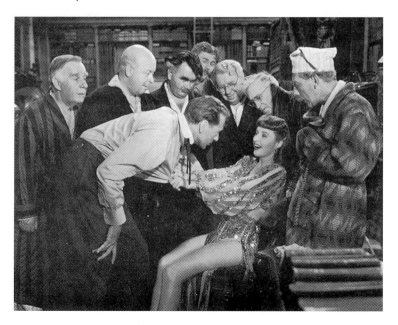

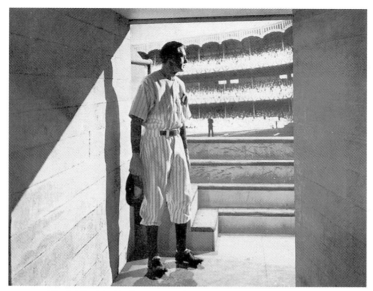

ABOVE: *The Pride of the Yankees*, 1942, Gary Cooper. BELOW: *Up in Arms*, 1944, Danny Kaye.

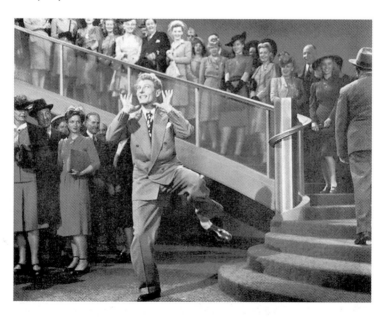

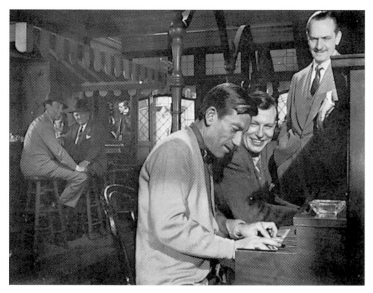

ABOVE: *The Best Years of Our Lives*, 1946, Hoagy Carmichael, Harold Russell, Fredric March, and Dana Andrews (in background, on the telephone). BELOW: *The Bishop's Wife*, 1947, Cary Grant, David Niven, and Loretta Young.

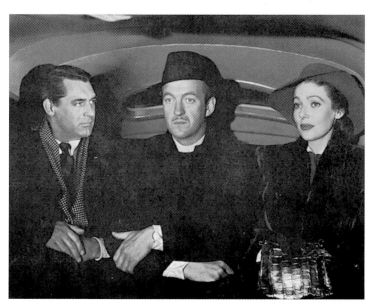

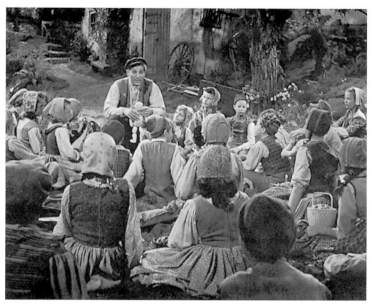

ABOVE: *Hans Christian Andersen,* 1952, Danny Kaye. BELOW: *Guys and Dolls,* 1955, Frank Sinatra, Vivian Blaine, Jean Simmons, Marlon Brando, and Stubby Kaye.

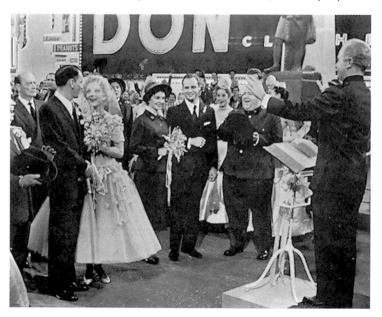

While Sam consistently shook his son's confidence, Frances infused him with fear. From her mother, Frances's feelings about Jews became more confused. She was perfectly comfortable being married to one, but she never let up in reminding her baptized son that he had to beware because he was Jewish. Just before Sammy began dating, he had wanted to attend a dancing school at the Riviera Country Club in Pacific Palisades. "You can't go there," Frances warned him; "they don't allow Jews." When Sammy reeled off the names of several Gentile friends who were going there, Frances said, "That's fine for them, but you're different." A few years later, Sammy broke his nose, leaving a slight bump in the middle of his otherwise Aryan features. "Mother," he remembered, "was horrified I'd carry these scars for the rest of my life."

Frances's paranoid reactions were little more than an extension of her mother's continually bizarre behavior. Bonnie McLaughlin was still able to tyrannize Frances. She tried to create trouble for the Goldwyns at every turn, even though she lived off an allowance provided by her son-in-law. On her holiday visits to Laurel Lane, she never failed to wear a big feather in her hat, knowing Frances still feared birds. More than once she reported Sam to the police for some imagined crime. She still wished Frances had married someone else; and a present to Sammy one year revealed who that was. She gave him a box of bookplates that read: "Ex libris: George Goldwyn."

Sammy entered what he later described as "a very bad year." Suddenly Sam and Frances had an adolescent before them, and they had absolutely no idea how to handle him. To compensate for their years of inattention, they began to monitor his every move. "I got stubborn and resentful," their son remembered, "My parents were right on top of me. It became important for me to get out, and nobody knew how to cope with it. There comes a point when a person just must get out."

One night, Sammy ran away. He did not get much farther than a friend's house on a neighboring knoll in Beverly Hills. Sam's first response was to call the police; Frances feared that her son had been kidnapped and said, "Nobody must know. *They* must never find out." She called Ira Gershwin's wife, Leonore, who calmed them through the night. At sunrise, the boy reappeared. Frances never figured out what had prompted his flight. Sam, the former teenage fugitive, was even more perplexed. "Can you imagine," he asked Lee Gershwin, "running away from *this* house?" Just when there seemed no way the three Goldwyns could peacefully co-exist under one roof, a mysterious stranger entered their lives.

Hilde Berl was a small Austrian woman, whose dark brows accentuated her piercing blue eyes. A trained graphologist with psychological training and extraordinary insights into human behavior, she spent a few weeks each year in New York. Many people found her a "charlatan," but at least as many had benefited from her almost mystical gifts. The Goldwyns met her in 1938 at a large party hosted by a mutual friend, and Frances said, "I hear you do such remarkable work. It is ridiculous to exploit you at a party." Miss Berl said "Yes," ending their conversation. A few months later, she appeared at a gathering in Los Angeles at which the Goldwyns were present. This time, Frances asked if she could write something for Miss Berl to examine. She said "Yes" again, and Frances wrote a few sentences. "Your only trouble," Hilde Berl said upon analyzing her high cursive, full of big loops and cut-off endings, "is you can't handle your son."

Frances froze, then uttered, "Can you tell me more?" Her eyes burning into Frances's, Miss Berl asked, "Do you love him?" Frances reared in indignation and walked away.

A few minutes later, she returned with her husband. Sam took Hilde Berl's hand and said, "Listen, why do you go back to New York? We need you here." She explained that her life was in Europe, but that she was spending the summer at the Beverly Hills Hotel. Frances asked if she could call on her. "She was very serious about it," Hilde Berl remembered. "She wanted to know what she could do. She wanted to show she really loved her son." At their first meeting in her hotel suite, Miss Berl asked, "Are you ever with him alone?" Several sessions followed Frances's negative response, and then Miss Berl asked to see her husband.

Before they even spoke, Miss Berl examined her subject. She saw "great pain" in Goldwyn's face, which he masked by detaching himself from those around him. His clothes revealed his obsession with his image. "So you use him as an amusement," she said, starting right in, "—to entertain your friends, right? What impression do you think you make?" The suddenness of Hilde Berl's approach surprised Goldwyn, but he stayed to talk. "That boy," he said more than once, "look at what he has. Much more than I started out with." Goldwyn came back a few days later. "He was feeling plenty sorry for himself," Miss Berl said, "but he was willing to talk about it."

Goldwyn's pain originated from what he considered his mother's early loss of interest in him, her seeming not to care when he ran away for America. Hilde Berl immediately turned the image around in Goldwyn's mind. She proposed that young Schmuel was, in fact, his mother's favorite child, the smartest and strongest. Miss Berl reminded Samuel Goldwyn of the pogroms Hannah Gelbfisz had lived through and the absolute poverty. "Perhaps," she said to Goldwyn, "she thought one of her children could get out, would not have to be exposed to what she had endured. And that's why she wanted him to go. She felt he was the only one capable of reaching that world out there and surviving on his own."

Before leaving Los Angeles, Miss Berl asked Sam and Frances to visit her together. They arrived in a state of anxiety, sorry she was leaving, afraid of where she was leading them in their treatment of Sammy. "If you really love him," Hilde Berl said to the boy's mother, "you must send him away." Frances would not hear of it. Miss Berl turned to Sam and asked, "How much do you think this boy can take?" She pointed out that everything Goldwyn had perceived as his son's advantages—his money and his name—were the boy's heaviest baggage. She urged the Goldwyns to enroll Sammy in a new private academy called Fountain Valley School of Colorado—"where there were sons of more famous men than Sam Goldwyn, and richer men too."

"I can't," said Goldwyn, for no apparent reason other than not wanting to let go. "How much longer," she asked, "are you going to make that boy suffer?" Goldwyn said, "Nobody speaks to me like that."

"Well, I do," replied Hilde Berl. "And if you don't wish to hear it, let's not waste each other's time any longer." The Goldwyns exited.

The following year, Frances learned that Miss Berl was to be in New York when they were. She called to say she was investigating the school in Colorado. From that day forward, only geography kept the Goldwyns and the therapist apart. Over the next decade, they saw each other regularly if infrequently.

Fountain Valley School, in Colorado Springs, was founded by a group of educators eager to emulate in the West the best of the eastern preparatory schools. In the shadow of Pikes Peak, on a 1,600-acre hacienda-style ranch, the ten-year-old institution was a sheltered world unto itself for its one hundred pupils. "From the moment I walked in that place," an adult Sam Goldwyn, Jr., recalled, "I sensed I belonged there. It was the kind of education I'd never dreamed existed, a master-student relationship, in which you could just go to the master for instruction. It was the first time anyone treated me with respect as a student." Sammy saw his parents only during Christmas, Easter, and summer vacations. "I never really came back home after that," he recalled, "and it became the turning point in my relationship with my father. We began to have a personal relationship."

Hilde Berl worked another wonder on the Goldwyn family. Ruth Capps answered her phone one afternoon and heard a voice completely foreign to her. "This is Frances Goldwyn," said the cultured voice. "Don't you think it's time your father and you got together?" The rift between Sam and his daughter troubled Frances. "She was experiencing her own pain—loneliness," suggested Hilde Berl; "and she knew what it was like to grow up without a father." After one of her sessions with Miss Berl, she invited Ruth and her husband to Laurel Lane for dinner; then she invited them for holidays. Ruth never felt that Frances was taking a real interest in her, only that Frances was carrying out Goldwyn's unspoken wishes, taking hold of a situation too emotional for him to handle; nonetheless, Frances performed with aplomb. The gatherings were uncomfortable, but Frances did her best to see that conversation ran smoothly. Sammy and Ruth delighted in discovering each other. Father and daughter were always civil, keeping their feelings at a polite distance. From then on, Sam hurt her only unconsciously, excluding her in ways he was not even aware of. On one occasion, he bragged of having recently hosted the President's wife, saying how much Ruthie would have enjoyed meeting her. "He was right," Ruth admitted many years later; "I would have given anything to have met Mrs. Roosevelt, but it would never have even occurred to my father to have invited me."

When in 1939 Ruth gave birth to her second child, a son named Alan, she was startled to awaken in a private room—with coffee brewing, an air conditioner, and her own full-time nurse. She was flabbergasted when Frances walked into her room—with Sam, who had ordered and paid for the deluxe accommodations. Mac Capps handwrote his father-in-law a letter of thanks, noting that "more than the considerable physical benefits of your visit," Ruth "is more touched that you should have thought of them at all. . . . I wish I could tell you how happy your visit and solicitude have made Ruthie." In a postscript, Mac Capps explained that he had not put a salutation on his missive because after seven years of marriage, "you've never told me what to call you."

The economics of the thirties brought every Gelbfisz relative out of the woodwork, as well as several pretenders. Goldwyn rewarded most those who demanded least. He sent checks to his father's three siblings in Poland and monthly allowances to his sisters Mania (in Warsaw) and Sally (who had become a dressmaker in Birmingham, England). Early in the decade, he had loaned several thousand dollars to each of his American siblings. Ben and Bernard (they had changed their last name to Fish), who worked as salesmen for their brother, used the money as down payments on houses. So did their sister Nettie (who had married a wholesale-grocery salesman named Leo Sherman and moved from Chicago to central Los Angeles). One day, without explanation, Goldwyn canceled their debts.

Ben idolized Sam and spent his life staying in his good graces. He was so discreet in his motion picture sales and distribution career that few knew he was Sam Goldwyn's brother. Bernard moved to San Francisco, where he became a Christian Science practitioner, and Sam never saw or spoke to him again. In fact, he denied having a second brother. Nettie made constant demands on Sam for money, which were met by angry letters, then silence. In all her time in the United States, even when she lived a few miles away in Los Angeles, Sam never saw her. In June 1935, she had been rushed to the hospital with what doctors suspected was peritonitis. From her bed, she cried out to her daughter, Sally, "I want to see my brother Sam." The girl got through to him on the telephone and pleaded with Goldwyn to visit. "I hate hospitals," he said. "When Eddie Cantor was sick in the hospital, I didn't even visit him."

"But this isn't Eddie Cantor," she said, "it's your sister." Goldwyn sent a get-well letter signed by his secretary. A few days later, Nettie Sherman died. When Sally called to inform him of the funeral, she got a similar response: "I don't go to funerals." But he did show up at the burial and stood alone. Afterward he approached his teenaged niece and said, "Don't you worry; I'll always take care of you." From that day forward, he sent her a check for fifty dollars every month; when she got engaged, the checks stopped. Except for one chance meeting in a theater, they never spoke again.

Sam's sister Mania and her husband, Abraham Lebensold, sensed that Poland was no place for Jews in 1939. They prepared to move to England that fall. Goldwyn heard of these plans and sent $2,500 to the Home Office in London as a token of faith that he would provide for them if they were allowed to enter England. But the Lebensolds "took a cure" every summer in Krynica, a Polish spa, and 1939 would be no exception. While they were enjoying the waters that September, German troops marched into the country and ordered them back to Warsaw. Confined to the ghetto, the Lebensolds plotted their escape. Lebensold worked in a Nazi munitions plant for several months, handing over most of his wages to guards who promised to help him and his wife steal out of the country. Then, instead of abetting the Lebensolds, they arrested them, packing them off to Treblinka, where they were killed.

Goldwyn and his brothers tried to get their remaining relatives out of Poland. But it was too late. Those who had not already left were subsequently sentenced to concentration camps, where they all perished. Sam sent monthly allowances to his three surviving nieces in England; but he never gave anything to his nephew Fred Lebensold, who migrated on his own to Canada and became a prominent architect.

Nobody knew what the Holocaust cost Goldwyn emotionally. Like most of the Hollywood moguls, he wore an American flag on his sleeve to cover the yellow armband; he never discussed his family's losses. In late 1940, the religious feelings he had long concealed were put to another test.

Joseph P. Kennedy, after serving almost three years as ambassador to Great Britain, tendered his resignation to President Roosevelt and toured the country on a "peace crusade." In a series of off-the-record talks with Americans of influence he voiced many of the sentiments of the America First Committee, a popular isolationist organization. When Kennedy reached Hollywood on November 13, his rhetoric took some unusual twists, revealing several of his own prejudices. Fifty of the town's power brokers gathered for lunch at Warner Brothers, Sam Goldwyn among them. After dessert, Kennedy rose to report unofficially on London after its first few months of the blitz. He said that America should limit its aid to Britain so as not to jeopardize itself in the event of an Axis victory. Then he filled the room with the fear of God by telling them to "stop making anti-Nazi pictures or using the film medium to promote or show sympathy to the cause of the 'democracies' versus the 'dictators.'" He said that anti-Semitism was growing in England and that the Jews were being blamed for the war; any Jewish outcries, he said, would "make the world feel that a 'Jewish War' was going on." The audience sat stunned. Kennedy told them that Hitler liked movies and would want America to continue producing them; but, the ambassador added, "You're going to have to get those Jewish names off the screen."

The comments utterly dumbfounded most of those present. "As a result of Kennedy's cry for silence," observed Ben Hecht, "all of Hollywood's top Jews went around with their grief hidden like a Jewish fox under their Gentile vests. In New York, the influential Jews I met had also espoused the Kennedy hide-your-Jewish-head psychology."

Goldwyn burrowed deeper into his work. His salary was now $200,000 a year. Still fighting United Artists, he hesitated to start another picture until he realized he could use it to win that war. With his ranks reduced to one movie star and one director, Goldwyn rushed into production the only project he had in development that might suit them both. It was called *The Westerner.*

Jo Swerling and Niven Busch wrote most of the script about the legendary Texas lawman Judge Roy Bean. Lillian Hellman and Oliver La Farge did rewrites. William Wyler saw an opportunity to do right by his years of directing western quickies and could hardly wait to get started, but Gary Cooper wanted nothing to do with the film. Goldwyn meant for him to play the saddle tramp who rides into town; but it was plain to the actor that the starring role was Judge Roy Bean. The producer already intended to cast Walter Brennan as the flea-bitten old varmint, and Cooper knew he would end up stealing every scene. He wired Goldwyn that he did not approve of the material. "Goddamned Cooper is trying to kill me," the producer ranted.

Over the next few weeks, Goldwyn assured Cooper that his part was being fattened . . . and that if he failed to report for work, he would be sued for all the expenses incurred on the project to date—$400,000. Cooper showed up for his wardrobe fitting. Two weeks later, he read the final shooting script and wrote Goldwyn, "After careful and reasonable consideration I regret to advise you that the character, Cole Harden, is still inadequate and unsatisfactory for me, in my opinion, as is the story." Cooper went on to state that the script's inferiority violated both the spirit and the letter of their working agreements. "Like you," he wrote, "I have a position to uphold. My professional standing has been jeopardized from the beginning."

But Cooper never thought of himself as anything but a gun for hire. While Goldwyn's means of intimidation were "unprecedented" in Cooper's years in the picture business, he said he would "bow to your threats since normal reasoning and friendly relations mean little, if anything to you." He agreed to report for work and "to perform my services . . . to the fullest of my ability, with the express understanding that I am doing so under protest." But he was fed up with Goldwyn. This latest action, he wrote, only "serves as confirmation that my experience since the beginning of the contract has been consistently unsettled, insecure, lacking inspiration and enthusiasm and it is, therefore, best for you to realize that our association is incompatible, holding small hope for any mutually happy solution and I fail to see how we can profitably continue this strained relationship."

"I disagree with your conclusion that our situation holds small hope for any mutually happy solution," Goldwyn wrote back. ". . . There is no reason, Gary, why we can not both be very happy in our relationship. I will certainly do everything possible to bring this about, and if you are willing to go part way toward this end there is no reason why our association can not be a most pleasant one for each of us." Goldwyn conceded nothing.

Cooper grumbled his way through the filming of the million-dollar production on location outside Tucson. The introverted Cooper and the extroverted Brennan proved to be excellent foils for each other, no matter who was scoring the most points. Brennan also developed the best vocal impersonation of Sam Goldwyn of anyone in Hollywood. More than once, he telephoned Cooper and chewed him out in the producer's voice. "You goddamned son-of-a-bitch," he would say, "you're so lousy I want Brennan to have top billing in this picture." The film would bring Brennan his third Supporting Actor Oscar within five years.

Goldwyn liked *The Westerner* enough to announce that he was not going to distribute it through United Artists, despite his legal obligation. He interested Warner Brothers in releasing the film, until UA warned them they had better prepare for a lawsuit. None of the other studios in town would become Goldwyn's stalking horse in his battle with UA.

So Goldwyn returned to court, filing a new bill of complaint. He would let United Artists distribute *The Westerner,* but he was suing them for damages in delaying its distribution. In more than 150 pages, he listed the rest of his grievances, ranging from his partners' malicious attempt "to drive him out of business" to withholding moneys due and releasing "misleading statements to the press intimating that Goldwyn was a contract-breaker." Goldwyn's latest action did not intimidate his partners. Knowing he wanted to leave the company, they intended to fight to the finish. The longer the case dragged through the judicial quagmire, the better for them. The next year, Goldwyn's lawyer, Max Steuer, died, further delaying the case.

Goldwyn ceased to develop projects, loath to put any pictures into production so long as his distribution situation was unresolved. United Artists was prepared to sit him out, for they could always find product to release. Besides, they realized, even with his recent increase in output, Goldwyn had not provided a big hit since *The Hurricane.* He was counting on Oscar night to bring some badly needed luster to his name.

The evening of February 29, 1940, at the Cocoanut Grove in the Ambassador Hotel started promisingly enough for Samuel Goldwyn. The winner of the New York Film Critics Award had reason to believe he might win his first Oscar at the twelfth presentation of the Academy Awards. The results in the first six categories did not indicate a *Gone With the Wind* sweep, and Gregg Toland won for his black-and-white cinematography on *Wuthering Heights.* But the Los Angeles *Times* had broken its vow with the Academy not to publish the names of the winners until after the ceremony, and word of the remaining winners began to spread from their sunset edition to every table in the room. By the time the major awards were presented, first-time master of ceremonies Bob Hope was able to quip, "What a wonderful thing, this benefit for David Selznick." Clark Gable lost the Best Actor trophy to Robert Donat, but *Gone With the Wind* grabbed everything else. Goldwyn worried that one day his friend Selznick would have to pay a heavy price for the film's extravagant success; but the next morning he wired only his sincerest congratulations. Selznick wrote back, "I have long felt, and often said, that the day must come, as it should have years ago, for the industry officially to give recognition publicly to what everyone feels privately: that you are one of the few men who is forever fighting to raise the level of our industry and one of the few men who has never deserted his ideals."

The next year, David Selznick's *Rebecca* became box-office champion and took home another Best Picture statuette, the first time an independent studio had won the grand prize two years in a row. Sam Goldwyn felt the also-ran. He was no longer even the town's leading independent producer.

The Westerner would not be released until September 1940, nine months after *Raffles*. It was the longest lag between Goldwyn pictures since he had been producing. Worse still, he had nothing slated to go before the cameras for almost another year. *Samuel Goldwyn and Samuel Goldwyn, Inc.* v. *United Artists Corporation* was stagnating in the courts. His career was stuck.

One day in early 1941, somebody, at last, took action. Frances Goldwyn made a phone call, got in her car, and drove herself up Summit Drive to Pickfair. The mistress of the house met her in the foyer. Frances Goldwyn said that all this legal stalling was not doing anybody any good. Then she broke down in tears, flung herself prostrate on the floor, and pleaded with Mary Pickford to let Sam out of his United Artists contract. "I beg for my husband and child," she said.

Somehow these two women grasped the situation in a way that none of the moguls and their lawyers did. "Don't do that," said Mary Pickford. "I'll settle. But for God's sake, get up, Frances."

On March 11, 1941, United Artists canceled Goldwyn's distribution contract. They allowed him to cash in his stock for $300,000, and he received another $200,000 from the Silverstone Plan.

"THEY called me the lone wolf, and I have been called some other things, too," Goldwyn said years later in an interview. "I had partners but I discovered I was spending more time trying to explain to them what I was doing than in making pictures." As Hollywood's "only individual who owns and operates his own studio," Goldwyn would continue producing out of his plant on Formosa Avenue. But not since his beginnings in the film business had he been so devoid of properties and stars. For the first time in almost fifteen years, he lacked a distributor. More than ever, he lusted for the public approval and professional acknowledgment that persistently eluded him—a blockbuster hit at the box office and an Oscar.

Once again he was starting over, on his own.

PART
THREE

ENTRANC
SAMUEL GOLD
PRODUCTIONS

17 "We Did It Before and We Can Do It Again"

H E WOULD OFTEN come to moments of self-despair," Samuel Goldwyn, Jr., observed of his father over the years, "—moments in which he would sit with a faraway look in his eyes and contemplate the doom that lay ahead." The start of the 1940s marked one of those periods. Sammy remembered trying to argue with his father that "perhaps somewhere, somehow, there was sunshine. But he would even more soundly show me the illogicality of hope. Finally, when he had won the day and I agreed with him that all was lost, he would sit back in his chair, get a twinkle in his eyes, stick his jaw out and say, 'Yes, it's pretty bad. I just thank God I've still got Goldwyn.'"

Samuel Goldwyn, Inc., had virtually shut down for almost a year, but his settlement from United Artists and his salary from the preceding year alone netted Goldwyn close to one million dollars. Since going independent in 1923, he had produced fifty-eight pictures; except for the two he produced for Art Cinema, he owned them all outright. One cataclysm after another had threatened to wipe him out ever since his entering motion pictures—the First World War, the oligopoly of the studio system, the advent of talkies, the Depression; and he had withstood them all. The global conflagration heating up would be just another storm he would have to survive. "You should be quite accustomed to [this]," said David Niven in bidding Goldwyn farewell, as he became Hollywood's first star to enlist.

"You were through the last war, weren't you?" "Yes," Goldwyn said wearily, "I was at Fort Lee."

From the second-floor northeast-corner office of the Samuel Goldwyn Studios, the commandant himself sounded reveille. He drafted his favorite public relations man—Lynn Farnol—to alert the press that "there are going to be Goldwyn pictures again." Farnol was ordered to emphasize "that the chain and continuity of hit pictures, of quality pictures, interrupted and broken by the law suit, starts again," and that Goldwyn should be presented as a man "with renewed vigor and vitality—eager to go—full speed ahead."

For several weeks after his settlement with United Artists, Goldwyn looked around for a distribution deal. The recent acceptance by the five major film companies of a consent decree outlawing "block booking" had opened new outlets to independent producers. The "majors" were selling individual pictures for outside producers on a percentage basis. Frank Capra had recently struck such an arrangement with Warner Brothers, as had Howard Hughes at Fox. Both those studios appealed to Goldwyn, until he learned that they would not grant him preferential distribution rates. Neither would Paramount. He would not even consider the industry's colossus, MGM, as long as Louis B. Mayer was there. It looked as though Goldwyn had painted himself into a corner, his former partners appearing to be his only alternative. "AFTER IT'S ALL BEEN SAID AND DONE," read a *Variety* headline on March 26, 1941, "GOLDWYN MAY RELEASE THROUGH UA."

Then he zeroed in on the one studio in town that needed him as much as he needed them. Radio-Keith-Orpheum had been a breeding ground for talent and speculative investment since its creation in 1928, but financially it had never taken root. In January 1940—after reaping its share of profits from the great harvest of 1939—the studio had earned its way out of receivership and trumpeted a "new RKO." But the company was burdened with a new strain of film moguls whose interests were in business more than motion pictures, in distribution rather than production. Except for Walt Disney's feature-length cartoons of the early forties (*Fantasia, Pinocchio, Dumbo,* and *Bambi*), there was no consistency to the RKO product, as all their important producers, directors, and stars left them. RKO was so desperate to distribute Goldwyn's films, they agreed to all his terms, including a 17.5 percent distribution fee—less than Goldwyn had paid United Artists. It was so low that RKO barely stood to profit, even from his successes. As the producer approached his thirtieth year in motion pictures, they were banking on Goldwyn's best work's still lying before him.

. . .

AFTER Lillian Hellman's *The Little Foxes* proved to be a Broadway hit in 1939, Goldwyn decided he wanted the rights. "But Mr. Goldwyn," cautioned his story editor Edwin Knopf, "it's a very caustic play."

"I don't give a damn how much it costs," Goldwyn snapped back. "Buy it!"

Miss Hellman had recently finished the third year of her three-year contract with the producer; but because of extensions upon her refusing inferior material he offered her, it had almost another two years to run. She began adapting her play about greed in the industrializing South on February 28, 1940. To his dying day, Goldwyn referred to the property as "The Three Little Foxes."

Lillian Hellman had based her well-made play on the maternal side of her family. Her first three versions had detailed the marriage between Regina Hubbard and Horace Giddens, a syphilitic Southerner. After ten drafts, Hellman had changed the venereal disease to a coronary condition, and the domestic drama of infidelity corroded into one of rapacity: Regina blackmails her way into a deal with her two shady brothers, who are attempting to take over a cotton mill they intend to run on cheap labor. Her scrupulous husband stands in their way, until she causes his death. Their daughter, Alexandra, disgusted to learn of her conniving, leaves Regina a loathsome victim of her own cupidity.

As much as he liked the play, Goldwyn felt the average moviegoer would have trouble relating to the viperous Regina. He asked Miss Hellman to conventionalize the story without diminishing its impact. After two months, the playwright had not only opened up the script—creating scenes outside the Giddens house wherever possible—but also invented a new character, a newspaperman named David Hewitt, who became a love interest for Alexandra. After Willy Wyler read the script of *The Little Foxes*, his next assignment, he wrote Goldwyn: "I believe the main difficulty—in fact the only serious difficulty that confronted us with the play has been solved because Lillian was able to find, and add, the delightful character of David, who, together with Alexandra, make up a romance of the most delightful kind—a romance of two charming, kind, attractive and normal people, and . . . together they contrast the somewhat abnormal characters of the story."

Everybody else Goldwyn listened to disagreed. Edwin Knopf argued that each scene with the new character caused Regina to lose "the sharp bitter materialistic quality that made her so great upon the stage." Jock Lawrence agreed that too much love story detracted from the central themes of the play; but he thought the way to refortify Regina was in strengthening David, making him the dissenting voice of justice. Goldwyn borrowed bits of everybody's thinking and told Lillian Hellman that in her next draft he wanted less love story but more bite to it. "By that time," she recalled years later, "I had written over a dozen versions of 'The Little Foxes,' and I was through with it." Her thoughts had also turned to a play about resistance against German fascism, called *Watch on the Rhine*. She recommended that three friends complete the rewrites—her former husband, Arthur Kober, Alan Campbell, and his wife, Dorothy Parker. Goldwyn understood that Hellman was written out on the subject, and he hired the trio. When Goldwyn realized they were boondoggling, he ordered the latest of his young story editors, Niven Busch, Jr., to dismiss them. "I'd rather cut my heart out than tell you what I'm about to tell you," the polished Princetonian said upon entering Miss Parker's office. "Niven," she interrupted, "let me stop you. If you act on your first suggestion, no one will care less than I."

Wyler was excited about directing another Hellman work, the most literary screenplay he had ever been assigned. He regretted only that he had to make the film for Goldwyn, for he was starting to squirm under the producer's thumb. His recent loanouts to other studios had felt like paroles. Directing *Jezebel* and *The Letter* at Warner Brothers had not only resulted in some of his finest work (both Academy Award nominees for Best Picture) but had been pleasant experiences. Warner Brothers reflected their pride in having Wyler direct for them in all their billing and publicity.

When Wyler returned to his home studio, his ill will toward Goldwyn festered. He hired a publicity man of his own; and he told several friends that the theme of exploiting cheap labor in *The Little Foxes* interested him so much because it was the story of Sam Goldwyn. He eyed Warner Brothers longingly. In addition to the nicer treatment there, they had Bette Davis—his favorite actress, former lover, and the only person he could envision playing the role of Regina on the screen.

Realizing that Wyler had become his most important piece of manpower, Goldwyn instructed Lynn Farnol to start drumming up publicity for him, plenty of write-ups about his upcoming assignment on *The Little Foxes*. Goldwyn took to inviting Wyler to play gin rummy with him, foolproof pocket money Wyler could never resist. He also agreed to amend the director's much-extended contract, taking him off the weekly treadmill for a new two-year deal; it guaranteed him $75,000 for each of two pictures annually, plus 10 percent of the profits. And Goldwyn went to Jack Warner to borrow Bette Davis.

The very idea was ridiculous. Ever since she had challenged her contract in court in 1936, Warner Brothers had improved the quality of the roles they offered Miss Davis, and they firmly refused ever to loan her out. Warners' policy may have cost her many good parts, but they had turned her into the current champion at the box office and at the Academy Awards. Goldwyn's request, like all of its kind in the past five years, was denied.

Jesse Lasky had just hit bottom of the biggest dip of his roller coaster career. Nothing kept him going except his eternal optimism and one good idea—the life story of Alvin C. York, a mountaineer from Tennessee who went off to the Great War a conscientious objector, only to return its "greatest civilian soldier." Ever since Sergeant York's ticker-tape parade up Fifth Avenue in 1919, Lasky had envisioned a film of his story; but the soldier told the producer that his life was not for sale. With America about to become the great arsenal for democracy, Lasky approached him again, this time changing York's way of thinking with a $50,000 check, enough to finish the Bible school York was building back home. There was only one actor Lasky could see in the role, probably his only means of securing a production deal in town—Gary Cooper.

Lasky borrowed $25,000 on his life insurance to cover the check he had written York and peddled his story to the major studios, promoting the possibility of Cooper's being involved. All except one turned him down, declaring war pictures dead. Harry Warner, a superpatriot, insisted that his brother make a deal.

Then Jack Warner told Lasky to think of some other actor for the part. During Goldwyn's production hiatus, Cooper had appeared in *Meet John Doe* for Frank Capra at Warners, and the studio head said there was no way Sam Goldwyn would ever agree to loan Cooper out for a second Warners picture. Feeling nobody else could pull off the role, Lasky humbly went to his former brother-in-law; he knew full well that Sam had not forgiven him for his actions twenty-five years earlier. To his astonishment, Sam assured him that he had no objection to loaning Cooper for the part. Lasky returned triumphant, and he later remembered Jack Warner's reaction as one of incredulity. Warner got Goldwyn on the telephone. "Sam," Lasky overheard, "I understand you're loaning us Gary Cooper for the York picture. . . . That's wonderful, Sam—I can't express my appreciation for . . . I can? . . . How? . . . You're kidding! . . . Bette Davis is our biggest star! I can't do it!" Whereupon Warner hung up.

In a note as well-timed as it was cordial, Goldwyn then reminded Warner of a recent $425,000 gambling debt. "The wolf has hit me very hard," Jack Warner wrote back. "I would like to settle the deal for $2,500.00 [their code for $250,000]. I will appreciate it if you will do this. Someday I will do the same for you. . . . Nothing to do with the above. If you are willing to trade Cooper for Bette Davis, I am working on this in your behalf—the deal to be that you pay Cooper and we pay Davis." Goldwyn agreed to both halves of Warner's offer. It would be Bette Davis's only loanout from Warner Brothers between 1937 and the expiration of her contract in 1949.

Jock Lawrence tried to talk Goldwyn into letting Bette Davis play two roles in the film, Regina and her daughter. The producer resisted, because he had to think beyond this picture. He had no female stars under contract, and Alexandra had been made into a choice enough role to launch a young actress's career. Recently there had been much talk in Hollywood of Teresa Wright, a fresh-faced ingenue debuting on Broadway in a small role in *Life with Father*. The next time he was in New York, Goldwyn caught a performance of the Clarence Day play at the Empire Theater. While the actors were still taking their curtain calls, Goldwyn went backstage and awaited the twenty-year-old. "Miss Wright was seated at her dressing table when I was introduced, and looked for all the world like a little girl experimenting with her mother's cosmetics," Goldwyn would remember. "I had discovered in her from the first sight, you might say, an unaffected genuineness and appeal." He offered her a contract that night.

In signing, Miss Wright joined a company of Broadway veterans, most of the original cast of *The Little Foxes*. Regina's wheelchair-ridden husband, Horace, would be played by Herbert Marshall, who had just played Bette Davis's husband in *The Letter*. On the set, Goldwyn paid particular attention to the ingenue, ensuring that the film captured Miss Wright's freshness. "Teresa," he called out from behind the camera one day in an effort to loosen her up, "let your breasts flow in the breeze!"

Wyler and Gregg Toland, after four pictures together, had never collaborated so closely. Several of their scenes were to become classics because of their staging. "Movies are primarily visual, and 'Little Foxes' was very talky," Wyler said years later, in one of his few explications of his work; "and so I tried to make the audience see ordinary things in a different way. With all the talk going on, I just wanted to draw them into the scene." The opening sequence, around the dining room table, for example, is full of small character twitches, every one of which is picked up by a roving camera. Carl Benton Reid and Dan Duryea later discuss Horace's safe-deposit box while they are in a bathroom: Father and son are shown shaving back-to-back, catching glimpses of each other in their opposing mirrors, sudden close-up reflections of each man punctuating the dialogue.

Toland's camera was most potent during the climactic scene in which the helpless Horace begs Regina to fetch his heart medicine. She refuses.

The primary action in the scene is the struggling man, forced to totter from his wheelchair up the stairs; but according to Wyler, "what is interesting here is the wife. The scene is her face, what is going on inside her. You could have him out of frame completely, for example, just hear him stagger upstairs, coughing, whatever. It was, of course, more effective to have him in the background *out of focus* trying to get upstairs." Toland—just back from loanout to Orson Welles, for whom he photographed *Citizen Kane*—had been experimenting with a technique called "deep focus," in which the camera could record both a near and a far area at once. It allowed the director to achieve the effect he wanted, of making audiences "feel they were seeing something they were not supposed to see. Seeing the husband in the background made you squint, but what you *were* seeing was her face." Years later, Lillian Hellman admitted that much of the film—that scene in particular—worked better than the play, all because of "Willy's vision."

Precisely that created the most violent arguments ever on a Goldwyn picture. This time, however, Sam Goldwyn played referee. Weeks before the first day of shooting, Bette Davis developed her own ideas about the playing of Regina, which were in direct opposition to Wyler's. "We fought bitterly," the actress later acknowledged in describing her third collaboration with the director. "I had been forced to see Tallulah Bankhead's performance. I had not wanted to. A great admirer of hers, I wanted in no way to be influenced by her work. It was Willy's intention that I give a different interpretation of the part." But after seeing the Bankhead version—"etched in acid"—Davis insisted that that was the only way to play the part. Wyler thought Regina was a complex character, still full of the charms that had attracted her husband in the first place. He believed the actress secretly resented playing the mother of a seventeen-year-old and was trying to distance herself from the role by overdoing her makeup and resisting any subtleties in the character that might humanize her. Wyler had had the same experience with Ruth Chatterton when she played Fran Dodsworth; but this time he was up against the screen's quintessential bitch-goddess.

Fur flew. Wyler resorted to his standard routine of repeated takes to break down his actress, but she would not bend. If anything, Miss Davis's performance became more venomous. They were heard screaming at each other on the set and off, their disagreements assuming the stridency of lovers' quarrels. Goldwyn could barely assert himself between these two iron wills: He could but remind Davis that Wyler had already helped her deliver her best performances; and he told the director that "she must know what she's doing, because she's made a damned good career out of playing these bitches." After a few weeks of standing up to her director, the star phoned in sick.

"Hollywood was licking its chops this morning over rumors and counter-rumors regarding Bette Davis," Hedda Hopper clucked on her May 21, 1941, radio broadcast of movieland news. "Some say she isn't ill, and she's definitely out of 'Little Foxes' because she's rowing with director Willy Wyler. . . . Others claim she's going to have a baby, and still more say she's having trouble with her husband." Miss Hopper adopted the studio's party line and dismissed the gossip as nonsense. For the next three weeks, Wyler shot around the absent star.

Miss Davis returned to the picture more vigorous than ever. The passionate arguments were over, but the basic disagreement about the character was not. For the most part, Davis got her way, until one afternoon, when she refused to reshoot a scene Goldwyn wanted filmed again. Miss Davis went to her dressing room and changed into her street clothes. Goldwyn stomped onto the set and suggested that she phone her lawyer. He warned her that the rest of the cast would remain in costume until she returned and that he would sue her for all costs until they resumed work. She disappeared for a few minutes, apparently to consult with her attorney and accountant. Minutes later, she was back before the cameras.

Goldwyn tied his impeccable production together with a score by an Iowan who had almost no film-composing experience. That Meredith Willson—who had once toured with John Philip Sousa's band—had recently written some of the score to Chaplin's *Great Dictator* was recommendation enough to Goldwyn.

The Little Foxes was a great success. Lines formed outside Radio City Music Hall and every other theater where it played. The press was unanimously enthusiastic, almost all critics rating it higher than the play. One of the most respected members of the new wave of young film critics, James Agee in *Time*, quibbled over Bette Davis's mimicking Tallulah Bankhead's performance so closely, and wrongly blamed Wyler. But almost everyone else marveled at the film. The Motion Picture Academy nominated *The Little Foxes* for nine Oscars—including Best Picture, Director, Screenplay, Actress, and two for Supporting Actress (Patricia Collinge and Teresa Wright)—the most Goldwyn had ever received for a single production. He was back at his former cruising altitude, but still no higher. His film took home no trophies that year.

After five Goldwyn films—not counting *The Winning of Barbara Worth*—Gary Cooper was at the acme of his popularity; but his most successful roles had all been off the Goldwyn lot. In the last year alone, he had limned two of his most memorable characters—the near-suicidal hero in Frank Capra's *Meet John Doe* and Sergeant York, for which he won an Oscar. Goldwyn constantly berated his story department for failing to find exciting material for Cooper. He needed a quick fix of pure inspiration.

Billy Wilder—born Samuel Wilder in 1906 in Galicia, not far from Sam Goldwyn's birthplace—had become a name to every producer after only five years in America. The former free-lance writer (and occasional gigolo) in Vienna, then Berlin, fled Germany while the Reichstag was still smoldering. He arrived in Hollywood in early 1934 with an offer to write a screenplay from one of his stories for $150 a week. His English vocabulary then consisted of little more than popular song lyrics, but his affection for American jargon made learning the language easy for him. He and his collaborator, Charles Brackett, specialized in sophisticated farce, brittle humor that was hard on the outside and romantic within. By the end of the decade, he was writing some of the slyest English dialogue ever to make its way onto the screen—including Garbo's in *Ninotchka*. After a particularly frustrating experience watching one of his scripts get mangled at Paramount, Wilder decided it was too frustrating to write material that he could not direct.

Just then, Goldwyn called the head of Paramount's story department, William Dozier. "Y'know, Bill," he said, "I'm thinking it's time you and I started doing each other favors." That sounded good to the bright thirty-two-year-old. "Let's start," Goldwyn added, "by you doing me one. . . . I'd like to borrow Brackett and Wilder."

Dozier said that was impossible. Then the powers at Paramount realized they might use the writers to ransom Gary Cooper for their upcoming production of *For Whom the Bell Tolls*. Goldwyn also got them to throw in some cash, plus the future services of Bob Hope, who had recently made a big hit opposite Bing Crosby and Dorothy Lamour in *The Road to Singapore*, the first in a successful series of silly, often improvised comedies.

Brackett and Wilder waded through the piles of scripts and treatments Goldwyn had been considering for Gary Cooper. Their assignment of finding something seemed futile until Wilder remembered a story sitting in his own European trunk, called "From A to Z." It was an adult variation on "Snow White and the Seven Dwarfs," in which a stripteaser falls in with some scholarly professors writing a new encyclopedia. Upon reaching the "S" volume, Professor Bertram Potts gets stuck with the entry "Slang." The pussycat agrees to move into the owls' aerie and educate him, unwittingly implicating them all in her imminent marriage to a gangster. Brackett liked the story enough for Wilder to submit it to Goldwyn. "I'll talk to you tomorrow," Goldwyn told Wilder, upon receiving the pages.

It might have been a stretch to imagine Gary Cooper as an aging professor specializing in linguistics, but as Goldwyn understood it, the part called for a shy, romantic lead. The next day, he called Wilder to say, "Frances read the story. She likes it. How much?" Wilder said ten thousand dollars. Goldwyn thought that was too high but said, "I'll tell you what. I give you seventy-five hundred now. If we ever get it made, I give you another twenty-five hundred." Wilder agreed, so long as he could stand on the set to observe every shot of the film, his final phase of training before becoming a director himself.

Wilder's tutor would be the master of rapid-fire romantic comedies, Howard Hawks. Goldwyn felt uneasy about working with Hawks a third time, less because of his experiences with him on *Barbary Coast* and *Come and Get It* than because of a basic flaw in the man. Goldwyn thought Hawks had "no character." He threw money away, was obsessed with betting on the horses, and was always involved in real estate schemes; worst of all, he did not always make good on his gambling IOUs. Movies seemed a means to support his bad habits; but with *Bringing Up Baby, Only Angels Have Wings, His Girl Friday,* and *Sergeant York* as the most recent notches on Hawks's belt, Goldwyn had to admit there was no director better suited for drawing the best out of Gary Cooper or from Brackett and Wilder's charming script.

Ball of Fire crackled with what *Time* called "some of the juiciest, wackiest, solid American slang ever recorded on celluloid." It also contained such enchanting scenes as Sugarpuss O'Shea giving her bachelor hosts conga lessons. The climax of the film hinged, literally, on a loose screw, when Potts enters the wrong room at an inn because the number 9 on the door has slipped around to a 6. "It was a silly movie," Billy Wilder admitted forty years later. "The writer was still young and innocent . . . but I guess so were the audiences then."

Goldwyn's first choice for the female lead was Ginger Rogers—brassy and blond, she could sing and dance. But she had just got herself out of Fred Astaire's shadow by playing Kitty Foyle, for which she won an Oscar; she was looking for a less frivolous role. Goldwyn sent the script to Jean Arthur; she liked the part but was under contract to Columbia, which would not loan her out. Goldwyn turned to Carole Lombard. She wished him much success in the venture, but wrote back that she was "not interested in the character or the plot . . . after all everyone has their own prerogative of his likes and dislikes." Goldwyn had not been so hard up for a female lead since casting *Stella Dallas*. Again, his last resort, Barbara Stanwyck, carried the day, delivering another Academy Award—nominated performance.

She and Cooper created enough sparks to ignite everyone around them. Hawks proved to be unusually efficient, his direction clean and sharp. Goldwyn gave Dana Andrews his first big break in one of his films, the tough-guy role of Joe Lilac. "PREVIEWED BALL OF FIRE LAST NIGHT," Goldwyn wired Gary Cooper in Sun Valley on October 29, 1941. "IT WENT OVER LIKE A BALL OF FIRE."

After the film's success, Billy Wilder telephoned the producer and said, "Mr. Goldwyn, I see the picture is a hit." Goldwyn jubilantly concurred. "Well, Mr. Goldwyn," Wilder added, "where's the money you promised?" Goldwyn, appearing to have no recollection of the $2,500 bonus he had offered when he bought the story for $7,500, said, "If I promise, I promise on paper." Wilder angrily hung up on him. Ten minutes later, Wilder's phone rang. It was Goldwyn. "Billy," he said, "I just talked to Frances. She don't remember it either." Wilder was so furious he told Goldwyn that from that moment forward they should just pretend they did not even know each other—that if "you don't remember the deal and Frances doesn't remember the deal, the hell with both of you." Wilder slammed the phone down. Ten minutes later, it rang again. It was Goldwyn, with a contrite tone in his voice. "Look, Billy," he said, "I don't want people going around Hollywood saying I'm not honest. Come on over, right now . . . and pick up the fifteen hundred dollars."

"He was a titan with an empty skull," Wilder said of Goldwyn in retrospect, "—not confused by anything he read, which he didn't." But his "instinct for the better things" made Goldwyn, in Wilder's eyes, "an absolutely, totally dedicated man—like a passionate collector." Wilder liked him and they became friendlier over the years. But he never saw the last thousand dollars.

After watching the rushes on *Ball of Fire* one day, Goldwyn had announced to Wilder that he was looking for a big picture and that he wished the writer would come to him with some big ideas. Realizing Goldwyn was not about to hire him to direct a film, as he hoped, Wilder made an appointment with the producer just to tweak his nose. "Mr. Goldwyn," he said at the meeting, "why not do a picture about Nijinsky?" Goldwyn looked puzzled. Wilder explained that Nijinsky was the single most famous ballet dancer in the world, a Russian with a "marvelous, touching story." Wilder proceeded to talk about this peasant with a passion to dance who met Diaghilev, the impresario of the Bolshoi, and of their becoming homosexual lovers. "Homosexuals! Are you crazy?" Goldwyn interrupted. But Wilder proceeded, insisting the story got better. He told of Nijinsky's going insane, and that every day, while exercising in a Swiss asylum, he believed he was a horse. "A homosexual! A horse!" Goldwyn interrupted again, rapidly losing interest. But Wilder plowed through to the end of the story, detailing Nijinsky's marriage to a woman, Diaghilev's revenge, and Nijinsky's neighing for the rest of his life. Goldwyn shooed Wilder from the office, shouting at him for wasting his time on such a miserable story. On his way out the door, Wilder poked his head in with an afterthought. "Mr. Goldwyn," he said, "you want a happy ending? Not only does Nijinsky think he's a horse. But in the end . . . he wins the Kentucky Derby."

THE first week of December 1941, Sam Goldwyn was on a train leaving New York, where he had arranged for the opening of *Ball of Fire* at Radio City Music Hall. On Sunday the seventh, while the Super Chief clacked its way out of Chicago, a nation huddled around its radios and thumbed through atlases, trying to locate Pearl Harbor. It was a crisp morning in Los Angeles, where *The Great Dictator, Sergeant York,* and *Citizen Kane* were playing in downtown theaters. Louis B. Mayer had recently reprimanded Willy Wyler, in the middle of directing *Mrs. Miniver* on loanout to MGM, for the extreme nastiness with which he had told Helmut Dantine to play a young Nazi flier shot down over the English countryside. He had reminded the director that Loew's had theaters all over the world, including Berlin. "We don't make hate pictures," he told Wyler. "We don't hate anybody. We're not at war."

On December 8, 1941, Congress declared war on Japan. Days later, the United States was committed to smiting the other Axis powers as well. "Since yesterday afternoon we live in another world," read a letter from Albert Lasker waiting on Goldwyn's desk. "What it will bring forth no man knows. It makes one feel deeply that this homeland of ours must be preserved, though it takes not merely our fortunes but our lives." Louis B. Mayer asked Wyler back into his office and told him to film *Mrs. Miniver* as he wished, portraying the young German "as a typical Nazi son of a bitch."

Hollywood rallied, and Goldwyn marched to the fore. In the previous two years alone, he and the other big-money powers had been besieged with dozens of requests for financial aid—such causes as Bundles for Britain, the Greek War Relief Association, Russian War Relief, United China Relief, Fight for Freedom, and the Red Cross War Emergency Drive. Goldwyn gave generously—anywhere from $500 to $5,000 to each of them—but he also contributed an idea that would augment Hollywood's impact on the philanthropies of the nation. He proposed forming the Permanent Charities Committee of the Motion Picture Industry, in which all war charities would be pooled into one Hollywood fund. Goldwyn thought the plan would result in heavier donations and lighter paperwork; and, as he announced at the founders' meeting on June 28, 1940, "We as an industry want to show what we can do as a united body. Therefore, the industry must get credit for it." Goldwyn was named chairman of the organization, which would expand throughout the war years and beyond, raising millions of dollars.

With America and the Jews sharing a common enemy for the first time, Hollywood began to find its true religion. One by one, Jewish moguls came out of the closet. More than the age-old charitable tradition of *tzedaka* drove them; it was the feeling of guilt that, as Ben Hecht said, "blooms in the soul of the immigrant Jew who turns into an American nabob."

In early 1942, Hecht became co-chairman of the Committee for a Jewish Army of Stateless and Palestinian Jews. He called on David Selznick to lend his name to the cause. Selznick refused, saying, "I'm an American and not a Jew." Hecht asked if Selznick would become a sponsor if he could prove that he was a Jew; his litmus test was to call three friends of Selznick's choice and ask them one question: "What would you call David O. Selznick, an American or a Jew?" If any one of them said "American," Hecht agreed to back off. Selznick accepted the challenge. Martin Quigley, publisher of the *Motion Picture Exhibitors' Herald,* said Selznick was a Jew; writer Nunnally Johnson said the same. Casting the decisive vote, Leland Hayward replied, "For God's sake, what's the matter with David? He's a Jew and he knows it." Selznick got converted.

Sam Goldwyn was no different. After quietly contributing to Jewish charities over the years, he agreed to listing his name in the United Jewish Welfare Fund's yearbook along with the twenty thousand other supporters. In 1943, he contributed $5,000, a figure topped by only a handful of wealthier Angelenos—such as Jack Warner, Harry Cohn, Louis B. Mayer, and Joe Schenck. The last had less ability just then to donate $10,000, but much more reason.

By 1941, a trade union protected practically every studio employee, from screen actors to janitors. The Screen Writers Guild tended to be the most vocal, its members having the most direct access to the American consciousness. But only one segment of the Hollywood work force had muscle nationwide, the International Alliance of Theatrical Stage Employees, known as "Yatsy." Al Capone's mob eventually took over IATSE (which included every motion picture projectionist in America); and an underling named Willie Bioff became its man in Hollywood. He induced the studio heads to corral the ten thousand still unorganized studio workers into

IATSE; then he demanded that the studios pay protection to him to keep the machinery greased. Joseph Schenck, as president of Twentieth Century–Fox, became the conduit through which Bioff was bought off.

There is no evidence of Sam Goldwyn's having paid the $25,000 required of small studio heads (half the dues the majors had to pay), but it is safe to assume he was tithed like everybody else in town. Within a few years, the Screen Actors Guild exposed IATSE. A tough New York district attorney, Thomas Dewey, created his reputation by investigating industrial rackets and busting the mob; Bioff was convicted of extorting a million dollars from the film industry. Joe Schenck, the only Hollywood mogul without children, volunteered to take the rap for the rest of the industry. He was sentenced to a year and a day in Danbury prison on a charge of income tax evasion.

Goldwyn dined with Schenck on the eve of his entering prison, in May 1942, and wrote him regularly while he was behind bars. His letters were full of local news and constant reminders of "how proud I am of your friendship and what it means to me." When Schenck came up for parole, Goldwyn wrote an impassioned letter to the Department of Justice, emphasizing Schenck's active involvement in charities and affirming "with the utmost sincerity that I have never known a finer man than Mr. Schenck." Goldwyn's friend of thirty-one years was released in September and was the guest of honor at a small dinner at Laurel Lane marking his return to Hollywood.

During Schenck's brief absence, Hollywood went to war. Clark Gable later won the Air Medal for bombing missions over German-held territory; Jackie "The Kid" Coogan flew a glider behind Japanese lines in Burma; Douglas Fairbanks, Jr., won the Silver Star for service at Salerno. Tyrone Power enlisted in the Marines, Henry Fonda in the Navy. James Stewart became a colonel in the Air Force, winning the Distinguished Flying Cross.

Those who could not fight could still serve. The United Service Organization had begun producing camp shows even before Pearl Harbor. That idea of taking live shows to the boys abroad quickly spread around the world. Ingrid Bergman sang Swedish folk songs to hospitalized men in Alaska; Al Jolson crooned outside Palermo; Kay Francis and Martha Raye toured North Africa; Paulette Goddard played the China-Burma-India theater; singer Martha Tilton, harmonica player Larry Adler, and Jack Benny entertained in the Southwest Pacific. As in the First World War, movie stars proved to be the most persuasive promoters of war bonds. Had Carole Lombard accepted Sam Goldwyn's offer to appear in *Ball of Fire*, she very likely would have been at the Radio City opening of the film on January

16, 1942, instead of taking off on a bond-selling tour. Her plane crashed into Table Rock Mountain, just outside Las Vegas; there were no survivors.

Within days of America's entry into the war, studios volunteered all their services and facilities for producing training films. A number of moviemakers joined the Signal Corps. Frank Capra was assigned to Washington, where he created a series of propagandistic "orientation" films called "Why We Fight." Later, he saw action on several fronts, which he captured in documentary films. Directors George Stevens, Anatole Litvak, and John Huston signed up for similar duty. Walt Disney produced everything from health education films to morale builders. In *The New Spirit,* Donald Duck helped the public understand the government's demand for higher taxes.

The editors of *Look* magazine found grass-roots Hollywood was "just another town at war," sacrificing just like the rest of the country. Within twenty-four hours of Pearl Harbor, studio trucks were transporting army troops and equipment. Air-raid shelters were built on studio lots. Sets were built that could be modified and reused in other pictures; hairpins were inventoried, sterilized, and reused. Gas-guzzling car-chase scenes were virtually eliminated.

Hollywood's greatest contribution to the war effort was in maintaining the steady flow of its standard product, adapting American movies to the times. "A few producers saw that they could render a priceless service by making a certain number of pictures that were not only entertaining, but which could interpret the war for our own people and other people of the world," noted Lowell Mellett, chief of the Bureau of Motion Pictures of the Office of War Information, looking back on those last weeks of 1941.

The OWI took great pains not to interfere with the motion picture industry. The government was so mindful of the evils of censorship that Mellett told the MPPDA bluntly that "you are free to make pictures your government does not like." But he also recognized that Hollywood was run almost completely by first-generation Americans, patriots all, and "that since you are as zealous as our government in our desire to win the war you do not want to do anything to harm the war effort." He asked film producers to submit treatments, scripts, and films to the Bureau of Motion Pictures for "information and objective opinion . . . that makes no comments on the theatrical aspects of a film" but points out anything that might be harmful in world relations. In the early months of 1942, for example, Goldwyn's *The Real Glory*—in which the Moros were portrayed as villains—was still in distribution around the world. Yesterday's enemies had become today's allies, and further screenings of that film could only foster ill will. Once Mellett's office pointed this out to Goldwyn, he took another look at the picture, then yanked it from further distribution.

While the OWI discouraged certain types of films, it encouraged others. At a gathering of producers at the Beverly Wilshire Hotel, Mellett explained the government's targets:

"We would like to see pictures that dramatize the underlying causes of the war and the reason why we fight," he said. "Unless the public understands these, the war may be meaningless." RKO responded with *This Land Is Mine,* directed by Jean Renoir, in which a Nazi-occupied village fights for freedom; Warner Brothers made *Mission to Moscow,* the story of U.S. Ambassador Joseph E. Davies; Alexander Knox played the title role in *Wilson* for Twentieth Century–Fox, a film that so stirred Goldwyn he bought full-page ads for it. Studio head Darryl F. Zanuck put a dozen war-theme pictures into the works—from *Secret Agent of Japan* to *Berlin Correspondent*—before enlisting.

To "provide better understanding of our partners in this war," MGM adapted Pearl S. Buck's *Dragon Seed,* with Katharine Hepburn and Walter Huston as Chinese peasants taking on the Japanese. Sam Goldwyn believed Noel Coward's *In Which We Serve* would "do more to build up good will in America than any propaganda sent out of England since the war began."

Above all, Mellett emphasized, "We would like to see more and more true pictures of America. . . . You know it is true and you know also, I am sure, that the real America is a better sort of place and real Americans are perhaps a little better people than their average in the pictures that foreigners see." Warners' life of George M. Cohan, *Yankee Doodle Dandy,* was the quintessential flag-waver of the day—in Sam Goldwyn's opinion, "by far the best musical show ever made."

Goldwyn chalked the first picture on his slate after Pearl Harbor upon receiving an indirect message from the President himself that America needed a film about Russia. Lowell Mellett and New Dealer Harry Hopkins had been the links between Pennsylvania Avenue and Formosa Avenue. On December 10, 1941, Goldwyn wired Mellett that he wished to proceed with a documentary film that he would release commercially. Days later, Hitler's army marched within miles of Moscow. "The Russian news was very bad that winter of 1942," Lillian Hellman remembered of the time when Sam Goldwyn first discussed his notion with her, "but all of America was moved and bewildered by the courage of a people who had been presented to two generations of Americans as passive slaves." She was "wild" to do a picture about the Soviet Union. So was William Wyler, who had just wrapped on *Mrs. Miniver.*

Wyler and Hellman went to Washington to see the Soviet ambassador, Maxim Litvinov. He said making such a film would be impossible without the complete cooperation of the Russian government. The next day Stalin's foreign secretary, Vyacheslav Molotov, approved the idea.

An excited director and writer returned to New York, where they met with Sam Goldwyn at the Waldorf Towers. He agreed that they should make a quick trip to Russia to see what sites could be photographed. "Because of the enormous American admiration for the Russians in those days," remembered Miss Hellman, "we were an almost guaranteed success before we started. Goldwyn recognized that, of course, and knew that a large part of the cost of the picture—planes, camera crew, extras—would be supplied by the Russians." The meeting was the most harmonious Goldwyn's creative team had ever had with him—until Wyler said that while he was in Russia, he wanted his salary paid in monthly installments to his wife. "This simple request," Miss Hellman observed, "caused Goldwyn's face to change, and I remember knowing immediately that something was going to happen." Hellman said she wanted her salary paid in two chunks—"half on the day we started photography, half on the day I arrived home, even if I came back in a coffin." Then Goldwyn blew his top.

For the next twenty minutes, he challenged Hellman and Wyler on their political convictions. "You say you love America, you are patriots you tell everybody. . . . Now it turns out you want *money* from me, from *me* who am sacrificing a fortune for my government because *I* love my country." Wyler said he did not understand Goldwyn's point. "This picture is being made for commercial release and you intend to profit on it as you profit on any other movie," he said. "You're not putting up a nickel for 'your government.' The Russians, as a matter of fact, are giving you most of a free ride." Hellman said the entire discussion was nonsense; they should be paid on this as they would be on any picture. *"Nonsense?"* Goldwyn exclaimed, rising to his feet. "You call it *nonsense* to take money away from your government?" Wyler was all for prolonging the argument; but Hellman saw that Goldwyn had lost his sense of reason. "Sam," she said, "your problem is that you think you're a country . . . and that all the people around you are supposed to risk their lives for you!"

Hellman and Wyler both knew all along that Goldwyn had every intention of paying them, that he was just looking for a way to shave their salaries. In the weeks before everybody was again talking amicably, Goldwyn heard from the director's attorneys that Wyler had, in fact, filed on December 9, 1941, with the War Department for a commission in the Signal Corps and that the vigorous thirty-nine-year-old had subsequently passed his two physical examinations at Fort Monmouth. "I DO NOT KNOW

HOW MUCH OF THIS INFORMATION IS CORRECT AND NATURALLY HAVE NO
DESIRE TO ATTEMPT, EVEN INDIRECTLY, TO INTERFERE WITH WYLER'S
INDUCTION," Goldwyn wired Lieutenant Colonel Darryl Zanuck of the
Signal Corps, "BUT ON THE OTHER HAND, I DON'T WANT HIM TO USE
THE ARMY AS AN EXCUSE TO AVOID A COMMITMENT WITH ME. WOULD
APPRECIATE YOUR CHECKING FACTS AND ADVISING ME AS PROMPTLY AS
POSSIBLE WHETHER THESE REPRESENTATIONS ARE CORRECT."

In late spring 1942, Wyler went on official leave to the United States
Army to make a documentary called *The Negro Soldier.* In short order, he
was a major in the Army Air Force, filming bombing missions over Europe. By then Gregg Toland had also left his post at Goldwyn Studios,
becoming a Navy lieutenant in Hawaii.

Neither Goldwyn nor Hellman wanted to abandon the Russian project.
After more discussion, they agreed she should write what she called a
"semi-documentary," to be shot in Hollywood, for which she would be
fully paid. It would be months before Goldwyn would have anything to
film, and by then the thinning ranks under his command were all but
depleted. "Actors, directors and writers are fast joining the armed forces,"
Goldwyn wrote Joe Schenck in July 1942. "Fifty-six men in my studio
have left. . . . The same proportion applies at the other studios. It looks
to me as though we are in for a long war, but I have every confidence in
the world that in the long run we are going to win."

Were it not for the government's cry for patriotic pictures, Goldwyn
most likely would never have even considered what became his next project, a baseball story. "It's boxoffice poison," he told story editor Niven
Busch, without even hearing the specifics of the plot. "If people want
baseball, they go to the ballpark."

Busch nonetheless proceeded to recommend a story about the life of Lou
Gehrig, who had recently died at the age of thirty-seven. On July 4, 1939,
the New York Yankees herculean star of 2,130 consecutive games had appeared on the diamond of Yankee Stadium for the last time, to bid his
public farewell; he was suffering from amyotrophic lateral sclerosis. "I've
been walking on ball fields for sixteen years, and I've never received anything but kindness and encouragement from you fans," he said. After ac-
knowledging his teammates, past and present, the sportswriters, his team
managers, his parents, and his wife—"a companion for life . . . who has
shown me more courage than I ever knew"—the "Iron Man" began to lose
control. "People all say that I've had a bad break," he found the strength
to add; "but . . . today . . . today I consider myself the luckiest man on
the face of the earth."

Busch ran the newsreels of "Lou Gehrig Appreciation Day" for his boss.

When the lights came on in his screening room, Goldwyn was mopping his eyes. "Run them again," he said.

After the second viewing, a fully composed Goldwyn barked, "Get Mulvey in New York. We'll get the rights." In an instant, Goldwyn was talking to his senior associate—whose wife, Marie "Dearie" McKeever, had recently inherited a one-quarter interest in the Brooklyn Dodgers from her father. "Mulvey," he said, "call Mrs. Gehrig. Tell her there's a remote possibility that we might be interested in the story of her husband." For some $30,000, she sold the rights.

While Goldwyn was negotiating with publicist and sports enthusiast Christy Walsh for the services of Babe Ruth and other real New York Yankees, Busch realized the extent of Goldwyn's ignorance about the game. After a particularly grueling bargaining session, Goldwyn pulled Busch aside and quietly asked him what position Lou Gehrig played. "First base," Busch replied. "First base?" Goldwyn asked, making sure he got it right. "*First* base," Busch underscored, emphasizing it in such a way that "I think he got the idea that there were ten bases and one worked his way up to first." Negotiations continued that afternoon until the round of Goldwyn screams that customarily closed each session. "You're robbing me!" Goldwyn yelled at Walsh. "I'm not going to pay through the ass for just some lousy . . . THIRD baseman!"

Busch assigned Paul Gallico to write the story for the film, called *The Pride of the Yankees.* Knowing the climax of the picture, Gallico worked backward, fleshing out the people Gehrig had referred to in his valedictories. He told the story of the immigrant Gehrigs, especially Lou's mother, who had worked as a cook at a fraternity at Columbia University so her son might get an education and become an engineer. When she suddenly needed an operation, Lou did not tell her he obtained the money for it by accepting an offer from the Yankees. Then Gallico followed Gehrig's rise to the major leagues and his rivalry with Babe Ruth. The centerpiece of the film would be the love story between the bashful athlete and the sophisticated Chicago socialite Eleanor Twitchell—their cute courtship, his untying himself from his mother's apron strings, and the Gehrigs' final acceptance of his fatal illness. Jo Swerling and Herman Mankiewicz wrote a screenplay that landed right on the foul line between earnest and maudlin. The *New York Times* would later note that "without being pretentious," it was "a real saga of American life—homey, humorous, sentimental and composed in patient detail."

Goldwyn saw Gary Cooper in the lead from the start. It was the last commitment he had from the actor under his present contract, and it was the first time Goldwyn had offered him a role commensurate to his screen status. Niven Busch successfully pushed Goldwyn to give Teresa Wright, whom he was soon to marry, her first starring role, as Eleanor. Walter Brennan played yet another Cooper sidekick, a sportswriter friend. The no-frills Sam Wood was hired to direct. It was "a tough picture to produce," Goldwyn admitted to Joe Schenck upon the film's completion, "as there are so many people throughout America who knew Gehrig that his biography had to be handled with the greatest of care." The biggest problem grew from Gary Cooper's being as unfamiliar with baseball as Sam Goldwyn was.

Except for his years in England, Cooper had spent most of his childhood on a horse in Montana, and he had never held a bat in his hands. To make matters worse, he was right-handed, and Gehrig was one of the most celebrated southpaws in the history of the game. Sam Wood could cover certain running and fielding moves by filming a double in long shots, but there was no escaping Cooper's having to step up to home plate and take a convincing whack at the ball. The actor went into spring training with several ballplayers and learned to throw, catch, slide, and bunt properly. He even developed a strong, steady swing, but he just could not master it left-handed. Film editor Danny Mandell saved the day with an ingenious idea. He suggested to Goldwyn that they allow Cooper to bat right, but have him run to third base, not first. If the costumer reversed the letters and numbers on the players' uniforms in those few shots, Mandell could simply flip the film over, giving the impression of a lefty running to first base.

Goldwyn later admitted that his major challenge on the film was "to watch my baseball so that it didn't get the best of the personal story. As the picture now stands, the baseball is purely a background and the love story is the dominant factor." To ensure that *The Pride of the Yankees* ended up a picture for the millions of women left at home as much as a sports movie, Goldwyn insisted on a nightclub sequence, featuring the dance team of Veloz and Yolanda. The Gehrigs' favorite ballad, Irving Berlin's "Always," wafted through the film. Goldwyn's heavy dose of romance proved the secret to the film's success.

Charles Skouras—whose brother Spyros had moved that year from managing the Fox Metropolitan Theaters in New York to the presidency of the parent company, Twentieth Century–Fox—liked *The Pride of the Yankees* enough to pass on several recommendations. Goldwyn followed his advice of exhibiting the picture at as much as 25 percent over the regular general admission price of movies "and in no event at less than fifty-five cents general admission." Skouras also suggested creating a word-of-mouth campaign by premiering the picture in just one city. After New York, the picture moved across the country, capped by a benefit at the Pantages Theater in Hollywood that raised $5,000 for the Naval Aid Auxiliary. "From what I understand," Goldwyn wrote Joe Schenck, "it will be the last opening that Hollywood will be allowed to have for the duration of this war. As you know they are stopping night baseball and all outdoor sports at night. Nor can we shoot any more scenes at night. From now on all this is 'verboten.'"

Goldwyn made more money off *The Pride of the Yankees* than from any film he had yet produced. Several thousand dollars came from such producers as Pandro Berman and Buddy DeSylva, who had bet that the film would not gross more than $3 million, the benchmark those days for blockbuster business.

The reviews rivaled the receipts, particularly those of several individuals whose opinions Goldwyn greatly respected. Eleanor Gehrig said the film was all she could hope for and that she was "completely happy with it." Wendell Willkie, whom Goldwyn had supported for President in 1940—told him, "Sam, you have done something very important here. You help democracy everywhere by showing what opportunities there are in America." Goldwyn replied, "Why shouldn't I—who knows better than I do the opportunities in America?" The picture was nominated for eight Academy Awards, including Best Picture, Best Actress, and Best Actor. Goldwyn assumed that all the film's glory would clinch Gary Cooper's resigning with him.

Instead, the actor resigned. Goldwyn's one leading man could hardly wait to end his relationship with the producer. After his experience with Goldwyn, Cooper chose to become an actor for hire, making his lucrative deals one at a time and proceeding to enjoy more than a decade of solid hits. One year younger than the century, Cooper had been too old to enlist in the armed services, but in 1943 he went on a five-week tour of American bases in New Guinea. The movie actor had little he could perform on a stage beyond striking an unaffected pose and reciting Lou Gehrig's farewell speech. That invariably brought the men to tears, then to their feet in inspired applause.

Teresa Wright won an Oscar that year, but not for *The Pride of the Yankees*. She had also been nominated as Best Supporting Actress in *Mrs. Miniver* and collected her statuette for playing Greer Garson's daughter. That picture's award sweep included a first Oscar for Major William Wyler, then flying somewhere over Europe. Goldwyn had not counted on Miss Wright's becoming such a sensation so quickly, and he had no starring roles ready for her. In fact, the only part he saw available was in the ensemble of his Russian picture.

Lillian Hellman had recently taken her friend Willy Wyler to task for making "such a piece of junk" as *Mrs. Miniver.* She claimed to have walked out of a screening in tears because it was "a lot of sentimental crap—soft and saccharine, really beneath him." Writing her Russian story that summer, she vowed to keep her film from becoming such a marshmallow. Her first draft, completed in August 1942, was more bitter but no better.

"The time of the picture is the morning of June 21st, 1941, the day before the German invasion of the Soviet Union," Miss Hellman wrote on page one of *The North Star.* "The opening of the picture takes place in a small village—the village of a collective farm—near the Soviet border." Over the next one hundred pages, the playwright interwove the stories of the peasant neighbors on "the last morning of peace." A group of young people at the start of their summer vacation from school, Tanya and Damian and their friends, are about to set off on a walking trip to Kiev for their first glimpse of the big city. For seventy-five pages, the script tracks the happy vagabonds as they prepare for their trip and take to the road. Wise old Karp warns the youths not to go—"because the morning smells bad." But they proceed, only to have a squadron of Nazi bombers interrupt their journey. The last quarter of the film details the farm's mobilization as the village comes under attack. "Comrades," good farmer Rodion tells his neighbors, who have elected him their soviet representative, "this is not a time for mourning. It is a time for revenge."

Goldwyn was so gung ho about the project that he rushed it into production. Miss Hellman raged to her dying day that Sam Goldwyn "phonied" up her film. In truth, the very premise of *The North Star*—all its characters drawn in broad strokes and primary colors—was as subtle as a propaganda poster.

With the war thinning the ranks of Hollywood's directors as well as of its leading men, Sam Goldwyn considered himself lucky to engage Lewis Milestone, who had directed the World War I masterpiece *All Quiet on the Western Front.* But Milestone's talent had gone off of late, as he turned out several stale comedies and the soggy *Edge of Darkness,* about the Nazis storming Norway. Upon reading the first draft of Hellman's script, he announced that he "had very little criticism to offer." Almost everyone else who had read the script had great reservations, but Goldwyn's patriotic fervor for this project made the readers feel that voicing them would have been tantamount to treason.

Over the next few months, Milestone suggested several ideas to Miss Hellman. He wanted the film to show the Nazi atrocities she had only suggested. At his urging, the writer blinded one character and maimed another. The role of a doctor was invented, someone to challenge his German counterpart in the occupational army. The German doctor would be played by Erich von Stroheim, enjoying a brief renaissance in his acting career now that movies needed a man "you love to hate." In this picture he would bleed the local children for plasma. He says he is sorry about the deeds he must perform, but he is only one helpless man in a changing world. Hellman appreciated most of Milestone's notes for the first fifty pages.

The next fifty were another matter. Milestone rewrote much of the dialogue into what Miss Hellman would later call "a sort of Gregory Ratoff patois." Bigger changes followed. "I understood that you were satisfied with the script and would not begin to add to it your own particular director's imagination and knowledge," Hellman wrote Milestone on February 19, 1943. "I was, therefore, shocked to find that you are evidently not satisfied with the script, and that you seem to feel no hesitancy in basically changing not only the sequence of the story, but its characters, and its plot." Miss Hellman said, "just such goings-on is the reason why decent writers don't like to work in Hollywood. It is an ugly and insulting conception of writing. Art is not made by democratic meetings, with contributions."

Each day on "the Russian story" lessened Hellman's faith in both the project and the producer. "My letter may not have dampened his enthusiasm," she wrote Goldwyn about Milestone, ". . . but his 'suggestions' have definitely dampened mine. They weren't 'suggestions': they were basic changes, and as I wrote Milly [Milestone] it was not so much that he should have wanted to make them, as it was the nature of the ones he wished to make." In her growing disinterest, Miss Hellman, atypically, almost never fought a single point to the finish. Goldwyn even sent her several telegrams egging her on to disagree whenever she felt her script was being harmed. "I LOVE YOU TOO MUCH TO DO ANYTHING YOU FEEL SO STRONGLY AGAINST," he wired. "AND I LOVE YOU TOO MUCH TO TELL YOU ABOUT IT IN A TELEGRAM," she replied, then sat on her hands.

Miss Hellman attended the picture's casting sessions but failed to protest any of the choices until after the film was released. Walter Huston and Ann Harding, whom Warners had just starred in *Mission to Moscow,* headed an all-American company of actors. A handsome, dark-haired newcomer, just seventeen, named Farley Granger was hired to play Damian opposite Teresa Wright. Only days before filming—after rehearsals and costume fittings—Goldwyn's only contract star broke it to the producer that she was pregnant. Goldwyn always suspected Niven Busch, whom he had recently fired, of inseminating her just so she would not have to play so small a part in the picture. Goldwyn borrowed Darryl Zanuck's latest discovery, Anne Baxter, for the role. He hired Aaron Copland to write the music and Ira Gershwin the lyrics for several folk songs. Again Miss Hellman expressed nothing less than pleasure at the choices. She would have been welcome on the set, to speak her piece at any time; but Hellman stayed away for the entire shoot.

At the end of production, Goldwyn saw an assembly of a scene he felt needed to be reshot and rewritten. He asked Frances to contact Miss Hellman. After three weeks with no response to her letter, Frances asserted herself more aggressively. "WE FEEL VERY STRONGLY THAT A FEW SCENES SHOULD BE ADDED IN ORDER TO CLEAR UP LAST PART OF PICTURE," she wired on July 10. "COULD YOU POSSIBLY COME OUT IMMEDIATELY TO SEE IT. YOU WILL THEN I'M SURE SEE WHAT'S NEEDED AS I KNOW IF YOU DO ONE WEEK'S WORK THIS WILL BE THE BEST PICTURE YOU OR SAM EVER HAD."

Hellman went west. Forty minutes into the rough cut of the film, she started to cry, first quietly to herself, then histrionically. "Shut up, shut up, shut up!" Goldwyn yelled. "How dare you cry!"

"Don't tell me when to cry," Hellman replied. "You've turned it into junk." Over the next few minutes, the film still running before them, the two argued so violently that the projectionist came out of his booth to prevent mayhem. "You let Milestone turn this into a piece of junk!" she screamed. "It will be a huge flop, which it deserves to be." She insisted she was through listening to Goldwyn ever again. She returned to her hotel room, where, as she remembered, she cried all day.

At five o'clock, Goldwyn's secretary called Miss Hellman to say her boss had gone home and wished to see her. A taxi drove her to Laurel Lane and waited for her in the large courtyard. As she entered the house, Goldwyn shouted, "I hear you tell people that Teresa Wright was your discovery!"

"What does this have to do with anything?" she asked.

"Answer my question," he demanded.

"No," she said. "I will not answer any questions. I told you this afternoon, I take no more orders from you. Ever."

Goldwyn commanded her to leave. "I will not get out of this house," she said, "until you have left this room." All the color draining from his face, he reissued his order. She restated hers. They stared each other down, and he blinked first, crying out for Frances. She ran into the room, trying to make peace, and he stormed up the stairs. Upon his exit, Hellman walked out the front door.

A few weeks later, many people walked out of the preview of *The North Star* in Inglewood. But that did not shake Goldwyn's confidence in the film. He pleaded with Charles Skouras to help him get bookings in Los Angeles theaters before the first of the year, because "THIS PICTURE HAS GREAT CHANCE OF RECEIVING ACADEMY AWARD." In setting up a screening for Arthur Sulzberger in New York, he unabashedly referred to the film as a "classic."

The North Star opened in early November 1943, at a time when political convictions often ruled reviewers' sensibilities. Most of the New York press found the picture moving enough to compensate for what Bosley Crowther in the *New York Times* called its "departures from reality." Henry Luce was mad for the picture, and *Time* called it a "cinemilestone."

The film critic at *The Nation,* James Agee, found the documentaries being produced as part of the Army Orientation Series far more effective.

In its basic design Lillian Hellman's script could have become a fine picture: but the characters are stock, their lines are tinny-literary, their appearance and that of their village is scrubbed behind the ear and "beautified"; the camera work is nearly all glossy and overcomposed; the proudly complicated action sequences are stale from overtraining; even the best of Aaron Copland's score has no business ornamenting a film drowned in ornament: every resourcefulness appropriate to some kinds of screen romance, in short, is used to make palatable what is by no remote stretch of the mind romantic.

Agee, who later wrote the screenplay of *The African Queen,* conceded that the "picture represents the utmost Hollywood can do, within its present decaying tradition, with a major theme."

"I don't care if this picture doesn't make a dime," Goldwyn said when *The North Star* was released, "just so long as every man, woman, and child in America sees it." He tried to rally support for the film by appealing to his eighty-year-old friend, William Randolph Hearst. Goldwyn was still in disfavor with Hearst for having voiced his pleasure with *Citizen Kane,* and he tried to get back in his good graces by shipping a print of *The North Star* to him at Wyntoon, the ranch to which he had retreated when he was told that San Simeon was an obvious target in the eventuality of a Japanese attack on California. "YOU ARE A VERY GREAT PRODUCER SAM BUT I THINK A GOOD AMERICAN LIKE YOURSELF OUGHT TO BE PRODUCING PRO-AMERICAN PROPAGANDA INSTEAD OF PRO-RUSSIAN PROPAGANDA," wired WRH after viewing it. "THANK YOU FOR YOUR WIRE AND FOR THE COMPLIMENT," Goldwyn replied. "I ASSURE YOU THAT 'THE NORTH STAR' WAS NOT MADE AS PROPAGANDA FOR ANYTHING BUT PURELY AS ENTERTAIN-

MENT AND THE LOCALE MIGHT JUST AS WELL HAVE BEEN POLAND, HOL-
LAND OR ANY AMERICAN FARM COMMUNITY." Even though several Hearst
critics liked the film, all favorable reviews of it were pulled from his syndicate. He issued an order not to print a word about the film, except to
smear it as red propaganda.

The North Star had its fans, seemingly in proportion to their involvement in the war effort. A special screening in Washington for a dozen
senators was a success; and Lowell Mellett heartily endorsed it. But after a
big opening week, the public showed no interest in it. For the first and
last time in his career, Goldwyn sold off the rights to one of his films. By
then he would kid, "When Stalin got depressed, he ran that picture."
Later, as the cold war heated up, twenty-two minutes' worth of sympathetic references to the Soviets were deleted and stock footage of the
Hungarian revolt of 1956 was inserted, turning *The North Star* into an
anti-Communist action picture.

Lillian Hellman never stopped bemoaning the bastardization of her
script. After *The North Star* opened, she aired all her grievances in a long
interview in the *New York Times*. In her memoirs twenty-five years later,
she maintained that her screenplay "could have been a good picture instead
of the big-time, sentimental, badly directed, badly acted mess it turned
out to be."

More than the botching of this one movie had been bothering her. Lillian Hellman felt Sam Goldwyn had played dirty pool with her three-year
contract, then entering its eighth year. After *The North Star*, Goldwyn
scavenged his larder of unproduced properties and sent one to the writer
as her next assignment. "I don't agree with this method of handling the
Hellman situation," James Mulvey wrote Goldwyn on the subject. "Hellman we know will not agree to do [it] and I feel you have no intention of
doing it or wanting her to do it." Goldwyn proceeded all the same.

During the resultant contract extension, Hellman bumped into Joe
Schenck in the dining car of the Twentieth Century, where they discussed
her bondage to Goldwyn. Schenck said he would help secure her release
by signing a new contract with her. He handed Miss Hellman a menu and
told her to write on the back of it the terms she wanted. The next morning, over breakfast at the Blackstone Hotel in Chicago, Schenck signed it.
Neither fully believed in the menu's legality, but it carried enough weight
to put her release in motion.

"I was the first writer ever to pay my way out of a contract to Sam
Goldwyn," said Lillian Hellman. "I owed him one more script and he said
he'd let me out for forty thousand dollars. It was the meanest goddamned

gesture I'd ever heard of." On September 18, 1944, Lillian Hellman signed a three-page document that officially terminated her Goldwyn contract (which dated back to January 1936) once the sum of $27,500 had been paid. Goldwyn and Miss Hellman hardly saw each other ever again.

In the saber-rattling spirit of 1943, *The North Star* picked up six Academy Award nominations, mostly in the crafts. It took home no trophies. Most Oscars that year went to more romantic evocations of war: *For Whom the Bell Tolls* and the year's big winner, *Casablanca*. The Best Actress Oscar went to Jennifer Jones in her first starring role, *The Song of Bernadette*. It was a kind of annunciation of the wave of immensely popular religious films (such as *Going My Way* and *The Bells of St. Mary's*, with Bing Crosby) that would console the war-worried nation during the next few bloody years.

Between March and September of 1942, the Office of War Information tallied 260 feature films dealing with some aspect of the war, at home or abroad. The OWI still wanted "war aims and war progress impressed and re-asserted on America's conscience"; but it discouraged "the industry's undue emphasis on the exciting, blood-and-thunder phrases of the war and its sloughing of equally significant problems in civilian life as well as of the basic issues of the struggle and what is implied in the peace after victory." *Boxoffice* editor Maurice Kann said the nation's exhibitors felt the same. Their new cry was: "Give us light stuff. Give us comedies, slanted with the war if you like. Give us serious war pictures, of course, but please, Mr. Producer, exercise a little restraint."

After thirty years of considering comedies as but the mortar between his dramatic works, Goldwyn made them the building blocks of his career. He continued to develop movies about the fighting on each of the fronts, even one about the Army band; but over the next four springs, he produced only *The North Star* and five comedies. He began talking to reporters about the need for "escapist" pictures—to "give people an opportunity to forget for an hour and a half the troublesome and perturbed world we live in."

Wartime Washington became a popular venue for motion picture plots. Basil Rathbone, in his sixth outing as Sherlock Holmes, cemented ties between the two English-speaking powers by solving a 1943 spy mystery there; Jean Arthur, Joel McCrea, and Charles Coburn made the most of the housing shortage in the nation's capital that year in George Stevens's *The More the Merrier*. And Sam Goldwyn bought a story from Leonard Spigelgass and Leonard Q. Ross called "The Washington Angle." Its sinuous plot involved a bungling ex–foreign correspondent who tries to win back his job by cracking a spy ring. Goldwyn sent a draft of the absurd script to Charles MacArthur, hoping he could dress it up enough for Cary Grant—who had become Hollywood's most debonair leading man.

"I happen to think that farce needs more solid foundation than comedy and the present structure seemed shaky to me and badly motivated here and there," MacArthur wrote Goldwyn in refusing the project. He also questioned Goldwyn's choice of casting. "My vote," he said, "would be Bob Hope, because I think he can get away with more inconsistencies than Grant, whom I prefer to see." Goldwyn completely rethought his movie by drawing a bead on the comic talent fast becoming the most popular in the world.

Goldwyn negotiated with Y. Frank Freeman, who ran Paramount, for the release of Bob Hope as the balance of payment on their Gary Cooper–Billy Wilder trade the year before. He hired a series of gag writers to plant punch lines throughout the script. Wishing some of the success of the recent *Road to Morocco* might rub off on him, Goldwyn also drafted that film's director, David Butler, and the series' leading lady, Dorothy Lamour. Austrian-born director Otto Preminger played the Nazi heavy, one of his few screen roles before embarking on a controversial directing career.

The film ended up being called *They Got Me Covered*. Its bang-up business softened the blow of the reviews, which mostly shifted the spotlight from the producer to the star.

Goldwyn could not resist developing another Hope picture, this time applying the "Goldwyn touch." In order to get the most out of the $133,500 he was paying Paramount for twelve weeks of the star's services, he intended to back him up with $2 million worth of Technicolor, fairy-tale art direction by Ernst Fegte (a German refugee Goldwyn called "Faggoty"), a rich score by David Rose, and plenty of pulchritude. He also invested heavily in the script, which was pulled together by Don Hartman, a forty-year-old collaborator on several "Road" pictures and the latest "genius" to join Goldwyn's staff, as a writer and associate producer.

The Princess and the Pirate was custom-made for Bob Hope. He played Sylvester Crosby, a loud-mouthed vaudevillian of the 1740s, who boards a merchant ship in the West Indies and finds himself in the company of a princess, running out on the marriage her father has arranged for her. Brigands seize the ship and the princess and Sylvester. One-liners and desperate schemes again rescue the star, in a plot all but identical to his preceding venture—except for the ruffled shirts, the sea battles, the mutinies, and the treasure map tattooed on Sylvester's chest. He even does a quick turn at the Bucket of Blood Tavern, performing with "Ye Goldwyn Girls." Ninety-five minutes later, the princess's father sails to the rescue, then permits her to marry any man she chooses. Sylvester winds up for a romantic clinch at the fade-out, only to have the princess walk right past him and hurl herself at one of the king's mariners—Bing Crosby. "I work my brains out for nine reels," Hope says to the camera, "and some bit player from Paramount comes over and steals my girl. That's the last picture I'll ever make for Goldwyn."

It was, but not for lack of success. It became one of the year's biggest hits. Paramount kept their star on a short leash after that, limiting him to movies on their own lot when he was not back at the front lines. Goldwyn was riding too high to be upset. He was taking in so much money, his accounting firm of Olvany, Eisner & Donnelly in New York recommended liquidating Samuel Goldwyn, Inc., and establishing "collapsible corporations" for each new picture. The goal of these maneuvers was "to convert ordinary income into capital gains," with its more favorable tax schedule, and to benefit from certain depreciation tactics. Just by pushing paper around, Goldwyn made $800,000 from his studio property in 1942 alone. On top of his six-figure salary, there were now big profits from his pictures. His stock portfolio thickened. His net worth climbing past $10 million— $3 million invested in war bonds—he handily met his 1944 income tax bill of $578,020.15. What was more, Goldwyn had just signed a man he believed was the greatest discovery in motion pictures since Eddie Cantor.

Goldwyn had pursued Danny Kaye for several years, ever since seeing him perform his zany antics and patter songs at the Martinique in New York. At the start of 1941, Kaye all but stole the reviews from Gertrude Lawrence in *Lady in the Dark,* in which he sang a breathless number called "Tchaikowsky"—reciting the tongue-twisting names of forty-nine Russian composers in about as many seconds. By late October, he had left the cast to headline in another show, *Let's Face It.*

Goldwyn kept trying to sign him to a motion picture contract, but the new star stalled, weighing several studio propositions. "Danny must make his own choice," wrote agent John Hyde from Hollywood to his boss, William Morris, in the New York office. "We here would very likely favor Goldwyn because as an individual he would be Danny's employer, producer and sponsor. Furthermore, Goldwyn is ripe and eager to make stars with comparative unknowns, and of course we believe with Goldwyn's help Danny must reach the top in movies." After two years of patience and persistence, Goldwyn got his commitment to make movies for him.

There was never any question of Danny Kaye's phenomenal talent as a singer, dancer, or comedian. But once Goldwyn had him in Hollywood, he realized why none of the other studios had signed him. The dark-haired triple threat (born David Daniel Kaminsky), with his wild eyes and pronounced nose, photographed badly. "In that first screen test," Frances Goldwyn later remembered, "Danny's face was all angles and his nose so long and thin it almost was like Pinocchio's. More tests were made. Then more. In each a new makeup was tried and different lightings. And none was good." Some people suggested he looked too "sinister," a euphemism for Jewish. The uninhibited Harry Cohn at Columbia said he had not signed Danny Kaye because "he looked like a mountains comic."

Goldwyn had Kaye's big musical debut in the works, when all his most trusted associates urged him to "take the loss in pride and money and call the picture off—to forget Kaye." For nights, Sam argued with himself, refusing to say die. One hot morning in the summer of 1943, Sam and Frances were watching "those endless Danny Kaye tests" for the umpteenth time, when Goldwyn grabbed the telephone and called for the studio hairdresser. "I've got it! I've got it!" he shouted into the phone. "Expect Kaye in ten minutes. He's having his hair dyed blond!" Makeup finished the job, completely brightening Kaye's screen image.

The actor willingly accepted the cosmetic changes; but he and his wife resisted Goldwyn's efforts to remodel his comic character. More than the composer of the star's clever specialty numbers, the petite Sylvia Fine Kaye was the savviest judge of what material worked for her husband and what did not. The moment they arrived in Hollywood, the Kayes saw that Goldwyn was trying to duplicate his great success with musicals in the thirties by recycling Cantor's material. "Everybody, Sam Goldwyn included, thought a comedian who wasn't cruel or bombastic had to play a nebbish," Mrs. Kaye explained. "But that's not who Danny was. He played the eager beaver. That's quite different. He'd trip himself up in enthusiasm." For months, every time Sam Goldwyn passed Danny Kaye on the lot, he would greet the performer with a big smile and an enthusiastic "Hello, Eddie!"

Goldwyn put Owen Davis's 1925 comedy, *The Nervous Wreck*—the source material for *Whoopee!*—under Don Hartman's supervision. Several writers updated the story to the present, preserving little more from the original material than its hypochondriacal hero. In *Up in Arms*, Danny Kaye would play a "kid" named Danny, a pill-popping elevator operator (in a medical building, so he could be close to his doctors) who gets drafted along with his buddy Joe Nelson. Danny is secretly in love with a WAC, who is in love with Joe; her best friend secretly admires Danny. In a series of mishaps, the girls wind up on the boys' ship as it heads overseas. The situation allows for several big musical numbers and plenty of physical comedy, as Danny tries to hide the stowaways. On a Pacific island, he is thrown into a guardhouse, which gets captured during a Japanese raid.

Through his buffoonery, he manages to turn his captors into prisoners, marching them at gunpoint into camp, where he is hailed a hero. The Kayes were unhappy with Goldwyn's obvious attempt at reproducing Eddie Cantor with that moth-eaten twenties plot. But it had holes big enough for a few Danny Kaye specialty routines—notably a patter song known as "The Lobby Number" (a satire on motion picture spectaculars, officially titled "Manic-Depressive Pictures Presents") and a scat song from *Let's Face It* called "Melody in 4F"—both by Sylvia Fine.

Kaye was still performing in New York when Goldwyn called the star's wife into his office to announce that he had a test of the actress he had settled on for the picture. "She's just great. Wait till you see her," he said, full of enthusiasm, inviting Sylvia Fine to what he called his "projecting room." Moments later, she sat looking at a pretty blonde, with big blue eyes slightly close together—rather like Frances Goldwyn's. "Oh my God," Mrs. Kaye said to herself. "That's the girl who worked with 'Pansy the Horse'!"

Mrs. Astor's Pet Horse was a revue Billy Rose produced at his Diamond Horseshoe in New York. One night in late 1942, he invited the Goldwyns and Mrs. John Hertz to visit his nightclub, where he pointed out the girl in the "Pansy" act—two comedians in a horse costume who joked, sang, and danced with the curvy straight woman. Her name was Virginia Jones, but she borrowed her brother-in-law's surname—Mayo. Lelia Alexander, the Goldwyn studio researcher, was convinced that her boss's entire sense of beauty had sprung from "a poor little boy's dream of a fairy tale princess." Nobody personified that image more than Virginia Mayo. Within a moment of her leaving the stage, Goldwyn asked Billy Rose if he would object to the girl's going to Hollywood. So long as she completed the run of the show, Rose said he was happy to have been part of her discovery. She signed a seven-year contract.

For all her natural beauty and ability to sing and dance, Samuel Goldwyn saw in Virginia Mayo only the next in a long line of women he hoped to mold into his first female star. He provided her with acting lessons, voice lessons, speech lessons, and dance lessons. Twice a week, Hollywood's leading "charm coach," Eleanore King, instructed her in posture and appearance. A nutritionist put her on a diet. A masseuse "contoured" her face after Miss King pronounced Virginia Mayo's cheeks "too fat for screen work." Goldwyn himself called her every night at nine o'clock, inquiring if she was keeping up with her lessons and if she had brushed her hair one hundred strokes.

After six months of this regimen, Virginia Mayo had improved in every department. But one problem remained. Every time a motion picture camera turned her way, she froze. The experience of each test warmed her up a little; but as Sylvia Fine Kaye watched her latest tests, she could only think of "that poor girl talking to two guys in a horse costume." She knew her husband would never stand for it and said everything she could to dissuade Goldwyn from hiring her for the lead in *Up in Arms.*

Goldwyn cast Constance Dowling and Dinah Shore as the two WACs in *Up in Arms.* Dana Andrews played the best friend. Like all the Goldwyn leading men before him, he realized, five years into his contract, that the only worthwhile jobs he was picking up were off the lot; Fox would give him his first important role in the 1944 film *Laura.* Virginia Mayo was sent down to the chorus, becoming one of the thirty-six new Goldwyn Girls.

Another producer might very well have sent her back to New York, especially in those days when the images of the nation's sex goddesses were changing radically. As men in films assumed a new wartime virility, their female counterparts matched them in femininity. Virginia Mayo was a definite throwback to the former beauty queens, pretty tame alongside such new screen sirens as Lana Turner, Hedy Lamarr, Ava Gardner, Veronica Lake, and Lauren Bacall—who had recently flunked a screen test for Sam Goldwyn.

Musicals, as *Up in Arms* illustrated, also changed in the forties. Gold diggers and babes on Broadway became "jills" in jeeps, pin-up girls, cover girls, and "oomph" girls; white tie and tails were replaced by khaki. The public wanted to see red-blooded boys and plenty of cheesecake. Fred Astaire glided off the screen for a few years, making room for the more gymnastic Gene Kelly. Alice Faye and Ruby Keeler and Ginger Rogers stepped aside for the likes of Betty Grable and Rita Hayworth. Movie music swung.

Agnes de Mille had just revolutionized dance on Broadway with her choreography in *Oklahoma!* Goldwyn was so determined to hire her for *Up in Arms,* he interrupted her honeymoon to offer her the job. After she turned him down, he signed Danny Dare, who had just worked on Paramount's *Holiday Inn.* Dare staged an exhilarating "Jive Number," composed by Harold Arlen, which showed off Danny's Kaye's considerable dancing abilities. A dream sequence—inspired by the success of *Lady in the Dark*—allowed Dare to parade the chorus girls in scanty costumes instead of their drab uniforms.

Sam Goldwyn was confident that his entire two-million-dollar investment could be seen on the screen; but he feared he would not see a return on his money. For all his victories in the battles of production and distribution, Goldwyn was still waging his Thirty Years' War with exhibitors.

Paramount, Loew's, Warners, Twentieth Century–Fox, and RKO owned most of the nation's important theaters. In the 92 American cities with populations over 100,000, at least 70 percent of the first-run theaters were affiliated with one or more of the "big five." RKO had stuck to its distribution contract, which gave Goldwyn final approval of every rental deal they negotiated; and they gave him favorable terms when they ran his films in their theaters. But in those territories in which RKO had no houses, Goldwyn was forced to accept whatever terms the other "majors" dictated.

Warners and Paramount theaters were Goldwyn's leading foes. They usually consented to show Goldwyn's films only for a flat rental fee, with no additional percentage of receipts if a film's business exceeded that sum. Even on those occasions when the big five's theaters agreed to pay bonus "coverages," they would play the Goldwyn product at off hours, always accommodating home-studio product over his. As a result, a Goldwyn picture in a Warners theater sometimes earned as little as one eighth what it might have made elsewhere. If this sort of business was not illegal, Goldwyn thought it should be.

Such apparent antitrust violations became the top priority of the Society of Independent Motion Picture Producers, an organization whose membership included William Cagney, Chaplin, Disney, Sol Lesser, Mary Pickford, David O. Selznick, Edward Small, Hunt Stromberg (who had been a major producer at MGM for sixteen years), Walter Wanger, Orson Welles, and Sam Goldwyn. For years, they had tried to build a case against studios that owned their own theaters. On July 20, 1938, *United States of America* v. *Paramount Pictures, Inc. et al.* (a suit that named Columbia, Universal, and United Artists in addition to the five majors) had been filed in the District Court of the United States, but it was moving toward trial with glacial speed. Sam Goldwyn felt he could push it along by dramatizing the problem.

T. & D. Theatres in Reno, Nevada, had been a thorn in Goldwyn's side for years. In 1944, he decided to take them to task and ended up taking on the whole town. Goldwyn rented Tony's El Patio Ballroom, alongside the Southern Pacific right-of-way in Reno, and announced that he would screen *Up in Arms* there instead of in a theater. When the local fire department declared Goldwyn's portable projection booth in violation of local safety laws, his crew moved into the parking lot, where they planned to construct a canvas theater. The town commissioners said that did not comply with local building ordinances, that all seats had to be fastened to a floor. The Goldwyn team moved indoors again, securing chairs to the dance floor and building a platform outside one of the ballroom windows, through which they could project the film. T. & D. took out angry notices in the Reno newspapers, threatening suit "because the platform blocked the sidewalk"; they bemoaned that the good people of Reno had to suffer the indignity of "uncarpeted floors . . . the whistle of freight trains . . . static in the sound system." Goldwyn tried turning public sentiment in his favor when he announced the receipts from his show's opening night would be donated to the Reno Red Cross. He went to Nevada for the occasion, gathering photographers and reporters as he nailed the last chair into the floor.

On the night of August 22, the ballroom at Tony's El Patio was packed almost to capacity. The crowd applauded Goldwyn as he vowed to fight what he called "a monopoly which has been able to keep the productions of independent producers from showing their films unless the producers are willing to pay 'prohibitive percentages.'" To drive the message home, he introduced a special guest—his former partner at United Artists and one of his most bitter enemies for close to three decades, Mary Pickford.

"America's Sweetheart" herself spoke to the assembly, and was broadcast over Reno radio:

To produce "Up in Arms," Mr. Goldwyn spent a whole year of intensive work and $2,000,000 of his own money. This is a lot of time and a great deal of money. But to what avail? Only to be told upon completion that he shall not be permitted to show his picture except as dictated by monopoly.

I would prefer to sit on a wooden chair, bench or even on the floor to see a fine film than to rest upon plush covered opera chairs and be forced to witness a dull, stupid and boring film in the finest movie palace in the country.

. . . I say it is not merely the question as to whether this one or dozens of Goldwyn's pictures do or do not play in Reno or the entire state of Nevada. It's rather the question of whether he or I, or other Americans, are to be given opportunity to carry on our lives and businesses openly and honestly.

Every major magazine and wire service carried the story. The United States attorney in Reno monitored the event from start to finish. Within months, *United States of America* v. *Paramount Pictures, Inc., et al.* was being argued in the courts. Not until its decision of December 31, 1946, did the district court enjoin "the five majors from expanding their present theatre holding in any manner." The solicitor general of the United States teamed with the attorney general in appealing the decision, claiming that relief had been inadequate. The following year, the Supreme Court sided with them and ordered complete theater divorcement, a process that would take several more years and lawsuits. Sam Goldwyn's own case against Fox West Coast Theatres in 1950 would drag on until 1961, at which time he was awarded $300,000 in damages.

All the fanfare over *Up in Arms* fanned fires at the box office. Besides becoming one of Sam Goldwyn's biggest moneymakers, the film marked one of the most auspicious debuts in motion picture history. Frank Quinn of the New York *Daily Mirror* wrote, "Not since Greta Garbo made her cinematic bow has there been anything so terrific as the inimitable Danny." The rest of the critics fell over themselves reaching for more glowing adjectives.

Goldwyn believed he had two stars on his hands. After the beautiful Virginia Mayo "straighted" so well as princess to Bob Hope's pirate, Goldwyn felt confident that she could play opposite Danny Kaye. Goldwyn and his associate Don Hartman minted two original musical comedies in annual succession for this new screen team.

Wonder Man was a silly story about a pair of twins—a swinging nightclub entertainer named Buzzy Bellew, who is about to marry his dance partner, and a bookworm named Edwin Dingle, who is in love with a librarian. Buzzy has witnessed a gangland murder; and on the eve of his marrying, the mob rubs him out to keep him from testifying. But Buzzy comes back to haunt the body of his brother until the thugs are brought to justice.

The film was another wildly successful showcase for the star. Virginia Mayo held her own as the librarian. And Goldwyn seemed to have made yet another discovery in pretty Vera-Ellen Westmeyr Rohe. A nineteen-year-old singer and dancer who had just appeared in a revival of Rodgers and Hart's *A Connecticut Yankee*, she received outstanding notices using just her first name.

The next Kaye musical employed the same cast in another recycling of an Eddie Cantor hit, *The Kid from Spain*. This time, Danny Kaye played a milkman mistaken for a prizefighter. *The Kid from Brooklyn* grossed over four million dollars, one of the most profitable films on the Goldwyn books.

Rather than enjoy the success, Frances became obsessed with the war; she could not prevent herself from hoarding enough provisions to get her and Sam through it. Every year at the Thanksgiving table, she said, "I thank God for this house."

In the peace and quiet of the Quaker-run Fountain Valley School in Colorado—away from his parents' self-involvement—Samuel Goldwyn,

Jr., at last had a chance to find himself. Besides taking an active interest in his studies, Sammy came into his own in the theater. He produced and directed several plays, always arranging for his parents to visit on the weekends of his shows. It was an easy train ride on El Capitan to Colorado Springs. But, Sammy recalled years later, "There'd always be a telegram at the last minute." Not once in his two years at the school had either of his parents visited.

The family communicated through the mails. Frances wrote to her son twice a week, and Sam dictated a letter approximately every ten days. Each letter read like the carbon copy of its predecessor: He would bawl out Sammy for some financial imprudence and describe how he was clearing up the mess. Then he would issue briefs on the strength of his work despite the weakness of his health. There followed some paternal platitudes coupled with some unreasonable expectation, so that the boy could hardly fail to disappoint him. In closing, he would wax effusive about how much he missed his son.

> What is worrying me right now is getting away from the studio around the first of June. . . . However, your graduation means everything to me as I have only one son and I love him very much— so I will manage somehow.

Sammy wrote home religiously once a week. After enthusing about school, he would try to include himself in his father's life, first by praising *him* and sympathizing with *his* being overworked.

With Sammy's graduation less than three weeks away, he still had not received a telegram. A letter from Frances in mid-May broke the news. The boy was heartbroken, but he had long since learned how to channel his own hurt into ministering to his father's chronic need for sympathy. "I am really awfully sorry," Sammy wrote back to his father. "Is there any chance that you could fly here Tuesday morning and go back ten minutes after the services? But I understand how busy you must be with your two pictures and not having a capable director must make things much tougher. You must be working dreadfully hard." At least Frances appeared at the graduation, carrying a letter from her husband. It read in part:

> . . . God bless you and help you; and remember that while I am not present, I am with you in spirit and pray for you every minute. You are my only boy, and outside of Mother, you mean more to me than anything in the world. I know you are not going to disappoint me, and will live up to all the things I hope for you.

After the graduation ceremony, Sammy went home for eight days. Then he left for the East Coast, where he entered the University of Virginia.

Sam did not know that his six-foot-three-and-one-half-inch, seventeen-year-old college freshman was harboring a great desire to join the Army. "My attitude toward college," he recalled later, "was it was a waiting point between Fountain Valley and the service. I wanted to be an officer." He took examinations to take part in the V-12 program, accelerated training for officers. "I don't quite know what you are referring to when you say you want to join the V-12," Goldwyn wrote after Sammy dropped his first mention of his plans to enlist. "I am agreeable to anything you want to join," he wrote, "—but I certainly feel that you should not miss getting that college education, as it is something that will stand you in good stead for the rest of your life."

Sammy enrolled at Charlottesville, and immediately felt at home on campus. He took a particular interest in psychology classes. Letters between parents and son duplicated the missives of earlier years. He never stopped urging Sammy to stick to his studies, as "I want my dreams about your education to come true." And in matters of Sammy's financial malfeasance, Goldwyn could turn on a dime:

I have today changed my will and left you absolutely nothing [he wrote on September 30, 1943]. I have also notified the trustees that the interest I gave you in the profits of my two pictures, THE NORTH STAR and UP IN ARMS, is to revert to me; for I have come to the realization that I cannot rely upon you. It's not that I love you less, Sammy—but from now on you're going to have to stand on your own feet, and accept the responsibility for your conduct. You will be either a good citizen, or, plainly speaking, a bum. That's a choice and a decision you will have to make for yourself and I cannot live your life for you.

Shortly before turning eighteen, Sammy enlisted, passing the qualifying examinations for the Army Specialized Training School. He would stay at Virginia until called, at which time he wanted to apply for Military Intelligence.

For the first time, the Goldwyns were not together for the holidays. It was lonely for all three of them. Sammy spent a blue Christmas in New York with the Irving Berlins. Sam and Frances offered no resistance to their son's decision to join the military.

"Sammy is now in the Army—he was very anxious to join and we did not want to stop him," Goldwyn wrote in a surprising letter to his daugh-

ter, Ruth; "so pretty soon you will have a General as a brother." Perhaps
envisioning Christmases yet to come, a somewhat reformed Goldwyn also
sent "all my love to the children, yourself and Mac." What was more, over
the next few years Goldwyn hired his son-in-law as an assistant art director
on several films and even allowed him screen credit. Sam invited the two
Capps children to swim and play tennis at Laurel Lane, but he hardly got
to know them.

Sammy marked time at college the rest of that term, awaiting orders
from the Army and running up bills beyond his $175 monthly allowance.
"With the exception of a little mistake like me you have plenty to be
thankful for as does Mother," Sammy wrote his father on their nineteenth
wedding anniversary. "Each of you got a fine deal in the other. I don't
think that any son ever had a finer Father & Mother. I have plenty to be
proud of." Goldwyn replied that it was

> very comforting to hear that at last you realize how much we mean
> to you. You mean just that much to us. You are what we live for, and
> what I am working for. My great hope in life is that eventually you
> will be able to take over. When you do I know you will make a great
> success of it, as I have great faith in you. You are intelligent and
> understanding, and I know you will be a much greater man than I
> ever was. You'll have a much better background than I had, and I
> know you are going to use it.

Not having seen his son for most of a year, he raised his allowance to $250
a month.

"When I see some of your pictures I realize all that I have got to learn,"
Sammy wrote his father. "I only wish this war would get over. The day I
get my discharge from the Army, I want to start." More immediately, he
studied hard for his first-year examinations, and planned to celebrate his
Army induction with a junket to New York City. His parents talked for
weeks of joining him there for a round of theater and parties with the
Berlins, the Sulzbergers, and the Harrimans. This time they kept their
word.

"I can't tell you what a pleasure it was for me to spend those few days
with you in New York last week," Sam wrote Private Goldwyn on July 5,
1944.

> I had the best time I've ever had in New York. You are so nice to be
> with, and are such a good companion. And it made me very proud
> to see how much everyone who met you liked you. . . .

I know that you're going to be a great soldier, and that everyone will like you, wherever you are.

God bless you, my boy, and all the luck in the world to you.

With all my love—

Daddy

Sammy reported to Camp Walters, thirty miles from Fort Worth, Texas, outside a town called Mineral Wells. Just eighteen, he set his sights on officer candidate school, armed for the first time with his father's admiration.

The young man had evidently known exactly what he was doing just a few years earlier when he had tried to run away from home. As Sammy later admitted, "The best thing I ever did was get out of that house."

18 Best Years

ASOLDIER'S MOTHER, Frances Goldwyn became a fiend for news, addicted to every newspaper and magazine she could get her hands on. With keen interest she read the August 7, 1944, number of *Time*, featuring Heinz Guderian, the new Nazi chief of staff, on the cover. Frances kept flipping to the "The Nation" section, where the lead article that week was called "The Way Home."

Beneath a large photograph of soldiers hanging out of an old train— "Home Again!!" chalked on its side—ran a story about 370 members of the 1st Marine Division, home for a thirty-day furlough after twenty-seven months of battle. En route from San Diego to the East Coast, the *Time* reporter captured the thoughts of the marines and the "strange embarrassment" of their return. "Somebody's making money, and it isn't us," said a red-haired sergeant from Rochester after paying forty cents for a beer. Another marine asked, "Your wife know you're coming?" to which his comrade replied, "Sure, I wired her from Chicago." One proud holder of the Silver Star, awarded for killing seven hundred Japanese on two successive nights, talked of his prewar life as a cabdriver. Many of the men discussed casualties.

"I was very moved," Frances later recalled after reading that piece in *Time*, "and I thought, 'What's going to happen to these boys when they get back to their hometowns?' I told Sam he should make a picture treating the readjustments of veterans."

Frances remembered Sam's balking for months. Ever since *The North*

Star, he had been gun-shy of any serious war-related project. Still, every few days she reminded him of all "the drama that was inherent in the situation of veterans returning home," until at last he told his wife "flat out he'd never do it." In fact, on August 5, 1944, Goldwyn sent an inter-office communication to his story editor Kay Brown, asking her to register two titles for a possible motion picture: "Home Again" and "The Way Home."

That season, Goldwyn learned from an agent that no less a writer than MacKinlay Kantor was passing through town and that he was poking around for a Hollywood assignment. Kantor was the author of two Civil War novels and was serving as a London-based correspondent, flying in combat missions with the U.S. air forces and the R.A.F. over enemy territory. Goldwyn saw signs all around of the story Kantor should write. John Hersey's *A Bell for Adano,* a story that tolled the imminent end of the war in Europe, had just been sold to the movies; Hersey had another story in the marketplace, called "Joe Is Home." David Selznick's current release was a moving film called *Since You Went Away,* about an American family's adapting to the head of the household's being away at war. It struck Goldwyn that the time was ripe to prepare that story of the soldiers coming home.

Goldwyn told Kantor his idea for a *post*war picture. "Returning soldiers! Every family in America is part of this story," he said. "When they come home, what do they find? They don't remember their wives, they've never seen their babies, some are wounded—they have to readjust." Goldwyn showed him the *Time* article and said he wanted Kantor to write the story however he saw fit—"the story you have to tell from your own knowledge." Goldwyn offered him $20,000—$7,500 for a screenplay treatment, the rest for the story itself. On September 8, Kantor signed a contract and went to New York to write. It was one of the few times Goldwyn had ever given a writer carte blanche. He pinned no special hopes to the project, especially when he learned that Kantor intended to tell his story in free verse.

Goldwyn turned his attention to more promising projects. He spent months negotiating for the life story of the man he would forever revere as the greatest hero of the twentieth century, Dwight D. Eisenhower. When Goldwyn learned that two other producers attached to the film refused to donate their profits to some charity, as he and the Supreme Commander of the Allied forces intended to do with theirs, he dynamited the whole deal. So began a cordial friendship that would last the rest of their lives. "In my father's eyes," Samuel Goldwyn, Jr., later remarked, "Eisenhower could do no wrong."

Goldwyn also grabbed at such commercial properties as *Arsenic and Old Lace* and *Life with Father*, but they slipped through his fingers. He never even had a chance at such best-sellers as *The Razor's Edge, A Tree Grows in Brooklyn, The Seventh Cross, The Song of Bernadette,* and *Forever Amber.* His difficulties in searching for story material were compounded by "the technical problem of casting"—as he explained to *Stella Dallas*'s author, Olive Higgins Prouty, who gave him first crack at her latest novel, *Now, Voyager.* He had to let that go to Jack Warner for Bette Davis, simply because "it was unsuitable for the people whom we have under contract at the present time." Fearfully Goldwyn watched a whole new generation of young stars—Gene Kelly, Jennifer Jones, Lauren Bacall, Van Johnson, Gene Tierney, even the ice-skating sensation Sonja Henie—capture more attention than his lineup of Danny Kaye, Teresa Wright, Virginia Mayo, and Dana Andrews.

The war had made America more prayerful, and a host of "angel" stories was descending upon Hollywood. Such films as *Here Comes Mr. Jordan, I Married an Angel,* and *The Horn Blows at Midnight* had all succeeded at the box office. Frank Capra would send Henry Travers down from the stars as Clarence, an angel in quest of his wings, who helps James Stewart discover his worth in *It's a Wonderful Life.* Goldwyn wanted such a story for himself. With rumors of David Niven's imminent return to Hollywood, Goldwyn's story advisers found just such a project for him and Teresa Wright among the heap of Hollywood rejects—Robert Nathan's 1928 best-seller, *The Bishop's Wife.*

Goldwyn also needed material for Danny Kaye. Pat Duggan, a Goldwyn story editor, put out feelers to James Thurber, who said he would be willing to sell "The Secret Life of Walter Mitty" for $25,000. Goldwyn was incensed. "The character is worth about $2,500, or at the top, $3,500," he wrote Miriam Howell in his New York office. He ended up shelling out $15,000 for the rights, and $10,000 more for another Thurber favorite, "The Catbird Seat."

Goldwyn was also able to obtain the rights to a book that had attracted him while it was still in galleys. Few others saw the film possibilities of Gwethalyn Graham's *Earth and High Heaven,* because it dealt with a subject almost never discussed in fiction or motion pictures.

Anti-Semitism became a festering problem in the United States in the 1940s—"worse than it has been in years," Goldwyn noted in a letter to Jack Warner. Rabbi Edgar Magnin suggested that "the country needed a scapegoat for the pain it was suffering, and so a lot of people said to themselves, 'If there were no Jews, there'd be no Hitler.'" *Earth and High Heaven* was directed at that backlash. It was the story of a well-born Canadian

Protestant girl and a poor but talented Jewish lawyer who want to marry; her anti-Semitic father disapproves. Goldwyn purchased the rights for $100,000 and considered it an investment in something greater than financial returns. "Personally," he wrote his son, "I believe it is a great love story—and as for the conflict over the Jewish question, it's something that has never been done before and that's a contribution I want to make for the screen and I think it can be done through this great love story."

Ring Lardner, Jr., was the first to take a crack at it—shortly after co-writing the screenplay for *Woman of the Year,* the first of nine pictures that would team Spencer Tracy with Katharine Hepburn. Howard Koch, after writing *Casablanca,* completed four drafts before throwing in the towel. Elmer Rice, whose *Counsellor-at-Law* had touched on similar themes a decade earlier, wrote three versions himself. From the start, Goldwyn had envisioned casting a tall, dark-haired newcomer, Gregory Peck. In 1947, however, Darryl Zanuck bought the rights to an even bigger book on the subject of anti-Semitism, *Gentleman's Agreement,* and Elia Kazan directed Peck in the film version. Goldwyn gradually lost interest in his project and after six years junked it. Not making that one film haunted him more than most of his failures.

The only Goldwyn project that showed steady progress was MacKinlay Kantor's novel in verse. "Just now I am extremely grateful to you for having instigated this story," he wrote Goldwyn in October, seventy manuscript pages in; "I should not have begun writing it at this time except for your enthusiasm and compulsion." By January, he was writing the screen treatment from his completed novel.

Glory for Me follows three servicemen, honorably discharged for medical causes, who return to the same hometown. In peacetime Boone City (modeled after Cincinnati), they had come from different walks of life and not known each other; now the lives of the three veterans become enmeshed.

The novel's central figure is Fred Derry—"twenty-one, and a killer of a hundred men"—a former soda jerk, now an Air Force lieutenant decorated many times over. Joining him is Homer Wermels, seaman second class, who had left home engaged to the girl next door, only to return a drooling and convulsing spastic. The third passenger in the homeward-bound B-17 is Alton Marrow Stephenson III, Harvard '24, assistant vice president of the Cornbelt Trust and Savings, and now a sergeant. He returns to his wife, Milly, and their two grown children, and finds himself uncomfortable with their cushy lives.

Kantor's book is a cynical tale of readjustment. In chronicling but a few events—the arrival of each veteran at his home, being reunited with his family, a drunken night on the town—Kantor reveals the psychological problems peculiar to the men who had been overseas. The most significant plot development involves Fred's discovering his wife, Marie—whom he had known less than two weeks before he married her and shipped out— with another man. He leaves her at the beginning of the novel and is drawn to Al's daughter, Peggy, by the end. The rest of the 268 pages are bitter impressions of life for the returning warriors.

The only writer Goldwyn thought could possibly translate the text into drama was Robert Sherwood. Unfortunately, Sherwood had given up screenwriting after *Rebecca* in 1940. Since then he had become a presidential aide and speechwriter and head of the overseas division of the Office of War Information. There had been rumors that he was eager to leave the government, so Goldwyn sent him Kantor's treatment. He was impressed but said he was more interested just then in writing a war play of his own, "The Rugged Path." Goldwyn told Sherwood he would wait until it was completed before assigning anyone else to the script. Pride, even more than practicality, made Goldwyn wait for the three-time Pulitzer Prize winner. Goldwyn had become rich during the war, almost entirely off escapist comedies, but the serious trophies of his profession still eluded him. At sixty-five, he believed his only chance for realizing his dreams was in embracing the character who had carried him this far, that self-invention that stood for quality, "the Great Goldwyn."

As he became one of Hollywood's leading purveyors of comedies during the war, so too did he become the number one butt of the town's jokes. Goldwynisms—as his colorful misuses of English were popularly referred to—abounded. With so many gag writers working for him, hardly a lunch in Hollywood went by without somebody's concocting a malapropism and passing it off as something Sam Goldwyn had just said to him. No Hollywood column was complete without a risible reference to Goldwyn. Myriads of funny sayings were thus falsely attributed to the producer: "We've passed a lot of water since then," he purportedly told a long-lost friend; "I've been laid up with intentional flu"; "I would be sticking my head in a moose"; "Anything that man says you've got to take with a dose of salts." Upon being informed that a sundial told time by the sun, Goldwyn was alleged to have remarked, "My God, what'll they think of next?" Garson Kanin was certain his former boss never said, "A verbal agreement isn't worth the paper it's written on." Chaplin took credit for sticking an old music hall gag on Goldwyn: "I can answer you in two words. Im possible." At least a dozen different people have claimed Goldwyn uttered "Include me out" in their presence—on twelve different occasions. Averell Harriman often used the phrase during diplomatic negotiations and always credited his friend.

In 1943, while Sammy was in college and the object of considerable ribbing from his schoolmates because of his father's clownish image, Goldwyn sought somebody to clean up his act. Albert Lasker recommended one of his disciples—Benjamin Sonnenberg, a short, shiny-domed New Yorker with a walrus mustache, who had become the leading figure in the burgeoning business known as public relations. "You must understand this was Tycoon Territory. Big shot stuff," Sonnenberg later recalled of those early days. "It was like the Cabots and the Lodges. Lasker spoke only to Goldwyn and Goldwyn spoke only to Lasker." Sonnenberg and Goldwyn met on Labor Day at the beach house of Harry Warner's daughter Doris and agreed on a thousand-dollar-a-week deal, guaranteed for two years. Sonnenberg's task, he said, was "to transform him from Mr. Malaprop into an English don."

The first step in making Goldwyn over was to write "a definitive brief" entitled "Samuel Goldwyn—The Man Versus the Legend." It was a twenty-three-page report that presented the "basic publicity line which I was anxious to have used in all stories to be published about you." It stressed the uniqueness of Goldwyn, his independent stands and his attraction to fine writing. Of the countless gags circulated about his "alleged peculiarities of speech," Sonnenberg said: "At first they were amusingly tolerated by Mr. Goldwyn in a spirit of sportsmanship—something like the way old Henry Ford laughed at the old 'tin lizzie' jokes."

Then Sonnenberg tried "to get space in organs of quality." For several months, he got Hedda and Louella, Winchell and Lyons, to lay off the Goldwynisms with promises of scoops. He arranged for profiles of Goldwyn to appear in magazines whose readers would ordinarily look down on articles about motion picture people.

Over the next few years, a slew of articles expounding high-minded positions toward motion pictures appeared under Samuel Goldwyn's byline. Frances Goldwyn wrote several pieces about her life in service to this great man. The Goldwyn name appeared everywhere, from the Congressional Record to Muriel Stafford's handwriting analysis column in the New York *Mirror,* in which she said his "altruistic f and y" revealed "he's very romantic and warm-hearted." After a year of Sonnenberg's services, the two men dissolved their agreement. Goldwyn saw that he could generate as much positive publicity as he wanted by himself. Sonnenberg later admitted he had learned as much from Goldwyn as from anybody else "in my black magic racket."

But Sonnenberg worked periodically for Goldwyn over the next few years, making occasional contacts for him and offering his New York town house when Goldwyn needed a special place to entertain. Shortly after he went off the payroll, Sonnenberg remembered, "I was telling Goldwyn he didn't really need me, that he should just be himself." Goldwyn's eyes burned into him, and then he roared with laughter. "For that," he said, "I had to pay fifty thousand dollars!"

With their charming absence of malice, Goldwynisms made a permanent comeback, though most people in Hollywood had not realized they had ever left. In time, everybody would hear that in trying to console Billy Wilder after one of his films flopped, Goldwyn told him not to feel too bad: "You gotta take the sour with the bitter." Walter Winchell reported Goldwyn's winning a recent argument, saying, "We are dealing in facts, not realities!" Walking from the dining room at Laurel Lane into the den one night, Goldwyn asked Myrna Loy, "Whatever happened to that little guy in Ethiopia—Hail Salesia." Goldwyn was quick to laugh along with anyone who tittered at the malapropisms in his presence, but in one session with Hilde Berl, his eyes teared as he blurted a tormenting truth—"I hate my mouth!"

Hilde Berl pointed out that the Goldwynisms were not going to disappear, no matter how good his public relations. She reminded him that these gags were good publicity, and actual or not, they were invariably clever and affectionate. "So I asked Sam Goldwyn," she recalled, "whether he wanted to be a master of these Goldwynisms or slave to them." It was a simple question of self-esteem.

At one of Elsa Maxwell's next parties, the guests played a parlor game in which each had to write his own epitaph. Sam jotted three words: "Include me out."

Except for his new sense of relaxation about his speech, Goldwyn marched through his day with as much precision as the vagaries of his profession would allow. He generally rose just before dawn and immediately reached for the bedside telephone, a private line he used only for talking to James Mulvey in New York. After discussing every foreseeable piece of business for the day and grosses of the night before, he performed an hour of rigorous calisthenics. His breakfast tray arrived, carrying the Los Angeles newspapers, the trade papers, two strips of bacon, two boiled eggs, orange juice, coffee, and an assortment of pills. He enjoyed a visit from a doctor, who would get him through one more day.

He showered, then dressed his firm, barrel-shaped body—a forty-one-inch chest and forty-inch waistline. His suits were all smartly tailored Savile Row, woolen weaves, usually in gray. T. Hodgkinson Ltd., in St. James's, made his shirts, Sulka his ties and handkerchiefs. Lobb of London made his shoes; and, observed Irene Mayer Selznick, "He was the best shod man in town." Goldwyn carried nothing in his pockets—no wallet, no money, no keys; friends commented that "he didn't want to ruin the line of the clothes." He smelled faintly of The Gentleman's Knize Ten, a sweet fragrance of sandalwood.

By eight forty-five, he was out the door, striding down Laurel Lane toward Sunset Boulevard, then east onto the Strip as far as Holloway, which cut down to Santa Monica Boulevard—three miles. There the chauffeured Cadillac that had been tailing him picked him up and drove him the rest of the way to the studio. With Frances reporting to the studio every day for work as well, he sometimes varied the routine. They would drive together from the house and walk the last half hour of the trip, arriving in their respective offices by nine-thirty, in later years at ten.

Goldwyn would enter his office through the back stairs, then buzz his secretary when he was ready to begin work. He insisted the temperature be a steady seventy degrees, often difficult to regulate because his outside door was to be kept open except in extremely cold or rainy weather. No windows were permitted open. Goldwyn relied on natural light; lamps were to be lit only on especially gloomy days. His secretary was expected to check the thermostat several times a day.

A procession of highly efficient women served as Goldwyn's secretary, each lasting many years on the job. The secret to holding the position lay in anticipating the boss's whims. Goldwyn would see no visitors from off the lot without appointments, except for those people the secretary presumed he would want to see. These included the top agents in town—Charles Feldman, Abe Lastfogel from William Morris, and Bert Allenberg. "Mr. Goldwyn likes his desk kept as clean as possible, inside as well as on top," one secretary instructed her successor. He did not want to be bothered with any mail that was less than essential. Registered letters—generally presaging legal trouble—were always refused unless the secretary was "absolutely certain it is something the company will want to accept." His secretaries learned to inspect his wastebasket every night to be certain he had not thrown out something that belonged in the files. Because he was obsessive about ridding the office of rubbish, they frequently cleaned the cabinets. One secretary asked if it was all right to discard a large batch of yellowing files. Goldwyn said yes—"just so long as you make copies of everything."

Three telephones sat on the secretary's desk. Two connected with Goldwyn's phone; the third connected with Frances Goldwyn's office, down the hall. Before a call would be announced to Goldwyn over the Dictograph, the other party had to be holding on the phone—"as Mr. Goldwyn will not wait." Beside the secretary's typewriter in the outer office were earphones; she was expected to monitor his conversations and make notes.

"One drawback to this," one of them noted, "is that Mr. Goldwyn automatically expects you to know *everything* that is going on, forgetting that you can't, for instance, listen in when he is home or in his dressing room." The sole exception to the secretary's eavesdropping on calls was whenever the Goldwyns were talking to each other. Another private telephone sat in a cabinet in Goldwyn's office; nobody but him was ever to touch it—"no matter how often or how long it rings." It was another hot line to Mulvey.

Goldwyn went to his private suite for lunch a little after noon. His dining room could seat as many as twelve, but generally served one or two important guests or a handful of his most important staff members. His own chef prepared a hearty hot meal, light on sauces. Josephine Berger, his cook of many years, could always delight him with his favorite dishes, Hungarian goulash or pot roast with potato latkes. Goldwyn counted calories, but he never pushed away Miss Berger's pastries or a dish of ice cream. His body weight of 175 pounds almost never changed over his entire adult life.

Luncheon was over by two o'clock, at which time employees excused themselves and returned to work. Almost nobody knew what Sam Goldwyn did until three o'clock every afternoon. No meetings were scheduled, and his secretary told all callers that he was in private conference. In fact, Goldwyn retired to a room off the dining room, where he completely disrobed, hung up his clothes, put on a pair of pajamas, and napped until his secretary telephoned him one hour later.

Goldwyn would work until five forty-five, then begin his journey home. The driver would take him as far as the Beverly Hills border, where Doheny Drive met Sunset Boulevard, and Goldwyn would walk the rest of the way. Because he carried no keys, he entered the house through the delivery entrance near the kitchen, never the front door. He would bathe and change clothes before dinner.

Guests would be invited for seven-thirty. Cocktails (one finger of Old Ben Ledi Scotch for Goldwyn) were served for twenty-five minutes. Then the hosts made their way into the dining room—whether their guests had arrived or not. William Dozier remembered being invited to dine with the Goldwyns in 1946, just before he married Joan Fontaine. He and Miss Fontaine (whom Goldwyn was trying to interest in *Earth and High Heaven*) arrived at Laurel Lane exactly at the appointed hour, only to discover the driveway completely empty and no signs of life coming from the house. They concluded they were either early or had arrived on the wrong night, so they drove down the hill to the Beverly Hills Hotel for a drink. They returned to the Goldwyns' a little after eight, but instead of being ushered into the living room, they were led directly to the dining room, where the

Goldwyns sat eating soup with one other couple and two empty chairs, place settings before them. (The Kirk Douglases had the same experience the first time they were invited to 1200 Laurel Lane.) Other hostesses in town knew to notify Frances if they did not expect to have food on the table by eight o'clock, so that she could feed Sam a sandwich beforehand. The Goldwyns served wine at their table, but he never drank any. In fact, he did not believe one should drink anything while eating, not even water. He took a cup of coffee after every meal and water (without ice) in between. After dinner, he would light a cigarette, puff it two or three times, and hold it while the ash grew long. Frances, with her fear of fire, used to grind out her cigarette in an ashtray, then pour the crushed remains into an envelope, which she would put back in the ashtray for a servant to clear. After a party, she would spend an hour checking every room for any un-extinguished cigarettes.

On nights out, Goldwyn liked to be home by eleven, but he was no stick-in-the-mud. "Sam Goldwyn had the best time at a party," observed George Cukor. "He acted as though every party were given just for him, and he was always on his best behavior in public." At a party at the Lewis Milestones' in 1944, Arthur Hornblow, Jr.,'s wife, Leonora, witnessed a rare instance in which Goldwyn lost his composure and a lot more. A simple buffet was set up next to a lot of bridge tables for the dozens of guests. Mrs. Hornblow noted:

Sam was the first back at his table with a plate *laden* with food. Although I was looking at him, I'll never know how it happened, but he must have tripped, as he certainly lost his balance and fell right into the bridge table which, of course, collapsed. The glasses were broken and Sam was soaked. A chicken leg stuck like a flower behind his ear. All the china on the table was broken as well as the glasses. There were quite a few glasses as they served two kinds of wine as well as water. The women's purses were drenched as was the rug. Sam and the entire collapsed table had to be taken away. The horror note is that everyone burst into wild, uncontrollable and un-ending laughter, especially me. And Sam unable to bear the idea that he had been so clumsy turned upon me and said, "You pushed me."

Goldwyn sulked for days if he heard about a glamorous party to which he had not been invited; it made him feel like just another pawn on the Hollywood chessboard.

In their separate bedrooms, Sam and Frances were each sleeping a little more soundly those days. He was contributing $60,000 a year to more than fifty different charities. His donation to the United Jewish Welfare Fund soared to $25,000. He never lost his itch to gamble, but the fever had broken. In lieu of the all-night poker games, he seemed just as happy settling for smaller bets—on anything. The only way he found baseball games tolerable was in betting on each pitch. In July 1944, he bet socialite Evalyn Walsh MacLean $500 (to her $250) that FDR would not run again. Weeks later, he wrote Sammy, "While I have never voted for him, as you know, and while I'm as bitterly opposed to a fourth term as I was to a third, I feel it would be a mistake to change governments at this time."

Goldwyn actively supported the Roosevelt-Truman ticket. In addition to the $5,000 he and Frances each contributed to the Democratic National Committee, he solicited more than $50,000 from others in town. He sent congratulatory messages to the President after each major speech, assuring him of his faith and support. On December 1, President Roosevelt wrote Goldwyn "just . . . to tell you how deeply I appreciate the loyalty and confidence which prompted you to work so hard in my behalf." In January, Goldwyn wrote the President again to congratulate him on "the happy occasion of the inauguration of your fourth term and the equally happy occasion of your birthday." He asked national committeeman Edwin Pauley if the President would autograph a picture for him.

In February 1945, Roosevelt's administrator of the Federal Economic Administration asked Goldwyn to proceed to England on a confidential mission as special adviser. The government wanted him to inspect battle-torn Britain and report on the country's economic circumstances, specifically in terms of Reverse Lend-Lease and Mutual Aid. On the seventeenth, the Army's Air Transport Command flew Goldwyn from New York to London, where he bivouacked at Claridge's. Over the next three weeks, he visited aircraft, motor, and munitions plants engaged in war work; he also inspected hospitals and various bombed parts of the city. He had a two-and-a-half-hour lunch with Winston Churchill. "That was really the high spot of my visit to England," Goldwyn wrote his longtime friend Colonel William Paley afterward, "as I found him tremendously interesting." He told one reporter that he thought Churchill would make a good film star because he was "the greatest poisonality" in Britain.

On February 28, Goldwyn went to Coventry, where the mayor escorted him through the ruins of their great cathedral. Goldwyn said it was "the saddest thing I have ever seen in my life." The next morning, he left for Oxford, where he took tea at Balliol College and delighted his capped and gowned audience when he said he was so impressed with the university that "you can include me in."

Goldwyn made time in his busy schedule to visit with J. Arthur Rank, who in the mid-thirties founded a distribution company and committed himself to the revitalization of the British film industry. Within a decade, the Rank Organisation owned several English film studios, Denham and Pinewood among them. Its trademark of a squat, muscular man beating a gong sounded the advent of an ambitious new generation in British cinema. Rank distributed the successful Alec Guinness comedies made at Ealing Studios, as well as the early works of such directors as David Lean (*Great Expectations* and *Oliver Twist*), Carol Reed (*Odd Man Out* and *The Fallen Idol*), and Laurence Olivier, who produced, codirected, and starred in *Henry V*. (Its success encouraged him to proceed with a film version of *Hamlet*.)

Goldwyn's report to the FEA recommended a program of documentary films that would capture England's present circumstances and show the "two-sidedness" of Lend-Lease.

"For the present," the London journal *Picture Post* reported Goldwyn as saying, "the film industry is taking a breath . . . before its plunge into the future." No doubt thinking of his having put *Glory for Me* in abeyance, he said, "What the public wants now is escapist films—melodrama, entertainment. The great films about the war won't come for another five years at least."

A series of distractions contributed that spring to the calm that Goldwyn had predicted. An endless succession of parties celebrated each piece of favorable war news. The Goldwyn organization in New York was settling into new offices in the RKO Building at Rockefeller Center. In Hollywood, two unions warring for jurisdiction over a group of set decorators made it practically impossible to hire any draftsmen or painters on the lot. And on April 12—a photograph still waiting to be signed and sent to Goldwyn from the Oval Office—Franklin Roosevelt suffered a cerebral hemorrhage. Goldwyn sent two telegrams to Washington that afternoon— one to Mrs. Roosevelt, the other to Harry Truman at the White House. "IN THIS HOUR OF OUR SORROW MAY WE WISH YOU STRENGTH AND THE BLESSINGS OF HEAVEN IN THE WORK THAT LIES AHEAD OF YOU. WE PLEDGE YOU OUR SUPPORT AND OFFER YOU OUR PRAYERS," he wired the new President. "I have confidence that Truman will make a success of his job," Goldwyn later wrote Sammy, then working through OCS at Fort Benning, Georgia. "I like him very much, and he has some very fine people around him."

After nine days of mourning, the Goldwyns threw themselves a party in honor of their twentieth wedding anniversary. Forty people arrived at Laurel Lane for dinner, and another forty afterward, Under Secretary of State Archibald MacLeish among them. Some of the guests stayed until six in the morning. Mrs. Goldwyn gave her husband a watch, inscribed: "April 23, 1945 meaning twenty happy years. Love Frances." Sam gave her a gold necklace and earrings. "I've never seen her look as lovely as she did Saturday night," he wrote Sammy of the occasion. "I'm very proud of her and the twenty wonderful years we've had together—and I'm just as proud of my son." He was also "very pleased that our marriage is considered one of the most successful in Hollywood." (The following year, Goldwyn's anniversary present to his wife was a legal document—a gift of pictures and associated rights that he owned, with the wish that "your ownership of these pictures [may] bring to you a small portion of the happiness which these twenty-one years have brought to me.")

Conforming to the President's wishes, there was no national holiday on May 8, 1945, V-E Day—only a hiatus of a few minutes during Truman's speech to the nation. The smell of victory in the air, Sammy contemplated his escape from the service. He told his father on the telephone that "if Japan suddenly surrendered I would resign. The reason being that my chances of getting out would be very much better as an enlisted man than as an officer." The father of Private Goldwyn, then just a few months away from becoming an officer, was greatly disturbed. "I feel that you ought to keep on trying just as hard to graduate as you did when you first went in," he wrote Sammy on July 31, 1945. "Never start a thing unless you can finish it—and you should make that apply to everything you do."

"Don't get the idea that I'm a quitter," Sammy wrote back, standing up to his father for the first time. "That really hurts coming from you. I never asked you to help me get a soft job did I? I took whatever I got and I've done it on my own. . . . I'm proud of that but once I get out of here the Army is going to be strictly passe. But it really hurts me for you to say things like you did in your last letter. My life has a lot more to offer me than being an Army man all my life. As long as there is a war on I'll do my best at whatever I'm assigned but afterward I want out but quick."

Three months later, the Japanese bowed down. America went on a thirty-six-hour spree from "V" Hour on Tuesday, August 14, when the Allies accepted Japan's unconditional surrender, through the following day. Studio employees were paid for their holiday. Each week brought the return of more soldiers, but Sammy stuck it out and graduated to second lieutenant, Company D, 112th Infantry Training Battalion, at Camp Robinson, Arkansas. During the months it took the Army to muster out its troops, he thought about Special Service. His father urged him not to "hesitate to call on me. After all, the war is over and any lift I can give you would seem to me to be perfectly legitimate." Sammy gave the high sign and through Goldwyn's contacts got assigned to the Public Relations

Division in the European Theater within weeks. Stationed in Germany, he worked on a number of projects, producing Army shows and writing press releases.

Hollywood war casualties seemed mercifully few, and the return of most of its leading men was an occasion in itself. MGM's 1945 release *Adventure* would be forgotten long before its advertising copy: "Gable's back and Garson's got him." Goldwyn's professional family came home virtually unscathed. Gregg Toland was back in time to photograph *The Kid from Brooklyn*. David Niven returned a hero, having served king and country from Dunkirk to Normandy; his other liege, Sam Goldwyn, had permitted him to appear in a number of service films during the war, as well as a few commercial ventures he thought might keep the actor's name before the public. Niven never got over the telegram from Goldwyn mentioning the possibility of his playing one of J. M. Barrie's most popular fictional heroes: "THINK CAN GET YOU ADMIRAL CRICHTON WITH PARAMOUNT," Goldwyn dictated to his secretary. Niven did not end up playing the Admirable Crichton, but Goldwyn loaned him out for several pictures before he had a movie of his own for his biggest, though not fully proven, star. A huge banner—"WELCOME HOME, DAVID"—was strung across the main gate of the Goldwyn lot, and a black-tie dinner was thrown in his honor.

No such tantara greeted Goldwyn's most anxiously awaited veteran. In 1944, Lieutenant Colonel William Wyler had made a highly praised documentary called *Memphis Belle*, the story of a Flying Fortress on its twenty-fifth mission over Germany. Wyler was furloughed when the film was released, and visited his wife at the Plaza Hotel in New York. The unusual way in which they met, coming toward each other down a long corridor, got indelibly etched in his memory.

Wyler returned to Europe to film another documentary, *Thunderbolt*, about the one-seat fighter planes that had helped liberate Italy. His photographer had not captured Rome and the Italian coastline exactly as he wanted it, so Wyler wedged himself in the waist of a plane and ran his own camera during a flight from Rome to Grosseto. The blasts of wind and engine noise had knocked Wyler's hearing out before, but this time it did not pop back in. His auditory nerves suffered severe damage. In time, partial hearing returned only to his left ear. He was shipped stateside by boat, then went through several Air Force hospitals, where doctors offered little hope. Lillian Hellman saw Wyler before he took the train home to Los Angeles. "I never saw anybody so thoroughly depressed in all my life," she remembered. "He was sure his career was over."

Fortunately, Wyler discovered that if he wore an earphone that hooked up to the sound engineer's equipment, his hearing was good enough to discern even the actors' inflections. The contract he had signed with Goldwyn before going overseas lessened his resentment over having to deliver one more picture to him. He was to receive $2,500 per week, plus 20 percent of its profits.

Wyler browsed along the shelf of Goldwyn's unproduced properties and found that only MacKinlay Kantor's *Glory for Me* excited him. He and Goldwyn agreed that nobody but Robert Sherwood could adapt such difficult material, that he was one of the few writers "able to present his political and economic ideas in a very solid, commercial form." In August 1945, when he learned that the playwright had completed *The Rugged Path*, Goldwyn arranged a meeting in Hollywood with Sherwood and Wyler. On the fourteenth, Sherwood signed the contract to write the film.

His play going into rehearsals, Sherwood returned to New York, in conflict over *Glory for Me*. He wrote Goldwyn that he had been thinking a great deal about the material and had concluded that, "in all fairness, I should recommend to you that we should drop it. This is entirely due to the conviction that, by next Spring or next Fall, this subject will be terribly out of date." Sherwood said he found Kantor's story fundamentally concerned with men who were medically discharged before the end of the war, which rendered them "somewhat lonely figures as veterans in a civilian community." He was sure the national picture would be "radically different when every American city has tens of thousands of soldiers and sailors who have returned to civilian life and who will already have passed through the first stages of readjustment before this picture can be released." He even thought the picture would arouse "considerable resentment" in suggesting that the neuroses of the minority of veterans were typical of all returning servicemen. To prove he was not simply reneging, Sherwood told Goldwyn he would gladly work on some other story for him. A volley of calls did not change Sherwood's mind.

A telegram from Sam Goldwyn on September 4 did. "DEAR BOB," he wired:

I HAVE BEEN THINKING OVER THE TELEPHONE CONVERSATION WE HAD THE OTHER NIGHT AND I WANT TO RESTATE MY FEELINGS ABOUT THE STORY. I HAVE MORE FAITH IN IT NOW THAN I HAD SIX MONTHS AGO BECAUSE I FEEL THE SUBJECT MATTER WILL BE EVEN MORE TIMELY A YEAR FROM NOW THAN IT IS TODAY. AS YOU SAID, THERE WILL BE SEVERAL MILLION MEN COMING HOME NEXT YEAR, AND MORE OF THEM THE YEAR AFTER AND TO RELEASE A PICTURE AT THAT TIME PRESENTING THEIR PROBLEMS SEEMS TO ME TO BE HITTING IT RIGHT ON THE NOSE. . . . YOU HAD THE RIGHT AP-

PROACH TO THE CIVILIAN POINT OF VIEW IN THE STORY AND THIS,
COUPLED WITH YOUR DESIRE TO INJECT SOME GOOD AMERICAN HU-
MOR THROUGHOUT, SHOULD MAKE IT ONE OF YOUR OUTSTANDING
WRITING JOBS. THIS IS THE STIRRING, EMOTIONAL STORY I WOULD
LIKE TO PRODUCE, AND THE POINT OF VIEW YOU EXPRESSED WHEN
YOU WERE OUT HERE CONVINCED ME THAT IF WE KEEP THE PROPER
ENTHUSIASM FOR OUR PROJECT IT CAN BE THE IMPORTANT PICTURE
OF THE YEAR.

Sherwood agreed that as soon as his play had opened, he would attack the material. The Goldwyns went to New York to celebrate.

HIS thoughts turning to his first autumns in America, Goldwyn took Frances upstate to what had been the capital of luxury during his salad days—Saratoga Springs. There, thirty miles from Gloversville, Sam Goldfish had gone whenever he had been able to scrape together the trolley fare. In those days, he could only afford to go for a few hours, just long enough to imagine possibilities.

Goldwyn's arrival made local headlines—"ONE TIME GLOVE SALESMAN, NOW CINEMA GREAT." When the program chairman of the men's club of the Kingsborough Avenue Presbyterian Church in Gloversville heard that the town's favorite son was nearby, he hand-delivered an invitation to speak at the group's meeting that Tuesday night. Goldwyn refused—until he received a call from his first employer in the glove business, Albert Aaron. Goldwyn made a dinner date with him and agreed to address the men's club afterward.

Frances Goldwyn had never seen her husband in such a state of nerves as he evidenced on October 30, 1945. He went back and forth through his suits in the hotel room closet, trying to decide which to wear. He did the same with his ties. Then he started on Frances's wardrobe. Three times along the road to Gloversville, Goldwyn told the chauffeur to pull over so that he could run into the bushes.

The car at last reached the town's tower of splendor. The Kingsborough Hotel was somewhat the worse for four decades of wear, but the marble floors and mahogany walls Sam Goldfish had remembered all those years still gleamed. He paused to look at the large plate-glass windows that had once fascinated him. Well-wishers jammed the lobby of the hotel. As Goldwyn entered, old glove moguls who had known Goldwyn when—Albert Aaron, Theodore Lehr, Adam Klopot—swarmed around him. Another man approached Goldwyn and touched his arm, saying that in the far end of the lobby was someone who wanted to know if he remembered Hamburg.

Goldwyn froze. "Looking startled," Frances recalled, "you headed across the lobby. I followed. In one of those leather chairs I'd heard so much of was a very old man. You stared at him hard, then said, 'Why, of course . . . of course.' And you put your arms around him." It was Jacob Liebglid—now spelled Libglid—who had taken in the teenage runaway Schmuel Gelbfisz back in Hamburg and helped him get to his aunt in England. Amazingly, just months after Sam Goldfish had left Gloversville for New York City in 1906, Libglid left Germany for Gloversville. The two men had not seen each other since the old country. Libglid was living in the hotel, still working in the local industry. Goldwyn, his eyes moistening, asked if he needed anything. Libglid said, "No, I'm a pretty good glove maker."

"Good?" Albert Aaron interrupted. "He's the best in my plant, the best in America."

Some sixteen people, Libglid included, went into the dining room, where the hotel served its finest meal. Everybody reminisced, then talked about the declining state of the local industry. From the way her husband joined in, Frances realized he could "still manage fairly well in gloves."

They all walked into another room for the club meeting. Frances was the only woman there. She chose a seat in the back row, which was empty except for one man. He looked her over, looked again, and hurried away. Goldwyn went to the front of the hall, where he was introduced. He was so nervous that he forgot to put his hat down—he just fidgeted with it throughout his short speech. "Gentlemen," he said, "this is the most exciting moment of my life. Gloversville to me and coming here tonight is like coming home. I have a great affection for this town. This is the place that gave me my first start in life."

He said that Gloversville was where he got his first job and his citizenship papers—"which is perhaps the greatest gift to any man to become a citizen of this great country."

"When I was a boy my one outstanding ambition was to get enough money to have dinner in the Hotel Kingsborough," he said. "And after that I wanted to stroll through the lobby, back and forth, in front of the window and watch the pretty girls as they walked up and down the street. I realized my ambition, but couldn't resist the impulse to do it again tonight while I was in the lobby." He told of his reunion with Jacob Libglid, and how that man had raised the money so that Goldwyn might continue on to America. Still fussing with his hat, he said, "Gentlemen, I would like to stay here all night and just talk to you, but that is impossible. I want to thank you from the bottom of my heart for allowing me to come here to talk to you. God bless you all."

By the time Sam had finished, the man who had eyed Frances so closely had returned to his seat. He poked her with a small package containing a pair of white kid gloves. "Put them on," he whispered. "In a minute you're going to be shaking hands with the club members." Frances did not understand at first, until the man pointed out that Frances's gloves were cotton—"for all sorts of reasons perfectly satisfactory," she realized, "except for wearing in Gloversville." That moment, she later told her husband, made her "understand something about Gloversville—and something more about you." The Goldwyns returned to Saratoga Springs, and a few days later to Los Angeles.

Within a month, Tiffany's sent a round gold pocket watch with Roman numerals—valued then at two hundred dollars—to the New Kingsborough Hotel (as it had been renamed). It was inscribed: "JACOB LIBGILD [*sic*]. A FRIEND INDEED. SAMUEL GOLDWYN." Libglid carried it with him everywhere he went. Locals remember his pulling it out on any occasion to call out the time, then regaling everyone around him with an amazing tale from an earlier time. Over the next few years, Libglid's health deteriorated. Goldwyn sent money regularly, right up to the octogenarian's death in 1950.

HOME from his sentimental journey, Goldwyn became consumed with adapting *Glory for Me.* After *The Rugged Path*'s short Broadway run, Robert Sherwood and his wife arrived in Los Angeles in early December 1945, with more than one hundred pages of screenplay. Sam and Frances put them up at Laurel Lane. They were free to come and go as they pleased; but for weeks Sherwood sequestered himself in the downstairs guest room before a typewriter. The two couples usually dined together, but Goldwyn made it a rule not to discuss the story. "Bob worked hard all day and I felt that he should relax and see a picture or meet people at night," Goldwyn later told Sherwood's biographer, John Mason Brown. "But during dinner one evening he said he would like to talk to me when we were through. After dinner he said, 'Sam, I feel I have failed you. I just can't get this story—something blocks me.'" Goldwyn told him, "I have had writers fail me before. Let's see what the trouble is."

Sherwood kept on talking, Goldwyn remembered, while his wife, Madeline, packed and Frances tried to get plane reservations for them to go home. After a couple of hours, Sherwood said, "Madeline, don't pack—and don't bother about the reservations. I'm going to my room and think about this." The next morning at seven o'clock, Goldwyn got word that Sherwood wanted to have breakfast with him. At the table, Goldwyn recalled, "he told me the story, scene for scene, just as it was finally put on the screen."

Sherwood had suddenly realized how he could turn MacKinlay Kantor's tone poem into a fugue, interweaving the three stories and transposing the entire piece from a minor to a major key. The secret lay in developing one dominant story line—the relationship between the banker's daughter, Peggy, and Fred Derry. Instead of allowing the former soda jerk to discover his wife with another man at the start of the piece, as Kantor had done, Sherwood imposed a more traditional three-act structure over the material. He allowed Fred to come home to his wife and try to pick up where his marriage had left off; then he would discover that neither of them loved the other; and not until the end of the film would he decide to leave her. At the same time, Sherwood needed to enlarge on the character of Peggy— so that Fred could meet the girl, lose the girl, then get the girl. In return for Sherwood's working three months on the script without any contractual obligation, Goldwyn pledged that "there would be no changes in or rewriting of his script."

Sherwood made all the other stories in the revised screenplay serve that central love story. The pivotal scenes in which Fred and Peggy meet, and when Fred breaks off their budding romance, would occur at a bar owned by Butch, the uncle of the spastic Homer. Fred and Peggy would finally come together at Homer's wedding to Wilma, the girl next door.

Goldwyn saw opportunities for all his young contract players. Dana Andrews would play Fred Derry; and Virginia Mayo had been progressing enough in her acting lessons to pull off the role of his floozy of a wife. Farley Granger could play the spastic, Homer, and Goldwyn's latest discovery, Cathy O'Donnell, could play Wilma. Teresa Wright would be Peggy Stephenson. Goldwyn had hoped to sign Fred MacMurray and Olivia de Havilland to play her parents, Al and Milly, but they found the roles too inconsequential; "third banana," said MacMurray. Leland Hayward suggested two of his clients, Fredric March and Myrna Loy. March's days as a leading man were over, and Goldwyn knew he would eagerly accept the role. Myrna Loy's popularity in "The Thin Man" series had made her the movies' "perfect wife" and kept her a star. Even though Goldwyn doubted she would ever accept so small a role, it took only one dinner at Laurel Lane to discover that her arm needed no twisting. "I had read the book," Miss Loy remembered, "and when Sam Goldwyn asked if I would play the part, I said, 'Yes'—fast." Though it was not the largest role in the film, hers was the biggest name and, accordingly, got top billing.

The only change in casting occurred because neither Wyler nor Sherwood thought spasticity was suitable for the screen. They figured any actor's accurate portrayal would be too grotesque to watch, and anything less than that would look phony. Wyler and Sherwood were visiting veterans' hospitals looking for character details when the director suddenly recalled an Army Pictorial Service documentary he had seen about a young sergeant who had lost both his hands. *Diary of a Sergeant* had been produced to help other amputees readjust to their lives. The star of the film was a former meat cutter named Harold Russell, who—as he explained—"got into an argument with a block of T.N.T. and lost. The score was two hands off about six inches above the wrist." He was fitted with a set of steel claws controlled by a shoulder harness and moved by elastic bands. More than Russell's mastery of his "hooks" interested Wyler; it was his acceptance of his disability. "That was just the attitude required for the role," said Wyler, "because in our story, Homer, in spite of his physical disability, makes a better adjustment than the other two veterans . . . who both had emotional disturbances caused by the war but no physical injuries." Harold Russell got the role intended for Farley Granger.

Sherwood spent the next few months rewriting. He credited Goldwyn for steering him from the politics of the drama toward more human interest. "I don't want you to think of this as a Hollywood picture," the producer told him. "I want something simple and believable."

On April 9, 1946, Sherwood submitted his final screenplay, which ran twice the length of a normal script. The plight of readjusting veterans and observations of postwar America were inherent in every scene, but the 220 pages proved to be a timeless drama about love and marriage. Sherwood found a new title, one full of hope and irony, in a phrase Marie Derry tossed off just before walking out on Fred on page 201: "The Best Years of Our Lives." Goldwyn found it cumbersome, but it would stand until something better came along.

Although he had exhibited extreme bravery over enemy skies during the war, Wyler promptly suffered a recurrence of nerves. He protested that the script was not ready, and he refused to proceed. Goldwyn explained that the entire cast had been put on salary and called to rehearse the next day. "They'll be here every day until you show up," Goldwyn warned him, thinking of the expense in delaying the production any further, "and you'll pay the difference." Before Wyler became paralyzed by his own fears, Goldwyn sent for the director's business manager and said, "I hope Mr. Wyler's got deep pockets."

Wyler showed up the next day, but the animosity between him and Goldwyn surfaced almost every morning after that in a clangorous fight, hammer and anvil pounding out some point or other—rages of the equally inarticulate that got their juices flowing. They played gin rummy together every Sunday.

Shooting began on April 15, with the Goldwyn team of Wyler and Toland and editor Mandell at the peak of their powers. Wyler was as demanding as ever, knowing exactly what he wanted once he had seen it. Gregg Toland observed that the war had affected his director's style in subtle ways. "Willy . . . had seen a lot of candid photography and lots of scenes without a camera dolly or boom," he noted. "He used to go overboard on movement, but he came back with, I think, a better perspective on what was and wasn't important." Black-and-white film enhanced the picture's realism. Toward that end, Wyler asked the costume designer, Irene Sharaff, not to create any fashions for the actors, but to take them to department stores where the characters would have shopped and have them wear the clothes for several weeks before showing up on the set.

Filming would continue for more than one hundred days. The first moment Wyler deviated even slightly from the Sherwood script—as he did in late May, deleting a phrase of dialogue—Goldwyn called him on it. In a letter of gentle reprimand, he reminded Wyler that he had vowed to Sherwood that the script would be filmed precisely as written, and that he wanted it "clearly understood . . . that there are to be absolutely no rewrites, no changes of any nature whatever in dialogue . . . without my approval in advance." Wyler obeyed.

He still had to suffer the usual indignities from his employer, but Wyler knew that Goldwyn had never given a director such free rein. The producer hardly even appeared on the set. The cast could remember few episodes in which the two prewar antagonists went after each other publicly. Harold Russell did recall one morning when Wyler did not arrive on the set until eleven. "That son of a bitch!" he fumed when he finally appeared. "He would like the credits to read Sam Goldwyn presents Sam Goldwyn in a picture called 'Sam Goldwyn,' Produced by Sam Goldwyn, Directed by Sam Goldwyn, Written by Sam Goldwyn!"

Goldwyn maintained his distance, and the result was the most realistic-looking film he ever produced. "You know, every so often we do pictures, we don't know our subject well enough," Wyler explained; "in this case . . . I knew my subject. I learned it the hard way and . . . somehow when you get personally involved in the story something gets on the screen that makes it human and real and improves the picture somehow and you can't put your finger on what it is, you know, but it's the director's personal involvement." Wyler explained that elusive quality in one word: "Truth."

The Best Years of Our Lives begins at Welburn Air Terminal, where three

GIs meet and board the same plane for Boone City. Homer is promptly introduced having to sign a piece of paper; his hooks prove to be no problem for him or for the soldiers around him. Within minutes, the audience witnesses Homer's reunion with his parents, younger sister, and Wilma:

He bends down and picks up the sea bag with his hooks. This is too much for Mrs. Parrish. She has tried to maintain her composure, but her heart is breaking, and she is forced into a great sobbing release of tears.

MED. CLOSE—MRS. PARRISH
She cannot control herself. Homer, greatly disturbed, comes close to her, and tries to comfort her.

HOMER
It's all right, Ma—don't cry.

MRS. PARRISH
It's—it's nothing, Homer—

MR. PARRISH
(gently taking Homer's arm)
It's just that your Ma is so glad to see you home.

Harold Russell performed a number of tricky scenes, designed to show his compensating for his handicap in the most unassuming way. During one shot in which he was having a drink with Fredric March, the old pro warned him, "When I say my lines, keep those goddamned hooks down! Don't lift that bottle of beer, because I want people listening to what I'm saying, not watching you drink beer."

"We got lucky with Harold Russell," said Wyler, "because he was an absolute natural." Goldwyn had enrolled him in acting classes, but the director insisted he ditch them. In the end, Russell compensated for lack of technique with integrity, which shone through his entire performance, even the love scenes.

Although everybody in the film got to perform a star turn, the strength of *Best Years* lay in its ensemble acting. Dana Andrews, as Fred, has several tough but touching moments with his father and stepmother—actors Roman Bohnen and Gladys George—who live on the wrong side of the tracks. In his scenes with Virginia Mayo, he shows a man fighting to maintain his dignity. And he proves to be especially tender opposite Teresa Wright, who was grateful to play her first "homewrecker" instead of the simpering ingenue roles in which she was getting typecast, roles that made Wyler call her "the best cryer in the business."

In preparing the film, Wyler had discovered in Ontario, California, a plane "graveyard"—an endless lot of row upon row of stripped-down bombers that had been constructed too late to see action. He described it to Sherwood. The writer immediately grasped its potential, how it could become the scene of Fred Derry's epiphany. Juxtaposed with his father's proud reading of Fred's citation for the Distinguished Flying Cross, Sherwood wrote of Fred's walking among the battered veteran bombers, stopping at one, its name painted on the nose:

> There are also four or five Nazi flags, and several rows of bomb symbols, records of missions. The engines have been taken out. Fred stops to look at this emasculated plane with nostalgic affection.
>
> He looks around, then climbs up into the fuselage.

Wyler created a scene of a bombing mission—the heavy sounds of flak and fighters and machine gun fire—entirely in Fred's imagination. Dana Andrews's facial expressions and the sound effects evoke the disturbing moment. It was enhanced by the music, largely an atonal representation of the sounds of the plane, starting with the revving of each engine.

To score *Best Years*, Goldwyn went as he always had to Alfred Newman, even though he had headed Twentieth Century–Fox's music department for the past five years. Newman recommended Hugo Friedhofer, a San Francisco–born musician who had gotten his first chance to score a picture when Newman suggested that Goldwyn hire him to write the music for *The Adventures of Marco Polo*. "I think Goldwyn still somehow thought Al was working for him," Friedhofer said years later. "This was years after Al had been head of music at Fox. Anyway, Goldwyn took his advice without question and I got the job even though William Wyler and others didn't want me."

The most conventional story in *Best Years* was that of Al Stephenson, the banker who comes home to find his family getting along perfectly well. Fredric March pulled out all his acting stops in quiet domestic moments with Myrna Loy and Teresa Wright as well as a few comic arias. His biggest scene is a drunken toast he makes at his bank's salutatory dinner for him.

March also became the focal point of one of the most ingenious shots ever printed on film. Al has met Fred at Butch's and told him he wants this extramarital dalliance with Peggy to stop. Fred agrees to telephone her right away. As he goes to the booth to make the call, Homer enters. He and Butch, played by songwriter Hoagy Carmichael, sit at a piano and perform a duet of "Chopsticks." Through the mastery of Gregg Toland, Wyler was able to stage both scenes in a single shot. Using deep focus, Toland enabled Wyler to situate Dana Andrews at the top-left-hand corner of the frame and the other three around the piano in the lower right. The camera eye was kept on Fredric March, and an audience could absorb both pieces of drama, understanding Fred's call to Peggy without having to hear a word of it, just by seeing him in the distance as Al did.

Even Goldwyn, who was never interested in the mechanics of filmmaking, understood that Toland's cinematography in this picture was exceptional. He rewarded him with his own full frame in the credit titles, and he displayed Toland's name in most of the advertising posters.

Yet another moment in the film captured the spirit of the entire nation as it came home from the war in all its pain and glory: It practically summed up the decade. Fredric March arrives at his apartment, his children answer the door, and he shushes them, asking where their mother is.

INT. LIVING ROOM

It is small, but attractively, comfortably furnished.

We are looking out through open French windows to a small terrace, where MILLY is setting the supper plates on a card table. It is just about sunset. There are three chairs. Milly looks young and alluring and very much alive.

MILLY

Who was that at the door?
                (she turns to look in the living room)
Peggy! Rob! Who was . . .

Suddenly, instinctively, she knows. Throughout these years, Al has always been there, in her mind, and she has been thinking of the moment when he would walk in that door.

She puts down a plate, hard, and goes to the French windows leading into the living room. She sees Al, as he comes through the door from the corridor on the other side of the room.

For a while, both of them just stand there, looking at each other, appraisingly, almost suspiciously, as though they were strangers. Their silence is strained, intense. . . .

Wyler recalled his own reunion with his wife at the Plaza Hotel, their walking down the corridor toward each other, and he staged it exactly that way. The emotion of every wife awaiting her husband's return could be read on Myrna Loy's face. Teresa Wright told the actress she thought it was so effective a moment because there was "real love in that scene." Later Miss Loy revealed the "motivation" that made it work. She said, "They just can't wait to get into the sack."

Halfway through filming *Best Years*, Wyler panicked. His doubts this deep into the picture started to rub off on Goldwyn. They both liked everything that had been filmed so far, but they feared that the scenes were not building to a climax. They grew anxious for Sherwood to write new pages that would punch up the end of the movie. Sherwood was not concerned. He believed all the characters arrived at dramatic and logical conclusions and that the three men meeting at Homer's wedding to Wilma, with the suggestion of Fred and Peggy pursuing their romance, was a resounding finale. For days, frantic communiqués between the two coasts filled Goldwyn with qualms. Wrestling with the script one midnight, he instinctively reached for the phone and dialed Sherwood in New York, oblivious of the time differential. As soon as Sherwood picked up the receiver, Goldwyn started in with his latest thoughts—stopping only when a groggy Sherwood asked, "Sam, do you have *any* idea what time it is?" The next thing Sherwood heard was Goldwyn's calling out, "Frances, Frances . . . Bob wants to know what time it is!"

Sherwood stood by his script as written, talking Goldwyn and Wyler through the remaining scenes so they might appreciate the impact of the simple ending and all its implications. What Sherwood could not convince Goldwyn of, the Breen Office could. It found the film's ultimate message more than potent. It was poison.

The Production Code Administration, under Joseph I. Breen's iron hand, had many objections to the script of *The Best Years of Our Lives*. They suggested that the scenes having to do with the breakup of the marriage between Fred and Marie be rewritten, "in order to get away from any suggestion of a condonation of this tragedy." A subsequent letter from Breen's office said that Peggy's home-wrecking intentions would have to be eliminated. The rest of the Breen Office litany cited such cinematic sins as a "passionate" kiss between Milly and Al, a "vulgar" belch after Al downed a Bromo Seltzer, and any scenes involving alcoholic beverages. Producers were "free to accept or disregard any observations or suggestions" made by the Breen Office, but the Motion Picture Association fined a producer $25,000 for releasing any picture without the seal of approval of the Production Code Administration.

As late as sixty days into production, the Breen Office was still trying to impose its morality on the film—what Ben Hecht called "Mother Goose platitudes and primitive valentines . . . [where] there are no problems of labor, politics, domestic life or sexual abnormality but can be solved happily by a simple Christian phrase or a fine American motto." Goldwyn replied that he would make no alterations—"since we believe this ending is honest, true, and within the bounds of decency and good behavior." When it realized Goldwyn had no intention of backing down, the Breen Office retired its objections, leaving an irreparable chink in the code.

Best Years wrapped on August 9, 1946—with 400,000 feet of film "in the can." While the Goldwyns vacationed at the Moana Hotel at Waikiki Beach, Danny Mandell, in concert with Wyler, assembled a rough cut of the film that was 16,000 feet, about twice the length of most movies. Goldwyn knew that two hours and forty minutes of motion picture was too long to release, but when he watched it upon his return, it never felt long. On October 17, they sneak-previewed the film in a small neighborhood house, the United Artists Theater in Long Beach, hoping the audience would indicate where they might cut an hour out of the film. Goldwyn's staff sat in the back of the theater with stopwatches, at first timing between audience responses, then discovering long patches of rapt silence. Danny Mandell said "people stopped chewing their gum." There was a pregnant hush after the lovers' clinch at the finale, then a burst of applause that did not quit for several minutes. The audience's response cards were overwhelmingly favorable, almost unanimous in unqualified praise. Out on the curb, the Goldwyn staff held its conference—Sam and Frances, Mandell, production head Leon Fromkess, and a dozen others. Wyler approached them and asked if they could release a film that long. Goldwyn said they had no choice, that there seemed to be but one hundred feet to trim at most. After each test screening that followed, someone would timidly suggest a scene that might be sacrificed. "If I'd listened to them all," Goldwyn commented later, "the only thing left would have been the credits."

Goldwyn's decision to release the film in its entirety was more than a $2.1 million gamble. Theaters would be naturally loath to exhibit the film not only because of its unusual subject matter but also because its length would dictate half the number of usual screenings. He secured a booking at the Hollywood Pantages Theater for January 1947 and looked forward to opening it in New York shortly after that. When Wyler learned of these plans, he lit a fire under his producer. He suggested that *Best Years* would almost certainly get nominated for some Academy Awards, and they stood a better chance if they opened in Los Angeles before the year-end deadline for qualification, rather than waiting until the following year and risking its being forgotten.

A New York tycoon named Robert Dowling owned the Astor, which prided itself on screening prestigious films; his approval was needed before he would run a film. Goldwyn took a print to New York to show to him. In exchange for a pair of theater tickets, he rented Ben Sonnenberg's Gramercy Park house for the night and ran the film in his private screening room. When the Sonnenbergs returned, they all drank champagne to celebrate the November 22 opening of *Best Years* at the Astor. While Dowling was still awestruck by the film, Goldwyn finagled one of the best rental agreements out of him he had ever gotten from any theater—40 percent of the gate. The producer used that to finesse other favorable contracts across the country.

In his $400,000 worth of advertising, Goldwyn created an air of distinction about *Best Years*. Certain theaters, like the Astor, would sell tickets only on a reserved-seat basis, some for as much as $2.40. Goldwyn arranged a screening of the film for Norman Chandler, publisher of the Los Angeles *Times,* and got him to promote the film in the paper's news section if the first night's Los Angeles proceeds were turned over to charity. The managing editor of the rival Hearst paper, the *Herald-Examiner,* said it would do the same if Marion Davies's pet charity was the recipient. The *Reader's Digest* announced a symposium—"Which are the Best Years of Our Lives?"—and Lynn Farnol lined up a team of famous writers to contribute responses. A representative from Louisiana took the floor of the House and said *The Best Years of Our Lives* should be "required seeing for every American. It is a credit to the United States, and I should like this made a matter of record in Congress." Virginia Mayo and Teresa Wright were photographed for covers of *Life.* Hoagy Carmichael plugged the film on his radio show; and it seemed as though all the other radio stars in America wanted Myrna Loy or Fredric March or Dana Andrews to appear on their shows.

Bob Hope wanted Goldwyn on his show. A few days before his appearance, Goldwyn asked one of his writers, Harry Tugend, what he ought to say on the air. Tugend wrote an exchange that Hope's writers liked. The comedian would say, "Well, Mr. Goldwyn, how have things been going since I left your studio?" Goldwyn would reply, "I'll tell you, Bob. Since you left, we've had the best years of our lives." Exactly as rehearsed, Goldwyn stood before the NBC microphone and Hope fed him his line: "Well, Mr. Goldwyn, how have things been going since I left your studio?"

"I'll tell you, Bob," he said confidently. "Since you left, things are better than ever."

The Best Years of Our Lives opened as scheduled at the Astor in New York and Christmas week at the Beverly Theater in Los Angeles. Goldwyn was petrified after the first noon show at the Beverly, which played to an almost empty house. For reasons he never figured out, a crowd gathered three hours later, and the evening show was packed. "The public doesn't know what they want until they see it," Goldwyn often said; "but it's a mystery to me [why they're drawn in the first place]—they smell it." In selling a picture, Goldwyn was ultimately certain of but one thing: "You can't beat the word of mouth."

He received unparalleled notices. Abel Green of *Variety* called the film "one of the best pictures of our lives." The *New York Times* said the film "sets the highest standards of cinematic quality and meets them triumphantly." *Newsweek* spoke of it as "epic" art; *Time* said Goldwyn had put together "a sure-fire hit . . . with good taste, honesty, wit—and even a strong suggestion of guts." James Agee grudgingly doled out words of praise on a story he found inherently pat and timid. He granted that "this is one of the very few American studio-made movies in years that seem to me profoundly pleasing, moving, and encouraging." In a follow-up article two weeks later in *The Nation,* he wrote: "I can hardly expect that anyone who reads this will like the film as well as I do. . . . But it is . . . a great pleasure, and equally true, to say that it shows what can be done in the factory by people of adequate talent when they get, or manage to make themselves, the chance." After the film had its Christmas-week qualifying run in Los Angeles, Goldwyn pulled the picture until its nationwide opening in the spring—at which time he hoped to garland the advertisements with Oscar nominations.

Best Years grossed close to ten million dollars in its first year of release. It became the second-biggest moneymaker in talking-picture history to date, bettered only by *Gone With the Wind.*

For months, letters both adulatory and congratulatory crossed Goldwyn's desk—from René Clair to General Omar Bradley, who told Goldwyn, "You are helping the American people to build an even better democracy out of the tragic experiences of this war." Secretary of the Navy James Forrestal said it was "a credit to both you and Industry." War correspondent Bill Mauldin said it was "the first real, honest-to-God sincere thing I've seen about the war and its aftermath."

The film had a healing effect on the wounds of the nation and, it seemed, of every citizen who saw it. No message moved Goldwyn more than the seventeen words Western Union relayed on the night of November 21. "I HAVE JUST SHED THE BEST TEARS OF MY LIFE. YOUR LOVING AND VERY PROUD DAUGHTER, RUTH." "When it is all said and done,"

Goldwyn wrote her back, "it's what our own think of us that really counts, and I don't mind admitting that I love being told you are proud of me, and I will always do my best to keep things that way."

On December 14, 1946, he and Frances had sailed from New York on the *Queen Elizabeth* for England. The Goldwyns spent the holidays with Sammy and arranged the London bookings of *Best Years*. The film opened there in the spring and played to crowded houses for over a year, grossing as much in its twenty-second week as it did in its second. It became a similar phenomenon everywhere in the world, from Sydney to Rio de Janeiro. It received the British Academy's award for the best foreign or domestic picture of the year, and several international equivalents—the French "Victoire," the Danish "Filmprisen," the Japanese "Hannya."

The Goldwyns returned to New York on the same ship, ringing in 1947 with the news that the New York Film Critics had voted *Best Years* the best picture of the year. On January 6, Goldwyn picked up a bronze plaque from the Newspaper Guild of New York, their Page One Award for his "outstanding presentation of the responsibilities of society to the returning servicemen." The Hollywood Foreign Correspondents Association presented him with their "Golden Globe."

Upon returning to Los Angeles, Goldwyn learned that he was for the seventh time in the running for the one prize that still remained beyond his grasp. *The Best Years of Our Lives* led that year's Academy Award nominations with eight—Best Picture, Best Actor (Fredric March), Best Supporting Actor (Harold Russell), Best Director, Best Screenplay, Best Sound Recording, Best Scoring of a Dramatic Picture, and Best Film Editing. *The Jolson Story* received six nominations and *The Razor's Edge* four, including Best Picture. The three other competitors for the top honor were Olivier's *Henry V*, Frank Capra's *It's a Wonderful Life*, and *The Yearling*. Goldwyn was not the favorite. *The Yearling* and *The Razor's Edge* were products of major studios, MGM and Twentieth Century–Fox, which voted in blocks; and Darryl Zanuck had already made it known that he intended to campaign hard for his Oscar.

NOVELIST Robert Nathan said, "Sam Goldwyn was so busy taking bows that year he didn't pay much attention to his other projects—my book among them." Goldwyn had two promising literary adaptations in the works that suffered from neglect, but he was leading a charmed life those days.

He had bought "The Secret Life of Walter Mitty" only because it sounded like a vehicle for the protean Danny Kaye. Its milquetoast of a hero was reminiscent of the old Eddie Cantor roles; and his daydreams would allow the star to play several different characters, sometimes in song. Goldwyn already envisioned the film in Technicolor, with a dozen Goldwyn Girls.

In order to make the four-thousand-word Thurber story work as a Danny Kaye picture, writers Ken Englund and Everett Freeman had to invent more than adapt. They changed Walter Mitty from a middle-aged henpecked husband into a younger bachelor hopelessly tied to his mother's apron strings. They made him a drudge in a publishing house of pulp fiction—a proofreader whose fantasies make it difficult for him to separate reverie from reality. To keep such a plot in motion, Mitty had to get involved in an actual melodrama more fantastic than any he had ever dreamed—one involving a foreign dignitary and his mysterious but beautiful daughter, spies, precious jewels, and a sinister psychiatrist.

In November 1945, Goldwyn brought the one-hundred-sixty-page script of *The Secret Life of Walter Mitty* to New York. He told Thurber the first sixty pages were all right and asked him not to read the last one hundred pages, because they were too "blood and thirsty." Thurber did read the entire script, and—as he later said—"I was horror and struck. Mr. Goldwyn expected me to remove the blood and thirst without reading it but somehow to preserve the melodrama. It was a task for wizards, stated in the wondrous dialectics of Oz."

Ken Englund also consulted with Thurber in New York. The former wanted to preserve as much of the flavor of the original story as possible, and the latter understood that the screenwriter had only been following orders. "We could not take out the melodrama," Thurber reported later of their ten days of work together, "but we could attempt to cover it up with additional dream scenes and other devices. . . . I wrote that a courtroom dream and a firing squad dream like those in my original story, together with a dozen other suggestions I made, might obscure or at least dilute the melodrama." Among these suggestions were several bits of physical comedy that struck Goldwyn as nothing more than rusty Keystone Kop routines. He decided Thurber had nothing more to say that was worth listening to.

The star's wife, on the other hand, did. Sylvia Fine felt too many of these new dream sequences "slowed up the story" and got in the way of the musical numbers she had prepared for her husband—material Thurber dismissed as "git-gat-gittle songs." The most famous of these to sneak into the film was her "Anatole of Paris," which demanded that Mitty become a French fashion designer in one of his fantasies.

One morning, some twenty people sat around a conference table to dis-

cuss the production of *Walter Mitty.* Goldwyn entered promptly at nine
o'clock to begin the meeting. Counting heads, he saw everybody from
Danny Kaye to propman Irving Sindler—everybody except Kaye's wife.
"Where's Sylvia?" Goldwyn asked. "She'll be here a little late," Kaye explained. "In the mornings she goes to the psychiatrist." Goldwyn turned
red and exploded, "Anybody who goes to a psychiatrist—should have his
head examined!"

Again Goldwyn made Virginia Mayo the beautiful object of Danny's
affections, this time rewarding her with co-star billing. Boris Karloff
played the villainous Dr. Hugo Hollingshead. Thurber was so embarrassed
by the production that he felt it necessary to defend himself publicly. He
vented his spleen in the pages of *Life,* where the editors reported that he
"grows almost profane when he thinks of how his story has been cor-
rupted." One psychiatric scene in particular, which Thurber had hoped
would be deleted, "had not only been restored," Thurber wrote, "but it
finally contained a bathing girl incident which will haunt me all the days
of my life."

"As I need not tell you, the original story, 'The Secret Life of Walter
Mitty,' is a pure gem, which added great luster to the little magazine in
which it was first published," a ghostwriter for Goldwyn wrote the *Life*
editors in retort. "However, in order to convert such a gem into a feature
length motion picture it is necessary first to elaborate it into a screenplay."
Author and producer debated for weeks.

The reviews pronounced the film solid entertainment, despite its devia-
tion from the source material. The public adored the movie, making *The
Secret Life of Walter Mitty* one of the year's biggest hits. Goldwyn heard
from dozens of people he respected, including Robert Sherwood, who
wired him that "with the exception of two or three spots," he thought the
film was "wonderfully good" and Kaye's performance "really brilliant."

Thurber had already accepted ten thousand dollars from Goldwyn as an
option payment on his story "The Catbird Seat." Five thousand dollars
more were due upon submission of a motion picture treatment, and another forty thousand dollars if Goldwyn produced a film of the story. Thurber returned the ten-thousand-dollar option payment with the hope that
Goldwyn would tear up their contract. The author told Miriam Howell
that he had "only the kindliest of feelings" toward Goldwyn personally; he
just could not endure another such adaptation of his material. If Goldwyn
chose to accept Thurber's terms, James Mulvey suggested that he send
Thurber a check for $2,500 to cover his legal and agents' fees. Gold-
wyn did.

"I defy every convention," Goldwyn told an interviewer that year. "I make a picture to please me—if it pleases me there is a good chance it will please other people. But it has to please me first." He admitted he was difficult but said he could not help that: "That's the way I make pictures. . . . Usually when people are happy making a picture it's a . . . *stinker.*" If the converse were true, Goldwyn's next picture had all the makings of a huge success.

Leonardo Bercovici's screenplay of *The Bishop's Wife* retold Robert Nathan's story of Henry Brougham—a bishop so desperate in his attempts to raise money from wealthy parishioners for a new cathedral that he has woefully neglected everybody else in his life, especially his wife, Julia. After a particularly discouraging meeting with his leading benefactress, Henry prays for help. From heaven arrives a devil-may-care angel named Dudley, whose miracles are more in the nature of prestidigitation. He wreaks change on the lives of everybody he encounters—including Henry, whom he makes jealous of his relationship with Julia. The bishop's love rekindled, Dudley realizes his work on earth is done and disappears, leaving neither trace nor memory of his visit, except for everybody's new acts of charity and love. Goldwyn thought the script lacked the whimsy of the source material.

He tried to entice his Oscar-nominated team to patch it up. William Wyler would have no part of it. As soon as he had completed his work on *Best Years,* Wyler had fulfilled all legal obligations to Sam Goldwyn. He would never deny that Goldwyn had sparked his career, but after ten years of the scourge, Wyler wanted nothing more to do with him beyond receiving his 20 percent of the profits on that final film. He joined a production company Frank Capra had organized for directors eager to be their own bosses. It was aptly named Liberty Films. The company lived long enough to see only its founder release pictures with its trademark of a huge tolling bell—*It's a Wonderful Life* and *State of the Union;* but over the next ten years, Wyler became his own producer, creating a string of important (though occasionally bloated) films, which included *The Heiress, Roman Holiday, Friendly Persuasion,* and *The Big Country.* Wyler never failed to invite Goldwyn to an early screening of each film—anxious for his approval, eager for his advice. "Nobody," Wyler claimed to the end, "knew how to market a picture like Sam."

Robert Sherwood found all the bones of *The Bishop's Wife* in place but thought its heart and soul were missing. "I THINK IT NEEDS FAR MORE THAN A QUICK POLISHING JOB," he wired Goldwyn in October 1946. "THE MOST SERIOUS DEFECT IS THAT THE BISHOP IS NOT A HUMAN BEING. HE IS A DREARY STUFFED SHIRT WHOM IT WOULD BE IMPOSSIBLE FOR AN INTELLIGENT WOMAN TO LOVE AND I DOUBT THAT EVEN DAVID NIVEN

COULD MAKE HIM SYMPATHETIC. . . . BELIEVE THE STORY CAN BE FUN-DAMENTALLY GOOD BUT IT REQUIRES AN ENTIRELY NEW APPROACH." Over the telephone, Goldwyn talked Sherwood into finding just that.

Although it remained to be seen whether David Niven could deliver an audience, Goldwyn drew up a new contract—with a hefty raise—for his newly arrived star. The Hollywood press corps had kept his name alive over the years, constantly reporting on his military heroics; and the insouciant actor seemed to have matured considerably over the last few years. Upon signing his new agreement, Niven wrote his producer "that so long as I am in your employment you will have my complete loyalty in all things and that I shall bend every effort to give you full value for your money." He read the new script of The Bishop's Wife and "adored" it. Unfortunately, he thought he was to play the role of the angel. When he learned otherwise, he protested so much that Goldwyn threatened to keep him out of the picture altogether.

Goldwyn had considered but one actor to play Dudley—Cary Grant. He called Grant's agent, Jules Stein—a former ophthalmologist from Kansas City, who was quickly turning his Music Corporation of America into one of the most powerful agencies in show business. Stein said there was no way Cary Grant could take the part, that his next four films were lined up. Goldwyn said he would pay anything to have him. Stein said it was a matter not of money, just of time. Unable to let go of the idea, Goldwyn phoned the agent repeatedly. (Many found Goldwyn masochistic in his persistent courting of rejection.) Then, on the day he finally had to cast the role, Goldwyn called one last time, only to learn that Cary Grant's next picture had suddenly fallen through, leaving the actor with an immediate hole in his schedule. Goldwyn paid him almost half a million dollars—the biggest check he had ever signed for an actor. Grant found the character a "rather conceited, impudent, high-handed magician" and had no genuine desire to play the part.

Teresa Wright's costumes for the title role were all made when she announced that she was pregnant again. Goldwyn substituted Loretta Young, whose career had progressed steadily since he had cast her in The Devil to Pay in 1930. She had just played the lead in the film that would win her an Oscar, The Farmer's Daughter. Self-conscious about the length of her neck, she told designer Irene Sharaff she needed costumes to shorten it; she also liked to wear powder and paint. Goldwyn explained to her that "A bishop's wife is not a glamour girl," and he did not "like those three layers of make-up." She grudgingly went along with the producer's wishes but did not speak to him for weeks.

Goldwyn no longer had any directors under contract, and none of any

quality seemed to be available. Charles Feldman, an agent Goldwyn could
seldom resist, sold him William Seiter, a director who muttered for days
that he was not up to the task. With three disgruntled actors on his hands,
he never took command of the picture. Three joyless performances began
showing up on the screen. After several weeks—and an investment of
$900,000—Goldwyn fired Seiter and announced he was starting the pic-
ture over.

"It was killing Sam Goldwyn," Robert Sherwood observed, "not to have
Willy on the picture." Frances put feelers out to Wyler but got no response. The sudden postponement of Twentieth Century–Fox's production
of *The Time of Your Life* freed its director; Henry Koster, whose biggest
credits to date had been Deanna Durbin movies, leapt at this opportunity.

"Would you like to work with Laurette Taylor?" Goldwyn asked Koster,
in interviewing him for the job. "I'd love to," the director said. "She's a
great actress. But she's dead." Goldwyn looked at Koster as though he were
an idiot. "She's not dead!" he cried. "She was just in here two hours ago,
sitting in the same chair you're sitting in, and I talked to her." Koster
insisted that was impossible, as she had died the year before. Goldwyn
buzzed his secretary and barked into the box, "Who was that lady who was
just sitting here two hours ago? That actress." Came the secretary's reply:
"Loretta Young."

"See," said Goldwyn, slapping his hand on his desk. "What did I tell
you? She's not dead."

Koster was offered *The Bishop's Wife* and accepted it. Goldwyn never did
get the leading lady's name right. The closest he came was in calling her
"Miss Yeng." That did not faze Koster, whom Goldwyn called "Kester."

After shutting down for six weeks, *The Bishop's Wife* began shooting
again. A new script and Koster's hand leavened it somewhat, but tension
still prevailed on the set. Cary Grant as the angel was more detached than
Goldwyn liked. It posed a problem for Goldwyn, because Grant had just
done him an enormous favor: Despite the actor's reputation for being
money mad, he had taken himself off payroll during the six-week layoff.
Nonetheless, somebody had to deal with the ineffective way Grant was
playing the angel. Goldwyn came to the set and discussed the matter with
him. "You want me to be happy, don't you?" Grant asked the producer. "I
don't give a *damn* if you're happy," Goldwyn replied. "You're going to be
here for only a few weeks, and this picture will be out for a long time. I
would rather you should be unhappy here, and then we can all be happy
later."

A little later, Koster came to film a love scene, and "Miss Yeng" bridled
at being photographed from the left side. Cary Grant refused in kind,

making it impossible for Koster to stage the two people facing each other. So he placed the actors at a window, staring out at the stars, Cary Grant stepping in behind her and placing his hands on her shoulders. "What the hell happened to the love scene?" Goldwyn demanded of Koster when he saw the rushes. "I don't want people looking out the window," he said; "I want them looking at each other." Koster explained the problem to Goldwyn, who marched onto the set with his own solution. He asked "Miss Yeng" if Koster's explanation about her "bad side" was true. She said it was. "Fine," he announced. "From now on, I can only use half your face, you only get half your salary."

The Bishop's Wife previewed to generally favorable audience response, but it fell in the middle and never bounced back. Goldwyn telephoned Billy Wilder—hotter than ever after *Double Indemnity* and *The Lost Weekend.* "Wilder," he said, "we're in terrible trouble."

Appealing to Wilder as a friend, the producer asked if he and Charles Brackett could not look at *The Bishop's Wife* and at least identify the problem. The pair watched the film and immediately pointed out a few scenes that needed some "frosting." Goldwyn offered them $25,000 to fix them. Wilder and Brackett worked all weekend and delivered the pages to Goldwyn and Koster, who had to reshoot the sequences Monday morning. The next preview worked like a charm.

Goldwyn asked Brackett and Wilder to lunch with him to discuss their compensation. On their way, the two writers decided their entire weekend of work was a lark. "Let's be generous," Wilder said to Brackett. "We'll have to pay ninety per cent of that money in taxes anyway, so why not just tell Goldwyn it was our pleasure?" They arrived at the studio and met the producer in his private dining room. "Now about the money—" Goldwyn started to say, when Brackett interrupted him. "Mr. Goldwyn," he said. "Billy and I have discussed it, and we have come to the conclusion that we don't really want any."

"That's funny," Goldwyn replied. "I've come to the same conclusion."

With what seemed like another hit picture (and contender for an Academy Award) in the can, Goldwyn threw a party at Laurel Lane for the talent who had worked on *The Bishop's Wife.* The stars were all there, along with Gregg Toland and the Henry Kosters. It was a sumptuous meal, served with bottles of a fine Lafite-Rothschild. The Kosters were the last to leave, a little after eleven o'clock. Halfway out the driveway, Mrs. Koster realized she had left her gloves in the house. Her husband went back to the front door, rapped lightly, and let himself in. Nobody seemed to be around, so he quietly made his way to the dining room to pick up the gloves. As he entered the room, Goldwyn was standing at the far end of the table, carefully pouring what remained in one of the wineglasses back into the bottle.

AFTER presenting its annual awards at Grauman's Chinese Theater for the past three years, the Academy of Motion Picture Arts and Sciences moved its nineteenth ceremony to the mammoth Shrine Auditorium in downtown Los Angeles. With 6,700 seats to fill, the Academy opened the event to the public for the first time, a chance to watch the proceedings from the balcony. Most of the Hollywood community, in evening dress, sat on the main floor, nominees close to the center aisle, where a spotlight could catch winners as they mounted a few steps to the stage. Cedric Gibbons had designed the ten-thousand-dollar neoclassical set—a pylon with six Greek columns forming a semicircle behind a five-foot gilt plaster replica of the Oscar. Presenters and winners would stand at a microphone in the center, then exit stage left to the pressroom. Jack Benny got the proceedings under way at eight forty-five on the night of Thursday, March 13, 1947.

The president of the Screen Actors Guild, Ronald Reagan, began the evening with a brief "Parade of Stars," a montage of Oscar-winning films. Then Academy president Jean Hersholt presented four special awards, three of them apparent consolation prizes: to Laurence Olivier for "outstanding achievement" in his production of *Henry V;* to Claude Jarman, Jr., the juvenile star of *The Yearling;* and to Harold Russell, "for bringing hope and courage to his fellow veterans through his appearance in *The Best Years of Our Lives.*"

Rex Harrison presented three crafts awards, and by the time he left the stage, there was still no indication of the evening's big winner. Danny Mandell won for editing *Best Years,* but Columbia's *Jolson Story* beat Goldwyn's Gordon Sawyer for the Sound Recording award. The English *Blithe Spirit* won in Special Effects, suggesting there might be a wave of wins for the eleven foreign films among the year's nominations—which included France's *Children of Paradise,* Italy's *Open City,* and six British entries.

Lana Turner announced that Hugo Friedhofer won for his score of *Best Years;* but *Anna and the King of Siam* and *The Yearling* won for best art direction (black-and-white and color, respectively), then again for cinematography—two categories in which Goldwyn did not even have a nominee. Van Johnson presented the Best Song award to Harry Warren and Johnny Mercer for "On the Atchison, Topeka and the Santa Fe" (beating out Hoagy Carmichael, who had written "Ole Buttermilk Sky" that year).

A little after ten-thirty, a trend emerged. Robert Montgomery handed the award for Best Screenplay to Robert Sherwood. Then Billy Wilder, calling *Best Years* "the best-directed film I've ever seen in my life," presented a statuette to William Wyler. (Virginia Mayo would later insist she won Wyler's Oscar for him—"because everyone said, 'My God! If he can do *that* with Virginia Mayo . . . '")

Eric Johnston, Will Hays's successor as president of the Motion Picture Association of America, appeared before the microphone to announce the winner of the Best Picture. Twentieth Century–Fox's *The Razor's Edge* was considered the evening's favorite. MGM, which had waged its own strong campaign in the trade papers, seemed a close second with *The Yearling*. *It's a Wonderful Life* was the choice of the softhearted, and *Henry V* had the intellectuals' vote. But the winner was *The Best Years of Our Lives*.

Goldwyn, one of his staff observed, "danced up the aisle with a big smile on his face." He simply thanked the principals involved. He carefully got through his entire list without a flub . . . until he reached the end and commended "Hugo Carmichael."

Donald Nelson, head of the War Production Board, appeared to present the tenth miniature bust of Irving Thalberg to the producer with "the most consistent high quality of production" that year. He called Sam Goldwyn from the wings to accept that as well. The recipient was visibly choked up.

The biggest surprise of the evening followed, when the Best Supporting Actor award went not to a veteran scene-stealer such as Charles Coburn, William Demarest, Claude Rains, or Clifton Webb, but to the scene-stealing veteran. Harold Russell became the first actor ever to win two Oscars for the same role. "I'll never forget coming off the stage for press pictures after being given my second award," Russell remembered, "and having Cary Grant . . . lean over and whisper, 'Where can *I* get a stick of dynamite?'"

Best Years had no nominee in either the supporting or leading lady categories, leaving a single opportunity to get within one of *Gone With the Wind*'s record of eight Oscars. Joan Fontaine did the honors, citing the performances of Laurence Olivier, Larry Parks, Gregory Peck, James Stewart, and announcing that the winner was Fredric March. The actor was in New York, so Sam Goldwyn made the most of the moment by sending Cathy O'Donnell before the crowd of six thousand to accept the trophy. Goldwyn forever thereafter counted his Thalberg Award and Harold Russell's honorary Oscar in *Best Years*' final tally, so he could boast that his picture set the record for most Academy Awards, with nine.

RKO president Peter Ravthon hosted a festive party at his house, which ran into the small hours of the morning. Goldwyn and Willy Wyler did not even greet each other, and they gravitated to different corners of the room all night. But what Goldwyn regarded as Wyler's ungrateful defection was not going to spoil the evening. Frances observed that her husband acted "like a child who'd got absolutely everything he wanted at Christmas."

The chauffeur drove them home and Frances carried herself upstairs to bed. After several minutes had passed and Sam still had not ascended, she padded about the house, looking for him. She found him sitting on the edge of a couch in the dark living room, his Oscar in one hand, his Thalberg in the other. His head bowed down, he was sobbing.

19 The Plague

H E WAS EUPHORIC for days.
David Selznick, Darryl Zanuck,
and Jack Warner were among the first
to send congratulations on March 14, 1947. "YOU DESERVED EVERYTHING
YOU GOT," wired Joseph Schenck. MGM's executive producer Lawrence
Weingarten wrote Goldwyn that "last night's presentation was one of the
few times that the Thalberg Award achieved its real purpose." Thalberg's
widow, Norma Shearer, seconded those sentiments in her telegram. "OF
COURSE WE SHALL ALL GET A BONUS SHANT WE?" asked David Niven in
his wire. "I AM PROUD OF YOU," said Farley Granger in his. Mack Sennett
paid his respects, saying, "MY HAT'S OFF TO A PIONEER WHO IS STILL
PIONEERING." Sammy cabled felicitations from London. Harry Arthur,
one of the most hardfisted exhibitors in the country, told Goldwyn he was
now willing to pay *him* for the honor of running the film in his theater. A
Los Angeles *Times* editorial asserted that "Hollywood can be proud of the
picture it selected. 'The Best Years of Our Lives' represented the better
American spirit. It deserves to be seen by people throughout today's cha-
otic world."

The rest of the year brought so many fan letters for *Best Years* that
Goldwyn had time to read only pages of typed excerpts that his secretary
served with the morning mail. The nation's periodicals covered every aspect of the film. *Forbes* magazine gathered the "50 Foremost Business Leaders Today" for a banquet in New York; and by dint of Goldwyn's recent
acclaim, they selected him as the most illustrious ambassador from Hol-

lywood. He sat among such household surnames as Dow, Firestone, Ford, Gimbel, Kaiser, Luce, Mellon, Rockefeller, and Sarnoff. The crowning piece of publicity that year was a ten-page spread in the October 27, 1947, issue of *Life*. Ben Sonnenberg had arranged the in-depth profile of Goldwyn, which traced his entire career in the motion picture business.

Goldwyn was not about to start eating lotus. His latest success only reminded him of the philosophy to which he had long held: "The higher you climb, the farther you can fall." Just months after his triumph at the Academy Awards, he told *Life* reporter Roger Butterfield, "It is not good enough to be good. I never was bad on purpose in my life. Suppose next time I make a stinker? I'm worrying about that."

Other problems weighed heavily on Goldwyn as well. The nation was going through its own postwar identity crisis. As always, movies reflected the shifts in taste. Motion picture attendance dropped radically. A survey indicated that the public would much rather watch Ingrid Bergman, Greer Garson, Rita Hayworth, Jennifer Jones, Lana Turner, Gene Tierney, and June Allyson than such longtime favorites as Joan Crawford, Ginger Rogers, and Myrna Loy. Gregory Peck and Alan Ladd had become more popular than Clark Gable. Garbo, away from the screen for five years, was staging a comeback—a film about the French courtesan Madame de Lenclos. She and James Mason had already made wardrobe tests for producer Walter Wanger, but at the last minute the financing fell through.

Congress passed the Taft-Hartley bill in 1947, imposing restrictions and responsibilities on labor unions. "The lush economic days of the immediate past are over," Goldwyn warned the President, who vetoed the bill; "and unless the productivity of both labor and capital increases, we cannot expect to meet what the future holds forth." Picket lines outside studio gates were a common sight.

On top of labor's demands, efforts to force the major studios to divest themselves of theaters cost the independent motion picture producers a small fortune. Big studios lost that much and more in complying with the court orders. Great Britain—which accounted for 85 percent of an American film's foreign income—announced a new tax of 75 percent on American film earnings in its theaters. "Of 123 pictures sent into the foreign market," *Daily Variety* reported, "only 19 paid their negative costs in the domestic market." Studio net profits in 1946 of $121 million fell off $35 million the next year, another $40 million the year after that. Most studios let go of half their contract talent, putting another 12,000 laborers on the streets. Goldwyn slashed the salaries of his studio's executives by 50 percent, starting with his own.

Amid these statistics, George Gallup's Audience Research, Inc. ("The Gallup Pool," as Goldwyn called it), reported that 70 percent of New York City's moviegoers had seen at least one television program. Of those, only a handful were considered "regular televiewers"; but by August 1947, 30,000 television sets had been sold in the greater New York viewing area alone.

In the summer of 1947, a new specter haunted Hollywood, one far more ominous than television's fuzzy images. It had been in the winds since February 1944, when a group of vigilantes formed the Motion Picture Alliance for the Preservation of American Ideals. "We believe in, and like, the American way of life," they told the press:

> . . . the freedom to speak, to think, to live, to worship, to work and to govern ourselves, as individuals, as free men; the right to succeed or fail as free men, according to the measure of our ability and our strength.
>   Believing in these things, we find ourselves in sharp revolt against a rising tide of Communism, Fascism and kindred beliefs, that seek by subversive means to undermine and change this way of life.

With director Sam Wood leading the charge, Walt Disney, John Wayne, Robert Taylor, Gary Cooper, Adolphe Menjou, Charles Coburn, Ward Bond, and Hedda Hopper, among others, pledged themselves "to fight, with every means at our organized command, any effort of any group or individual, to divert the loyalty of the screen from the free America that gave it birth."

William Randolph Hearst seemed to be behind the effort, if not igniting this torch for liberty then at least blowing the flames. No sooner had the Motion Picture Alliance been announced than an editorial in Hearst's Los Angeles *Examiner* boosted the organization, condemning the "patriotic majority in the motion picture industry" for being "slow to organize and to assert its principles and exercise its influence."

> Consequently, the subversive minority in the industry has connived and contrived to produce a long succession of insidious and evil motion pictures to the discredit of the industry and to the detriment of the country. . . .
>   It has made pictures glorifying Communistic Russia, ignoring the oppressive and tyrannical character of Bolshevism and inventing virtues for it that have never existed.

The "red-baiters" never did single out a film, or even a line of dialogue, that could clearly be considered anti-American, pro-Communist propaganda. (The closest they got were *Mission to Moscow* and Goldwyn's *The North Star,* both of which had been made at the President's urging.)

The time was ripe for an anti-Communist takeover of America. The country's spiritual leader for most of a generation was dead, and the reins of power were up for grabs. A labor force in turmoil was looking for scapegoats. The Congress found itself with a new crop of young anti-Communists alongside a number of veteran Republicans, glad at last to have the chance to turn the political tide. Many of them referred to "liberal" Roosevelt-like thinking as "pink," or, worse, "red."

In 1938, Congressman Martin Dies of Texas had chaired a temporary Special Committee of the House of Representatives on Un-American Activities. Seven years later, his colleague John Rankin of Mississippi moved to make it a permanent standing committee. The motion carried, and the gavel passed to Representative J. Parnell Thomas of New Jersey. His most eager colleague was freshman representative Richard M. Nixon of California. Each of the committee members had his own hidden agenda in Congress, recognizing the committee as an opportunity to enhance his financial or political fortunes. "There was no doubt in my mind," said Rabbi Edgar Magnin, "that the committee was out to get Jews." Those Americans who blamed Jews for "creating the war" now wanted their pound of flesh. "Anti-Communism" may have been on their tongues, but anti-Semitism was on many of their minds. To give impetus to their cause, they turned not to that industry most riddled with Communists but to one almost exclusively dominated by Jews, one guaranteed to draw headlines.

In May 1947, the House committee (dubbed HUAC) and Sam Wood's Motion Picture Alliance joined hands. Representatives Parnell Thomas and John McDowell convened special sessions of their committee in Los Angeles's Biltmore Hotel. Such well-known faces as Robert Taylor and Adolphe Menjou testified before them in secret. "Volunteers of information," Thomas called them—"friendly witnesses." Inevitably, parts of their testimony leaked to the press. *Variety* reported former Eminent Author Rupert Hughes had testified that the Screen Writers Guild was "lousy with Communists today." Ginger Rogers's mother, Lela, was rumored to have testified that her daughter had refused to speak the line "Share and share alike" in one picture. The MPA pasted a "red label" on such all-American goods as *Margie* and *The Best Years of Our Lives.*

The congressmen returned to the Capitol and kept quiet for weeks. Their ominous silence bred more rumors. By summer's end, it was announced that HUAC would open hearings on the "Hollywood situation" on September 23, 1947, in Washington. "This is the big show the Honorable J. Parnell Thomas and Company have been whipping into shape for the past several months," read an editorial in the September number of the Screen Writers Guild's official magazine; ". . . we must prepare ourselves for it, and we must fight it."

Over forty members of the Hollywood community were subpoenaed to appear before the committee—mostly actors, writers, and directors. Half were members of the Motion Picture Alliance; most of the remaining nineteen were Jews who were well known for their leftward leanings. A few industry giants—famous Americans whose presence would lend gravity to the proceedings—were also called. Samuel Goldwyn received his subpoena on September 25.

The public hearing did not get under way until the third week of October. By that time, Chairman Thomas and his cohorts had assembled all the players they needed for their passion play. They also decided to keep the program of events a secret, so nobody knew from one day to the next who was scheduled to appear. This allowed the committee to make any last-minute substitutions they wished for dramatic effect.

The committee's first witness signaled the tenor of the hearings that would follow. Instead of Eric Johnston, whose moderate views the committee well knew, Chairman Thomas called the blustery Jack Warner. Without even being asked, he offered information about his own "Americanism" and the names of a dozen "Communists" he insisted he had fired the moment he learned of their politics. To follow Warner with RKO's liberal Dore Schary or even Louis B. Mayer—who loved his country but loathed this committee—might have indicated a broad-minded investigation of sedition in the United States.

Chairman Thomas turned instead to the chorus of "friendly witnesses," the membership of the Motion Picture Alliance. Several writers and directors were glamorously supported by Robert Taylor, Robert Montgomery, Ronald Reagan, Gary Cooper, and George Murphy. Within a week, the committee had few to hear from except those targeted as "unfriendly," whom the committee intended to slaughter or make squeal. All the producers on the list of potential witnesses released to the press eventually got called—except Goldwyn. He was supposed to leave the country for the Royal Command performance of *The Bishop's Wife;* but his House orders forbade his departure. He went to New York, where he could leave for Washington or London at a moment's notice.

Back in Los Angeles, William Wyler, John Huston, and writer Philip Dunne felt that all the razzle-dazzle of the hearings was diverting the public's attention from the most important issue. They formed the Committee for the First Amendment, an organization committed to the freedoms of speech and assembly, the individual's right, said Wyler, "to keep his political beliefs to himself." At Ira Gershwin's house, they gathered most of the liberals in town, including Judy Garland, Edward G. Robinson, and Billy Wilder. They proposed that a petition be sent to Washington, holding that the hearings were "morally wrong" because:

> Any investigation into the political beliefs of the individual is contrary to the basic principles of our democracy;
>
> Any attempt to curb freedom of expression and to set arbitrary standards of Americanism is in itself disloyal to both the spirit and the letter of our Constitution.

Five hundred people signed it. Huston, Dunne, Ira Gershwin, Danny Kaye, Gene Kelly, Paul Henreid, John Garfield, June Havoc, Evelyn Keyes, Jane Wyatt, Sterling Hayden, Humphrey Bogart, Lauren Bacall, and a few others delivered it.

John Howard Lawson—one of the writers on Goldwyn's *They Shall Have Music*—was the first "unfriendly witness" called to the stand. He had hoped to read an introductory statement, a courtesy afforded the friendly witnesses, but he was refused. The committee wanted only one question answered: "Mr. Lawson, are you now or have you ever been a member of the Communist Party of the United States?" Between the constant poundings of Chairman Thomas's gavel, he tried to have his say. After a dozen interruptions, Thomas ordered guards to remove Lawson from the premises.

When Eric Johnston was asked to testify, he admonished the committee for their tactics, then astonished the very motion picture community he was representing when he advocated the exposure of Communists. The hearings became a free-for-all.

From that moment on, the only unity among witnesses came from the most hostile of those called, ten who banded together and refused to testify. Scrutiny of their screenwriting, in fact, would reveal neither a trace of Communist propaganda nor even any great influence in town. As Billy Wilder noted, "of the Unfriendly Ten, only two had any talent, the other eight were just unfriendly."

While the fates of the "Hollywood Ten" were being sealed, Sam Goldwyn paced his tenth-floor suite at the Sherry Netherland Hotel, impatient at not being called. Lillian Hellman later suggested that he posed a threat to the committee just then, because he was "too much of a wild card. You never knew what was going to come out of his mouth, and he probably wouldn't have gone along with the committee's script." While dressing for the theater on October 29, he talked to a reporter from the *New York Times*. "I was subpoenaed some time ago and I have been here awaiting their pleasure," Goldwyn said. "But so far they have not called me and in the meantime I am tied up by the subpoena." He explained that all his business was being thrown into disarray. "What is the matter?" Goldwyn asked. "Are they afraid to call me?"

The next day, Goldwyn was ready to testify, whether the committee was or not. With the help of George Slaff, Goldwyn's general counsel, ghostwriter, and most trusted adviser, he released his own statement to the press, and got national coverage:

> As an American, I have been astounded and outraged at the manner in which the committee has permitted our industry to be vilified by gossip, innuendo and hearsay. I had hoped that a Committee of Congress would be sufficiently aware of the traditions and background of American democracy so that it would not permit itself to be used as a sounding board for a smear campaign intended to destroy public confidence in the integrity of an industry which so many of us have spent the best years of our lives in building up.
>
> The most un-American activity which I have observed in connection with the hearings has been the activity of the Committee itself. The purpose of these hearings seems to have been to try to dictate and control what goes on the screens of America. I resent and abhor censorship of thought. I assure you that as long as I live no one will ever be able to dictate what I put on the screen so long as I continue to honor and obey the laws of our country.

Ruth Capps had been hurt by the recent *Life* profile of her father because, for all its detail, it made no mention of her existence; but she was impressed enough with his recent statement to put her feelings aside and commend him for making "a very courageous and just evaluation of the whole thing. I only wish the other producers," she wrote, "had taken their cue from you instead of being stampeded by this ridiculous and shocking committee."

On November 14, Goldwyn met President Truman and told him, "There never has been, and there never will be, any Communism in our pictures." He said the "Thomas Committee has been un-American in the

RIGHT: New York, 1946. Two years after Frances Goldwyn urged her husband to read a magazine article about returning soldiers, the billboard for his greatest production went up in Times Square. BELOW LEFT: At the New York City opening—November 1946—of *The Best Years of Our Lives.* William Wyler with his wife, Talli (left), and Lillian Hellman. BELOW RIGHT: Frances sits with William S. Paley, who had once tried to talk her into leaving Sam, and with socialite Mrs. William Rhinelander Stewart.

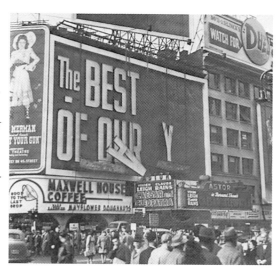

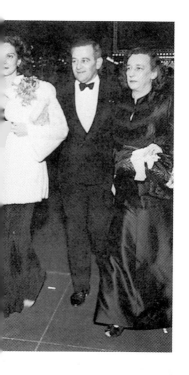

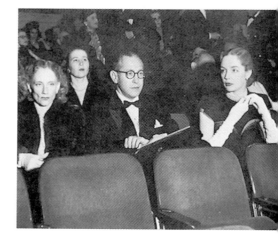

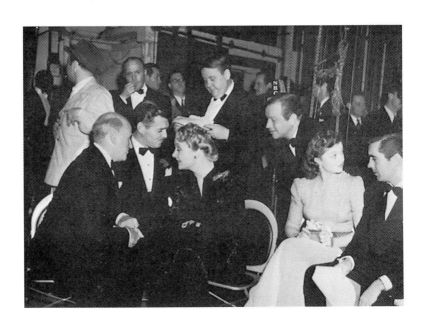

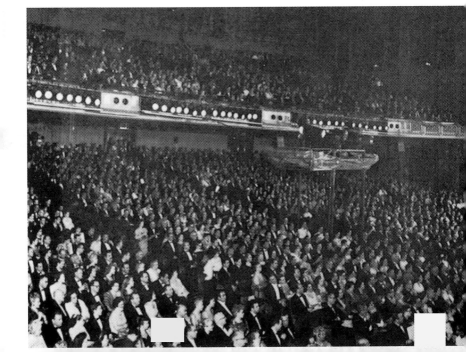

OPPOSITE: Hollywood, c. 1940. Left to right: Goldwyn, Jack Benny, Clark Gable, Carole Lombard, Charles Laughton, Melvyn Douglas, Myrna Loy, and Tyrone Power.

RIGHT: Academy Award winners, March 13, 1947. Left to right: Anne Baxter (*The Razor's Edge*), Goldwyn (*The Best Years of Our Lives*), Olivia de Havilland (*To Each His Own*), and Harold Russell (*The Best Years of Our Lives*)—a first-time actor who won two Oscars for the same performance.

BELOW: Triumph, after sixty-seven productions and thirty-four years.

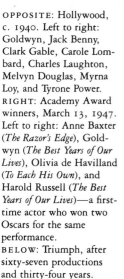

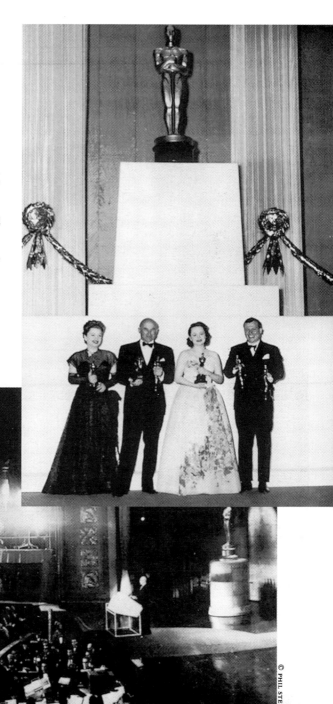

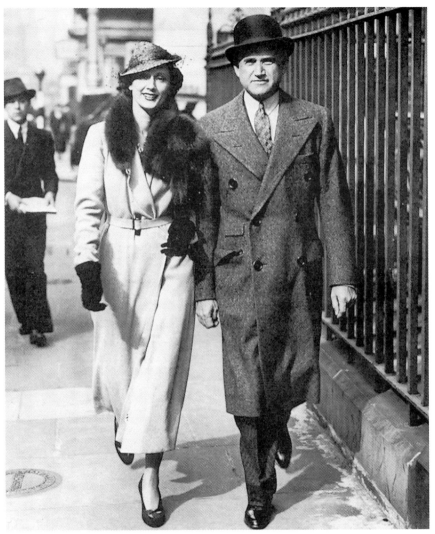

Mr. and Mrs. Samuel Goldwyn, London, 1946.

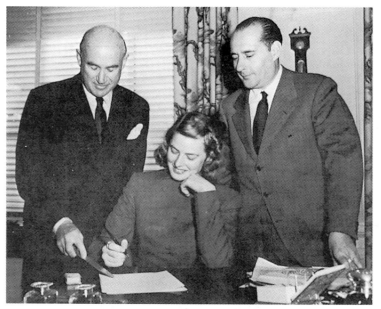

ABOVE: Goldwyn signs Ingrid Bergman and Roberto Rossellini to a contract, 1949. Once Goldwyn got the publicity he wanted, he let the deal fall apart. BELOW: David Niven returns from the war to the studio and receives his fan mail, December 1945. He became Goldwyn's biggest postwar star.

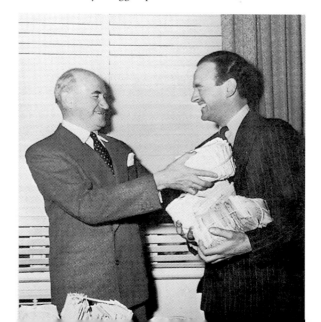

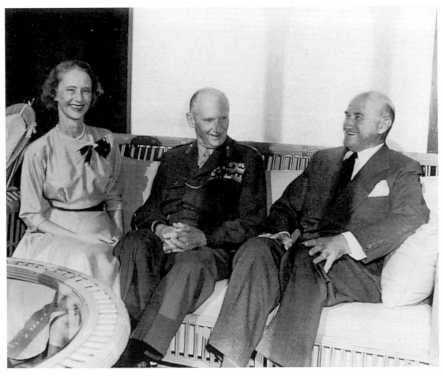
The Goldwyns entertain Field Marshal Montgomery at Laurel Lane, 1954.
At a dinner of Hollywood luminaries, Goldwyn introduced his guest of honor
as "Marshall Field Montgomery."

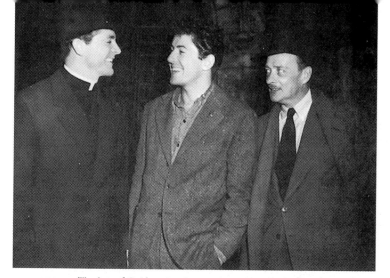

ABOVE: The last of Goldwyn's contract players—Dana Andrews, Farley Granger, and Robert Keith—on the set of *Edge of Doom,* the nadir of Goldwyn's career. BELOW: Sam and Frances visit "The Little Mermaid" in Copenhagen while promoting *Hans Christian Andersen.*

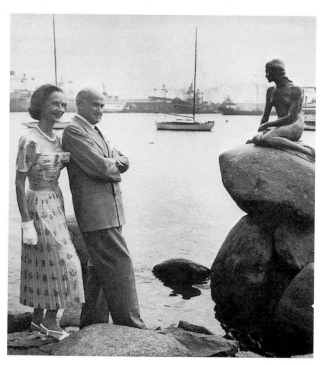

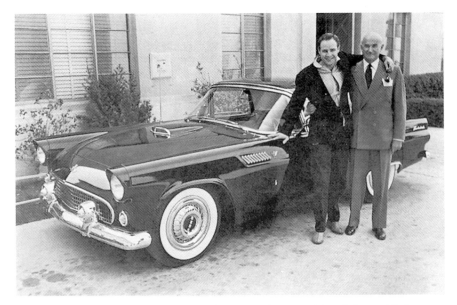

ABOVE: Goldwyn with Marlon Brando in 1955 after the making of *Guys and Dolls*. The Thunderbird was Goldwyn's gift to Brando for his model behavior during the production. BELOW: Goldwyn Girls rehearse a number from *Guys and Dolls*.

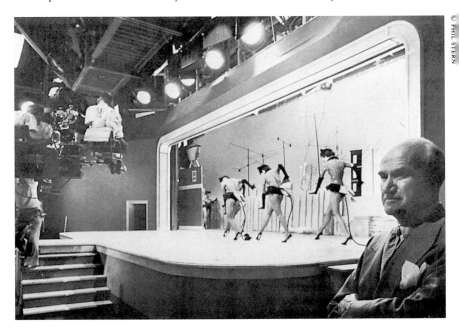

way it has handled this," and that "Thomas is seeing this through pink-colored glasses."

So were many religious, educational, and veterans' groups. Theaters running films with "unfriendly" supporters faced boycotts. The manager of the Orpheum Theater in Kansas City, Missouri, forwarded to Goldwyn a letter he had received from an irate patron who had walked out on *The Secret Life of Walter Mitty;* the moviegoer said he and his three companions "heartily disapprove of the actions of this man [Danny Kaye] at the hearing recently held in Washington, D.C., and we will certainly not go to see any shows in which he appears or any of the other nine or ten people." Goldwyn took the trouble to reply, insisting that "Danny Kaye is a fine American, who, after being rejected by the Army on grounds of physical disability, travelled many thousands of miles in the war zones entertaining our troops overseas. In going to Washington recently as he did, he was exercising an old-fashioned and fundamental American right of expressing his opinion to the elected representatives of the people. This right was prized so highly by the founders of our nation that they embodied it in our Constitution." Independent Sam Goldwyn could afford to make such statements. Most of the other producers of motion pictures in America had to answer to board chairmen and stockholders.

Furthermore, Lillian Hellman later suggested, most of the studios' founding fathers who were still active were then in their fifties and early sixties; they had grown "older and wearier" and less inclined to tackle the mailbags of protest letters they were receiving. "Threats that might once have been laughed about over a gin rummy game," she wrote in *Scoundrel Time,* "now seemed dangerous to their fortunes. Movie producers knew full well that the Communists of Hollywood had never made a single Communist picture. . . . But they told themselves the voice of America was speaking, and to some extent it was."

The industry's leading executives announced a meeting at the Waldorf-Astoria Hotel for November 24, 1947. Corporate sentiment was swaying them toward the endorsement of measures that were punitive and preventative: The Hollywood Ten must be fired; and no known Communists must be hired. The day before the conference, Sam Goldwyn (at sixty-eight, one of the oldest people in the room) formulated a policy statement he thought his colleagues should adopt:

The men just cited by the Congress will have their day in court. The question of their rights will be taken to the Supreme Court of the United States. After the Supreme Court has spoken, we will know definitely whether they were within their rights or not, in acting as they did. Until then we are reserving judgment and suspending action. . . .

Eric Johnston, like most of the conferees, did not think that was any kind of action at all. After patriotic speeches by several studio heads, only one man, as Dore Schary remembered it, "was bold enough to suggest that there was an air of panic in the room."

Goldwyn, ramrod straight, bald headed, and with a slightly Oriental slant to his eyes, spoke sarcastically and irritated Johnston, who responded with an angry speech concluding with the cliché question asking us whether we were mice or men. He insisted that if the motion-picture business wanted to earn the respect of the American public, the ten men who had appeared plus any known, or believed to be, communists had to be discharged.

Schary protested that such punishment outweighed what had not yet been determined a crime. Goldwyn said he "would not be allied to any such nonsense." He and Schary and Walter Wanger were the only producers in the room who protested. Lillian Hellman contended that Goldwyn's dissension was not "a vote for freedom," more "that he always voted against any group decision." The producer's consistent behavior in the line of fire, however, suggested greater conviction than that.

The consensus of the room was that the longer the hearings dragged on, the longer the Committee would encroach on the business of Hollywood. It was agreed that a committee of its own should draft a resolution that would assure the country that Hollywood would police itself.

The result was an eight-paragraph statement that effectively blacklisted the Hollywood Ten and any "Communist or a member of any party or group which advocates the overthrow of the Government of the United States by force or by any illegal or unconstitutional methods." Loyalty oaths became standard means for smoking out more Communists.

In 1951, HUAC resumed its investigation of Hollywood under new leadership. Representative John Wood had replaced J. Parnell Thomas, who had been found guilty of financial malfeasance while in office. The Hydra-headed committee was no longer fooling around. It wanted names. Some people tried to save face, some their skin. The committee managed to char the careers of scores of actors and writers (the latter had the small advantage of pseudonymity) throughout the fifties and beyond. Lillian Hellman was willing to talk about herself under oath, but when it came to informing on others, she said, "I will not cut my conscience to fit this year's fashions." That cost her employment in Hollywood for more than a decade. Because of the untimely deaths of two Supreme Court justices, the new, more conservative high bench refused to hear the cases of the Hollywood Ten, who all served prison sentences. In looking back on that dark time, the blacklisted Dalton Trumbo said, "it will do no good to search for villains or heroes or saints or devils because there were none; there were only victims." The only suggestion of justice Ring Lardner and his jailmate Lester Cole saw upon their arrival at the Federal Correctional Institute in Danbury, Connecticut, was that J. Parnell Thomas was already an inmate there.

After a year of the most devastating havoc ever to hit Hollywood, Sam Goldwyn set out to prove that he had not been afflicted with what he called "the Academy Award disease"—the paralysis that seized David Selznick for four years after the release of *Rebecca*. (Sam had also recently chided his debt-ridden friend for committing the worst mistake of his life—selling his interest in *Gone With the Wind* for not even $500,000. "David," Goldwyn told Sammy, "hasn't got his head on the ground.") Goldwyn had not put a single project into production in the nine months since the rewards of *Best Years* had come pouring in—his longest hiatus in production since leaving United Artists. On Sammy's next visit home from abroad he found his father depressed, "strange and moody." Goldwyn was having trouble falling asleep at night, and he talked about death routinely. He wanted Sammy near him, but the young man instinctively felt it was best to keep his distance, returning only one month a year. Sammy felt he could always cheer up his father by talking about the Best Picture Oscar—until the day when Goldwyn yelled, "Don't mention that goddamned award! It's nothing but trouble to me."

The strains at home increased as Sam tried to regain his confidence by milking all the extra publicity for *Best Years* that he could—including credit for its creation. His gains in self-esteem were Frances's losses. Unacknowledged for her role in conceiving the project, Frances tussled with her own secret feelings of worthlessness. Ironically, they surfaced at what should have been the most secure moment in her life: Hitler was dead; her son was grown; and her husband was making more money than she had ever counted on—enough to ensure her family's comfort for the rest of their days. Feeling unneeded, Frances at last surrendered to the curse of her forefathers, the behavior she had resisted for so long. She began to drink alcoholically.

She found one other form of release. In late 1947, Frances, in her forties, went to the small third-floor office of Assistance Unlimited, an odd-jobs agency on the corner of Selma and Vine in Hollywood. Having called ahead to inquire about their rates for typing, she left three short chapters of a novel, ten badly typed pages corrected in blue pencil. She gave neither her name nor her phone number, saying only that she was "out a lot" and would return in a few days with more to be typed. For several weeks she came around with pages of an insider's look at Hollywood, a novel sprinkled with real names of stars; she asked if the secretaries could help her get an agent. They speculated about the identity of their "mystery lady." Just as the tenth chapter was being typed, *Life* published pictures of a Hollywood party their reporters had attended, and there, among the celebrities, was Frances Goldwyn. The women at Assistance Unlimited were delighted to have unmasked the mystery lady; word quickly spread through the building's secretarial grapevine. Within days Walter Winchell's column reported that Mrs. Samuel Goldwyn was writing a semi-autobiographical novel. Her anonymity broken, she never returned to the typists' office. Before proceeding any further with the venture, she did show her pages to her husband. They were either quite embarrassing or so promising that he feared she might launch a career of her own. Whichever, he told her they were terrible. She discarded them and abandoned the project.

Alcohol-induced changes in Frances's behavior—sudden depression and provocative comments—added to Sam's anxiety. But he chose never to confront her about her drinking. That was her private affair. His insomnia worsened. He needed somebody to talk to without having to watch what he was saying; and he got considerable relief from May Romm, an eminent psychiatrist who had proved extremely helpful to several of Hollywood's elite. After a few sessions, Frances made him stop. She said, "Psychiatrists break up marriages," and pointed to Dr. Romm as the culprit behind the recent divorce of David and Irene Selznick. Knowing he should not, Sam obliged her.

With tensions persisting, Goldwyn called on Hilde Berl, the therapist who had proved so helpful in dealing with the family's crises during Sammy's adolescence. He told her he had made more money than he had ever dreamed, but that he was not deriving any pleasure from it. She suggested he buy paintings.

"Paintings?" Goldwyn asked incredulously. She said his entire outlook would change, starting with the atmosphere in which he lived. Beyond that, she said, it would be like learning a wonderful new language, one without words. Goldwyn hesitated after pricing some paintings, but he began to notice that many of the important people he respected most collected art. Hilde Berl nudged him to look first at the French Impressionists. In 1948, he purchased a Matisse called *Les Anémones* for $13,500. A

Braque followed, then a Picasso still life from 1938 for $10,000. When Lillian Ross came to town to chronicle for *The New Yorker* John Huston's filming of *The Red Badge of Courage*, she overheard a conversation in which a roly-poly man said, "I'm at Sam Goldwyn's last night and he says he's got a new painting to show me. So he takes me over to the painting and points to it and says, 'My *Toujours* Lautrec!'" Paintings became favorite gifts between Sam and Frances. They amassed an impressive collection, mostly works by famous names.

OVER the next three years, Goldwyn stepped up his production to its prewar level, two pictures a year. But the seven films he released between October 1948 and December 1951 revealed only a gradual diminution in his powers of judgment. "I think the old guy was hurting," said Alfred Crown, one of the new recruits to the Goldwyn organization. "I think it's a sure sign your imagination is starving when you start living off your reputation and feeding off yourself."

The first film of this cycle was a remake of his 1942 hit *Ball of Fire*. Even the story's creator, Billy Wilder, admitted the inherent creakiness of the plot; to haul it out again only seven years later suggested desperation. The writer wanted nothing more to do with it.

Goldwyn approached the original film's director, Howard Hawks, even though each had vowed never to work with the other again. He hounded him to think of a new approach to the story of the shy professor who falls in love with the stripper. Hawks resisted, until the producer offered him $25,000 a week. The eight encyclopedists writing about "Slang" became a muster of musicologists analyzing "Jazz." Harry Tugend accepted the screenwriting assignment, which involved little more than plugging musical references into the Brackett and Wilder script. No accommodations were made for the new cast: Danny Kaye and Virginia Mayo would simply stand in for Gary Cooper and Barbara Stanwyck. Goldwyn spangled the movie with "stunt casting"—jazz artists Louis Armstrong, Tommy Dorsey, and Lionel Hampton. Benny Goodman played one of the professors.

A Song Is Born, as the remake was titled, miscarried. With close to twenty jazz numbers crammed into the film, *Time* said, the plot served "only as a link between jam sessions." There was no room for a single Kaye specialty number; and to make matters worse, Danny and Sylvia Kaye temporarily separated during the filming. The star, Howard Hawks remembered, was reduced to "a basket case, stopping work to see a psychiatrist twice a day. . . . He was about as funny as a crutch." Goldwyn forced Virginia Mayo to watch *Ball of Fire* over and over until she could mimic

Barbara Stanwyck's every movement. Goldwyn made her appear even more artificial by hiring another singer to dub the musical numbers. Hypersensitive to the politics of the period, the studio asked Hawks not to "get the Negroes and the white musicians too close together." The director made a point of never seeing this second version.

Goldwyn received the worst critical clobbering of his career. Danny Kaye fans felt shortchanged, and so did the star. In his five pictures for Sam Goldwyn, Kaye thought, he still had not fully expressed his identity on film. In the meantime, he had become one of the most beloved performers in concert halls around the world. When Jack Warner learned his Goldwyn contract was expiring, he approached him with a comedy (*The Inspector General*), and Kaye left. Warner also grabbed Virginia Mayo, whom Goldwyn had seldom used as anything more than a decorative foil for Kaye. Instead of pairing them again, Warner put her in a number of dramatic roles, opposite the likes of James Cagney, Alan Ladd, Ronald Reagan, and newcomer Burt Lancaster. Vera-Ellen, who was receiving more fan mail than either Kaye or Mayo, found herself sitting out the rest of her contract because Goldwyn never saw her as anything more than a supporting player. She held her own with no less than Gene Kelly and Fred Astaire on loanouts to MGM; "but after Mr. Goldwyn set me up in pictures," she said late in life, "he really ruined my career." Goldwyn's next film, released two months after *A Song Is Born*, fared no better with the public and cost him his two remaining lead actors.

The discriminating public savored a number of serious English pictures after the war—David Lean's *Great Expectations*, Laurence Olivier's *Hamlet*, and an adaptation of English novelist Rumer Godden's *Black Narcissus*. Sam Goldwyn chased the trend. He secured the rights to the latest of Godden's moody novels, *Take Three Tenses*. Playwright John Patrick, who had written *The Hasty Heart*, adapted the Godden book, also a wartime love story.

The house at 99 Wiltshire Place narrates the film, introducing viewers to an old retired general, Sir Roland Dane, his great-niece, Grizel, and the Canadian flier in love with her. Their arrival unlocks the memory of Roland's thwarted first love, which ultimately brings the young couple into each other's arms. Beneath bursting bombs they declare their love, as the Dane mansion is shelled, killing the general inside.

Goldwyn had cast Niven in but one picture since his return from the war, but he kept him constantly employed. After a disastrous eight months making *Bonnie Prince Charlie* against his will in London for Alexander Korda, Niven told Goldwyn he needed a vacation before returning to Hollywood. Goldwyn refused. "David," he wrote, "don't for a minute think that you have reached the stage where you are so big on the screen that you can afford to disregard your contract and your studio's instructions. While I am doing everything possible to build you up to the position that I would like to see you reach, you should for your own sake be doing your share instead of trying to throw a monkey wrench into what we are doing." Niven complied, pleased to be given the lead in *Take Three Tenses,* retitled *Enchantment.*

The part required him to age from a young guardsman in love to the old, melancholy Dane. Teresa Wright played his love interest and Farley Granger the Canadian flier. Goldwyn surrounded them with fine actors, including a child named Gigi Perreau. Her performance was so moving that crew members applauded her on the set after her most dramatic scenes. To play Grizel, Goldwyn sprang Harry Cohn's newest star, Evelyn Keyes, from her Columbia contract. "Ahhh!" Goldwyn boomed every time he saw her. "My favorite actress!" He hired Irving Reis, triumphant from his RKO hit, *The Bachelor and the Bobby-Soxer,* to direct.

In its profile of Goldwyn, *Life* had quoted Darryl Zanuck on the subject's "instinctive talent"; but "as a publicity expert, at getting attention and newspaper space for Goldwyn," Zanuck said,

> he is absolutely a past master—a genius—the greatest in the business.
>
> If he doesn't have any significant pictures to release, if he is putting out some little musical comedy or other, he will issue a statement that it's Hollywood's job to brighten the lives of the people and not worry them about serious issues. And then, when he has a significant picture to release—something like "The Best Years of Our Lives"—he will wait until just a day before it comes out and issue a statement saying that Hollywood isn't producing enough significant pictures!

So it was with *Enchantment.* Preview cards indicated that audiences found the picture "confusing" and "slow moving," with a "want-to-see factor" much lower than the average Goldwyn movie. But the producer boldly wrote Julius Ochs Adler of the *New York Times* that he began planning *Enchantment* as

> something which might counteract the trend of tough, hard, gangster pictures and others of a similar type . . . springing up again after the war. . . . I wanted to say in "Enchantment" that there was

more to life than bitterness and disillusionment or escape through slam-bang crime stories.

Enchantment did not deliver the promise of its title. Most critics dismissed it as a manipulative tearjerker. "The picture flopped," said Evelyn Keyes. "Sam stopped calling me his favorite actress. He had to blame somebody, and he owned all the other players."

Not for long. Teresa Wright was announced for his next picture, but ill health stepped in the way. She had made four films for Goldwyn and had dropped out of as many. When the latest private survey from George Gallup showed her "marquee rating" stuck where it had been for the better part of a decade, Goldwyn canceled her contract.

He called David Niven to his office and told him that he, on the other hand, was very lucky: He was being loaned to Korda again, to make *The Elusive Pimpernel.* Niven said he did not mind local loanouts, but he could no longer tolerate the constant uprooting from his family. Goldwyn reminded the actor that he had picked him up "out of the gutter." Niven replied that the producer had been repaid a thousand times over. Goldwyn said failure to appear in this picture would result in his suspension; Niven said he looked forward to a holiday, and besides, he had "plenty of money in the bank." Goldwyn pressed the switch on his intercom and said, "Find out how much money Niven has in the bank." Three minutes later, the intercom spoke back: "One hundred and eleven dollars."

After *The Elusive Pimpernel,* Goldwyn loaned Niven out to play opposite Shirley Temple in *A Kiss for Corliss.* Meantime, other studios were telling Niven they would have important properties for him if he were a free lance. Niven made an appointment to see his boss. "Look, Sam," he said, "we don't see eye to eye anymore. I have two years left of my contract. How about releasing me?" Niven never forgot Goldwyn's unflinching eyes as he flicked his intercom lever and said, "Give Niven his release as from today . . . he's through." As the actor slid into a career slump for several years, he got to thinking that Goldwyn actually held the power to blackball him in the industry forever.

For Goldwyn, there was a greater, irreplaceable loss upon the completion of *Enchantment.* In September 1948, forty-four-year-old Gregg Toland took to his bed for a week, then died suddenly from a coronary thrombosis. Toland was the highest-paid cameraman in Hollywood; he had photographed most of Goldwyn's talking pictures—thirty-seven in all. The producer was furious not to see a single star among the crowd at Toland's funeral.

Goldwyn's story purchases over the next few years were all in service of promoting his two remaining stars, Dana Andrews and Farley Granger. The stories ranged from lachrymose to grim, reflecting his darkening mood. "Something happened in the organization," Granger recalled. "Goldwyn was suddenly making movies that could have been done by anyone. The other studios were developing their new young stars—Rock Hudson, Tony Curtis, and the MGM kids [Elizabeth Taylor, Peter Lawford, June Allyson]. I begged him to split my contract with Fox, because doing one film every year or two for him made me dependent on loan-outs for my career." But Goldwyn refused. After Granger received fine notices in two unusual films—Nicholas Ray's *They Live by Night* and Hitchcock's *Rope*—Goldwyn starred him in a film for the first time.

It was based on a novel about America's most famous feuding families, the Hatfields and the McCoys. *Roseanna McCoy* was an Appalachian version of *Romeo and Juliet,* in which the young title heroine falls in love with the hot-blooded son of her clan's rivals. With Teresa Wright, it might have assumed greater stature. Even Cathy O'Donnell might have made a go of it, but Goldwyn lost interest in her career when she suddenly married Willy Wyler's brother Robert. Goldwyn launched a nationwide star search and became smitten with a slightly pudgy teenager named Joan Eunson. The Goldwyn publicity department changed her surname to Evans and built her and Farley Granger up as one of the screen's great new love teams. Frances Goldwyn, who had been cultivating friendships with important agents and writers on both coasts, persuaded novelist John Collier to write the screenplay.

Farley Granger remembered Collier's having captured much of the mysticism of the mountains in his version of *Roseanna McCoy,* but it was too literary for Goldwyn. Several other writers, Ben Hecht among them, whittled it down to hokey melodrama and hillbilly clichés. Director Irving Reis was sent to the Sierra Madres to film even before the script was finished. He spent several days shooting action sequences of his principals before shutting the production down while the screenplay was completed. The film ended up with a lot of kissing scenes in the woods and Johnse Hatfield forcing himself upon the reluctant Roseanna McCoy.

The Goldwyn studio churned out a pulpier movie on a neighboring soundstage. It drew even sharper criticism, probably because it sprang from a higher source. At the urging of Julius and Philip Epstein, twins who had written *Casablanca* and *Mr. Skeffington,* Goldwyn purchased the rights to a *New Yorker* short story called "Uncle Wiggily in Connecticut," by the literary sensation of the day, J. D. Salinger. It was a spare tale of an afternoon between two former college roommates, one a lush who—it is implied—had entered her loveless marriage without revealing her pregnancy by another man. In the Epsteins' version, more than had ever been suggested would be shown, resulting in a "four handkerchief" movie with a farfetched plot. For the alcoholic central character, Goldwyn borrowed Susan Hayward from Universal. Dana Andrews would play the unsuspecting father of her child (another role for Gigi Perreau). Mark Robson had just impressed the town directing *Champion* and *Home of the Brave;* Goldwyn thought they were so "brilliant" he signed him to direct three pictures, starting with this one—*My Foolish Heart.* Goldwyn hired one of the schmaltziest melodists in Hollywood, Victor Young, to score the picture and write a title song. His Oscar-nominated title tune ran through the picture and became a big hit.

John McCarten, *The New Yorker* reviewer, said *My Foolish Heart* was so "full of soap-opera clichés . . . it's hard to believe that it was wrung out of a short story . . . that appeared in this austere magazine a couple of years ago." Robert Sherwood could not help telling Goldwyn how "phony" he found the picture, the victim of "that old long arm of coincidence." A few months later, Goldwyn expressed interest in buying the screen rights to Salinger's latest work, *The Catcher in the Rye,* only to learn that the author refused to sell them. Hollywood's interest in those rights never waned over the years, but as a result of the bastardization of "Uncle Wiggily," Salinger resolved never "to sell any more of his works to the screen regardless of financial sacrifice" to himself.

The national election of 1948 did nothing to lift Goldwyn's spirits. Although he continued to write the occasional letter of praise to the President, Goldwyn wanted Truman out of the White House. Billy Wilder remembered attending a rollicking Election Night party at the Goldwyns' that November, dozens of their friends toasting with champagne as the radio announced Governor Dewey's apparent victory. A little after midnight, Wilder left to pick up his future wife, a nightclub singer named Audrey Young. By the time they returned to Laurel Lane, Wilder discovered the house awash in gloom. "Sitting in the living room on the carpet, with their backs to the wall," he remembered, "were Charlie Brackett, Mary Pickford, and Louella Parsons—all dissolved in tears." They were bemoaning the sudden change in events. "We're leaving the country. Truman won. The Reds are taking over," they cried. "Goldwyn," recollected Wilder, "was just staring into space, completely pale. Now, believe me, I lived through Hitler being appointed Chancellor, and we took it better than that."

Sic transit gloria mundi:

Charlie Chaplin's first film in seven years, *Monsieur Verdoux,* flopped miserably; and his personal life had finally turned the press against him.

Agents from the Federal Bureau of Investigation, the Treasury Department, and Immigration were dogging him; so was Mary Pickford, who saw United Artists going down the drain. The Hearst papers said this "moral nonentity" should be denied the privilege of being even "a paying guest" in the United States. The FBI questioned Goldwyn about Chaplin's rumored political activities, but he could offer no evidence of his old friend's being a Communist. "Charlie would never join the Party," Goldwyn later quipped to friends; "he's too cheap to pay the dues."

Adolph Zukor still held the title of chairman of Paramount's board, but the 1948 Supreme Court decision forcing their theaters to split from the producing companies threw Paramount into turmoil. A special Academy Award to Zukor—"a man who has been called the father of the feature film in America, for his services to the industry over a period of forty years"—in March 1949 was Hollywood's way of handing him a gold retirement watch. Zukor would live almost another thirty years—to 103. His influence declining with each passing day, "old creepy," as his employees called him, retired to his fabulous estate in New Jersey. "Zukor," Goldwyn told Alfred Crown, "stole more money from this business than anybody who ever lived."

Billy Wilder would never forget a 1948 dinner with the Goldwyns at Romanoff's that was perhaps the most telling illustration of Hollywood's entering a new age. They were seated in one of the booths to the side of the bar when a very tall gray-haired gentleman came right up to Goldwyn and brandished his long index finger. "Here you are, you son of a bitch," he growled drunkenly; "I ought to be making pictures—" Before he could say another word, Frances scared him off by hissing, "Get away from here, you silly man." Sam just sat there agape, and Frances asked who that was. Looking as though he needed a drink himself, he said, "D. W. Griffith." A few months later, the medium's first titan was dead. At the request of the Motion Picture Academy, Goldwyn attended Griffith's memorial service at the Hollywood Masonic Temple as an honorary pallbearer. Wilder's next picture would be a mordant elegy to the silent-picture era, *Sunset Boulevard*.

In 1950, American box-office receipts fell off one quarter of a billion dollars—the disappearance, Goldwyn figured, of some fifteen to twenty million once regular customers. Goldwyn's only solace was that all of Hollywood was in a tailspin.

A sharp production executive named Buddy Adler carried Columbia into a new era of respectability with such successes as *All the King's Men* and *Born Yesterday*. Jerry Wald, who had been a writer for a decade, produced *Johnny Belinda* and *The Glass Menagerie*. Still in his thirties, Stanley

Kramer began tackling human issues in such realistic films as *Champion, Home of the Brave,* and *The Men,* as well as a widely admired production of *Cyrano.*

After twenty-five years, United Artists could pretend no longer. Grosses in 1950 were half what they had been in 1946. Pickford and Chaplin averted bankruptcy for their brainchild by surrendering it to a pair of New York attorneys, Arthur B. Krim and Robert S. Benjamin. In 1955, the courts ordered the auction of the United Artists lot—what an erstwhile partner had baptized the Samuel Goldwyn Studios. Only two bids were submitted: $1,501,000 from Goldwyn; $1,525,000 from Mary Pickford. The studio was hers, unless James Mulvey on Goldwyn's behalf could better her price. There were fifteen raises in open court, then Goldwyn won the lot outright for $1,920,000. After thirty years of quarreling, Mary Pickford had no reason to talk to Sam Goldwyn ever again. She shook hands with Mulvey, then told the press, "I want to forget business for a while."

In 1948, Howard Hughes bought RKO. Production executive Dore Schary could not conform to his new boss's nocturnal hours and felt uncomfortable because, he later noted, "I knew more about motion pictures than he." Schary became a vice president at MGM. Within three years, he was head of the studio, after the Loew's management asked Louis B. Mayer to "resign." Goldwyn rejoiced at Mayer's dismissal.

Motion picture contracts became more complicated, as stars demanded bigger pieces of the profit pie; many directors as well as actors established independent production companies. Their agents gathered more power as they became more resourceful. Myron Selznick had died in 1944, and his partner, Leland Hayward, sold their agency to start a career as a Broadway producer; Charlie Feldman became a motion picture producer. That left the town wide open for big dealmakers to hang out their shingles—such agents as Phil Berg, Bert Allenberg, and Sam Jaffe. There was a young powerhouse at the Famous Artists Corporation named Ray Stark. Abe Lastfogel helped build up the William Morris Agency. No organization of artists' representatives enjoyed greater success than the Music Corporation of America. Within Jules Stein's expanding empire, agents Lew Wasserman, Jennings Lang, and Taft Schreiber were fast becoming important figures in their own right. "I have to give Sam Goldwyn credit for helping me get a foothold out here," said Jules Stein shortly before his death in 1981, when his empire had grown to be worth more than a billion dollars. "Sam was the one who introduced me to all the right people." Stein formed a separate friendship with Frances, who explained to him the less obvious power games in town.

A new wave of foreign filmmakers invaded Hollywood. Michael Powell and Emeric Pressburger's British production of *The Red Shoes* gave Americans an intimate look at the international world of ballet; the French exported Jean Cocteau's *The Eternal Return* and *Beauty and the Beast,* and Jean-Louis Barrault's *Children of Paradise.* The Italians made the greatest impact, starting with Roberto Rossellini's semidocumentary *Open City,* the first film in a foreign language to be nominated for an Academy Award—for its Sergio Amidei and Federico Fellini screenplay. The next year, Vittorio De Sica's *Shoeshine* was nominated in the same category.

Goldwyn detested the Italian postwar realism but began issuing statements about how much "we have . . . to learn from the terrible experiences which the European countries were suffering." In February 1949, he and Roberto Rossellini announced a business partnership that would include Ingrid Bergman, then at the peak of her fame. They told the press they were going to make a picture called *Stromboli,* in which Miss Bergman would be the only professional actress. At their joint press conference, Rossellini expounded at great length on his revolutionary new method of filmmaking, in which he and his cast and crew would just appear at a location with more of an outline than a script and improvise the scene. As Rossellini enthusiastically carried on, Goldwyn leaned over to George Slaff and whispered, "New? That's the way we made pictures thirty-five years ago!" Sam Goldwyn, Jr., insisted that his father was never genuinely interested in partnering with anyone—"certainly not Rossellini. It just seemed like the best way to get some good publicity just then." Before Rossellini left Hollywood to start *Stromboli,* Goldwyn had withdrawn from the project.

In an article under his byline in the Winter 1949–50 issue of *Hollywood Quarterly,* Goldwyn asked if the industry could survive "the most difficult competition imaginable," that "form of entertainment in which all the best features of radio, the theater, and motion pictures may be combined." The American population—with its sudden boom in new parents and students on the GI Bill—was getting used to staying home for its nightly entertainment. There were already close to one million television sets installed. America's rooftops became metal forests.

Sam Goldwyn saw the future of the medium as early as February 1949, when one of the nation's advertising magnates, Roy Durstine, wrote him that General Electric, General Motors' Chevrolet Division, Philco, and Texaco had already pledged at least one million dollars apiece to television advertising; Admiral, Sanka Coffee, Motorola, Emerson Radio, and American Tobacco were not far behind. Before the coaxial cable had linked together nationwide networks, before the new medium's programming had been determined, Goldwyn accurately described the kinds of programs the new industry would be producing. He also speculated that the "greatest potentialities" for audiences and producers lay in an experimental device called "Phonevision." This form of pay television, he said,

> is a system by which any television-set owner will be able to call his telephone operator, tell her that he wishes to see "The Best Years of Our Lives" (if I may be pardoned for thinking of my favorite picture), or any other picture, and then see the picture on his television set. The charge for the showing of the picture will be carried on the regular monthly telephone bill.

At age seventy, Goldwyn put two pictures in the works, contemporary stories he thought would speak to the changing American audience. With the vast majority of the country's moviegoers under thirty, Hollywood tried to lure them out of their new suburban houses with the subject it thought would interest them most—the American family. While most "family films" still embraced motherhood and America, audiences were growing allergic to pasteurized scenarios. Movies were successfully exploring social issues; race and religion were no longer cinematic taboos. People wanted to see that the "typical American family" did not exist, that every family had its troubles.

Screenwriter F. Hugh Herbert approached Goldwyn with an original idea about an American family. *Our Very Own* offered plenty of roles for Goldwyn's young contract players, plus a plot that was at once simple and controversial: The happy Macauley family is upset on the eve of daughter Gail's high school graduation when she learns that she was adopted. Goldwyn borrowed Ann Blyth to play the lead. Farley Granger would play her boyfriend (who installs television antennas), Joan Evans a younger sister who lets the skeleton out of the closet. Eleven-year-old Natalie Wood, still in pigtails, would play a third daughter, and Jane Wyatt their mother, good preparation for her future television role as the quintessential American mother. To play Gail's best friend, a victim of a wealthy but broken home, Frances Goldwyn urged her husband to cast a nineteen-year-old actress she had seen in a play in Philadelphia—Phyllis Kirk.

On Frances's say-so alone, Sam began negotiating with Miss Kirk's agent, Paul Small—who was Dore Schary's brother-in-law. Their dealings in New York were interrupted when Goldwyn suddenly had to undergo prostate surgery. The operation at Manhattan's Harkness Pavilion was routine; but Goldwyn was having trouble getting the reluctant Miss Kirk to sign a contract. Recovering among three dozen bouquets of flowers (and greetings from another fifty famous well-wishers), Goldwyn grew so anxious he told Small, "If you get her to sign . . . when you're ready for this operation, I'll pay for it."

Phyllis Kirk came to Hollywood in late 1949 and was surprised to see the lack of activity at the Goldwyn Studios. It reminded her "of Asbury Park about to be boarded up for the season." Frances Goldwyn, thriving on her increasing responsibilities, tried to "protect" her by suggesting where she might live. The young actress found Frances "colder than ice, full of pretensions and airs, a real duchess"; preferring privacy, Miss Kirk rented a small flat in town and often drove up the coast to Zuma Beach, where she would sleep in her red convertible, returning to Hollywood just before sunrise for her six o'clock makeup call. There, on the deserted lot, she regularly bumped into a disheveled man in baggy khakis, who worked on the second floor at the end of the main building on Formosa Avenue. Every morning at daybreak, they shared coffee and a doughnut. He became Miss Kirk's only friend.

David Miller, who had just directed *Love Happy*, the last of the Marx Brothers movies (distinguished most for its featuring blond hopeful Marilyn Monroe), directed *Our Very Own*. The film did respectably at the box office, cashing in on its young stars and elevating Farley Granger to "teen fave" status; but it was one of the most synthetic films ever to carry the Goldwyn label.

Although Phyllis Kirk had a $15,000 contract for eight weeks' work on her next picture, Goldwyn had nothing else ready for her. In the meantime, Paul Small insisted that she keep an appointment at RKO, which had suddenly become interested in signing her. She was led into an executive office that was pitch black, except for a pool of light barely illuminating a pair of long-fingered hands resting on the desk. Groping in the dark, she found a chair and sat. When Howard Hughes said, "Good morning," she recognized the voice. It was that of the man with whom she shared coffee and doughnuts. Even though Hughes owned an entire studio, he preferred tinkering on his films at night in the privacy of the small cutting room he kept on the Goldwyn lot. He offered the young actress a contract, but she refused; she figured she was "not exactly Jane Russell"and that she would be paid just to sit around and do nothing. She did no better by Sam Goldwyn, who never worked with her again.

Goldwyn chose to exploit Joan Evans instead, teaming her with his headliner, Dana Andrews, and Farley Granger. The film was *Edge of Doom*, and as Granger later noted, "That's where it brought all our careers." It was based on a dismal novel that delved into the psyche of a delivery boy, Martin, who in a rage over the death of his mother kills a priest for refusing to provide her with a fancy funeral. The parish's new priest investigates his predecessor's death, playing cat and mouse with Martin and his conscience. At last Martin confesses, freeing himself with the truth. Such somber material had never interested Goldwyn in the past, but a new force on the Goldwyn lot had become its leading advocate.

Frances Goldwyn no longer hid her power. While her husband wallowed in his worst funk since his expulsion from the old Goldwyn Company in 1922, Frances saw an opportunity to assert herself. She kept the studio under tight rein, and she delighted in her own efficacy. She became Goldwyn's chief scout for talent and material; she worked on every speech and article he put before the public; she had all but his ultimate word on production matters, from script to costumes. On business trips, she carried their money and a small notebook, in which she entered even the pettiest cash outlays. She assumed much of his correspondence, including the persistent financial requests from his relatives in England. "If you continue bothering Sam for extra moneys," she wrote his sister Sally in August 1950, "your allowance will be instantly cut off." On their next trip to London, the Goldwyns cordially greeted Sam's nieces in their suite at Claridge's; the instant he left the room, Frances turned to the younger, Pola, and insisted she had no reason to dun him any longer, because she had become a pretty woman. Said Frances, "You can walk the streets."

While protecting her husband's fortune, Frances swaddled herself in Catholicism. Indeed, she had recently told Lillian Hellman she thought she would become a nun after Sam died. She converted half her bedroom at Laurel Lane into a "nun's cell," furnished with little more than her narrow bed, a crucifix on the wall, and a nightstand, on which sat rosary beads and a small picture of her friend of thirty years, George Cukor—with whom she spoke on the telephone every day. (Their relationship had deepened in the 1940s, as he suffered personal and professional humiliations. Frances was always there for him, though he kept most of his private life from her. She did know, however, that he was, as she said, "unlucky in love" and that he had been cruelly taunted in the Army for being homosexual. No longer a staff director at MGM, where he had become known as Hollywood's leading "woman's director," he had a seesaw career over the next thirty years—with several forgettable films in between such classics as *Born Yesterday, Pat and Mike, A Star Is Born,* and *My Fair Lady.*) Until she was ready to make a further commitment to God, Frances served Sam Goldwyn. She read the galleys of *Edge of Doom* and was desperate to turn it into a film. She convinced him it was the story of a man fighting for redemption of his soul, and every bit as compelling as *The Informer.*

Mark Robson would direct it as the second film under his contract, but

Goldwyn had a difficult time finding anyone to adapt the dreary material. Philip Yordan, who had written an unpretentious film about another murderer, *Dillinger*, for "B"-movie factory Monogram Pictures, took the job. The psychological bones of the story were removed, and all that remained, as Walter Winchell commented, was "raw meat."

At the first sneak preview, in Santa Barbara, half the house gave the film its lowest rating, "poor." Most of the audience found the film "depressing" and "morbid." The Pasadena crowd the next night was less kind. After several months of editing, *Edge of Doom* opened at the Astor Theater in New York. Critics crucified it. It played next door to the Victoria, where *Our Very Own* had opened the week before. This meant Goldwyn's name and product could be plastered for an entire block overlooking Times Square. By the second week, not even Farley Granger (whose presence at the Boston opening required police to control the mob of bobby-soxers) could draw crowds into the Astor.

Goldwyn was desperate to breathe life into the stillborn picture. Jock Lawrence reminded him how they had "saved" *Wuthering Heights* by adding a narration. Using that same technique and adding two scenes to bookend the film, they could turn *Edge of Doom* into the story of a priest who makes good rather than a boy who went bad, thus underscoring its uplifting message—redemption through faith. Doctoring a film that had already opened was practically unheard of, but Goldwyn hired Charles Brackett and Ben Hecht. Even with their new scenes, *Edge of Doom* seemed beyond salvation.

Goldwyn was chewing out his staff one day for not creating a successful advertising campaign for the film. "I don't know what's the matter with you," he said to them. "This is a simple story about a boy who wants a fine funeral for his mother, so he kills a priest." Upon hearing his own words, he suddenly grasped the fundamental problem with the movie. With his next breath he said, "Let's not spend another dime."

After a three-year string of losers, Goldwyn was furious, having to concede, as he did to Alfred Crown, that "we won't even get our money back for prints, advertising and distribution costs. . . . The slowness with which these pictures are played—and that goes for all the pictures—is enough to bust anybody!" More than the profits and losses of a few films were at stake; there was his company's future to consider. He had built a library of seventy-five films, which he and his wife owned outright, and Sammy had reached his majority. In the wake of Frances's recent failure with *Edge of Doom*, Sam took a new look at their son.

After his hitch in the Army, Sammy elected to stay in Europe. He left Wiesbaden for London, where he sought a job in motion pictures. Gold-

wyn fought with himself over his son's blooming independence, then tried
to lure Sammy home. "I think I ought to tell you that a good percentage
of the Goldwyn Company stock is laid away in trust for you," he wrote
before his son had made any commitments abroad; "and your big interest
in the future is going to be in the Goldwyn Company as between you and
Mother you will own most of the business. Therefore, I agree with you
that you should learn as much as you can about the picture business. As I
have always told you, my own interest now is for you and all the organizing I am doing and everything else for that matter is for the day when you
will come in and carry on, as I personally do not care to work any longer
than I have to."

Sammy chose to remain in England. The J. Arthur Rank film company
hired him as an associate producer. At first, his father expressed nothing
but "every faith in you and all the confidence in the world that you will
make a great success of your new undertaking." Then Goldwyn became
obsessed with his namesake's reflecting badly on him.

He encouraged his son to make his own decisions but constantly prof-
fered unsolicited advice. He berated him for not volunteering more about
his work, then criticized the decisions Sammy wrote home about. He took
pride in hearing that the Goldwyn name had become a magic carpet into
London society for his son; but when Sammy's name appeared in the social
columns once too often, Goldwyn reminded him: "you are the son of a
Hollywood producer and as such you are very vulnerable. . . . I should
hate to see you go to London and start going around to cafes and behaving
like a rich man's son."

George Cukor went to England at that time and wanted to introduce
Sammy to such friends as Cecil Beaton and Somerset Maugham, whom
young Goldwyn greatly admired. "I would love to do more to help
Sammy," Cukor told Frances; but, thinking of the sexual implications, he
said, "It would look bad if I did it." Instead, he neatly arranged for
Maugham to invite the young man to lunch.

The harder Sammy worked to create a life for himself in London, the
harder Sam worked to get him home. In October 1946, he wrote: "It's
very hard on mother and me to have you so far away as you know you're
all we have—and you mean more to me than anything in this world outside of mother; my entire life is wrapped around you." And in May 1947:

. . . I feel very strongly that you should come home—that by being
here with me for a month you will take back with you things that
may help you in your future work there. . . .

As I told you on the phone, one of the things that bothered me

about your coming home was the fact that you might come back here
and start going back to your old routine; but after thinking it over
and analyzing your activities abroad, I have great faith that you are
on a different footing now and that you fully realize your responsibilities—so I am not as much worried about this as I was.

Goldwyn established a trust fund for his son, which would provide him
with an annual income, more than $25,000 in the next year alone.

The twenty-one-year-old was determined to stay abroad, if only to prove
his mettle to himself. After resisting his father for a year, Sammy gently
declared his independence. In late April 1948, he wrote:

You know how badly I want to carry on the name and the tradition
of quality for which it stands. I can only do that by being a fine
director-producer. I couldn't get along on the basis of your fine work.
I must do my own. I don't want people to say he's good but his father
was better. I want to be better than you and I hope someday to have
a son who'll be even better than I hope to be. Please try and understand this, Daddy. I love you and Mother very dearly. . . . Please try
and see that what I am doing is what I feel is right.

Goldwyn immediately telephoned his son, then recorded his sentiments
in a letter. "I want you to do what you feel is best for yourself," he insisted.
"You never need accept my advice unless you feel like taking it." Within
weeks, he warned James Mulvey that Sammy was likely to try borrowing
money from the trust. Under no circumstances, said Goldwyn, were any
more funds to be released to him. "He is on his own," Goldwyn said, "and
if he wants to fool around Europe, it is up to him to take care of himself. . . . I feel he has no right to hang around over there when he can be
earning money here."

Sammy stayed abroad through most of 1948, working on several small
pictures and producing a play in London. After two years with the Rank
Organisation, he moved to France with a friend, Blaine Littell. By the end
of the year, he had come to accept his father's assurances of independence
and opportunity in Los Angeles. If he would just come home, Sam and
Frances guaranteed he could produce a picture. After being away most of
a decade, he returned, leaving behind $7,000 in debts, which his father
paid. Goldwyn was so delighted to have his son back, he threw in a bonus
of a $100-a-week allowance. Sammy got a job as associate producer to
Leonard Goldstein at the newly merged Universal–International, on a picture starring James Mason, called *One Way Street.*

At Laurel Lane, Sammy's parents subjected him to their constant criticism of old. He moved into his own apartment, but still they quarreled with everything he did. They disapproved of practically every girlfriend he presented to them; and, recalled Ira Gershwin's wife, Lee, "Frances did everything she could to bust the important relationships up."

On March 8, 1950, the studio publicity department released the story Goldwyn had dreamed of for a quarter of a century: His son was joining the company as a producer. Goldwyn junior's first production, the announcement said, would be an idea of his own, which he would write with Blaine Littell, then working for the Denver *Post.* Called *No Time Like the Present,* it was the story of an American soldier in the occupational army in Germany who befriends a family there. For the first time in three years, Goldwyn seemed to be coming out of the dumps.

Sammy chose that moment to spring on his parents the news that he intended to marry a girl with whom he had reacquainted himself, a cousin of his friend Blaine Littell. Jennifer Howard had grown even more attractive in the few years since he had first met her, and she had proved herself most gifted on the New York stage. The daughter of Sidney Howard and his first wife, actress Clare Eames, and raised among the Damrosches, America's most distinguished musical dynasty, she seemed a perfect match for the handsome young producer. The senior Goldwyns demurred. She was older than Sammy; she was an actress; and she had already been married. More to the point, George Cukor noted, "Frances wasn't about to approve of anybody Sammy wanted to marry."

The twenty-four-year-old was determined to cut the cord. To Lee Gershwin, the boy's fervent desire to marry and start his own family was inevitable: "Sammy had nobody, just his parents . . . and I think he had to plant some roots, and surround himself with children." Jennifer, both of whose parents were deceased, had the same desire. Sam and Frances had been in New York for the unsuccessful opening of *Edge of Doom,* and there was a question of their getting to California for the small wedding celebration. They flew in the day before.

By the time Sammy returned to Los Angeles from his brief honeymoon in Carmel, his father's dreams of working with him were disappearing. North Korean troops, equipped with Soviet-made weapons, had already rumbled across the thirty-eighth parallel to invade South Korea. A picture about the peacetime army suddenly seemed anachronistic, out of touch. "Sam, Jr."—as his father had taken to calling him in business—informed the defense authorities in Washington that *No Time Like the Present* was being put on ice.

One night that summer, Sammy arrived at Laurel Lane with Jennifer,

flashing a letter that had arrived that afternoon. Second Lieutenant Goldwyn, on inactive duty in the Army Reserve, had been called up. "He could
see no reason why, with all the able-bodied young Americans there were
who had never seen service," his father later related, "he had to be singled
out to go back." Goldwyn agreed, railing that he, too, "was being discrim-
inated against." Frances said it did not seem fair to her either. The family
groused long after dinner—all except the newest addition, who sat in
polite silence.

At last Jennifer spoke up. She turned to Sammy, Goldwyn remembered,
and said, "Lord knows I don't want to see you go—but why shouldn't
you? You stayed in the Reserve because you thought that was the right
thing to do. Now they've called you, so what are you kicking about? They
probably won't ship you overseas right away, and till they do, I can be
near your camp. Lots of wives have done it. I can too." Nobody liked the
situation, but she said, "Maybe we ought to be thankful for what we've
got and can keep instead of griping about what we have to give up!"

Goldwyn did not sleep that night, only partly out of paternal concern.
He awakened Frances at three o'clock to tell her he had a new idea for a
motion picture. He wanted to "tell a story of the effect of America's rearm-
ing on the lives of the American family today." He saw a film of universal
significance and artistic importance.

Goldwyn went directly to Robert Sherwood. "YOU HAVE A WONDERFUL
IDEA AND IT SHOULD OBVIOUSLY BE CARRIED THROUGH AT THE EARLIEST
POSSIBLE MOMENT," Sherwood wired; but he begged off developing it,
citing Broadway commitments. Irwin Shaw, who had just published his
first novel, *The Young Lions,* agreed to write the screenplay of what became
a multiple love story. He tore its title right off the Uncle Sam enlistment
posters—*I Want You.*

As in *Best Years,* this picture told the story of three men, this time all
in the same family. World War II veteran Martin Greer lives with his wife
and runs the family construction business with his father, a World War I
veteran still bragging of his military heroics, and his younger brother,
Jack, just graduated from high school. The Greer household is thrown into
turmoil when Jack gets drafted and does everything he can to dodge it. In
the end, Jack goes into the service, and the army makes a man of him; his
father is exposed as a fraud who had been but a general's orderly in the
Great War; and Martin, after wrestling with his own conscience, reenlists,
leaving his wife, his mother, and his brother's girlfriend patriotically
awaiting the return of their soldiers. Years later, Shaw admitted he had
been "whoring" when he wrote the script, which he rationalized by saying,
"I just gave Sam what he wanted."

The screenplay, with all its American stereotypes, contained big roles for Goldwyn's two leading men, Dana Andrews (in his last picture under his Goldwyn contract) and Farley Granger (in another unsympathetic part for the twenty-five-year-old teen idol). It failed to attract any major stars to support them. Goldwyn borrowed Dorothy McGuire from Selznick and gave her second billing.

I Want You was one of Goldwyn's most trouble-free productions. From its opening, with an aerial introduction to a small American town, to its nuptial finale, Goldwyn resolved any problems by duplicating what had worked in *Best Years of Our Lives*. Everything came easier this second time around. Mark Robson put up none of the interference Goldwyn had come to expect for so many years from William Wyler. Richard Day, who had not designed sets for Goldwyn since the thirties, returned to create a look *Newsweek* would note "has all the exaggerated realism of a painting by Norman Rockwell"—just the way Goldwyn liked it.

Ironically, the catalyst for the picture was nowhere near its production. Sammy had transferred his commission to the Signal Corps, where he would direct and produce documentaries; he accompanied Dwight Eisenhower on his return mission to Western Europe as supreme commander of NATO's defense forces. By the time *I Want You* previewed in Santa Barbara, cease-fire negotiations in Korea had already begun. The audience reaction that September night was tepid. Goldwyn was nonetheless committed to an all-out promotional attack, for reasons that went beyond business.

Goldwyn had turned hawkish. In 1951, he became one of the nation's leading supporters of the Committee on the Present Danger, an organization committed to the belief "that we can compel peace through the sheer force of United States strength." Goldwyn believed "the most important single thing which we, as a nation, can do at this time is to build our own defenses by supporting the military and economic defense of the free world as proposed in the Administration's foreign aid program." With this cinematic statement of his philosophy, he intended to reclaim the summit he had held four years earlier.

Goldwyn made up for any artistic inferiority in the picture with advertising superiority. He pegged every article, letter, and interview about *I Want You* to its being no mere movie but a statement of national importance. He likened the film at every opportunity—whether it was a letter to General Eisenhower or to General Adler of the *Times*—to *Best Years*. Because it was a Goldwyn production, critics did not dismiss *I Want You* out of hand; but they stopped just short of describing it as a cartoon.

Goldwyn remained obsessed with topping *Best Years*. He realized he had failed to find any new trend in movies as show business entered the television age. He had miscalculated seven times in a row, and his biggest question was which way to proceed.

On March 20, 1952, he got his answer. Danny Kaye hosted the twenty-fourth presentation of the Academy Awards, at the RKO Pantages Theater in Hollywood. *A Place in the Sun* and *A Streetcar Named Desire* were the evening's favorites for top honors; *Quo Vadis* was a contender, while *The African Queen* and *Death of a Salesman* were expected to pick up awards along the way. Because musicals, even more than comedies, had long been dismissed as too frivolous to win the grand prize, Jesse Lasky startled most of the motion picture community when he opened the Best Picture envelope and announced *An American in Paris*. It was as far afield as one could get from the American primitives Sam Goldwyn had been producing. Arthur Freed's sophisticated spectacle, directed by Vincente Minnelli, was a two-hour depiction of an expatriate painter, which climaxed with a seventeen-and-one-half-minute ballet: In and out of sets in the style of Dufy, Renoir, Rousseau, Toulouse-Lautrec, Utrillo, and Van Gogh, 120 dancers moved to the Gershwin symphonic suite that gave the film its title.

It was the same piece of music George Balanchine had choreographed for *The Goldwyn Follies* in 1937, which Goldwyn had struck from the picture.

20 Dinosaurs

B Y 1950, American consumers had spent more than one billion dollars on television sets. That figure more than doubled in 1951. Over a six-year period, this new mania hooked enough people to keep movie attendance in its postwar decline, plunging from seventy-six million to fifty million patrons a week. Five thousand theaters closed. "My father was suddenly dealing in a world of great changes, which he didn't always grasp," said Sam Goldwyn, Jr., about his father in the fifties, when television took hold of American life.

Show business suddenly found itself with a new set of rules. Many former vaudevillians and nightclub performers found that their acts played better on the small box. Tuesday nights, most American families adopted a favorite "uncle," Milton Berle. Radio favorites Burns and Allen, Jack Benny, and Arthur Godfrey found themselves no less at home on their own television shows. Goldwyn's scouts urged him to sign a versatile comic named Sid Caesar—"the funniest guy alive," said Lynn Farnol—to a picture contract. Before an offer could be put on the table, television came unto Caesar and made him one of the most innovative forces in entertainment. He was hailed every Saturday night. Syndicated newspaper columnist Ed Sullivan became ringmaster of a variety show that ran every Sunday for twenty-three years.

With the promise of more celebrity in a single night than it took most movie stars a decade to attain, some performers preferred visibility on television to what the movies offered. One former Goldwyn Girl, a redhead who seldom got her name on a theater marquee, found the perfect arena for her talent in a Monday-night half-hour situation comedy. By the end of 1951, everybody in America loved Lucy.

Bob Hope starred in regular television specials. The Marx Brothers broke up as a screen team, and Groucho became a television quizmaster. Only five years after winning her Oscar for *The Farmer's Daughter*, Loretta Young hosted a weekly series of original dramas, many of which she starred in. Charles Boyer, Dick Powell, and David Niven (who had not yet found his footing after Goldwyn gave him his walking papers) formed a television production company called Four Star Television, Inc. (even though they were unable to persuade a fourth star to join them in the venture).

Over the next decade, every studio sought to capitalize on motion pictures' greatest strength; they developed techniques for making their larger-than-life images even larger. Screens were widened, new sound systems were developed, and color was enhanced. In 1952, Spyros Skouras bought the rights to a French patent that Twentieth Century—Fox christened CinemaScope; this wide-angle process proved commercially successful in its debut, the otherwise routine biblical epic *The Robe*. There were experiments in three-dimensional, stereoscopic photography (what *Variety* called 3-D), in which images seemed to protrude right out of the screen. Goldwyn was wary of all the new effects, cautious of "novelty in place of real values."

"Goldwyn used to say, 'You're only as good as your next picture,'" recalled Alfred Crown. Upon the failure of *I Want You*, he had half a dozen projects in development: a few domestic dramas; a western; a Broadway hit about the twenties, called *Billion Dollar Baby;* and an adaptation of the Mary Poppins books. But he chose to resurrect a project he had buried years earlier, the only one that might match the charm and sophistication of *An American in Paris*. Goldwyn lost interest in everything else. Noted Sam Goldwyn, Jr., "My father got compulsive about producing each picture as though it were his last. *That* was the one he would go out on, the one he'd be remembered for."

Although he had first put writers on the assignment in 1938, the time never seemed more ripe for a king-sized, colorful musical based on Hans Christian Andersen. He suddenly realized this when Paramount tried to buy one of the scripts he had commissioned on the subject. It blended Andersen's life with several of his fairy tales; and Goldwyn thought it could somehow conclude with a Balanchine ballet featuring Moira Shearer, the star of *The Red Shoes*. Danny Kaye heard about Goldwyn's intentions to get the film made. Even before there was a satisfactory script, he saw it as a wonderful vehicle for himself and made it clear to Goldwyn that he was "crazy to do the picture." It cost the producer close to $200,000 to get his former contract player.

For another $75,000 and 5 percent of the net profits, Goldwyn hired Moss Hart, the author of *Lady in the Dark,* the musical that first brought Kaye to the public's attention. He sent Frances to New York with two earlier treatments of the material, in the hope of enticing the crowned heads of Broadway, Richard Rodgers and Oscar Hammerstein II, to write an original score. "This has been a long labor of love," Goldwyn explained in a letter to the songwriters, "because if ever I loved anything in my entire career, this has been it." After they turned him down, Goldwyn appealed to Frank Loesser, who had composed the theme song for *Roseanna McCoy* before writing *Guys and Dolls,* then in its second year on Broadway. Loesser accepted.

In trying to pull a script together from the thirty-two versions Goldwyn owned, Moss Hart leaned most heavily on the 1938 treatment by Myles Connolly. Concluding that Andersen was a rather drab, often unsympathetic, character, Connolly had outlined the film as a "sort of fairytale" of the writer's life, illustrated with Andersen's stories. Hart and Loesser selected those best suited for setting to music—"Thumbelina," "The Ugly Duckling," "The Emperor's New Clothes," and "The Little Mermaid"; then the writer had to string those songs into a story.

Hart's version of Hans Christian Andersen is a completely fictitious account of a moonstruck cobbler who delights the children of Odense with his charming tales to the point of distraction and to the utter dismay of the local elders. Banished from town, he journeys with his apprentice (Peter, an unexplained young ward) to Copenhagen, where he hopes to ply his trade. Almost immediately upon arriving in the capital, however, he is incarcerated for unwittingly violating a town ordinance. Imprisoned, he sings a story to a little girl outside his cell window ("Thumbelina") while Peter hides out at the Royal Theater. There he overhears Doro, a temperamental ballerina, shrieking for a cobbler. Peter suggests Hans, who is released from jail so that he can make her slippers. Hans falls in love with her, unaware that she is married to her equally temperamental ballet director.

Hans pines for her, and masks his deep feelings in a story called "The Little Mermaid"—a tale of misplaced love. It accidentally lands in the hands of the dancer, who mistakes the billet-doux for a ballet plot. Peter tells Hans of the mishap. He chastises the youth and rushes to Doro to proclaim his love for her, only to find that the ballet company has left town.

In her absence, Hans opens his shop, but incurably reverts to his old ways of charming children with his tales. "The Ugly Duckling" so comforts the bald-headed child to whom it is sung that his father, a newspaper editor, prints it. Hans becomes a famous writer. The ballet company returns, performing "The Little Mermaid," but Hans does not get to see it because the dancer's husband locks Hans in a closet. The next day, he declares his love for Doro, only to be told the truth—that she is married and, for all the marital strife, loves her husband. Returning to Odense with Peter, Hans is welcomed a hero by all the admirers of his stories, young and old alike.

Within ten weeks, Moss Hart had the screenplay on paper. Over the next ten weeks, he moved into the guest suite on Laurel Lane and wrote five more drafts. He stretched the plot everywhere possible to accommodate another half-dozen Loesser songs—including "Inchworm," "I'm Hans Christian Andersen," "Wonderful Copenhagen," "No Two People," and a bewitching ballad called "Anywhere I Wander." He paced the story fast enough to move the audience from one tune to another without their paying too much attention to the plot. Alfred Crown suggested that Goldwyn was so anxious to get a film in production—"he thought it might blot out the memory of that string of losers"—that he did not notice how nonsensical the story was. It was a case of "The Emperor's New Clothes": Everybody was afraid to tell the leader that he had bought a bum bill of goods. Only Farley Granger, cast under protest in the unsympathetic tertiary role of the ballet master, spoke up. He said the script was so "ridiculous" that it was becoming a joke around town. "Look at that plot," he said. "Boy meets girl; boy loses girl; boy gets boy."

The four-million-dollar spectacle started shooting several months later than Goldwyn had originally expected. The delays cost him several important elements. George Balanchine could not change his schedule with the New York City Ballet, and Moira Shearer got pregnant. She was replaced by Renée Jeanmaire, prima ballerina with the Ballet de Paris, the dance company of her husband, Roland Petit. He was hired to choreograph *Hans Christian Andersen*. Directors' prior commitments forced Goldwyn to go far down his list of choices until he got to Charles Vidor, whose most notable films had been *Cover Girl* and *Gilda,* with Rita Hayworth. Filming on Richard Day's gingerbread-house sets—about as realistic a depiction of Denmark as the plot was true to Andersen's life—was scheduled to last more than four months, through the spring of 1952.

Age seventy-three, Goldwyn was a new man. "Things are getting very exciting around the studio these days," his secretary wrote Sammy. "Some of the sets are nearing completion and they are truly magnificent . . . gorgeous costumes are in work—tests are being made—and a million other things seem to be going on at the same time. Mr. Goldwyn is working very hard but is thriving on it. He is in the best of health and seems to enjoy every minute of the day." The producer could not keep himself away from the set; for months he hummed "Thumbelina."

Goldwyn unleashed his most elaborate promotional campaign. The film's publicist, David Golding (whom he called "Goulding"), urged him to spend $25,000 on the world-class photographer Gjon Mili; his extraordinary shots in lieu of the usual production stills resulted in several extravagant magazine layouts. Goldwyn tapped into television everywhere he could. Dinah Shore sang "Anywhere I Wander" on her program; Ed Sullivan presented a retrospective of the producer's life and work. George Burns and Gracie Allen threw in an exchange about the film in the short routine that closed their program. Edward R. Murrow used the production as a window into "the new Hollywood" on his program of on-the-spot journalism, *See It Now.*

Months before the film's fall opening, Danes protested that Samuel Goldwyn was desecrating their national monument. Andersen scholars insisted that Danny Kaye bore no resemblance to the actual storyteller; the Danish foreign ministry railed in both the American and the Danish press that "the setup is so crazy and is . . . more Mexico than Denmark." Goldwyn screened an early cut of the film for Mogens Skot-Hansen, the United Nations representative to the motion picture industry. He publicly announced that it could only "promote the interest for Andersen's fairy tales not only in the U.S.A. but also in Denmark when it is released." Skot-Hansen told his countrymen only to worry about where they would "find room for the millions of tourists" whom the film would attract.

Danny Kaye visited Denmark in July 1952. From the airport he went straight to the statue of Andersen in one of Copenhagen's central parks, to lay flowers. More than fifty policemen were needed to escort him through the throngs who awaited him at the memorial. "I came here to see if you would murder me," he said, only to be assaulted with cheers. He climbed the statue and embraced Andersen, then had to be carried on policemen's shoulders past the thousands of fans. Kaye performed a special concert of the film's score, broadcast on radio across Europe, before a live audience of 250 Danes who had been selected from 75,000 applicants for tickets.

By attaching a disclaimer, Goldwyn spiked the guns of any critics who might attack his film's lack of authenticity. The film began by stating, "Once upon a time there lived in Denmark a great story-teller named Hans

Christian Andersen," and that this film was not a biography "but a fairy tale about this great spinner of fairy tales." Most viewers of the film played along, subordinating their objections to the plot and character to the many charms of Danny Kaye's silver-throated renditions of the Loesser songs.

Hans Christian Andersen opened Thanksgiving week 1952 and became an immediate box-office champion. From his room at the Sherry Netherland Hotel, Goldwyn could look down on the long line of New Yorkers waiting to see his movie at the Paris Theater. "That's what I've got to be thankful for," he told his son. It earned more than six million dollars in its initial run—the most of any Goldwyn film to date except for *Best Years*; and it was nominated for six Academy Awards (music, song, sound, cinematography, costumes, and sets). Cecil B. DeMille won the Best Picture Oscar that year with his version of circus life, *The Greatest Show on Earth*. That victory was something of a message to the public, that the struggling medium of motion pictures could still deliver something television could not.

Goldwyn felt that both he and his industry had survived yet another debacle. "It all proves to me that this business of ours is still a great and healthy one," he wrote one critic. "If you make your pictures for the whole family, the whole family will make a bee-line for the theatre."

The most fractious reaction to *Hans Christian Andersen* came from Farley Granger, who was fed up with yet another inferior role. In New York, the Actors Studio was teaching a naturalistic acting technique that grew out of Stanislavsky's precepts; its "method" was preparing several new talents for the screen who almost single-handedly were changing the image of American leading men: Marlon Brando led this pack of movie "rebels"; Montgomery Clift was a sensitive, introspective version; and in but three films, James Dean would capture the social unrest of his age and come to symbolize an entire generation. Even such conventional newcomers as Tony Curtis, Robert Wagner, and Tab Hunter threatened to eclipse Farley Granger's time in the sun.

The restless twenty-seven-year-old actor reacted to his disappointment with bad deportment, occasionally disappearing for weeks at a time. In his tenth year under contract, and on suspension again, Granger wrote Goldwyn, "our relationship seems to be going downhill and getting worse rather than better." He asked Goldwyn to release him. Goldwyn replied with an accounting of all the unrequired boosts in salary and career he had offered the young actor. "We are often our own worst enemies," he counseled, "and I sincerely believe that your present attitude can only be harmful to yourself. The only way out is not 'divorce' as you put it, but to live up to your agreement in all respects." A short time later, Goldwyn realized he had no future plans for him, and he let Granger—the last of his contract stars—go.

For the first moment in his life, Goldwyn found himself with time on his hands. He discovered unforeseen bliss on July 11, 1951, when Jennifer gave birth to a girl, named Catherine Howard Goldwyn. She and Sammy called her Cricket. Before the child was three months old, Frances sailed to France, where the family was living on a farm outside Paris. She sent Sam a report of her inspection tour, glowing in every department—from Sammy's job heading SHAPE's photographic office of the Motion Picture Division to the baby's blue eyes and red hair "and features any one can see must grow into a beautiful face."

Goldwyn established a trust for his granddaughter, which he started by signing over the rights to one of his most successful films, *The Hurricane.* He kept a photograph of the baby on his desk, and snapshots of her with her father, mother, or grandmother in every room of the house. "I just love the looks of that baby," he wrote Sammy.

Back in mufti, Sammy moved with his family to Central Park West in New York. He launched a show business career of his own in television, working for Edward R. Murrow. Within a few years, he had returned to Los Angeles, where he produced feature films. The first, *Man with the Gun* in 1955, starred Robert Mitchum. In the ten years after Cricket's arrival, Jennifer gave birth to three sons—Francis Sidney Howard in 1954, John Howard in 1958, and Anthony Howard in 1961. The doting grandparents showered them with presents; and for a few hours on holidays, Sam Goldwyn became a sentimental family man. (He and Frances's mother even found it in their hearts to raise flowery toasts to each other.) Like most of the Goldwyns' friends, Leonora Hornblow observed that "Sam poured into his grandchildren all the love he had withheld from Sammy." (Meantime, Sam expressed token interest in Ruth's children: When Blanche Capps married a dentist, Ralph Stern, Goldwyn did help outfit his office; but Goldwyn did not even notice his grandson Alan's growing interest in photography. When Ruth found the courage to ask her father if he could find even the most menial studio job for her son, Goldwyn only snarled, "Everybody doesn't have to be in the movies!")

Besides his son's sons, Goldwyn came to see charity as a way to perpetuate his name. In 1951, he offered the University of California one million dollars for the construction of a hospital on the Los Angeles campus. When the university was unable to meet the financial demands entailed in erecting the Goldwyn Pavilion, he created a scholarship at UCLA for medical students. In 1954, he established the Samuel Goldwyn Award in Creative

Writing, to be presented annually. (Francis Ford Coppola would take first place eight years later.) The Samuel Goldwyn Award, $2,500 for "the best painting by a Southern California artist," was funded in 1957. A $75,000 contribution to the Permanent Charities Committee in 1956 made possible the purchase of a lot and the erection of their new headquarters, the Samuel Goldwyn Building. Goldwyn also served as president of the United Jewish Welfare Fund, and when the state of Israel achieved its independence, Abba Eban invited him to introduce the new nation's president, David Ben-Gurion, at a fund-raising gala. (Although Goldwyn never stopped supporting Israel, he did have limits. One day Edward G. Robinson went up to Laurel Lane to discuss the idea of helping the young country start its own movie industry. "My God," said Goldwyn. "There are enough rotten Jews in Hollywood!")

Aside from Ronald Reagan (the former Warners star who became host of television's *General Electric Theater*), Hollywood claimed few political supporters more active than Sam Goldwyn. In October 1951, he had written General Eisenhower ex cathedra: "I can tell you without reservation that every single bit of evidence which comes to me from all parts of the country demonstrates beyond doubt that the American people unreservedly want you to serve them. . . . The people want you. The people will continue to want you. And, unless I have no knowledge whatever, the people will demand you!" Goldwyn bombarded the general with similar cables and letters until he accepted the nomination of the Republican party. "TO ME," Goldwyn wired the new candidate in July 1952, "THIS IS A DREAM COME TRUE." One of Ike's biggest contributors and fund-raisers, he attended the inauguration and became the President's most diehard constituent. Over the years, they became friends, with Goldwyn sending flattering messages after every important presidential speech. The only time he questioned the President was in the dog days of 1954, at which time he expressed his opinions to Chief of Staff Sherman Adams. "Day by day I grow more and more concerned with the evil which McCarthy works upon our country," he wrote. "Unfortunately, he was elected as a Republican and, as a party, we will remain cursed with the stigma of McCarthy unless he is repudiated unqualifiedly." He suggested the President take aggressive action, but Eisenhower maintained silence.

For the greater part of the two years following *Hans Christian Andersen*, Goldwyn enjoyed his leisure. He and Frances traveled to Hawaii, weekended in Palm Springs, and even indulged in a three-week visit to the Austrian spa of Bad Gastein. They spent close to six months touring the capitals of Europe. Goldwyn became a hound for publicity, especially in his absence, when there was no news to report. "If a day went by without something about him in the paper," Dave Golding remembered, "he'd say, 'You bastard, Goulding—you let me die.'"

Back at the office, he was walking in circles. One of his brightest executives, William Dozier, had quit because "Goldwyn just didn't seem interested in making pictures. He wasn't buying anything." He had an early crack at Robert Anderson's *Tea and Sympathy* but resisted because the suggestion of adultery in the plot would prevent the film from getting the Motion Picture Association's seal; at the same time, he wrote to Eric Johnston, insisting that the industry update its production code. Goldwyn contented himself contemplating remakes and meeting with representatives of several new companies that were offering large sums of cash to motion picture studios for the license to distribute their films on television. Danny Mandell cut down two dozen Goldwyn pictures so that they might air in hour-long versions; but then he refused to sell. Robert Sherwood and Willy Wyler, both between projects, discussed the idea of getting together with Goldwyn on another one, but—as Wyler said—"it seemed like too much bother for everybody."

Instead, Goldwyn rereleased *The Best Years of Our Lives,* modified to play on a wide screen. It opened with all the hoopla of a new picture, including a gala premiere in Washington, D.C., on February 3, 1954, with Sherman Adams, five Supreme Court justices, two cabinet members, and twenty-four senators in attendance. "As far as I am concerned, what counts is what is in the picture, not when it was made," Goldwyn told the press. "A literary classic is just as important in its 10th or 20th or 100th edition as it was when it was first written, and the public accepts this as a matter of course. The same should be true of motion pictures." With a quarter-million-dollar campaign advertising it as "The Most Honored Picture of All Time," *Best Years* grossed another million dollars. "I am not yet ready to make a specific announcement about my next picture," Goldwyn was telling the press, "but when I do you can rest assured that it will be one worth hearing about." It was.

A golden age of the Broadway musical was climaxing—a decade and a half in which the art form's leading practitioners were creating the greatest works of their careers. Hollywood's recent success in enhancing size, sound, and spectrum made motion pictures feel they were at last fully able to do those works justice. Between 1955 and 1958, four Rodgers and Hammerstein classics reached the screen—*Oklahoma!, Carousel, The King and I,* and *South Pacific* (which Goldwyn called "Southern Pacific"). Invigorated by the success of *An American in Paris,* MGM attacked the genre in the fifties with all the artillery the big studio could muster. They filmed Cole Porter's *Kiss Me, Kate* in 3-D in 1953, Lerner and Loewe's *Brigadoon* in CinemaScope the following year, *Kismet* the year after that. When Hollywood ran out of recent Broadway hits, it turned out original musicals and revived old favorites by Berlin, the Gershwins, and Jerome Kern.

Frank Loesser's *Guys and Dolls* had opened at the 46th Street Theater on November 24, 1950. Before the second-act curtain had fallen that night, Samuel Goldwyn later noted, "I made up my mind to bring that show to the motion picture screen." Unfortunately, so did practically every other Hollywood producer there. After its three-year run, the show's owners auctioned the property. On March 3, 1954, Sam Goldwyn found himself bidding against MGM, Paramount, and Columbia. He won with an offer of one million dollars (against 10 percent of the picture's worldwide box-office gross)—the highest figure yet paid for a story property in motion picture history.

Guys and Dolls was based on a Damon Runyon short story, "The Idyll of Sarah Brown," with several of his other touts and tinhorn characters thrown in. Screenwriter Jo Swerling laid the groundwork for the play, and Abe Burrows (formerly a radio gag writer) finished it; Frank Loesser wrote a dozen original songs. The musical tells two love stories—one between Nathan Detroit (proprietor of "the oldest established permanent floating crap game in New York") and Miss Adelaide, a nightclub performer with a persistent "bad, bad cold," the psychosomatic result of their fourteen-year engagement. The other lovers are Sky Masterson, a freewheeling smoothie who will bet on anything, and Sarah Brown, a volunteer at the Save-a-Soul Mission. All of them take a chance and wind up winners at a double wedding ceremony in Times Square.

It was a peculiar moment to produce *Guys and Dolls*. Hollywood, in its attempts to attract crowds, had split itself along generational lines. The old guard believed in making pictures bigger still, more fantastic. (Such new box-office champions as *Quo Vadis*, *Cinerama Holiday*, and *The Robe* supported their case.) The Young Turks saw the effectiveness of realism on the silver screen, using the camera as a kind of microscope. Mumbling young men in black leather jackets (*The Wild One* and *Rebel Without a Cause*) were fast becoming the screen's heroes of preference; gritty slums (*The Blackboard Jungle*) proved exciting screen locations. Smaller, psychological works full of sexual tension—William Inge's *Come Back, Little Sheba*, *Picnic*, and *Splendor in the Grass* and Tennessee Williams's *The Rose Tattoo* and *Suddenly Last Summer*—spoke to a new generation of moviegoers. Even in directing *Oklahoma!* Fred Zinnemann strove for realism, shooting much of the action outside the confines of the soundstage, in actual cornfields. For Goldwyn, these trends were ill winds. As his son noted, "Now he was living in a world he didn't like."

"One day, around 1954," Mrs. William Wyler later observed, "there was a whole crowd of new faces in town." Many were a breed of young television executives who saw their medium as the dominant communication and entertainment force of the future. Other Hollywood tenderfoots made up a new generation of movie executives, men with little stake of their own in the industry. Directors, actors, agents, and new independent producers were building businesses from chips of the crumbling studios. The very concept of an independent producer would soon seem outmoded—and a misnomer. As studios began to phase out their supervisors (executive producers), "independent" came to designate anyone with an idea who went to a studio in search of backing—making him, in fact, an extremely dependent producer. Those few, like Goldwyn, who still financed themselves, struck most of the industry as archaic. Hollywood was falling into the hands of men who had no passion for the "garments" they manufactured, no feel for the material.

Sam Goldwyn was one primordial producer not ready to trudge into extinction. He drew strength from Cecil B. DeMille, who was just then moving heaven and earth to produce the greatest spectacle of his career, a remake of his 1923 *The Ten Commandments.* (Jesse Lasky, the third in that triumvirate of Hollywood pioneers, was reduced to writing his memoirs to pay his bills.) Goldwyn grew determined to produce *Guys and Dolls* as the ultimate film musical, an epic. He would demonstrate for the world that none of his powers had diminished, the cost be damned. Every element of the film was "special ordered," to the extent that the handiwork drew attention to itself. Goldwyn spent $5.5 million overproducing the movie.

He started by hiring one of Hollywood's most prodigious talents to write and direct *Guys and Dolls,* even though the twenty-five-year veteran of motion pictures had never made a musical. Joseph L. Mankiewicz had, however, won back-to-back pairs of Oscars—for writing and directing *A Letter to Three Wives* in 1949 and for *All About Eve* in 1950. Mankiewicz was one of the most intellectual moviemakers ever to succeed in Hollywood. He felt the libretto of *Guys and Dolls* was thin, and so he wrote an entire script that could have played without any music at all. "My primary, almost only, objective in this writing," he explained to Goldwyn, "has been to tell the story as warmly and humanly as possible—and to characterize our four principals as fully as if their story were going to be told in purely dramatic terms." With songs, the film would have run four hours. Goldwyn knew the script was long but liked Mankiewicz's deepening of the characters and creation of more "romantic interest." He told him, "You write with great warmth and charmth."

Goldwyn and Mankiewicz considered almost every leading man in Hollywood for both male leads. The roles had been rendered practically indistinguishable, different only in Sky's being required to sing the show's serious songs while Nathan had to play the more comic scenes. They thought first of Gene Kelly, but MGM refused to loan him out. Then they discussed Tony Martin, Kirk Douglas, Robert Mitchum, and Burt Lancaster. Bing Crosby wanted the role of Sky so much that he sent his attorney to plead his case before Goldwyn. Clark Gable's agent pushed hard for his client. In a moment of wild inspiration, Goldwyn thought of a team that had proved unusually successful in the last five years, Dean Martin and Jerry Lewis. Mankiewicz put the kibosh on that idea.

Although nobody knew if he could even carry a tune, one name kept surfacing in every casting session for the role of Sky—Marlon Brando. The hottest actor in films, since his 1950 debut in *The Men,* he had been nominated for four Best Actor Oscars in his next five roles; he won for *On the Waterfront.* Because of Brando's strong aversion to the press, he had been vilified as a "bad boy"; but Mankiewicz, who had directed him in *Julius Caesar,* considered him the consummate actor. When Goldwyn heard that Brando's hesitation in taking the part was not his ability to sing so much as the size of the role, he urged Mankiewicz to win him over. "WANT VERY MUCH TO HAVE YOU PLAY SKY MASTERSON," the director wired. "IN ITS OWN WAY ROLE AS I WOULD WRITE IT FOR YOU OFFERS CHALLENGE ALMOST EQUAL OF MARK ANTONY. YOU HAVE NEVER DONE A MUSICAL NEITHER HAVE I. WE NEVER DID SHAKESPEARE EITHER. I AM CONFIDENT THIS WOULD BE EXCITING GRATIFYING AND REWARDING EXPERIENCE FOR BOTH OF US."

In the midst of negotiations, Frank Sinatra's agent got hold of the script. His client insisted on being in the picture. There would be no conflict in the fact that Goldwyn was about to sign Brando; Sinatra was desperate to play Nathan Detroit. Mankiewicz thought Sinatra was all wrong for the part; in fact, he still hoped to talk Goldwyn into signing Sam Levene, who had created the role on Broadway. But he met the singer at the Beverly Hills Hotel and found that "Frank was just in love with it." Even though Brando and Sinatra were better suited for each other's roles, Goldwyn liked the ring of the stars' names. Brando received top billing and $200,000 for fourteen weeks. Thinking of MGM's advertising on Garbo's first talking picture, Goldwyn thought they might promote *Guys and Dolls* with two words: "Brando Sings." When Harry Cohn, who was then working with Abe Burrows, heard this casting news, he said, "Good for Goldwyn, bad for the picture."

Goldwyn wanted Grace Kelly for Sarah Brown, the missionary. In the three years since he had first heard about her, she had made two films for Hitchcock, played Gary Cooper's leading lady in *High Noon,* and won an Academy Award for her performance in *The Country Girl.* She would make but a few more films before playing in *The Swan* (a remake of Frances Howard's farewell to the silent screen before marrying her "prince"). When she turned this part down because of prior commitments, Goldwyn tried Deborah Kerr, who was also booked. The third choice was Jean Simmons, who had just played Desiree to Brando's Napoleon.

With Betty Grable unavailable to play Miss Adelaide, Goldwyn hired Vivian Blaine, who had originated the role onstage. A chorus of new Goldwyn Girls was recruited. Michael Kidd was asked to re-create his original choreography, and Goldwyn rounded up several members of the Broadway cast—including Stubby Kaye (whom Goldwyn called "Stubby Toe").

A septuagenarian producing his seventy-ninth film, Sam Goldwyn had the enthusiasm of a neophyte. No detail of the production escaped his Argus eyes. One afternoon, Mankiewicz and Loesser were supposed to discuss with Goldwyn the placement of a new song in the picture. "We didn't want to argue in front of him," the director later recounted; "it's better to be a unified front." So on their way to his office, they stopped at a supply closet and hid inside. "We were discussing the situation," said Mankiewicz, "when suddenly the door opened. There was Sam. We both felt awful. A couple of shits. Like we were stealing from him or something. Sam just looked at us with a look of hurt dignity and said, 'I want you to know—I'm not the kind of producer who shoves the money under the door.'"

Irene Sharaff, who designed the costumes, discovered Goldwyn's basic passion for his work as well. She would long remember the day she quietly laughed behind Goldwyn's back when she overheard him tell Mankiewicz he wanted a "close-up" of Brando in one of the dance numbers, "with his feet"; but she also never forgot the day just before they were to film the wedding finale. He and the director had already approved of the dress Jean Simmons was to wear, but as Goldwyn and Sharaff were walking along, he suddenly grabbed her arm and said, "How about the uniform and holding the bouquet instead of the wedding dress?" Ordinarily, the designer later said, "I would have put such a query down to his shrewd budget-paring, but in this instance he was absolutely right. The incident, brief and beyond the film of no consequence, won me over."

Despite the public's new taste for slice-of-life realism, Goldwyn still believed movies should make magic. "People don't want to pay good money," he told Alfred Crown, "to see somebody else's kitchen." So the sets of *Guys and Dolls* were nothing like the streets of New York—not even as Stanley Donen had colorfully captured them in *On the Town*. Keeping his films stage-bound, Miss Sharaff suggested, was "his way of maintaining control." In this case, Oliver Smith's sets were a vivid mixture of scenery both realistic and stylized. "As a result," wrote Stephen Sondheim in *Films in Review,* "they have the disadvantages of both, and these disadvantages work against the very special nature of Runyonesque story-telling." They added a dimension of phoniness to the proceedings, offering little wit or irony.

Joseph Mankiewicz's direction did not help. Sam Goldwyn, Jr., suggested that the director had become so taken with the spectacle of production numbers that he was inclined to keep the camera still, often producing a static quality. Furthermore, the film felt padded, its songs often proving redundant alongside the protracted nonmusical scenes. Orson Welles told Abe Burrows, "They put a tiny turd on every one of your lines."

Vivian Blaine and Stubby Kaye (particularly in his rousing rendition of "Sit Down, You're Rockin' the Boat") recaptured the essence of the show. Nobody found Frank Sinatra noteworthy, but with the addition of a new song, "Adelaide," he sang enough to satisfy his fans. For Goldwyn, the most unexpected surprise proved to be the beautiful Jean Simmons, whose sweet voice and strong acting made him think the love story worked better in the film than onstage. "I'm so happy," he said, bustling toward her after seeing the rushes one day, "that I couldn't get Grace Kelly."

The first time the Goldwyns heard the recording of Brando's songs, Frances tried to make the best of a painful moment. "He sounds like . . . a young Astaire," she offered. Frank Loesser rolled his eyes skyward. Gordon Sawyer and his crew of sound engineers worked hard to patch together respectable versions of his numbers. In the end, Goldwyn was so pleased with Brando's performance onscreen and off that he rewarded him with a white Ford Thunderbird. Seeing no strings attached, Brando accepted it.

"Faithful in detail, the picture is false to the original in its feeling," read the November 14, 1955, *Time* review of *Guys and Dolls,* stating the objections of practically every other critic.

Predictably, Goldwyn ordered his biggest promotional push ever. Richard Avedon took publicity photographs, Ed Sullivan featured numbers on his show, and even the reclusive Brando (feeling indebted to Goldwyn for the new car) gave interviews and attended the film's premieres. When he finally had enough, he announced at one press conference that the film was "nothing to get on your tricycle about."

After more than a decade of profitably releasing his films through RKO, Goldwyn changed distributors. The Howard Hughes film enterprise was in a corporate tailspin, and by 1958 would be run into the ground. Goldwyn found the best terms for himself at MGM, which, since the expulsion of Louis B. Mayer, had been nosediving as well. Nicholas Schenck, the president of Loew's Inc., the studio's parent company, made much of Goldwyn's at last joining the organization that had long borne his name. Goldwyn privately delighted in the fact that after all those years, he could make that claim and the exiled Mayer could not. *Guys and Dolls* did over thirteen million dollars in business, becoming the number one box-office attraction of the year.

The film also received Oscar nominations in the three visual categories—sets, costumes, and cinematography—but it won no awards. For the third year in a row, the Academy's grand prize want to a smaller-screen, black-and-white $350,000 production, *Marty*—the story of a lonely butcher that had originated as a live television drama. "It is neither high, wide, nor handsome, and it has been photographed with a camera designed to present films of the type we used to know and love before CinemaScope opened new and lunatic vistas for enjoyment," said *The New Yorker* review. *Marty* also won trophies for Best Director, Best Screenplay, and Best Actor, and it grossed in the millions.

Goldwyn continued to back his style of Hollywood entertainment. He sent the Goldwyn Girls on a world tour, from Australia to South America; and *Guys and Dolls* became a huge international hit, rivaling MGM's overseas records set by *Gone With the Wind*. Sam and Frances resumed their globe-trotting, to preside at as many foreign openings of the picture as possible, traveling as far as Tokyo. When he learned that Marlon Brando was in Japan filming *Teahouse of the August Moon* at the time of the *Guys and Dolls* premiere there, Goldwyn asked him to attend. Brando refused, saying, "I've done enough for that white Thunderbird." The film grossed almost half a million dollars in that country alone, twenty thousand dollars in Venezuela, over one million dollars in England.

Box-office receipts, increased holdings in stocks and bonds, investments in gushing oil wells, and swelling trust funds were still not enough to make Frances feel completely secure. She was never comfortable enough with her wealth to splurge. One friend said, "The only reason Frances even went along with buying all that art was because she knew it was a good investment. It's why she also preferred jewels to clothes." Wherever she stayed—in her stateroom on the *Queen Mary* or at Claridge's in London—she traveled with her own tin of Sterno, a jar of Maxwell House instant coffee, and a teakettle. Sam, on the other hand, had at last allowed himself to loosen his belt. On vacations, he indulged in rich food, and once he went through an entire tray of pastries. The Goldwyns booked an apartment for a month at the Grand Hôtel de l'Europe in Bad Gastein.

Goldwyn needed a pastime. Sammy suggested croquet, which had become the rage on several Long Island estates. Louis Jourdan, a French actor who had come to America under contract to David Selznick, was generally regarded as the best player in town; he also set the pace for the weekenders at Darryl Zanuck's Palm Springs house. A game with that much social cachet and so few physical demands appealed to Goldwyn. Although it was far more complicated than he ever took time to learn—"It's like playing chess on a lawn," explained Jourdan—he became an overnight devotee.

In 1953, the lot across the street from the Goldwyns and the Firestones, crowning Laurel Lane, had come up for sale for $50,000. Leonard Firestone suggested the two families buy the property jointly, agreeing that if either left the cul-de-sac, the other would have the right to buy the half-interest for $25,000; until such time, the neighbors agreed that no additional dwelling could be constructed on it. As a birthday present for her husband a few years later, Frances bought the Firestone share of the parcel (extravagant, but a good investment) and converted the property into one of the finest croquet courts in the country, complete with gazebo for spectators. Then, "rather like casting 'Best Year,'" suggested Louis Jourdan, "he surrounded himself with the best players he could find." Besides the handsome Frenchman, George Sanders, restaurateur Michael Romanoff, writer Casey Robinson, Howard Hawks and his brother Bill, Gig Young, and director Jean Negulesco became regulars all day Saturday and Sunday. (Humphrey Bogart occasionally played there; in fact, his last outing before succumbing to cancer in 1957 was to watch some old friends play on the Goldwyn court.) The proprietor had cards printed up for his special guests, making them life members of the "Goldwyn Croquet Club." On the back were printed the organization's three rules:

1. Don't get excited.
2. Correctly remember balls you are dead on.
3. Have patience with fellow members who are not as good as you are.

His club members gave Goldwyn a handicap: Generally he was excused from hitting through the center wicket, and he was entitled to a consultant during play. Neither helped much. Nobody ever wanted to be Goldwyn's partner, because he neither listened nor improved. Goldwyn just wanted to win—to hit his ball through the wickets and smash his opponents' balls to kingdom come. He cheated by moving his ball whenever he thought nobody was looking, and he often made up house rules that were to his immediate advantage.

Playing on the Goldwyn court was not about advancing one's career. Curiously, there was not even any betting. "Even tempers, polite memory, and noble unselfishness were our guiding spirits," recounted Negulesco. "Until we walked onto the court. Then the spirit of Hollywood croquet exploded." One time when George Sanders was about to smash Sam's ball, Goldwyn pleaded, "If you don't do it, George, I'll buy you a Rolls-Royce." Sanders said he already owned one and sent the ball sailing. Another time, writer Charles Lederer found himself playing singles with Goldwyn and noticed him heading for the third wicket without having passed through the second. Lederer called him on it, and they argued back and forth until Lederer quietly said, "Sam, you go to the third wicket and I walk out of this court and *never* come back." With high-pitched indignation, Goldwyn turned on his opponent and said, "What's the matter with you? Are you for Stevenson or something?" Louis Jourdan, with whom he was generally partnered, used to try reasoning with Goldwyn, Socratically asking questions in an effort to teach him the fine points of the game. "I was being too impeccable," Jourdan realized. "And one day when I went too far, he could take it no longer; and he said, 'Where are we . . . a court of law?'"

Goldwyn established an annual tournament, complete with awards. Louis Jourdan generally took home the loving cup, and Goldwyn developed an especially warm relationship with him. Otherwise, Sam kept his relationships casual, so that the games could be what Jourdan said were "four or five hours of total escape for him." He talked as little business as possible; and what advice he tendered those days was platitudinous. More than once, he explained to Jean Negulesco the secret to being a successful producer. "You get yourself a great story," he would say. "Then you get the best writer available. Then you get the best director. Then you hire a first-class cast, the right cast, and a great cameraman. . . ." The first time Negulesco heard this wisdom, he started to laugh. A dead-serious Goldwyn stopped him, saying, "I mean it. It is the only way."

Some eighteen months followed the release of *Guys and Dolls* before Goldwyn went sniffing for his next project. He had become so finical that almost nothing appealed to him anymore. One night, Goldwyn and playwright John Patrick saw *Cat on a Hot Tin Roof* together. As they exited the theater, Goldwyn asked what he thought of the Williams play. Patrick said it was not his "kind of thing" and that he was, in fact, offended by much of the dialogue and the subject matter. "I feel the same," said Goldwyn. "And I'm no Polly Adler."

There would have been no genuine search for new material had Frances not become her husband's eyes and ears. She solicited properties from all quarters, and any idea for a motion picture needed her approval before Sam heard about it. She was among the first to see the movie possibilities of *The Naked and the Dead, Anastasia,* and *The Birdman of Alcatraz* (as early as 1953); but in her job as story editor, she found herself as stymied as her paid predecessors had been. All dreams of producing another Robert Sherwood script ended in November 1955, when the critic, dramatist, screenwriter, and presidential speechwriter, and one of Goldwyn's closest friends, died. Francis put pencil to paper, helping her husband write a eulogy.

A year later, Goldwyn seized upon an idea for a film with William Wyler, *The Diary of Anne Frank.* Goldwyn thought the successful Broadway adaptation of the young Jewish girl's journals was "one of the finest dramatic presentations I have witnessed in a considerable time." The one-set play seemed an unusual departure from Goldwyn's "blockbuster" mentality at the time; but, as his son explained, "he knew it would make an important picture."

Goldwyn sent Wyler to New York, and not even the director's ambivalence toward the material dissuaded Goldwyn from proceeding. He figured he could talk Wyler out of his reservations. Then Frances spoke up. "Mother was desperately opposed to it," Sam junior remembered. Because it was a Jewish story, "she was afraid it would lose a lot of money." Goldwyn considered throwing the project Sammy's way, but Frances put her foot down. She could live with her husband taking such a chance, but she said, "Sammy's just starting a career; I don't want it to be something that will fail."

Goldwyn won Wyler over, then lost the property because of his own vanity. Anne Frank's father, who did not know one Hollywood producer from another, controlled the rights to his daughter's story. He was not willing to sell them to anybody without script approval. Goldwyn took this as an insult. A short visit to Europe, a telephone call, even a letter explaining his intentions, would probably have won Mr. Frank over. Instead, Goldwyn rode away from the project on his high horse. George Stevens eventually produced and directed the film. A few years later, looking back over almost sixty years in motion pictures, Goldwyn told his son his biggest disappointment had not been one of the films he had made; it was *The Diary of Anne Frank,* the one that got away.

Goldwyn and Wyler became closer for the experience, bringing their relationship to a level of mutual respect; "and the best part," Wyler said, "is that I didn't have to work for him." When the director needed advice on his next offer, he went directly to his former producer. MGM had decided to remake *Ben-Hur,* hoping the stupendous epic could bail out the scuppered studio, just as the silent version had thirty-five years earlier. Goldwyn urged his friend to take the job, arguing that it would be an opportunity for Wyler to make more money than ever before. He even helped negotiate his contract, assuring Wyler hefty profit participation.

In 1957, James Mulvey suggested that Mr. Goldwyn (as he still called him after thirty years) act on his fondest dream and make a film of *Porgy and Bess.* The Gershwins had long refused to sell the film rights; then they got trammeled up with one Robert Breen, who had been directing the opera around the world for years. Mulvey saw a clear way to the rights by paying Breen off.

In the twenty-two years since it was first performed, Ira Gershwin had counted more than ninety film producers who expressed interest in *Porgy and Bess.* The recent revolution over racial injustice in the United States heightened people's awareness of blacks and incited new interest in this musical version of the crippled black beggar in love with a two-timing woman. Arthur Freed, Hal Wallis, L. B. Mayer, Anatole Litvak, Buddy Adler, and Dore Schary all made offers. (Gershwin never seriously considered Harry Cohn's proposal, once he said he hoped to produce the film with a white cast in blackface—Al Jolson as Porgy, Fred Astaire as the Harlem fast-talker Sportin' Life, and Rita Hayworth as Bess.) In May 1957, Goldwyn obtained the rights for $650,000 against 10 percent of gross receipts and announced that Robert Breen would be associate producer of the picture. Breen was hardly heard from again. Goldwyn pledged the profits from the film to charity, to be dispensed through his foundation.

Applying the formula for great picturemaking that he had spelled out to Jean Negulesco, Goldwyn got the best writer available. He cast a wide net, starting with Langston Hughes. He tried to interest Paul Osborn (who had recently written the screenplays of *East of Eden* and *Sayonara*), Frances Goodrich and Albert Hackett (*The Diary of Anne Frank*), Sidney Kingsley, and the successful team of Jerome Lawrence and Robert E. Lee. They all turned him down, praising the material but citing other commitments. Clifford Odets was given the rush over a private dinner at Laurel Lane, but he, too, passed on the opportunity. Sammy, who was producing a western called *The Proud Rebel,* starring Alan Ladd, recommended one of television's young writing sensations, Rod Serling. Goldwyn got lucky when "out of the blue," as Frances put it, came N. Richard Nash, the author of *The Rainmaker*. By Christmas 1957, he had written a hefty first draft. After two major revisions, he put Goldwyn at ease, assuring him that *Porgy and Bess* was a good twenty-five pages shorter than *Guys and Dolls*.

Then Goldwyn went after the best director. Elia Kazan, Frank Capra, and King Vidor (who had directed the all-black musical *Hallelujah* in 1929) were his first choices. He settled on Rouben Mamoulian, absent from films for nine years until the 1957 production of *Silk Stockings*. Goldwyn did not need reminding that Mamoulian had directed not only the original stage version of *Porgy and Bess* but also the play, *Porgy*, on which the musical work was based.

Getting "a first-class cast, the right cast" proved to be Goldwyn's most formidable task on the film. Because black actors had, de facto, long been barred from Hollywood's major studios—except to tap-dance and play maids and shuffling lazybones—few had the opportunity to become stars. The café-au-lait Lena Horne had come closest to acceptance by white audiences, but her roles in films were mostly "guest appearances," numbers that could be snipped out of prints playing in southern theaters; it looked for a moment as though James Edwards, who portrayed the victimized soldier in *Home of the Brave*, might make it, but he did not catch on. Most recently, a fine-featured West Indian named Harry Belafonte was crossing the color line with his performances in *Carmen Jones* and *Island in the Sun*.

To the generation of young black actors trying to break through, the movie screen of the late fifties became as crucial a battleground in the fight for equality as the buses of Montgomery. *Porgy and Bess* struck many of them as a giant step backward—a story of fornication, drug addiction, and murder, all told in heavy dialect, that did nothing but reinforce negative stereotypes of blacks. Harry Belafonte flatly turned down the lead, and several actors refused other roles. Only Sammy Davis, Jr.—an extremely successful nightclub performer, especially in the new desert playground of Las Vegas—campaigned for a role, that of Sportin' Life. One night at a party at Judy Garland's, he came in and sang several numbers. "Swear on your life you'll never use him," said Lee Gershwin, turning to Goldwyn. "Him?" he replied incredulously. "That monkey?"

"I represent the greatest Negro actor in the whole world," Lillian Schary Small wrote Goldwyn upon learning of his intentions to make *Porgy and Bess*. The actor's name was Sidney Poitier. He was a strapping Bahamian with decidedly Negroid features and dark skin; just thirty, he had picked up a few movie roles since his debut in 1950, then in 1957 worked in three films back-to-back. "He is not a singer," Mrs. Small wrote, "but that is never too much of a problem where the part requires a fine actor." For one of the few times, Goldwyn saw an actor's work that equaled an agent's claims. He made a firm offer of $75,000 for Poitier to play Porgy.

Mrs. Small was not actually Poitier's agent. Martin Baum in New York was, and she was but an independent agent on the West Coast with whom Baum sometimes associated himself. She promised to deliver the actor, even though she had not even discussed the role with him. Unfortunately, as Poitier later noted, "I had a considerable aversion to 'Porgy and Bess' because of its inherent racial attitudes." He flatly refused the part. By that time, however, Goldwyn had announced to the press that he had signed Poitier.

Mrs. Small might have cleaned up the mess by admitting she had committed her client to the role without authority. Instead, she was determined to make good on her word. Goldwyn went to the press again. He leaked the situation to Leonard Lyons, who wrote in his column that Poitier's friends were urging him "to change his mind and agree to do 'Porgy and Bess' for Sam Goldwyn, without a script-approval clause," because Goldwyn was "far more sensitive and sensible about such matters than any one in motion pictures." Then Lyons quoted his friend, Ralph Bunche, the Nobel Prize–winning diplomat, who stated that the play was "a classic, and ought to be preserved on film."

"I was being nudged hard because Sam Goldwyn's nose was publicly out of joint," Poitier recalled. At last even his New York agent insisted that the actor owed the producer a meeting. Poitier realized failure to do so would result in his name being smeared in Hollywood.

The meeting at Laurel Lane could not have been more cordial. After several minutes of pleasantries, Poitier voiced his objections to the material. "I understand how you feel, Mr. Poitier, but I disagree with you," replied Goldwyn, "—this is one of the greatest things that has ever happened for the black race." The remark was not lost on Poitier, who was impressed that this old glove drummer should have resorted to "such an outrageous bullshit statement." At the end of the meeting, Goldwyn insisted that he did not want Poitier to do anything against his will. He asked only that the actor give it "some more honest thought. Man to man."

While he was thinking, Poitier met with Stanley Kramer, who wanted him for a film called *The Defiant Ones*. It was the story of two escaped convicts of different races who hate each other but are chained together. Exactly the sort of realistic role Poitier had been aching for, it made *Porgy and Bess* look archaic. Kramer said he was prepared to draw up a contract—once he had a release from Goldwyn on this *Porgy and Bess* deal he had heard about. Even if there were no papers between Goldwyn and Poitier, Kramer said he could not start a picture with the actor if he thought Goldwyn might bring suit and shut down the production. Poitier said there was no problem; he instructed Lillian Small to tell Goldwyn he had thought about it, and he was not going to do *Porgy and Bess*.

Poitier believed she never delivered the message. Goldwyn said he was holding him to the agent's promise; and Martin Baum reminded Poitier of Goldwyn's power to blackball the actor. "As I saw it," Poitier later wrote, "in my career there was a real beginning for a breakthrough—not only for me, but for other blacks in films." He and his agent closed their contingency deal with Kramer, then went to Goldwyn. "I know that I'm caught in a bind," he told Goldwyn, "—I want to do Kramer's picture. I know you know about the Kramer deal. I understand that you're not going to let me off the hook from the promise my agent gave you. If that is correct, then I'll do 'Porgy and Bess.'"

Goldwyn said, "I don't want you to do 'Porgy and Bess' unless you're going to do it the best way you know how. It's no good me spending all this money if you're not going to come in with team spirit and a feeling of participation." Poitier replied that he was a "professional actor," and as such he would "do the part to the best of my ability—under the circumstances." Goldwyn welcomed him to the project. On December 10, 1957, he introduced Poitier to a corps of newsmen, and Poitier explained the reasons for his turnabout. They were, he said, "pure and honest."

> I have never, to my conscious knowledge, done anything that I thought would be injurious to anyone—particularly to my own people. Now this is a personal choice. I do not pretend to be the conscience of all Negroes.
>
> I am happy to say that my reservations were washed away by Mr. Goldwyn and Mr. Mamoulian in their plans for "Porgy and Bess." I was convinced irrevocably that it will be a great motion picture and tremendous entertainment and that it will be enjoyed by everyone—little and big—people of all races and creeds. . . . I'm happy that I met with Mr. Goldwyn and Mr. Mamoulian—and I found them almost as sensitive as I am.

Goldwyn contributed one thousand dollars to the National Association for the Advancement of Colored People.

Controversy over Goldwyn's all-Negro production raged. For the first time, such criticism came from the black community. It had proved so difficult to find players for the film that Goldwyn's staff had gone scouting in the sports world, considering Jackie Robinson and Sugar Ray Robinson.

Once Sidney Poitier was signed, the rest of the cast fell into place. While the actor was making *The Defiant Ones,* Dorothy Dandridge, the sultry star of *Carmen Jones,* changed her mind and agreed to play Bess; Pearl Bailey said she would take part, as long as the costumer, Irene Sharaff, understood that she refused to wear a bandanna, because it smacked of Aunt Jemima. Brock Peters was cast as the wicked Crown, and a young beauty with a fine voice, Diahann Carroll, was given the part of Clara, whose "Summertime" sets the tone for the entire piece. Goldwyn tried hard to get Cab Calloway to play Sportin' Life, but complications threw the part to Sammy Davis, Jr. Most of the cast were professional singers, but almost all their songs were dubbed by others.

Goldwyn hired Andre Previn to be music director. Born in Berlin in 1929, Previn had moved with his family to Los Angeles when he was ten. MGM began hiring this wunderkind as an arranger while he was still a schoolboy; at nineteen, he was given his first composing assignment. Over the next ten years, he scored two dozen films for the studio, including some of their biggest musicals. Not yet thirty, he had just completed work on *Gigi,* for which he would win an Academy Award.

Goldwyn gave Previn complete control over the music of *Porgy and Bess.* His only edict was that all the singers heard in the film had to be black. Goldwyn had hoped Leontyne Price would perform Bess's songs, but she told him, "No body, no voice." The original soprano he hired had to be paid off and sent away after a test was made of Dorothy Dandridge, because Goldwyn decided she did not sound the way the star looked.

The art directors created the worst sets money could buy. At Goldwyn's insistence, the streets of Catfish Row in the Charleston, South Carolina, wharf district looked clean enough to eat off. This ghetto reeked of studied shabbiness. Irene Sharaff was restricted in the amount of wear and tear her costumes could show. When the women singers in the chorus lined up for the first costume review before the final dress parade, Miss Sharaff recalled, Pearl Bailey "created havoc by screaming, 'No one is going to wear a bandanna in any picture I'm in!'" There ensued "a discussion somewhat like an international conference—and a compromise was reached whereby only a few of the women at a time would wear bandannas." The incident later struck the costumer as "ridiculous, particularly since shortly afterwards many black women took to wearing bandannas as symbols of what they were fighting about."

After six months of travail, *Porgy and Bess* was scheduled to shoot just after the Independence Day weekend. On Tuesday, July 1, 1958, Sam and Frances toured Stage 8 (one of the two largest stages in Hollywood, 400 by 800 feet), making a final inspection of the set and costumes and props. A complete dress rehearsal for the Technicolor and Todd-AO spectacle was called for nine the next morning. More than two million dollars' worth of materiel stood ready to go.

A little after 4 a.m. that Wednesday, a blaze broke out on Stage 8. Flames were leaping 300 feet into the air when the fire department arrived. The entire north wall of the structure fell inward, producing a thunderous roar. Within hours, the stage was reduced to rubble.

Frances received word at Laurel Lane but kept it to herself until she heard Sam stirring. She ordered his breakfast tray, then gently broke the news that the entire set and all the costumes had been destroyed. Years earlier, a similar fate had befallen Adolph Zukor, and Goldwyn had been impressed with his first reaction; he had simply asked, "Was anybody hurt?" Forty years later, Sam, without batting an eye, reached for his tray and asked the same question. Nobody was.

Frances placed the difficult phone calls. Smoke was billowing when set designer Oliver Smith, art director Joe Wright, and the studio's general manager, Milton Pickman, arrived. Irene Sharaff burst into tears. Irving Sindler watched flame and water wipe out thirty years of props he had accumulated and stored in the lower part of the soundstage. Mamoulian was especially supportive, Frances noted, standing "rocklike" beside Sam. Telegrams and calls of support streamed in for days. Frank Freeman at Paramount, Loew's Joseph Vogel, and Jack Warner each offered use of his studio. David Selznick expressed great concern, as did Willy Wyler, who wired from Rome that "STAGE EIGHT HELD GREAT AND FOND MEMORIES FOR ME." The most touching message came from Cecil B. DeMille, who was at Cedars of Lebanon, recovering from a heart attack that struck him after he completed *The Ten Commandments*. "Tell Sam," he said, "the phoenix arose from the ashes of a great fire and so will you with your great strength."

Recent events gave Goldwyn reason enough to question whether he should even try. At the presentation of the thirtieth annual Academy Awards that March, he had become the second recipient of the Jean Hersholt Humanitarian Award. He could have retired that night and remained for a quarter century the only producer ever to win that award as well as the Thalberg and Best Picture trophies. Another special Oscar given at the same ceremony went to Gilbert M. Anderson. The latter's name meant almost nothing to the thousands sitting in the Hollywood Pantages, but it meant everything to Sam Goldwyn. Anderson was none other than "Broncho Billy," the star of the western that had lured Goldwyn off the streets of Times Square in 1913 and into motion pictures. Broncho Billy had bowed out of films in the twenties, his extant two-reelers the only fossils that marked his place in Hollywood's prehistory.

Perhaps worse than Anderson's obscurity was the passing in ignominy of three of Goldwyn's peers, once-mighty patriarchs who had not known when to quit: In October 1957, Louis B. Mayer had died, in studio exile. Just months earlier, Goldwyn had heard of his plotting a comeback to the troubled MGM and immediately bought a block of shares in the company; waving his receipt before Sammy, he said with glee, "Here are 10,000 votes against him."

Less than three months later, Jesse Lasky died, penniless. Goldwyn's former brother-in-law and first partner in the motion picture business had just minutes earlier been promoting his unsuccessful book of memoirs. Although he continued to revile Lasky, Goldwyn chipped in several thousand dollars (with Cecil DeMille) so that Bessie Lasky could hold on to her house.

In February 1958, Harry Cohn, who had run Columbia Pictures since its creation in 1920, died. When a member of the Wilshire Boulevard Temple asked Rabbi Magnin if he could not think of "one good thing to say" about the deceased, the rabbi paused and said, "He's dead."

If Goldwyn was looking to abandon *Porgy and Bess* without losing face, the studio fire had provided the opportunity. Instead, he sent a wire back to his oldest friend in the industry: "DEAR CECIL: YOUR MESSAGE WAS VERY SWEET AND IT IS JUST LIKE YOU TO ALWAYS WANT TO HELP. YOU REMEMBER THE EXPERIENCE WE HAD ON 'THE SQUAW MAN.' THAT WAS EVEN WORSE AND WE CAN TAKE IT BETTER NOW THAN WE COULD THEN." For weeks, the town buzzed that the fire had been the work of black arsonists trying to shut down the picture. Goldwyn publicly denounced the theory and stuck to the explanation that an unextinguished cigarette had been the cause; but studio insiders held to the arson theory. In shrugging off the disaster as just one of those things endemic to motion picture production, Goldwyn told one reporter, "Well, there's *always* a crisis. If it's not me, it's Israel." Goldwyn ordered the sets of *Porgy and Bess* rebuilt and the costumes resewn; the cast was told there would be but a six-week delay. Before the film's completion, Cecil B. DeMille died.

During the weeks of reconstruction, director Mamoulian tried to impose on the film ideas that had not gone over before. Goldwyn argued for strict adherence to the original Gershwin score; Mamoulian wanted to use the jazzier arrangements that Breen had used in his production. The director also said the script begged "for more visual and action build-up" and that the production should not be shackled to the set. He often made snobbish remarks about Goldwyn's lack of understanding, even his inability to read. Not until the director hired his own press agent did Goldwyn fire him; and then, said Sam Goldwyn, Jr., "it was for colossal indecision." Willy Wyler volunteered to direct the picture, if Goldwyn was willing to postpone the production for a few months. Goldwyn did not want to wait. He paid Mamoulian his full $75,000 salary and hired Otto Preminger, who had worked for Goldwyn only once, as an actor in *They Got Me Covered*. Except for a polite announcement to the press, Goldwyn refused to discuss his decision.

Mamoulian was incensed that after working for eight months preparing the script, hiring and rehearsing the cast, prerecording the music, and supervising the sets and costumes—all to the producer's approval—Goldwyn should then dismiss him for "frivolous, spiteful or dictatorial reasons not pertinent to the director's skill or obligation." He brought his case to the Directors' Guild of America, which brought action against the producer, notifying all guild members—including Preminger—"that they may not enter into a contract with Samuel Goldwyn."

That brought the Screen Producers Guild into the fray, protesting "with shock and dismay the hysterical assaults upon the dean of American producers, Mr. Samuel Goldwyn, for exercising his prerogatives as an employer by changing directors on 'Porgy and Bess.'" They pointed out that Goldwyn had honored the contract with Mamoulian to the letter, paying him off in full; they said he was "completely within his rights in refusing to present his side of the story to a kangaroo court."

The influence of a French film review called *Cahiers du Cinema* was just breaking on American shores those days, especially its promotion of the "auteur theory." This philosophy spotlighted directors as the true stars of the medium and emphasized the thematic consistencies of their works. Community sympathy tilted toward Mamoulian.

The director stepped up his charges against Goldwyn. He claimed that the producer had not properly informed him of the termination of his services. Then his press agent, Russell Birdwell, called a special news conference, at which he presented an old black actor who had played a small role in both the original play and the musical of *Porgy*. Leigh Whipper said he was withdrawing from this production in support of Mamoulian because he believed *Porgy and Bess* had fallen into hands "unsympathetic" to his race. He aspersed Preminger specifically, calling him "a man who has no respect for my people." This brought about a flurry of reaction from almost every member of the movie's cast, many of whom had worked with Preminger on *Carmen Jones*. At last, even Mamoulian's agent, Irving Paul Lazar, thought his client had gone too far; he informed *Variety* that the director had grossly misrepresented the facts in the case. After three weeks of nasty press, Goldwyn was completely exonerated, even praised. Said Goldwyn in the end, "I'm the only one in this thing who's exhausted from not talking."

Goldwyn and his new director got off to a peaceable start. Preminger asked for changes in the script, the set, the rehearsal schedule, and insisted on shooting the central picnic sequence on location—Venice Island, near Stockton, California. Goldwyn agreed to everything. In negotiating Preminger's contract, they bickered only on the director's share of the profits. Goldwyn offered 10 percent, and Preminger was accustomed to 50. In a kindly moment, the director told his brother (and agent), Ingo, "Look, let's leave it to Goldwyn. When the picture is finished and he sees it he can decide what my percentage should be." Taken aback by such trust, Goldwyn promised to be fair.

From that moment on, Goldwyn had a more difficult time with the director than he had ever had with Mamoulian. He liked Preminger's strength, but their styles clashed. They argued about practically everything, particularly Preminger's treating the songs as extensions of scenes, not musical numbers. The director also favored the jazz arrangements, and he thought the producer was spending money on the wrong things. "Look," he said, "you've got a two-dollar whore in a two-thousand-dollar dress." Their daily shouting matches became the talk of the studio. Preminger remembered, "People used to gather under the open window of my office to hear me bellow at him on the telephone."

The set was a hotbed of tension. Preminger told his cast at the start, "I want you to know that I grew up in Europe. For me there is no difference between black and white people. So if you behave badly I will be just as tough with you as I would be with white actors." He proved to be an equal-opportunity tyrant, more than once reducing the fragile Dorothy Dandridge to tears. The day he laced into Sidney Poitier, the actor walked off the set with quiet dignity, unwilling to return until he received an apology. Pearl Bailey busied herself raising the black consciousness of her fellow players. Sammy Davis, Jr.—a recent convert to Judaism—created a small stir when he announced that he would not be showing up one morning because it was Yom Kippur. The night before Miss Dandridge was to play the scene in which Crown rapes Bess, she told Preminger that he simply had to recast Brock Peters, because, she stammered, "he's so black." Throughout the shooting, various civil rights organizations and the minority press regularly tarred Goldwyn for his anachronistic attitudes toward blacks. "The only thing left," said Goldwyn upon completion of the most troubled shoot of his career, "is for me to go to jail."

One afternoon, Goldwyn invited the Ira Gershwins and a few guests to a projection room, where they sat and just listened to the sound track. For forty-five minutes, Andre Previn's arrangements of the Gershwin score burst through the finest high-fidelity sound equipment. Everyone was moved. Goldwyn, almost in tears, walked over to young Previn, put his hand on his head, and tousled his hair. "You should be goddam proud, kid," he said. Then he added, "You should never do another thing in your life."

Porgy and Bess did not perform so well with the picture added. The two-and-a-half-hour production (with intermission) felt leaden. Columbia released the film with less than enthusiasm. One of their executives predicted a tough sell because of its downbeat ending and suggested a new one, in which Porgy gets up from his cart and walks. In his efforts to remain true to the material, Goldwyn risked further box-office failure by forbidding any references to the film with the word "musical" as either adjective or noun; he ordered it advertised as an "American folk opera." Just before the release of *Porgy and Bess,* Ingo Preminger asked Goldwyn what profit percentage he had settled upon for his brother. "You left the participation to me," Goldwyn announced. "So there is no participation."

It was a moot point. Goldwyn figured *Porgy and Bess* would have to gross twice its $7 million cost to show a profit. "Today a fine picture makes more than it ever did," Goldwyn told one reporter. "You have to pay $3 and you can't get in. But there is great competition. You have to have the goods. Television has changed it all. Hollywood used to make 600 pictures a year, now it's only 300. Soon it will be less, and they all better be good." He intended to take his time exhibiting *Porgy and Bess,* opening it in New York on June 24, 1959, on a reserved-seat basis.

Porgy and Bess earned half its cost. By the time Goldwyn opened the film in the South, it had become the target for public attacks by uprising black organizations. He pulled the picture from several parts of the country indefinitely, waiting for the militant social climate to change. He could take some pride in the film's being nominated for three Academy Awards (including sound and costumes). Only Andre Previn and Ken Darby won, for Best Scoring of a Musical Picture, making it the first Goldwyn production to take home a trophy since *The Bishop's Wife.* Almost every other award that year went either to *The Diary of Anne Frank* or to *Ben-Hur;* the latter became the new Oscar champion by winning eleven statuettes, including Wyler's third.

On August 27, 1959, Goldwyn called a press conference in his office. The occasion of his seventy-seventh birthday (in fact, he was eighty) was newsworthy enough to capture headlines in the newspapers and on page one of *Daily Variety*. He and Frances posed for the cameras. She said she had given him a suitcase, suspenders, and some shirts—all of which he could use because they planned to spend most of the next year traveling abroad. "No one is waiting breathlessly for my next picture," he granted. "They may retire me," he vowed to the battery of reporters, "but I am never going to retire." It was exactly the posture the newsmen had come to expect from the man who, as Loudon Wainwright had recently written in *Life*, was "left standing alone as the last of the great Hollywood moguls. . . . a unique relic of a vanished species: the one-man gang."

LATE one night, the lone survivor wanted the next day's newspaper. He asked Frances for some change, but all she could find was a twenty-dollar bill. He took it, got in the Cadillac, drove himself to the drugstore in the Beverly Wilshire Hotel, double-parked, went in, bought the paper, and came out again. Back behind the wheel, he felt a knife blade against his neck. The mugger said he wanted all of Goldwyn's money, or else he would kill him.

Goldwyn drove home and related the story to Frances. Then he handed her a ten-dollar bill.

21 A Slow Fade to Black

HOLLYWOOD SNICKERED in the late fifties at a joke about the Goldwyns. As Joseph Mankiewicz remembered it, young Frances Howard married Sam Goldwyn, looking forward to his timely demise and her long, merry widowhood. But ten years pass, and she's thirty to his fifty-seven; she's fifty, he's a hale seventy-seven. And, as the story goes, she's a broken-down ninety and he's still hanging on, at one hundred seventeen. "There he is, at last, on his deathbed," recounted Mankiewicz, "and Frances finally says everything she's been longing to get off her chest all this time: 'For seventy years I have served you,' she says. 'Every time you touch me, my skin crawls. Every time you kiss me, I want to vomit. Every time you make love to me, I want to die.'" After Frances has spoken her piece, Goldwyn calls out to the crowd of mourners waiting in the hall. "Guess what!" he cries. "Frances wants me to marry again!"

For those who saw the Goldwyns regularly, the anecdote was not so funny. Sam's pink face and powerful physique seemed hardly to have changed in all the years of their marriage. His gait had slowed only slightly. Frances, on the other hand, had lost weight over the years. The sleeves on her dresses billowed over her bony arms; her azure eyes sank deeper into her heavily lined face; her hennaed hair and the always-fresh gash of lipstick made her complexion look pasty. Through it all, she remained faithful to her marriage contract, eager to please her husband. "Poor Virginia Zanuck . . . having to live with such a monster," she once

489

said to Leonora Hornblow. "Nobody," Mrs. Hornblow noted, "ever said that of Frances Goldwyn."

Sam Goldwyn was her entire life. Frances maintained few friendships—Mrs. Fred Astaire and Mrs. Irving Berlin, both of whom she telephoned once a week, and her favorite sister, Dede, with whom she talked of spending her future widowhood. Her mother had gone almost completely mad but still maintained a strange emotional hold over the daughter who had never stopped supporting her. Bonnie continued to cook up unguents and potions, she read extreme-right-wing literature, and she told everybody she was growing a third set of teeth! She raised turkeys indoors and refused Frances entrance into the feather-filled rooms—which continued to be paid for by the very man she had once sworn would never marry her daughter. George Cukor and Frances still spoke at least once a day.

Although the Goldwyns entertained less often, Frances could still turn on the perfect dinner party. She never lost her regal bearing. "Of all the social queens," noted Mrs. Billy Wilder, "she was the classiest. She was also the most fun . . . and supportive." Frances always paid attention to her husband; she took to calling him "Mr. Goldwyn" in front of others. As he grew impatient with chitchat, she discouraged lingering in the dining room, so they all might get on with that night's screening.

Sexual liberation in the sixties turned the motion picture screen into an orgiastic playground, and most of Hollywood's latest product turned Goldwyn off. His private screening of *Blow-Up* in 1966 was going just fine until the scene in which David Hemmings cavorts with a couple of young girls. "Oh God," Goldwyn cried out, calling a stop to the screening; "this is a goddamned dirty picture!" Not long after that, Goldwyn complained to Billy Wilder that he had seen an even more disgusting display—*Hello, Dolly!* Wilder was puzzled—not only because he could not imagine anything scurrilous in that harmless musical but also because Darryl Zanuck had not released it yet. Goldwyn insisted he knew what he saw, and it was one of the filthiest pictures he had ever seen. Wilder asked him to recite the plot. "Sam," he interrupted upon hearing about the drug-taking and sex lives of three aspiring actresses, "I think you're referring to *Valley of the Dolls*." "That's just what I said," Goldwyn insisted. "*Valley of the Hello Dollies.*"

The Goldwyns tried to stay in touch with the new names in the industry, but Frances was less interested than her husband in the recent crop of films. No sooner would a picture begin than she would be at the bar, where she kept a private batch of martinis. Audrey Wilder noticed she would throw back the first one, then down another four during the course of a film. With a few people, Frances would allow herself to reveal a bawdy sense of humor, occasionally even joke at herself. At one big post-premiere party at Romanoff's, she sat next to Audrey Wilder and ordered a pink gin—straight gin and bitters. "The drink of the London whores," Frances said, stifling a giggle that threatened to shake her rigid back.

On one of their recent trips east, the Goldwyns called on Irene Mayer Selznick, who upon divorcing had uprooted herself from Beverly Hills and moved to the Pierre Hotel in New York. There she forged a new life for herself as the producer of such Broadway hits as *A Streetcar Named Desire*, *Bell, Book and Candle*, and *The Chalk Garden;* she also bought forty acres with ponds and waterfalls in Bedford Village, an hour north of the city. Sam and Frances visited her house, surrounded by stone walls, dogwoods, and pungent lilacs. One afternoon, coming in from a walk, Frances stopped in her tracks, stared at the idyllic setting, and burst into tears. She was happy to see that the very house she had long dreamed of for herself did in fact exist. "I'm glad you have it," she conceded to her old friend. The place made Sam melancholy as well. After a long hike through the adjacent wildlife sanctuary, he stopped Irene on the dusty dirt road leading back to the house and placed his hands on her head. "I'll tell you what I want," he said, his eyes glistening. "I want to live longer." Tears rolling down his cheeks, he added, "I just want to live to see Cricket married."

" MY father liked the idea of a dynasty," said Sam Goldwyn, Jr., "but he was never sure how it would work. It was a subject of great ambivalence for him. Part of him believed, 'Après moi le déluge'; but then he'd reveal his obsession that his name endure and he'd say, 'We've got to continue.'" The way Jules Stein multiplied his interests into the largest empire in show business elicited Goldwyn's admiration but not his envy. "He was afraid if he built too strong an organization," Sam Goldwyn, Jr., added, "he would have to watch out all the time." The result was a net worth of some twenty million dollars, one tenth what the MCA founder amassed in half the time. "I could've been worth many times more than I was," Goldwyn admitted, "but I wouldn't have survived." His son said, "Even when his picture-making instincts started to go, he just wanted to be in command of a ship. He didn't care how big or if it went down."

After establishing trust funds for his family, Goldwyn abdicated the real decisions about the future of his family's involvement in his business to his wife. "When [the] time comes," Frances told a newspaper interviewer in late 1959, "I hope my son will take over. I won't. I'm involved in things at the studio because I'm interested in my husband's career, but I don't want the same things for myself. I'm a woman. But don't get the idea I'll sit around and knit. Not on your life. I'm going to WRITE."

After abandoning her attempt at a Hollywood novel, Frances took a stab at one other book—a biography of her husband. She wrote two pages and quit. Over the next few years, she showed no signs of losing interest in the operation of the studio, nor in involving Sammy. She persisted in economizing at every turn—fixing her own cigarette holder filters with swabs of cotton, shopping for fabric to re-cover an umbrella that could not have been worth more than five dollars in the first place. Billy Wilder remembered Frances's asking if he had received one of those wartime Oscars, which had been made of some inferior alloy that tarnished badly. Wilder had (for directing and writing *The Lost Weekend*) and recommended a man he had found who shined each trophy up for eighty dollars. Frances thanked him. A week later, she told him she had found somebody to do the job for twenty-five. "I've lived through three generations of the very rich here," she took to saying. "I'd like to live through a fourth."

Just before one of the Goldwyns' next visits to Hawaii—an annual trip between their vacations to Bad Gastein with the Wilders and their retreats to Palm Springs—Frances made an appointment with Claudette Colbert's husband. Dr. Joel Pressman was a highly respected nose and throat doctor on the staff at UCLA Medical Center, who also performed cosmetic surgery on many Hollywood personalities. Frances had her face lifted. At the same time, she stopped dying her hair (which had in fact lost its natural color when she was twenty-one). Frances stepped off the boat from Hawaii a month later sporting a new look. It was a shocking metamorphosis, which most of her friends said made her look twenty years younger—rested and vigorous beneath her cap of snow-white hair. With a figure in vogue for the fashions of the sixties, she dressed more with the times, sometimes trendily.

Her robust husband had at last become the model of the American success story he had long dreamed of, that character he began inventing back in Warsaw. He rested more and more on his laurels, as his survival of each additional year warranted some new accolade. In 1959, the Producers Guild of America presented him with their Milestone Award—even though he did not belong to the organization. The next year, the Emperor of Japan bestowed on him the Order of the Rising Sun for "contribution to the cultural understanding between our two countries." In 1961, the state of Israel specially commended Goldwyn for "two decades of service to world Jewry through the United Jewish Welfare Fund." The Hollywood Foreign Correspondents Association christened their Golden Globe for the Best Foreign Picture the Samuel Goldwyn International Film Award; the

American Council for Nationalities Service presented Goldwyn their first Golden Door Award.

Goldwyn reduced his daily appointments to official audiences with the press and important powers in town. Lunch every ten days would be with somebody of current prominence—Jonas Salk or Alfred Hitchcock or David Ben-Gurion or Julie Andrews. Otherwise he dined with his immediate studio staff, almost always including his new general manager, Jack Foreman—a sharp, go-getting alumnus of the University of Southern California's school of cinema, who had served ten years at CBS. As the once lengthy log of telephone calls during the day shortened to a few influential names, Goldwyn usually found himself going home after his midday nap for a round of croquet or an appointment with one doctor or another. A slip on the croquet lawn resulted in a knee operation; a kidney stone had to be removed; otosclerosis demanded ear surgery and a hearing aid. In lieu of Christmas cards, well-wishing form letters were typed and sent to fifty powerful friends in business and industry (Howard Hughes, Arthur Sulzberger, Walter Annenberg, Norman Chandler, William S. Paley, etc.). No actors or writers made the Goldwyns' list; in fact, most of the show business names were heads of companies. Goldwyn's secretary wired another twenty messages to such special acquaintances as Lord Beaverbrook, Averell Harriman, Sherman Adams, and the Eisenhowers.

In the summer of 1960, Goldwyn met Senator John F. Kennedy—in Los Angeles for the Democratic National Convention—at Charles Feldman's. Goldwyn would never forget Joseph Kennedy's anti-Semitism, a trait he assumed the senator had inherited; he also thought young Kennedy was too much of a playboy to be President. Goldwyn became a staunch supporter of Richard Nixon, and later ticked off for the press the tough world issues that his man was most qualified to tackle: "The defense budget, the U.S. foreign policy mess, Castro," Goldwyn said. "And that H-bomb. That's dynamite!"

After the election, Goldwyn congratulated the President-elect. He invited the also-ran to a private luncheon—just Nixon and Dorothy Schiff, publisher of the New York *Post,* in his studio dining room. Goldwyn said the television debates had cost Nixon the election and told him, "I'd have gotten you a make-up man." For several hours, Goldwyn gave Nixon a piece of his mind. Nixon did not know his host was thinking of his own track record when he said, "Only one thing is important—to survive. If you can survive 51% of the time . . . you're a winner."

Twelve hundred people filled the International Ballroom of the Beverly Hilton Hotel on Sunday night, August 26, 1962, to dine on roast beef, asparagus, and a flaming ice cream cake—all in honor of Samuel Gold-

wyn's "eightieth birthday." The dais alone held more than two dozen celebrities, from Jack Benny to Mayor Sam Yorty, with such as Senator Jacob
Javits, Danny Kaye, Leonard Firestone, and William Wyler in between.
Toastmaster George Jessel conducted the ceremonies, noted the Los Angeles *Times*, "as if they were half-men's smoker and half-religious 'shab-
bas.'" President Kennedy sent a telegram of congratulations. Richard
Nixon (whom Goldwyn was actively supporting for governor) said Goldwyn was "one of those who began with nothing but his own ability, and
achieved greatness on just that." Frank Sinatra and Eddie Fisher sang,
Loretta Young kissed Goldwyn to prove she "wasn't afraid of him any
more," Harpo Marx spoke, and Jimmy Durante stole the show with a
rendition of "Inka Dinka Doo." Along with messages from former Presidents Eisenhower and Hoover, Goldwyn received one hundred fifty congratulatory telegrams on the occasion and another one hundred cards and
letters; dozens of flowers; a pair of shoes from Fred Astaire; and an enco-
miastic editorial in the *New York Times*.

The next morning, Goldwyn announced to the press his plans for a
sweeping new code of ethics for Hollywood. It was an extensive program
that called on all branches of the industry to:

> (1) provide fine entertainment, (2) see to it that the money which
> goes into making pictures and which comes from the public is not
> squandered and (3) restore standards of conduct—personal and busi-
> ness—to the highest possible levels.

With Hollywood currently plagued by "runaway production" (the abandonment of Los Angeles soundstages for cheaper locations elsewhere), soaring salaries, and several companies on the verge of bankruptcy, Goldwyn
said, such a plan was "the only way this industry is going to be saved."
When asked if he had sounded out other studio heads about his proposed
code, Goldwyn said, "I don't sound out anybody. I do it."

He continued to use each birthday to summon the press and talk more
about the state of the business than about his own affairs. When Ben
Hecht came to him with a new idea for a film, Goldwyn told him outright, "As things are right now, I am not taking on any obligations to
produce any pictures." Two years later, he was telling people he had "decided to wait until the climate is a little better for picture making."

What Goldwyn had taken out of Hollywood, he began putting back,
in increasing amounts. A $250,000 donation to the Motion Picture Coun-
try House and Hospital in Woodland Halls resulted in the Samuel Goldwyn Plaza, sixteen cottages and a large recreational area. Dorothy Chandler

confidentially assured him that the center stage of Los Angeles's new theater compound would be named the Samuel Goldwyn Theater in return for his $100,000 donation; the chagrined Mrs. Chandler had to renege when the Ahmanson Foundation offered one million dollars for those nominal rights.

On November 21, 1963, an invitation was mailed from the White House—the President requesting the pleasure of Mr. Goldwyn's company at lunch three weeks thence. The next day, Goldwyn's secretary rushed into his office, where he was meeting with Jack Foreman, and announced that the President had been shot. "We turned on the TV," Foreman remembered, and "Sam cried like a baby." For the next three days, he sat glued to the television at Laurel Lane. He wrote condolence letters to Kennedy's widow and his mother.

"Goldwyn played both sides of the street," said William Paley, "wherever the power was." He supported Lyndon Johnson in 1964, before swinging back to support Republican actors playing new roles in California politics—George Murphy (whom Goldwyn had brought to Hollywood) and Ronald Reagan. The Goldwyns contributed more than $15,000 to Nixon's 1968 presidential campaign.

"Conservatism became an important philosophy in Goldwyn's life," observed Jack Foreman. "I felt he thought he'd never produce again." Goldwyn focused most of his attention on his catalogue of eighty films, fifty-three of which were marketable to television. "Protect those pictures," he told Sammy repeatedly, "and they'll protect you."

A "flamboyant wheeler-dealer" named Matthew "Matty" Fox was among the first to approach Goldwyn with the idea of buying his old films for resale to television. "He'd come around with a check for one million dollars made out to Samuel Goldwyn," Foreman remembered, "and he'd wave it under his nose." Goldwyn sneezed at it. By the sixties, all the studios had unloaded their theatrical film libraries on television, and Goldwyn knew television would devour them instantly. NBC's *Saturday Night at the Movies* could gobble up the best product of an entire studio in a single year. Keeping his films off the air could only make them more valuable. For years, he flirted with several television syndicates and networks. One afternoon, Dan Seymour, the future chairman of the J. Walter Thompson advertising agency, asked Goldwyn how much money he was looking to make from the sale of his film library. "I don't know," said Goldwyn, tapping his index finger against his temple, "but when I hear the number, I'll know it."

In 1960, Goldwyn's representative reported that he had gathered bids as high as five million dollars from stations in the United States and abroad. Goldwyn and Foreman decided to separate the blockbuster musicals of the fifties and license the rest as a package on a limited basis. In 1964, Goldwyn commanded one million dollars for two runs of *Hans Christian Andersen*; he got the same terms for *Guys and Dolls*.

Through all the dealings, the head of CBS hung fire. Foreman said, "It hurt Sam when he announced he was releasing films for TV and Bill Paley didn't come forward." Paley knew better. "Sam Goldwyn wants me to buy some of his films," he quietly announced to some people one weekend in Sands Point, "and I know the day I do will mark the end of our friendship."

In late 1964, Goldwyn at last released his library—to five of CBS's privately owned and operated outlets (known as O & O's), in New York, Los Angeles, Chicago, Philadelphia, and St. Louis. Paley kept himself so far removed from the arrangements that he did not even know negotiations had been concluded. Goldwyn waited for a phone call from his old friend, and when none came, he placed one. "Well, I hope you're happy with the deal," he said to Paley, who could not make out what he was talking about. "Don't you know," said Goldwyn, playing along, "you've bought my pictures for television?" In truth, Paley did not know; the licensing of fifty old movies for five O & O stations was a routine matter for lower-echelon executives. "Come, come," said Goldwyn, unable to imagine the head of CBS having anything more important on his desk than the licensing of Goldwyn films. "That's very hard for me to believe."

Goldwyn scrutinized every detail concerning the broadcasting of his films. He announced the deal with his customary ruffles and flourishes, as if opening a new picture. At a press conference, he argued that "pictures worth showing shouldn't be denigrated" and pointed out that "fine plays are produced many times and they are never called oldies." He invited Cecil Smith, television critic of the Los Angeles *Times,* to a private lunch. "Well," Smith said later, "that was an invitation you couldn't turn down. But everything in the private dining room reminded me of my grandmother's—the food and the furniture. The whole meeting was like walking into another century."

Goldwyn kept his finger on Hollywood's pulse by renting out space at his studio, one of the best facilities in town. It became his plaything. Sam junior said, "He loved to up people's rents." Under Jack Foreman's supervision, the modest fortress at Formosa Avenue and Santa Monica Boulevard was billing close to four million dollars a year, leasing offices and stages to producers of television programs, commercials, and feature films. The studio's primary tenant since 1957 was the Mirisch Company, a successful independent production outfit started by three brothers. In the changing industry of smaller production companies, they quickly became preeminent. Much of their success lay in creating partnerships with important directors, starting with Billy Wilder on *Some Like It Hot*. John Sturges made *The Magnificent Seven* for them. In 1960, the Mirisch Company won Best Picture with Wilder's *The Apartment*, then repeated the honor the next year with Robert Wise's *West Side Story*. In 1964, they slated ten films for production, with such directors as Wilder, George Roy Hill, Blake Edwards, Melville Shavelson, John Frankenheimer, and Norman Jewison. Goldwyn got to know as many of the new talents as possible, inviting each of them to lunch or croquet.

The regular croquet game drifted apart. When he could not recruit any stray players, he would draft a studio underling or Sammy, pulling them away from their own work by insisting they spend the afternoon with him. Even looking the other way when Goldwyn moved his ball into better position, opponents invariably beat him; Goldwyn would throw his hands up and say, "Don't you have anything better to do with your time?"

"Life rolled along pleasantly enough," Frances recalled of the sixties, until her husband developed a fear of aging. "He saw so many of his contemporaries pass on that he became touchy on the subject of age. When someone at the studio jokingly called him a senior citizen, he was depressed for days." He sometimes lost his balance, but she almost always saw him quickly right himself. She tried to ignore his stray nonsensical comments, but on a few occasions she had to telephone agents and undo deals her husband had impetuously made.

In January 1962, Ben Fish died of a heart attack. To the end, he worshiped the brother who had brought him to this country and employed him for much of his life. Sam and Frances went immediately to the family's side and later to the funeral at Forest Lawn. Ben's widow, Augusta, practically a stranger to Sam, said how glad she was he was there. "Why shouldn't I be?" he said indignantly. "He was my brother." It was the first Jewish service Sammy had ever attended with his father. Every detail fascinated him, even though he hardly knew the deceased. The traditional recitation of the Kaddish, an Aramaic song of mourning, all but threw him into shock. He could barely believe his ears as that most solemn of all Jewish prayers pealed from his father's mouth.

The sudden death of Moss Hart at fifty-seven, and that of Edward R. Murrow (the same age, a few years later), also took their toll. Then Goldwyn suffered the worst loss of his life.

"David Selznick was really my father's son," conceded Sam Goldwyn, Jr. "I was more like the grandson." Since *The Third Man*, coproduced with Alexander Korda in 1950, Selznick had had his hand in but three films, all with his wife Jennifer Jones. The last was *A Farewell to Arms* in 1957.

After that he diligently prepared *Tender Is the Night,* a package with his wife that he ended up selling to Twentieth Century–Fox. The studio left him completely out of the production.

"Sam went to such extreme lengths to get David reestablished and able to function with sufficient freedom that David became really sentimental about him," Irene Selznick wrote in her memoirs. He practically begged several studios to give Selznick some kind of production deal. "I have known David since he was nine years old and have always found him to be a perfect gentleman and a man with great ability," Jack Warner wrote Goldwyn in January 1965; but like the rest of Hollywood, he wanted nothing more to do with him.

Amid his latest schemes and strategies, Selznick suffered a series of heart attacks. He admitted them to Irene but swore her to secrecy, especially in concealing his ill health from Goldwyn. If Sam knew, he suggested, "It'll kill him." On June 22, 1965, a fifth attack finished Selznick off.

That night, Goldwyn called his son and said he was "very depressed." Sammy was preparing to meet one of the Selznick boys at the airport, but his father said he would send a cab, that it was more important to "come and sit with me." Sammy drove to Laurel Lane at ten-thirty and met his father in the library. "For the next two and one-half hours," Sammy recalled, "my father poured out every mistake David had ever made, vilifying him. He paced back and forth saying, 'I tried to straighten that boy out.' When he finished he sat down and dissolved into tears and cried like a baby."

Goldwyn had another hard time three years later, at Harold Mirisch's funeral. The turnout appalled him. The first person he saw was Steve McQueen, sporting long hair. "You're not going to have long hair like that," he insisted to Sammy, whom he had pressed into accompanying him. When Zsa Zsa Gabor walked by, he came undone. "Whores, lawyers, and agents!" he cried. "That's all that showed up for this wonderful man." He made it clear to Sammy that he wanted his own funeral small and private.

Disaffections in the sixties ate at Sam Goldwyn even more than deaths. He viewed his career as nothing but the dispensing of opportunities, so it horrified him to find few who ever gave him anything back. Only two actors, he felt, properly appreciated him. One was Gary Cooper, who sent Goldwyn a photograph of himself—inscribed "To Sam/who made my career possible"—just before he died of cancer in 1961. The other was David Niven, whose film career had been resuscitated by *Around the World in 80 Days.* That led to an Academy Award for *Separate Tables* and another three decades in the picture business. On April 2, 1966—practically thirty years to the day since Goldwyn signed him to his first contract—Niven handwrote him a three-page letter from his château in Switzerland. "After thirty years of incredible good fortune," he concluded, ". . . I just had to sit down in my Swiss cuckoo clock after a good day's skiing and thank you once again from the bottom of my heart for all you did for me when it *really* counted." Except for Cooper and Niven, everybody else with whom Goldwyn ever did business seemed only to take from him.

William Wyler, who still played gin rummy with Goldwyn, was suing him. The director claimed $400,000, part of his 20 percent share of net profits on *Best Years,* which Goldwyn had withheld through creative book-keeping. Goldwyn felt betrayed; he had offered the profit participation to Wyler in the first place, and it had already paid off a jackpot close to $1.5 million. They settled out of court in 1962. "Just a word to tell you how pleased I am that our small financial differences have been amicably settled, and that they never had any effect on our regard and friendship for each other," Wyler wrote Goldwyn on October 16. But the relationship was not the same. Goldwyn never invited Wyler to lunch with him at the studio; and when *Best Years* played on television, Goldwyn asked his law-yers to see if there was any way to exclude Wyler from those profits. There was not.

Most of Wyler's remaining dealings with Goldwyn concerned Lillian Hellman, whom the producer considered most traitorous. In the fifties, Wyler had asked Goldwyn to permit a television production of *The Little Foxes* with Greer Garson, because the blacklisted Miss Hellman was then "desperate for money." Goldwyn granted the permission. In the early six-ties, Wyler returned on her behalf, this time to discuss *The Children's Hour.* In light of the changing mores, Wyler wanted to remake the movie for the Mirisches without bowdlerizing the lesbianism. Goldwyn said he would be happy to allow Wyler to proceed, but he no longer controlled the rights. He lied, saying they had been put in a trust and that those rights were held by his granddaughter. "But," Wyler spluttered, "there must be somebody we can talk to, somebody we can buy the rights from." "I don't know," said Goldwyn, slowly stroking one cheek, then the other; "Cricket wants a lot of money."

The Mirisches had to pay $350,000. Even though Miss Hellman re-ceived none of it, Goldwyn figured that a new version of her play was only to her benefit. But she soon brought suit against him, claiming that Gold-wyn had no right to sell the film of *The Little Foxes* to television, that through his authorizing the Greer Garson version of the play, his rights had reverted to the author. (She lost her case.) Goldwyn probably would never have seen Lillian Hellman again were it not for Frances, who heard she was in town. She called Miss Hellman at the Beverly Wilshire Hotel and invited her to dinner, insisting that they were all getting older and it was time for everybody to make up and be friends. On the promise that dinner would be a select group, she accepted.

The table was set for six—the Goldwyns, the Wylers, Miss Hellman, and her former husband, Arthur Kober. "Everything was going just fine," Miss Hellman remembered, until Bette Davis's name came up. "I had her in a very good picture I made," said Goldwyn, "'The Three Little Foxes.'" Hellman was more irritated than amused that after all this time, he still had not gotten the name of her play right. "Oh, really, Sam?" she said. "Well, I wrote the play and I wrote the movie."

"Of course you did," Goldwyn snapped back. "Who said you didn't write it? It was a great picture." Trying to recover, he turned to Wyler and asked, "Did you ever see it?" Keeping the lid on *his* temper, Wyler said that he had directed it. "Of course you did," insisted Goldwyn. "Who said you didn't direct it?"

Wyler began noticing other signs of age in Goldwyn. Of late, he always seemed to be recovering from some fall or another. (At Jack Foreman's urging, a discreetly enclosed Inclin-ator had been installed on the back stairs of Goldwyn's office.) When Miss Hellman came to town again a few years later, Wyler urged her to call on Goldwyn. She refused. He said people were not coming around to see Goldwyn so much anymore, and the least she could do was talk to him on the telephone. She rang up and got an appreciative Frances on the line. "Sam must have been sitting right there," Hellman remembered, "because I could hear her say, 'Sam, it's Lillian on the phone. She wants to talk to you.' And I heard him say, 'Tell her to go to hell.'" Frances put the phone back up to her mouth and said, "I'm terribly sorry, Lillian, but Sam can't come to the phone right now . . . but he says he misses you very much." That was her last conversation with the Goldwyns.

Then William Paley's worst fears about his friendship with Goldwyn were realized. Even before the premiere of the first Goldwyn movie on television, the producer saw that the deal was not all he had bargained for. In his mind, CBS would draw additional viewers for the prime-time airings of his pictures by advertising the Samuel Goldwyn name. He had not realized that CBS's O & O stations intended to run these films on their late shows, that each station could arbitrarily cut off the credits, and that Goldwyn would have no say in the advertising of the pictures. He began collecting evidence, poring over *TV Guide* each week, looking for omissions of his name in the ads for his films, staying awake into the wee hours to see if his name was on the screen. When he got no relief from his grievance letters to CBS executives, he took the matter up with William Paley himself. Goldwyn recited a long laundry list to him, bad-mouthing some of the network's finest men. Paley at last shut him up, saying, "Stop it! These are friends of mine."

Paley asked several people to see that Goldwyn's name somehow stood out in future advertising; and the next time he went to Los Angeles, he made a lunch date with Sam. But when he walked into Goldwyn's office, he found his friend of forty years "sitting straight as a ramrod," just staring. "He was hurt," Paley later said, "that his name wasn't large enough and that I had stood by my CBS friends." Over the years, Goldwyn would derive intense pleasure from the Nielsen ratings on his films as they broke in wider markets; Myrna Loy visited him in 1966, and she remembered the childlike giddiness with which he said, "Guess what! *Wuthering Heights* had a 72 percent rating in Pittsburgh!" But for years William Paley heard that Goldwyn was still "hurt" over what had happened between them. He said, "We were never good friends since."

Goldwyn blamed his general counsel, chief adviser, and spokesman of twenty years, George Slaff, for allowing CBS to get away with a contract like that. Then he and Slaff had stronger words over another longtime ally, Sylvan Ostreicher. A corpulent, white-haired attorney with a passion for tax law, Ostreicher had been the brains behind the many corporate reorganizations of Samuel Goldwyn, Inc., over the years, business maneuvers that had saved Goldwyn millions of dollars. When Ostreicher presented a bill for $250,000, Goldwyn went berserk. To make matters worse, Slaff said he thought Ostreicher was entitled to the money. Eventually he paid Ostreicher close to what he demanded. The ultimate price, however, was that the trust between Goldwyn and Slaff was broken. Slaff organized a private law firm and in August 1968 tendered his resignation.

Only one other defection left a larger void in Goldwyn's life. In the lull that followed *Porgy and Bess,* James A. Mulvey retired from the presidency of Samuel Goldwyn, Inc., to pursue his interests in baseball, having married years earlier into the Dodger organization. "He'd just had enough, always being at the end of the telephone," remarked George Slaff of the quiet, dapper Irishman who had been a bookkeeper before Sam Goldwyn had got hold of him. When Goldwyn went to buy him out of their partnership agreement, he felt he got the back of Mulvey's hand.

Goldwyn proceeded all according to law, paying what his accountants told him was the market value of Mulvey's share in the company. He well knew the figures were off by almost half. (He did the same for his brother Ben's estate, whose small percentage, they said, was worth $117,000.) Both parties balked at Price Waterhouse's lowball estimates. In 1967,

Mulvey slapped Goldwyn with a lawsuit, charging further that the producer's block sale of films to television violated antitrust laws, reducing Mulvey's profits on those hit pictures in which he participated. Augusta Fish sued too.

It was almost four years before each suit was concluded. The Fish estate received $200,000 for Ben's interests, Mulvey in excess of $1 million. By then, none of the litigants for either of the settlements was even present in court.

On Thursday, March 6, 1969, Mulvey's lawyer deposed the defendant. The next day, Goldwyn did not come to the office, stepping out of the house only for a visit with one of his doctors in Beverly Hills. He checked out remarkably well, especially for a man close to ninety. He spent a quiet weekend at home, the first in months away from Palm Springs. Sammy was on the tennis court with his sons John and Tony and a friend; he was leaving that night to scout locations for his next film, *Cotton Comes to Harlem.* From upstairs in the house, he suddenly heard his mother scream to him, "Come up and bring somebody with you!" Goldwyn had slipped and collapsed. Sammy and his tennis partner moved him into a bed and a doctor arrived in minutes to announce that Goldwyn had suffered a cerebral thrombosis. He explained how the aging process was largely the result of the gradual diminution of oxygen flowing through the body. Sammy reflected and counted what he now thought had been several small strokes, starting as far back as the year *Hans Christian Andersen* was released. How much the ensuing forgetfulness, falling, and fighting were the result of these strokes was anybody's guess.

There was no prognosis whether Goldwyn would regain all his faculties, but he appeared to have retained some powers of mobility. He did not lose his ability to speak, though he would submerge into deep recesses of silence. A male nurse was on duty at Laurel Lane before sunset. Frances's immediate concern was the public reaction. She still subscribed to the theory that "they must never know." Not until the next morning did she call studio manager Jack Foreman, and then it was just to say in a calm voice, "Sam won't be in today . . . and maybe not tomorrow."

Several days later, she imparted the whole truth. Word around town spread quickly. Most people kept a polite distance from Laurel Lane. Marvin Mirisch phoned Goldwyn's office on the eleventh, and Warren Beatty—the last call marked in Sam Goldwyn's appointment book—on the twelfth. By then, one part of the cloudy future seemed clear. Frances told Jack Foreman, "You just conduct the business the way you see fit." Sam Goldwyn never returned to his studio.

The house at 1200 Laurel Lane became bedlam. Goldwyn still had the strength of half his body, and the frustration of incapacitation doubled his ferocity. Though slurring his words, he could still holler. "He'd rage over nothing," said Foreman, "around the clock." Over the next two months, he went through fifteen nurses, men and women. Sammy—his eighteen-year marriage unraveled—commuted between coasts every weekend. When Dr. William Weber Smith saw Frances buckling under the strain, he suggested moving the patient to Las Encinas in Pasadena, a small convalescent hospital where many wealthy alcoholics dried out. Over the next two months, Goldwyn went through another dozen private nurses there. He took to imagining that people were plotting his murder. During a visit from his longtime friend David Rose, Goldwyn growled, "Get me out of this place!" Rose went to Frances and said, "Look—Sam Goldwyn . . . that he should end up here. You can afford to bring him home and set up as good or better facilities in the house." Besides, he pointed out, her drives out there twice a day were killing her. Dr. Jules Stein helped spring Goldwyn from the place.

On May 31, 1969, Dr. Judd Marmor, one of the city's eminent psychiatrists, consulted with the Goldwyn family, then began months of therapy with the patriarch. His counseling eased a lot of tension, and Goldwyn looked forward to his house calls from "Dr. Murmur."

He returned home July 2. Frances had a team of nurses in place and a precise schedule for everybody. That first afternoon, Goldwyn was sitting on a couch in the living room, when he was told it was time to go upstairs. In getting to his feet, he lost his balance and broke his fall by collapsing against a Chippendale end table, smashing it to smithereens. Frances just looked at David Rose, then to heaven, and exhaled audibly.

For several months, Goldwyn seemed to be coming around, responding well to both psychotherapy and physical therapy. He insisted each day that his nurse bring him downstairs for meals. Bathed and fully dressed (never in nightclothes), he sat at the table. One afternoon, he was having great difficulty getting the food from his plate to his mouth. When the nurse reached for a spoon to feed him, Goldwyn reared in indignation. "But, Mr. Goldwyn," the nurse said, "you need some help."

"Help?" Goldwyn cried. "How the hell do you think I got out of Poland?"

On October 16, 1969, Goldwyn's attorney petitioned in Superior Court to have his wife appointed as conservator of his $19.7 million estate. Goldwyn's medical condition and his yearly income of $650,000 were all entered into the public record. On November 3, Superior Judge Arthur K.

Marshall ruled that Goldwyn was too old and ill to manage his own affairs and that Mrs. Goldwyn had the authority to continue operation of his motion picture business.

"You're a goddamned fool," said Goldwyn to Sammy, who had helped effectuate the conservatorship. Sam knew that his wife did not fully grasp the business he had built over the last forty-six years; and he partially blamed his son for giving it away to her. "You have let a little bird out of the cage," he explained. "And it will fly to the ceiling, and hit the ceiling, and hit the ceiling . . . until it collapses." Jack Foreman urged Frances to work out of her husband's office.

Even when she sat behind Sam's desk, her mind was always back at Laurel Lane. Sixty-six-year-old Frances showed up at the studio with less frequency; in time, she stopped leaving the house altogether. George Cukor could lure her out for dinner with him and a few friends, but even that became a trial for her. Unbeknownst to almost everybody, she began suffering a series of small strokes herself.

"He is up a part of every day, walking around the house and garden, and there is still plenty of the old fight left in him," Frances wrote a friend in England in late 1969. Each day saw him wheeled more than he walked. He dabbled at painting, which his old friend Irving Berlin wrote him was "great therapy. It takes your mind off yourself which is good, and who can tell, you're liable to paint something that will be worth more in dollars than any picture you ever produced." Such old friends as Arthur Hornblow, Jr., and David Rose stopped by, but the visits became hard on everybody. Jack Foreman would patiently listen to his new delusion of the Mafia's taking over the studio. "I'd sit with him," George Slaff remembered, "and he'd start bawling." Goldwyn could still view movies at night. In May 1970, he saw *Easy Rider*. After a while, he wanted to see only films he had produced. Two in particular he would watch time and again—*Stella Dallas* and *Wuthering Heights*—and cry.

With both parents in steady decline, the pressure increased on Sammy. He remarried in August 1969, in Sagaponack, at the summer home of his childhood friend Mary Ellin Berlin and her husband, Marvin Barrett. The bride was Margaret Elliott Krutilek, a successful television writer from El Paso, who used the pen name Peggy Elliott. Sammy returned to Los Angeles and spent as much time with his father as possible. At one point, Sam and Frances had to check into St. John's Hospital in Santa Monica for their respective maladies, and Sammy would scurry between rooms. Even though he was stopping by three times a day, his father scolded him for never coming to see him.

Only one other nonmedical person paid regular house calls. Ruth would sit in the sun with her father on the back portico for hours at a time. Alone with her and his thoughts, Goldwyn would tearily hold her hand—and call her Blanche.

For four years, Goldwyn drifted, one day blurring into the next. He became a permanent resident of his bedroom, where the procession of strong male nurses were met almost daily by one doctor or another, attending Goldwyn's diminishing state. Drugs quelled his periodic irrational rages. Through it all, Frances kept her own frustration inside; she never stopped playing the family caretaker, no matter how arduous the role. She was understandably shaken on April 10, 1971, when her mother—after a lifetime of tormenting Frances—died in a Catholic rest home at the age of ninety-one. Helen Victoria Howard McLaughlin was quietly buried at Forest Lawn Memorial Park in Glendale.

Sam Goldwyn—only weeks apart in age from Bonnie—continued to rely on Frances, sapping her strength. On August 27, 1971—Sam's official eighty-ninth birthday—she tried brightening the pall that had descended upon the house by throwing two family birthday parties for him—one at lunch, the other in the afternoon. He ate cake at both meals. "Sam was delighted," she told the press.

By his next birthday, Frances looked completely worn out and seemed ready to throw in the towel. "Last year's was a fiasco," she confessed to Bob Thomas of the Associated Press. "It was simply too upsetting and exhausting for Sam, and he was days getting over it. This year I have told the family not to mention the birthday, and I'm praying that he doesn't know about it. Being a large year—90th—it would be worse than usual." Sick of masquerading, she allowed, "I don't lie any more. He has the heart and blood pressure of a young man—but nothing else seems to work. Except his appetite." When people asked how her husband was, she wearily said, "He's off on a long ocean voyage."

Only one other day in that long spell at sea stood out from the rest. On Friday, March 26, 1971, the phone rang at seven-thirty in the morning— "long distance," Frances remembered, "the White House wants to reach Mr. Goldwyn." She was sure it was a prank and hung up. At noon it rang again. This time a secretary said, "A little after eleven tomorrow, President Nixon plans to call on Mr. Goldwyn." "Oh, dear," Frances said, "is this true?" The voice at the other end said, "I swear it is."

The next morning, Frances went to her husband's room and instructed him to get "all dressed up" because the President was coming. Goldwyn coolly replied, "I'll be glad to see him." By nine-thirty, Laurel Lane was swarming with security men and news crews. Sammy and Ruth arrived. At exactly eleven, Goldwyn was wheeled into the living room, immaculately groomed and dressed. To those who had not seen him in years, he looked markedly different. For all the excess weight he was carrying for the first time in his life, he looked smaller. His wizened face had shrunk to a sour caricature. He did not appear to comprehend anything that was happening.

The President arrived and made a few minutes of small talk. Sitting beside Goldwyn, he said, "I'll never forget the first time I was defeated for the Presidency, you telephoned me and telephoned me and you insisted that I often lunch with you. Each time you said, 'Stay with it. You'll win.'" Goldwyn appeared comatose.

Then Nixon got to the business at hand. He had come to present Samuel Goldwyn with the Medal of Freedom, the nation's highest civilian honor. The President made a speech before hanging the medal around Goldwyn's neck, and the hollow rhetoric about the wholesomeness of the recipient's films made Sam junior suspicious. It rang of an old speech written for the late Walt Disney, and he guessed that Nixon was just doing some early electioneering, trying to win the support of the motion picture industry. Goldwyn's head nodded forward. In raising it, he tugged at the President's coat. The President bowed, putting his ear close enough to Goldwyn to hear him whisper, "You'll have to do better than that if you want to carry California."

The President jerked upright, hastily closed the ceremonies, and exited. Sam junior showed him to the door. In the foyer, Nixon asked, "Did you hear what your father said?" Sammy had, but to avoid any embarrassment, said he had not. The President's shoulders dropped in relief. "He said," Nixon boomed, "'I want you to go out there and beat those bastards!'"

Goldwyn returned to his nurses' care upstairs, where he was "ultimately reduced," said his son, "to a vegetable."

Late in the day of Monday, May 6, 1973, a second great fire broke out at the Goldwyn studio, destroying three soundstages. Sammy was in a projection room on the lot; and as soon as the alarms were sounded, he called his mother. "You mustn't bother me with that now," she said, her mind miles away; "George is coming to tea." Sammy explained that this was a major fire, which would soon be on television. "Oh," said Frances, "well, let's wait until George leaves."

Frances refused to acknowledge the two-million-dollar disaster until that Saturday, when Sammy insisted she visit the site. The chauffeur drove them to the studio, and Frances chatted nervously all the way. She said nothing as they inspected the charred ruins . . . until, with enormous relief, she sighed, "Oh, thank God this is all over." Sam was too far gone to know of the fire.

Later that year, Dr. Smith noticed that his patient was sprouting a new head of fine hair over that pate which had been bald for some sixty-five years. One of the nurses took credit, saying he massaged Goldwyn's scalp every day with Vaseline. With regular checkups showing no letup in the nonagenarian's vital signs, Dr. Smith mused for a moment that Goldwyn might miraculously be regenerating, that he might just live forever.

A little after two o'clock in the morning of Thursday, January 31, 1974, Schmuel Gelbfisz's ninety-four-year struggle "to be somebody" was over. Only a nurse was at his side. Frances was awakened and she sent for a doctor. Minutes later, she telephoned her son. "Sammy," she said, "he's gone."

Sammy arrived at the house, to find his mother in a state of shock. "She lived in fear of that moment for so long," he later noted, "that she didn't know what to do." Dazed, Frances turned to Sammy and the physician and asked, "Should we call a parson?" Sammy could not help laughing at the quaintness of the question; Frances and the doctor laughed too. Then Sammy said he wanted to make a speedy announcement to the media, but Frances insisted nobody must know and that they must not answer the telephones. "It was a knee-jerk reaction," Sammy observed; "she was far more concerned people would find out than that the event had happened." He persuaded her that her plan was impossible, that somebody would tip the press and trigger exactly the sort of havoc his father had dreaded. The news hit the front pages of newspapers around the world the next morning.

Within hours of the headlines, Sammy had completed the funeral arrangements. The huge front gates of Forest Lawn Memorial Park in Glendale were swung closed for the first time in the mortuary's fifty-seven years. For two hours, only the Goldwyn family and Rabbi Max Nussbaum of Temple Israel in Hollywood (whose performance at Harold Mirisch's funeral Goldwyn had liked) were allowed on the grounds. Their black limousines slowly drove a short way up Cathedral Drive to the nondenominational Wee Kirk o' the Heather. At that moment, all the film studios in Hollywood stopped to pay two minutes of private respect.

The rabbi, who did not know the deceased, eulogized him by saying, "He was a real man. His story of family devotion and dedication to an industry is without parallel. In this, he lived in the ideals of Judaism. With his contribution to the Jewish causes, he identified with his religion." Sammy paid more personal tribute, a few words about his father's indomitable will to survive—how no matter how bad things got, he would always say, "I just thank God I've still got Goldwyn."

"Well, he's gone," Sammy said of the man and of the character he had invented for himself, "but wherever he is, and whether we are wife, daughter, son, friend—even old enemies—we've had Goldwyn and it's always going to be part of us and we're damned glad of it."

The Goldwyns returned to their cars and followed the hearse up the winding roads of Forest Lawn to the highest slope, off Freedom Way. Behind two locked iron doors—accessible only by private key—they entered the walled Garden of Honor. In a serene corner was a gated plot eight by nine feet, the Little Garden of Constancy. A white marble bench sat to one side and a marble tablet, waiting to be inscribed, hung on the back wall. After Rabbi Nussbaum delivered the Kaddish, the casket was lowered into Crypt B—right next to his longtime nemesis, Bonnie McLaughlin. Later, Sammy asked Frances if his father had known of the burial plan. "I didn't always tell your father everything," she said, laughing.

SAMUEL GOLDWYN'S estate was appraised at $16,165,490.24. The figure is a small fraction of his legacy. Ownership of several dozen motion pictures, including many classics, would be placed in his son's hands. They became the bedrock for his own company, which would produce, distribute, and exhibit motion pictures. With the arrival of cable television networks, videocassettes, and methods of film exhibition yet to be invented, those movies alone assume a value in the tens of millions of dollars, the Samuel Goldwyn Company in the hundreds of millions. More than that, Samuel Goldwyn left a treasury of work—pictorial archives that reflect his dreams and permanent artifacts that reveal America in the twentieth century, fables that will enlighten in perpetuity.

Goldwyn's last will and testament, signed September 26, 1968, left his interest in Samuel Goldwyn Productions in trust for Frances. The restrictions on her controlling his fortune were, according to their son, "his way of running the business from the grave." He bequeathed gifts ranging from $5,000 to $25,000, according to years of service, to a dozen people in his household and studio employ, and left $1,000 to his barber of long standing. Each of Ruth's children received $50,000. Sammy's four children were given equal shares in a $400,000 trust fund, their mother a $50,000 trust fund of her own. Goldwyn provided Ruth with a $250,000 trust and Sammy with $1 million. The rest was left to the Samuel Goldwyn Foundation.

"My mother's life was over after Dad died," said Sam junior. Laurel Lane became her penitentiary. Except for visits with her closest friends, she shut herself in and practically starved herself, cutting the weekly grocery order to little more than cottage cheese, canned peach halves, frozen spinach, and some meat—ham butt, liver, or ground round. Once or twice a month, a guest was invited—usually George Cukor, to whom she would serve veal cutlets. She developed a smoker's hack, the result of her chain-smoking, a worsening habit she claimed began at age twelve in her efforts to kill the smell of her filthy convent school. For years, her face and skin had been erupting in rashes, angioneurotic edema—what she defined as "a short word for a wounded ego." All her suffering, suggested her son, was the result of the bargain she had struck when she married Sam Goldwyn, that devilish pact Hollywood had joked about for so long. Every time her skin broke out, Frances commented, "I can only have my vanity stepped on so many times."

The problem ran deeper than that. Unlike her husband, Frances never went to a doctor until a symptom proved unbearable. Even then she never fully disclosed all her ailments to any one physician. By the time one had recommended she see an ear-nose-throat specialist, she was suffering from an advanced state of cancer of the nose and trachea. Dr. Smith said they could operate, but it would mean cutting away much of her face. Frances refused treatment and swore her doctors to secrecy, especially in keeping her condition from her son. She devoted much of her time to prayer.

George Cukor was never less than loving and attentive, but repressed anger even toward him surfaced. One night, he and Frances attended a concert with another couple, a society lady whose husband was rumored to be homosexual. Both gentlemen excused themselves before the start of the performance and did not return to their seats before the intermission. Frances convinced herself that they were "doing something unspeakable." When she confronted him, she came uncorked, spewing out fifty years of frustration at not being able to share her life with the man she told friends was "the only person I ever truly loved."

Frances made Katharine Hepburn her rival. Not only did the actress enjoy a celebrated friendship with Cukor (the result of collaborating on eight pictures), but Hepburn had become a symbol of female indepen-dence, the unmarried woman who shaped her own destiny. Although Miss Hepburn always considered Frances his closest friend, Mrs. Goldwyn used to joke about "George's harem": "I'm really his second favorite," she would say; "Kate's his first." In making his father's funeral arrangements, Sammy had learned there was an extra crypt in the family plot for George Cukor. After the funeral, he raised the subject with his mother. A gentle smile broke across her lips; then she laughed sweetly and said, "Well . . . at least Kate won't get him there."

Frances spent the next year worrying about her estate and obsessing about her money. She was continually redrafting her will. Ultimately she decided to leave her beloved house and its contents to her son and designated that the studio should be auctioned, the proceeds going to the Motion Picture Country Home.

Frances deteriorated rapidly, her cancer spreading inward to the brain. Sammy remained devoted as she sank into helplessness. In the spring of 1976—fifteen months after his father's burial—he and his wife made their daily visit to Laurel Lane. Frances had become painfully frail, her breathing labored. Peggy summoned Monsignor Sullivan of the Roman Catholic Church of the Good Shepherd in Beverly Hills. Sammy ushered him to his mother's modest room—with only her rosary and her picture of George Cukor as a child within reach on her nightstand, and a crucifix above her on the wall. "I've come to see you, Frances," said the monsignor. "Father," said the drifting seventy-three-year-old, "I've been waiting for you." Sammy and Peggy waited downstairs while last rites were administered. Frances slipped into a coma.

Three months later—on July 2—Sammy made another of his visits. The nurse descended the stairs, and Sammy had only to look at her face to know the end had come. A funeral service was held the next afternoon.

PEGGY GOLDWYN surprised her husband on his fiftieth birthday—September 7, 1976—with a party upstairs at The Bistro in Beverly Hills. Two hundred friends and family members gathered. The most touching moment that night came when Sammy's oldest friend in the room was asked to make a toast. George Cukor stood and remarked on the fact that he was there at the wedding of Sammy's parents, that he was there the day Sammy was born . . . and, he added, "If circumstances had been different, I might well have been his father." Almost everybody in the room understood what he meant.

On January 24, 1983, George Cukor died at the age of eighty-three. Upon hearing the news, Sammy telephoned Cukor's executor to inform him that Frances had made arrangements for Cukor's burial. The executor said her plans had been stipulated in George's will. Cukor was interred in Crypt D of the Little Garden of Constancy, alongside Frances and Sam and Frances's mother in their still-unmarked tomb.

Below the quiet hill in which these four souls rest, the City of Angels stretches far away.

ACKNOWLEDGMENTS

NOTES AND SOURCES

INDEX

ACKNOWLEDGMENTS

More than forty years ago, Samuel Goldwyn first expressed a desire to have his biography written; but he told his son that he did not wish to be alive to see it.

In late 1978, Samuel Goldwyn, Jr., asked me if I wanted to write that book. One year later, we agreed that I should have unrestricted access to his parents' papers and the right to quote from them at will. He assured me that he would make himself available to discuss his mother and father and that he would exercise no control over the contents of the biography. He insisted that the book be "honest."

Toward that end, Samuel Goldwyn, Jr., gave me the keys to several vaults of material, and he sat for more than sixty hours of interviews. He answered every question put to him with unusual candor. Upon reading the manuscript, he limited his comments to the correction of facts, not the shaping of opinions. I am enormously grateful to him for his time and trust.

Samuel Goldwyn's daughter, Ruth Capps, was equally frank. From the moment I met her until the completion of this book, her straightforward remembrances have guided me and inspired me.

In an effort to avoid committing more mistakes to Hollywood's already error-riddled record, I have relied wherever possible on primary source material—the hundreds of thousands of documents in the Goldwyn archives, the Goldwyn films and their scripts, people who knew the Goldwyns. To those named below, and to many others who assisted me in the gathering, interpretation, and presentation of information, my most sincere thanks.

Goldwyn relatives who contributed to this portrait included: Adela and William Austin, McClure Capps, Allan Fish, Richard Fish, Patricia Gehrhardt, Aron Gutgold, Sally Sherman, and Paulina Tygiers. Special thanks to Peggy Elliott Goldwyn for innumerable kindnesses.

I am appreciative to the following citizens of Gloversville (and surrounding areas): Dr. Milton Feierstein, rabbi of Knesseth Israel Synagogue, Mrs. Lillian Pierson Cohen, Arthur Galinsky, Ruth Galinsky, Anthony Kaiser, Ed Lapos, Mrs. Bernard Libglid, Seymour Morris, Ralph Moses, Harry Pozefsky, Rosalind Schreiber, Miriam Sesonske, Stephen Sesonske, Mr. and Mrs. Ira Silverman.

For interviews, informative correspondence, legal permissions, supplying letters and other information pertaining to the life and motion picture career of Samuel Goldwyn, I am indebted to: Sir Max Aitken, Harry Alexander, Dana Andrews, Lelia Alexander Arensma, Mary Astor, Lauren Bacall, Jack Ball, Lucille Ball, Vilma Banky, Margery and Anthony Baragona, Mary Ellin Barrett, Joan Bennett, Josephine Berger, Beulah Bondi, Vanessa Brown, Nathan Burkan, Jr., Phyllis Kirk Bush, Mr. and Mrs. Frank Chatlos, Ina Claire, Henry W. Clune, J. J. Cohn, John and Jennifer Howard Colman, Rocky Cooper Converse, Alfred Crown, Bette Davis, Helen Dean, Agnes de Mille, Anne and Kirk Douglas, William Dozier, Marjorie Dye, Michael Feinstein, Mrs. A. Leon Fergenson, Jack Foreman, Martin Gang, Curt Gerling, Mr. and Mrs. Ira Gershwin, Edith Mayer Goetz, David Golding, Farley Granger, Anthony Haden-Guest, Chauncey Haines, Averell Harriman, Kitty Carlisle Hart, Helen Hayes, Jacob S. Hertz, Dorothy Hirshon, Jean Howard, Louis Jourdan, Danny and Sylvia Fine Kaye, Madge Kennedy, Evelyn Keyes, Edwin Knopf, Mary Lasker, Betty Lasky, Jesse Lasky, Jr., William Lasky, Justus Baldwin "Jock" Lawrence, Neill Lehr, Norman Lloyd, Myrna Loy, Rabbi Edgar F. Magnin, Daniel Mandell, Samuel Marx, Arthur Mayer, Virginia Mayo, May McAvoy, Joel McCrea, Roddy McDowall, Carmel Myers, Robert Nathan, Jean Negulesco, S. I. Newhouse, David Niven, Laurence Olivier, William S. Paley, Eleanor Perreau-Saussine, Thomas M. Pryor, Edward M. Reiskind, James Roosevelt, David Rose, Gordon Sawyer, Miriam Jasin Schubach, Caroline Seebohm, Russell Selwyn, Irene Sharaff, Leonard Shatzkin, Mrs. Robert Sherwood, Sylvia Sidney, Irving Sindler, George Slaff, Cecil Smith, Dr. William Weber Smith, John Springer, Barbara Stanwyck, Dr. and Mrs. Jules Stein, Anna Sten, Richard Stengel, Patricia Ziegfeld Stephenson, Iphigene Sulzberger, Blanche Sweet, George Towers, Vera-Ellen, Lew Wasserman, Mrs. Billy Wilder, Jeanne R. Woodbury, Mrs. William Wyler, and Vera Zorina. I am especially grateful to Hilde Berl Halpern and Mrs. Arthur Hornblow, Jr., for their vivid recollections.

I was privileged to have interviewed many writers and directors who worked for Samuel Goldwyn; my deepest regret is that so many of them did not live to see how helpful their contributions were. Heartfelt thanks to: Niven Busch, Jr., Henry Hathaway, Bruce Humberstone, John Huston, Garson Kanin, Henry King, Henry Koster, Mervyn LeRoy, Rouben

Mamoulian, Joseph L. Mankiewicz, and Billy Wilder. This would have been a woefully incomplete book were it not for the friendship and interest above and beyond any call of duty of George Cukor, Lillian Hellman, King Vidor, and William Wyler. *Requiescant in pace.*

Several libraries and their staffs proved especially helpful in my research—the Fulton County Historical Society and Museum in Gloversville, the YIVO Institute of Jewish Research, the Franklin D. Roosevelt Library, the Mid-Manhattan New York Public Library, the Library of the Performing Arts at Lincoln Center, and the library of the Academy of Motion Picture Arts and Sciences. Many film scholars and archivists were also extremely generous with their time, especially in my earliest days of research. Thanks to Thomas Bodley, John Hall, Miles Kreuger of the Institute of the American Musical, Richard Lamparski, Joseph McBride, Anthony Slide, Frederick Steiner (who let me read his unpublished dissertation on Alfred Newman), and David Shepard, one of film history's best friends. Seth Nasatir expertly catalogued the Goldwyn papers, making my journey through the millions of pages a smooth one.

The John Simon Guggenheim Memorial Foundation provided a generous grant, which enabled me to meet the expenses of my research.

When I began this book, David Michaelis promised to stand by me for however long it took to complete my "record stride." He kept his word, proving himself the very best of friends. I am also grateful to Joby Baker, Jon Bradshaw, Constance and Thomas B. Congdon, Jr., Leonore Fleischer, Evelyn C. Molesworth, and Dory Previn for their abundant interest and hospitality. Timothy Seldes of Russell & Volkening proved to be as valuable a friend as he is an agent, sorting out countless complications over the last decade. My parents, Barbara and Richard Berg, continued to provide their unshakable support at every turn; and it was a great comfort to know that Carlos Baker was still watching over me.

Despite Robert Gottlieb's recent shift in careers, he shepherded this book from inception to publication, providing insights on every aspect of its form and content. Victoria Wilson also edited the manuscript, with great skill and sensitivity; and she ingeniously transformed it into a book, making dozens of artistic decisions. The final results are very much better for her tasteful eye.

My deepest gratitude to those named on the dedication page. The boundless encouragement and generosity of Katharine Hepburn has been nothing less than electrifying, the spirit that sparked the writing of this book. Kevin McCormick has been my touchstone, against whose integrity I have tested every idea. Irene Mayer Selznick provided me with answers often before I knew the questions; she uncannily knew just when to suggest, correct, prod, and even scourge. I most heartily thank these three selfless friends for their love and their support. And their chocolate.

A.S.B.

Los Angeles
April 1988

NOTES AND SOURCES

Most of the documents cited below are part of the Samuel Goldwyn archives, which are the property of the Samuel Goldwyn Foundation in Los Angeles. The files generally include original manuscript letters as received by Samuel Goldwyn and carbon copies of his outgoing letters. The Goldwyn archives also contains countless clippings—many without sources, headlines, dates, or page numbers; this explains the occasional omission of such data.

Information obtained through interviews has been designated with an (I).

Other abbreviations are:

AL	Abe Lehr	LH	Lillian Hellman
ASB	A. Scott Berg	(M)	Memorandum
CC	Charles Chaplin	(NL)	Night letter
(DL)	Day letter	(R)	Radiogram
FG	Frances Goldwyn	RGC	Ruth Goldwyn Capps
GC	George Cukor	SG	Samuel Goldwyn
(IOC)	Interoffice communication	SGJ	Samuel Goldwyn, Jr.
JAM	James A. Mulvey	(T)	Telegram
JS	Joseph Schenck	(UN)	Unpublished notes
KV	King Vidor	WW	William Wyler

1 EXODUS

POLAND: FG, (UN); SG, Declaration for Naturalization, Oct. 3, 1899, Fulton County Courthouse, Johnston, New York; Jennifer Howard Coleman to ASB (I), Sept. 24, 1984; SG, (UN) for speech delivered in Denver, 1950; SG, (UN) for *Nation's Business*, Nov. 1966; Abraham Shulman, *The Old Country* (New York: Charles Scribner's Sons, 1974), p. 73; Irving Howe, *World of Our Fathers* (New York: Harcourt Brace Jovanovich, 1976), pp. 32–3; Frida Gelbfish to SG, July 15, 1947; Emanuel Nowogrodsky to SG, July 30, 1940; Shea Rubenstein to SG, Apr. 5, 1947; Adela Austin to ASB (I), Sept. 3, 1980; Paula Tygiers to ASB (I),

Sept. 3, 1980; SGJ to ASB (I), Oct. 11, 1983; Hilde Berl Halpern, Sept. 7, 1980; *Encyclopedia Judaica* (Jerusalem: Keter Publishing House), vol. 16, pp. 334–38; SG, *Behind the Screen* (New York: George H. Doran, 1923), p. 23.

HAMBURG: SG, "You Can Always Do Better," *American* magazine, July 1950, p. 124; SG, (UN) for *Nation's Business*, Nov. 1966; Mrs. Bernard Libglid to ASB (I), June 9, 1984.

ENGLAND: SG, "You Can Always Do Better," *American* magazine, July 1950, p. 124; SG, (UN) for *Nation's Business*, Nov. 1966; Adela Austin to ASB (I), Sept. 6, 1980; SGJ to ASB (I), October 11, 1983; Victor Savile, quoted in Arthur Marx,

Goldwyn (New York: W. W. Norton, 1976), pp. 15–16; FG, (UN) for *Woman's Home Companion,* Dec. 1950.

THE CROSSING: Passenger list for *Labrador,* Public Record Office, Kew, Richmond, Surrey, England TW9 4DU, call number BT27/Box 270, Nov. 26, 1898; Henry Fry, *The History of North Atlantic Steam Navigation* (London: Cornmarket Press, 1969—reprint of first edition, London: Sampson Low, 1896), pp. 198–203, 297–98, 303; Commander C. R. Vernon Gibbs, *British Passenger Liners of the Five Oceans* (London: Putnam, 1963), pp. 265–71, 535–42; N.R.P. Bonsor, *North Atlantic Seaway* (Prescot, Lancashire: T. Stephenson & Sons, 1955), pp. 243–52; Howe, *World,* p. 42; SGJ to ASB (I), Oct. 11, 1983; SG, (UN) for *Nation's Business,* Nov. 1966; Halifax Passenger Lists, Public Archives of Canada, Ottawa, Canada K1A ON3, call number C-4519; Hilde Berl Halpern to ASB (I), Sept. 7, 1980.

2 NEW YORK

ARRIVAL IN AMERICA: SG, (UN) for *Nation's Business,* Nov. 1966; GC to ASB (I), Sept. 11, 1979; SG to August Heckscher, president of American Council for Nationalities Service, Nov. 20, 1963; "Report of the U.S. Immigration Commission, vol. 15, 1911, pp. 476–77, quoted in Howe, *World,* p. 69.

GLOVERSVILLE AND GLOVEMAKING: Gloversville *Leader-Republican,* Oct. 31, 1945; Schenectady *Union-Star,* Aug. 19, 1955, p. 10; *Mayor's Message and Annual Reports: 1905* (Gloversville, 1905), Fulton County Historical Society and Museum [FCHSM]; *The Twin Cities Illustrated and Descriptive: Johnstown and Gloversville, New York—1907* (Kinderhook, N.Y.: National Illustrating Co., 1907), which also contains Earl B. Slack's "The Glove Center of the World," pp. 1–2, FCHSM; G. H. Cook, *The Industrial Advantages of Gloversville* (Gloversville: Geo. H. Cook, 1890), pp. 6–45, FCHSM; Adele S. Thompson, "Sacandaga," *Adirondack Life,* Spring 1976,

pp. 14–17; *Just for Fun* (no publisher: n.d.), illustrations of Gloversville citizens, FCHSM; *The Board of Trade of Gloversville New York: 1902* (n.p.: 1902), pp. 40–45, 59, 73, FCHSM; Barbara McMartin, "Fulton County's Glove Industry Tells the Story of Our County's Role in the Industrial Revolution," mimeographed sheet available at FCHSM; *Gloversville and Johnstown Directories* (Gloversville: Daily Leader Printing House), 1896–1916, vol. XXIII–XLIII, found in Gloversville Public Library; A. Jacob Sandler to SG, Sept. 29, 1947; Alva Johnston, *The Great Goldwyn* (New York: Random House, 1937), p. 37; SG, "The Summer Job I Had as a Boy," draft sent to *Esquire,* Oct. 28, 1957; Jules A. Higier to SG, Dec. 16, 1966; "Jewish History of Fulton County," in *Dedication Knesseth Israel Synagogue* (Gloversville: Privately printed 1963; available at social center of synagogue); Malcolm G. Hughes, "The Story of the Leather Glove," *The Glovers' Review* (Gloversville), Sept. 1909, pp. 10–15, available in Gloversville Public Library, special collections; John Dos Passos, "Hans Christian Goldwyn," New York *Herald Tribune,* Jan. 11, 1953, p. 11; Harry Pozefsky to ASB (I), June 8, 1984; Anthony Kaiser to ASB (I), June 8, 1984; Ralph Moses to ASB (I), July 30, 1984; Miriam Sesonske to ASB (I), June 8, 1984; Mrs. Bernard Libglid to ASB (I), June 9, 1984; Stephen Sesonske to ASB (I), June 8, 1984.

CITIZENSHIP: All documents pertaining to the citizenship of Samuel Goldfish, Bernard Goldfish, and Benjamin Goldfish were obtained from Fulton County Records, County Building, Johnstown, N.Y. 12095; Arthur and Ruth Galinsky to ASB (I), June 9, 1984.

SELLING GLOVES: SG, "What America Means to Me," *American Weekly,* Jan. 27, 1952, p. 2; Daisy Inch to SG, June 26, 1950; Mr. and Mrs. Forest E. Woodward to SG, Dec. 28, 1953; SG, (UN) for *Nation's Business,* Nov. 1966; SG, (UN) for "You Always Meet People the Second Time," *This Week,* June 20, 1961; Gloversville *Leader-Herald,* Mar. 29, 1971; *The Glovers' Review,*

July 1906, pp. 3, 16; Apr. 1906, pp. 10–11; Jan. 1907, p. 5; June 1907, p. 3; July 1907, p. 21; Jan. 1908, p. 15; June 1908, p. 25; Dec. 1910, p. 25; Jan. 1911, n.p.—all available in Gloversville Public Library, special collections; FG, (UN) for *Woman's Home Companion,* Dec. 1950; Anthony Kaiser to ASB (I), June 8, 1984; SG, "You Can Always Do Better," *American* magazine, July 1950, pp. 124–26; SGJ to ASB (I), Oct. 11, 1983; Jesse Lasky (with Don Weldon), *I Blow My Own Horn* (New York: Doubleday, 1957), pp. 76–9.

SG'S MARRIAGE: Jesse Lasky, Jr., to ASB (I), Sept. 8, 1980.

3 SYNAPSIS

NEWLYWEDS: SGJ to ASB (I), Oct. 11, 1983; Hilde Berl Halpern to ASB (I), Sept. 7, 1980; RGC to ASB (I), Oct. 13, 1979, and June 4, 1988; Lasky, *I Blow,* pp. 64–65, 67–72, 89; Samuel Waxman to SG, Dec. 1, 1938.

SALES MANAGER OF ELITE GLOVE CO.: *The Glovers' Review:* July 1912, p. 7; Nov. 1912, p. 13; Dec. 1912, p. 7; Mar. 1913, p. 7; April 1913, pp. 9–10; May 1913, n.p.

HISTORY OF MOTION PICTURES: Terry Ramsaye, *A Million and One Nights* (New York: Simon & Schuster, An Essandess Paperback, 1964), pp. xxxix–xl, 52, 58–60, 69, 73, 82, 164, 213, 215, 218, 227, 230, 231, 233, 251, 262, 270, 275, 278, 301–2, 318, 322, 328, 330, 341, 383, 385, 414, 420, 425, 453, 459, 462, 467, 474, 486, 494, 508, 511; Frederick A. Talbot, *Moving Pictures: How They Are Made and Worked* (Philadelphia: J. P. Lippincott, 1912), pp. 10–17; G. W. Bitzer, *Billy Bitzer, His Story* (New York: Farrar, Straus & Giroux, 1963), p. 66; John Drinkwater, *The Life and Adventures of Carl Laemmle* (New York: G. P. Putnam's Sons, 1931), p. 140.

SG ENTERS FILMS: SG, (UN) for *Nation's Business,* Nov. 1966; SG, (UN) re Cecil B. DeMille, Mar. 20, 1957; Jesse Lasky, (UN), "I Knew Him When," n.d.; SG, *Be-hind the Screen,* pp. 15–23; Johnston, *Great Goldwyn,* p. 40; Lasky, *I Blow,* pp. 89–93; Cecil B. DeMille, *Autobiography* (Englewood Cliffs, N.J.: Prentice-Hall, 1959), pp. 61–72; Agnes de Mille, *Dance to the Piper* (Boston: Little, Brown, 1951, 1952), p. 12; Bernard Rosenberg and Harry Silverstein, *The Real Tinsel* (New York: Macmillan, 1970), p. 326; Constance Friend Fergenson to ASB (I), Aug. 2, 1984.

EXPANDING GLOVE BUSINESS: *The Glovers' Review,* Jan. 1913, p. 31; Apr. 1912, p. 34.

4 DRAMATIS PERSONAE

ARRIVAL IN HOLLYWOOD; *THE SQUAW MAN: Moving Picture World,* vol. 18, Dec. 20, 1913, p. 1417; William de Mille, *Hollywood Saga* (New York: E. P. Dutton, 1939), pp. 42, 83; Agnes de Mille to ASB (I), Apr. 2, 1984; C. B. DeMille, *Autobiography,* pp. 76–8; Lasky, *I Blow,* p. 93; uncredited script for *The World's Greatest Showman,* Oct. 9, 1963; *Variety,* Feb. 29, 1914, p. 23; Agnes de Mille, *Dance,* pp. 13–15; Lillian Gish, *The Movies, Mr. Griffith, and Me* (Englewood Cliffs, N.J.: Prentice-Hall, 1969), pp. 84–6.

ZUKOR AND PARAMOUNT: Rosenberg and Silverstein, *Tinsel* (New York: Macmillan, 1970), pp. 70–3; Adolph Zukor, *The Public Is Never Wrong* (New York: G. P. Putnam's Sons, 1953), pp. 61–2, 66, 69, 71–3, 76, 79, 86–7, 93, 98; Blank "Agreement with *Paramount Picture Corporation,* 1914," p. 3.

STARS: SG (ghostwritten by Stuart Jacobson), "Golden Days of 'Glorifying,'" unpublished article; SG, *Behind the Screen,* pp. 30–1, 60, 66–72, 73–4, 81–90; SG, (UN) for *Nation's Business;* C. B. DeMille, *Autobiography,* pp. 77–85, 89–91, 92–3, 98, 101, 139, 140–45; William de Mille, *Saga,* pp. 42, 48, 53–84, 149–53; Rosenberg and Silverstein, *Tinsel,* pp. 70–3; CC, *My Autobiography* (New York: Simon & Schuster, 1964), pp. 137–38, 139, 144; Mack Sennett (as told to Shipp), *King of Comedy* (Garden City, N.Y.: Doubleday,

1954), pp. 76–9, 85; Ramsaye, *Million and One Nights*, pp. 494–95, 537–38, 577–79; Agnes de Mille, *Dance*, pp. 12–19, 22; Lasky, *I Blow*, pp. 93–106, 116–18; Lillian Gish, *The Movies*, pp. 78, 85, 91, 95–6, 100, 103, 111–13, 114–15, 119, 123; Lasky, "I Knew Him When," (UN), p. 4; Johnston, *Great Goldwyn*, p. 45.

SG VISITS MOTHER: Hannah Gelbfisz to SG, May 23, 1922.

PARAMOUNT: C. B. DeMille, *Autobiography*, pp. 124–25; Zukor, *The Public*, pp. 124–25; "Agreement," Famous Players Film Company with Paramount Pictures Corporation, March 1, 1915.

DIVORCE AND LASKY AGREEMENT: Supreme Court, New York County, Blanche Goldfish v. Samuel Goldfish, Final Decree, Mar. 14, 1916; Jesse L. Lasky with Sam Goldfish, "Agreement," Sept. 23, 1915.

5 MUSICAL CHAIRS

HOLLYWOOD: Agnes de Mille to ASB (I), April 2, 1984.

DIVORCE: Supreme Court, New York County, Blanche Goldfish v. Samuel Goldfish, Final Decree, Mar. 14, 1916.

TROUBLE AT LASKY COMPANY: Johnston, *Great Goldwyn*, pp. 45–6.

FAMOUS PLAYERS MERGER: C. B. DeMille, *Autobiography*, pp. 154–57; Lasky, *I Blow*, p. 122; Goldwyn, *Behind the Screen*, pp. 105–6.

JOAN THE WOMAN: C. B. DeMille, *Autobiography*, pp. 169–72, 175, 179, 180, 187; SG (ghostwritten by S. Jacobson) "Golden Days of 'Glorifying,'" p. 7; Ina Claire to ASB (I), Mar. 11, 1980.

BIRTH OF A NATION AND ITS INFLUENCE: Gish, *The Movies*, pp. 109, 161–62, 163, 164; Irene Mayer Selznick, *A Private View* (New York: Alfred A. Knopf, 1983), p. 28; Richard Schickel, *D. W. Griffith: An American Life* (New York: Simon & Schuster, 1984), p. 281; Bosley Crowther, *Hollywood Rajah* (New York: Henry Holt, 1960), p. 48; Ramsaye, *Million and One Nights*, pp. 559, 575–76, 585, 631, 635, 640, 648, 702, 708, 710, 712, 713, 715,

716, 718, 720, 731, 738, 741, 748, 749, 775.

THEATERS AND MUSIC: Ramsaye, *Million and One Nights*, pp. 723–25; David Naylor, *American Picture Palaces* (New York: Van Nostrand Reinhold, 1981), pp. 83, 216; Kevin Brownlow, *The Parade's Gone By* (Berkeley: University of California Press, 1968), pp. 338–39; C. B. DeMille, *Autobiography*, p. 134.

GOLDFISH LEAVES FAMOUS PLAYERS– LASKY: C. B. DeMille, *Autobiography*, pp. 176–77; Zukor, *The Public*, p. 179; Mary Pickford, *Sunshine and Shadow* (Garden City, N.Y.: Doubleday, 1955), pp. 107–8; Lasky, *I Blow*, pp. 123–24; Jesse Lasky, Jr., *Whatever Happened to Hollywood?* (New York: Funk & Wagnalls, 1975), p. 67; *Motion Picture News*, "Samuel Goldfish Resigns as Chairman of Lasky Directors," Sept. 30, 1916.

6 A NAME FOR HIMSELF

"FAMILIES" IN MOTION PICTURES: Richard Schickel, *His Picture in the Papers* (New York: Charterhouse, 1973), pp. 11–20; Gary Carey, *Doug & Mary* (New York: E. P. Dutton, 1977), pp. 32–3; CC's Jewishness related by Hilde Berl Halpern to ASB (I), Sept. 7, 1980; Lucille Ball to ASB (I), June 5, 1980.

ZUKOR LOAN: Zukor, *The Public*, p. 181.

BUYING OUT SG: Lasky, *I Blow*, p. 124; C. B. DeMille, *Autobiography*, p. 177; SGJ to ASB (I), Oct. 11, 1983.

SG AND FAMILY: Allan Fish to ASB (I), Dec. 28, 1979; Bernard and Ben Goldfish to SG, Nov. 17, 1916; Leo Sherman to SG, Dec. 6, 1916; Adele Austin to ASB (I), Sept. 6, 1980; RGC to ASB (I), Oct. 13, 1979.

THE SELWYNS: *New York Times*, June 23, 1958, "Arch Selwyn, 82, Stage Producer"; *New York Times*, Feb. 14, 1944, "Edgar Selwyn, 68, Producer, Is Dead," p. 17; Marguerite Tazelaar, "Edgar Selwyn, Heading West," prob. New York *Post*, Mar. 30, 1930; Russell Selwyn to ASB (I), July

5, 1985; Johnston, *Great Goldwyn*, pp. 47–8; SG, *Behind the Screen*, pp. 109–10; Margaret Mayo to SG, June 7, 1940, and Oct. 22, 1949; SG, (UN) for *American* magazine, July 1950.

EARLY GOLDWYN STARS: All dates and salaries were taken from unpublished contract books of the Goldwyn Company; Arthur Mayer to ASB (I), Aug. 2, 1980.

MABEL NORMAND: Sennett, *King*, pp. 47–52, 103, 137, 193–98, 199–201, 205; Minta Durfee Arbuckle, quoted in Walter Wagner, *You Must Remember This* (New York: G. P. Putnam's Sons, 1975), p. 34; Madge Kennedy to ASB (I), Feb. 6, 1980; KV to ASB (I), June 11, 1980; CC, *Autobiography*, pp. 153–56; Irene Mayer Selznick to ASB (I), Apr. 14, 1985; Blanche Sweet to ASB (I), Apr. 2, 1983; Arthur Mayer to ASB (I), Aug. 2, 1980; Mabel Normand to Mack Sennett, telegram, July 23, 1917, quoted in Betty Harper Fussell, *Mabel* (New Haven and New York: Ticknor & Fields, 1982), p. 105.

GOLDWYN CORPORATE PLANS: Contract books of the Goldwyn Company; Application of Goldwyn Pictures Corporation to the Committee on Stock List of New York Stock Exchange: A–5768—Goldwyn Pictures Corporation, Aug. 30, 1922; SG to staff (mimeo. bulletin), summer 1917.

MAKING MOVIES: J. J. Cohn to ASB (I), Feb. 11, 1980; Madge Kennedy to ASB (I), Feb. 6, 1980; *Fort Lee: Past and Present* (Fort Lee, N.J.: Fort Lee Chamber of Commerce, 1973), pp. 18–19; Hedda Hopper, *From Under My Hat* (Garden City, N.Y.: Doubleday, 1952), p. 100; SG, *Behind the Screen*, pp. 123–25, 131; Johnston, *Great Goldwyn*, pp. 50–1; Mary Garden and Louis Biancolli, *Mary Garden's Story* (New York: Simon & Schuster, 1951), pp. 229–33; Arthur Mayer to ASB (I), Aug. 2, 1980.

ADVERTISING AND NEW STARS: Howard Dietz, *Dancing in the Dark* (New York: Quadrangle/New York Times Book Co., 1974), pp. 38–9, 42–3, 54–5; Jock Lawrence to ASB (I), Oct. 17, 1982; Arthur Mayer, *Merely Colossal* (New York: Simon & Schuster, 1953), pp. 11–13; Arthur Mayer

to ASB (I), Aug. 2, 1980; SG, *Behind the Screen*, pp. 134–35, 143–44; SG, (UN) to unidentified interviewer, Dec. 8, 1952.

MABEL NORMAND: David Rose to ASB (I), Feb. 21, 1980; Mayer, *Colossal*, p. 13; Hopper, *Under My Hat*, pp. 93–5; Fussell, *Mabel*, p. 106; Madge Kennedy to ASB (I), Feb. 6, 1980; Sennett, *King*, pp. 209–11.

ACQUIRING TALENT: Quotes about Rex Beach, cited in Asa Don Dickinson, *The Best Books of Our Time: 1901–1925* (New York: H. W. Wilson, 1931); Samuel Marx to ASB (I), Feb. 24, 1984; Contract books of the Goldwyn Company; Muriel Elwood, *Pauline Frederick: On and Off the Stage* (Chicago: A. Kroch, 1940), pp. 77–86; SG, *Behind the Screen*, pp. 139–41; Leon Barsacq, *Caligari's Cabinet and Other Grand Illusions* (Boston: New York Graphic Society, 1976), pp. 197–98, 200–1; Lasky, Jr., *Whatever Happened*, pp. 10–11; Miriam Sesonske to ASB (I), June 8, 1984; Stephen Sesonske to ASB (I), June 8, 1984; Neill Lehr to ASB (I), July 13, 1983.

MARKETING GOLDWYN FILMS: SG to staff (unpub. bulletin), c. summer 1917.

WORLD WAR I: Ramsaye, *Million and One Nights*, p. 781; Sgt. Herbert H. Brin, *The Longhorn*, newspaper, Camp Walters, Tex., Dec. 29, 1944, p. 1; SG, "What America Means to Me," *American Weekly*, Jan. 27, 1952, p. 23; Kevin Brownlow, *The War, the West and the Wilderness* (New York: Alfred A. Knopf, 1979), p. 116; the quip from Edgar Selwyn appears in Hopper, *Under My Hat*, p. 100.

GOLDWYN FILMS DURING WAR; COPING WITH SHORTAGES: Various unsourced clippings, Lincoln Center Library—"Goldwyn Surmounts Difficulty," March 10, 1918; "'The Floor Below' Delightful Film," n.d.; "Pleasing Personalities in Human Domestic Comedy. Grab It," Oct. 13, 1918; "Dissolving Title Used in Kennedy's Latest," n.d.; Tallulah Bankhead, *Tallulah, My Autobiography* (New York: Harper & Brothers, 1952), pp. 54, 62–3; Harry Alexander to ASB (I), Aug. 2, 1980.

LOUELLA PARSONS: Louella O. Parsons,

The Gay Illiterate (Garden City, N.Y.: Doubleday, Doran, 1944), pp. 9, 29–30, 65–6; SG, (UN) (ghostwritten by George Slaff) for *Life*, Aug. 24, 1962.

SECOND YEAR OF GOLDWYN: SG, unpub. pamphlet for Goldwyn managers, c. summer 1918; Ramsaye, *Million and One Nights*, pp. 789–92; Arthur Mayer to ASB, Aug. 2, 1980.

NEAR-DEMISE OF GOLDWYN COMPANY: William Hebert to Roger Butterfield, Sept. 30, 1947; SG, *Behind the Screen*, pp. 110–18; Frances Marion, *Off with Their Heads!* (New York: Macmillan, 1972), p. 88; Anita Loos, in Fussell, *Mabel*, p. 114; Madge Kennedy to ASB (I), Feb. 6, 1980; Harry Alexander to ASB (I), Feb. 15, 1980; David Rose to ASB (I), Feb. 21, 1980; Johnston, *Great Goldwyn*, pp. 52–3.

SG CHANGES NAME: Court order, "In the Matter of the Application of SAMUEL GOLDFISH," Dec. 19, 1918; SGJ to ASB (I), Jan. 5, 1979; RGC to ASB (I), Oct. 13, 1979.

7 THE BUSINESS OF AMERICA

WILL ROGERS: Bryan B. Sterling and Frances N. Sterling, *Will Rogers in Hollywood* (New York: Crown Publishers, 1984), pp. 2–8, 17; Will Rogers, *The Autobiography of Will Rogers*, ed. Donald Day (Boston: Houghton Mifflin, 1949), pp. 58–68; Betty Rogers, *Will Rogers: His Wife's Story* (Norman: University of Oklahoma Press, 1941, 1979), pp. 143–44; Charles Higham, *Ziegfeld* (Chicago: Henry Regnery, 1972), pp. 108–9; contract books of the Goldwyn Company ("Rogers").

BUILDING OF THE STUDIOS: Marc Wanamaker, "Before Hollywood Was Hollywood," Los Angeles *Times*, "Calendar," Aug. 31, 1980, pp. 62–4; Wanamaker, "Historic Hollywood Movie Studios," *American Cinematographer*, Mar., Apr., and May 1976; Wanamaker, "Thomas H. Ince: Father of the Western," *The Movie* (London), no. 109, 1982, pp. 2170–72; Lloyd Morris, *Not So Long Ago* (New York: Ran-

dom House, 1949), p. 132; Drinkwater, *Laemmle*, pp. 170–71; contract books of the Goldwyn Company; Madge Kennedy to ASB (I), Feb. 6, 1980; Will Rogers, in Sterling, *Will Rogers*, p. 6.

BLANCHE LASKY'S REMARRIAGE AND RGC: Blanche Sweet to ASB (I), Apr. 2, 1983; Jesse Lasky, Jr., *Whatever Happened to Hollywood?* (New York: Funk & Wagnalls, 1975), p. 14; Jesse Lasky, Jr., to ASB (I), Sept. 8, 1980; George Edwin Joseph to Gabriel Hess, Dec. 22, 1919; Appeal No. 5414, Blanche Goldfish v. Samuel Goldfish, Supreme Court, Appellate Division, First Department, New York, October 1920; Nathan Burkan to George Edwin Joseph, Dec. 20, 1919; George Edwin Joseph to SG, Dec. 9, 22, 1919; Gabriel Hess to SG, March 21, April 2, 1919; Ruth Lasky to SG, May 1, 1919; Ruth Lasky to SG, May 3, 1919; Ruth Lasky to SG, n.d. [prob. summer 1919]; SG to Ruth Goldwyn, May 13, 26, June 16, July 22, Nov. 11, 1919.

ZUKOR, UNITED ARTISTS, AND LOEW: Ramsaye, *Million and One Nights*, pp. 793–95; Tino Balio, *United Artists: The Company Built by the Stars* (Madison: University of Wisconsin Press, 1976), pp. 27–9; Bosley Crowther, *The Lion's Share* (New York: E. P. Dutton, 1957), pp. 50–2.

SG AND EMINENT AUTHORS: Harry Alexander to ASB (I), Feb. 15, 1980; Arthur Mayer to ASB (I), Aug. 2, 1980; contract books of the Goldwyn Company ("Atherton," "Beach," "King," "Scott," "Rinehart," "Morris," "Hughes," "Eminent Authors"); Rupert Hughes, "My Adventures in Pictureland," *Photoplay*, Nov. 1919, pp. 72–3, 121; SG's "Statement of Assets and Liabilities," July 24, 1919; Felix F. Feist, open letter from Goldwyn Distributing Corporation to the trade, June 18, 1919; Felix Feist to resident managers, July 10, 1919; Goldwyn Distributing Corporation to All Managers, confidential letter, June 17, 1919.

GOLDWYN STARS: Contract books of the Goldwyn Company ("Farrar," "Frederick," "Kennedy," "Moore," "Normand," "Pickford, Jack," "Rogers"); Goldwyn, *Behind the Screen*, pp. 150–57; AL to SG, February 18, 1919; Elwood, *Pauline Frederick*, pp. 99–113; SG to AL, Feb. 11, 1919; Irene Mayer Selznick to ASB (I), May 31, 1985; Sennett, *King*, pp. 211–13, 218–22; Harry Alexander to ASB (I), Feb. 15, 1980; Sterling, *Will Rogers*, pp. 3, 35, 38; Clarence Badger's "Reminiscences" appear in *ibid.*, pp. 8–16; Rogers, *Autobiography*, pp. 62–3; Will Rogers to SG (T), Oct. 17, 1919; Elmer Rice, *Minority Report* (New York: Simon & Schuster, 1963), pp. 170–85; Rudy Behlmer and Tony Thomas, *Hollywood's Hollywood* (Secaucus, N.J.: Citadel Press, 1975), p. 104; *New York Times*, Oct. 24, 1921; "Report on Rogers" [c. late 1920].

EMINENT AUTHORS: Mary Roberts Rinehart, *My Story* (New York: Farrar and Rinehart, 1931), pp. 291–97; Gertrude Atherton, *Adventures of a Novelist* (New York: Liveright, 1932), pp. 543–44; Rex Beach, *Personal Exposures* (New York: Harper & Brothers, 1940), pp. 186–206; Mayer, *Colossal*, pp. 34–5.

EXPANDING OF GOLDWYN PICTURES CORP.: AL to SG, May 17, 1919; contract books of the Goldwyn Company ("Lehr"); SG to AL, June 9, 1919; Frank Joseph Godsol is referred to in Mayer, *Colossal*, pp. 39–44; Messmore Kendall, *Never Let the Weather Interfere* (New York: Farrar, Straus, 1946), p. 272; contract books of the Goldwyn Company ("Godsol"); Harry Alexander to ASB (I), July 27, 1988; Kevin Lewis and Arnold Lewis, "Include Me Out: Samuel Goldwyn and Joe Godsol," *Film History*, June/July, 1988, pp. 133–53. The du Pont fortunes are described in Gerald Colby Zilg, *Du Pont: Behind the Nylon Curtain* (Englewood Cliffs, N.J.: Prentice-Hall, 1974), pp. 168–70; Max Dorian, *The Du Ponts: From Gunpowder to Nylon* (Boston: Little, Brown, 1962), pp. 186–94; William S. Dutton, *Du Pont: One Hundred and Forty Years* (New York: Charles Scribner's Sons, 1951), pp. 246–51; SG to AL, Dec. 30, 1919; SG to AL, Dec. 17, 1919; SG, Annual Message to Goldwyn Managers and Salesmen [c. summer 1920]; the Goldwyn lot is described in "Application of Goldwyn Pictures Corporation to the Committee on Stock List, New York Stock Exchange," Aug. 30, 1922, p. 3.

CAPITOL THEATRE: Kendall, *Weather*, pp. 264–71; Ben M. Hall, *The Best Remaining Seats* (New York: Bramhall House, 1961), pp. 57–69; Naylor, *Picture Palaces*, p. 44; *Journal of the American Society of Heating and Ventilating Engineers* [n.d., n.p.—prob. 1920]; misc. unmarked clippings, Lincoln Center Library—"The Goldwyn Company" (1919 and 1920).

MAETERLINCK: Contract books for the Goldwyn Company ("Tarkington," "Maeterlinck," "Eminent Authors"); Dietz, *Dancing*, pp. 55–9; "Press Release—1920," reporting SG speech to exhibitors; Johnston, *Great Goldwyn*, pp. 60–4; SG, *Behind the Screen*, pp. 249–56; Mayer, *Colossal*, p. 36; Arthur Mayer to ASB (I), Aug. 2, 1980; Harry Alexander to ASB (I), Feb. 15, 1980.

SG TO EUROPE: SG to AL, Mar. 18, 1920; SG, *Behind the Screen*, pp. 256–60; Dietz, *Dancing*, p. 59; Mayer, *Colossal*, p. 10.

GOLDWYN COMPANY'S NEW MODE OF BUSINESS: SG to W. W. Laird, July 23, 1920; SG to AL, Jan. 13, 1920; Harry Alexander to ASB (I), Feb. 15, 1980; SG to AL, Mar. 19, 1920 (dated Mar. 18, 1920); SG to AL, Mar. 22, 1920; SG to AL, Mar. 24, 1920; F. J. Godsol to SG (T), Jan. 1, 2, 5, 1920; SG to F. A. Gudger (T), Feb. 13, 1920; AL to SG, May 24, 1920; Mayer, *Colossal*, p. 37.

SG RESIGNS AND RE-SIGNS: "Synopsis of Minutes of Board Meetings—1920"; SG to AL (NL), Sept. 3, 1920; SG to AL, Sept. 9, 1920; Crowther, *Lion's Share*, p. 68; Kendall, *Weather*, pp. 273–74; Harry Alexander to ASB (I), Feb. 15, 1980; Minutes of Sales Department Conference, Mar. 22, 1920; AL to SG, Apr. 11, 1921; SG to F. J. Godsol, May 18, 1921.

SG AS LAME DUCK PRESIDENT: Minutes of Board Meeting, Oct. 22, 1920; F. J. Godsol to SG, Jan. 7, 1921; Arthur Mayer to ASB (I), Aug. 2, 1980; SG to AL,

Feb. 15, 24, 1921; AL to SG, May 5, Oct. 13, 1921; Rae Lipnick to SG, Jan. 8, 1921; Richard Griffith, *Samuel Goldwyn: The Producer and His Films* (New York: Museum of Modern Art Film Library, 1956), p. 11; Carl Sandburg, "The (Chicago) Daily News," May 12, 1921, reprinted in Harry M. Geduld (editor), *Authors on Film* (Bloomington: Indiana University Press, 1972), pp. 47–9.

SG's "BREAKDOWN": Rae Lipnick to Mabel Normand (T), May 10, 1921; Rae Lipnick to AL (T), May 11, 1921; AL to Rae Lipnick (T), May 12, 1921; SG to AL (T), May 13, 1921; SG to Mabel Normand (NL), May 13, 1921; AL to SG (T), May 17, 1921.

COLLAPSE OF COMPANY: "Analysis of Disbursements and Receipts for 1921"; SG to AL (DL), May 19, 1921; Harry Alexander to ASB (I), Feb. 15, 1980; SG to AL, June 4, 1921; SG to AL (DL), June 6, 1921; SG to AL, June 9, 1921; AL to SG, June 10, 1921; SG to F. J. Godsol (T), July 31, 1921; SG to F. J. Godsol, July 11, 1921; SG to F. J. Godsol (NL), July 22, 1921; SG to F. J. Godsol (NL), July 28, 1921; George P. Bissell to SG, Aug. 3, 1921; AL to SG, Oct. 25, 1921; SG to AL, Oct. 3, 1921; AL to SG, Nov. 4, 1921; AL to SG, Nov. 16, 1921; SG to AL, Nov. 28, 1921; AL to SG (T), Feb. 14, 1922; SG to F. J. Godsol (T), Feb. 15, 1922; SG to AL, Mar 1, 1922; "Application of Goldwyn Pictures corporation to committee on Stock List of New York Stock Exchange," Aug. 30, 1922, p. 6; Mayer, *Colossal*, pp. 39–40.

8 ELBA

HOLLYWOOD AND ITS SCANDALS: Ramsaye, *Million and One Nights*, p. 815; C. B. DeMille, *Autobiography*, pp. 237–38; SG, *Behind the Screen*, pp. 247–48; Elinor Glyn, *Romantic Adventure* (New York: E. P. Dutton, 1937), pp. 150–51, 304–6; Ina Claire to ASB (I), Mar. 11, 1980; King Vidor, random notes, 1965; Madge Kennedy to ASB (I), Feb. 6, 1980; CC, *Autobiogra-*

phy, pp. 265–66; Kevin Brownlow, *Hollywood* (New York: Alfred A. Knopf, 1979), p. 157; Anita Loos, *A Girl Like I* (New York: Viking Press, 1966), p. 121; Adela Rogers St. John, *Love, Laughter and Tears: My Hollywood Story* (Garden City, N.Y.: Doubleday, 1978), p. 6; David Rose to ASB (I), Feb. 21, 1980; Marion, *Off with Their Heads!*, pp. 92–3; Carmel Myers to ASB (I), May 21, 1980; Lasky, *I Blow*, pp. 153–58; C. B. DeMille, *Autobiography*, pp. 238–39; King Vidor to ASB (I), June 11, 1980; "Sex on the Rampage," *This Week*, Los Angeles *Times*, Dec. 12, 1943, p. 5.

CLEANING HOUSE: Ramsaye, *Million and One Nights*, pp. 809–15, 820–21; Will H. Hays, *The Memoirs of Will H. Hays* (Garden City, N.Y.: Doubleday, 1955), pp. 323–27, 329–30, 344–45; Mabel Normand's writing to SG is referred to in a letter, AL to SG, June 6, 1922; a copy of the round-robin letter to Will Hays of December 2, 1921, appears in Ramsaye, *Million and One Nights*, between pp. 816 and 817.

REACTION TO SG'S OUSTER: SGJ to ASB (I), Oct. 11, 1983; SG to F. J. Godsol (NL), Feb. 15, 1922; AL to SG (T), Feb. 15, 1922; F. J. Godsol to SG, Mar. 9, 1922; SG to AL, Mar. 14, 1922; Arthur Mayer to SG, Mar. 9, 1922; George E. Kann to SG, Mar. 10, 1922; Howard Dietz to SG, Mar. 13, 1922; Rupert Hughes to SG (T), Mar. 12, 1922; SG to Rupert Hughes, (NL), Mar. 13, 1922; Goldwyn Studios Organization to SG (T), Mar. 13, 1922; SG to AL (T), c. Mar. 14, 1922; SG, *Behind the Screen*, p. 261.

SG SPRINGS BACK INTO ACTION: SG to AL, Apr. 10, 1922; Edward Wise to SG, Mar. 7, 1922; Blanche Sweet to ASB (I), Apr. 2, 1983; SG on two types of producers, quoted in Providence *Evening Bulletin*, Nov. 27, 1935; Neil S. McCarthy to SG (T), Mar. 29, 1922; the rights to *Ben-Hur* are discussed in Crowther, *Lion's Share*, pp. 92–3; SG to Halle & Stieglitz, Apr. 19, 1922; AL to SG, June 6, 1922; SG to AL, June 24, 1922; SG to AL, Apr. 10, 1922; SG to AL, May 26, 1922; AL to SG, May 16, 1922; AL to SG, June 30, 1922; SG to

AL, July 12, 1922; AL to SG, Oct. 13, 1922; AL to SG, June 6, 1922.

SG "WRITES" MEMOIRS: SG to AL, May 26, 1922; Johnston, *Great Goldwyn*, p. 81; Arthur T. Vance of *Pictorial Review* to SG, June 5, 1922; Arthur Vance to SG, June 9, 1922; Arthur Vance to Paul Block, June 9, 1922; Arthur Vance to SG, June 5 and 12, 1922; AL to SG, June 6, 1922; SG to AL, May 26, 1922; AL to SG, July 11, 1922; AL to SG, July 12, 1922; SG, *Behind the Screen*, pp. v, vii, 23, 24, 106, 107, 183–84, 262–63; Dennis F. O'Brien to Arthur Vance, Oct. 14, 1922; AL to SG, July 12, 1922; AL to SG, Aug. 11, 1922.

As of SG's March 31, 1924, royalty report, *Behind the Screen* had sold 6,739 books at $2.50: JAM to SG, July 21, 1924; JAM to AL, Aug. 23, 1924.

SG AT GREAT NECK: Robert W. McCully (veterinarian) to SG, Mar. 29, 1922; Johnston, *Great Goldwyn*, pp. 80–1; SG to AL, Aug. 12, 1922; Rupert Hughes to SG, July 16, 1922; SG to AL, July 12, 1922; AL to SG, July 19, 1922; SG to AL, Aug. 12, 1922; AL to SG, Aug. 11, 1922; Douglas Fairbanks to SG, Jan. 10, 1923; Douglas Fairbanks to Jack Coogan, Jan. 10, 1923; David Rose to ASB (I), Feb. 21, 1980; regarding CC, AL to SG (T), Nov. 18, 1922; CC, *Autobiography*, p. 295; Hilde Berl Halpern to ASB (I), Sept. 7, 1980.

DIRECTORS: KV to ASB (I), June 11, 1980; Byron Haskin, in Brownlow, *Hollywood*, pp. 204–5; William A. Wellman, *A Short Time for Insanity* (New York: Hawthorn Books, 1974), pp. 118, 146–49; FG to Richard Griffith, Aug. 16, 1955; King Vidor, *A Tree Is a Tree* (New York: Harcourt, Brace, 1953), pp. 67–8, 69–70, 71, 106–7; WW to ASB (I), Apr. 1, 1980; Neil S. McCarthy to SG, Nov. 7, 1922.

SG RESUMES PRODUCTION: Montague Glass, "Potash and Perlmutter: Their Origin and Their Originator," *The Glovers' Review*, Feb. 1910, pp. 15–19; SG to Ruth Goldwyn, May 14, 1923; SG, memorandum re *The Eternal City*, c. Jan. 1923; SGJ to ASB (I), Oct. 11, 1983; Marquis James and Bessie Rowland James, *Biography of a*

Bank: The Story of the Bank of America (New York: Harper & Brothers, 1954), pp. 245–47; Balio, *United Artists*, p. 52; C. B. DeMille, *Autobiography*, pp. 242–45; JS to SG, c. Oct. 30, 1931; Griffith, *Goldwyn*, p. 16; SGJ to ASB (I), Oct. 11, 1983; Henry King to ASB (I), May 28, 1980; Arthur C. Miller's escape from Italy is recounted in Liz-Anne Bawden, ed., *The Oxford Companion to Film* (New York and London: Oxford University Press, 1976), p. 468.

SCREENWRITERS: Anita Loos, *A Girl*, p. 71.

WAITING AT SARANAC LAKE: SG to Ruth Goldwyn, Aug. 13, 1923.

SG PRESENTS HIS FIRST FILMS: *New York Times*, Sept. 24, 1923, p. 5.

THE MERGER: Crowther, *Lion's Share*, pp. 70–4, 79–81; statistics on American business cited in Rebecca Brooks Gruver, *An American History* (New York: Appleton-Century-Crofts, 1976), p. 895; Upton Sinclair, *Upton Sinclair Presents William Fox* (Los Angeles: published by the author, 1933), p. 69; accounting (M), probably JAM to SG, "'The Eternal City,' February 28, 1925"; SGJ to ASB (I), Oct. 11, 1983.

F. J. Godsol's death was alluded to in *New York Times*, May 2, 1935, p. 23. He left $250,000 to his cousin, Mrs. Al H. Woods.

SG often referred to himself as a "lone wolf"; here he is quoted from (UN) for (I) with George Slaff, c. June 1959, in preparation for a five-part series on SG in Los Angeles *Times;* see also Alvin H. Marill, *Samuel Goldwyn Presents* (South Brunswick, N.J., and New York: A. S. Barnes, 1976), p. 23.

9 LEADING LADIES

BEAUTY AND STARS: SG quoted in William Fadiman, *Hollywood Now* (London: Thames and Hudson, 1973), p. 98; Selznick, *Private View*, pp. 60–1; John Mason Brown, *The Worlds of Robert E. Sherwood: Mirror to His Times, 1896–1939* (New York: Harper & Row, 1965), p. 187.

CYTHEREA AND *IN HOLLYWOOD WITH POTASH AND PERLMUTTER*: R. A. Rowland to SG (T), Mar. 22, 1924; SG to R. A. Rowland (T), Apr. 16, 24, 1924; R. A. Rowland to SG (T), Apr. 24, 1924; "Goldwyn Seeking Screen Vampire," prob. Los Angeles *Herald-Examiner*, c. Mar. 19, 1924, enclosed in letter from Neva Sylvester to SG, Mar. 21, 1924; SG to George Fitzmaurice (T), Feb. 9, 1924; George Fitzmaurice to SG, April 4, 1924; for details about Technicolor, see *Oxford Companion to Film*, p. 681.

SG'S SOCIAL LIFE: SG's secretary Valeria Belletti calls her boss a "chaser" in a letter to her friend Irma Prina, Feb. 27, 1925; John Mason Brown refers to one of the caricatures in *Sherwood*, p. 168; another is reproduced in Marion Davies, *The Times We Had: Life with William Randolph Hearst* (Indianapolis/New York: Bobbs-Merrill, 1975), p. 262; CC, *Autobiography*, pp. 227–28, 289; CC to SG (T), Aug. 25, 1921; SG to CC (NL), Aug. 27, 1921; David Rose to ASB (I), July 26, 1983; KV, *A Tree*, p. 99; KV to ASB (I), June 11, 1980.

SG AND RGC: SG to Sadie Robinson (secretary), c. Apr. 5, 1924; RGC to ASB (I), Oct. 13, 1979; Nathan Burkan to SG, Jan. 20, 1920; Gabriel Hess to Nathan Burkan, Jan. 21, 1920; Nathan Burkan to SG, June 8, 1921; SG's secretary to AL, Jan. 13, 1920; SG to Gabriel Hess (T), July 11, 14, 1921; Gabriel Hess to SG (NL), July 12, 1921; SG to Mrs. Hector Turnbull, Feb. 23, 1922; SG to Ruth Goldwyn, Aug. 24, 1922; Ruth Goldwyn to SG, c. June 6, 1923; SG to Ruth Goldwyn, June 10, 1923; SG to Ruth Goldwyn, May 14, 23, Aug. 13, Sept. 14, 28, 1923; Ruth Goldwyn to SG, c. Oct. 12, 1923; SG to Ruth Goldwyn, Oct. 22, 1923; Ruth's note calling her father on his neglectful behavior does not exist but is referred to in SG to Ruth Goldwyn, Nov. 28, 1923; Ruth's "sweet letter" is referred to in SG to Ruth Goldwyn, Dec. 12, 1923; Ruth Goldwyn to SG (T), Dec. 21, 1923; the baked potato incident: RGC to ASB (I), Sept. 18, 1978;

SG to Ruth Goldwyn, Feb. 5, 1924; SG to Nathan Burkan, Feb. 29, 1924; SG to Nathan Burkan, Mar. 7, 1924; AL to SG (T), Aug. 27, 1924.

LETTER FROM SG'S MOTHER: Hannah Gelbfisz to SG, May 23, 1922.

SG-MARION-FITZMAURICE PICTURES OF 1924: SG to Nathan Burkan (T), Feb. 27, 1924; SG to George Fitzmaurice (T), Apr. 8, 1924; George Fitzmaurice to SG (T), Apr. 10, 1924; May McAvoy to ASB (I), July 30, 1983; Blanche Sweet to ASB (I), Apr. 2, 1983; "Estimated Production Cost, No. 3" for *Tarnish*; A. H. Giannini to SG (T), June 27, 1924; JAM to SG, Oct. 16, 1924; SG to AL (T), Oct. 17, 1924; Marion, *Off with Their Heads!*, p. 123; "Foreign Sales" accounting, c. Oct. 30, 1924.

SG TO EUROPE: Adela Austin to ASB (I), Sept. 6, 1980; Hilde Berl Halpern to ASB (I), Sept. 7, 1980; Aron Gutgold to ASB (I), June 1, 1985.

Details of Hannah Gelbfisz's death are in a letter from her doctor, Henryk Higier, to SG, June 6, 1935.

VILMA BANKY: SG, (UN), Dec. 8, 1952; Vilma Banky to ASB (I), July 2, 1984; SG to Vilma Banky (R), March 9, 1925; Will Hays to JS (T), Aug. 18, 1925; SG discusses Vilma Banky (and the early troubles with her wardrobe) in Leonard Lyons, "The Lyons Den," *New York Post Magazine*, August 4, 1967, p. 3; SG to Louella Parsons, March 9, 1925; Al Wilkie to AL (IOC), n.d.

Condé Nast's apartment is described in Caroline Seebohm, *The Man Who Was Vogue: The Life and Times of Condé Nast* (New York: Viking Press, 1982), p. 2; other details of his parties were supplied from the Condé Nast Archives: "Party Breakdowns," "Things That Can Be Done a Day or Two Before a Big Party"; "Table Arrangement" (New York: Condé Nast Publications).

MEETING FRANCES HOWARD: Coudert Nast's interest in Constance Howard was told by her daughter, Patricia Gerhardt, to ASB (I), Sept. 29, 1984; SG, "What America Means to Me," *American Weekly*, Jan. 27,

1952, p. 23; SG's reminiscences, as reported to Leonard Lyons, loc. cit.; Johnston, *Great Goldwyn*, p. 54.

FRANCES HOWARD'S BACKGROUND: Patricia Gerhardt to ASB (I), Sept. 29, 1984; Henry W. Clune to ASB, Sept. 17, 1984; SGJ to ASB (I), Oct. 17, 1983, and May 21, 1988; Billie Burke (with Cameron Shipp), *With a Feather on My Nose* (New York: Appleton-Century-Crofts, 1949), pp. 197–98, 199; GC to ASB (I), Sept. 11, 1979, Nov. 27, 1981; GC, rough notes dictated Dec. 18, 1970, and written up as a short profile called "Frances Goldwyn," by the Goldwyn office, Jan. 7, 1971; A. Winfield Chapin (fellow actor in Knickerbocker Players) to FG, Feb. 1, 1974; Irene Mayer Selznick to ASB (I), July 29, 1985; Katharine Hepburn to ASB (I), Apr. 9, 1983; Lasky, *I Blow*, p. 141; Gavin Lambert, *On Cukor* (New York: G. P. Putnam's Sons, 1972), pp. 25–6; Curt Gerling, *Never a Dull Moment* (Webster, N.Y.: Plaza Publishers, 1974), pp. 26–8; FG, early draft for "Dear Sam: Do You Remember?," *Woman's Home Companion*, Dec. 1950; Vilma Banky to ASB (I), Aug. 31, 1984.

VILMA BANKY GOES TO HOLLYWOOD: SG to AL, Mar. 27, 1925.

SG's COURTSHIP OF FG: FG, in Wagner, *You Must Remember*, pp. 105–6; Hilde Berl Halpern to ASB (I), Sept. 7, 1980; GC to ASB (I), Sept. 11, 1979; FG, early draft for "Dear Sam: Do You Remember?"; AL to SG (T), Apr. 15, 1925; Vilma Banky to SG (T), Apr. 16, 1925; SG to Vilma Banky, Apr. 16, 1925; Johnston, *Great Goldwyn*, pp. 55–6; "Motion Pictures," *The New Yorker*, Apr. 25, 1925, p. 31; Carl Brandt, "The Celluloid Prince," ibid., pp. 13–14; Vic Shapiro to SG, Aug. 26, 1959; *Jersey Journal*, Apr. 24, 1925.

10 CANAAN

FG AND SG ARRIVE IN HOLLYWOOD: FG, in Wagner, *You Must Remember*, pp. 105–6; Carl Brandt, "Celluloid Prince"; FG, "Dear Sam: Do You Remember?," pp.

42–44, 71; more on building of theaters in Los Angeles in Naylor, *Picture Palaces*, pp. 83–7, 216; Gernot Kuehn, *Views of Los Angeles* (Los Angeles: Portriga Publications, 1978), pp. 106–9; Morris, *Not So Long Ago*, p. 132; Irene Mayer Selznick to ASB (I), August 7, 1985; GC to ASB (I), Sept. 11, 1979; FG, draft of "Company's Coming," *Los Angeles Examiner*, Dec. 9, 1959, sec. II, 1; KV to ASB (I), June 11, 1980; Carmel Myers to ASB (I), May 21, 1980; Gish, *The Movies*, p. 281; Valeria Belletti to Irma Prina, June 26, 1925.

BEVERLY HILLS AND SANTA MONICA: Joe Shea, "Beverly Hills: Then & Now," and a facsimile of the "Chain of Title from the King of Spain to the City of Beverly Hills," appear in *Goldbook* (Beverly Hills: Goldbook, 1983), pp. 35, 37, 41; Sandra Lee Stuart, *The Pink Palace* (Secaucus, N.J.: Lyle Stuart, 1978), pp. 26–32; CC, *Autobiography*, p. 200; Charles Lockwood, *Dream Palaces* (New York: Viking Press, 1981), pp. 100–23; AL to SG (T), Jan. 9, 1925, informed SG that Marion Davies had bought the Lexington Road house; Marion Davies, *The Times*, pp. 32, 34, 101, 103; Clinton H. Anderson, *Beverly Hills Is My Beat* (Englewood Cliffs, N.J.: Prentice-Hall, 1960), p. 23; Parsons, *Illiterate*, p. 89; Selznick, *Private View*, pp. 71–2, 81–2; FG, in Wagner, *You Must Remember*, pp. 107–8.

FG's ROLE IN SG's LIFE: FG, "Dear Sam: Do You Remember?," p. 71; GC to ASB (I), Sept. 11, 1979; RGC to ASB (I), Oct. 13, 1979; Louella Parsons, "The Real Mr. Goldwyn," *Los Angeles Herald-Examiner Pictorial Living*, Feb. 22, 1959, p. 42.

STUDIO LIFE: Valeria Belletti to Irma Prina, Feb. 19, n.d. (c. Mar.), n.d. (c. Apr.), May 6, June 6, 1925. (N.B.: Valeria Belletti's letters are not part of the Goldwyn archives; they are privately owned.)

LEAVING FIRST NATIONAL: Nathan Burkan to SG (T), May 28, June 7, 1924; JAM to SG, June 11, 1924; SG to R. A. Rowland, May 29, 1924; R. A. Rowland to SG (T), June 6, 1924; SG to Nathan Burkan (T), Sept. 22, 1925; SG to AL (T), Nov. 1, 1925; AL to JAM, Aug. 19, 1925; SG to Nathan Burkan (T), July 1, 1925; SG to AL (T), Nov. 7, 1925; Nathan Burkan to SG (T), Apr. 30, 1925.

JOINING UNITED ARTISTS: SG's difficulties finding a new distributor are discussed in JS to SG, n.d. (c. Oct. 30, 1931); Balio, *United Artists,* pp. 49–60; Gloria Swanson, *Swanson on Swanson* (New York: Random House, 1980), p. 264; SG to Nathan Burkan, June 1, 1925; Nathan Burkan to SG (T), June 9, 1925; A. H. Giannini to SG, May 22, 1925; United Artists deal memorandum, "Samuel Goldwyn Contract," dated July 1925; "Agreement Between Samuel Goldwyn and United Artists Corporation," dated Aug. 29, 1925; Valeria Belletti to Irma Prina, June 6, 1925.

THE DARK ANGEL: KV, *A Tree,* pp. 112–15; *Variety,* Oct. 14, 1925, p. 42; information on George S. Barnes was obtained from a "Biography of George Barnes," at the Academy of Motion Picture Arts and Sciences Library; KV to ASB (I), June 11, 1980; Marion, *Off with Their Heads!,* p. 123; Irving Sindler to ASB (I), May 22, 1980.

BANKY PUBLICITY AND HOLLYWOOD GOSSIP: Valeria Belletti to Irma Prina, Aug. 21, Sept. 26, 1925; Victor Shapiro to C. F. Bertelli, July 28, 1925—includes English versions of the telegrams to be sent from Imre Lukatz to Vilma Banky, Sept. 1, 1925, and her reply to be cabled to the baron at the Hotel Crillon, Paris, Sept. 5, 1925; news clipping in SG files, n.d. (poss. *New York Times,* c. Sept. 10, 1925); Louella O. Parsons to SG (T), Sept. 2, 1925; Louella O. Parsons to SG, Feb. 12, 1929; the quotes of acclaim for Vilma Banky were excerpted and collected in several pages for SG; Guy Bolton to SG, Oct. 15, 1925; Quinn Martin, "Magic Lantern," *Motion Picture World,* Oct. 25, 1925; a monthly tally of Vilma Banky's fan mail—"Total Banky Fan Letters"—is in the SG files; Marion, *Off with Their Heads!,* pp. 123, 126.

STELLA DALLAS: Griffith, *Goldwyn,* p. 17; SG to Nathan Burkan, Feb. 29, 1924; JAM to AL, Oct. 2, 1924; Marion, *Off with Their Heads!,* pp. 112–23; Henry King to ASB (I), May 28, 1980; SG to Fannie Ward, May 16, 1924; Fannie Ward to SG, c. June 1, 1924; Belle Bennett to SG, "Monday," c. Feb. 1925; Valeria Belletti to Irma Prina, June 26, 1925.

Marion, *Off with Their Heads!,* p. 122; SG to A. H. Giannini, May 26, 1925; Henry King to ASB (I), May 28, 1980; Griffith, *Goldwyn,* p. 16; Valeria Belletti to Irma Prina, Sept. 5, 1925; KV to ASB (I), June 11, 1980; "Mr. Goldwyn Describes Try-Outs of Pictures," *New York Times,* Oct. 25, 1925; JS's opinion of *Stella Dallas* is mentioned in Hiram Abrams to SG (T), Sept. 26, 1925; SG to Victor Shapiro, Sept. 3, 1925; "Mr. Goldwyn suggests following changes on folder for Stella Dallas advertising" (M), (c. Sept. 5, 1925).

REACTION TO STELLA DALLAS: Ethel Barrymore to SG, n.d. (c. Oct. 9, 1925); Elinor Glyn to SG, Oct. 7, 1925; Douglas Fairbanks to SG, Oct. 9, 1925; CC to SG (T), Oct. 31, 1925; John Barrymore to SG (T), Oct. 9, 1925; Cecil B. DeMille to SG, Oct. 6, 1925; Harold Lloyd to SG, Oct. 10, 1925; Montague Glass, "Samuel Goldwyn: Motion Picture Producer," souvenir program for *Stella Dallas* (New York: Commanday-Roth, 1925), p. 2; the details of Hearst's reaction appear in (M) from FG to George Slaff, May 23, 1958, which he incorporated in an article allegedly written by SG, "If You Like It, Give a Cheer!," *This Week,* Oct. 19, 1958, p. 2; W. R. Hearst to Arthur Brisbane, n.d. (c. Oct. 8, 1925); SG to W. R. Hearst, Oct. 8, 1925; W. R. Hearst to SG, Nov. 15, 1925; Mordaunt Hall, "The Screen," *New York Times,* Nov. 17, 1925, p. 30.

COLMAN AND BANKY: Ronald Colman to SG, n.d. (c. Oct. 1925); *Photoplay,* May 1926, p. 35; Lasky, *I Blow,* p. 195; "Total Colman Fan Letters"; FG, "Dear Sam: Do You Remember?"; Rod La Rocque discussed his early career in Rosenberg and Silverstein, *Tinsel,* pp. 236–47; Cecil B. DeMille to SG (T), Jan. 12, 1926; SG to Cecil B. DeMille (T), Jan. 13, 1926; details about DeMille Studios appear in Valeria Belletti to Irma Prina, March 31, 1926; Vilma Banky to ASB (I), July 2, 1984.

STARTING BARBARA WORTH: Quotations from the synopsis and statistics about the book appear in the souvenir program of *The Winning of Barbara Worth* (© SG; Lord Printing Company, 1926), pp. 1, 7, 10, 11; SG to AL (T), Feb. 3, 1926; SG to AL (T), Feb. 18, 1926; SG to AL (T), Feb. 16, 1926.

SG'S FINANCES (1926): "SG—Loans Outstanding Nov. 29, 1926"; SG to Max Radt of Capitol National Bank, March 17, 1926; Max Radt to SG, March 18, 1926; SG to Jules Brulatour, Apr. 26, 1926; SG to Nathan Burkan, Aug. 28, 1926; SG to Nathan Burkan (T), Oct. 27, 1927; Nathan Burkan to SG (T), Dec. 5, 1927; SG to Nathan Burkan (NL), Dec. 5, 1927.

FILMING BARBARA WORTH: KV uses the Abe Stern quotation as both title and epigraph of his memoirs; "Making the Film," souvenir program, pp. 12–14; SG to Hiram Abrams (T), Apr. 21, 1926; SG to A. H. Giannini, June 21, 1926.

GARY COOPER: Valeria Belletti to Irma Prina, June 26, 1925; Gary Cooper (as told to Dorothy Spensley), "The Big Boy Tells His Story," *Photoplay,* Apr. 1929, pp. 64–5, 133–35, and May 1929, pp. 70–1, 84–5; Gary Cooper (as told to George Scullin), "Well, It Was This Way," *Saturday Evening Post,* 8-part series, Feb. 18, 1956, to Apr. 7, 1956; Homer Dickens, *The Films of Gary Cooper* (Secaucus, N.J.: Citadel Press, 1970), pp. 2–3, 6–7; Valeria Belletti to Irma Prina, July 15, 1926; Gary Cooper, filling out "Samuel Goldwyn Productions—Biographical Record," June 13, 1926; "Artist's Contract" between Gary Cooper and SG, June 5, 1926; Brownlow, *Parade,* pp. 114–17; Henry King to ASB (I), May 28, 1980. Irving Sindler to ASB (I), May 22, 1980; Nan Collins to R. B. McIntyre, July 2, 1926; AL to SG (T), July 17, 1926; SG to AL (T), July 29, 1926; AL to SG (T), Aug. 2, 1926; Gary

Cooper to SG (T), Aug. 2, 1926; SG to Garry [*sic*] Cooper, Aug. 3, 1926; Marion, *Off with Their Heads!,* pp. 126–27; Valeria Belletti to Irma Prina, July 15, and Nov. 3, 1925; SG's comments appear in (UN) from spring 1959 in preparation for Jack Smith's Los Angeles *Times* profile.

DEATH OF VALENTINO: SG to Rudolph Valentino (T), Aug. 18, 1926; SG to JAM (T), Aug. 23, 1926; JAM to SG (T), Aug. 23, 1926.

BANKY-COLMAN FILMS: Untitled clipping (poss. Los Angeles *Examiner*), Aug. 26, 1926; another unsourced clipping, "Vilma Banky Trampled After Fall from Horse," Aug. 2, 1926; Marion, *Off with Their Heads!,* pp. 145–46.

UNITED ARTISTS GROWING PAINS AND SG'S FORTUNES: Balio, *United Artists,* pp. 61–71; *Variety,* Dec. 2, 1925, p. 27; JS to Trustees in the Dissolution of Art Cinema, May 20, 1935; Sinclair, *William Fox;* Nathan Burkan to SG, Apr. 4, 1927; "SG, Inc.—Summary of Pictures Released," cost and profit accounting, Aug. 1, 1931; "Royalty Statement—'Stella Dallas,'" Mar. 29, 1930; Henry King to SG, Aug. 20, 1926; SG to Henry King, Aug. 25, 1926.

BIRTH OF SGJ AND JEWS IN L.A.: Rabbi Edgar F. Magnin to ASB (I), May 27, 1983; SGJ to ASB (I), Oct. 11, 1983; GC to ASB (I), Sept. 11, 1979; Irene Mayer Selznick to ASB (I), Nov. 18, 1984; Carmel Myers to ASB (I), May 21, 1980; on Mary Pickford's anti-Semitism, David Rose to ASB (I), Feb. 21, 1980; Pickford, *Sunshine,* pp. 213–14.

SPECTERS IN HOLLYWOOD (1926): Swanson, *Swanson,* p. 283; SG writes of censorship troubles in a letter to William Curley (of the Chicago *Evening American*), May 18, 1927; Robert Osborne, *50 Golden Years of Oscar* (La Habra, Cal.: ESE California, 1979), pp. 2–3; Miles Kreuger, "Vitaphone: 1926–1976," *The 50th Anniversary of Vitaphone* (New York: Institute of the American Musical, 1976; the Institute is now located in Los Angeles), p. 3; Hays, *Memoirs,* pp. 390–92; Sinclair, *William*

Fox, pp. 73–4, 103–6; Parsons, *Illiterate*, pp. 117–18; Ramsaye, *Million and One Nights*, p. 514; Fred Niblo, JS, et al. to SG (T), Oct. 7, 1926; *Constitution and By-Laws* (Hollywood: Academy of Motion Picture Arts and Sciences, 1927), p. 1; Henry King to ASB (I), May 28, 1980.

RITES OF HOLLYWOOD; BANKY WEDDING: FG, "Dear Sam: Do You Remember?," pp. 80–1; Rod La Rocque, in Rosenberg and Silverstein, *Tinsel*, pp. 247, 251; Vilma Banky to ASB (I), Aug. 31, 1984; Mayfair dances described in Selznick, *Private View*, p. 95; Cecil B. DeMille to SG (T), Apr. 7, 1927; SG to Cecil B. DeMille (T), Apr. 8, 1927; various clippings, newspapers unidentified, including "Banky Wedding Program Told," June 9, 1927; "Screen Stars Get License," June 18, 1927; Rev. Michael Mullins to SG, June 27, 1927; SG's secretary to Dr. Louis Furedi, June 30, 1927; SG said the wedding cost him $25,000, in interview for Jack Smith's Los Angeles *Times* profile of Gary Cooper, spring 1959; "2nd Front Page," Los Angeles *Herald-Express*, Oct. 31, 1951, shows original front-page coverage of the Banky-La Rocque wedding; SGJ to ASB (I), June 10, 1980; May McAvoy to ASB (I), July 30, 1983.

THE JAZZ SINGER: May McAvoy to ASB (I), July 30, 1983; George Jessel, in Wagner, *You Must Remember*, pp. 89–90.

SG MADE DIRECTOR OF UNITED ARTISTS: SG to JS (T), Oct. 11, 1927.

11 INTERREGNUM

THE JAZZ SINGER AND TALK OF TALKIES: SGJ to ASB (I), Oct. 31, 1983; GC to ASB (I), Sept. 11, 1979; Jack Warner to SG (T), Dec. 20, 1927; *Variety*, Oct. 12, 1927, p. 7; *Variety*, Oct. 19, 1927, p. 23; *Variety*, Nov. 16, 1927, p. 7; *Variety*, Dec. 7, 1927, p. 7; D. W. Griffith quoted in Stuart Berg Flexner, *Listening to America* (New York: Simon & Schuster, 1982), p. 404—see also D. W. Griffith, "The Movies 100 Years from Now," *Collier's*, May 3, 1924, p. 7; Mary Pickford

quoted in Flexner, *Listening*, p. 405; *Variety*, Oct. 5, 1927, pp. 1, 58.

CURSE OF TALKIES: Sam Warner's obituary appears in *Variety*, Oct. 12, 1927, p. 11; Marcus Loew memorial issue of *Variety* was Oct. 19, 1927; Samuel Marx, *Mayer and Thalberg: The Make-Believe Saints* (New York: Random House, 1975), p. 100; Rogers, *Autobiography*, p. 187.

WIRING FOR SOUND: Balio, *United Artists*, pp. 77–80; William Fox to SG, Aug. 21, 1928; memorandum and "Routine for Preparing Prints for Synchronization," H. D. Buckley to Producers of United Artists Pictures, Oct. 29, 1928; Gordon Sawyer to ASB (I), Apr. 30, 1980; Zukor, *The Public*, pp. 253–54.

PLIGHT OF THE ACTORS: "Too Many Picture Actors," *Variety*, Nov. 30, 1927, p. 1; Zukor, *The Public*, pp. 253–54; Budd Schulberg, *Moving Pictures: Memoirs of a Hollywood Prince* (New York: Stein and Day, 1981), p. 176; Parsons, *Illiterate*, pp. 118–19.

THE AWAKENING: *Variety*, Jan. 9, 1929; Arthur Hornblow to SG (T), Mar. 9, 1928; more discussion of theme songs appears in Ethan Mordden, *The Hollywood Musical* (New York: St. Martin's Press, 1981), pp. 18–19; Irving Berlin to SG (T), Sept. 17, 19, 1928; cost and profit figures appear on "Summary of Pictures Released," Aug. 1, 1931.

THE RESCUE: Ronald Colman to AL, Aug. 5, 1928 (N. B.: This letter has been reproduced with the salutation reading "My dear Sam"; in fact, the latter was addressed to AL); SG to Pete Smith (T), Apr. 20, 1928; Lynn Farnol to SG (T), May 8, 1928; (M) marked "Important Please," from Barrett C. Kiesling to Robert McIntyre, May 17, 1928; cost and profit figures appear on "Summary of Pictures Released," Aug. 1, 1931.

OUT WITH THE OLD, IN WITH THE NEW: Stephen Harvey, "'Queen Kelly' Opens—More Than 50 Years Late," *New York Times*, Sept. 22, 1985, sec. H, pp. 17, 32; the activity at Paramount's Astoria studios is discussed in Lasky, *I Blow*, pp. 219–

20; Robert Montgomery's screen test is described in Johnston, *Great Goldwyn*, pp. 88–9; Lambert, *On Cukor*, p. 28; GC to FG (T), n.d. (c. Oct. 12, 1926); AL to SG (T), Oct. 13, 1926; GC to ASB (I), Nov. 27, 1981; C. B. DeMille, *Autobiography*, pp. 304–5; Valeria Belletti to Irma Prina, Dec. 15, 1928; early musicals are discussed in Mordden, *Hollywood Musical*, pp. 18, 21, 22.

NEW GENERATION OF FILMMAKERS: The "corned beef and cabbage" joke comes from Bruce Humberstone to ASB (I), Mar. 11, 1984; "Columbia, the 'Germ' of the Ocean" is a chapter title in Frank Capra, *The Name Above the Title* (New York: Macmillan, 1971), pp. 81–99; GC to ASB (I), Sept. 11, 1979; an "interview" with Harry Cohn, recorded Mar. 26, 1928, in Bob Thomas, *King Cohn: The Life and Times of Harry Cohn* (New York: G. P. Putnam's Sons, 1967), p. 47–8; layoffs at the studios are mentioned in a letter from Valeria Belletti to Irma Prina, Jan. 16, 1928.

RESETTLING OF THE STUDIOS: Wanamaker, "Before Hollywood Was Hollywood," pp. 62–4; Sinclair, *William Fox*, p. 75; Richard B. Jewell (with Vernon Harbin), *The RKO Story* (New York: Arlington House, 1982), pp. 8–10; Lasky, *I Blow*, pp. 196–97; among those who referred to the United Artists studio as "Doug and Mary's" was Irving Sindler to ASB (I), May 22, 1980; lists of films released by United Artists, grouped by both year of release and producer, appear in Balio, *United Artists*, pp. 245–79.

HORNBLOW: Brooke Hayward, *Haywire* (New York: Alfred A. Knopf, 1977), pp. 80–1; Mrs. Arthur Hornblow, Jr., to ASB (I), Oct. 19, 1982; Julia Benita Colman, *Ronald Colman: A Very Private Person* (New York: William Morrow, 1975), pp. 79–80.

SG ENTERS TALKIES: "'Westerns' Dying in U.S.," *Variety*, Jan. 18, 1928, p. 1; *Variety*, Jan. 25, 1928, p. 52; "Kidding Kissers in Talkers Burns . . . ," *Variety*, Oct. 30, 1929, pp. 1, 63; KV to ASB (I), June 11, 1980; FG, "Dear Sam, Do You Remember?," p. 44.

THIS IS HEAVEN: Hope Loring, *This Is Heaven* (screenplay); (George Marion, Jr.), "Dialogue—'This Is Heaven,'" pp. 1–2; SG to Sime Silverman (unsent T), Jan. 21, 1929.

SG SEARCHING FOR NEW MATERIAL: SG to Robert Sherwood (then film critic for *Life*), Aug. 2, 1926; *Arms and the Man* was first suggested as a vehicle for Colman and Banky, JS to SG (T), Jan. 23, 1926; Arthur Hornblow to SG, Dec. 28, 1927; Jesse A. Levinson to SG (T), Sept. 27, 1927; SG to Louella Parsons (T), Nov. 4, 1924.

BULLDOG DRUMMOND: Colman, *Colman*, pp. 83–7; Wallace Smith, *Bulldog Drummond*—"Silent Version" and "Sound Version," Scenes 1, 8–10, 296–300; "Weekly Negative Cost Report, 'Bulldog Drummond,'" Nov. 28, 1931; Arthur Hornblow to SG (T), Oct. 27, 1928; GC to ASB (I), Sept. 11, 1979; Monta Bell, "The Director: His Problems and Qualifications," *Theatre Arts Monthly*, Sept. 1929, quoted in Richard Koszarski, *Hollywood Directors, 1914–1940* (New York: Oxford University Press, 1976), pp. 228–33; John Gillett, *International Encyclopedia of Film* (New York: Crown, 1972), p. 361; Barsacq, *Caligari*, pp. 142–43, 227; Joan Bennett to ASB (I), Nov. 15, 1983; SG discussed rehearsing *Drummond*, in Griffith, *Goldwyn*, pp. 19–20; Johnston, *Great Goldwyn*, pp. 92–3; the story about the word "din" was verified by Mrs. Arthur Hornblow, Jr., to ASB (I), Oct. 19, 1982.

FATE OF BANKY: Mrs. Arthur Hornblow, Jr., to ASB (I), Oct. 19, 1982; SG talked of Vilma Banky to Leonard Lyons, New York *Daily News*, July 1, 1950; AL to SG (T), June 4, 1929; Edward G. Robinson (with Leonard Spigelgass), *All My Yesterdays* (New York: Hawthorn Books, 1973), pp. 103–4; SG, (UN) for Jack Smith's articles in Los Angeles *Times*, Spring 1959; "Hungarian Actress to Quit Films," prob. Los Angeles *Examiner*, May 2, 1930; Schulberg, *Moving Pictures*, p. 176.

FORTUNE OF COLMAN: Colman, *Colman*, pp. 86–7; "Summary of Pictures Released," Mar. 29, 1930, Aug. 1, 1931;

statistics about the Academy Award are from Osborne, *50 Golden Years*, pp. 15–16; Joan Bennett to ASB (I), Nov. 15, 1983; Arthur Hornblow, Jr., to SG (T), Oct. 27, 1928.

HOLLYWOOD COMES OUT OF SPIN: Hays, *Memoirs*, p. 394.

CAMINO PALMERO: "Historic Resources Inventory" for 1800 Camino Palmero, Lots 18, 19, and 20 of the Las Colinas Heights Tract (prepared by Bureau of Engineering, City of Los Angeles); SGJ to ASB (I), Mar. 7, 1984, Feb. 24, 1988; Lasky, *I Blow*, p. 240.

THE CRASH: "Wall St. Lays an Egg," *Variety*, Oct. 30, 1929, pp. 1, 64.

12 MAKING WHOOPEE

REVERBERATIONS OF THE CRASH: SG's finances are recorded in "SG, Inc. and Subsidiary Companies Reconciliation of Surplus Account," Mar. 29, 1930, and JAM to AL, Apr. 30, 1928.

IDENTITIES OF THE STUDIOS: Behlmer and Thomas, *Hollywood*, pp. 42–3; Sinclair, *William Fox*, pp. 116–17; Charles Higham, *Warner Brothers* (New York: Charles Scribner's Sons, 1975), p. 85; *Oxford Companion to Film*, p. 717; SG to A. H. Giannini, Apr. 10, 1930; SG on MGM's formula, SGJ to ASB (I), Oct. 20, 1983; Lasky, *I Blow*, p. 240; WW to ASB (I), Apr. 1, 1980.

SG AND *CONDEMNED*: SGJ to ASB (I), Oct. 17, 1983; Arthur Hornblow, Jr., to SG (T), Oct. 22, 1928; Flexner, *Listening*, p. 434; "Weekly Negative Cost Report for Production #20—'Condemned,'" Nov. 28, 1931; "Production Cost—'Condemned to Devil's Island,'" Jan. 11, 1930.

RAFFLES: SG's line about the "day of the director," in Marill, *Goldwyn Presents*, p. 91; KV to ASB (I), June 11, 1980; Bruce Humberstone to ASB (I), Mar. 11, 1984; Colman, *Colman*, p. 95; John Springer and Jack Hamilton, *They Had Faces Then* (Secaucus, N.J.: Citadel Press, 1974), p. 110; Winona B. Meyer, "Ronald Colman Present at Fox for Big Preview," New York *Evening*

Telegram, Apr. 22, 1930; the reviews of the film were sent in a long telegram, Lynn Farnol to SG, July 25, 1930; "Weekly Negative Cost Report for Production #21—'Raffles,'" Nov. 28, 1931; SG to AL (M), Oct. 2, 1930; the Eisenstein story appears in Leon Moussinac, *Sergei Eisenstein: An Investigation into His Films and Philosophy* (New York: Crown Publishers, 1970), p. 167. Jay Leyda, film critic and associate of Eisenstein, was present at the time Goldwyn made the remark, and he confirmed it, according to Stephanie Winston to ASB, Nov. 17, 1979.

THE DEVIL TO PAY: Terms of the Lonsdale deal appear in Reeves Espy to SG (IOC), July 11, 1939; SG to Frederick Lonsdale (T), June 30, 1930; Frederick Lonsdale to SG (T), July 1, 1930; SG to Frederick Lonsdale (T), July 1, 1930; Lonsdale's arrival and stay are discussed in: SG to Frederick Lonsdale (T), July 17, 18, 1930; R. B. McIntyre to SG (M), July 18, 1930; Frederick Lonsdale to SG (T), Aug. 9, 1930; replacement of Constance Cummings appears in Colman, *Colman*, pp. 100–2; Loretta Young's experiences are chronicled in ibid., pp. 103–6; Mordaunt Hall, *New York Times*, Dec. 19, 1930, p. 30; "New York charges to 5/2/31" (a memorandum attached to "Weekly Negative Cost Report for Production #24—'The Devil to Pay,'" Nov. 28, 1931; SG Inc., "Royalty Statement—Frederick Lonsdale," Dec. 31, 1932; SGJ to ASB (I), Oct. 20, 1983.

ZIEGFELD AND MUSICALS: SGJ to ASB (I), Oct. 20, 1983; Eddie Cantor, *Take My Life* (Garden City, N.Y.: Doubleday, 1957), pp. 11–13, 122, 123–24, 153, 161; Burke, *Feather*, pp. 221–22; Lasky, *I Blow*, p. 194; Bob Thomas, draft of article for Associated Press, after interview with SG, Feb. 4, 1963, pp. 2–3; SG to Nicholas Schenck, Aug. 19, 1930; Mordden, *Hollywood Musical*, pp. 17–18; Bruce Humberstone to ASB (I), Mar. 11, 1984.

FINANCING AND PRODUCING SG'S 1930 pictures: Evelyn Laye, *Boo, to My Friends* (London: Hurst & Blackett, 1958),

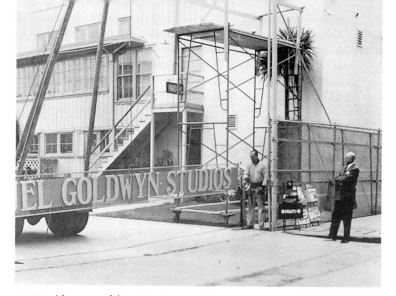

ABOVE: After years of disputing the ownership of the United Artists studio, Goldwyn outbid Mary Pickford in court. The new landlord watches the rechristening of the studio, April 21, 1955. BELOW: Writer N. Richard Nash, Goldwyn, and director Rouben Mamoulian at work on *Porgy and Bess*. 1958. Within months, the film's main set would burn down, Mamoulian would be fired, and the NAACP's protests against the film would kill any chances for its success. It was Goldwyn's eightieth and last picture.

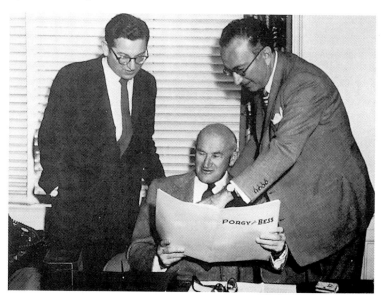

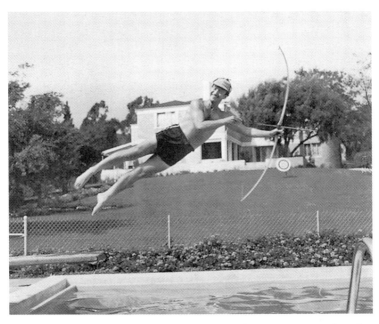

ABOVE: David Niven. According to Goldwyn, he and Gary Cooper were the only actors who expressed proper gratitude to him for their careers. BELOW: Lucille Ball, after she had risen to stardom in television, 1950s. Goldwyn offered her advice on the expansion of her show business empire.

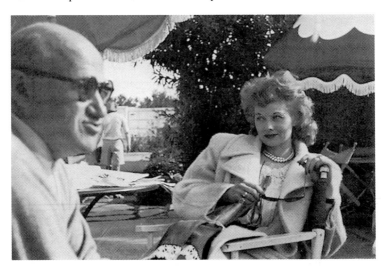

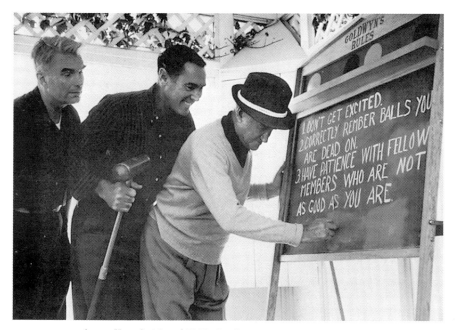

On the blackboard:

GOLDWYN'S RULES

1. DON'T GET EXCITED.
2. CORRECTLY REMBER BALLS YOU ARE DEAD ON.
3. HAVE PATIENCE WITH FELLOW MEMBERS WHO ARE NOT AS GOOD AS YOU ARE.

ABOVE: Actors Kent Smith and Philip Reed review the Goldwyn rules of the Goldwyn Croquet Club. As at cards and backgammon, Goldwyn cheated shamelessly. BELOW: George Sanders, restaurateur Michael Romanoff, and Goldwyn, c. 1960.

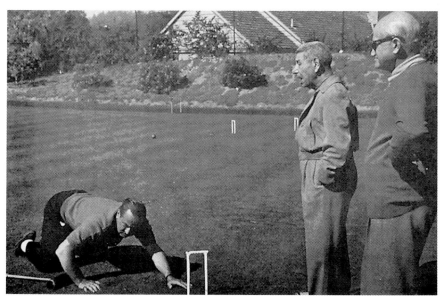

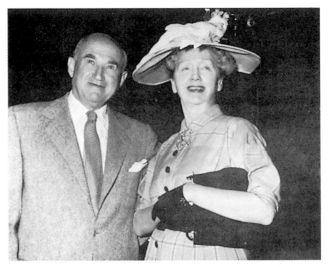

ABOVE: Goldwyn with Hedda Hopper. Although she had acted in silent pictures for him in Fort Lee, New Jersey, Goldwyn preferred leaking stories to her rival, Louella Parsons. BELOW: Three generations of Goldwyns: Sam junior, his daughter, Cricket, and Sam.

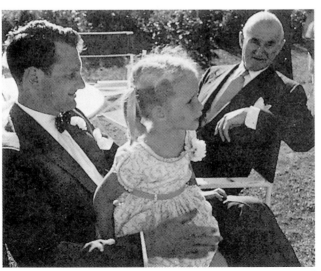

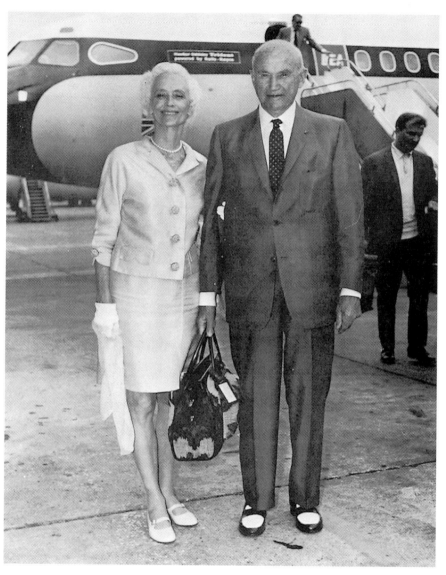

Sam looked the same decade after decade, but Frances made changes (she let her hair grow white and had a face lift).

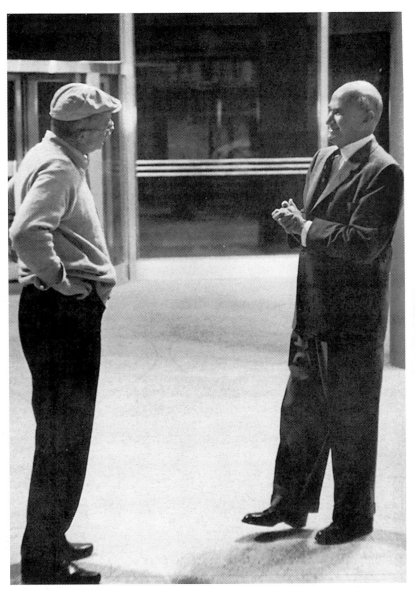

Billy Wilder with Goldwyn, 1960.

RIGHT: Jesse Lasky, Sam Goldwyn, and Cecil B. DeMille, fifty years after *The Squaw Man* launched their careers. Goldwyn outlived his former partners by fifteen years.
BELOW: The wedding of agent-producer Charles Feldman and Clotilde Barot, 1968. Gray eminence Sam Goldwyn stands with his arm around Warren Beatty; Jules Stein pokes his head over Goldwyn's shoulder; Ray Stark, Louis Jourdan, and David Brown stand in the center at rear; Robert Evans, Billy Wilder, Mike Romanoff, Frank Sinatra, and Richard Zanuck to the right; Irving Lazar at right front.

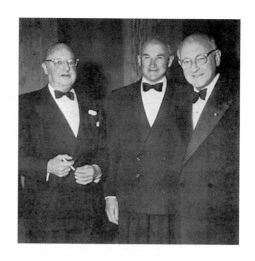

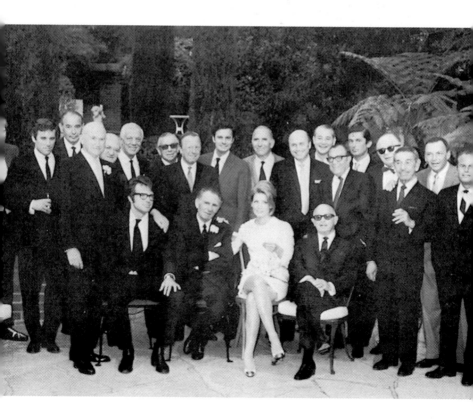

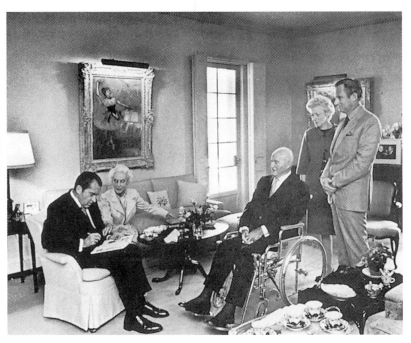

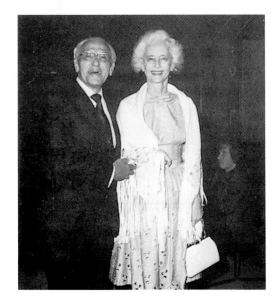

ABOVE: Richard Nixon, then President, awards Goldwyn the Medal of Freedom. Frances sits on the couch. Ruth and Sam junior stand behind Goldwyn, March 27, 1971. RIGHT: Frances and George Cukor, loving friends to the end.

p. 115; JS to SG, Mar. 26, 1930; A. H. Giannini to SG, Apr. 1, 1930; SG to A. H. Giannini, Apr. 10, 1930; Johnston, *Great Goldwyn*, pp. 87, 94; Arthur Hornblow to SG, "A Plan for the Preparation and Production of 'Whoopee,'" Mar. 6, 1930.

Z & G PRODUCTIONS: SG to Florenz Ziegfeld (T), Feb. 8, 1930; Burke, *Feather*, p. 223; SG to Florenz Ziegfeld (T), Mar. 3, 1930; SG to Florenz Ziegfeld (unsent letter), Feb. 28, 1930; SGJ to ASB (I), Oct. 20, 1983; Florenz Ziegfeld to SG (T), Mar. 4, 1930; Florenz Ziegfeld to SG (T), Mar. 5, 1930; SG to Eddie Cantor (T), Feb. 4, 1930; SG to Florenz Ziegfeld (T), Jan. 31, 1930; SG to Florenz Ziegfeld (T), Mar. 3, 1930; Arthur Hornblow, Jr., to Lynn Farnol (T), Feb. 8, 1930; Florenz Ziegfeld to SG (T), Mar. 5, 1930.

SCRIPT AND COSTUMES OF *WHOOPEE!*: Eddie Cantor to SG (T), Feb. 17, 1930; Eddie Cantor to SG, Feb. 12, 1930; Cantor, *Take My Life*, pp. 136–37, 153–54; SG to Lynn Farnol (unsent T about Busby Berkeley's drinking), Feb. 28, 1930; Lynn Farnol to SG (T), c. Feb. 28, 1930; Lynn Farnol to SG (T), Feb. 20, 1930; Florenz Ziegfeld to SG (DL), Mar. 4, 1930. Costumes are discussed in Florenz Ziegfeld to SG (T), Feb. 27, 1930; AL to JAM (T), Mar. 14, 1930; Florenz Ziegfeld to SG (T), Mar. 19, 1930; SG to Florenz Ziegfeld (T), Mar. 20, 1930; SG to Florenz Ziegfeld (T), Apr. 12, 1930; Burke, *Feather*, p. 217; Patricia Ziegfeld, *The Ziegfelds' Girl* (Boston: Little, Brown, 1964), pp. 202–3.

GOLDWYN GIRLS: SGJ to ASB (I), Oct. 20, 1983; "The Goldwyn Girls Come Back," unsigned typescript of article, *Parade*, Jan. 20, 1952; Johnston, *Great Goldwyn*, p. 87; Jean Howard to ASB (I), July 20, 1983; Bruce Humberstone to ASB (I), Mar 11, 1984.

RICHARD DAY: Barsacq, *Caligari*, pp. 51, 53, 57, 204.

ALFRED NEWMAN: Tony Thomas, *Music for the Movies* (South Brunswick, N.J.: A. S. Barnes, 1973), pp. 54–5; Frederick Steiner, *The Making of an American Film Composer: A Study of Alfred Newman's Music in the*

First Decade of the Sound Era (unpub. MS.), pp. 21–62, 63–99, 110–16; "Alfred Newman," *Look*, Feb. 19, 1946, p. 86; Gordon Sawyer to ASB (I), Apr. 30, 1980.

FILMING OF *WHOOPEE!*: Eddie Cantor to SG, Feb. 8, 1930; Cantor, *Take My Life*, pp. 154, 155; Florenz Ziegfeld to SG, July 22, 1930; "Weekly Negative Cost Report for Production #22—'Whoopee,'" May 2, 1931; Bruce Humberstone to ASB (I), Mar. 11, 1984; SGJ to ASB (I), Oct. 20, 1983.

ONE HEAVENLY NIGHT: Laye, *Boo*, pp. 114, 116–17; SG to A. H. Giannini, Mar. 24, 1930; Louis Bromfield to SG, Wednesday, Aug. 1930.

SG'S SOCIAL LIFE: Cardplaying anecdotes and Joseph P. Kennedy's remark are reported in Richard Meryman, *Mank* (New York: William Morrow, 1978), pp. 134, 183; SGJ to ASB (I) Oct. 17, 1983, Jan. 20, 1984, Mar. 26, 1988, and May 21, 1988; Jean Howard to ASB (I), July 20, 1983; Bruce Humberstone to ASB (I), Mar. 11, 1984; Marjory Dye to ASB (I), Jan. 20, 1984; Irene Mayer Selznick to ASB (I), Oct. 9, 1985; Selznick, *Private View*, pp. 160, 367.

RESULTS OF *WHOOPEE!* AND *ONE HEAVENLY NIGHT*: "Z & G Motion Picture Corp., Royalty Statement," Nov. 28, 1931; "Weekly Negative Cost Report for Production #23—'One Heavenly Night,'" Nov. 28, 1931; "One Heavenly Night—N.Y. Charges to 11/28/31" (M); "SG, Inc., Detailed Cost of Pictures," Nov. 28, 1931; "SG, Inc., Summary of Pictures Released," c. 1932; *Whoopee!* was reviewed in *Variety*, Oct. 8, 1920, p. 22; the other reviews of *Whoopee!* appeared in a memorandum, "New York Press Reports of 'Whoopee,'" prob. Lynn Farnol to SG, c. Sept. 30, 1930; SG to Nicholas Schenck, Aug. 19, 1930.

FATE OF ZIEGFELD: "Z & G Motion Picture Corp.—Stocks, Sept. 30, 1931"; Florenz Ziegfeld to SG, July 14, 1931; Florenz Ziegfeld to SG (T), Aug. 16, 1931; SG to Florenz Ziegfeld (T), Aug. 17, 1931; Jean Howard to ASB (I), July 20, 1983; Florenz Ziegfeld to SG (T), July 11, 1930;

Ziegfeld, *Ziegfelds' Girl*, pp. 202–3; Florenz Ziegfeld to SG (T), Mar. 23, 25, 1932; GC to ASB (I), Jan. 8, 1981; Katharine Hepburn to ASB (I), Apr. 5, 1983; Burke, *Feather*, pp. 241–42, 249.

13 COMING OF AGE

HOLLYWOOD BELLIES UP: Balio, *United Artists*, p. 96; Samuel Marx, *Mayer and Thalberg*, p. 265; Sinclair, *William Fox*, p. 117; Jewell, *RKO*, pp. 32, 44; Higham, *Warner Brothers*, pp. 100–1; Zukor, *The Public*, pp. 261–62; Lasky, *I Blow*, pp. 242–43; Stanton Griffis, *Lying in State* (Garden City, N.Y., Doubleday, 1952), p. 84.

STREET SCENE: Theodore Dreiser, "What Are America's Powerful Motion Picture Companies Doing?," *Liberty*, June 11, 1932, pp. 6–11; SGJ to ASB (I), Oct. 17, 1983; SG to Joseph P. Bickerton (T), Nov. 22, 1930; KV to ASB (I), June 11, 1980; Schulberg, *Moving Pictures*, pp. 351, 353–56; Sylvia Sidney to ASB (I), Apr. 4, 1983; JS to SG (T), May 25, 1931; Paul Rotha, *The Film Till Now* (Feltham, Middlesex: Hamlyn Publishing Group, Spring Books, 1967), p. 371; KV, *A Tree*, pp. 202–5; Beulah Bondi to ASB (I), Apr. 27, 1980; Helen Hayes to ASB (I), July 22, 1984; SG to JS, July 2, 1931; Mr. Codd to SG and AL (IOC), July 15, 1931, re cost of *Street Scene*; Siegfried Kracauer, *Theory of Film: The Redemption of Reality* (New York: Oxford Press, 1960), p. 139; René Clair, *Cinema Yesterday and Today* (New York: Dover, 1972), p. 132; Max Steiner's comments, "Scoring the Film," appear in *We Make the Movies*, ed. Nancy Naumburg (New York: W. W. Norton, 1937), p. 218; Steiner, *American Film Composer*, pp. 127–32, 240–49; Lynn Farnol, "Street Scene Opens Tonight," Press Release #6547, n.d.; Harpo Marx to SG (T), Aug. 27, 1931; Lynn Farnol to SG (IOC), Aug. 25, 1931; Elmer Rice to SG (T), Aug. 27, 1931.

TONIGHT OR NEVER: Irene Sharaff, *Broadway & Hollywood* (New York: Van Nostrand Reinhold, 1976), p. 16; Guy Croswell Smith to SG, June 5, 1931; Gloria Swanson to SG, Mar. 16, 1931; Lynn Farnol to SG (T), Mar. 4, 1931; SG to Lynn Farnol (T), Mar. 5, 1931; SG to Mlle Chanel (T), Mar. 4, 1931; SG to Lynn Farnol (T), Mar. 3, 1931; Lynn Farnol to SG (T), Mar. 3, 1931; Lynn Farnol to SG (T), Mar. 4, 1931; SG to Mlle Chanel (T), June 25, 1931; Swanson, *Swanson*, pp. 412–19; Helen Gahagan Douglas, *A Full Life* (Garden City, N.Y.: Doubleday, 1982), pp. 88, 94–5, 97, 103–4; Mervyn LeRoy (as told to Dick Kleiner), *Mervyn Leroy: Take One* (New York: Hawthorn Books, 1974), p. 103; Mervyn LeRoy to ASB (I), Feb. 7, 1980; Mordaunt Hall, *New York Times*, Dec. 18, 1931, p. 29.

THE GREEKS HAD A WORD FOR THEM: Arthur Hornblow, Jr., to SG (IOC), Feb. 12, 1931; Sidney Howard, "Notes for Screen Treatment of 'The Greeks Had a Word for It,'" n.d. (c. Feb. 12, 1931); Ina Claire to ASB (I), Mar. 11, 1980; SG to JS (T), May 22, 1931; SG to JS (T), May 28, 1931; "Final Shooting Schedule on 'The Greeks Had a Word for It,'" Aug. 21, 1931; Carole Lombard to SG, n.d. (c. Sept. 1, 1931); SG to JS (unsent letter), June 25, 1931; Ina Claire to SG, Jan. 15, 1932; AL to SG (IOC), Jan. 28, 1932; SG to AL (IOC), Feb. 1, 1932.

THE UNHOLY GARDEN: Colman, *Colman*, pp. 109–10; Ben Hecht, *Charlie: The Improbable Life and Times of Charles MacArthur* (New York: Harper & Brothers, 1957), pp. 174–78; Arthur Hornblow, Jr., to Leland Hayward (T), May 20, 1931; Ben Hecht to Arthur Hornblow, Jr. (T), May 21, 1931; Arthur Hornblow, Jr., to Leland Hayward (T), May 21, 1931; Ben Hecht to SG (T), May 22, 1931; Ben Hecht, *A Child of the Century* (New York: Simon & Schuster, 1954), p. 343; the reviews were sent from Lynn Farnol to SG (T), Oct. 29, 1931; "SG, Inc. Royalty Statement, 'Unholy Garden,'" Dec. 29, 1934.

ARROWSMITH: Griffith, *Goldwyn*, pp. 20–1; Helen Hayes to ASB (I), July 22, 1984; Colman, *Colman*, pp. 111–12; Dan Ford, *Pappy: The Life of John Ford* (Englewood Cliffs, N.J.: Prentice-Hall, 1970), pp. 65–6; Sidney Howard, *Arrowsmith* (Sound version—Aug. 3, 1931), pp. 4, 8, 35, 96; rave notices reported by AL to SG (T), Feb. 4, 1932; Mordaunt Hall, "Arrowsmith," *New York Times*, Dec. 8, 1931, p. 36; SG to Irving Thalberg, Jan. 29, 1932.

COLMAN TROUBLES: Colman, *Colman*, pp. 117–20; FG, unpub. draft for "Dear Sam: Do You Remember?" contains the anecdote about SGJ and Harpo Marx; "Ronald Colman Sues Goldwyn for Millions," *Los Angeles Herald-Express*, Sept. 13, 1932, p. 1; SG (UN) (prob. to George Slaff), Dec. 8, 1952; William Randolph Hearst to SG, Nov. 29, 1932; Relman Morin, "Cinematters," *Los Angeles Record*, n.d. (c. Sept. 15, 1932); "Colman Plumb Set on Quitting," *St. Louis Globe Democrat*, Jan. 10, 1933; Ronald Colman to JS, Aug. 18, 1933; JS to Ronald Colman, Sept. 6, 1933.

CANTOR MUSICALS: Cantor, *Take My Life*, pp. 155–59; "SG, Inc. and Subsidiary Companies Summary of Pictures Released," June 4, 1932; Royalty Statements for Eddie Cantor on *Palmy Days* and *The Kid from Spain*, both dated Dec. 30, 1933; LeRoy, *Mervyn LeRoy*, p. 102; souvenir program, *The Kid from Spain*, n.d., pp. 2–5, 16; SGJ to ASB (I), Oct. 20, 1983; "Mr. Cantor in the Bullring," *New York Times*, Oct. 30, 1932, sec. VIII, p. 6; James and James, *Biography of a Bank*, p. 429; Lynn Farnol to SG (IOC), Jan. 23, 1933; Eddie Cantor to SG (T), Jan. 23, 1933; SG to Eddie Cantor, Feb. 3, 1933.

SG'S FINANCES: "SG, Inc. and Subsidiary Companies—Notes Payable," Nov. 28, 1931; "Consolidated Balance Sheet," June 4, 1932; "Consolidated Profit and Loss Statement," June 4, 1932; "SG—Life Insurance," July 8, 1932; SGJ to ASB (I), Mar. 7, 1984; the Goldwynism to Leo McCarey is quoted in George Oppenheimer, *The View from the Sixties* (New York: David McKay, 1966), p. 97.

RGC'S SETTLEMENT: RGC to ASB (I), Oct. 13, 1979, Jan. 30, 1988; Lasky, Jr., *Whatever Happened*, pp. 76–7; "BLANCHE GOLDFISH against SAMUEL GOLDFISH," Mar. 3, 1932; SG to JAM, May 29, 1933; RGC to SG, May 24, 1933; SG to JAM, May 31, 1933; McClure Capps to SG (T), June 24, 1933; SG to JAM (T), June 26, 1933, 9:30 a.m.; SG to JAM (NL), June 26, 1933; AL to JAM (T), Sept. 12, 1933; SG to JAM (IOC), Sept. 23, 1933; "AGREEMENT between SG and RUTH TURNBULL CAPPS," finally agreed and signed Nov. 29, 1933; SGJ to ASB (I), October 7, 11, 20, 1983.

14 "THAT LITTLE SOMETHING EXTRA"

DISCOVERY OF ANNA STEN AND PRE-PRODUCTION OF *NANA*: GC to ASB (I), Nov. 27, 1981; Kyle Crichton, "The Kid from the Ukraine," *Collier's*, Mar. 31, 1934, pp. 32, 52; "Making the Breaks for the New Stars," proofsheets, *Everyweek* magazine (NEA Service, Inc.), Nov. 26, 1933, p. 5; Phil Gersdorf, "The Passionate Peasant," unpub. article written for SG Productions, in five parts, n.d.; John Kobal, *People Will Talk* (New York: Alfred A. Knopf, 1985), pp. 129–41; Lynn Farnol to SG, Mar. 7, 1932; Anna Sten to ASB (I), Oct. 25, 1980; SG, "Do We Pay Our Picture Stars Too Much?," *Saturday Evening Post*, Feb. 17, 1934, pp. 8–9, 90–2; SG, transcript of radio broadcast, KMTR, Los Angeles, Oct. 24, 1934, 7 p.m.; RGC to ASB (I), Oct. 13, 1979; SG to Lynn Farnol (T), Mar. 19, 1932; Lynn Farnol to SG (T), Mar. 27, 1932; SG to Lynn Farnol (T), Mar. 28, 1932; SG to Guy Smith (T), Apr. 6, 1932; Guy Smith to SG (T), Apr. 11, 1932; SG to Lynn Farnol (T), Apr. 15, 1932; Lynn Farnol to SG (T), Apr. 18, 1932; Lynn Farnol to SG (T), Apr. 19, 1932; Fred Kohlmar to SG (IOC), Dec. 29, 1932; Oppenheimer, *View*, pp. 95–6, 103, 109–11; SG to Cole Porter (T), June 5, 1932; Cole Porter, "Anything Goes," refrain 3, as printed in *Cole*, ed. Robert Kimball (New York: Holt, Rinehart & Winston, 1971), p. 127.

NATIONAL CRISIS AND STEN'S PAY

CUT: Balio, *United Artists*, pp. 97–9; carbon copy of letter from Arch Reeve to Charles E. McCarthy of Fox Film Corp., sent to SG, Mar. 8, 1933; SG to AL (T), Mar. 9, 1933; AL to SG (T), Mar. 9, 1933; AL to SG (T), Mar. 10, 1933; SG to AL (T), Mar. 11, 1933; Anna Sten to SG, Mar. 11, 1933; SG to Anna Sten (T), Mar. 13, 1933; Anna Sten to SG, Mar. 15, 1933; AL to SG (T), Mar. 16, 1933; AL to SG (T), Mar. 17, 1933; AL to Anna Sten (T), Mar. 21, 1933.

PROMOTION OF ANNA, PRODUCTION OF *NANA*: SG to Lynn Farnol (IOC), Jan. 20, 1933; Lynn Farnol to SG (IOC), Jan. 24, 1933; Condé Nast to SG, Jan. 18, 1934; Oppenheimer, *View*, pp. 109–11; Kobal, *People*, p. 135; AL to Robert Fairbanks, Sept. 19, 1933; Gersdorf, "Passionate Peasant," part 5, pp. 1–5; GC to E. J. Mannix, Sept. 8, 1933; GC to ASB (I), Nov. 27, 1981; Gerald Peary and Karyn Kay, "Interview with Dorothy Arzner" in *The Work of Dorothy Arzner: Towards a Feminist Cinema*, ed. Claire Johnston (London: British Film Institute, 1975), pp. 19–29; "Dorothy Arzner Is Dead at 82," *New York Times*, Oct. 12, 1979, sec. II, p. 79; Mollie Merrick, "Goldwyn Has Faith in Soviet Actress," *Buffalo Evening News*, Oct. 21, 1933; "SG's Bright New Star from Red Russia!" brochure, Department of Advertising and Publicity, United Artists Corporation; the Sten advertisements with a different adjective each day ran in the Los Angeles *Times* and the *Herald*, Feb. 22–28, 1934; SG to AL (T), Jan. 16, 1934; SG to William Randolph Hearst (T), Jan. 19, Feb. 5, 1934; W. R. Hearst to SG (T), Feb. 6, 1934; SG to AL (T), Feb. 1, 1934; Alfred Newman to SG (T), Feb. 2, 1934; SG to Alfred Newman, Feb. 5, 1934; AL to SG (DL), Feb. 6, 1934; *Literary Digest*, Feb. 17, 1934, p. 47; the story about Zola's heirs appeared in *Hollywood Reporter*, May 18, 1934, p. 1.

WE LIVE AGAIN: SG to John Balaban of Balaban & Katz Corp., May 17, 1934; SG to Leland Hayward (T), Dec. 2, 1933; Leland Hayward to SG, Dec. 30, 1933; Sidney Howard to Arthur Hornblow, Jr., Mar. 16, 1933; George Oppenheimer to SG (IOC), Dec. 13, 1933; SG to George Oppenheimer (IOC), Dec. 16, 1933; "Tolstoi's Heirs Can't Complain," undated newspaper clipping; "Cinema," *Time*, Nov. 12, 1934, p. 42; Rouben Mamoulian to ASB (I), May 15, 1984; Willard Mack to SG, n.d. (c. Jan. 1, 1934); Willard Mack to SG, Jan. 14, 1934; Willard Mack to SG, "Wednesday," n.d. (c. Feb. 1, 1934); James Curtis, *Between Flops* (New York: Harcourt Brace Jovanovich, 1982), pp. 95–6; Sidney Howard to SG (T), June 5, 1934; Oppenheimer, *View*, pp. 111–12; laundry list of writers' requests appears in Nancy Lynn Schwartz, *The Hollywood Writers' Wars* (New York: Alfred A. Knopf, 1982), p. 30; "Preview—We Live Again," *Variety*, Sept. 22, 1934; GC to ASB (I), Nov. 27, 1981.

THE WEDDING NIGHT: Edwin Knopf to ASB (I), June 1, 1980; AL to SG (IOC), Aug. 22, 1934; KV, *A Tree*, pp. 205, 207–9; Rocky Cooper Converse to ASB (I), June 14, 1984; KV to ASB (I), June 11, 1980; *Newsweek*, Mar. 23, 1935, p. 29; Paul Holt, "Anna Sten Walks Out," London *Daily Express*, May 21, 1935, p. 1; Kobal, *People*, pp. 140–41; Rouben Mamoulian to ASB (I), May 15, 1984.

GOLDWYNS AT HOME: GC to ASB (I), Nov. 27, 1981; FG's secretary to Cartier, Oct. 27, 1932; SGJ to ASB (I), Oct. 17, 20, 1983, Mar. 7, 1984; Anna Sten to ASB (I), Oct. 25, 1980; SG to Richard Jaeckel of H. Jaeckel & Sons, Nov. 19, 26, 1934; SG to Jules Glaenzer of Cartier (T), Apr. 14, 1937; Rocky Cooper Converse to ASB (I), June 14, 1984; FG, "Dear Sam: Do You Remember?," p. 81; FG, menu books; SG's secretary, "Guest list—New Years Eve party—December 31, 1935"; Katharine Hepburn to ASB (I), Apr. 8, 1983; Dorothy Hirshon to ASB (I), June 12, 1984; William S. Paley to ASB (I), June 13, 1983; Averell Harriman to ASB (I), May 3, 1982; LH to ASB (I), Nov. 15, 1981; F. Scott Fitzgerald, *The Last Tycoon* (New York: Charles Scribner's Sons, 1941), p. 3; Hilde Berl Halpern to ASB (I), Sept. 7,

1980; Neill Lehr to ASB (I), July 13, 1983; SGJ is quoted in "The risky business of Samuel Goldwyn, Jr.," *Women's Wear Daily*, Feb. 20, 1986, p. 16; Mary Ellin Barrett to ASB (I), Oct. 1, 1980.

MUSICALS AND *ROMAN SCANDALS*: "SG will make a radical departure . . . ," press release, c. 1932; transcript of interview between Howard Teichman and SG, May 2, July 17, 1962; George S. Kaufman to SG, Jan. 10, 1932; John Mason Brown, *Sherwood*, p. 297; "Supreme Court of the State of New York, County of New York, Robert Sherwood, Plaintiff, against SG, Inc., Defendant," Jan. 8, 1934; identical papers were filed with George S. Kaufman as plaintiff; SG to Charles Schwartz, May 26, 1933; George S. Kaufman to SG, Oct. 19, 1933; SG to George S. Kaufman, Oct. 30, 1933; Oppenheimer, *View*, pp. 91, 99–103; SG to Louella Parsons, May 18, 1933; Lucille Ball to ASB (I), June 5, 1980; SG to Lynn Farnol (IOC), Dec. 1, 1933; Cantor, *Take My Life*, p. 160; "Memorandum of substance of conversations between Mr. Goldwyn, Mr. Berkeley and Mr. Zanuck," n.d.; Bruce Humberstone to ASB (I), Mar. 11, 1984; "Two Producers Quit Hays Group," *New York Times*, Oct. 24, 1933, p. 23; "Assails Salary Stand," *Variety*, Oct. 27, 1933, pp. 1, 6; "My resignation from the Association of Motion Picture Producers . . . ," press release, c. Oct. 28, 1933; SGJ to ASB (I), Feb. 21, 1988; JS to SG, Apr. 10, 1934.

KID MILLIONS: Eddie Cantor to SG (T), Feb. 24, 1934; SG to Eddie Cantor, Feb. 26, 1934; Cantor, *Take My Life*, p. 160; Oppenheimer, *View*, pp. 97–8; Ethel Merman (with George Eells), *Merman, an Autobiography* (New York: Simon & Schuster, 1978), pp. 65–66; Eddie Cantor to SG, Nov. 26, Dec. 6, 1934.

STRIKE ME PINK AND CANTOR RIFT: Merman, *Merman*, p. 77–78; Cantor, *Take My Life*, pp. 160–61; SG to Eddie Cantor (T), Jan. 22, 1935; Eddie Cantor to SG (T), Jan. 23, Sept. 14, 1935; SG to Eddie Cantor, Sept. 14, 1935.

DARK ANGEL, OBERON, AND KORDA: SG to Murray Silverstone (T), Dec. 18, 1934; a source who swears he paid $100 to spend the night with Merle Oberon and who wishes to remain anonymous, to ASB (I), 1980; Charles Higham and Roy Moseley, *Princess Merle: The Romantic Life of Merle Oberon* (New York: Coward-McCann, 1983), pp. 17–26; Michael Korda, *Charmed Lives* (New York: Random House, 1979), pp. 17–24; 35–47, 51, 78–89; JS to SG (T), Aug. 7, 1934; FG and SG to JS (T), Aug. 7, 1934; RGC to ASB (I), Oct. 13, 1979; Merle Oberon to Alexander Korda (T), Jan. 11, 1935; Merle Oberon to SG (T), Feb. 13, 1935; Merle Oberon to Alexander Korda (T), Mar. 6, 1935; JS to SG (T), Jan. 17, 1935; SG to Alexander Korda (T), Jan. 11, 1935; JS to SG, Jan. 30, 1935; Alexander Korda to Merle Oberon (T), Mar. 5, 1935; Alexander Korda to SG (T), Jan. 16, 1935; SG to Alexander Korda (T), Mar. 6, 1935; Alexander Korda to SG (T), Mar. 9, 1935; SG to JS (unsent), Mar. 12, 1935; JS to SG, Mar. 14, 1935; Alexander Korda to SG (R), Oct. 4, 1935; SG to Alexander Korda (T), Oct. 7, 1935; Alexander Korda to SG (T), Jan. 4, 8, 1936; two worksheets, headed "Our Proposal" and "Korda's Proposal"; Al Kaufman of Myron Selznick & Co., Inc., to SG, Aug. 14, 1936; LH to ASB (I), Nov. 16, 1981; Lillian Hellman, *Three: An Unfinished Woman, Pentimento, Scoundrel Time* (Boston: Little, Brown, 1979), pp. 466–67; Sidney Franklin to SG (T), Mar. 11, 1935; JAM to SG (IOC), Jan. 14, 1935; the director who said "Goldwyn wanted everything clean about Merle . . ." WW to ASB (I), Jan. 8, 1981.

OTHER NEW PLAYERS AND *BARBARY COAST*: SG, (UN) for interview, Dec. 8, 1952; David Niven, *The Moon's a Balloon* (New York: G. P. Putnam's Sons, 1972), pp. 183–93; Joseph I. Breen to SG, Aug. 27, 1934, in which he points out: "The ruling of the Code . . . is quite clear—'Sexual immorality . . . should never be introduced as subject matter unless *absolutely essential* to the plot. . . . It must not be presented as attractive and beautiful . . .

and it must not be made to seem right and permissible . . ."; Joel McCrea to ASB (I), Apr. 30, 1980; Robinson, *Yesterdays*, pp. 156–61; Joseph McBride, *Hawks on Hawks* (Berkeley: University of California Press, 1982), pp. 106–9; Ben Hecht and Charles MacArthur to SG (T), June 14, 1935.

ACADEMY AWARDS: Osborne, *50 Golden Years*, pp. 10–11, 15; Marion, *Off with Their Heads!*, p. 241; SGJ to ASB (I), Oct. 20, 1983.

THE GAY DECEPTION: Joel McCrea to ASB (I), Apr. 30, 1980.

15 "THE GOLDWYN TOUCH"

WW: Joel McCrea to ASB (I), May 13, 1980; WW to ASB (I), APR. 1, 1980; LH to ASB (I), Nov. 15, 1981; Axel Madsen, *William Wyler* (New York: Thomas Y. Crowell, 1973), p. 116.

SIGNING LH AND *THESE THREE*: Richard Layman, *Shadow Man: The Life of Dashiell Hammett* (New York: Harcourt Brace Jovanovich, 1981), p. 135; LH, *Three*, pp. 456, 465–66, 467–68; *A Code to Govern the Making of Motion and Talking Pictures* (New York: Motion Picture Association of America, 1948), p. 7; LH to ASB (I), Nov. 15, 1981; Joseph I. Breen to SG, July 31, 1935; Frank S. Nugent, review of *These Three*, *New York Times*, Mar. 29, 1936, p. 22; WW to ASB (I), Apr. 1, 1980; Thalberg's reference to WW as "Worthless Willy" was often told by SG to SGJ, who related it to ASB (I), Oct. 26, 1983; "Agreement" between WW and SG, Sept. 19, 1935; "Agreement" between LH and SG, Jan. 4, 1936; Hecht, *A Child*, p. 482.

GOLDWYN STAFF AND "GOLDWYN TOUCH": LH, p. 468; Scott Meredith, *George S. Kaufman and His Friends* (Garden City, N.Y.: Doubleday, 1974), pp. 193–94; SGJ to ASB (I), Oct. 20, 1983; WW to ASB (I), Apr. 1, 1980; Johnston, *Great Goldwyn*, pp. 15, 23; LH, *Three*, p. 468; SGJ to ASB (I), Mar. 7, 1984.

MAKING *THESE THREE*: Merritt Hulburd to SG (IOC), Oct. 30, 1935; WW to ASB (I), Apr. 1, 1980; LH to ASB (I), Nov. 16, 1981; Madsen, *Wyler*, p. 137; Joel McCrea to ASB (I), Apr. 30, May 13, 1980; Daniel Mandell to ASB (I), May 5, 1980.

The anecdote whose punch line is "Since when are we making pictures for kids?" is one of the most popular Goldwyn stories, told by many people who claimed to have been there when SG said it. Garson Kanin said it occurred during the making of *Dead End;* director Henry Hathaway remembered Goldwyn's saying it to him during the making of *The Real Glory;* SGJ recalls a similar scene during the making of *The Adventures of Marco Polo*. Alfred Newman to SG (IOC), Feb. 22, 1936; Graham Greene, "These Three," *The Spectator,* May 1, 1936.

UNITED ARTISTS POWER SHIFT: Balio, *United Artists*, pp. 125, 127–41; Irving Thalberg to SG and Mary Pickford, Feb. 7, 1936; David Rose to ASB (I), July 26, 1983; *Fortune* research files, for article on SG and UA published Dec. 1940.

SG'S SEARCH FOR MATERIAL: "Memo: From G.B.S. to S.G.," unidentified clipping, poss. *Variety*, Sept. 27, 1936; George Bernard Shaw to Mary Grey, Oct. 25, 1932; SG to Murray Silverstone (T), Oct. 31, 1934; SG to Murray Silverstone (T), Oct. 11, 1934; SG to George Bernard Shaw, Aug. 6, Sept. 14, 1936; Oppenheimer, *View*, pp. 112–14; unsigned (M), "Marco Seeks 'Oz' Yarns for Screen," discussed purchase price by SG; Moss Hart to SG (T), Oct. 18, 1933; Vincent Youmans to SG (T), Mar. 15, 1934.

COME AND GET IT: Edna Ferber to SG (T), Oct. 28, 1936; Julie Goldsmith Gilbert, *Ferber* (Garden City, N.Y.: Doubleday, 1978), p. 332; many of Miss Ferber's feelings about the script appear in Merritt Hulburd to SG (IOC), Nov. 6, 1935; McBride, *Hawks*, pp. 10, 78, 96–8; Frances Farmer, *Will There Really Be a Morning?* (New York: G. P. Putnam's Sons, 1972), pp. 160–65; Joel McCrea to ASB (I), May 13, 1980.

SG PREPARES TO SAIL FOR EUROPE: JAM to Betty Goldsmith (IOC), Jan. 23,

1936; KV to ASB (I), June 11, 1980; Ernest C. Fishbaugh, M.D. to SG, "Diet and General Directions," Feb. 6, 1935.

DODSWORTH PREPRODUCTION: WW to ASB (I), Apr. 1, 1980; Johnston, *Great Goldwyn*, p. 23; "Themes from 'Dodsworth,'" n.d.; Sidney Howard to Ann Watkins, Oct. 5, 1935; Sidney Howard to SG, Oct. 6, 1935; Merritt Hulburd to Ann Watkins (T), Oct. 5, 10, 1935; Max Gordon (play's producer) to SG, Oct. 4, 1935; Sidney Howard to SG, July 19, 1935; Merritt Hulburd to SG (T), Nov. 16, 1935; R. B. McIntyre to SG (T), Mar. 4, 1936; Merritt Hulburd to SG, Oct. 21, 1935; Sidney Howard to Merritt Hulburd, Mar. 14, 1936.

OBTAINING *DEAD END*: Merritt Hulburd to SG, Nov. 22, 1935; WW to ASB (I), Apr. 1, 1980; Johnston, *Great Goldwyn*, p. 23.

GOLDWYNS' TRIP TO EUROPE; SG LANDS IN HOSPITAL: FG, "Dear Sam: Do You Remember?," pp. 81, 88; FG to Douglas Fairbanks (T), Apr. 17, 1936; SGJ to ASB (I), Oct. 26, 31, 1983, Feb. 20, 1988; Neill Lehr to ASB (I), July 13, 1983; RGC to ASB (I), Jan. 30, 1988; SG to A. H. Giannini (T), May 7, 1936; Mary Pickford to FG, May 9, 1936.

PRODUCTION OF *COME AND GET IT*: Merritt Hulburd to SG c/o FG (T), Apr. 30, 1936; McBride, *Hawks*, p. 106; AL to FG (T), June 8, 1936; JAM to AL (T), June 9, 1936; Merritt Hulburd to FG (T), June 5, 1936; Merritt Hulburd to SG c/o FG (T), Apr. 30, 1936.

PRODUCTION OF *DODSWORTH*: Sidney Howard to Merritt Hulburd, Mar. 14, 1936; Sidney Howard to George Haight, Mar. 22, 1936; Sidney Howard to Merritt Hulburd, Apr. 21, 1936; Merritt Hulburd to Sidney Howard, Apr. 7, 1936; WW to ASB (I), Jan. 8, 1981; Niven, *Moon*, pp. 199–200; Mary Astor, *A Life on Film* (New York: Delacorte Press, 1971), pp. 118–22, 125.

SG REACTS TO *COME AND GET IT*: McBride, *Hawks*, p. 85; SG to Edna Ferber, Oct. 27, 1936; Joel McCrea to ASB (I),

Apr. 30, 1980; WW to ASB (I), Apr. 1, 1980; "Mr. Wyler does the retakes . . .," unsigned memorandum, n.d.; Jock Lawrence to SG (IOC), Aug. 21, 1936; Edna Ferber to SG, Oct. 31, 1936; Merritt Hulburd to SG (IOC), Sept. 30, 1936.

MARY ASTOR SCANDAL: Astor, *A Life*, pp. 125–27, Mary Astor, *My Story: An Autobiography* (Garden City, N.Y.: Doubleday, 1959), pp. 166–71.

DODSWORTH KUDOS; THALBERG DEATH: Sinclair Lewis to SG (T), Sept. 18, 1936; SGJ to ASB (I), Oct. 31, 1983; Samuel Marx, *Mayer and Thalberg*, pp. 248–51; Rabbi Edgar I. Magnin to ASB (I), May 27, 1983; WW to ASB (I), Jan. 8, 1981; SG to Norma Shearer (T), Sept. 14, 1936; Miriam Hopkins to SG (T), Sept. 15, 1936.

BELOVED ENEMY AND AL'S DEPARTURE: Merritt Hulburd to JAM (T), June 10, 1936; *Variety*, Aug. 25, 1936, p. 1; *New York Times*, Aug. 25, 1936, p. 23; Neill Lehr to ASB (I), July 13, 1983.

"REIGN OF TERROR": SGJ to ASB (I), Feb. 20, 1988; SG's secretary to Raymond F. Stevens (manager of Sun Valley Lodge), Dec. 4, 1936; Samuel Marx to ASB (I), Feb. 24, 1984; Garson Kanin, *Hollywood* (New York: Limelight Editions, 1984), pp. 1–8; Garson Kanin to ASB (I), June 13, 1984; Joshua Logan, *Movie Stars, Real People, and Me* (New York: Delacorte Press, 1978), pp. 23, 34–41; Joshua Logan to SG, Aug. 1, 1957 (with separate cover letter to FG, same date); Niven, *Moon*, pp. 201–2; WW to SG (T), Sept. 24, 1936; "Woman Chases Man," *Time*, May 31, 1937, p. 26; WW to ASB (I), Jan. 8, 1981; Joel McCrea to ASB (I), Apr. 30, 1980; WW to SG (T), Nov. 9, 1936.

DEAD END: Merritt Hulburd to Sidney Howard, Sept. 30, 1936; Sidney Howard to Merritt Hulburd (T), Oct. 14, 1936; Merritt Hulburd to Sidney Howard, Oct. 5, 1936; Lewis Milestone to SG (T), Sept. 3, 1936; SG to LH, Oct. 16, 1936; LH to ASB (I), Nov. 16, 1981; LH to SG, Nov. 5, 1936; Fred Kohlmar to SG (IOC), Oct. 23, 1936; Sylvia Sidney to ASB (I), Apr. 4, 1983; WW to ASB (I), Jan. 8, 1981; AL is quoted in Reeves Espy to SG (IOC), July 25, 1936; Lewis Yablonsky, *George Raft* (New York: McGraw-Hill, 1974), pp. 97–8; Sidney Kingsley, *Dead End* (New York: Random House, 1936), pp. 84–5; "'Dead End,' Comparison of Estimate & Cost," July 13, 1937; FG, "Dear Sam: Do You Remember?," p. 88.

STELLA DALLAS: Joel McCrea to ASB (I), May 13, 1980; Zeppo Marx is quoted in Paul D. Zimmerman and Burt Goldblatt, *The Marx Brothers at the Movies* (New York: G. P. Putnam's Sons, 1968), p. 98; Fred Kohlmar to Reeves Espy (IOC), Nov. 23, 1936; KV to ASB (I), June 11, 1980; KV, *A Tree*, p. 210; KV to SG (T), July 23, 1937; Marion Davies and W. R. Hearst to SG (T), Aug. 10, 1937; Olive Higgins Prouty to SG (T), July 27, 1937; Henry King to ASB (I), May 28, 1980.

THE HURRICANE: John Ford to SG (T), Oct. 31, 1936; Ford, *Pappy*, pp. 100–1, 102; Charles Nordhoff to SG, Feb. 1, 1936; Jock Lawrence, *Show* (privately printed magazine promoting *The Hurricane*), vol. 3, 1937–38, pp. 3–5, 9–11, 21; SGJ to ASB (I), Oct. 31, 1983; Hecht, *A Child*, p. 488; Joel McCrea to ASB (I), Apr. 30, 1980; Jock Lawrence to ASB (I), Oct. 17, 1982; Astor, *A Life*, pp. 134–35; "The Hurricane," *Life*, Oct. 25, 1937, p. 107; Ira Gershwin (through Michael Feinstein) to ASB (I), June 23, 1983.

PLANNING THE GOLDWYN FOLLIES: Griffith, *Goldwyn*, pp. 31–2; SG to Murray Silverstone (T), Aug. 7, 1936; SGJ to ASB (I), Oct. 26, 1983; Archibald Selwyn to SG, Feb. 11, 1936; George Gershwin to Isaac Goldberg, May 12, 1937, quoted in Edward Jablonski and Lawrence D. Stewart, *The Gershwin Years* (Garden City, N.Y.: Doubleday, 1973), pp. 276, 282; SG to Freddy Kohlmar (IOC), Jan. 3, 1936; Fred Kohlmar to Reeves Espy (IOC), Aug. 29, 1936; Vera Zorina to ASB (I), Mar. 19, 1984; LH to ASB (I), Nov. 15, 1981.

UA TAKEOVER ATTEMPT: Balio, *United Artists*, pp. 142–55; David Rose to ASB (I), July 26, 1983; Neil S. McCarthy to Douglas Fairbanks, Mar. 18, 1938; JS to Mary Pickford, Mar. 16, 1938; *Fortune* research files, 1940.

FIRING ASSISTANTS: Kanin, *Hollywood*, pp. 13–14, 16–22, 258; Samuel Marx to ASB (I), Feb. 24, 1984; Garson Kanin to ASB (I), June 13, 1984.

PRODUCING THE GOLDWYN FOLLIES: Jablonski and Stewart, *Gershwin*, pp. 289–96; Mrs. Ira Gershwin to ASB (I), July 2, 1983; Vernon Duke, *Passport to Paris* (Boston: Little, Brown, 1955), pp. 350–58; "Tough Break for Goldwyn," London *Daily Mail*, Aug. 2, 1937; Kanin, *Hollywood*, pp. 108–9; Jock Lawrence to ASB (I), Oct. 17, 1982; Vera Zorina to ASB (I), Mar. 19, 1984; LH to ASB (I), Nov. 15, 1981; SGJ to ASB (I), Oct. 26, 1983; GC to ASB (I), Nov. 27, 1981.

RGC remembered FG's boasting of SG's "private list" of women, to ASB (I), Oct. 13, 1979.

Sam Marx to SG (IOC), June 1, 1937; David O. Selznick to SG, June 1, 1937; Ben Hecht to SG, n.d. (c. late 1937).

THE GREAT GOLDWYN: Johnston, *Great Goldwyn*, pp. 94, 99; WW to ASB (I), Apr. 1, 1980.

16 ANNUS MIRABILIS

BEATON: SGJ to ASB (I), Mar. 25 and 26, 1988; Frank Crowninshield, "The New Left Wing in American Society," *Vogue*, Feb. 1, 1938, pp. 72–73, 165–67; Seebohm, *Man Who Was Vogue*, pp. 209–212; Irene Mayer Selznick to ASB (I), Mar. 27, 1988.

THE STATE OF THE INDUSTRY: Will H. Hays, "Enlarging Scope of the Screen," Annual Report to the Motion Picture Producers and Distributors of America, Inc. (MPPDA), New York, Mar. 27, 1939, pp. 1–8; SG to CC (unsent letter), Mar. 2, 1938; SGJ to ASB (I), Oct. 31, 1983; Rocky Cooper Converse to ASB (I), June 14, 1984.

Universal's founder, Carl Laemmle, died in September 1939.

SG'S PROPOSED PROJECTS: SG to George Bernard Shaw, Mar. 3, 1938; George Bernard Shaw to SG, Mar. 29, 1938; Miriam Howell to SG (IOC), Nov. 4, 1938; David O. Selznick to SG (T and letter), Jan. 24, 1939; SG to David O. Selznick, Jan. 25, 1939; SG to LH, Aug. 15, 1939; Edwin Knopf to SG (IOC), Apr. 21, 1939; LH to SG (T), Apr. 24, 1939; LH to ASB (I), Nov. 16, 1981; Miriam Howell to SG (IOC), Sept. 22, 1938; Katharine Hepburn to ASB (I), Apr. 6, 1983; Edwin Knopf to SG, Nov. 29, 1939; SG to Katharine Hepburn (T), Jan. 6, 1940; Sidney Howard to SG, Feb. 20, 1939, and Feb. 14, Mar. 1, Mar. 2, 1939; SG to Edwin Knopf (T), Dec. 12, 1939; Edwin Knopf to SG (T), Dec. 14, 1939; Miriam Howell to SG (T), Jan. 17, Feb. 22, 1939; Edwin Knopf to SG, Dec. 1, 1939.

ADVENTURES OF MARCO POLO: David Rose to ASB (I), Feb. 21, 1980; Douglas Fairbanks to David Rose (T), Oct. 30, Nov. 2, 1936; SG to Merritt Hulburd (T), Dec. 8, 1936; Douglas Fairbanks to SG, Mar. 19, 1937; David Rose to JAM (IOC), Nov. 4, 1936; Lana Turner, *Lana* (New York: E. P. Dutton, 1982), pp. 32–3; Jock Lawrence to SG (IOC), Mar. 14, 1938; "'The Flower of Flatbush' Makes Good," *Life*, Apr. 18, 1938, p. 29; Jock Lawrence to SG (IOC), press release for trade papers, June 21, 1937; WW to ASB (I), Jan. 8, 1981; SG, Inc., "Estimated Loss—'Marco Polo,'" c. Mar. 1, 1939.

THE COWBOY AND THE LADY: Kanin, *Hollywood*, pp. 82–96; Jock Lawrence to ASB (I), Oct. 17, 1982; Rocky Cooper Converse to ASB (I), June 14, 1984; WW to ASB (I), Jan. 8, 1981; SG, Inc., "Estimated Loss—'Cowboy and the Lady,'" c. Mar. 1, 1939.

THE REAL GLORY: Henry Hathaway to ASB (I), Feb. 5, 1980; David Rose to ASB (I), July 26, 1983.

WUTHERING HEIGHTS: Hecht, *Charlie*, p. 228; Sylvia Sidney to ASB (I), Apr. 4, 1983; Helen Hayes to ASB (I), July 22,

1984; Emily Bronte, *Wuthering Heights* (New York: Triangle Books, 1939), published in conjunction with the release of the film, contained Currer Bell's introduction, p. xxiv; (UN) in *Time* and *Life* morgue, "SG," Nov. 12, 1952; SGJ to ASB (I), Oct. 31, 1983; WW to SG (T), Apr. 2, 1938; Bette Davis to ASB (I), Jan. 19, 1983; WW to ASB (I), Apr. 1, 1980; George Mitchell, "A Great Cameraman," *Films in Review*, Dec. 1956, pp. 508–9; John Huston to ASB (I), Mar. 9, 1980; Jock Lawrence to Reeves Espy (IOC), May 31, 1938; Ben Hecht to SG (T), May 5, 1938; Laurence Olivier to Melvyn Bragg (transcript of interview presented on *South Bank Show*); Laurence Olivier to ASB (I), Mar. 26, 1980; Merle Oberon to Laurence Olivier (T), June 6, 1938; WW to SG (T), July 7, 1938; SG to WW (T), July 12, 1938; WW to SG (T), Aug. 20, 1938; SG to WW (T), Aug. 24, 1938; WW to SG (T), Aug. 25, 1938; Laurence Olivier, *Confessions of an Actor: An Autobiography* (New York: Simon & Schuster, 1982), pp. 106–9; WW to SG (R), Aug. 31, 1938; SG to WW (T), Sept. 12, 1938; Jack Warner to SG, Dec. 15, 1938; SG to WW (T), Aug. 22, 1938; Niven, *Moon*, pp. 203–7; SG, Inc., "Summary of loss . . . due to the illnesses of Merle Oberon and WW"; SG to WW (unsent letter and IOC), Dec. 20, 1938; SG to Merle Oberon, Feb. 17, 1939; SGJ to ASB (I), Oct. 31, 1983; SG, Inc., "Daily Production Report," Feb. 27, 1939; SG to Laurence Olivier, Mar. 23, 1939; Jock Lawrence to SG (IOC), "Wuthering Heights Billing," Dec. 30, 1938; Alfred Newman to SG, Oct. 16, 1937; Steiner, *Film Composer*, pp. 370–411; Jock Lawrence to ASB (I), Oct. 17, 1982.

THEY SHALL HAVE MUSIC: SG to Jascha Heifetz, Oct. 1, 1937; SG to Miriam Howell (T), July 28, 1938; Miriam Howell to SG (IOC), Nov. 7, 1938; (M) of stipulations in Heifetz deal, n.d.; WW to ASB (I), Jan. 8, 1981; Miriam Howell to SG (T), Dec. 13, 1938; SG to Miriam Howell (T), Dec. 21, 1938; Miriam Howell to

SG (T), Dec. 21, 1938; Joel McCrea to ASB (I), Apr. 30, 1980; SG to Jascha Heifetz (T), June 7, 1939; SG's advertising orders appear in Jock Lawrence to Ben Washer (IOC), July 10, 1939; Deems Taylor, *Jascha Heifetz* (New York: United Artists Corporation, 1939), pp. 8–12; SG to R. J. O'Donnell of Interstate Theatres (T), Sept. 16, 1939; Iphigene Sulzberger to ASB (I), Mar. 31, 1983; Thomas A. Pryor to ASB (I), Mar. 19, 1984; Bosley Crowther, "They Shall Have Music," *New York Times*, July 26, 1939, p. 7.

HIRING JAMES ROOSEVELT; OPENING OF *WUTHERING HEIGHTS*: James Roosevelt to ASB (I), July 9, 1984; David Rose to ASB (I), Feb. 21, 1980; James Roosevelt, "For Monday A.M. Release" (press release), n.d.; "James Roosevelt, Film Official, Is on the Job—Looking for It," New York *World Telegram*, Jan. 3, 1939; "Begins His Film Job," New York *Sun*, Jan. 3, 1939; Julia McCarthy, "Jimmy, Goldwyn V.P., Sphinx About Movies," New York *Daily News*, Jan. 4, 1939; John Hay Whitney to SG (T), Dec. 5, 1938; David O. Selznick to SG (T), Dec. 5, 1938; FG, "Dear Sam: Do You Remember?," p. 81; Frank Nugent, "Wuthering Heights," *New York Times*, Apr. 14, 1939, p. 28; SGJ to ASB (I), Oct. 31, 1983; WW to ASB (I), Apr. 1, 1980.

Among the many newborns named Cathy that year was Wyler's daughter.

SG to Mrs. Franklin D. Roosevelt (T), Mar. 27, 1939; Kate Cameron to SG (T), Dec. 27, 1939; SG to Ben Hecht (T), Dec. 27, 1939.

LOSING STARS; ELEVATING NIVEN: The Merle Oberon story about copies of her films was related by Robert Osborne to ASB (I), Nov. 25, 1981; Joel McCrea to ASB (I), April 30, 1980; SG to Bertram Block (IOC), Aug. 23, 1939; Reeves Espy to SG (IOC), Aug. 21, 1939; SG to JAM (IOC), Aug. 16, 1939; Edwin Knopf to Sam Wood (IOC), Aug. 18, 1939; Edwin Knopf to SG (IOC), Nov. 3, 1939; Niven, *Moon*, pp. 217–23; Dana Andrews to ASB (I), June 24, 1980; R. B. McIntyre to Mr. [Al]

Evens (IOC), "Test Option for Dana Andrews," Oct. 21, 1938; Frances Kroll Ring, *Against the Current: As I Remember F. Scott Fitzgerald* (Berkeley, Cal.: Creative Arts Book Company, 1985), pp. 55–6; Fitzgerald's quote about SG appears in his notes for *The Last Tycoon*, Princeton University Library; Gary Cooper to SG (T), Sept. 6, 1939; SG to Gary Cooper (T), Sept. 6, 1939; WW to ASB (I), Jan. 8, 1981; SGJ to ASB (I), Feb. 21, 1988; David Niven to SG, n.d. ("Sunday," c. Sept. 15, 1939); "Movies aren't enough . . ." is a quote Irving Hoffman was going to run in his column but did not: Irving Hoffman to W. R. Wilkerson, Oct. 10, 1939.

SG BATTLES UA: Balio, *United Artists*, pp. 155–57; Walker, "*Fortune* Research—United Artists story," Oct. 4, 8, 1940 (*Time/Life* files); "Statement to be Presented by Mr. James Roosevelt at a Meeting of The Board of Directors of United Artists Corporation," Jan. 13, 1939; Reeves Espy to SG (IOC), May 9, 1939, discusses changing the name of the studio; SG to Sam Harris of *Cinema Publication* (T), Dec. 16, 1940.

SG AND UNPOPULAR STANDS: SG, untitled press release, "SG, always two-fisted in his scanning of the celluloid scene . . . ," n.d., 4 pp., discusses block booking; SG, "Hollywood Is Sick," *Saturday Evening Post*, July 13, 1940, pp. 18–19, 44, 48–49; SG to W. W. Clark of *The Cinema*, n.d.; SG, "I Believe in Colour, but—TELEVISION IS NEARER," *Film Weekly*, Oct. 5, 1934, p. 7; much of SG's intelligence about television was obtained from Reeves Espy to SG (IOC), Feb. 4, 1939; SGJ to ASB (I), Oct. 31, 1983; SG talking to the *Time* photographer comes from a *Time* office memorandum, Peter Stackpole to J. S. Billings (in *Time* morgue), Mar. 29, 1939.

SG AND FAMILY LIFE: GC to ASB (I), Sept. 11, 1979; SGJ to ASB (I), Oct. 26, 31, 1983, and May 21, 1988; Mrs. Albert Lasker to ASB (I), June 15, 1984; SG to SGJ, July 17, 1934; LH to ASB (I), Nov. 16, 1981; Mrs. Ira Gershwin to ASB (I), July 2, 1983; Hilde Berl Halpern to ASB

(I), Sept. 7, 1980; "The Promise of the Future Begins Today," brochure of Fountain Valley School of Colorado, Colorado Springs; RGC to ASB (I), Oct. 13, 1979; McClure Capps to SG, n.d.; SG to Ben Fish, July 20, 1934; Richard Fish to ASB (I), Oct. 5, 1984; Sally Sherman to ASB (I), Oct. 8, 1984; Adele Austin and Paula Tygiers to ASB (I), Sept. 3, 1980; SG to Under Secretary of State, Home Office, London, Apr. 25, 1939; Sally Linden to SG (T), Nov. 28, 1939; "Tale of a City" (Washington, D.C.: U.S. Government Printing Office, 1942); SG to Bernard Fish, Mar. 13, 1940.

JOSEPH P. KENNEDY: SGJ to ASB (I), Feb. 24, Mar. 25, 1988; Douglas Fairbanks, Jr., to Franklin D. Roosevelt, Nov. 19, 1940 (FDR Library, PSF: DIPLOMATIC: GREAT BRITAIN: KENNEDY); Hecht, *A Child*, p. 520; Richard J. Whalen, *The Founding Father: The Story of Joseph P. Kennedy* (New York: New American Library, 1964), pp. 346–47; Michael R. Beschloss, *Kennedy and Roosevelt: The Uneasy Alliance* (New York: W. W. Norton, 1980), pp. 223–26.

THE WESTERNER: Jock Lawrence to SG (IOC), Sept. 15, 1939; WW to ASB (I), Jan. 8, 1981; SG to Gary Cooper (T), Nov. 2, 1939; Reeves Espy to Gary Cooper (T), Nov. 2, 1939; SG to Gary Cooper, Oct. 19, 1939; Gary Cooper to SG, Nov. 18, 1939; SG to Gary Cooper, Nov. 29, 1939; SGJ to ASB (I), Feb. 21, 1988; that Walter Brennan did the best SG impersonation was confirmed by Joel McCrea to ASB (I), April 30, 1980; Reeves Espy to SG (IOC), Oct. 13, 1939; Dimitri Tiomkin to SG (T), Apr. 25, 1940; *Daily Variety*, Jan. 4, 1940, p. 4; Walker, *Fortune* research files, 1940; SG and SG Inc. v. United Artists Corporation, United States District Court for the Southern District of New York, 1940.

SG, A "LONE WOLF" AGAIN: SG to David O. Selznick (T), Mar. 1, 1940; David O. Selznick to SG, Mar. 8, 1940; SGJ to ASB (I), Mar. 7, 1984; the "lone wolf" quote comes from an unpublished interview conducted by George Slaff c. June 1959 in

preparation for Jack Smith's five-part series on SG in the Los Angeles *Times*.

17 "WE DID IT BEFORE AND WE CAN DO IT AGAIN"

SG REENTERING PRODUCTION: SGJ, unpublished "Eulogy," c. Feb. 1, 1974; the "Fort Lee" anecdote comes from the files of Irving Hoffman, sent in a letter to W. R. Wilkerson, Oct. 10, 1939, then forwarded to SG; Lynn Farnol to SG (IOC), Feb. 14, 1941; Thomas Brady, "Mr. Goldwyn Bows Out," *New York Times*, Feb. 16, 1941, p. 29; "After It's All Been Said and Done, Goldwyn May Release Through UA," *Variety*, Mar. 26, 1941; David Rose to ASB (I), Feb. 21, 1980; Jewell, *RKO*, pp. 18–19, 140–43, 144, 156.

THE LITTLE FOXES: Edwin Knopf to ASB (I), June 1, 1980; JAM to LH, Oct. 26, 1939; LH to ASB (I), Nov. 15, 1981; LH, *Three*, pp. 473–75; WW to SG, May 6, 1940; Reeves Espy to SG (IOC), May 3, 1940; Edwin Knopf to SG (IOC), May 3, June 10, 1940; Jock Lawrence to SG (IOC), n.d. (c. May 10, 1940); Niven Busch, Jr., to ASB (I), Aug. 31, 1981; WW to ASB (I), Apr. 1, 1980; Bette Davis to ASB (I), Jan. 19, 1983; Rudy Behlmer, ed., *Inside Warner Bros. (1935–1951)* (New York: Viking Penguin, 1985), p. 121; James Roosevelt to SG (discussing WW's new contract), Feb. 2, 1940; Lynn Farnol to SG, Mar. 18, 1941; Bernie Harrison, "Director Wyler Here; Will Film 'Little Foxes,'" Washington, D.C., *Times Herald*, Mar. 19, 1941; Lasky, *I Blow*, pp. 252–60; Joel McCrea to ASB (I), April 30, 1980; SG to Jack Warner, June 6, 1940; Jack Warner to SG, n.d. (c. June 10, 1940); Reeves Espy to Harry Warner, Aug. 16, 1940; Jack Warner to SG, July 31, 1940; Jock Lawrence to SG, Mar. 8, 1941; Lynn Farnol to SG (T of press release re Teresa Wright), March 14, 1941; SG (ghostwritten unpub. article), "I Never Stop Looking," Sept. 2, 1948; Niven Busch to ASB (I), Aug. 31, 1981; WW to ASB (I), Jan. 8, 1979; Madsen, *Wyler*, pp. 209–10; Bankhead, *Tallulah*, p. 237; "Hedda Hopper's Hollywood," transcript, May 21, 1941; Leonard Lyons, "The Lyons Den," *New York Post*, May 16, 1965; Lynn Farnol to SG (T), Aug. 22, 1941; James Agee, *Time*, Sept. 1, 1941, pp. 86–7.

BALL OF FIRE: Edwin Knopf to SG, Dec. 13, 1939; Billy Wilder to ASB (I), July 8, 1983; William Dozier to ASB (I), Mar. 11, 1984; William Dozier to SG, July 3, 1942; SGJ to ASB (I: re Hawks), Oct. 26, 1983; *Time*, Jan. 12, 1942, p. 70; Jean Arthur to SG, n.d. (c. June 1941); Carole Lombard to SG, June 6, 1941; McBride, *Hawks*, p. 82; SG to Gary Cooper (T), Oct. 29, 1941; Billy Wilder to ASB (I), Dec. 2, 1982.

PEARL HARBOR: WW to ASB (I), July 23, 1981; Albert Lasker to SG, Dec. 8, 1941.

WARTIME CHARITIES: "J. Hutchings detailed notes" (unofficial minutes of meeting of Permanent Charities Committee), June 28, 1940; Hecht, *A Child*, pp. 538–40; *Dawn of Liberation: Year Book of the United Jewish Welfare Fund of the Los Angeles Jewish Community Council* (Los Angeles, 1944), pp. 30, 44, 69, 96.

Even Mary Pickford contributed to the UJWF—$25.

JS'S TROUBLES: F. E. Pelton to SG, "Confidential—Report of Producers' Labor Negotiating Committee," Sept. 4, 1941; Albert Fried, *The Rise and Fall of the Jewish Gangster in America* (New York: Holt, Rinehart & Winston, 1980), pp. 129–41, 169–71, 228n; Schwartz, *Writers' Wars*, pp. 113–14, 124–25, 131–32; SGJ to ASB (I), Nov. 3, 1983; SG to JS (T), Apr. 24, 1941; Marcia Winn, "Bioff's Shadow Is Still a Cloud on Hollywood," Chicago *Daily Tribune*, July 28, 1943; SG to JS, May 7, 1942; SG to Arthur D. Wood, examiner of parole board, Aug. 10, 1942; Arthur D. Wood to SG, Aug. 15, 1942; SG to JS (T), Sept. 24, 1942.

HOLLYWOOD GOES TO WAR: Editors of *Look*, *Movie Lot to Beachhead* (Garden City, N.Y.: Doubleday, Doran, 1945), pp. 5,

59, 82–95, 228–29; Lowell Mellett, transcript of address delivered Feb. 17, 1943; several letters concerning "The Real Glory" appear in *Harrison's Reports* (New York, 1942), vol. XXIV, no. 38, p. 1; SG to Noel Coward (T), Nov. 19, 1942, SG to Secretary of the Navy, n.d. (c. Nov. 20, 1942); SG to Jack Warner, July 3, 1942.

START OF "THE RUSSIAN PICTURE": "Unproduced Story material," Dec. 14, 1942; SG to Lowell Mellett (T), Dec. 10, 1941; LH, *Three*, pp. 135–39; LH to ASB (I), Nov. 15, 1981; WW to ASB (I), Jan. 8, 1981; SG to Darryl Zanuck, Mar. 25, 1942; Gregg Toland to SG, Mar. 22, 1942; SG to JS, July 2, 1942.

PRIDE OF THE YANKEES: Niven Busch, Jr., to ASB (I), Aug. 31, 1981; *New York Times*, July 16, 1942, p. 23; Louella Parsons to SG, July 22, 1941; SG to JS, June 4, 1942; Daniel Mandell to ASB (I), May 5, 1980; Charles P. Skouras to SG, June 30, 1942; SG to Sam Wood (T), July 16, 1942; SG to JS, Aug. 12, 1942; SG to Abel Green, editor of *Variety*, Jan. 19, 1943; SG to Paul Gallico, June 1, 1942; SG, "What America Means to Me," *American Weekly*, Jan. 27, 1952, p. 2; "Goldwyn-Gary Unrenewed Yet," *Variety*, July 22, 1942, p. 2; Rocky Cooper Converse to ASB (I), June 14, 1984.

THE NORTH STAR: LH to ASB (I), Nov. 15, 1981; LH, untitled first-draft screenplay of *The North Star*, Aug. 24, 1942; pp. 1, 61, 81; Don Hartman to SG, Oct. 22, 1942; Lewis Milestone to ASB (I), Feb. 4, 1980; Collier Young to SG, Oct. 22, 1942; LH, *The North Star* (revised final draft), Feb. 16, 1943, p. 126; SG to LH, July 15, 1943; LH to Lewis Milestone, Feb. 9, 19, 1943; SG to LH (T), Feb. 24, 1943; LH to SG, Feb. 27, 1943; SG to LH (T), Feb. 9, 1943; LH to SG (T), Feb. 10, 1943; LH to SG, Oct. 16, 1942; Ira Gershwin to ASB (I: through Michael Feinstein), June 28, 1983; LH quoted in Theodore Strauss, "The Author's Case," *New York Times*, Dec. 19, 1943, sec. II, p. 5; SG to LH (T), Dec. 3, 1942; LH to SG, Dec. 4, 1942; FG to LH, June 24, 1943; FG to LH (T), July 10,

1943; LH to ASB (I), Nov. 16, 1981; LH, *Three*, p. 139.

SG, LH PART COMPANY: JAM to SG (IOC), Oct. 19, 1942; JAM to SG (IOC), June 4, 1942; LH to ASB (I), Nov. 15, 1981; JS to SG, July 17, 1943; SG to JS, July 28, 1943; "Agreement" between SG and LH, Sept. 14, 1944 (signed by LH on Sept. 18, 1944).

RELEASE OF *NORTH STAR*: "Hollywood Inside," *Daily Variety*, Sept. 23, 1943, p. 2; Terry McDaniel to Charles P. Skouras, Sept. 16, 1943; Dick Mears (manager of The Academy theater in Inglewood, Cal.) to SG, Sept. 15, 1943; SG to Charles Skouras (T), Nov. 10, 1943; SG to Arthur Sulzberger, Sept. 20, 1943; Bosley Crowther, "The North Star," *New York Times*, Nov. 5, 1943, p. 23; "The New Pictures," *Time*, Nov. 8, 1943, p. 54; James Agee, *Agee on Film* (New York: McDowell, Obolensky, 1958), pp. 56–8; the Goldwynism about this picture not making a dime was related by several people, LH to ASB (I), Nov. 16, 1981, among them; SG to W. R. Hearst, Sept. 29, 1943; W. R. Hearst to SG (T), Oct. 5, 1943; SG to W. R. Hearst (T), Oct. 6, 1943; SG to William Hebert (T), Nov. 9, 1943; Mrs. Hugo Black to SG, n.d. (c. Nov. 1943); WW to SG, Nov. 18, 1943.

SWING TOWARD ESCAPIST PICTURES: Maurice Kann, "How Far with War Films?," *Boxoffice*, Sept. 26, 1942 (tear sheet); SG to Joseph Bernhard, May 19, 1941.

THEY GOT ME COVERED: Charles MacArthur to SG, Mar. 25, 1942; John Steinbeck, "Bob Hope Idol of War Camps, New York *Tribune*, July 27, 1943; Editors of *Look, Movie Lot*, p. 84.

THE PRINCESS AND THE PIRATE: "Salaries," Dec. 14, 1942; comments about Don Hartman appear in "Statement of Samuel Goldwyn—Questions by Grant B. Cooper," May 17, 1944.

SG'S FINANCES: M. Eisner to SG, Nov. 19, 1942; Ellsworth C. Alvord (of Alvord and Alvord), "Memorandum re Tax Consequences of Separate Incorporation of Pic-

tures," Apr. 10, 1943; SGJ to ASB (I), Aug. 27, 1984; Commissioner of Internal Revenue v. SG, "Petition to Review a Decision of the Tax Court of the United States," No. 12,037, June 20, 1949; Sylvan Ostreicher to Head, Appellate Division, Bureau of Internal Revenue, n.d. (c. Feb. 1952); SG's assets in "investments, cash, etc." were valued in a report of Price Waterhouse & Company of Dec. 31, 1944, and sworn to in a deposition of SG when he agreed to sponsor his niece Pola Tajtel, July 23, 1946; "Exhibit 'A'—SG Income Tax Payments on 1944 Income"; some of SG's "collapsible corporations" include: Avalon, Regent, Beverly, and Trinity Productions.

SIGNING DANNY KAYE; *MAKING UP IN ARMS*: John Hyde to William Morris, May 5, 1941; SG to Danny Kaye (T), Oct. 29, 1941; SG to Danny Kaye, Dec. 5, 1941; FG, "Dear Sam: Do You Remember?," p. 88; Sylvia Fine Kaye to ASB (I), Oct. 7, 1983; Danny Kaye to ASB (I), Oct. 18, 1980; SG to Irene Lee (T), June 26, 1942; Irene Lee to SG (T), June 27, 1942; Billy Rose to SG (T), Jan. 5, 1943; Lelia Alexander Arensma to ASB (I), May 20, 1980; Virginia Mayo to ASB (I), May 27, 1980; SG to Billy Rose, Jan. 6, 1943; Billy Rose to SG, Jan. 12, 1943; Eleanore King to SG (IOC), May 13, 1943; Eleanore King, "Memo for Virginia Mayo," n.d. (c. Sept. 1943); Dana Andrews to ASB (I), May 20, 1980; SG's appraisal of Lauren Bacall appears in Goldie Arthur to Robert McIntyre (IOC), Mar. 18, 1943; Agnes de Mille to ASB (I), Apr. 2, 1984.

THE THEATER WARS: "United States v. Paramount Pictures, Inc., etc.," Petition, Equity No. 80-273, filed July 20, 1938; "Petition and Brief of the Society of Independent Motion Picture Producers as Amicus Curiae," Dec. 12, 1945; part of the Supreme Court's decision is quoted in Gerald Mast, ed., *The Movies in Our Midst: Documents in the Cultural History of Film in America* (Chicago: University of Chicago Press, 1982), pp. 509–604; JAM to Loyd Wright, Sept. 1, 1944; Thurman Arnold to SG Productions, Inc. (M), n.d. (c. Oct.

1944); John C. Flinn to Loyd Wright, Nov. 4, 1943; Ben Fish to JAM, May 7, 1943; Louella O. Parsons, "Goldwyn Puts on Reno Show in Ballroom," Los Angeles *Examiner*, Aug. 23, 1944; "An Explanation and Statement of Facts by the T. & D. Theatres of Reno," advertisement, Reno *Evening Gazette*, Aug. 23, 1944; "The Battle of Reno," *Time*, Sept. 4, 1944, pp. 78–80; "Goldwyn's Crusade," Reno *Evening Gazette*, Aug. 30, 1944, p. 4; "FBI Probes Goldwyn Charge," *Daily Variety*, Aug. 29, 1944, pp. 1, 9; "FBI Probing Goldwyn's Charges of Chain Control; Tieup with Decree," *Variety*, Aug. 30, 1944, p. 7; "Trade Views," *Hollywood Reporter*, Sept. 5, 1944, p. 1; Lee Garling, "Divorcement Only Solution, Government Says in Appeal," *Boxoffice*, Feb. 1947; Mary Pickford to SG, Dec. 16, 1944.

SUCCESS OF KAYE MUSICALS: SG to Arthur Dent, Apr. 4, 1944; Frank Quinn, "Up in Arms," New York *Daily Mirror*, c. Aug. 2, 1944; Pat Duggan to SG (IOC), Dec. 23, 1943.

SGJ COMES OF AGE: SGJ to ASB (I), Oct. 31, 1983, Mar. 26, 1988; SG to SGJ, May 5, 1943; SG to SGJ, Mar. 11, Apr. 29, 1943; SGJ to SG, n.d. (c. Mar. 18, May 1, 15, 1943); SG to SGJ, Mar. 22, May 18, 27, 1943; SGJ to SG, June 30, 1943; SG to SGJ, July 6, 30, Aug. 19, 23, Sept. 30, Dec. 23, 30, 1943; SG to RGC, Oct. 30, 1943; Dean George Ferguson, Jr., to SG, Jan. 12, 1944; SG to SGJ, Feb. 10, 1944; SGJ to SG, Mar. 16, 1944, and n.d. (c. Apr. 20, 1944); SG to SGJ, Apr. 25, 1944; SGJ to SG, n.d. (c. May 20, 1944) and June 8, 1944; SG to SGJ, July 5, 1944.

18 BEST YEARS

GERMINATION OF *BEST YEARS*: "The Way Home," *Time*, Aug. 7, 1944, pp. 15–16; SG, "An Open Letter to Darryl F. Zanuck," n.d., in *Daily Variety* and *Hollywood Reporter*, Aug. 8, 1944; FG is quoted in Wagner, *You Must Remember*, p. 109; SG to Kay Brown (IOC), Aug. 5, 1944; SG to George Slaff in preparation for Jack Smith's

June 1959 interviews in Los Angeles *Times*; William S. Cunningham, "Big Producers Men of Brain and Vision, Columbus, Ohio, *Citizen*, Jan. 15, 1936, p. 21; SGJ to ASB (I), Oct. 26, 1983; SG to SGJ, Sept. 8, 1944; SG to Irene Lee, Sept. 29, 1942; Miriam Howell to SG (T), Nov. 2, 1944; Documentary Unit of CBS, "The Hollywood Picture" (unpublished script), Nov. 3, 1948; Pat Duggan to Al Evens (IOC), Dec. 12, 1944; Maurice "Red" Kann to SG, Sept. 7, 1944; SG to Maurice Kann, Sept. 14, 1944.

EISENHOWER FILM: Milton Eisenhower to Jules Levey and Leo Morrison, Nov. 22, 1944; Milton Eisenhower to SG, July 13, 1945; SG to Jules Levey, June 20, 1945; Jules Levey to SG, June 21, 1945; SG to Milton Eisenhower (T), July 13, 1945; Dwight D. Eisenhower to SG, July 22, 1945; SG to Dwight D. Eisenhower, Aug. 8, 1944; SGJ to ASB (I), Nov. 3, 1983.

DIFFICULTY FINDING STORIES: SG to Irene Lee (IOC), Jan. 5, 1943; SG to Kay Brown (IOC), Dec. 16, 1943; SG on buying best-sellers for the screen, (UN) for interview with Edwin Schallert, July 14, 1947; *Hollywood Reporter*, Jan. 23, 1941, p. 1; Olive Higgins Prouty to SG, Oct. 15, 1941; SG to Mrs. Lewis Prouty, Oct. 21, 1941; SG to Pat Duggan (IOC), June 19, 1943; SG referred to the "new stars" in a letter to Lester Markel of the *New York Times*, Jan. 16, 1945; Pat Duggan to SG (IOC), May 21, 1943; SG to Miriam Howell (IOC), Dec. 27, 1944.

EARTH AND HIGH HEAVEN: SG to Jack Warner, Nov. 9, 1943; Rabbi Edgar Magnin to ASB (I), May 27, 1983; SG to SGJ, Apr. 4, 1945.

PROGRESS ON *GLORY FOR ME* (*BEST YEARS OF OUR LIVES*): MacKinlay Kantor to SG, Oct. 6, 1944; Pat Duggan to SG (IOC), Oct. 24, Dec. 14, 1944; MacKinlay Kantor, *Glory for Me* (New York: Coward-McCann, 1945), pp. 3, 13, 42, 194, 268; Miriam Howell to SG (T), Apr. 4, 1945; Pat Duggan to SG (IOC), May 31, June 15, 1945.

SG AND HIS IMAGE: Kanin, *Hollywood*,

pp. 342–48; Anthony Haden-Guest (UN of interview with Benjamin Sonnenberg), n.d.; Benjamin Sonnenberg to SG, Feb. 11, Sept. 8, 1944; Muriel Stafford, "Your Handwriting and You," New York *Sunday Mirror Magazine*, Jan. 9, 1944, pp. 19; Averell Harriman to ASB (I), May 3, 1982; Billy Wilder to ASB (I), July 8, 1983; Walter Winchell, Los Angeles *Evening Herald-Express*, Oct. 19, 1943; Myrna Loy to ASB (I), Mar. 30, 1983; Hilde Berl Halpern to ASB (I), Sept. 7, 1980; FG validates the "Include me out" epitaph story in Wagner, *You Must Remember*, p. 107.

SG's DAY: SGJ to ASB (I), Dec. 1, 1983; SG to T. Hodgkinson, Oct. 6, 1950; FG to T. Hodgkinson, July 18, 1944; SG to T. Hodgkinson (T), Feb. 9, 1944; T. Hodgkinson to Helen Kirk (secretary to SG), Oct. 18, 1932; SG's secretary (prob. Francis Inglis), "Instructions and Suggestions," n.d. (c. 1951); Wagner, *You Must Remember*, p. 111; Josephine Berger to ASB (I), May 17, 1980; William Dozier to ASB (I), Mar. 11, 1984; GC to ASB (I), Sept. 11, 1979; Leonora Hornblow, unpub. diary entry, April 4, 1944 (sent to ASB, July 24, 1984).

SG's SOCIAL AND POLITICAL CONNECTIONS: "Donations—1945"; "Mr. Goldwyn's Bets," July 5, 1944; SG to SGJ, Mar. 30, 1944; Edwin W. Pauley to Franklin D. Roosevelt (M), Nov. 5, 1944; SG to Edwin Pauley, Nov. 11, 1944; Pat Duggan to SG (IOC), Nov. 8, 1944; Robert Hannegan to SG, Nov. 10, 1944; Franklin D. Roosevelt to SG, Dec. 1, 1944; SG to Franklin D. Roosevelt, Jan, 18, 1945; SG to Edwin Pauley, Nov. 3, 1944.

SG's TRIP TO ENGLAND: "US AAF Air Transport Command," Feb. 17, 1945; SG to William Paley, Apr. 24, 1945; Ministry of Information, "Program of Visits by Mr. SG," for Feb. 23, 28, 1945, Mar. 1, 1945; Guy Ramsey, "Sam Would Sign on Churchill as Star," London *Daily Mail*, Feb. 27, 1945; "U.S. Film Chief Wants to Show the World Coventry's Blitz Scars," Birmingham, Eng., *Evening Dispatch*, Feb. 28, 1945; "Sam Without Goldwynisms," Not-

tingham *Journal*, Feb. 27, 1945; "Mr. Goldwyn Looks at Oxford," Oxford *Mail*, Mar. 2, 1945; Sir Max Aitken to ASB (I), Sept. 5, 1980; SG to Leo T. Crowley, administrator, Federal Economic Administration, Mar. 12, 1945.

THE "LULL" OF 1945: Elsa Maxwell to SG and FG (T), Aug. 14, 1944; SG to Jan Masaryk, May 4, 1945; A. H. Evens to Goldie Arthur (IOC), Dec. 23, 1944; SG to Edwin J. Pauley, May 3, 1934; SG to Mrs. Franklin D. Roosevelt (T), Apr. 12, 1945; SG to Harry Truman (T), Apr. 12, 1945; SG to SGJ, May 7, 1945; SG to SGJ, Apr. 16, 1945; SG to SGJ, Apr. 24, 1945; SG to SGJ, May 7, 1945; SG to FG, Apr. 23, 1946; John C. Flinn to SG (T), May 2, 1945; "Policy for payment of payroll—'V' Day," Aug. 22, 1945; SGJ to SG, Aug. 3, 1945; SG to SGJ, July 31, 1945; SG to SGJ, Aug. 31, Sept. 12, 1945; Col. Clarence E. Lovejoy to SG, Dec. 4, 1945; SGJ to ASB (I), Oct. 26, 1983; David Niven, *Moon*, p. 273, and *Bring on the Empty Horses* (New York: G. P. Putnam's Sons, 1975), p. 134; SG to David Niven (T), Jan. 15, 1941; Agee, *Film*, pp. 88–9; WW to ASB (I), Jan. 8, 1981; LH to ASB (I), Nov. 15, 1981.

SIGNING WW AND SHERWOOD TO *GLORY FOR ME* (*BEST YEARS*): Marvin Ezzell to WW, Aug. 25, 1943, Oct. 23, 1945; WW to ASB (I), Apr. 1, 1980; Pat Duggan to SG (IOC), June 15, 1945; Robert Sherwood to SG, Aug. 27, 1945; SG to Robert Sherwood (T), Sept. 4, 1945.

SG VISITS GLOVERSVILLE: FG, "Dear Sam: Do You Remember?"; "Goldwyn, One Time Glove Salesman, Now Cinema Great, Visits Home City," Gloversville *Leader-Republican*, Oct. 31, 1945; Arthur and Ruth Galinsky to ASB (I), June 9, 1984; Anthony Kaiser to ASB (I), June 8, 1984; Vern Steele to SG, Aug. 1, 1947; SG to Jacob Libglid, Aug. 8, 1947; Vern Steele to SG, Aug. 14, 1947.

MAKING *BEST YEARS OF OUR LIVES*: SG to John Mason Brown, June 27, 1957; SG to WW, May 29, 1946; Griffith, *Goldwyn*, pp. 37–41; Pat Duggan to SG, Nov.

21, 1945; SG to Pat Duggan (T), Nov. 28, 1945; Pat Duggan to SG (T), Nov. 28, 1945; SG to Leland Hayward (T), Nov. 29, 1945; Leland Hayward to SG (T), Nov. 29, 1945; Myrna Loy to ASB (I), Mar. 30, 1983; Robert Sherwood, *The Best Years of Our Lives* (screenplay), Apr. 9, 1946, pp. 28–9, 33, 173–74, 195–96, 201, 206; Harold Russell to Ben Washer, Nov. 26, 1945; WW, "Introduction," to Harold Russell (with Dan Ferullo), *The Best Years of My Life* (Middlebury, Vt.: Paul S. Eriksson Publisher, 1981), p. 10; Lester Koenig, "Gregg Toland, Film-Maker," *Screen Writer*, Dec. 1947, pp. 27–33; Irene Sharaff to ASB (I), Feb. 10, 1984; Irving Sindler, "The Best Years of My Life" (unpub. MS.); Russell, *Best Years*, pp. 37–49; WW to ASB (I), July 24, 1981; Dana Andrews to ASB (I), June 24, 1980; Virginia Mayo to ASB (I), May 27, 1980; Bernard Herrmann to SG, July 30, 1945; Hugo Friedhofer is quoted in Thomas, *Music*, p. 153; WW to Robert Sherwood (T), June 6, 1946 (repeated in T from SG to FG on same date); dictates from the Breen Office are quoted in Documentary Unit of CBS, "The Hollywood Picture" (unpub. script), Nov. 3, 1948; Hecht, *A Child*, p. 469.

RELEASE OF *BEST YEARS*: Daniel Mandell to ASB (I), May 5, 1980; "'The Best Years of Our Lives'—1st Preview" (tally sheet), Oct. 17, 1946; Leonard Lyons, *New York Post*, May 16, 1965; WW to ASB (I), Apr. 1, 1980; Benjamin Sonnenberg (UN) of interview by Anthony Haden-Guest, n.d.; William Hebert to SG (IOC), Nov. 16, 1946; Lynn Farnol to SG (IOC), June 27, Oct. 14, 1946; Harry Tugend story, as retold by WW to ASB (I), Jan. 8, 1981; James Agee, "What Hollywood Can Do," *The Nation*, Dec. 7, 14, 1946, in Agee, *Film*, pp. 229–33; Omar Bradley to SG, Dec. 5, 1946; Bill Mauldin to SG, Jan. 3, 1946; James Forrestal to SG, Dec. 13, 1946; RGC to SG (T), Nov. 21, 1946; SG to RGC, Nov. 25, 1946; SG to David Golding, Nov. 9, 1946; Frances (Inglis) to SG, note, Oct. 25, 1948.

SECRET LIFE OF WALTER MITTY: Rob-

ert Nathan to ASB (I), Mar. 27, 1982; SG to Miriam Howell (IOC), May 9, 1946; "Goldwyn vs. Thurber," *Life*, Aug. 18, 1947, pp. 19–22; Irving Sindler to ASB (I), June 12, 1980; Sylvia Fine Kaye to ASB (I), Oct. 7, 1983; George Slaff to ASB (I), Feb. 25, 1984; Benjamin Sonnenberg to SG, Aug. 21, 1947; Robert Sherwood to SG (T), July 11, 1947; JAM to SG (IOC), June 28, 1946; SG to James Thurber, July 31, 1946.

THE BISHOP'S WIFE: SG quoted in Roger Butterfield, "Sam Goldwyn," *Life*, Oct. 27, 1947, p. 127; William Hebert to Roger Butterfield, Sept. 30, 1947; WW to ASB (I), Jan. 8, 1981; Robert Sherwood to SG (T), Oct. 21, 1946; David Niven to SG, July 20, Sept. 14, 1945; Leland Hayward to SG, July 18, 1946; Goldie Arthur is quoted in Marx, *Goldwyn*, p. 323; Cary Grant's reservations appear in Pat Duggan to SG (T), Jan. 2, 1947; Sharaff, *Broadway*, p. 68; Sherwood spoke of SG's yearning for WW to SGJ, who retold ASB (I), May 11, 1984; Henry Koster to ASB (I), July 12, 1983; "'Bishop's Wife'—Preview Cards," Sept. 16, 1947; Billy Wilder to ASB (I), July 8, 1983.

ACADEMY AWARDS, 1946: "20th Annual Awards—Instructions to Academy Award Nominees," Mar. 20, 1948, included a diagram of the set, which had been used the year before; Virginia Mayo to ASB (I), May 23, 1980; Russell, *Best Years*, p. 47; WW to ASB (I), Jan. 8, 1981; FG, "Dear Sam: Do You Remember?," p. 88; SGJ to ASB (I), Nov. 3, 1983.

19 THE PLAGUE

BEST YEARS AFTERGLOW: Darryl F. Zanuck to SG (T), Mar. 14, 1947; Ann and Jack Warner to SG (T), Mar. 14, 1947; David O. Selznick to SG (T), Mar. 14, 1947; JS to SG (T), Mar. 14, 1947; Lawrence A. Weingarten to SG, Mar. 14, 1947; Norma Shearer to SG (T), Mar. 14, 1947; Mack Sennett to SG (T), Mar. 14, 1947; SGJ to SG (T), Mar. 14, 1947; "A Picture About the Real America," Los Angeles *Times*, Mar.

15, 1947, sec. II, p. 4; B. C. Forbes, "Today's 50 Foremost Business Leaders," *Forbes*,
Nov. 15, 1947, pp. 37–48, 150, 152,
154; Butterfield, "Sam Goldwyn," pp.
126–42; Jennifer Howard Coleman to ASB
(I), Sept. 24, 1984; Roger Butterfield to
SG, June 9, 1947.

BEST OF TIMES, WORST OF TIMES:
SGJ to ASB (I), Dec. 1, 1983; Dore Schary,
Heyday: An Autobiography (Boston: Little,
Brown, 1979), p. 150; Butterfield, "Sam
Goldwyn," p. 142; "Continuing Audit of
Marquee Values" (Hollywood: Audience
Research, Inc., Dec. 1946), pp. 2, 5; Gar-
bo's inability to get financing was told by
Roddy McDowall to ASB (I), Feb. 8, 1988;
SG to Harry S. Truman, June 12, 1947; SG
to *Variety* (statement for advertisement),
Aug. 11, 1947; Irving Bernstein, *Holly-
wood at the Crossroads: An Economic Study of
the Motion Picture Industry* (Hollywood: Hollywood AFL Film Council, 1957), pp. 17–
18, 23–24, 31–2; "Goldwyn Slashes His
Top Salaries," *New York Times*, Feb. 11,
1948, sec. II, p. 2; Beverly Jones (of Audience Research, Inc.) to William Hebert,
Oct. 29, 1947; SG, "Hollywood in the
Television Age," *Hollywood Quarterly* (Winter 1949/1950), quoted in Mast, *The Movies*, pp. 634–39.

HOLLYWOOD BLACKLIST: Credo of Motion Picture Alliance and Hearst editorial
were reprinted in Red Kann, "On the
March," *Motion Picture Herald*, Feb. 19,
1944, p. 26; Walter Goodman, *The Committee* (New York: Farrar, Straus & Giroux,
1964), pp. 173–74; Rabbi Edgar Magnin
to ASB (I), May 27, 1983; J. Edgar Hoover
quoted in Eric Johnston, statement before
committee on Un-American Activities,
Mar. 27, 1947; Rupert Hughes, in *Variety*,
May 16, 1947, p. 3; Lela Rogers, in Robert
Vaughan, *Only Victims* (New York: G. P.
Putnam's Sons, 1972), pp. 75–117; Larry
Ceplair and Steven Englund, *The Inquisition
in Hollywood: Politics in the Film Community,
1930–1960* (Garden City, N.Y.: Anchor
Press/Doubleday, 1980), pp. 255, 258–71,
275–98; Victor S. Navasky, *Naming Names*
(New York: Viking Press, 1980), pp. 78–

85; Martin Gang to ASB (I), Mar. 6, 1984;
Editorial, *Screen Writer*, Sept. 1947, pp.
34–5; SG to Paul V. McNutt (T), Oct. 29,
1947; SG to J. Parnell Thomas (T), Oct.
29, 1947; WW to ASB (I), Apr. 1, 1980;
Committee for the First Amendment peti-
tion quoted in Lauren Bacall, *By Myself*
(New York: Alfred A. Knopf, 1979), p.
174; Ring Lardner, Jr., *The Lardners: My
Family Remembered* (New York: Harper &
Row, 1976), pp. 319–22; the opening
statements of the Hollywood Ten appear in
Vaughan, *Victims*, pp. 315–34; Will Lis-
ner, "Goldwyn Is Eager for Inquiry Call,"
New York Times, Oct. 30, 1947, p. 4; SG,
press release, Oct. 30, 1947; RGC to SG,
"Thursday" (prob. Oct. 30, 1947); SG to
RGC, Nov. 13, 1947; SG's comments to
Truman appear in teletype copy, Nov. 14,
1947; C. E. Blomquist (irate patron) to
Orpheum Theater, Nov. 19, 1947; SG to
C. E. Blomquist, Nov. 28, 1947; LH,
Three, pp. 636–39; SG, draft of statement,
Nov. 23, 1947; Schary, *Heyday*, pp.
164–66, 369–70 (Waldorf Conference
statement).

WW later asked SG to hire one of the
Hollywood Ten, but the producer refused,
saying it would be "dishonorable" because
he had, after all, signed the Waldorf Conference statement and had to stand behind
his signature (WW to ASB [I], Apr. 1,
1980).

FIGHTING "ACADEMY AWARD DIS-
EASE": SGJ to ASB (I), Dec. 1, 1983, Apr.
4, 1988; Hilde Berl Halpern to ASB (I),
Sept. 7, 1980; Jeanne Race Woodbury to
ASB (I), Apr. 6, 1988; SG to Fifth Avenue
Bank, Mar. 24, 1948; Paul Rosenberg &
Co. to SG (receipt), Dec. 3, 1951; René
Haas of Arthur Lenars & Co. to SG, June
19, 1950; SG to J. M. Musgrave (IOC),
April 19, 1954; Sam Salz, Inc., to SG (re-
ceipt), March 26, 1954; Lillian Ross, "Pic-
ture," in *Reporting* (New York: Dodd,
Mead, 1981), p. 249; Alfred Crown to ASB
(I), March 28, 1984.

A SONG IS BORN: McBride, *Hawks*, pp.
85–7; *Time*, Nov. 1, 1948, p. 92; William
Hebert to SG (IOC), Aug. 29, 1947; Vera-

Ellen to SG, June 27, 1947; Vera-Ellen to ASB (I), Feb. 2, 1981.

ENCHANTMENT AND NIVEN'S DISEN-CHANTMENT: SG to David Niven, Jan. 5, 1948; Eleanor Perreau-Saussine to ASB, Nov. 18, 1980; Evelyn Keyes, *Scarlett O'Hara's Younger Sister* (Secaucus, N.J.: Lyle Stuart, 1977), p. 137; Butterfield, "Sam Goldwyn," p. 139; "Tabulation of Preview Cards," Oct. 14, 1948; "Preview Profile Report," Oct. 23, 1948; SG to Julius Ochs Adler, Dec. 7, 1948; Beverly Jones (Audience Research, Inc.) to SG, Sept. 3 and Oct. 16, 1947; Niven, *Moon*, pp. 287–89; Pat Duggan to SG (IOC), May 21, 1945; Frances Inglis to Frank Toland, Oct. 12, 1948.

SLUMP CONTINUES: Billy Wilder to ASB (I), July 8, 1983; SG to George Bernard Shaw, April 15, 1948; G. B. Shaw to SG, April 20, 1948; Pat Wallace to SG, Dec. 30, 1947; SG to Laurence Olivier, May 5, 1948; Farley Granger to ASB (I), June 13, 1984; Y. Frank Freeman is quoted in SG to JAM (IOC), Sept. 19, 1950; SG to Stanley Kramer (T), Apr. 7, 1949; SG called *My Foolish Heart* a "four handkerchief" movie in "Kup's Column," Chicago *Sun-Times*, Jan. 24, 1950, p. 27; John McCarten, *The New Yorker*, Jan. 28, 1950, p. 75; Robert Sherwood to SG, Oct. 28, 1949; Alice Young to FG (IOC), Aug. 7, 1951; David Unger to SG, Jan. 19, 1961; J. D. Salinger quoted in *New York Times*, Jan. 15, 1961, sec. VII–2, p. 38; 1950 box-office figures in SG, "Is Hollywood Through" (proofs), *Collier's*, Sept. 21, 1951; grosses from *Variety*, Jan. 4, 1950, p. 59.

SIC TRANSIT GLORIA MUNDI: "Chaplin Should Be Taken at His Word and Barred From U.S.," Los Angeles *Herald-Express*, April 15, 1947, reprinted in David Robinson, *Chaplin: His Life and Art* (New York: McGraw-Hill, 1985), p. 546; Iphigene Sulzberger recalls a night with the Goldwyns when the FBI questioned them about CC, in Susan Dryfoos, *Iphigene* (New York: Dodd, Mead, 1981), pp. 212–13; SG's quip related by SGJ to ASB (I), Dec. 8,

1983; Alfred Crown to ASB, Mar. 28, 1984; Billy Wilder to ASB (I), July 8, 1983; Mrs. WW to ASB (I), Apr. 15, 1983; Balio, *United Artists*, p. 283; "Goldwyn Acquires UA Studio Lot," Los Angeles *Times*, Apr. 21, 1955; Schary, *Heyday*, p. 172; SG, press release, Feb. 2, 1949; William Hebert, press release, Feb. 2, 1949; Dr. P. A. Lindstrom to SG, Feb. 15, 1949; George Slaff to ASB (I), Feb. 25, 1984; SGJ to ASB (I), Dec. 1, 1983; "Goldwyn Quitting Johnston Agency," *New York Times*, Jan. 19, 1949, p. 34; William Hebert, press releases, Jan. 18, 19, 1949; SG, "Hollywood in the Television Era," *Hollywood Quarterly* 4 (Winter 1949), pp. 145–51; Roy Durstine to SG, Feb. 26, 1949.

OUR VERY OWN AND *EDGE OF DOOM*: Phyllis Kirk Bush to ASB (I), Sept. 26, 1984; SG to F. Hugh Herbert, Aug. 2, 1950; Farley Granger to ASB (I), June 13, 1984; FG to Sally Linden, Aug. 29, 1950; Paulina (Pola) Tygiers to ASB (I), Sept. 3, 1980; LH to ASB (I), Nov. 15, 1981; Walter Winchell, quoted in Jock Lawrence to SG (IOC), July 12, 1950; "'Edge of Doom'—First Sneak Preview," Feb. 22, 1950; "'Edge of Doom'—Second Sneak Preview," Feb. 23, 1950; SG to Charles Brackett, Aug. 21, 1950; Charles Brackett to SG, Aug. 21, 1950; SG to Ben Hecht (IOC), Aug. 17, 1950; "Quotes on 'Edge of Doom,'" July 20, 1950; SG to Alfred Crown (IOC), Mar. 20, 1951; SGJ to ASB (I), May 21, 1988.

SG'S DYNASTIC DREAMS; SGJ COMES HOME: SGJ to SG, April 28, 1946; SG to SGJ, May 9, July 16, Aug. 16, Oct. 1, 1946, April 7, 1947; SG to David MacDonald, Feb. 18, 1947; SG to SGJ, May 17, May 28, 1947; H. M. Bardt (v.p., Bank of America) to SG, Oct. 11, 1947; JAM to SG (IOC), Feb 14, 1949; SGJ to SG, n.d. (rec. May 5, 1948); SG to SGJ, May 5, 1948; SG to JAM (IOC), May 29, 1948; JAM to SG (IOC), Apr. 4, 1949; SG to JAM (IOC), Mar. 23, 1949; Mrs. Ira Gershwin to ASB (I), July 2, 1983; "SGJ Joins Goldwyn Productions as Associate Producer" (press release), Mar. 8, 1950; GC to ASB (I), Sept. 11, 1979; SG to John J. McCloy, July 14, 1950.

KOREA AND *I WANT YOU*: SG, notes on "Dateline Korea," July 15, 1950; Jock Lawrence, "Confidential—Korea Story Analysis," July 26, 1950; SG, "To Jenny . . . with Love," *This Week*, Nov. 18, 1951, pp. 10, 18; Robert Sherwood to SG (T), Oct. 17, 1950; SG to Irwin Shaw (T), June 15, 1951; SG to Irwin Shaw (T), July 18, 1951; Sid Garfield to JAM (IOC), June 11, 1951; SG to William Paley, Sept. 20, 1950; "'I Want You'—First Sneak Preview," Oct. 25, 1951; "Highlights from General Donovan's Statement," March 6, 1951; SG to Gen. Dwight D. Eisenhower, Sept. 28, 1951; SG to John Shaw Billings, July 19, 1951; SG to Gen. Julius Adler, July 12, 1951; SGJ to ASB (I), Dec. 1, 1983.

20 DINOSAURS

CHANGES IN HOLLYWOOD: SGJ to ASB (I), Oct. 26, Dec. 1, 1983; Alfred Crown to ASB (I), Mar. 28, 1984; SG, transcript of interview with Edward R. Murrow, broadcast Apr. 6, 1951; SG, "Billion Dollar Baby" (revised typescript, ghostwritten by George Slaff), Feb. 8, 1950; SG, press release, Sept. 17, 1953; Lynn Farnol to SG, Sept. 18, 1950; Niven, *Moon*, p. 299; SG, press release, Mar. 3, 1953.

HANS CHRISTIAN ANDERSEN: William Dozier to SG (IOC), May 9, 1951; Henry Koster to Bert Allenberg (T), Nov. 9, 1950; SG to Robert Sherwood, Dec. 8, 1950; Robert Sherwood to SG, Dec. 6, 1950; SG to Noel Langley (N), Dec. 18, 1950; Noel Langley, "Supplementary Notes on 'Hans Anderson [*sic*],'" n.d.; Noel Langley to SGJ (T), Dec. 20, 1950; Moss Hart's deal confirmed in Irving Paul Lazar to SG (T), June 19, 1951; SG to Oscar Hammerstein II and Richard Rodgers, June 11, 1951; SG to SGJ, June 28, 1951; Myles Connolly to SG, May 1, 1952; Kitty Carlisle Hart to ASB (I), Oct. 22, 1982; Alfred Crown to ASB (I), Mar. 28, 1984;

Farley Granger to ASB (I), June 13, 1984; Frances Inglis (SG's secretary) to SGJ, Jan. 15, 1952; SG to Danny Kaye, June 5, 1951; Gunhild Gansing (American editor of the Danish weekly *Tidens Kvinder*), letter to *Christian Science Monitor*, Mar. 29, 1952; Jean Hersholt to SG, Feb. 22, 1952; SG to Jean Hersholt, Feb. 25, 1952; Mogen Skot-Hansen's comments are quoted in notes for press release, Apr. 4, 1952; "Danes Okay Kaye, Who Feared Kayo," *New York Times*, July 22, 1952, p. 21; "Danes Surrender to Kaye-Andersen," *Film Daily*, July 23, 1952, p. 8; SG to SGJ, Oct. 6, 1952.

GRANGER DEPARTS: Farley Granger to ASB (I), June 13, 1984; Farley Granger to SG, Oct. 14, 1952; SG to Farley Granger, Oct. 15, 1952; SG expresses his relief over *Hans Christian Andersen* in letter to Frank Scully, Nov. 28, 1952.

SG AND FAMILY: FG ("Grandparents") to Jennifer Goldwyn (T), July 11, 1951; FG to SG, Oct. 10, 1951; Irene Mayer Selznick to ASB (I), Oct. 9, 1985; SG to SGJ, Oct. 20, Nov. 21, 1951; Mrs. Arthur Hornblow, Jr., to ASB (I), Oct. 19, 1982; SG to Alan Capps, Jan. 12, 1953; FG to RGC, Nov. 16, 1953; SGJ to ASB (I), Feb. 24, May 21, 1988; RGC to ASB (I), June 4, 1988.

CHARITY AND POLITICS: Robert G. Sproul to SG, Feb. 26, 1951; SG to Dr. Stafford L. Warren, June 6, 1951; SG to board of regents, UCLA, Feb. 25, 1953, July 27, 1954; proposed press release for SG Award for painting, Mar. 13, 1957; Willis Goldbeck (pres., Permanent Charities Committee) to SG, Jan. 12, 1956; Abba Eban to SG, Apr. 23, 1951; SG, introduction of David Ben-Gurion, May 24, 1951; SGJ to ASB (I), Aug. 21, 1988; SG to Gen. Dwight D. Eisenhower, Oct. 12, 1951, and (T) July 11, 1952; SG to Sherman Adams, Aug. 9, 1954.

Through Eisenhower, SG met Field Marshal Montgomery at a White House dinner, and they became friends. SG was his host for several nights in 1954, throwing him a black-tie dinner party on November 30; the guests included the James Masons, the

Gary Coopers, the David Nivens, and two dozen others. Goldwyn introduced the guest of honor as "Marshal Field Montgomery."

BETWEEN PROJECTS: David Golding to ASB (I), Mar. 3, 1984; William Dozier to ASB (I), Mar. 11, 1984; SG to Audrey Wood (re *Tea and Sympathy*), Feb. 11, 1954; SG to Eric Johnston, Dec. 24, 1953; SG to George T. Bye, Sept. 30, 1953; Robert Sherwood to SG, Sept. 11, 24, 1953; Ray Stark to SG, Feb. 25, 1953; SG to Robert Sherwood, Sept. 17, 1953; Danny Mandell to SG (IOC), Dec. 10, 1953; David Golding to SG, Jan. 31, 1954; SG (transcript of press conference), n.d. (c. Nov. 1953); James Mulvey to SG (IOC), Aug. 12, 1954; SG (transcript of press conference), n.d. (c. Nov. 1952).

GUYS AND DOLLS: SG, quoted in press release, n.d. (c. Nov. 1955); "'Guys' to Goldwyn for Million," *Hollywood Reporter*, Mar. 4, 1954, pp. 1, 4; "Cinema," *Time*, May 9, 1955, p. 106; SGJ to ASB (I), Dec. 1, 1983, Mar. 7, 1984; Mrs. WW to ASB (I), Apr. 15, 1983; Joseph L. Mankiewicz to SG (IOC), Nov. 2, 1954; Joseph L. Mankiewicz to ASB (I), June 6, 1983; Abe Burrows, *Honest, Abe* (Boston: Atlantic Monthly Press/Little, Brown, 1980), pp. 291–95; JAM to SG (T), June 24, 1954; SG to Bing Crosby, July 30, 1954; Lew Kerner to SG (T), May 26, 1954; SG to Joseph L. Mankiewicz, June 3, 8, 1954, and (T), July 22, 1954; Joseph L. Mankiewicz to SG (T), June 8, 1954; Joseph L. Mankiewicz to Marlon Brando, n.d. (c. July 23, 1954); Robert V. Newman to SG (IOC), Aug. 9, 1954; SG to Miriam Howell, June 1, 1954; Deborah Kerr to SG, Jan. 5, 1955; "Stubby Toe" was recalled by David Golding to ASB (I), Mar. 3, 1984; Irene Sharaff to ASB (I), Feb. 10, 1984; Irene Sharaff, *Broadway*, p. 93; Alfred Crown to ASB (I), Mar. 28, 1984; Stephen Sondheim, *Films in Review*, Dec. 1955, pp. 523–25; Jean Simmons (through Geoffrey Barr) to ASB (I), May 30, 1986; Brando is quoted in Harry Bacas, "Brando Lets Off Steam on Duty Visit Here," Washington,

D.C., *News*, Nov. 14, 1955; Howard Dietz to SG (T), Mar. 7, 1955; SG to Nicholas Schenck, Mar. 30, 1955; Earl Wingard, proposed release regarding foreign business, June 1, 1956; "'Guys and Dolls'—Estimated Gross," Oct. 16, 1956.

CROQUET AND LEISURE BETWEEN PICTURES: Friend of FG who wishes to remain anonymous, to ASB (I), 1983; Mrs. Arthur Hornblow, Jr., to ASB (I), Oct. 19, 1982; FG to A. J. Dunne of Lehman Brothers, June 11, 1958; SGJ to ASB (I), Oct. 26, 1983; Louis Jourdan to ASB (I), Aug. 11, 1983; Leonard K. Firestone to SG (R), July 1, 1953; FG to George Slaff, July 1, 1953; SG to John Jaques & Son, Ltd., Mar. 10, 1958; Jean Negulesco to ASB (I), Aug. 17, 1983; Lauren Bacall to ASB (I), June 13, 1984; Jean Negulesco, *Things I Did and Things I Think I Did* (New York: Linden Press / Simon & Schuster, 1984), pp. 159–63.

NEW PROJECTS: Maurice Revnes to SG, Apr. 11, 18, 28, 1955; SG to Maurice Revnes, Apr. 14, 1955; the John Patrick incident was related by Cecil Smith to ASB, May 20, 1980; FG to McKay Morris, Sept. 25, 1953; FG to George Landy, Oct. 9, 1953; Miriam Howell to FG, Jan. 6, 1955; FG to Bennett Cerf, Dec. 12, 1955; SG, press release on the death of Robert Sherwood, Nov. 14, 1955; SG, advertisement for *Diary of Anne Frank*, n.d. (c. Mar. 1956); SGJ to ASB (I), Oct. 26, 1983; Frances Goodrich and Albert Hackett to SG, Oct. 7, 1956; WW to ASB (I), Jan. 8, 1981.

PORGY AND BESS PREPRODUCTION: SGJ to ASB (I), Dec. 1, 1983; Ira Gershwin to James Goodrich (Hollywood editor, Johnson Publishing Co.), Apr. 8, 1958 (in private collection of Mrs. Ira Gershwin); Ira Gershwin (through Michael Feinstein) to ASB (I), June 28, 1983; SG Prod., press release, May 9, 1957; Langston Hughes to SG, July 8, 1957; Paul Osborn to SG, July 3, 25, 1957; Frances Goodrich and Albert Hackett to SG, Sept. 30, 1957; Clifford Odets to SG, July 9, 1957; SGJ to SG (IOC), July 10, 1957; FG to Miriam Howell, Oct. 14, 1957; N. Richard Nash to SG, Feb. 17, 1958; Arthur Pincus to SG (re Elia Kazan), June 4, 1957; Abe Lastfogel to SG (re Frank Capra), Aug. 5, 1957; KV to SG (T), Aug. 22, 1957; Garson Kanin to SG, May 27, 1957; Mrs. Ira Gershwin to ASB (I), July 2, 1983; Lillian Schary Small to SG, May 15, Oct. 30, 1957; Lillian S. Small to Sidney Poitier, Nov. 11, 1957; Sidney Poitier, *This Life* (New York: Alfred A. Knopf, 1980), pp. 205–13, 220–24; Leonard Lyons, "The Lyons Den," New York *Post*, Nov. 21, 1957; Dorothy Kilgallen, "The Voice of Broadway," New York *Journal American*, Nov. 12, 1957, p. 13; SG and Sidney Poitier, transcript of press conference, Dec. 10, 1957; Rev. Maurice A. Dawkins (pres., L.A. NAACP) to SG, Jan. 13, 1958; Jackie Robinson to SG, Dec. 9, 1957; Eddie Jaffe (agent for Sugar Ray Robinson) to SG, Feb. 5, 1958; Sharaff, *Broadway*, pp. 94–5; Loudon Wainwright, "The One-Man Gang Is in Action Again," *Life*, Feb. 16, 1959, pp. 103–16; "American Classic Sings Anew," *Life*, June 15, 1959, pp. 70–82; Irene Sharaff to ASB (I), Feb. 10, 1984.

STUDIO FIRE; RESUMPTION OF *PORGY AND BESS*: "Goldwyn Studio Fire Razes $2,000,000 Set," Los Angeles *Times*, July 3, 1958, p. 1; Wainwright, "One-Man Gang"; Zukor's reaction to the fire at the old Famous Players studio is recorded in SG, *Behind the Screen*, p. 29; Irving Sindler to ASB (I), June 12, 1980; FG to N. Richard Nash, July 7, 1958; SG to Y. Frank Freeman, July 7, 1958; Joe Vogel to SG (T), July 3, 1958; Jack Warner to SG (T), July 2, 1958; David Selznick to SG (T), July 4, 1958; WW to SG (T), July 10, 1958; SG to WW, July 10, 1958; DeMille's message was sent from Milton E. Pickman to SG (IOC), July 2, 1958; SGJ to ASB (I), Dec. 6, 1983; David Selznick to SG (T re Bessie Lasky), Feb. 11, 1958; Bessie Lasky to SG, June 25, 1958; a member of the Wilshire Boulevard Temple who wishes to remain anonymous, to ASB (I), Nov. 12, 1982; SG to Cecil B. DeMille (T), July 2, 1958; Irene Sharaff to ASB (I),

Feb. 10, 1984; Rouben Mamoulian to SG (NL), Feb. 3, 1958; "Statement Issued by Screen Directors Guild" (c. Aug. 1958); "Confidential—Proposed Statement from the Screen Producers Guild" (c. Aug. 1958); Russell Birdwell, press release, Aug. 5, 6, 1958; Irving Paul Lazar to Joe Schoenfeld (of *Daily Variety* [T]), Aug. 11, 1958; Otto Preminger, *Preminger* (Garden City, N.Y.: Doubleday, 1977), pp. 136–39; Sammy Davis, Jr. (with Jane and Burt Broyar), *Yes I Can* (New York: Farrar, Straus & Giroux, 1965), pp. 475–77; Otto Preminger to SG (T), Sept. 27, 1958; Stephen Longstreet, "*Close-up* Demands That Samuel Goldwyn Shelve 'Porgy and Bess,'" *Hollywood Close-up*, Aug. 28, 1958, pp. 1, 3, 7; Al Tamarin to *Porgy and Bess* personnel (IOC) (c. Dec. 1958); "Porgy Chased Off Screen," Charleston, S.C., *News and Courier*, Mar. 16, 1961), p. 10a.

"LAST OF THE MOGULS": "Sam Goldwyn Happily Observes 77th Birthday," Los Angeles *Times*, Aug. 28, 1959, sec. III, p. 1; James Powers, "Goldwyn, 77, Maps New Pic," *Daily Variety*, Aug. 28, 1959, pp. 1, 4; Wainwright, "One-Man Gang," p. 103; Norman Lloyd to ASB (I), May 28, 1980.

21 A SLOW FADE TO BLACK

SG RETIRES, FG DECLINES: Joseph L. Mankiewicz to ASB (I), June 6, 1983; Mrs. Arthur Hornblow, Jr., to ASB (I), June 14, 1984; Louella Parsons, "The Real Mr. Goldwyn," Los Angeles *Examiner*, Feb. 22, 1959, pp. 34–5, 42, Mar. 1, 1959, pp. 34–5; Mrs. Ira Gershwin to ASB (I), July 2, 1983; Mrs. Billy Wilder to ASB (I), July 14, 1983; SGJ to ASB (I), Nov. 3, 1983; Billy Wilder to ASB (I), July 8, 14, 1983; Irene Mayer Selznick to ASB (I), Apr. 4, 1987; SGJ to ASB (I), Oct. 26, 1983; "Mrs. Goldwyn Plans to Write in Future," Los Angeles *Herald-Express*, Aug. 19, 1959, p. D6; GC to ASB (I), Sept. 11, 1979.

SG HONORS AND POLITICS: Screen Producers Guild, press release on occasion of Milestone Award, Jan. 21, 1959; Jean

Howard to ASB (I), July 20, 1983; SG quoted in "People," *Time*, Mar. 28, 1960, p. 42; Jack Foreman to ASB (I), July 29, 1983; SG to Pres. Dwight Eisenhower, Jan. 16, 1961; "H'wood Gives Massed Stellar Tribute to Samuel Goldwyn on 80th Birthday," *Variety*, Aug. 29, 1962, pp. 2, 16; Philip K. Scheuer, "They Came to Praise Sam—and Rib Him," Los Angeles *Times*, Aug. 29, 1962, p. 11; "Transcript of Speeches at Samuel Goldwyn's Testimonial Dinner," Sept. 14, 1962 (*Time/Life* files); Joe Hyams, "After Goldwyn Birthday—A Plea for Code," New York *Herald Tribune*, Aug. 28, 1962, p. 8; SG to Ben Hecht, Oct. 3, 1960; SG to John F. Royal, Sept. 4, 1962; "Tribute Paid Goldwyn at Dedication," Los Angeles *Valley Times*, June 27, 1966, pp. 1, 3; SG to Mrs. Norman Chandler, June 24, 1963; Mrs. Norman Chandler to SG, Aug. 6, 1963, Jan. 3, 1966; William S. Paley to ASB (I), June 13, 1983; Gen. Dwight Eisenhower to SG, June 24, 1966.

THE STUDIO AND SELLING PICTURES TO TV: Jack Foreman to ASB (I), July 29, 1983; SGJ to ASB (I), Nov. 22, 1983; story about Dan Seymour was related by Jack Ball (who was also at the meeting) to ASB (I), Dec. 2, 1987; "Despite $5,000,000 Sales, Goldwyn Changes His Mind on Pix-Into-TV," *Variety*, Nov. 9, 1960, p. 24; William S. Paley to ASB (I), June 13, 1983; "CBS Stations Giving Goldwyn Films Colorful Videbut," *Daily Variety*, Dec. 29, 1964, p. 6; Cecil Smith to ASB (I), May 20, 1980; SG Productions, "Comparative Summary of Income and Expense Excluding Film Rentals," n.d. (c. Dec. 1959); Wagner, *You Must Remember*, pp. 112–13.

DEATHS AND DEFECTIONS: Wagner, *You Must Remember*, p. 113; Richard Fish to ASB (I), Oct. 5, 1984; SGJ to ASB (I), Oct. 17, Dec. 1, 7, 1983; Selznick, *Private View*, p. 380; Jack Warner to SG, Jan. 7, 1965; Irene Mayer Selznick to ASB (I), Nov. 18, 1984; David Niven to SG, Apr. 2, 1966; George Slaff to ASB (I), Feb. 25, 1984; "Wyler-Goldwyn Suits Set for Sept.

11," *Daily Variety*, May 4, 1962, p. 1; WW to SG, Oct. 16, 1962; WW to ASB (I), Jan. 8, 1981; Samuel Rosenman to George Slaff, Feb. 26, 1965; George Slaff to SG (IOC), Mar. 1, 1965; LH to ASB (I), Nov. 15, 1981; William S. Paley to ASB (I), June 13, 1983; Myrna Loy to ASB (I), Mar. 30, 1983; the Pittsburgh ratings of *Wuthering Heights* also appear in SG to Donald H. McGannon (T), Feb. 10, 1966; George Slaff to SG, Aug. 5, 1968; SGJ to ASB (I), Oct. 26, Nov. 22, 1983.

SG'S STROKE: SGJ to ASB (I), Oct. 11, Dec. 8, 1983; Dr. William Weber Smith to ASB (I), Feb. 23, 1983; Jack Foreman to ASB (I), July 29, 1983; Mrs. Ira Gershwin to ASB (I), July 2, 1983; David Rose to ASB (I), July 26, 1983; "Goldwyn Asks for Conservator," Los Angeles *Times*, Oct. 17, 1969, p. 2; "SG Ready to Step Down," Los Angeles *Herald-Examiner*, Oct. 17, 1969, sec. A, p. 5; "Court Rules on Estate of Goldwyn," Los Angeles *Times*, Nov. 4, 1969, sec. II, p. 8; GC to ASB (I), Sept. 11, 1979; FG to Jympson Harmon, Nov. 19, 1969; Irving Berlin to SG, May 19, 1970; Mrs. Arthur Hornblow, Jr., to ASB (I), Oct. 19, 1982, June 14, 1984; George Slaff to ASB (I), Feb. 25, 1984; SGJ to ASB (I), Sept. 18, 1978; Bob Thomas, press release, c. Sept. 1, 1971; Bob Thomas, "Goldwyn Turns 90 Sunday," Los Angeles *Times*, Aug. 26, 1972, sec. II, p. 9; Philip K. Scheuer, "Frances Goldwyn Talks, in Retrospect, About Sam," *Calendar* (Los Angeles *Times*), July 25, 1971, p. 20.

SECOND FIRE: SGJ to ASB (I), July 28, 1988.

SG'S DEATH: SGJ to ASB (I), Dec. 8, 1983, and May 21, 1988; Albin Krebs, "Samuel Goldwyn Dies at 91," *New York Times*, Feb. 1, 1974, pp. 1, 34; "Sam Goldwyn Eulogized," Los Angeles *Herald-Examiner*, Feb. 2, 1974; SGJ, unpublished eulogy; Last Will and Testament of SG, probate package #P600467, Los Angeles County Archives.

DEMISE OF FG: SGJ to ASB (I), Oct. 17, Nov. 3, 22, Dec. 1, 8, 1983; GC to ASB (I), Sept. 11, 1979; Dr. William Weber Smith to ASB (I), Feb. 23, 1984; story of FG blowing up at GC related by Mrs. Ira Gershwin to ASB (I), July 2, 1983; Katharine Hepburn to ASB (I), Feb. 12, 1984; Irene Mayer Selznick to ASB (I), Nov. 18, 1984; George Slaff to ASB (I), Feb. 25, 1984, and May 21, 1988.

CUKOR'S DEATH: SGJ to ASB (I), Feb. 25, 1988; George Towers to ASB (I), Mar. 7, 1988.

INDEX

PERMISSIONS ACKNOWLEDGMENTS

Grateful acknowledgment is made to the Samuel Goldwyn Foundation, Samuel Goldwyn, Jr., and Ruth Goldwyn Capps.

Very special thanks to everyone who granted permission to include the following previously unpublished material: Excerpt from an August 18, 1933, letter by Ronald Colman is reprinted by permission of Juliet Colman Toland; excerpts from a November 18, 1939, letter by Gary Cooper are reprinted by permission of Veronica B. Cooper; a December 4, 1942, telegram, an excerpt from a February 19, 1943, letter, and an excerpt from a February 27, 1943, letter by Lillian Hellman are reprinted with permission of the copyright proprietors, the Literary Property Trustees under the Will of Lillian Hellman; excerpt from an April 4, 1944, memorandum to herself is reprinted by permission of Leonora Hornblow; excerpt from an August 27, 1945, letter by Robert Sherwood is reprinted by permission of Madeline H. Sherwood; a November 9, 1936, telegram and an excerpt from a May 6, 1940, letter by William Wyler are reprinted by permission of Margaret T. Wyler; excerpt from a March 5, 1930, telegram by Florenz Ziegfeld is reprinted by permission of Patricia Ziegfeld Stephenson.

Grateful acknowledgment is made to Warner/Chappell Music, Inc., for permission to reprint an excerpt from "Anything Goes" by Cole Porter. Copyright 1934 by Warner Bros. Inc. (Renewed). All rights reserved. Used by permission.

All photographs not otherwise credited are courtesy of the Samuel Goldwyn Foundation.

A NOTE ON THE TYPE

The text of this book was set, via computer-driven cathode-ray tube, in Garamond No. 3, a modern rendering of the type first cut by Claude Garamond (1510–1561). Garamond was a pupil of Geoffroy Troy and is believed to have based his letters on Venetian models, although he introduced a number of important differences, and it is to him we owe the letter which we know as old style. He gave to his letters a certain elegance and a feeling of movement that won for their creator an immediate reputation and the patronage of Francis I of France. Composed by Graphic Composition, Inc., Athens, Georgia. Printed and bound by Fairfield Graphics, Fairfield, Pennsylvania. Inserts printed by Halliday Lithographers, West Hanover, Massachusetts.